Reviewer's Speak

An engaging manual with realworld examples, cases and hands-on projects to give a comprehensive understanding about business analytics. A valuable reference for professionals wanting to make a career in business analytics.

Dr. Sanjay Modi
Executive Dean, Lovely Professional University

A prospective comprehensive book on Business Analytics that promises to coverthe concepts and applications well.

Prof. D. PGoyal, Professor of Information Systems, MDI, Gurgaon

An engaging encyclopedia filled with real world examples, cases and hands-on projects—a wonderful insight into the world of analytics.

Dr. Bhimaraya Metri
Dean (Academic)
International Management Institute (IMI)

Business analytics which seems to sound as a complex subject is made simple and easy to understand in this book. The author provides a deep insight into the world of business analytics which is further substantiated by its various real world examples.

Dr. Harsh Vardhan Samalia
Assistant Professor
Rajiv Gandhi Indian Institute of Management, Shillong
Academic Chair – Strategic Management Area

Filtering the relevant information and its analysis is the key to organizational success. This book provides the tools and techniques to use more of data and less of intuition to build and sustain in the business. Highly recommended for managers and entrepreneurs.

Dr. Parveen Gill
Professor & Program Coordinator
The Business School, Humber College ITAL, Canada

The availability of literature on business analytics has been a problem in recent times. Coming up with a title on this topic which covers most of the concepts that need to be addressed and that too in a simple, detailed and updated manner is most heartening.

Dr. Gagan Deep Sharma
University School of Management Studies
Guru Gobind Singh Indraprastha University
New Delhi

BUSINESS ANALYTICS

Sahil Raj

School of Management Studies,
Punjabi University, Patiala

Cengage

Australia • Brazil • Canada • India • Mexico • Singapore • United Kingdom • United States

Cengage

Business Analytics

Sahil Raj

For product information and technology assistance, contact us at **asia.infoindia@cengage.com**

For permission to use material from this text or product, submit all requests online at **www.cengage.com/permissions**

ISBN-13: 978-81-315-2788-7
ISBN-10: 81-315-2788-3

Cengage Learning India Pvt. Ltd.
T-303, 3rd Floor
DAV Complex, Plot 3
Mayur Vihar Phase 1
Delhi-110091

Cengage is a leading provider of customized learning solutions with employees residing in nearly 40 different countries and sales in more than 125 countries around the world. Find your local representative at **www.cengage.com**

Cengage is committed to creating inclusive and diverse products, including perspectives that represent the diversity of people across all backgrounds, identities, opinions, and experiences. If you have any feedback related to this, please contact us at **support.cengage.com**

To learn more about Cengage products, platforms and services, visit at **www.cengage.co.in**

Printed by:
Saurabh Printers Pvt Ltd
67A-68 Ecotech Ext-I Greater Noida, Tel-0120-2341180

Printed in India
Print Number: 09 **Print Year:** 2024

Foreword

Back in the good old days of data processing, computers were an expensive luxury which not many companies could afford. The use of computers was mainly to aid the accountants to do their number crunching faster and more accurately. It was computerisation of manual tasks.

Eventually, when computers become more powerful, more applications were added to help not only the finance department but other departments as well. Applications like human resource management, order processing, customer record management, sales support management and so on, were added to make the company more productive and efficient. Nevertheless, computers were still mainly playing a support role.

In the early 1990s, computer services departments began to be called Information Services departments. This happened because many companies realised that computers or Information Technology can be used to extract useful information from the vast amount of data that has been collected from the transaction processing systems when the companies interact with customers. Such information can be used for helping management make tactical and strategic decisions in order to become more profitable and more competitive in the marketplace. So Information Technology began to move out of the Back Office to the frontline and a new breed of executives called the Chief Information Officers (CIOs) was born.

Since claiming their place at the frontline, Information Technology (IT) has enabled companies to be more competitive and more innovative. Systems like Customer Relationship Management systems, Supply Chain Management Systems, E-commerce applications and so on, have become invaluable tools for companies to serve their customers better and interact better with their suppliers. IT has given companies their competitive tools.

When is a competitive tool not a competitive tool? When everyone is using one, of course. As more and more of these tools become affordable through cloud service providers, companies have to find the next competitive tool to ensure that their market share does not become eroded.

Companies have collected vast amount of data through the use of the many Enterprise Application systems they have implemented in the last ten to fifteen years. Now is the time to apply analytics to these data to discover new insights into customer behaviour and customer preferences in order to improve products and services offered by the company. Data analytics combined with business analytics are helping companies to be more customer-focused, innovative and competitive. As a result, there is a huge demand for data analysts and data scientists worldwide.

This book is an invaluable guide to the information technologists who want to be part of the exciting revolution that is happening all around the world now.

Alex Siow
Professor of National University, Singapore
Director, Strategic Technology Management Institute, Singapore

Preface

As the organisations are collecting massive data in the form of structured, unstructured and semi-structured data, there is demand for those managers who can decipher the complex data. The future managers need to have analytical skills, and business analytics is one area which addresses all these issues. Business Analytics is a compelling subject of concern to all managers, practitioners, teachers and students who seek to broaden their horizon and wish to unlock the true potential of data. Cases and discussions presented in this book were drawn largely from the author's experience, and hence would address practical issues that may have to be considered while dealing with such situations. It is often seen that many books discuss theoretical aspects that students fail to relate practically. Considering this issue, this book includes hands-on projects with complete dataset in appendix so that students can practically apply all theoretical aspects discussed and realise the potential of analytics. It is time that budding managers visualised analysis beyond SPSS, and in this book a new dimension of analysis is presented in the form of multidimensional analysis by applying SQL Server. SQL Server is a user-friendly application which does not require programming to run the applications. The complete working of SQL Server is explained with the help of screenshots.

The book is organised into twelve chapters. Chapter 1 presents a detailed discussion on the overview of business analytics. After going through this chapter, readers will be able to understand the potential of business analytics in managing business.

Chapter 2 introduces the reader to one of the most important aspects of business analytics, i.e., data. As data is often termed as the lifeline of any analytical tool, it is important for the budding managers to understand the importance of data. Giving importance to the data not only means collection of data but also it is imperative to maintain its quality and integrity. All the aspects related to data integrity and data profiling are deliberated in this chapter.

Chapter 3 is a unique chapter highlighting the emergence of new type of data, i.e., unstructured data. As more and more people are using social media platforms to express their feeling, it is time that organisation acknowledged the importance of this type of data which is highly unstructured, i.e., data which do not fit into traditional format of rows and columns. This unique feature of unstructured data demands new approaches to view and analyse the data.

Chapter 4 has an extensive coverage of data warehouse and its applications in corporate scenarios. As organisations are steadily moving from traditional database to data warehouse, it is indeed critical for future managers to understand the importance and applications of data warehouse. All the aspects related to data warehouse including various architectural designs are deliberated in this chapter.

Chapter 5 has detailed discussions on the role of data modelling, particularly the role of relational data modelling. Going further in this chapter, issues regarding conceptual design, logical design and physical design are highlighted.

Chapter 6 highlights one of the most widely applied data modelling techniques, i.e., multidimensional modelling. Multidimensional models help to view data from different dimensions and hence are of great help to managers. All the concepts of multidimensional modelling like dimensions, attributes, measures and schemas are discussed in detail in this chapter. For better understanding of concepts of multidimensional modelling, hands-on project with screenshots of SQL Server is also given at the end of the chapter.

Chapter 7 is a comprehensive view on ETL. To build any multidimensional model, it is imperative to extract data from the right sources, transform the extracted data into one desired format and at last load the data into the cube to start analysis. All these aspects are discussed in detail in this chapter. For better understanding of concepts of ETL, hands-on project with screenshots of SQL Server is also given at the end of the chapter along with the dataset in the appendix.

Chapter 8 addresses critical concerns of the organisations regarding the limited functionality of OLTP. Realising this fact, organisations are steadily moving from OLTP to OLAP models because OLAP focuses on analysis of data rather than on transactions like OLTP, which enables the managers to view the data from different dimensions. This chapter deals with the important concepts of OLTP and OLAP. At the end of chapter, hands-on project is also given which helps students practically run and understand the importance of OLAP applications.

Chapter 9 stresses on the need of constant evaluation of the actions taken by the organisation in order to reach its objectives. In this chapter, all the techniques of evaluation like KPI, balanced scoredcards, KPI-based balance scorecards and dashboards are discussed in detail. For better understanding of concepts of KPI, hands-on project with screenshots of SQL Server is also given at the end of the chapter.

Chapter 10 highlights that mere reporting of the past events is not sufficient; rather organisations need to be innovatived in order to change its strategies to counter the dynamic environment; accordingly organisations are extensively applying predictive analytics. All the concepts of predictive analytics are explored in this chapter.

Chapter 11 gives a detailed account of data mining concepts. As data mining helps the organisations to mine relevant information from the data, it is of prime importance in the present time. In this chapter, the important tools and techniques of data mining are elaborated in detail.

Chapter 12 is a futuristic perspective of business analytics as this chapter throws light on the emerging areas where organisations have started applying analytics like facial analytics, retail analytics, and social media analytics and analysis of big data applying Hadoop.

Acknowledgement

I would like to sincerely express my gratitude to a number of individuals who have given me the impetus to complete a project of this magnitude. I wish to place on record my sincere thanks to Mr. Alex Siow for agreeing to review and forward this book. Mr. Alex Siow is truly an inspiration to me. Going by his achievements and his current profile as Professor, National University Singapore and Director, Strategic Technology Management Institute, Singapore, honestly I was a bit apprehensive when I approached him to review this book. But on the contrary, he readily not only agreed to review this book but also forwarded this book. Indeed his inputs have enabled me to view this subject from a completely different perspective.

Special acknowledgement goes to Shivinder Kaur and Tanveer Kajla who have contributed more directly to the contents of this book and have been of immense help to me.

I am extremely grateful to Dr. B.A. Metri, Dr. Sanjay Modi, Dr. Parveen Gill, Dr. D.P. Goyal and Dr. Harsh Vardhan Samalia who were instrumental in encouraging this endeavour and making this happen. I earnestly thank the editorial team of Cengage Learning for having faith in me and giving me opportunity to work with Cengage Learning India.

I am deeply indebted to my parents and grandparents for their unconditional love and support. This journey has been successfully treaded only with the abundance of love and support from my son and wife and I owe my heartfelt thanks and gratitude to both of them.

This book is my earnest attempt in articulating my understanding and experience towards inculcating analytical approach in budding managers. I seek feedback and suggestions (at dr.sahilraj47@gmail.com) to improve the approach and contents in all ways to enhance the value to every reader of this book.

Sahil Raj

Contents

CHAPTER 1

Introduction to Business Analytics

After going through this chapter, you will able to

- Understand the journey of information systems
- Understand the present scenario of Business Analytics
- Understand the applications of analytics
- Understand how to embed analytics in business
- Understand how to monitor and conduct competition analysis
- Understand OLAP and OLTP

INTRODUCTION

Before starting with the core concepts of business analytics, it is very important to discuss the changing paradigm in the recent past. As a student of business management, you must understand this fact that knowledge of Information Technology is very important for becoming a successful manager. Preferably, in the recent past, more and more organisations have been talking about business analytics. Even universities have either started a new course in business analytics or have included business analytics as a core paper. This is validation of the need for business analytics. But before leaping on the business analytics bandwagon, it is important to discuss the journey of the information systems from merely a transaction processing system (TPS) to providing a cutting competitive advantage by applying the concepts of business analytics. In this book, all the concepts of business analytics are discussed in an easy manner. Students need not have any specialised knowledge to understand the basic concepts and relevant case studies, and hands-on project are also given so that students can have a better understanding of the practical implementation of business analytics. In the following sections, the core concepts regarding the journey of information systems are discussed so that students can easily comprehend the advance concepts of business analytics.

Most people use statistics the way a drunkard uses a lamp post, more for support than illumination.

—Mark Twain

JOURNEY OF INFORMATION SYSTEMS

Information systems have evolved from simple TPS to DSS.

The first application of information systems in business organisations is the transaction processing system known as TPS. Initially, organisations implemented transaction processing system so as to automate the basic manual processes.

In TPS, the input is data and the output is also data, which means that managers cannot take any critical decisions applying TPS (Exhibit 1.1). But, as the organisations grew, the role of managers became more complex and demanding. The organisations felt the need for a specialised system which can provide relevant information to the managers so that the managers can take critical decisions at the right time. In this epoch, the organisations started implementing the management information systems (MIS) (Exhibit 1.2).

Exhibit 1.1 Transaction processing system

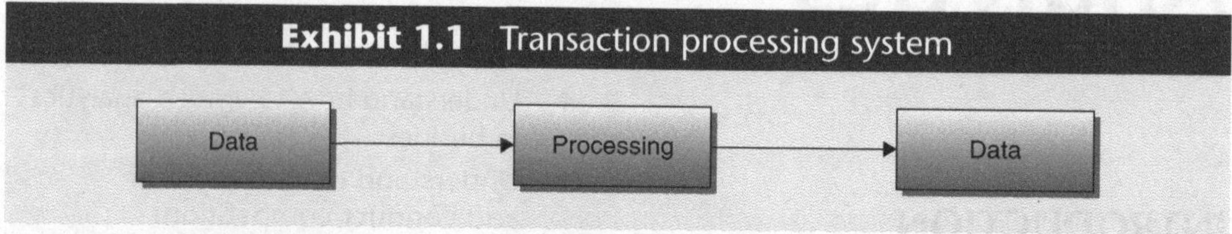

Exhibit 1.2 Management information systems

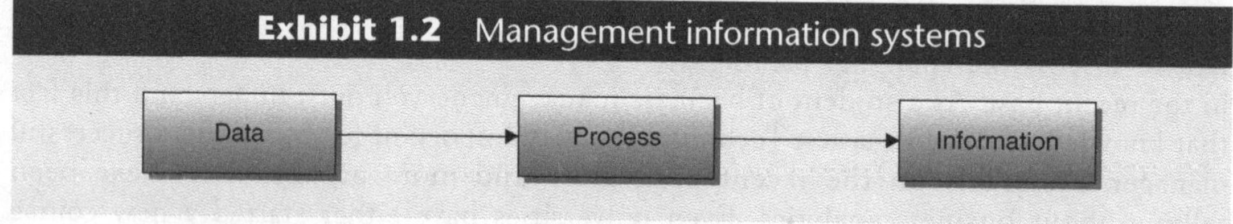

In MIS, the input is data and the output is information. The implementation of management information systems was rather a first step towards the journey of business analytics. The organisations for the first time started realising the true potential of information systems. Applying MIS, the managers could take right decisions on the basis of the right information which is provided at the right time. But with time, organisations felt that there was a need for proper segmentation of core business processes. Consequently, the organisations were split on the basis of the core business processes, i.e.,

1. Marketing
2. Finance
3. HR
4. Production

The output of TPS is data where as the output of MIS is information.

With the clear-cut segmentation in different functional areas, the organisations appointed the marketing manager, finance manager,

HR manager and production manager to manage these functional departments. With the segmentation of core business processes, each manager started managing independent profit centres. In this epoch, the organisations realised the need for a specialised information systems so as to cater to the different requirements of different managers. To facilitate the functional manager, the organisations started implementing various functional information systems such as

With the segementation of core business processes, the organisations started implementing functional information systems like

1. Marketing Information Systems
2. Finance Information Systems
3. Production Information Systems
4. HR Information Systems

1. Marketing Information Systems (Exhibit 1.3)
2. Finance Information Systems
3. Production Information Systems
4. HR Information Systems

Exhibit 1.3 Diagram of marketing information systems

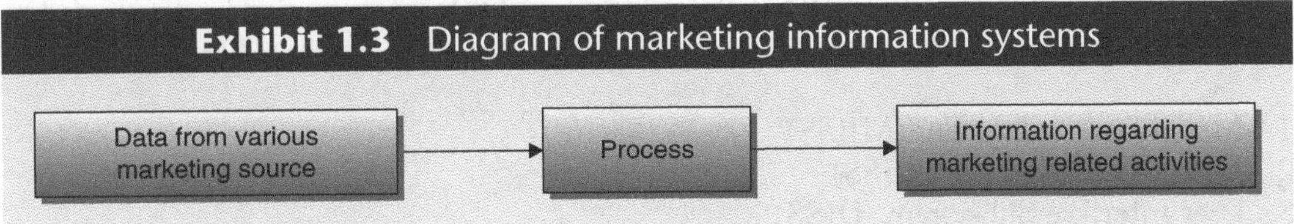

Although the functional information systems provided the much-needed information to all the functional heads, there was an urgent need for all the functional managers to interact with each other as one functional head is dependent on other functional heads. To solve this problem, organisations implemented ERP, i.e., enterprise resource planning (Exhibit 1.4).

ERP helped to integrate all the key functional areas in an organisation as a result of which all the functional heads are able to interact with each other.

Exhibit 1.4 Diagram of ERP system

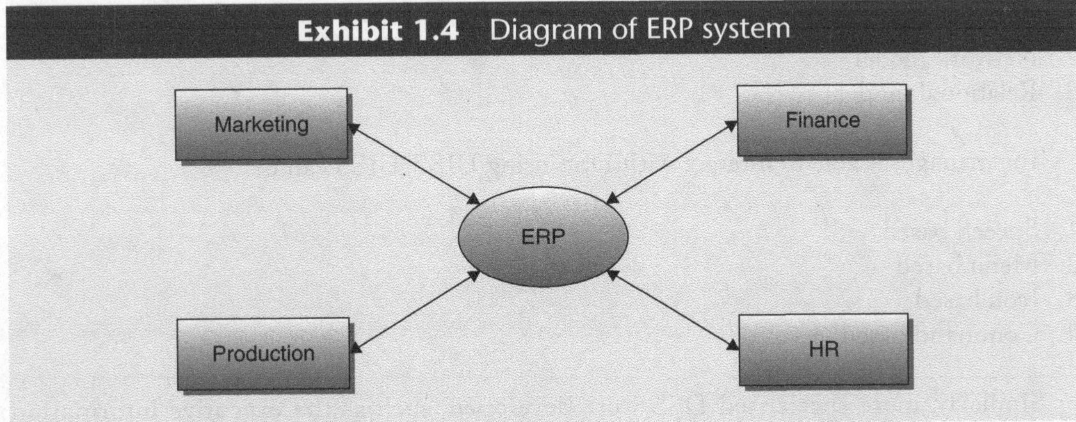

> The DSS provides the facility of What If analysis, i.e., DSS is interactive in nature. The DSS has three subsystems like
>
> 1. Model Base Subsystem (MBSS)
> 2. Database Subsystem (DBSS)
> 3. User Interface Subsystem (UISS)

ERP helped to integrate all the key functional areas in an organisation, as a result of which all the functional heads were able to interact with each other.

The information systems took another leap when organisations started implementing the decision support system (DSS). The need for DSS emerged from the fact that managers are working in a highly dynamic and unpredictable environment. Hence, it is important for managers to analyse the scenarios from different perspectives such as:

1. Decision making under certainty
2. Decision making under uncertainty
3. Decision making under risk

DSS provides the facility of What If analysis, i.e., DSS is interactive in nature. It has three subsystems:

1. Model Base Subsystem (MBSS)
2. Database Subsystem (DBSS)
3. User Interface Subsystem (UISS)

The MBSS helps the managers to relate the particular problem to the relevant scenario, and automatically a specific model is referred for answering the query of a manager. For instance, if the problem deals with the decision making under certainty, then automatically linear programming models (LPP) will be referred for fetching the results. Similarly for decision making under uncertainty, game theory models are referred and for decision making under risk, the program evaluation and review technique (PERT) and critical path method (CPM) models are referred. The DBSS provides the facility of proper storage of data. DBSS stores the data by selecting proper database models such as:

1. Hierarchical model
2. Network model
3. Relational model

The manager is able to interact with DSS using UISS. UISS can be:

1. Speech based
2. Menu based
3. Icon based
4. Command based

Similarly, more specialised DSS were developed, such as the executive information systems. Executive information systems were designed specifically for the top managers in an organisation. It helps the top managers to drill down the vast information and also allows the managers to have slice and dice facility to do an in-depth analysis considering various scenarios. Similarly, another specialised system was developed in this era, i.e., the expert systems. The expert systems provides expert knowledge to the manager. It has various sub-systems such as:

> Executive information systems helps the top managers to drill down the vast information and also allows the managers to have slice and dice facility in order to do in-depth analysis considering various scenarios.
>
> Expert systems provides expert knowledge to the manager.

1. Knowledge base
2. Inference base
3. User base
4. Updating facility

In the next phase, organisations realised the importance of knowledge for solving the problems. The organisations felt the need for developing a system where the managers can share their experience of handling specific problems so that in the future other managers can take help from the experiences recorded in the information systems which can be referred for similar future scenarios. Consequently knowledge management systems came into being.

PRESENT SCENARIO

Presently, there is immense pressure on managers. Although the end goals for any manager are the same, i.e., higher profit or lower cost, but the conditions under which these goals are to be achieved have changed drastically because the environment is so unpredictable, volatile and competitive. For example, the marketing manager needs to be proactive in deciding which product should come in the market at what time, how to market that product, which products should be marketed online and which product should be marketed offline; the finance manager needs to access the financial volatility in the environment so as to gauge the credit risk. The HR manager needs to recruit the right person and even needs to predict when a person is going to leave the organisation in the future. Similarly, operations manager needs to store optimum inventory which depends on the fact how he forecasts the future trend, which again is highly dynamic and volatile. Furthermore, unlike the past when there used to be scarcity of data, now organisations are flooded with data. The organisations are collecting not only huge amount of structured data, but also unstructured and semi-structured data.

> Although the end goals for any manager are the same, i.e., higher profit or lower cost, but the conditions under which these goals are to be achieved/fulfilled have changed drastically because the environment is so unpredictable, volatile and competitive.

Managers can not take rational decisions merely based on information. Traditional information systems just processes the data so that relevant information can be furnished to the managers. But considering the kind of dynamic environment under which the organizations are working, managers need to have insight knowledge of the data. Applying the traditional information systems, earlier managers can make reports and present these reports to the senior managers. The traditional information systems also provides the facility of knowing what is happening in the present time, i.e., manager is always aware of his present scenario. But the traditional information systems fail to provide the following solutions like

1. Why something happened in the past, i.e., reporting not only on past events, but also the causes of the issue
2. The best possible solution so that the present situation can be better handled, i.e., not only making aware of the present situation, but also guiding the managers to take best possible action
3. What are the favorable and unfavorable scenarios in future, i.e., not only extrapolation, but a prediction of the future events based on the proper analysis

Considering these facts, now organisations need not only focus on processing of data into information but also analyse the data; thoroughly so that managers can predict the future. This can be achieved by business analytics which helps the managers to analyse the voluminous data so that indepth knowledge can be gained to counter the dynamic environment and cut-throat competition.

"Nearly eight out of ten CEOs anticipate significant complexity ahead, but fewer than half feel prepared to handle it."

— IBM Global 2010 CEO Study

Business analytics is the combination of various applications which are applied by organisations to analyse the voluminous data so that managers can get in-depth knowledge from data to understand the current situation and also for the prediction of the future events. The main focus of business analytics is on multi-dimensional analysis of data so as to predict the future appropriately so that the managers can take timely actions. For the appropriate analysis of data, a business analyst takes help of various applications such as multi-dimensional modeling, ETL, data warehouse and data mining. It is high time that managers should optimally utilise the data. Organisations are collecting massive data and even processing the data, but not analysing the data for getting appropriate answers. The business analytics is indeed a necessity in the present time and is going to play even more important role in coming future. All these applications are explained in this book.

> Business analytics is the combination of various applications which are applied by organisations to analyse the voluminous data so that managers can get the in-depth knowledge from data to understand the current situation and also for prediction of the future events.

The market for worldwide business intelligence and analytics software, including BI platforms, corporate performance management suites, analytic applications and advanced analytics, totalled US$14.4 billion in 2013, up 8% from 2012 revenue of US$13.3 billion, according to new research from Gartner, Inc.

Exhibit 1.5 Diagram showing difference between MIS and business analytics

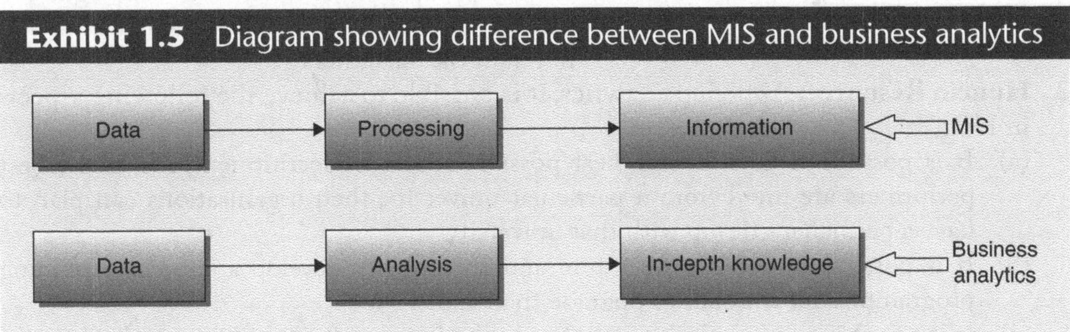

In the 2011 study, *Analytics: The widening divide*, the *MIT Sloan Management Review* and the IBM Institute for Business Value found a 57% increase—in a single year—in the number of organisations reporting that they apply analytics to create a competitive advantage.

(*Analytics: The widening divide: How companies are achieving competitive advantage through analytics*. IBM Institute for Business Value and *MIT Sloan Management Review*, 2011, page 2.)

APPLICATION OF ANALYTICS

In a recent report, Nucleus Research found that for every dollar a company spends on analytics, it gets back US$10.66.

(Nucleus Research. *Research Note: Analytics Pays Back $10.66 for Every Dollar Spent*. Document L122, November 2011, page 1.)

Analytics has a wide application in various fields, and in the following segment the application of business analytics is described in detail.

1. **Marketing**: Presently, marketing is the key functional area. The organisations are spending huge amount of money to market its products; applying the business analytics it is possible for an organisation to:

Analytics is widely applied in the areas of

1. Marketing
2. Human Resource
3. Production and Inventory
4. Finance

(a) identify the loyal customers
(b) identify the first-time customers
(c) recognise the attributes of customers who are repeat purchasers
(d) predict the changing trends and needs of customers
(e) design appropriate advertisement campaigns
(f) identify the most appropriate touch points so as to retain the customers

2. **Human Resource**: Applying analytics, it is possible to achieve the following aspects in HR:
   (a) It is possible to identify the best possible source of recruitment, i.e., if the best performers are hired from a particular university, then organisations can plan to have a permanent tie-up with that university.
   (b) It is possible to predict the future and accordingly develop appropriate training programmes for the staff to upgrade their skills.
   (c) It is possible to recognise the employee who is going to leave the organisation and also the reasons for future attrition.
3. **Production and Inventory**: The analytics can be applied in the following areas of production and inventory:
   (a) It is possible to forecast the future and accordingly plan the production process for uninterrupted manufacturing of the products.
   (b) It is possible to plan the future manpower requirement for smooth handling of the production process.
   (c) It is possible to plan future machine requirements.
   (d) It is possible to optimise the inventory levels.
   (e) It is possible to analyse which transportation method will be best suited for a particular product.
4. **Finance**: The analytics can be applied in the following areas of Finance:
   (a) It is possible to predict the future defaulters of a particular loan.
   (b) It is possible to give a loan to the most appropriate borrower.
   (c) It is possible to predict the uncertain future and to guide the finance manager to optimally manage the financial resources.

In Practice

Excellence University: Analytically Strategising

This case intends to provide an orientation to the students regarding different kinds of information that business analytics can provide to a business or an analytics user. The Excellence University is a State University offering courses in the field of MBA, MCA and Engineering. The Excellence University has more than 20,000 students and it has its main campus in the leading city of North India. As most of the states have passed the private university bill, there are many private universities coming up. Excellence University is facing a stiff competition from a number of private and other state universities. Although the infrastructure of Excellence University is by far the best, yet it is facing a tough time in the competitive environment. In the current year, the Excellence University faced many problems regarding admission, and more than half of its seats are vacant. The Excellence University had implemented a conventional information systems, but of late the management has realised that applying the conventional information systems, it is not possible to get insight into the data. The Vice Chancellor (VC) called a meeting with the various Heads of Departments and Dean (Admission) to find the reasons behind fewer admissions. The VC wanted to know in-depth information regarding the following aspects.

(a) To know the status of the number of national students and international students
(b) The reason why the students in the previous year left the course in between
(c) The key attributes of those students who are not doing well in studies
(d) The key attributes of those students who are getting good campus placements
(e) The reason why a certain number of students are not getting placed
(f) The particular industry which should be targeted on the basis of the skillset of students
(g) The future requirement of the faculty
(h) The training which should be imparted to the teachers on the basis of the industry requirement

Although the Dean (Admission) and heads of various departments had the data with them, they did not possess the tool for analysing the available data. To overcome the problem, the Excellence University implemented Business Analytics software. Applying Business Analytics software, it is possible for the Dean (Admission) and heads of various departments to get insight into the data. The management based on the complete analysis of the data framed the following strategies:

(a) Applying the Business Analytics software, it is possible to recognise the source of students, and it was analysed that in the current academic year there are few international students particularly from the African countries.
(b) The knowledge of the reason why previous-year students left the course in between has helped the management to rectify the problems. For example, most of African students had left the course in between and when analysed more precisely by applying analytics, it was found that African students are facing many problems in speaking English, and hence the management decided to start a special programme to impart English-speaking skills to African students and that will be free of cost.
(c) It was found out that students from rural background felt very hard to come up with the pressure of MBA curriculum, especially seminars and presentations. So special emphasis was given to these students.

(d) It was analysed that students coming from good private schools are getting placed.
(e) It was also found that even if a student who is good at studies but is weak in communication skills was not getting any placement in the MBA course. Although for engineering students, this is not applicable.
(f) It was analysed that presently there are many requirements from banking, IT and retail industries, so special subjects were included in the MBA course so that students can get more placement opportunities. Similarly, in the case of engineering, the students having knowledge of Database Management are more in demand, so special industry-oriented projects were started.
(g) It was analysed that going by the demand from the industry the faculty with the knowledge of IT (especially Business Analytics) should be hired.
(h) Even the in-house faculty, both in Engineering and MBA, dealing with the subjects of IT, special Business Analytics training should be imparted.

Applying the above strategies, the Excellence University received overwhelming response from students and the industry.

EMBEDDING ANALYTICS

Although business analytics gives the in-depth knowledge and analytical results in an organisation, but at the same time it should be kept in mind that business analytics demands a drastic change in executing a business strategy. This drastic change compels that organisations should first select an area or a particular target from where the analytics could be embedded in an organisation. This target area may arise from an unforeseen business scenario or a chance opportunity. The management then can take the help of analytics to find the solution. This not only helps the organisations to come out of the problem but also helps the managers to have hands on experience of the capabilities of analytics. Once this target is achieved, the next phase is of embedding analytics in an organisation is the widening of the scope of analytics. For this purpose, particular organisation can analyse the industry scenario and can take a vital clue from the competitors as to how its competitors are utilising the analytics for gaining a competitive advantage. Although this step may not help in providing a competitive advantage, it is important for organisations to remain one step ahead of its competitors. To overcome this situation, it is important that an organisation should implement analytics in those areas wherein even its competitors have not implemented. For this aspect the organisation should examine its core business processes and then evaluate where analytics can be best applied for getting the competitive advantage.

Effective embedding of analytics in an organisation helps in the widening of the scope of analytics.

Once the business processes are evaluated and selected, the next part in embedding analytics in an organisation is preparing a blue print regarding how analytics can be applied in core business areas and what kinds of results can be achieved

> IBM asked more than 2,500 CIOs from 78 countries, 19 industries and organisations of all sizes participating in its 2010 Global CIO Survey to identify one or more of their visionary plans for enhancing their competitiveness, 83% answered "business intelligence and analytics."
>
> (*The Essential CIO: Insights from the Global Chief Information Officer Study*, IBM Institute for Business Value, 2011, page 6.)

from analytics. For example, if an organisation has selected the HR area where analytics should be embedded, then it is important to prepare a blueprint of the possible changes in HR activities that will occur when analytics will be applied. If a particular organisation is facing the problem of a high attrition rate, and it has decided to use analytics to solve the problem. The analytics will answer the following questions:

1. What is the cause of attrition?
2. What are the attributes of the employees such as gender, marital status, number of dependants and area of posting so forth who are leaving the organisation?
3. What could be done to avoid attrition, i.e., a proper recruitment model should be developed?

EFFECTIVE IMPLEMENTATION OF ANALYTICS

For the proper implementation of business analytics, firms need to constantly monitor the environment to adapt to the dynamics of it and also need to analyse its competitors to understand the analytical of competitors. Both these factors have been discussed in detail in the following section.

> Effective implementation of analytics require
>
> 1. Constant Monitoring
> 2. Competition Analysis

Constant Monitoring

With the changing environment, the organisations have to alter its strategies to counter the dynamic forces. As business analytics is applied by organisations to apply the set strategies, it is also imperative that when an organisation changes its strategy, it should also review the business analytical methods/models which may become redundant with the implementation of

> Business analytics is applied by organisations in order apply the set strategies. It is also imperative that when an organisation changes its strategy, it should also review the business analytical methods/models which may become redundant with the implementation of the new strategy.

the new strategy. Moreover, it is also important for organisations to reset the analytical target so as to adjust it according to the changing environmental needs and competitors.

As the environment is so dynamic and if a particular organisation keeps on applying same analytical model then the organisation will not be able to get the desired results from that analytical model. For instance,

1. With changed environment, sources and even quality of data may change which may demand different types of profiling and integration techniques.
2. Particular organisation, according to its need implement the business analytics software, but it is also important for organisations to constantly review the current software package and then take a decision whether to continue with the same package or to buy a new one.
3. The changing preferences of customers should be taken into account in reviewing the analytical approach of an organisation. As with time, customers' needs and wants also change. Hence it is imperative that organisations should also change its analytical approach.

Competition Analysis

Initially, a particular organisation may get competitive advantage by analytically reviewing the collected data. But with time, its competitors also start implementing same analytical review models/methods of the organisation and eventually the organisation loses its competitive advantage. Hence, in order to review own analytical methods/ models, it is important that organisations should firstly review the analytical position of its competitors. In the following section, competitive analytical capability model is described. Applying this model, the organisation can review the analytical capability of its competitors and also can evaluate the future potential of its competitors. Once the organisation reviews the present and future analytical capability of its competitors, then it is possible for the organisation to review its analytical capability and accordingly it can take appropriate decision to enhance its analytical approach.

According to competitive analytical capability model, there are four types of competitiors:

1. **Back Benchers:** The Back Benchers are those competitors who are not interested in applying business analytics to its business processes. These organisations are only applying the conventional information systems to do just the processing of data and traditional reporting of the events.
2. **Followers:** These competitors are ardent followers of your organisation; whatever methods/models you are applying, all those methods/models are diligently adopted/copied by these followers.
3. **Threats:** The next category of competitors is about threats. These competitors are not only following the business analytical methods/models of your organisation,

There are four types of competitors:

1. Back Benchers
2. Followers
3. Threats
4. Stars

but also constantly applying new methods/models to give a tough competition to your organisation.

4. **Stars:** These competitors are leaders. These organisations are very aggressive in their approach and apply business analytics in this core activity. These organisations apply business analytics to predict the uncertain future and are truly leading the race.

Competition Analysis Matrix

	Present	Future
Stars	C5	C4
Threats	C4	C3, C5
Follower	C3	C2
Back Bencher	C1, C2	C1

In the above matrix, five competitors are depicted as C1, C2, C3, C4 and C5.

1. ***C*1:** This competitor is Back Bencher in the present and is going by the commitment of management; even in the future it is going to remain as a Back Bencher.
2. ***C*2:** This competitor is Back Bencher in the present scenario, but of late the management has started recognising the analytical methods/modules of your organisation and in the future it can be a follower of your organisation.
3. ***C*3:** The C3 competitor falls in the category of followers, but in the future it has the potential of becoming a threat.
4. ***C*4:** The C4 competitor lies in the category of threat. But as the management is very committed to applying analytics to the core business activities, this can become a star in the future.
5. ***C*5:** The C5 competitor lies in the category of a star at present, but management seems to be complacent and is just not reviewing its analytical model and it may result that in the future C5 can slip in the category of threat.

KEY TO SUCCESS

For obtaining the best results from business analytics, the following aspects should be considered by the organisations.

Key to success include

1. Data
2. Method
3. Involvement
4. Training
5. Plan
6. Sharing

1. **Data**: Data are the base of any business analytical process. For getting appropriate results, it is important that appropriate data should be collected by the organisation. Although there is influx of data sources, it is essential that organisations should select appropriate data sources so that the right data can be collected.

Organisations should also segregate the data as structured, unstructured and semi-structured data.

2. **Method**: Business analytics helps to analyse the data in a proper manner, which can be done by applying various methods/models. Moreover, there are various software tools with which business analytics can be implemented. But, the organisation should do self-introspection to know its strength and weakness so that the appropriate method and tool of analytics can be selected.
3. **Involvement**: To get the best results from business analytics, it is imperative that the top management should be actively involved in embedding business analytics in an organisation so that employees should not view that business analytics is an isolated department or practice; rather it should be embedded in the basic functionality of an organisation.
4. **Training**: Embededness of business analytics in an organisation results in a drastic change in the way of functioning of employees in an organisation. To get the best results from business analytics, proper training should be imparted to the employees of an organisation. After selecting the proper tool (Step 2), it is necessary to impart training so that employees can understand the potential of analytics.
5. **Plan**: It is important to have a proper plan for embedding analytics in an organisation. In an organisation, there are various functional departments and some functional heads may be more interested in embedding business analytics; hence, the organisation can start implementation of analytics from that functional department. Then, through the iterative process the complete implementation of business analytics in other departments can be done in an organisation.
6. **Sharing**: It is important that an organisation should plan which aspects of business analytics will be shared with the customers and other business partners. Business analytics does give great results to an organisation, but it also provides crucial and confidential information regarding an organisation. Hence, it is important to draw a line that segments which aspects will be shared with customers and other business partners and which aspects will not be shared.

OLTP AND OLAP

While previously the organisations applied OLTP to analyse the online transactions, now as the environment is becoming more and more dynamic, the organisations are applying OLAP to analyse the complex data. OLTP or Online transaction processing systems are client server applications which are generally applied for transaction-oriented applications. It enables quick access to data to multiple users and finds extensive applications in areas where real-time information is required by business users such as banks, airlines, retail stores and other areas involving data entry. The underlying data model for OLTP is a relational data model.

> OLTP stands for online transaction processing system.
> OLAP stands for online analytical processing system.

OLAP or online analytical processing systems are utilised to conduct analysis of data rather than transactions such as OLTP. OLAP enables a multidimensional view of data, or analysis of data from different business perspectives. It not only aids in fast retrieval of data, but also can conduct several operations on data such as drilling down the data to the lowest level of data, or rolling up from the lowest level to the highest level of data. Besides, it also aids in reporting and pivoting of data. Each of these concepts has been discussed in detail in a complete chapter devoted to OLAP and OLTP.

CONCLUSION

From the above discussion, it is evident that business analytics is becoming imperative for the success of any firm. The firms have traversed through different types of information systems, which has led to a huge accumulation of data. Hence unlike the past where there used to be a scarcity of data, now organisations are flooded with data. The organisations are not only collecting huge amount of not only structured data, but also unstructured and semi-structured data. Considering this fact, now organisations not only need to focus on processing of data into information rather the organisations need to analyse the data, the managers need to accurately depict the present scenario so that future can be predicted. Business analytics helps the managers to analyse the voluminous data so that in-depth knowledge can be gained to counter the dynamic enviornment and cut-throat competition.

KEY TERMS

- Journey of Information Systems 2
- Transaction Processing Systems 2
- Management Information Systems 2
- Functional information systems 3
- ERP 3
- Decision Support Systems 4
- Executive Information Systems 4
- Expert Systems 5
- Knowledge Management Systems 5
- Business Analytics 6
- Application of Analytics 7
- Embedding Analytics 10
- Constant Monitoring 11
- Competition Analysis 12
- Key Aspects 13

SUMMARY

In this chapter, we studied about the journey of information systems from transaction processing systems to executive information and expert systems. The chapter also highlighted why there is a need for business analytics. Besides, a greater emphasis was laid on a discussion of application of analytics and how to embed analytics in business functions and processes. We understood that for successful implementation of business analytics, we need to constantly monitor the environment in order to understand the changing customer's preference, varied nature data and to gauge the analytical software capabilities and analyse our competitor's analytic strategy. For analyzing competitor's analytical capability, competitive analytical capability model is discussed in detail with the help of which an organisation can divide its competitors as Stars, Threats, Followers and Back Benchers. The chapter also stressed upon the fact that the present-day managers need to understand the role of data, method, involvement and training for successful implementation of business analytics in a firm.

MULTIPLE CHOICE QUESTIONS

1. The main application of the transaction processing system is
   a. To provide information b. To automate manual work
   c. To provide knowledge d. Decision making

2. Management information systems is designed
   a. To automate manual work b. To provide knowledge
   c. To perform what-if analysis d. To provide information

3. Choose the odd one out
   a. Decision making under certainty b. Decision making under uncertainty
   c. Decision making under stress d. Decision making under risk

4. Which of the following is not a subsystem of decision support systems
   a. MBSS b. DBSS
   c. UISS d SISS

5. Enterprise resource planning helps in
   a. Interaction of all functional information systems
   b. Collection of data
   c. Interpret data
   d. Expert knowledge

6. Which of the following is not a subsystem of expert systems
   a. Knowledge base b. Inference base
   c. Strategic base d. User base

7. Business analytics provides
   a. Data b. Information
   c. Strategic information d. Knowledge

8. Back benchers in competitive analysis are organisations who apply analytics
   a. Strategically b. Proactively
   c. Rarely d. Never

9. Followers in competitive analysis are organisations who apply analytics
   a. Strategically b. Proactively
   c. Copy your analytical approach d. Never any analytics

10. The organisations which are not only following your analytical model, but also applying analytical methods in new areas are known as
    a. Back benchers b. Followers
    c. Threats d. Stars

11. The organisations which are very aggressive in its approach and are applying business analytics in its core activities are known as
    a. Back benchers b. Followers
    c. Threats d. Stars

12. Which of the following is the most important factor for success of implementing business analytics in an organisation
    a. Data b. Hardware
    c. Software d. Trained staff

13. OLTP is applied for
    a. Analysis of data b. Provides knowledge
    c. Strategy formulation d. Transaction-oriented applications

14. OLAP is applied in organisation to
    a. Have a single-dimensional view of data
    b. Have two-dimensional view of data
    c. Have three-dimensional view of data
    d. Have multi-dimensional view of data

15. To have a complete multidimensional analysis of data which type of application is needed
    a. TPS b. MIS
    c. DSS d. Business analytics

REVIEW QUESTIONS

1. Discuss the journey of information systems from transaction processing systems to business analytics.

2. What is the need for business analytics in the present business scenario?

3. Discuss the applications of business analytics in the core areas of an organisation.
4. "Even the best Business Analytics Models need constant evaluation". Comment on this statement.

ASSIGNMENT

1. The topic of discussion is "Need to move from Management Information Systems to Business Analytics". Divide the class into two groups and one group should argue in favour of MIS and other group should highlight the limitations of MIS and need of business analytics.

CASE STUDY

ELKAN Medicine

ELKAN medicine is a pioneer firm in research in medicine. This company is constantly engaged in inventing new drugs, and over the years, it has emerged as a leading company in the field of research. ELKAN medicine was founded in 1995 with the sole aim of inventing new medicines for healthcare in India. Over the years, ELKAN medicines have also ventured into hospitals and presently it has more than 20 hospitals in leading cities of India. These hospitals are an excellent source of voluminous health-related data for ELKAN medicine. Because India is a diverse country with many variations in climate and eating habits among different regions, the data collected by ELKAN medicine from its hospitals located in different regions provide an exciting platform for healthcare analytics. Realising this, ELKAN medicine is focusing on proper analysis of the collected data. To analyse the data, ELKAN medicine has developed a **Healthcare Analytics Systems (HAS)** integrated with **Geographic Information Systems (GIS). GIS** stores, integrates, edits, shares, analyses and exhibits geographic information for appraising decision making. GIS applications facilitate decision makers or users to analyse geographical information and compare different areas to understand patterns between them. Although GIS is widely applied in oil exploration, transportation and e-governance, this property of GIS to track and aid in comparison of geographical areas finds extensive applications in HAS of ELKAN medicine.

ELKAN medicine has applied GIS technology in developing its Healthcare Analytics Systems. HAS is fetching all the data from ELKAN's hospitals. All hospitals at ELKAN medicine incorporate a standardised system to collect patient's data in a proper format such as name of person, age, gender, pin code and area name. All this information is then stored in a central database. To validate the pin codes and area specified by the patient, the data entry by the patient is cross verified by HAS. This is done through the application of GIS technology integrated in HAS. GIS is already a repository of geographical information about India, and hence it can crosscheck the entered area and pin codes. By applying mapping technology, even the longitude and latitude of the area are traced. To augment its analytical abilities, HAS has gone a step ahead and integrated census data into its system. All this information, namely, Patient data, GIS and Census data, serves as input to HAS. Using all this information, ELKAN medicine has not only been able to gain a competitive edge in the healthcare industry, but it is also a leader in serving the society in the best possible manner.

Exhibit 1.6 Healthcare analytics system

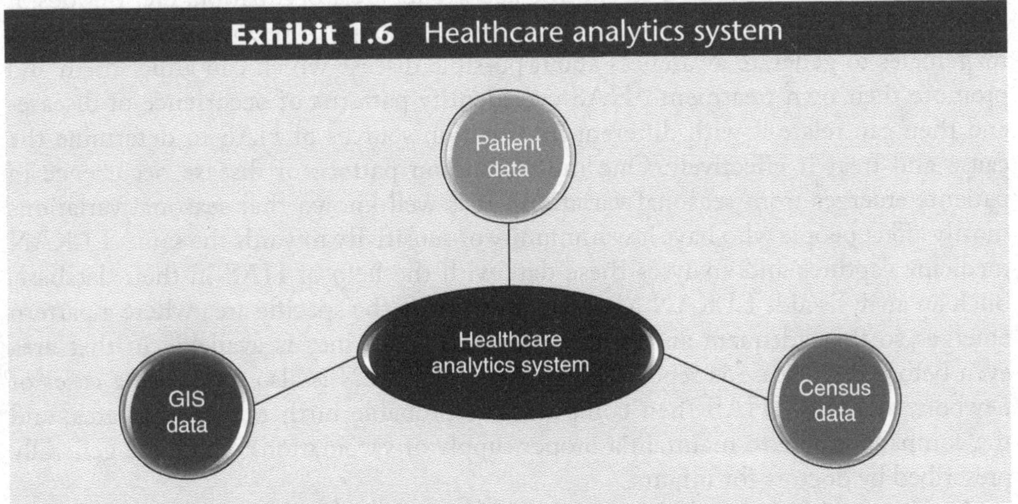

Application of analytics aids ELKAN medicine to perform a complete analysis of collected data and to yield various beneficial outcomes. HAS has made it possible, for ELKAN medicine to predict the possible outbreak of an epidemic in a particular area. For example, analytics can identify if large numbers of incidents are reported with the same disease from a given area. From the patient data entry and diagnosis stored in the system, HAS can tab the number of patients diagnosed with the same specific disease within a small time period coming from a particular area. This information can then be used as an indicator of some possible epidemic that can spread in that area. ELKAN medicine can then generate awareness in people in those areas to prevent the outbreak, or measures to be taken in case a person gets afflicted by the disease and can also monitor the supply of medicines required to treat that disease so that there is no shortage in the chance of an outbreak. Besides, it is also possible using HAS to know the attributes of the persons who are infected with a particular disease. This is because HAS at ELKAN tracks not only diseases, but also geographical information and census information. Census data contain demographic details categorised by geographical areas. ELKAN has been successfully able to map certain diseases to certain attributes of patients. For example, HAS suggests that diseases such as cardiac ailments, joint pains have high levels of occurrence in elder people. Ortho-related ailments have a high incidence of occurrence in females. This information has also been utilised by ELKAN to map to the lifestyle of people. Further, if a high number of people in a given area of a particular age group report backache, HAS maps area to census data which suggests the occupation taken by people in that area. If the mapping yields a similar occupational background for most of the people in that area, backaches can be probably attributed to that occupation. All this information helps ELKAN medicine to research for possible medicines to cure such diseases which are attributed to specific age group, area, occupation, etc. Besides, it also launches campaigns targeted at such specific groups of people such as for aged, for females to generate awareness about possible disease which can afflict them and promote their own treatments. HAS can identify patterns of occurrence of diseases and then can relate it with different information sources of HAS to determine the cause and treat it effectively. One most common pattern of disease occurrence in patients emerges from seasonal variations. It is well known that seasonal variations mostly affect people who have low immunity or sensitivity towards the same. ELKAN medicine captures and analyses these data with the help of HAS in their database. Such an analysis aids ELKAN Medicine to identify the specific area where a pattern emerges so that adequate and timely supply of medicines is available in that area even before the disease is reported by patients. ELKAN is also monitoring cases of newborn area-wise. HAS then computes the probable birth rate in that area, and the company is able to maintain a proper supply of vaccinations which are generally prescribed by doctors for infants.

Another application of HAS is identification of diseases prevalent in a particular area. Analysis of diagnosis by doctors of ELKAN hospitals for such specific diseases suggests contamination of natural resources, such as air, water, due to radiations or presence of harmful chemicals in the same. Careful monitoring of these diseases by ELKAN from regional perspective aids in pinpointing the specific geographical areas so that new medicines can be developed to treat such particular diseases. Recently, ELKAN medicine has also included the list of all the fast food joints, hotels and restaurants in a given area in their database. This information aids ELKAN to track possible eating disorders in a particular area, which can be the reason for diseases such as obesity, acidity, etc. in those areas. With the help of HAS software, it is possible to analyse the data of patients suffering from obesity, acidity, gastro-enteritis, etc. and to relate that information with eating joints present in that specific area to find out the eating habits of the people in that particular area. When analysis reveals high incidence of obese patients from an area which has a large number of eating joints as well, ELKAN Medicine has taken an initiative to open its own slimming centres at appropriate locations in such areas. Moreover, in these identified areas, doctors at

ELKAN Hospitals suggest their patients to follow a strict dietary regime and usage of weight loss shakes manufactured by ELKAN.

ELKAN Medicine also provides emergency services such as ambulances and first-aid services. Some areas are prone to accidents and in several cases of critically injured people chances of death are high as emergency services do not reach the accident spot in time. To avoid these kinds of circumstances, the company is applying HAS software to identify the accident-prone areas. It analyses the data regarding emergency accident cases reported at its own hospitals and other hospitals in the areas providing emergency services, where people were critically injured. This application of analytics has enabled ELKAN Medicine to identify accident-prone areas and to deploy ambulances 24×7 at such spots where chances of critical injury are higher. It also provides on-the-spot first-aid services at such locations to minimise the response time and increase the chances of survival of patients.

Questions

1. What do we understand by GIS? How did ELKAN implement GIS to develop a healthcare analytics system?
2. How does HAS at ELKAN aid in prediction of epidemic outbreaks?
3. How has ELKAN been able to provide timely emergency services?
4. What can possible advantages be gained by combining eating joints data with patients' data at ELKAN HAS?

PROJECT ACTIVITY

1. Visit a nearby retail store and discuss with the store manager that how he/she is doing the analysis of data. Prepare a report summarising the current analysis done by the store manager and identify the areas where analytics can be applied.

REFERENCES

Baars, H., and Kemper, H.G. (2008). Management support with structured and unstructured data—an integrated business intelligence framework. *Information Systems Management*, 25(2), 132–48.

Bhatt, G.D., and Grover, V. (2005). Types of information technology capabilities and their role in competitive advantage: an empirical study. *Journal of Management Information Systems*, 22(2), 253–77.

Davenport, T.H. (2006). "Competing on Analytics," *Harvard Business Review,* 84(1), 98–107.

Dekkers, J., Versendaal, J., and Batenburg, R. (2007). Organizing for business intelligence: a framework for aligning the use and development of information. Proceedings of the 20th Bled eConference eMergence, Bled, Slovenia, 625–36.

Evans, J.R. (2013). *Business Analytics: Methods, models, and decisions.* Upper Saddle River, NJ: Prentice-Hall.

"Guide to the IIBA Body of Knowledge: An Outline—Release 1.0, Version 1." www.iiba.com. 2005. International Institute of Business Analysis. 10 November 2005.

Gregor, S. (2006). The nature of theory in information systems. *Management Information Systems Quarterly*, 30(3), 611–42.

<http://www.iiba.com/pdf/bok/BOKRelease1.0Version1.0.pdf>

Kohavi, R., Rothleder, N.J., and Simoudis, E. (2002). Emerging trends in business analytics. Communications of the ACM, 45(8), 45–8.

"Managing Risk Using Business Analysis: Implementing Best Practices to Reduce analytics and competitive advantage: a review and a research agenda." Paper presented at the Fifth International Federation of Information Processing WG International Conference on Decision Support Systems, Lisbon, Portugal.

Project Risk. Participant survey during online presentation. ESI International: 22 March 2005, <http://www.esi-intl.com/public/news/20050322WebinarMangingRisk.asp>.

Sharma, R., Reynolds, P., Scheepers, R., Seddon, P., and Shanks, G. (2010). Business.

The Economist, The Data Deluge: Data data everywhere, Handling the cornucopia, New rules for big data, The open society, All too much, Clicking for Gold, Feb 2010.

Turban, E., Sharda, R., Aronson, J.E., and King, D. (2008). *Business Intelligence: A Managerial Approach*, Boston: Pearson Prentice Hall.

CHAPTER 2

Moving Ahead with Analytics

After going through this chapter, you will be able to

- Understand how *Business Analytics as Solution for Business Challenges*
- Understand the concept of Data Profiling
- Understand the concept of Data Integrity
- Understand the concept of Master Data Management
- Understand the Applications Areas of Business Analytics
- Understand the Prerequisites Requirements for effective Business Analytics
- Understand LOFT Effect
- Understand Future of Business Analytics

INTRODUCTION

At the present time, organisations are making data-driven decision making. But for taking data-driven decision making, it is very important to properly analyse the data. This analysis is done with the help of business analytics. Business analytics and business intelligence are often used interchangeably, but in this book we are dealing with business analytics. Business intelligence tells us what has happened, but business analytics tells the organisation that why it has happened. With the help of business analytics, organisations can perform three types of analyses.

- Descriptive Analysis—It is based on historical data
- Predictive Analysis—This helps in proper forecasting of the future events
- Prescriptive Analysis—It gives a proper prescription so that the same mistake will not be committed in the future

Data are the lifeline for any organisation. Managers need to analyse the data so that rational decisions could be taken by organisations. For this purpose, organisations need data-literate managers. In the IBM 2012 Partner World Conference, its CEO predicted that analytics will be the thread that weaves together front- and back-office systems to harness huge volumes of unstructured data for competitive business advantage. In other words, we can say that business analytics is that tool which brings data from different sources at one platform and helps organisations to use the data efficiently for achieving its business objectives. All the aspects related to the application of business analytics and pre-requisites for effective analytics implementation will be discussed in this chapter.

BUSINESS ANALYTICS AS SOLUTION FOR BUSINESS CHALLENGES

Organisations are working in a highly dynamic environment in which there is much uncertainty regarding the future. Organisations cannot apply hit and trial method to formulate strategies for gaining a competitive advantage. Organisations need to analyse the data precisely so that proper strategies can be formulated to overcome uncertainty in the future. The economic downfall has also compounded the problems for organisations. The growth is slow and the overall business scenario is not bright. But, there is some silver lining in the dark clouds; of late business is picking up and it is high time that organisations should not sit and wait for opportunities to come.

Rather, organisations should attempt to create opportunities by generating insights from the data available at hand. The competition is also increasing with each passing day. Organisations need to be very much innovative so as to attract and retain customers. As new organisations are entering the market with innovative ideas and business models, even well-established organisations with deep pockets cannot be complacent. Moreover, with the advent of the Internet, new organisations are using the technology to overcome the investment barriers. Yebhi.com and Flipkart.com are examples of two such firms which have just started business, yet powered by technology; they are giving competition to big retail stores. Hence, it is high time that organisations need to analyse the data so that it can overcome the intense competition. But to overcome competition, organisations need to have in-depth knowledge of competitors. In past, when competition used to be very minimal, organisations applied only simple information systems to analyze the limited data, but present scenario is completely opposite to the past and managers need to completely analyze voluminous data owing to cut throat competition in the market. This demands the application of business analytics so that managers can analyze complex voluminous data from various dimensions to formulate strategies in order to overcome the competition.

> Slow industry growth, Advent of Internet, Customer is emerging as major challenge; Dynamic environment calls for continuous innovation and voluminous growth of data are some of the key business challenges faced by all firms.

Customers are also a major force to reckon with as at the present time customers are not

Exhibit 2.1 Expert viewpoint

In 2013, expenditures on customer relationship management software increased by 13 percent to over $20 billion, according to Gartner. The technology is not going away anytime soon: Joanne Correia, research vice president at Gartner, notes "CRM will be at the heart of digital initiatives in the coming years. This is one technology area that will get funding because digital business is critical for companies to remain competitive."

loyal; consequently, organisations need to constantly change their strategies so as to retain customers. Organisations need to look for various reasons behind why the customer is purchasing the product of competitors, the timing of the purchase, pricing of the product, availability of the product, etc. To win the loyalty of customers is a very difficult task, but this task can be accomplished by proper analysing of the data. With business analytics, organisations can formulate those strategies which help organisations to retain their customers. But this process of application of business analytics should be an ongoing process. Organisations need to consistently devise new plans and products to win the confidence of customers; otherwise, organisations will not be able to survive in the competitive world. For example, Kodak used to be the market leader in the photographic print film but failed to read the pulse of customers as customers wanted a new technology with which they can store and share photographs. This was capitalised by Sony and Canon who brought digital cameras in the market. Similarly, Bajaj used to be the market leader in scooter, but it was failing to innovate and took the loyalty of customers for granted and paid a heavy price when Kinetic entered the market with gearless scooter and captured the entire market. These facts prove the point that organisations need to constantly innovate and managers need to apply those strategies which are based on a proper analysis of data. This analysis reveals the hidden secrets in the collected data. In the present time, the scenario is entirely different as there is flood of data. Organisations are collecting and storing huge volumes of data. These data are collected not only from Point of Sales, but with the advent of the Internet, organisations are capturing much data regarding what you have searched, the timing of the search, the products and even color and size of the product. Just imagine you have not purchased anything as you are just surfing and data are captured by the organisations. But, the real problem starts now. It is very important to properly analyse the captured data; otherwise, it is wastage of a crucial resource. With proper Business Analytics tool, organisations can decipher the secrets hidden in the captured data.

From the above discussion, it is quite evident that in the present time organisations need business analytics so as to counter the competition and to win the loyalty of the customers. Hence, you may think that organisations should have a business analyst so as to achieve the above-mentioned objectives. But, it should be kept in mind that merely appointing a business analyst will not deliver the required results. It is very important that the manager should have acquired Business Analytics skills so that he/she can understand and know the true potential of business analytics. Going one step ahead, the concerned manager should also get full support from top management to get the best results from business analytics. To achieve this objective, it is also important that top management should also value the business analytics as a mandatory tool in the present dynamic business scenario. Without the support and commitment of top management, the manager will face many difficulties and will not be able to deliver the results. The concerned manager also needs a team who understands the concepts of business analytics. It is the job of a manager to shortlist the goals and objectives of the business analytics team. This activity should be done by considering the overall goals and objectives of the organisation as the goals and objectives of the business analytics team should be in sync with the overall objectives of the organisation. The business analytics team requires specialised tools and technology to perform analysis of data. The organisations should provide the requisite tools and technology to the team.

Moreover, the tools and technology for business analytics are quite expensive; hence, the top management should not be in a hurry to recover all the cost in one go. The business analytics team should be given a considerable time to show its worth.

One of the most important requirements for the business analytics team is the data. Any unreliability in the data will lead to inaccurate analysis and results. Hence, it is very important that the business analytics team should get accurate and reliable data for further analysis of data. Data are usually spread all over the organisation. There are various departments in an organisation, and moreover an organisation is working in different cities or even in different countries. Hence, it is very important that all the concerned managers should work in coordination for the collection and storage of data at one place. This coordination also helps in checking data duplicity, which is very detrimental in business analytics.

The main role of a manager is to take rational decisions. Earlier with the help of information systems, managers used to get the required information for taking rational decisions, but considering the kind of environment in which organisations operate information provided by these information systems is not sufficient. The managers need to do an in-depth analysis of huge volumes of data from different perspectives, which is collected and stored by the organisation. This is possible with the help of business analytics. Business analytics provides the required knowledge to managers for taking rational decisions. As management is the combination of art and science, in the same manner, business analytics is the combination of art and science. Business analytics involves certain scientific applications such as Statistical analysis and predictive analysis, which gives an impression that business analytics essentially belongs to the scientific field. But for applications of these scientific principles, a manager has to apply his own skills such as judgment as to which tool is best suited at which situation and interpretation of results. These aspects are not based on any rule. Managers have to think and mould the applications of business analytics according to the particular situation. This perspective demands creativity and managerial capabilities of managers. But, business analytics is heavily dependent on the data and at the present time there is flood of data. These voluminous data have its own pros and cons. Organisations are gathering data from different sources, which is very much needed to apply any business analytics tool. But, on the hindsight, it is very difficult to ascertain the quality of these voluminous data. The bad quality of data will deliver inappropriate results. Here again, managers play a very important role to ensure proper quality of data. Various techniques, such as data profiling, data integrity and master data management, are applied by organisations to ensure the quality of data. In the following sections, all the fundamental concepts regarding data profiling, data integrity and master data management are discussed in detail.

DATA PROFILING

The process of examining the quality of data is known as data profiling. This examination of data should be done in a very systematic manner.

As the competition is becoming more and more intense with each passing day, organisations have realised that to remain in the market it is imperative to apply information systems. The result was the implementation of information systems right from TPS to MIS (DSS, ERP, CRM), etc. These technologies were applied by organisations so as to help managers in better decision-making. Although functionality of these information systems is different, one thing is common in all the systems, i.e., data. Even the success of business analytics is also dependent on data. If the quality of data is not appropriate, then it is not possible to get accurate results by applying any type of technology. In other words, we can say that if the quality of data is appropriate, then it will result in getting maximum benefits from any type of information system. Hence, it will not be wrong to say that it is data which are the heart of any type of information systems. But organisations have realised this aspect partially as presently organisations are collecting huge volumes of data with the hope that the mere collection of data will result in a better analysis and hence decision making. Organisations are also collecting different types of data, i.e., structured, semi-structured and unstructured data. But, organisations are not focusing on other important aspect of data, i.e., quality of data. The process of examining the quality of data is known as data profiling. This examination of data should be done in a very systematic manner. As organisations are collecting huge volumes of data, it becomes a very challenging job for any organisation to screen the data. Data profiling is very important because it helps organisations to know the quality of data, and accordingly, organisations can decide whether a particular data is fit for a particular application or not. Talking from the perspective of business analytics, it is the job of a business analyst (in coordination with a concerned manager) to check the quality of data to judge whether the data is fit for business analytics applications. As pointed out by the Gartner Group that through 2005 "more than 50% of Business Intelligence and CRM deployments will suffer limited acceptance, if not outright failure, due to lack of alternation to data quality issues". (A strategic approach to improving data quality", by Ted Fredem, Gartner Group, 19 June 2002).

In the light of the above discussion, the question arises as to how to do data profiling. In the following section, various techniques of data profiling are discussed.

1. **Composition Detail**: The business analyst first looks at the basic composition of the data. The analyst scans the columns and tries to visualise whether all the columns are filled with data or there are some null values or duplicity in data. The analyst at this stage also takes the help of metadata. Metadata has a detailed description of all the data such as data type, primary key, null count, max value, minimum value, etc. Metadata helps the analyst to see whether the data actually adhere to the metadata statistics or not.
2. **Format Detail**: As organisations are collecting data from different sources, even data regarding the same entity are collected from different locations, sometimes even from different countries; hence, it is very important to crosscheck the format of data. For example, in India the weight is generally measured in kilograms, whereas in USA it is measured in lb; similarly, data can be stored in different date formats such as 26/Dec/2008,

Data profiling techniques are:

1. Composition Detail
2. Format Detail
3. Statistical Analysis
4. Relationship Detail

26/12/2008, 26/12/08 and so on. It is important that data should be stored in one format; otherwise, it will give inappropriate results.

3. **Statistical Analysis**: Considering the amount of data which are collected presently, it is important that the analyst should take the help of statistics to check the quality of data. Even simple statistical techniques such as mean, max value, min value, median, standard deviation and standard error can give much-needed insights into the quality of data. For example, if the data are regarding marks and the analyst knows that marks vary from 0 to 100, various techniques of statistics can help to check the quality of data such as maximum value and minimum value in the data; mean can give the analyst an idea as to whether the data really lie between 0 and 100 and also the standard deviation can tell the variation in the data. Similarly, frequency count helps to know about how many times a particular entity has occurred in the collected data. For example, the same city Delhi can be recorded as DCH, DEL, DELHI and by applying frequency count even in a huge database comprising thousands of entries, the analyst can find out whether the same city is recorded in different formats and if yes then how many times and in which format.
4. **Relationship Detail**: Because organisations are collecting data from all possible sources, to manage the data for an effective analysis organisations store data in the form of a database. To manage databases, various types of relations among stored data are created. The business analyst should carefully analyse the nature of these relationships and also the corresponding entries in the database to match the relationships. The analyst should refer to metadata to find out the relationships. The analyst after judging the relationship then should analyse whether any relationship calls for a primary key/foreign key. The analyst then should also crosscheck the primary key to see whether the primary key is uniquely identified or not. All these aspects are taken care in detail in this part of data profiling.

DATA INTEGRITY

"Data integration tools are evolving towards the unification of structured and unstructured data and will begin to include semantic capabilities. Gartner envisions data services guided by an enterprise information management strategy to maximize the value and accessibility of information."

—Gartner

As data are the lifeblood for business analytics and any corruption in data can seriously hamper the results of business analytics, data integrity refers to maintaining the accuracy and consistency in the data. It is very important that the integrity of data should be maintained throughout the entire life cycle of data; otherwise, even the best analytics tools will not give accurate results.

Data integrity refers to maintaining the accuracy and consistency in the data.

Data integrity is divided into five parts.

1. **Physical Integrity**: Physical integrity refers to the storage and retrieval of data. Physical integrity deals with the structure of the data. Data can be corrupted or lost due to

hardware failure, power failure or natural hazards. It is important that due diligence should be given to store data accurately, for example,

- *Proper backup procedures should be adopted*
- *There should be uninterrupted power supply*
- *Proper provisions to safeguard the hardware equipments in case of any natural calamity*

> Data integrity includes:
>
> 1. Physical Integrity
> 2. Logical Integrity
> 3. Rule Integrity
> 4. Attribute Integrity
> 5. Concurrency Integrity

2. **Logical Integrity**: Logical integrity is rather the most important aspect regarding data integrity. Logical integrity deals with the rationality and consistency of the data. Logical integrity is maintained by
   (a) *Entity Integrity*: Entity integrity reinforces that there should be a primary key in the parent table. The primary key should have
      (i) No null values
      (ii) Values should be unique
   (b) *Referential Integrity*: Referential integrity reinforces the need for a foreign key. The foreign key column has the values that are present in the primary key column of the same or a different table. The table containing the foreign key is known as a child table or referring table and the table containing the primary key is known as a parent or referenced table. There are certain rules that should be followed to maintain the referential integrity:
      (i) Insertion: A row should not be inserted in the child table unless there is a matching entry in the parent table. Any type of insertion of values in the parent table should not cause referential integrity problems.
      (ii) Deletion Rules: Any row should not be deleted from the parent table if there are matching rows in the child table.
3. **Rule Integrity**: There are certain rules maintained by each organisation. The rule integrity refers to adhering to the rules set by an organisation. For example, the organisation gives specific rights to every manager and a particular manager can access data up to a certain level which depends on his job profile. The rule integrity enforces that these rights (limits) should be maintained so that every manager can only access data up to the limit set by the organisation policy.
4. **Attribute Integrity**: Attribute integrity deals with maintaining the integrity of the attributes of the entities, for instance there are certain attributes in the database which should not be null such as age. Hence, this attribute integrity should be maintained. Similarly, every attribute has a certain domain, i.e., a certain set of values which an attribute can take; for example, an attribute of an employee can take domains as M for Male and F for Female. The attribute integrity ensures that these domain values should be maintained in the database.
5. **Concurrency Integrity**: As the same data are being used for multiple transactions by multiple users, it is very important to maintain the consistency and accuracy of the data during different transactions. The concurrency integrity helps to enforce the integrity of the data during multiple transactions. This type of integrity is very important considering the kind of data that are being used in multiple transactions, for example, in banks or retail stores. The concurrency integrity is based on the ACID principle.

(a) *Atomicity*: Atomicity refers to the fact that each transaction is either completed fully or failed fully. This means that even if a part of the transaction is failed due to power cut or any other reason, then the entire transaction will be aborted.
(b) *Consistency*: It states that the database is always in the consistent state whether it is in the pre-transaction phase or it is in the post-transaction phase. The data during transaction should adhere to the integrity constraints set by each organisation so that the entire database should remain in the same consistent state.
(c) *Isolation*: As in any organisation there are a number of transactions taking place at the same time like in banks or retail store, isolation enforces that transactions should not interfere with each other.
(d) *Durability*: Durability enforces that when a transaction is completed it should remain in the database even if the power is switched off or the system crashes.

MASTER DATA MANAGEMENT

"MDM helping to understand and keeping track of all that data in terms of the unstructured becoming structured. And then the what: What are they talking about—again, uniquely identifying is it a product or service or which product, which service. So MDM enables big data analytics, and at the same time the big data analytics provides information that needs to be mastered and shared across certain organisations. So it's quite complementary and needed that big data work with MDM".

—Julie Langenkamp, Editorial Director of Information-Management.com

Before explaining the concept of master data management, it is important to discuss first the concept of master data. Master data is that data which holds the key information regarding the operations of an organisation. Master data is stored in different systems which are implemented in an organisation, for example, ERP, CRM, MIS, etc. As every department of an organisation is dependent on another department, the master data is also shared by disparate systems across the organisation. Master Data is very much different from metadata and transactional data. Transactional data describes the events that occur in the business operations of an organisation; for example, sales, billing, account receivable, account payable is an event. Transactional data is described by using verbs. Transactional data is highly volatile as it keeps on changing very rapidly (because it is based on events), whereas the master data holds the key information about business such as customer, products, etc. The master data is identified by nouns. Master data is not volatile (because it is based on entities and their attributes). The master data is quite distinct from metadata as metadata is data about data. It tells about the data type and size of attributes like metadata of account will be an integer with size 10, i.e., int (10), whereas master data holds the information regarding the entities. Hopefully, the concept of master data management is clear now to all the readers. The next aspect is the problems in master data. The main problem is that as different types

> Master data management comprises of all those rules and procedures which allow consistent recording, storage, and sharing of master data across an organisation.

of systems are applied in different areas of an organisation which results in giving different codes to the same entity. For example, ERP record the code of a customer as cust 1 and the CRM system can record the same customer as cust A. But it is important to manage the master data as master data hold critical information about an entity which is shared across the disparate systems implemented in an organisation. Master data management comprises all those rules and procedures which allow consistent recording, storage and sharing of master data across an organisation.

Gartner has given a seven-building block model which helps in the proper implementation of master data management.

Gartner's seven building block model:

1. Vision
2. Strategy
3. Governance
4. Approach
5. Processes
6. Technology
7. Metrics

1. **Vision**: There should be a proper vision for the management of master data. The master data management should be viewed as a key enabler and not as a stop gap management for providing instant solutions. This vision regarding the management of the master data should come from the top management. The involvement of top management helps in not only enhancing the credibility of master data management but also providing single vision for management of master data across the entire organisation.
2. **Strategy**: The proper strategy guides the organisation about how vision regarding the master data management will be implemented. The strategy provides proper and concrete actions for implementing the master data management vision. The strategy describes in detail that regarding the source of master data and end use of the data. The strategy helps the management to make a proper plan for implementing the master data management vision. This plan should have interconnected phases so that the entire plan can be implemented across the organisation.
3. **Governance**: Without proper governance, it is not possible for any organisation to do management of master data. Governance sets rules for collection and storage of master data. The governance helps for consistent retrieval of master data across the organisation.
4. **Approach**: In an organisation, each department's needs for master data are different. The unified approach for master data is rather difficult to achieve. So a proper organisational approach should be followed, for example the matrix organisational approach gives the best results for master data management. In the matrix organisation approach, data stewards are appointed so as to manage data requirements of different departments.
5. **Processes**: There should be a proper process for collection, storage and retrieval of master data. In the large organisation, it is rather difficult to establish processes in one go, so rather priorities are fixed for key domains, areas, sources and retrieval of master data. This prioritisation helps in creating processes.
6. **Technology Infrastructure**: To implement all the above-mentioned aspects, proper technological infrastructure is needed. It is important to decide which technology will be implemented, and if the external service provider is hired, then there should be proper criteria for selecting an appropriate service provider.
7. **Metrics**: It is important to measure the effectiveness of master data management. The organisation should develop proper metrics so as to measure the performance of master

Analytics has wide applications in the field of:

1. Marketing
2. Human Resource
3. Finance
4. Inventory

data management. Moreover, it is important that its metrics should be aligned towards the overall organisational metrics.

APPLICATIONS AREAS OF BUSINESS ANALYTICS

Business analytics has an extensive application in various functional areas of an organisation.

Marketing

Business analytics can be widely applied in various areas of marketing. At present, there is an intense competition and organisations are heavily relying on marketing activities to gain competitive advantage. The classic case of application of analytics in marketing is in retail industry as before opening any new store, the retail store manager should be able to answer various questions:

"The top five benefits being sought from location analytics are to improve the customer experience and customer satisfaction; gain competitive advantage; improve access to and value of existing information; improve organisational alignment and coordination; and deliver products and services faster".

—Mark is responsible for the overall business and research direction of Ventana Research and drives the global research agenda covering both business and technology areas

1. Which will be the proper location of the proposed store?
2. What will be the size of store?
3. What strategies will be used to target the selected customers?
4. How to win the loyalty of the customers (very difficult task!)?
5. What will be the price range?

Similarly, business analytics finds wide applications in the area of human resource, finance and inventory.

In Human Resource

"Given the radical shifts in demographics and technology, doubling down on the human capital practices of the past will not be enough to get the job done," Bersin said. "The research shows that organisations should re-imagine their approach to engaging people and move to re-engineer many of their HR practices. Attracting top talent has become a serious competitive issue that demands attention at the highest levels of the organisation."

—According to the Deloitte Global Human Capital Trends 2014 report

In human resource, the key job of the HR manager is to:

1. Finding the right person for the right job
2. Employee engagement
3. Job satisfaction
4. Reduction of attrition rate
5. Reasons for high attrition rate
6. Proper motivational strategies
7. Predicting future attrition and taking remedial actions

Finance

In financial matters, the key job of the finance manager is to:

1. Credit rating of the customers
2. Devising strategies to check default of loans
3. Preventing frauds

Inventory

The key job of the operation and inventory manager is to:

1. Find the product that will be in demand in the future
2. Set future quantity estimation of products
3. Decide the buying price
4. Estimating storage space

These questions cannot be answered by a simple analysis of data, by applying the conventional information system. Managers need to perform multidimensional analysis of data for getting the solution of above-stated questions. Business analytics provides the facility of a proper and multidimensional analysis of data to answer the above-stated goals. (In the second section of this book, all the advanced concepts of business analytics are explained in detail to understand how business analytics can be applied to have in-depth multidimensional analysis of data so as to accomplish above-stated goals.)

PREREQUISITES FOR EFFECTIVE BUSINESS ANALYTICS

Business analytics seems to be a magic pill. But before taking this pill the organisations need to do a thorough examination of certain critical aspects. It is very important to analyse the following aspects for getting the best results of business analytics. At the present time when the environment is very dynamic and economy is unstable, the direct implementation of the business analytics will not give good results. Rather, organisations need to be very vigilant before

> Prerequisites for effective Business Analytics are:
>
> 1. Mission Statement
> 2. Business Challenges
> 3. Involvement
> 4. Prioritize and Take Action

implementing the tools of business analytics. In this section, all those critical aspects are discussed which should be considered for successful implementation of business analytics.

1. **Mission Statement**: Before implementing the concept of business analytics in an organisation, it is very important to study the core mission statement of that particular organisation.
   For example, Mission Statement of IBM is "At IBM, we strive to lead in the invention, development and manufacture of industry's most advanced information technologies, including computer systems, software, storage systems and microelectronics. We translate these advanced technologies into value for our customers through our professional solutions, services and consulting business worldwide."
   The primary aim of business analytics is to help the organisation fulfil its goals and objectives. The mission statement is the basic building block for framing goals and objectives for any organisation. Business analytics should help the organisation to achieve its goals and objectives. Hence, a proper understanding of the mission statement helps in effective implementation of business analytics.
2. **Business Challenges**: In the present dynamic world, organisations are facing varied types of business challenges. Business analytics helps the organisation to overcome these varied business challenges. Sometimes, top management does not give enough importance to the business analytics team, and as a result of which the business analytics team has no idea about the possible business challenges that the organisation faces. The top management should not take business analytics as merely a supporting team; rather there should be proper involvement of the business analytics team so that it is possible to find out the business challenges faced by the organisation. The next question arises as to how to identify the business challenges so that an appropriate analytics tool can be applied for uncovering the hidden treasures (opportunities) from data in order to counter the business challenges.
3. **Involvement**: In order to identify the business challenges, it is imperative that the business analytics team should meet the representatives of various departments and then try to gauge the challenges faced by these departments. It is also important to make a list of challenges faced by an organisation. By making a list of challenges, the business analytics team makes a formal document on which it can be held accountable by the top management. For making the list of challenges faced by various departments, the business analytics team should interact with various departments such as
   (a) The business analytics team should meet the representatives of sales department to know the challenges faced by them in selling the product or services.
   (b) The business analytics team should also meet the representatives of the CRM team to know the problems faced by the customers of that organisation.
   (c) The business analytics team should also meet the representatives of the marketing department so that the business analytics team can understand the impact of various marketing strategies formulated by the marketing department.
   (d) The business analytics team should interact with the production department to know the problems faced by the production process and requirements of the production department.

(e) The business analytics team should interact with the HR department to know the process of recruiting the employees and also to know the training and development process of the organisation. The business analytics team should also get the idea of steps taken by the HR department to check attrition.

(f) The business analytics team should interact with the finance department to know the financial handling of the funds of that organisation.

After this process, the business analytics team makes a formal document, listing the various business challenges faced by these departments.

4. **Prioritize and Take Action**: Now when the list is ready, the next step is to prioritise the various challenges faced by the organisation. Suppose after meeting the various departments, the business analytics team makes a list of 25 business challenges. It is not possible for the business analytics team to provide an instant solution to all the 25 challenges; hence, it is very important to prioritise the list of challenges. This prioritisation process demands the involvement of the top management. With the help of the top management, the business analytics team prioritises the challenges and starts taking action according to the priority established. For example, if the CRM problem is given the highest priority, then the business analytics team first finds out the problems faced by the CRM department. With the help of various tools of business analytics (will be discussed in the later chapters), the business analytics team tries to provide the solution to the business challenges faced by the CRM department. After providing the solution, the business analytics team then focuses its attention on the next prioritised business challenge.

LOFT EFFECT

The implementation of business analytics is dependent on various factors. The business analytics is still an emerging field and organisations feel reluctant to spend money on analytics. Many a times, apart from careful, deliberate implementation of analytics, there are some other factors which result in the appropriate implementation of analytics. These factors are:

1. **Luck**: Luck plays an important role in the success of analytics in an organisation. Sometimes, luckily business analytics is introduced at that time when it is needed the most. As implementation of business analytics needs drastic changes in the organisation set-up and resources and when an organization is undergoing some change, then luckily that organisation also implements analytics in its core business strategy. This results in saving a lot of time and resources which eventually help the organisation to enhance its competitive advantages over its competitors.
2. **Opportunities**: Sometimes, an organisation gets just a right opportunity to introduce the analytics. As data are the lifeblood of analytics, sometimes just a right opportunity comes and analytics is applied in the best area where the data are present in right quantity and quality for application of business analytics.

LOFT:

1. Luck
2. Opportunities
3. Frustration
4. Threat

3. **Frustration**: As organisations are constantly trying to enhance their base whether on the terms of products or services, sometimes an organisation feels frustrated in that even by applying all possible measures, it is not possible to enhance its business. This frustration leads organisations to applying new technology for an in-depth analysis of data. This new technology is often business analytics.
4. **Threat**: Presently, organisations are working under an intense competitive environment, wherein organisations are always feeling the threat of being eliminated by its competitors. Organisations constantly need to re-innovate themselves so as to remain competitive in the market. This threat often leads organisations to taking the help of analytics for a better analysis of data so that they can remain ahead in this competitive era.

FUTURE OF BUSINESS ANALYTICS

The application of business analytics leads to an in-depth analysis of data. The business analytics also leads to a drastic change in the way of thinking, functioning of the organisation and even brings the cultural changes in an organisation. To discuss the future of business analytics, it is important to discuss the past and the present scenario to have a better idea of the future of business analytics.

1. **Phase I (Past)**: In the first phase, organisations worldwide started recognising the capabilities of analytics. In this phase, the data were structured and the application of analytics was very much limited. The analytics was primarily applied for getting more insights into structured data and also for reporting.
2. **Phase II (Present)**: Gradually, as organisations realised the importance of data, the analytics also gained considerable importance. At the present time, organisations are having much unstructured and semi-structured data apart from the structured data. Hence, presently analytics is widely applied for an analysis of all types of data. The multi dimensional analyses of data, cube rotation, slicing and dicing are some of the key applications of analytics at the present time. Organisations are applying analytics to build dashboards and KPIs. Some of the advanced applications of analytics in the present era are predictive analytics, text analytics and web analytics.
3. **Phase III (Future)**: In the future, analytics is going to play a very important role in organisations. Analytics will not be a separate entity; rather, organisations are going to apply analytics in their core business processes. Organisations are going to apply predictive analytics to counter the competitive forces operating in the market. For example, the retail sector is growing at the present time and holds the promising future and predictive analytics

> Phases of Business Analytics are:
>
> 1. Phase I (Past)
> 2. Phase II (Present)
> 3. Phase III (Future)

> Future of Business Analytics:
>
> 1. Newer models of predictive analytics
> 2. Advanced text analytics
> 3. Advanced visualization

will be widely applied by organisations to study the behaviour of customers and also for the market basket analysis. The market basket analysis will help retailers to associate with right products. In the future, more and more models of predictive analytics will be applied for predicting the customer's basket requirements and association of products in a particular basket. Moreover, the text analytics is going to be a major application of business analytics. Text analytics helps to decipher hidden information from the text-based content such as a word document. As the role of the Internet is going to be very significant in coming years, organisations are also going to use web mining to decipher the information from emails and other social networking sites. For example, an officer named XYZ Verma with belt number POP-125, dated 28 February 2014, suspected of illegal arms was stopped at a barricade while driving a white Maruti car no- ZZ-11-123 and was found in possession of brown sugar and a revolver (without a license).

Now, this email was sent by the local police station to the headquarter. Now, the headquarter wants to store only the relevant information from the above-mentioned email, so that in the future the record can be maintained. Applying text analytics and web mining, it is possible to store the important information in the following manner: the information will be mined

Officer code – POP-125
Date – 28/Feb/14
Name of Suspect – XYZ
Surname of Suspect – Verma
Vehicle mode – car
Vehicle make – Maruti
Vehicle Number – ZZ-11-123
Evidence 1 – Brown Sugar
Evidence 2 – Revolver (illegal)

In the future, we are also going to have advanced visualisation of data-applying analytics.

"Data Visualization goes beyond data integration; it can support multiple requirements, including "single version of truth", real time business intelligence, enterprise wide search, high performance transactional applications, federated views across multiple lines of business, and improved security for access to sensitive data."

—Forrester

"Data Visualization is now a mainstream technology with a significant number of major organisations employing it for a variety of purposes."

—Bloom Research

> IBM Many Eyes, a web community where various visualization experts, academics, and practitioners can share their knowledge and expertise regarding the visualization of data.

As analytics is applied to get an insight into the data and by having better visualization, it is easy to understand the data. Moreover, the analysis will be more interactive and meaningful. There are already various applications of advanced visualisation, which organisations are applying such as Tableau Software. Applying advanced visualisation, the analytics team will be able to present the data using less condensed lines such as spark lines instead of bar charts. Presently, data can be visualised by applying bullet graphs, heat graphs and decomposition trees. In the future, we are going to have more innovations in the field of Data Visualization. The importance of Data Visualization can be judged from the fact that IBM has created IBM Many Eyes, a web community where various visualisation experts, academics, practitioners can share their knowledge and expertise regarding the visualisation of data. Besides, several leading firms have already adopted this analytical platform. For example, the New York Times team used the data from Edison Research exit polls and the Associated Press to develop this amazing visual showing the shift in votes, where the blue dots indicate democratic votes and the red dots depict the republican votes.

Similarly, Health Infoscape is a compilation of 72 million electronic records of diseases and shows the connection of one disease with another. For example, when you catch the sore throat do you also end up getting an ear infection? GE, through its visualisation initiative, Health Infoscape, has the answer or at least an attempt to answer some of these questions. It also shows the strength of the connection and the likelihood of catching one disease due to the other, as shown below:

Exhibit 2.2 Visual showing of the shift in votes

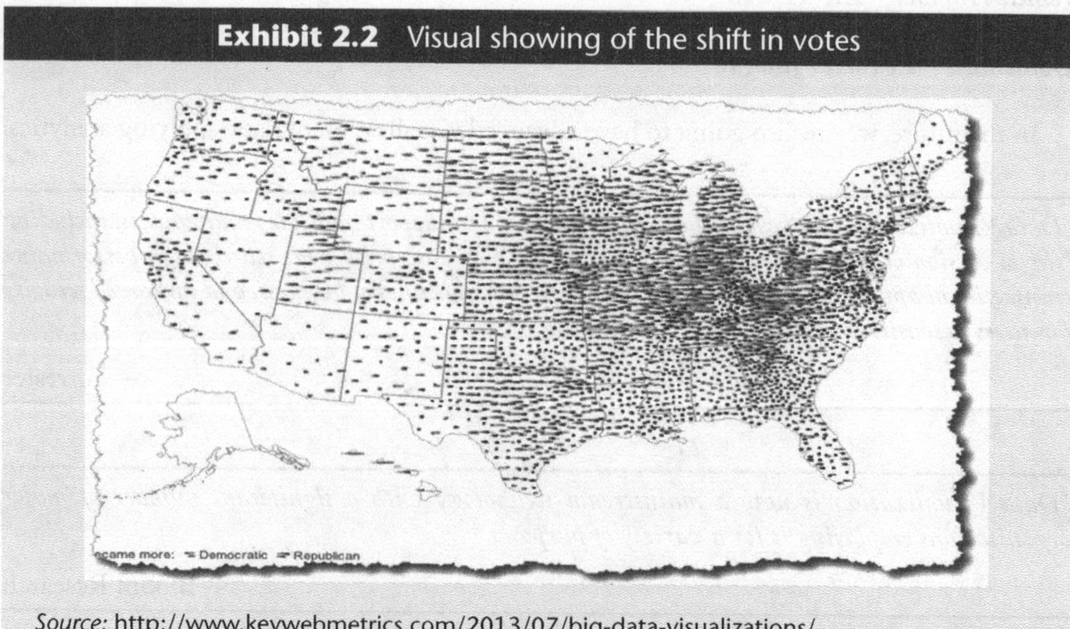

Source: http://www.keywebmetrics.com/2013/07/big-data-visualizations/

Exhibit 2.3 Health infoscape

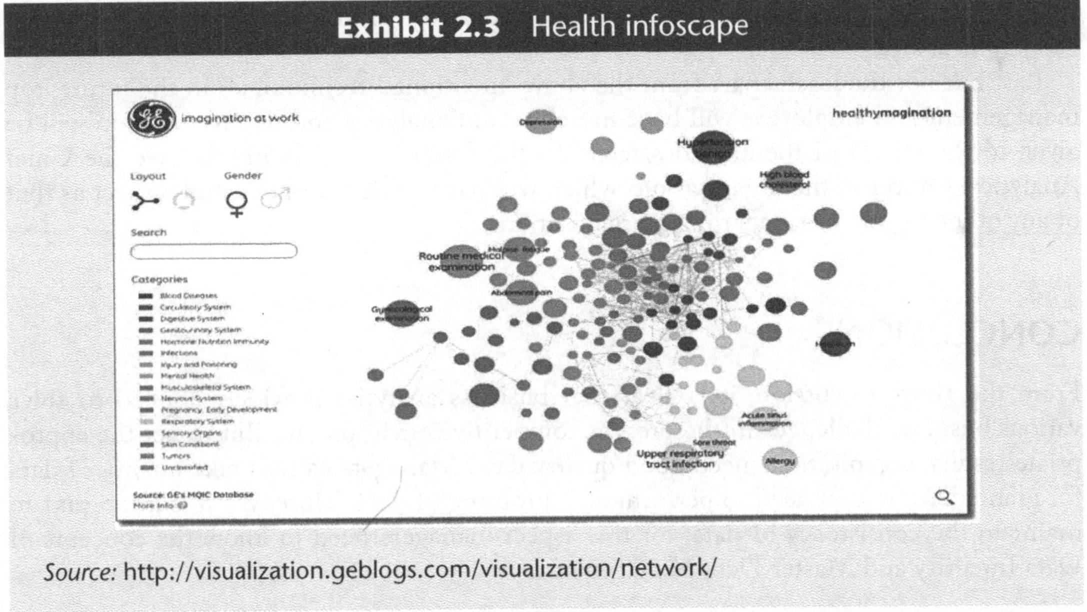

Source: http://visualization.geblogs.com/visualization/network/

Another interesting usage is by Facebook to depict the usage pattern of Facebook across different geographical areas. Instead of depicting plain figures and facts through tables, Facebook used data visualisation as shown below:

Exhibit 2.4 Visual depicting of the usage pattern of Facebook across different geographical areas

Source: http://sweb12.hciresearch.org/content/data-visualization-age-big-data

The intensity of the light indicates the popularity of the Facebook usage in that geographical area.

Last but not the least, apart from the above-mentioned technologies in the future, top management and employees will have more faith in analytics and due recognition will be given to the efforts of the analytics team. In the future, we are going to have the Chief Analytical Officer in the organisations which will have equal command and respect as that of any other top rank manager in an organisation.

CONCLUSION

From the above discussion, it is clear that business analytics is widely applied to solve various business challenges in the present competitive environment. But to get the appropriate results, organisations need good quality data. Managers cannot take quality of data for granted. Managers need to perform data profiling of data. Moreover, it is important to maintain the consistency of data; for this aspect managers need to know the concepts of Data Integrity and Master Data Management.

KEY TERMS

- LOFT 35
- Data Profiling 26
- Data Integrity 28
- Master Data Management 30

SUMMARY

In this chapter, we have studied that how business analytics is being applied in diverse functional areas. But as pointed out in this chapter, to get the best results from business analytics, there are pre-requisites for effective business analytics implementation in an organisation. This chapter also elucidates the LOFT factor for successful implementation of business analytics in an organisation. The chapter also highlighted that it is must for organisations to perform data profiling to examine the quality of data. Various techniques of data profiling are discussed in this chapter such as composition detail, format detail, statistical analysis and relationship detail. Moreover, as it is important to maintain consistency in data, in this chapter various aspects of data integrity are also discussed in detail. Last but not the least, this chapter also gives a detailed account of master data management. To have a better understanding of the concepts of business analytics review questions, assignment and project activity questions are given at the end of this chapter.

MULTIPLE CHOICE QUESTIONS

1. Which of the following is not a type of Data
   a. Structured Data b. Semi-Structured Data
   c. Semi-Formal Data d. Unstructured Data

2. Which is the most important aspect for getting the best results for analytics
   a. Data b. Technology
   c. Information d. Software

3. The process of examining the quality of Data is known as
   a. Data Cleanup b. Data Clear
   c. Data Testing d. Data Profiling

4. Composition Detail aspect in Data Profiling takes the help of
   a. Meta Data b. Master Data
   c. Mega Data d. Multi Data

5. Which of the following is not the technique of Data Profiling
   a. Composition Detail b. Format Detail
   c. Volume Detail d. Relationship Detail

6. The process of maintaining the accuracy and consistency of the data is known as
   a. Data Profiling b. Data Integrity
   c. Data Testing d. Data Checkup

7. Which of the following is not a part of Data Integrity
   a. Physical Integrity b. Logical Integrity
   c. Strategy Integrity d. Rule Integrity

8. Physical Integrity in Data Integrity checks
   a. Storage and retrieval of data b. Checks Primary key
   c. Checks Foreign Keys d. Checks Attributes

9. Which of the following is not a part of Logical Integrity
   a. Physical Storage of Data b. Entity Integrity
   c. Insertion Integrity d. Deletion Integrity

10. Concurrency Integrity is based on the principle of
    a. ACID b. LITMUS
    c. ALKALINE d. LOFT

11. The data which hold the key information regarding the operations of an organisation is known as
    a. Meta Data
    b. Mega Data
    c. Master Data
    d. Multi Data

12. LOFT effect does not include which of the following option
    a. Luck
    b. Opportunity
    c. Future
    d. Threat

13. The analysis, which helps the retailers to associate right products, is known as
    a. Market Analysis
    b. Retail Analysis
    c. Customer Analysis
    d. Market Basket Analysis

14. The analysis, which helps to decipher hidden information from the text based content, is known as
    a. Word Mining
    b. Text Mining
    c. Sentence Mining
    d. Paragraph Mining

REVIEW QUESTIONS

1. Discuss the need of business analytics in the current business environment.
2. What are the prerequisites for effective business analytics?
3. Discuss the role of LOFT effect in the implementation of business analytics.
4. Discuss the three phases, i.e., past, present and future of business analytics.
5. Discuss the importance and various techniques of data profiling.
6. What do you understand by data integrity?
7. Discuss the importance of master data management.

ASSIGNMENT

1. Choose a sector and then make an assignment discussing past, present and future of analytics in that sector (For example, banking sector).

PROJECT ACTIVITY

1. Visit a nearby organisation and study how that organisation is applying data profiling and data integrity concepts.

CASE STUDY

Swissotel and La Tienda Applying Analytics to Overcome Business Challenges

Swissotel, part of Fairmont Raffles Hotels International luxury, is a chain of hotels with the presence in leading cities of the world. Realising the intense competition in the hospitality sector, Swissotel invested in digital marketing, through which it offers its services and offerings digitally or electronically on the Internet. Although it was able to attract more visitors to its site through digital marketing, the outcome of this investment in terms of revenue generation was falling short of expectations of Swissotel. Management knew that something was amiss in its digital marketing strategy because Swissotel was offering the same digital marketing content to all visitors across the world such as US, UK and Australia. It realised that instead of offering the same digital content across the world, it needs to segment its visitors and then to target the promotional digital content. Barbara Pezzi, Director of Analytics & Search Optimization for Fairmont Raffles Hotels International said, "I use advanced segments to understand the behaviour of my paid visitors and to answer questions like 'What happened after paid visitors clicked on an ad?', and 'How does the behaviour of paid visitors differ from the behaviour of organic visitors from the same countries or markets?" For this, it needed to monitor its digital marketing content and in this pursuit, Swissotel took the help from Google Analytics. One of the key features of Google Analytics is the Adword Integration, which is the analysis of visitor behaviour in response to different adwords used in digital promotional campaigns. Such an analysis generates an insight into the Adwords which attract more visitors. After the application of analytics, it was seen by the Swissotel management that visitor response to digital content differs tremendously by countries. It was seen that visitors from countries such as US and Australia are significantly influenced by digital campaigns which contain Adwords regarding "Promotions" and "Package". The use of such Adwords in their promotional campaigns generated more traffic or attracted a larger number of visitors to Swissotel website hosting such digital campaigns. However, visitors from the UK showed a different kind of behaviour. They were spending more time on browsing rooms and checking out restaurants, rather than packages as compared with visitors from USA. Realising this segmentation among its visitors, the Swissotel management decided to specifically design different digital marketing campaigns for each country. For the UK, the campaign contained the Adword "Beautiful rooms and suites", while for Australian and US visitors, campaigns were designed containing "Great Deals" or "Discounts/Savers" as shown in Exhibit 2.5.

The results were overwhelming. There was a 70% increase in revenue, the majority coming from visitors clicking on "Beautiful rooms and suites". Barbara Pezzi testifies by stating that "By segmenting and refining our campaign, we were able to almost double our e-commerce conversion rate and, more importantly, to improve our per-visit value metric significantly."

Exhibit 2.5 Digital campaign of Swissotel offering discount

Source: http://www.swissotel.com/offers/category-results/?no-results=true

Founded in 1996, La Tienda is located in Williamsburg, Virginia. La Tienda offers authentic Spanish food like hand-crafted cheese, chorizos and pantry goods of Spain. It has warehouses in Williamsburg, Virginia and Alicante. The official website of La Tienda is www.tienda.com and La Tienda receives many online orders from its website. Buoyed by the positive response, La Tienda decided to expand its business and planned to deliver products in countries such as Canada and Australia. For this reason, it would require relying on ships to transport the products and to deliver the orders to places far from its warehouses. This would, however, add to the cost of the product due to additional shipping expenses. So, La Tienda wanted to know the impact of varying shipping rates on transportation and delivery of its orders. To solve this issue, La Tienda took the help of Web Strategies, which is a Virginia-based digital marketing company. It provides specialised services in the field of digital analytics. La Tienda started offering its products through its website in Canada and Australia at varying shipping rates. Web Strategies then applied digital analytics on the visitors of the La Tienda's website and tracked purchase patterns of each visitor. Based on this, the visitors of the company website were segmented into two groups. The first group consists of all the visitors who are close to the company's warehouse and hence do not have to bother about transportation expenses. The second group contained all those visitors who are far off from the company's warehouse and require transportation services. Then, drill-down techniques were applied to gain a better insight into purchasing patterns of visitors belonging to the second group. The order preferences and impact of shipping rates on orders of these visitors were analysed, and it was found that 48%

of the visitors are negatively affected by differential shipping cost. This implies that the visitors in the second group who are far from the company warehouses and are charged more due to additional shipping expenses have less inclination to order in the future. After this revelation, La Tienda decided to replace its differential shipping model with a less expensive flat shipping model, especially for the second-group visitors. The result of this whole exercise was a steep 70% increase in sales and that too from the second-group visitors. "For several years we were paying thousands and thousands of dollars for a complex analytics program that never quite gave us what we needed. With Analytics, we were able to access the data that we needed to run LaTienda.com, for free, and have it presented to us in an approachable format that gave us actionable data." - Tim Harris, CEO, LaTienda.com – The Best of Spain.

Questions

1. Before application of analytics, what kind of problems were faced by Swissotel and La Tienda?
2. How did Google Analytics aid Swissotel to overcome the problems? Discuss the role of Adwords in this.
3. How did web analytics segment users at LaTienda? What was the benefit to the firm?

REFERENCES

Briggs, L. L. (2010). "Why Data Quality Is a Measurable, Ongoing Effort," TDWIBlog, www. Tdwi.org.

Davenport T. H. and Harris, J. G. (2007). *Competing on Analytics: The New Science of Winning* (Cambridge, MA: Harvard Business School Press).

Diche J. and Levy, E. (2006). Customer Data Integration: Reaching a Single Version of Truth (Hoboken, NJ: John Wiley and Sons).

Duhigg, C. (2012). "How Companies Learn Your Secrets," New York Times, February 16.

Gartner Symposium Conference, "Infrastructure and Operations: Top 10 Trends to Watch, David Cappucio, October 2010.

Hopwood, P. (2008). "Data Governance: One Size Does Not Fit All", *DM Review Magazine.*

http://www.sjsu.edu/people/rakesh.ranjan/courses/cmpe272/s2/Team-Matrix-Google-Analytics.pdf, accessed May 12, 2014.

http://www.webanalisten.nl/wp-content/uploads/2012/09/webstrategies-latienda.pdf, accessed May 12, 2014.

Kouzes, J. M. and Posner, B. Z. (2007). The Leadership Challenge, 4th ed. (San Francisco, Jossey-Bass).

Manyika, J., Chui, M., Brown, B., Bughin, J., Dobbs, R., Roxburgh C. and Hun, A. (2011). Big Data: The Next Frontier for Innovation, Competition and Productivity (Mckinsey Global Institute).

MarkLogic On-Demand Webinar, "Managing the Information Explosion", July 27, 2011.

Plaza, B. (2011). "Google Analytics." Online 34.5 (2010): 33–37. *Academic Search Premier*. EBSCO. Web. May 9.

Ratekin, M. A. (2011). "What is the Current State of Customer Loyality?" Walker Information Group Blog.

Shwu-Min Horng. IEEE Paper-Analysis of Users' Behavior on Web 2.0 Social Network Sites: An Empirical Study.

Strategy Consulting Ltd., "Exploring Corporate Strategy Using M.S.O.T. Analysis".

www.google.co.in/analytics/customers/pdfs/swissotel.pdf, accessed May 12, 2014.

Zikopoulos, P. C. et al., (2012). *Understanding Big Data: Analytics for Enterprise Class Hadoop and Streaming Data* (New York: McGraw-Hill).

CHAPTER 3

Unstructured Data Analytics

After going through this chapter, you will be able to

- Understand the hidden facts regarding data
- Understand the need of data relevance
- Understand the concept of data representation
- Understand the concept of unstructured data
- Understand the characteristics of unstructured data
- Understand the analysis of unstructured data
- Understand the concept of semi-structured data
- Understand the characteristics of semi-structured data
- Understand the storage of semi-structured data
- Understand the querying techniques of semi-structured data

INTRODUCTION

The backbone of any business analytics application is data. Even for any simple application of information system, an organisation needs data. But over the period of time, organisations have become so fascinated with data that now organisations are collecting huge volumes of data to perform proper analysis. Organisations collect data from various sources, for example, telephone calls, websites, CRM softwares, surveys, etc. There is indeed a paradox for organisations as now organisations are facing the problem of managing the voluminous data rather the scarcity of data. It will not be wrong to say that organisations are investing a huge amount of money on collecting data, rather organisations are wasting a huge amount of money. Yes, indeed, as organisations have no clue about how to use the collected voluminous data. Moreover, the data collected by organisations are scattered and are in different forms. The data regarding an HR department have all the data related to HR processes. Similarly, the marketing department has all the data regarding the marketing function. But for taking strategic decisions, it is very important that the manager should have relevant consolidated data in one place. Hence, to get maximum benefit from data it is important to collect the right data, and to collect the right data the manager should first know the following aspects of data as detailed below.

Organizations are not utilising the true potential of data.

There are some interesting facts about data which a manager should know.

PRESENT SCENARIO

As of 2012, about 2.5 exabytes of data are created each day, and that number is doubling every 40 months or so. More data cross the internet every second than were stored in the entire internet just 20 years ago. This gives companies an opportunity to work with many petabyes of data in a single dataset—and not just from the internet. A petabyte is one quadrillion bytes, or the equivalent of about 20 million filing cabinets' worth of text. An exabyte is 1,000 times that amount, or one billion gigabytes.

—HBR

As discussed above, nowadays there is an explosion of data. Instead of a mindless collection of data, it is important to collect and store only meaningful data. This can only be possible if the manager knows the following facts about the data:

1. The most important fact, at the present time, about the data is that there is an explosion of data. As the data collected by organisations are huge, gone are the days when the collected data could be processed manually. Indeed, it will not be wrong to say that even the traditional information systems (TPS, MIS) are not able to process these massive datasets. The fact is that although organisations are collecting massive data, they have no idea of how to process these massive datasets.
2. The second important aspect is the changing nature of the data. The dynamic environment and intense competition make the collected data redundant in a very short period. Organisations need to collect fresh data so as to counter the competitive forces playing in the market. This fact implies that once the organisation has collected the data, it is very important that the it should quickly process that data; otherwise, the data will become obsolete.
3. The other aspect is the diversity of the data. Presently, organisations are collecting data of diverse nature. Gone are the days when organisations used to collect data from face-to-face interaction with customers. But now organisations are collecting data with the help of various media such as social networking sites, Wi-Fi tracking, videos, warehousing, etc.

GARBAGE IN, GARBAGE OUT

"It costs ten times as much to complete a unit of simple work when the data are flawed in any way as it does when they're perfect."

—Thomas Redman, "Make the case for better quality data", Harvard Business Review

Data governance means set of procedures that help to maintain the quality of data.

All the above facts make the data very unique and valuable. It also implies that for getting proper results from the collected data, organisations need to ensure the quality of data. Therefore, it becomes imperative that organisations should be very diligent while storing the data. All the above facts should be taken into consideration for maintaining the quality of data. If organisations are not going to pay attention to the above-mentioned facts, then the collected data will be of no use. Rather, the data will give disastrous results to the organisation. To ensure the quality of data, nowadays organisations are applying the concept of data governance. Data governance means a set of procedures that help to maintain the quality of data. Data governance ensures that organisations follow proper procedures to maintain the data, i.e., all the facts regarding the data are taken into consideration and moreover a proper team is appointed for data governance. This team is accountable for maintaining the quality of the data. In the following section, the PLEASE model is suggested to govern the data.

DATA RELEVANCE

As pointed out above, presently organisations are facing another type of problem. Earlier, there was the problem regarding the scarcity of data; as a result of which, managers were not able to take relevant decisions. But, in the present time, organisations are having a flood of data. Of late, organisations have realised the importance of data and as a result of which organisations are collecting data from each and every possible source. But, a mere collection of data is not going to solve the problem. In the following section, the solution to this problem is discussed in detail.

Earlier, when organisations had less data, everybody laid emphasis on the fact that organisations should collect more data in order to take decisions. But now when organisations are having massive amounts of data, managers are still facing the same problem, i.e., how to take rational decisions. The solution is not the mindless collection of data, rather it is very much important to collect relevant data. The relevance in the data depends on many factors. The relevant data can be collected by applying the PLEASE model. The data are very important for getting accurate results from the business analyst. But, the data should please the analytics team so that results can please the management. The PLEASE model helps to accomplish this objective (see Exhibit 3.1).

> The relevant data can be collected by applying PLEASE model.

Exhibit 3.1 PLEASE model various stages of PLEASE model

- *Problem identification*
- *Look for data*
- *Explain the data*
- *Act on the data*
- *Share knowledge*
- *Evaluate*

1. **Problem Identification**: For getting the accurate results, it is very important to identify the problem. As for any accurate treatment, it is very important to accurately diagnose the disease. Similarly, it is essential that the analytics team first should understand the problem thoroughly. Usually, the top management gives a vague problem to the analytics team; for example, the top management tells that there is a decrease in revenue in the second quarter. But, the analytics team should have an in-depth understanding of the problem. To achieve this objective, the analytics team should interact with all the relevant stakeholders to understand the problem. Any wrong understanding of the problem will have disastrous effects on the future of the organisation. For example, the above-stated vague scenario (decrease in revenue) should be analysed by an Analytics team in the following manner:
   - Which product, region or sales person has contributed to the decrease in revenue?
   - In which geographic areas is there a decrease in revenue, for example, in Northern, Southern, Eastern, Western regional branches, etc.?
   - What is the revenue of the competitors in the same time period?
   - Whether the policy decisions of government are affecting the organisation and its business?
   - What new marketing decisions are taken by the organisation that resulted in the decrease in the revenue?

   After analysing the above scenarios, the analytical team frames precise problem, but it is also important that the top management should crosscheck the problem identified by the analytics team. For this purpose, the analytics team should submit a properly documented file explaining the problem to the top management.
2. **Look for Data**: Once the problem has been accurately identified, the next step is to look for the relevant data that will help in solving the problem. Collecting massive data just for the sake of the collection will have rather yield inaccurate results for the organisation. So, it is imperative that an organisation should only collect relevant data. This will not only help in the better management of data, but also help in a proper analysis of the data. For example, in the above scenario, the business analytics team identifies the problem that the new marketing policy of the organisation has resulted in a decrease in revenue. So, the analytics team is only going to collect the data regarding the effects of the wrong marketing policy.
3. **Explain the Data**: Data collected by the analytics team are often technical in nature and need a careful analysis. The top management might not be in a position to understand the data collected in the second phase. Hence, it is very important to decipher the data in those terms which can easily be understood by the top management. The analytics team in this phase should explain the true meaning of data in a concise and simple manner. In this phase, the analytics team will provide answers to the critical questions raised by the management. It is advisable to use graphs and charts in this phase as the top management has a very limited time and graphs and charts provide an easy and quick understanding of data. For example, to show the difference in revenue in four zones or difference in revenue between your organisation and competitors in the form of graphs will save time and facilitate an easy understanding of the real scenario.
4. **Act on the Data**: After explaining the data, the next job of the analytics team is to suggest actions based on the data to overcome the business problem faced by the

organisation. As organisations are working in a dynamic and competitive environment, any decision taken by the organisation should be backed by proper data. So if the marketing team wants to implement new marketing initiatives, then the analytics team should provide them with various actions that can be taken by the organisation based on the collected data. For example, depending on the data the analytics team can suggest to the marketing team which brand ambassador should be hired by the organisation. As Thumbs Up has hired South Superstar Mahesh Babu because the maximum sales of Thumbs Up is in the South.

5. **Share Knowledge**: It is well known that knowledge is power. With the help of the above four stages, the analytics team acquires knowledge which helps to solve the business problem. But, it is very important to share this knowledge acquired to solve the problem. As every functional department is dependent on other functional departments, the different functional departments should work as a team to accomplish the goals and objectives of the organisation. The problem identified in the first stage might belong to the marketing department, but it is very important to share the knowledge (acquired to solve the problem) with other functional departments. In this phase, the analytics team shares the knowledge with other functional departments. The analytics team might use various techniques to accomplish this task, for example:
    - Meeting with other functional departments
    - Interacting with the help of Webinar
    - Using the organisational Intranet for sharing the newly acquired knowledge
6. **Evaluate**: Evaluation always helps in the improvement. This is also true for the analytics team. The actions suggested by the analytics team (Stage 4) are implemented by the organisation. Now, it is very important to crosscheck that whether the actions suggested by the team have resulted in solving the business problem accurately or not. If the actions suggested by the analytics team have not resulted in solving the business problem, then it is very important for the analytics team to find out the reasons for the wrong analysis. This evaluation helps the analytics team not only to rectify the problems and flaws, but also to acquire new knowledge. This, in turn, helps the analytics team to deliver accurate results.

DATA REPRESENTATION

In the previous sections, we have discussed about data in detail. In this part, we are going to discuss the next important phase in business analytics known as data representation. The third phase in the PLEASE model is about explaining the meaning of data. This is a very important phase as the actions (next phase) depend on the proper explanation of the data. For providing accurate meaning of data, the analytics team should follow the approach of data representation. Data representation is a technique of representation of data in such a way that it conveys the true meaning of the data. Data representation is done with the help of appropriate graphs and charts.

Data representation is a technique of representation of data in such a way that it conveys the true meaning of the data. Data representation is done with the help of appropriate graphs and charts.

New studies show that the way data are presented has a big impact—in particular, graphic representations and computer simulations can help.

—Robin Hogarth and EmreSoyer,
"A Picture worth a thousand numbers", The Magazine.

The main purpose of data representation is that it should convey the exact meaning of complex data to each and every stakeholder in the organisation and present the data in a uniform manner. As in the PLEASE model, for taking relevant actions it is very important to know the exact meaning of the data collected. Any misinterpretation of data will result in faulty actions. So, it is very important to decipher the data in an accurate manner. This is a very complex job, but with the help of the data representation approach it is possible to decipher the data and to take accurate actions. In the following part, the 6C Model is suggested for a proper representation of data (see Exhibit 3.2).

Exhibit 3.2 Various stages of 6C model

Various Stages of 6C Model

- *Content*
- *Candor*
- *Circumvent*
- *Center of attraction*
- *Crisp*
- *Communication*

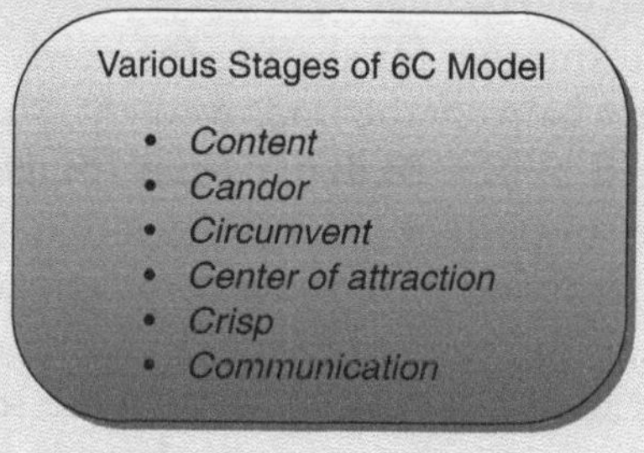

1. **Content**: Sometimes, the analyst goes overboard and uses inappropriate tools for showing the content of the data. Data representation is often misunderstood as representing the data using graphs and charts, but one important thing is often neglected, i.e., data representation should be done by choosing appropriate charts and graphs. Data representation should convey the true content of data. The graphs and charts should be selected in such a way that it helps to make data look simple and easily understandable. Hence, the careful use of various types of graphs and charts should be done in explaining the true meaning of the data.
2. **Candor**: Candor means honesty. Data representation using graphs is an excellent way to depict the data, but it is also a wonderful tool for deceiving the audience. Any technical person can play with the graph and can easily deceive the audience. Sometimes, the analytics team commits a mistake and collects inappropriate data (second stage of PLEASE model), and to cover their mistake the analytics team uses graphs to deceive the audience. This is unethical and can result in taking wrong action

based on misrepresentation of data. For example, the easiest way to deceive the audience is to use different scales to misrepresent the data.

3. **Circumvent**: The analytics team should circumvent the data. This means that only necessary data should be used to represent the situation. The use of unnecessary data will rather confuse the audience and will result in misrepresentation of data. Hence, the analytics team should focus on business objectives and then only use necessary data for representation of data to achieve overall business objectives and goals. But, sometimes the analytics team uses those data which have no relevance vis-à-vis overall goals and objectives for data representation. This results in confusion and leads to faulty actions.
4. **Center of Attraction**: For taking appropriate actions, it is very important to involve the top management. For this, the analytics team should convey the meaning of the data to the top management. This is generally done by giving a presentation to the top management. In this presentation, all the key members of the top management and the business analytics team should participate. Executives of the top management are generally non-technical persons and may not be well versed with the technical aspects of the analytics. Moreover, the top management has a very limited time and needs to take quick actions. So considering these facts, it is very important for the analytics team to represent the data considering these requirements in mind. The centre of attention should be the top management, and the whole of the presentation should be designed in such a way that it conveys the meaning to the top management. The analytics team should use appropriate graphs and also should do proper labelling to convey the meaning of the data. It is very important to get the response of the audience; hence, the presentation should be designed in such a way that it should evoke a response from the audience. Moreover, the analytics team should also take into consideration the nature of the audience—if the problem is of the marketing department, then the audience will be the head of the marketing team and key marketing team members along with other top management. Hence, the presentation should be prepared by taking the marketing team into perspective.
5. **Crisp**: As we have discussed earlier, the top management has very limited time and needs to take quick decisions. Hence, data representation should be crisp and to the point. The graphs and charts should not be loaded with unnecessary data. Also, the analytics team should straightway come to the core problem and should not waste time in describing unnecessary data which are of no use. The overuse or lengthy data representation leads to loss of interest of the audience and as a result of which the audience will not give their valuable suggestions for solving the business problem.
6. **Communication**: The true essence of data representation is a two-way communication. One part of data representation is the communication from the analytics team. The analytics team considering the above principles prepares a presentation. But, it is also very important that the audience should also communicate with the analytics team. The onus of two-way communication lies with the analytics team. It is very important that the analytics team should motivate or rather entice the audience to speak their mind. It is essential to take the feedback from the audience; hence, deliberately some questions should be put between the slides. For example, how long will we take to notice the decreasing customer loyalty? Questions of such nature will not only build the interest of the audience, but also encourage the audience to think and give their valuable suggestions. If there is no

Apart from structured data there are two other important types of data.

communication with the audience, then the analytics team will not be able to frame appropriate actions for the rectification of the business problem.

TYPES OF DATA

"IT organisations are managing more data than ever, data which has increasing business value and must be stored and protected for a long time. Most of this is unstructured file data, so there is a big opportunity to reduce storage costs through smart management, particularly archiving old files off to a less expensive tier."

—Robert Clark, senior vice president, Data Protection Group, Quantum

Data are the lifeline for any type of business analytics team. Without data it is not possible to apply an analytics tool. The manager should be very much careful about the data as data are of different types. Apart from structured data, there are two other important types of data. The knowledge of the proper type of data is very important for getting an appropriate result from the business analytics team. In the following section, two of the main types of data are discussed. Data are of the following types:

Exhibit 3.3 Types of data

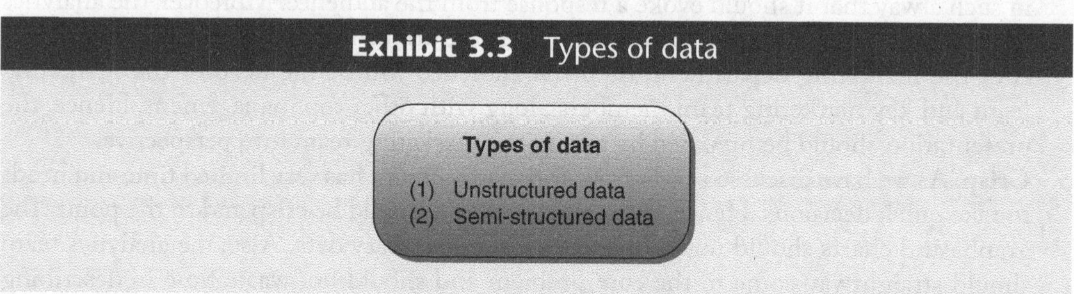

UNSTRUCTURED DATA

The Australian crime commission has 3.5 million records of unstructured data (most of which is text) and all efforts to add structure to the same and data warehousing proved futile. So the firm under the supervision of CTO Narelle Lovett is considering deployment of text analytics to mine the most out of the records. "Text is unbelievably difficult. It brings an enormous number of challenges. If you use Google to search something, how many times do you re-enter the phrase to try and pin down what you're trying to find? It's because what you're dealing with is primarily unstructured data. That's why data mining for text analytics is hard."

—Narelle Lovett, CTO, Australian Crime Commission

Unstructured Data: This is the most common form of data which any organisation possesses. This type of data is not present in the form of relational tables, i.e., rows and columns. As a result of which, it is very difficult to use these data for analysis. It is always easy to use those data which are properly organised, but the unstructured data are not properly organised; hence, it is not possible to apply rules of structured data for analysis of unstructured data. The examples of this type of data are shown in Exhibit 3.4.

> At the present time, there is explosion of unstructured type of data, as more and more people are using internet and expressing themselves in the form of Twitter, Facebook and other social networking platform.

Exhibit 3.4 Examples of unstructured data

(1) Images
(2) Spreadsheets
(3) Videos
(4) Feedback
(5) Power point presentations
(6) Call centre conversions
(7) Blogs
(8) Proposals
(9) Forums
(10) E-mails

At the present time, there is explosion of this type of data, as more and more people are using the Internet and expressing themselves in the form of Twitter, Facebook and other social networking platforms. For getting the customer's insights, it is very important for organisations to collect this type of data. Because generally before buying any product, people log on to the Internet to know the response of other people who have already purchased that product. Hence, for any organisation this type of data is very important, but the problem is that this type of data is not organised, i.e., it is unstructured. Organisations are spending huge amount of money on collecting and storing unstructured data, but organisations are not aware of how to use this type of data. It is very important that the concerned manager should have the in-depth knowledge of unstructured data for getting the best results using business analytics tools. The first task for any manager is to know the characteristics of the unstructured data.

The MS SQL Server provides a platform to handle unstructured data of many sorts, such as XML, text data and binary data. Some examples of unstructured data are video footage from retail stores, library deploying IT system for archiving, voice messages or other multimedia formats. The SQL Server offers FILESTREAM and BLOB to store unstructured data and integrates full text search in the database.

Characteristics of Unstructured Data

1. The unstructured data can be segmented into two types: one which is related to the core business processes such as Marketing, Production, HR, etc. and the other which supports the core business processes such as information regarding materials, manpower, etc.
2. Most of the unstructured data is in a casual form, for example, e-mails. No two e-mails will have the same type of layout. Each e-mail is different and it is very difficult to generalise the content on e-mail.
3. Most of the unstructured data are written by using different slangs, for example, with Short Message (SMS) the people write in different slangs to communicate to each other. Even on social networking sites people use different types of slangs which makes very difficult to formalise the unstructured data.
4. The unstructured data are present in huge volume; as a result of which, it is very difficult to store the unstructured data. The reason for the huge volume of unstructured data is that there are various sources of unstructured data, for example, e-mails, videos, Facebook chats, tweets on twitter, etc.
5. The shelf life of unstructured data is very short. As most of the unstructured data deals with the non-tangible attributes such as experience of customers, which keeps on changing very rapidly. Hence, it is very important to identify and discard the redundant unstructured data and to store the relevant unstructured data.
6. One of the most important attributes of unstructured data is that this type of data cannot be used directly in relational database because the unstructured data are not present in the form of rows and columns.
7. Unstructured data are not only presented in the form of a textual format, but it is also present in the form of images and videos. It will not be wrong to say that images and videos contribute a major chunk of unstructured data.
8. In most of the cases, unstructured data cannot be updated for example, once the e-mail has been sent then it is not possible to update the same e-mail.

Unstructured Data—Analysis Issue

The next important question is why unstructured data are so difficult to analyse. The following are the key features which make unstructured data very difficult to analyse.

1. **Format**: The unstructured data are presented in different formats. These include
   (a) *Text*
   (b) *Images*
   (c) *Videos*
   (d) *Spreadsheets*
   The availability of the unstructured data in different formats makes it very difficult to generalise and hence to analyse.
2. **Lack of Standardisation**: From the above point, it is clear that unstructured data are available in different formats. For storing the data in the relational databases, it is very

important that there should be similarity in the data (standardisation). But in the case of unstructured data there is no standardisation. You cannot standardise images and text. Even two e-mails cannot be standardised which makes the unstructured data very difficult to store in the form of relational database.

3. **Language**: The content of the unstructured data is generally written using informal language (slangs). When people communicate on Facebook, they use different slangs. Moreover, as organisations are working in different countries; as a result of which, organisations are collecting unstructured data in different languages which makes it very difficult to store and standardise the data.
4. **Volume of Unstructured Data**: Organisations store huge volumes of unstructured data. The huge amount of volume is attributed to the fact that organisations are collecting data from different sources. The advent of the Internet has resulted in an explosion of the unstructured data which makes it very difficult to store and manage the unstructured data.
5. **Ambiguity**: As the unstructured data are present in the form of text, images and videos, it is very difficult to understand the true meaning of the unstructured data. Somebody can interpret unstructured data in a different manner, whereas somebody else can visualise same unstructured data in a different manner. This can cause much ambiguity for any organisation.
6. **Security**: As most of the unstructured data are present in open sources such as the Internet, there is always an issue regarding security of the unstructured data. Moreover, as large volume of the unstructured data is available, it is very difficult to secure such a large volume of data.
7. **Storage**: The presence of huge amount of unstructured data makes it very difficult for organisations to store and manage the unstructured data. Moreover, the shelf life of the unstructured data is very short. Hence, for any organisation, it is not only important to store such a huge volume of data but at the same time also very important to delete obsolete unstructured data from the database.

Analysis of Unstructured Data

As from the above discussion, it is clear that the analysis of the unstructured data is a very difficult task, but there are some specialised techniques based on NLP (Natural Language Processing which is used to infer human–computer interactions based on principles of AI, linguistics and computer science) and statistical techniques which help in the analysis of the unstructured data. The techniques are:

1. **Logical Analysis**: This type of analysis helps to find out the meaning of a particular word. Even the same word may have different meaning in different situations. The logical analysis helps to find out the exact meaning of words, depending upon the kind of situation.
2. **Syntax Analysis**: In this type of analysis, the focus shifts from a single word to all words in a particular sentence. The syntax analysis helps to make or build a Parse Tree which depicts the relation of different words with each other in a particular sentence.

Exhibit 3.5 Techniques for analysis of unstructured data

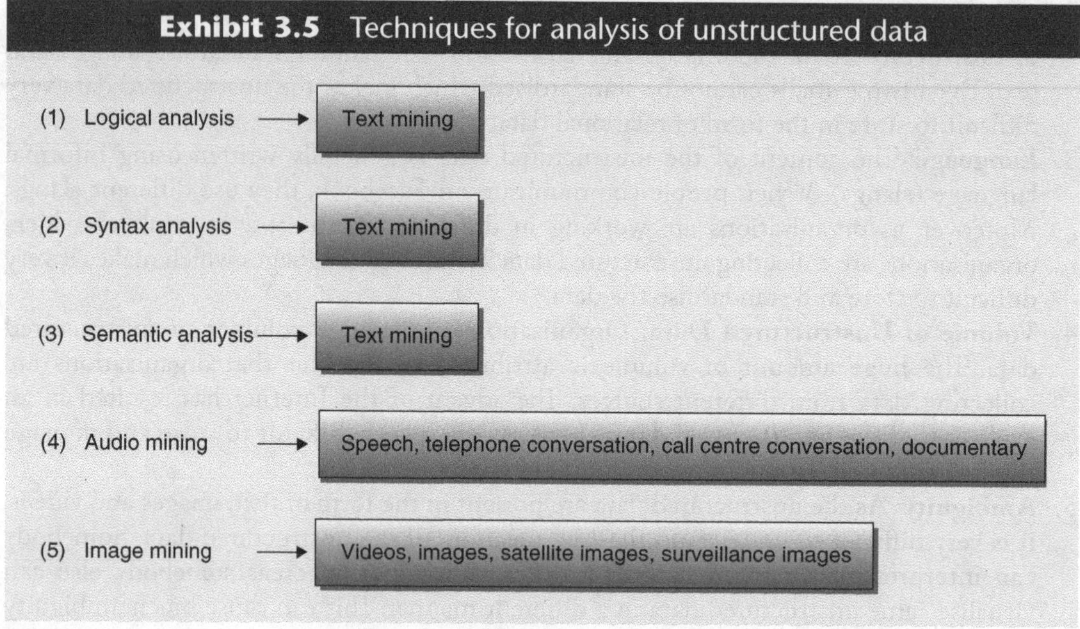

With the help of Parse Tree, one can easily find out subject, verb, object in a particular sentence.

3. **Semantic Analysis**: Once the logical and syntax analysis techniques are performed, the next and last step of text mining is semantic analysis. In the semantic analysis, focus is on the meaning of the entire sentence. After finding out the meaning of words and the exact position of words (subject, object and verb) using the above two techniques with the help of NLP in the semantic analysis, the text is mined to find out the exact meaning of the entire sentence.
4. **Audio Mining**: As the unstructured data are in different formats and if the data are in the form of the text format, it can be mined by using the above technique. But if the unstructured data are present in the form of speech or music, then for that aspect the audio mining technique is applied. The audio mining uses microprocessors and speech recognition algorithms to analyse (for example, in music industry) to find out various attributes of data, for example, in a music piece such as beats per minute and categorisation of music.
5. **Image Mining**: The unstructured data are also available in the form of video and images. Various softwares such as
   - *ORFEO*
   - *Monteverdi tool box*
   - *ROI-PAC*
   - *Music*

   are applied to find out various attributes of an image. This technique is very helpful in forecasting of weather and in forensic science

SEMI-STRUCTURED DATA

> Unlike the unstructured data, the semi-structured data is not the raw data but partly structured and has highly irregular pattern.

Semi-Structured Data: There is a thin line which divides unstructured data from semi-structured data. When we try to visualise the data very minutely, then another category of data comes into being which is known as semi-structured data. Unlike the unstructured data, the semi-structured data are not the raw data, but partly structured and have a highly irregular pattern.

> eBay has more than 100 million active users and 500 million auction listings implying 100 TB data per day. Data is stored in three systems which store structured, semi structured and unstructured data. For the purpose of analysis, a wide range of data tools such as MS Excel are used, and for reporting, KPIs and metrics and dashboards are used and a separate platform for uncommon problems which require deeper intervention.

Also, unlike the structured data, the semi-structured data do not fit into relational databases, i.e., not in the form of rows and columns, for example, EDI, paragraphs, sentences and chapters from books. Some fields are present in different formats and at the same time certain fields may be missing. In other words, there is no uniformity in the semi-structured data. Moreover, semi-structured data do not have any fixed schema and that is why this type of data is also sometimes referred to as schema less data. There is much focus on semi-structured data at the present time. The main reason for this is the presence of Internet. The Internet is the main source of semi-structured data. Organisations are collecting huge amount of data from various Internet sources. Also, not all the data available on the Internet follow a strict pattern. As a result of which, we categorise those data as semi-structured data.

"The rate at which semi-structured and unstructured data grows is very high. A single jet engine can generate 10TB of data in 30 minutes. It is critically important to develop a life cycle management strategy that includes archiving and deletion policies, business rules and IT automation."

—Maria C. Villar, Managing Partner, Business data leadership

Characteristics of Semi-Structured Data

1. **Irregular Pattern**: Unlike the structured data, the pattern of the semi-structured data is highly irregular. As pointed out above, some of the data may be missing or sometimes the data may be present in different formats. For example, at one place, date will be in the format 26/12/2008 and at some other place the format can be

2008/Dec/26. As a result of this irregular pattern, semi-structured data are very difficult to store and mine.

2. **Schema Less**: One of the most important attributes of semi-structured data is that it is schema less. In the case of structured data, there are proper structures, but in the case of semi-structured data there is no schema. In the case of structured data, there is a proper distinction between schema and data. But in the case of semi-structured data, there is no such distinction.
3. **Fast Changing**: The semi-structured data are fast changing data. Most of the semi-structured data come from various Internet sources; as a result of which, there is constant updating of the data which results in creating new updated data.
4. **Heterogeneous**: The semi-structured data are very much heterogeneous in nature. In other words, the semi-structured data are a mix of various types of data; rather it is a diverse mix of various types of data. The main reason behind this heterogeneity is the fact that most of the semi-structured data come from various Internet sources.
5. **No Strict Rule**: In the case of structured data, there are fixed schemas. A schema is a set of rules which data must adhere to. Any update which violates the basic nature of the schema is not permitted in the case of structured data. But the semi-structured data are schema less; as a result of which, there are no strict rules which govern the updating of the data.

Storage of Semi-Structured Data

From the above discussion, it is clear that semi-structured data are highly irregular and schema-less, which makes the storage of semi-structured data a key issue. There are two models which help in storage of semi-structured data.

1. ***OEM: Object Exchange Model***
2. ***DOM: Document Object Model***

1. **OEM**: The most popular model for storage of semi-structured data is the object exchange model (OEM). In the OEM model, the data are stored in the form of objects. The users develop new objects or can modify an existing object to create another new object. One of the main advantages of the OEM model is that there is no need for describing the schemas. Each object represented in OEM, it has its own schema. In an environment where it is often difficult to maintain consistency of the programmes or data representation and storage formats, such as in web-based technology, often OEM is used to represent complex data. OEM represents the semi-structured data in the form of graphs, rather than trees.

   In the OEM model to represent data objects, each object is characterised by the following attributes.

   (a) *Identifier*: Identifier helps to uniquely identify various objects across the system and is not visible to the end user.

   (b) *Label*: Label defines the meaning of the particular object. Labels are generally very informative as it helps to understand a particular object.

(c) *Type*: Type describes the data types shown with the help of OEM graphs, such as integer, real, string, etc.
(d) *The value*: Value defines the object in a more precise manner.

In OEM, an object can be

(a) *Atomic*: Atomic objects contain values in the form of some base data type (integer or string). They do not have any sub-component, for example, day or year or last name.
(b) *Complex Object*: The complex objects are, on the other hand, the collection of sub-objects or atomic objects. In the OEM terminology, complex objects are the collection of object identifiers.

The following example demonstrates this syntax of OEM text or object representation. Name of an individual is a complex object as it contains three other sub-components, viz., first name, last name and middle name. However, each of three components, viz., “first name”, “last name” and “middle name” is not further divisible. The user can therefore understand that name is a complex object with three atomic objects as components. So, the object “Name” can be encoded in OEM using the following syntax:

```
<Name {
<First Name “Ritu”>
<Middle Name “Kumar” >
< Last Name “Sen” >
} >
```

In this example, the complex object has the label “Name” and has three atomic OEM objects in its value. Therefore, while encoding, first the label of the complex object, viz., <Name appears, followed by curly brackets, as its value is complex. Each atomic object is encoded using “<”, followed by a label, for example, First Name, followed by a value which in this case is “Ritu”, ending with “>”.

Exhibit 3.6 Object exchange model

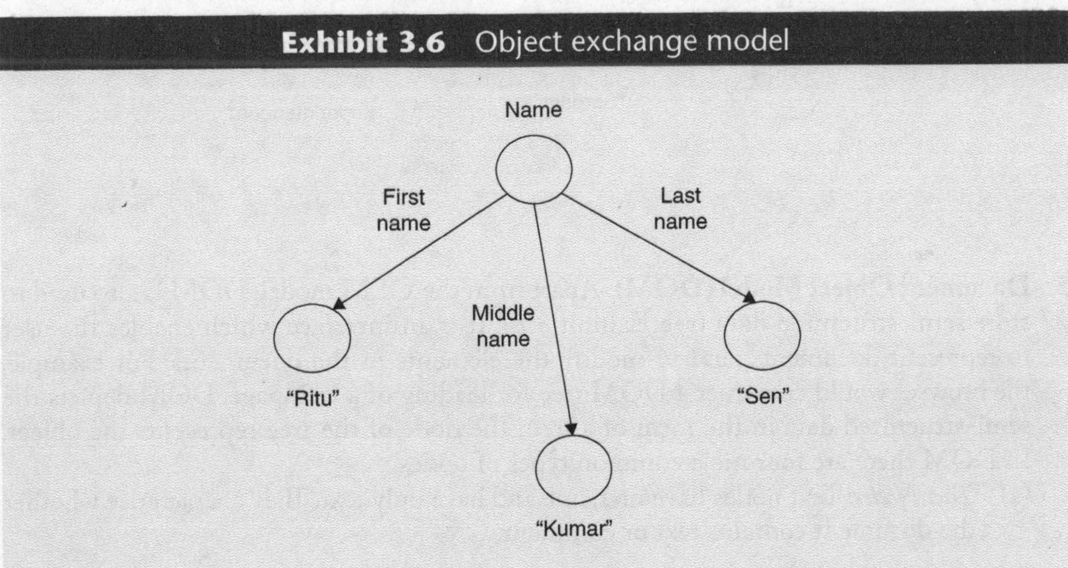

Here, the type identifier has been omitted, as the data types are intuitive. However, if we need to specify the same, then the syntax is changed as under <Age int 28>.

The same is represented in OEM graphically as well and is called a schema graph or a map object. The OEM map for the complex object "Name" is shown in Exhibit 3.6. Nodes represent objects and leaf nodes contain the value. In Exhibit 3.7, the details of the employees of a management college are shown using a schema graph. As is visible, different fields are maintained for different entries of data. This is why it is a semi-structured data. Each node represents an object such as faculty, staff, Management College and edges contain the object labels. There are two types of nodes:

(a) *Leaf Nodes*: It represents atomic objects and contains the value of the same. For example, "Head" is a value and a leaf node.

(b) *Non-Leaf Nodes*: It represents complex objects such as faculty or staff, which has several other fields.

Exhibit 3.7 Object exchange

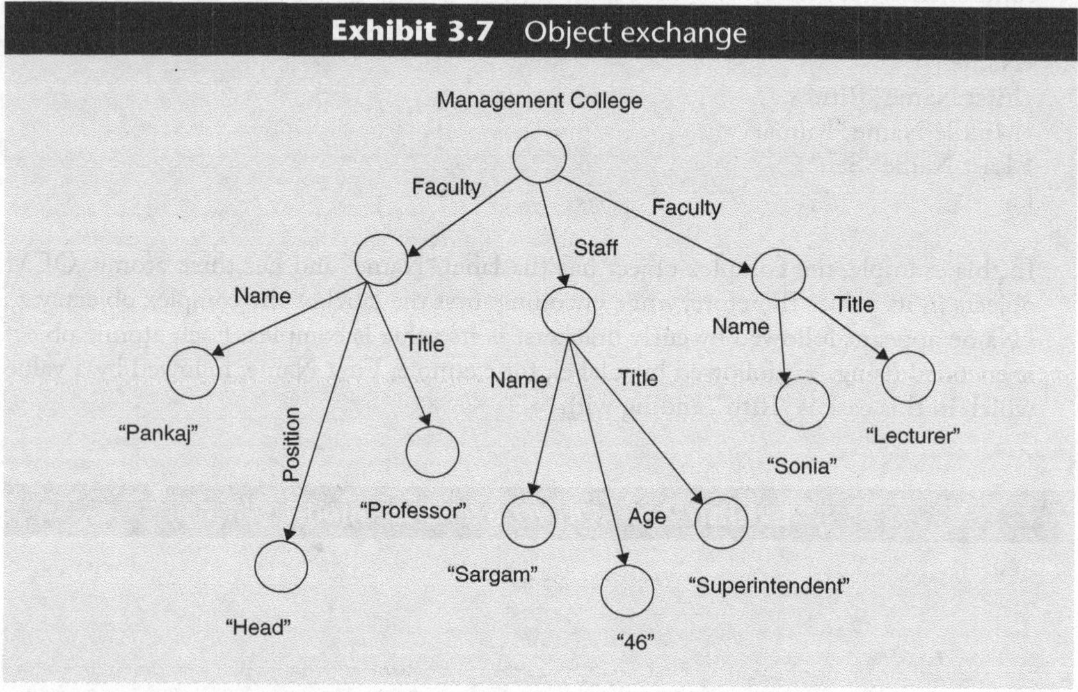

2. **Document Object Model (DOM)**: Apart from the OEM model, DOM is also used to store semi-structured data (see Exhibit 3.8). It is an interface which enables the user to represent documents, and to modify the elements of the documents. For example, the browser would construct a DOM tree for loading of a web page. DOM depicts the semi-structured data in the form of a tree. The node of the tree represents the object. In DOM there are four most common types of nodes.

   (a) *Text Nodes*: Text nodes have no name and have only text. They characterise whether the document contains text or comments.

(b) *Attribute Nodes*: Attribute nodes carry name and text. They specify the attributes of a given element or tag in the document. For example, "font" tag has "color", "size", "face" as attributes.

(c) *Element Nodes*: Element nodes have children. This specifies the different components of the document code such as <head>, <body>, <title> elements of the HTML documents.

Exhibit 3.8 Document object

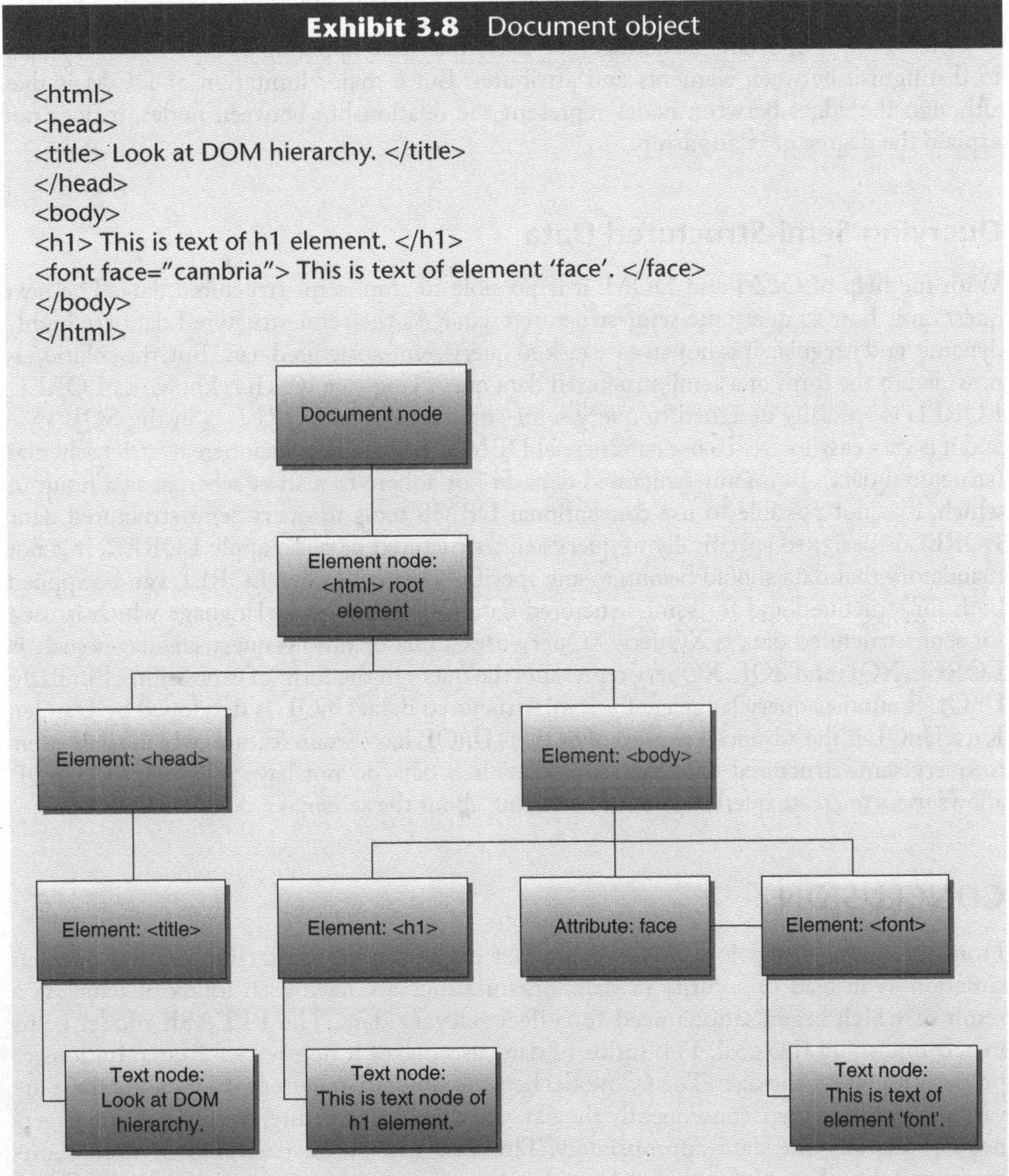

(d) *Document node:* Topmost node which identifies the document such as an HTML document.

The topmost node in the DOM tree is called the document node. It allows the user to access information in a direction that is from the parent to child node or vice versa. A simple representation of modelling of documents using DOM trees is shown as follows. A basic plain HTML document considered for this purpose is shown in the Box Exhibit 3.8.

One of the important advantages of DOM is that applying DOM it is very easy to distinguish between elements and attributes. But a major limitation of DOM is that although the edges between nodes represent the relationship between nodes, it does not explain the degree of relationship.

Querying Semi-Structured Data

With the help of OEM and DOM, it is possible to store semi-structured data. The next question is how to query the semi-structured data? As the semi-structured data are highly dynamic and irregular, it is not an easy task to query semi-structured data. But, the solution is provided in the form of a semi-structured data query language which is known as LOREL. LOREL is specially designed to query semi-structured data. LOREL is in the SQL style and it is very easy to use. To use commercial DBMS, the data should adhere to strict schemas (structured data). But, semi-structured data do not adhere to a strict schema; as a result of which, it is not possible to use conventional DBMS tools to query semi-structured data. LOREL is designed specifically to query semi-structured data. To apply LOREL, it is not mandatory that data should belong to any specific schema. Rather, LOREL can be applied both for structured and for semi-structured data. The other query language which is used for semi-structured data is XQuery. XQuery uses a mix of various query languages such as LOREL, XQL and SQL. XQuery represents the query in the form of expressions. Similarly, UnQL is another query language for semi-structured data. UnQL is developed by Damien Katz. UnQL is the advanced version of SQL as UnQL has certain features which allow users to query semi-structured data. As semi-structured data do not have schemas, the UnQL allows users to create queries without bothering about the schemas.

CONCLUSION

From the above discussion, it is evident that organisations are facing a rather peculiar situation as instead of security of data, organisations are having an influx of data. As a result of which organisations need to collect relevant data. The PLEASE model helps in accomplishing this goal. This influx of data also makes it necessary for organisations to properly represent the data. The 6C model helps to properly represent the data. As there are various sources of data, consequently the data also change its nature. Accordingly managers need to classify the data appropriately. The data can be unstructured or even semi-structured data. Knowledge of the data type is very important for a proper analysis of data.

In the next chapter, these concepts will be further applied to understand the fast-emerging area of business analytics, i.e., OLAP.

KEY TERMS

- PLEASE Model 49
- Data representation 51
- 6C model 52
- Unstructured data 54
- Semi-structured data 59
- OEM 60
- DOM 62

SUMMARY

In this chapter, various hidden aspects regarding data are discussed in detail. As earlier, there was the problem regarding the scarcity of data; as a result of which, managers were not able to take relevant decisions. But in the present time, organisations are having a flood of data; hence, it is very important to collect relevant data. The relevance in the data depends on many factors. The relevant data can be collected by applying the PLEASE model which includes the following stages

- ***Problem identification***
- ***Look for the data***
- ***Explain the data***
- ***Action***
- ***Share knowledge***
- ***Evaluate***

This chapter also discusses the important aspect of data representation. In this chapter, the 6C model is suggested for a proper representation of data. Various stages of the 6C model are discussed in detail. Moving forward, this chapter then discusses the two important types of data, i.e.,

Unstructured Data: This is the most common form of data which any organisation possesses. This type of data is not present in the form of relational tables, i.e., rows and columns. Then, various important aspects of unstructured data are discussed such as

- Characteristics of unstructured data
- Analysis of unstructured data

Semi-Structured Data: Unlike the unstructured data, the semi-structured data are not the raw data, but also unlike the structured data the semi-structured data do not fit into relational databases, i.e., not in the form of rows and columns. This type of data is not raw but has a highly irregular pattern.

This chapter also discusses various important aspects of semi-structured data such as

- Characteristics of semi-structured data
- Storage of semi-structured data
- Querying semi-structured data

The chapter closes with a case study and to have a better understanding of the concepts of unstructured data review questions and discussion questions are given at the end of this chapter.

MULTIPLE CHOICE QUESTIONS

1. Which of the following is not a characteristic of data in the present scenario
   a. Scarcity of data b. Explosion of data
   c. Diversity of data d. Velocity in data

2. The process of finding out right data is known as
   a. Data significance b. Data relevance
   c. Data invention d. Data innovation

3. Which of the following model is applied for data relevance
   a. PLEASE b. SMILE
   c. GLAD d. DISCOVERY

4. Which of the following is not a phase of PLEASE model
   a. Problem identification b. Explain the data
   c. Act on data d. Apply analytics

5. The process of a proper explanation of data is known as
   a. Data representation b. Data explanation
   c. Data versioning d. Data clarification

6. For data representation which model is applied
   a. 6C b. 6A
   c. 6B d. 6S

7. Which of the following is not a part of 6C model?
   a. Content b. Candor
   d. Crisp f. Clustering

8. The type of data which is present in the form of relational tables
   a. Unstructured data
   b. Structured data
   c. Formal data
   d. Casual data

9. Which of the following is not a type of data?
   a. Structured data
   b. Unstructured data
   c. Semi-structured data
   d. Semi-casual data

10. Which of the following is not an example of unstructured data?
    a. Images
    b. Tables
    c. Videos
    d. Feedback

11. Which of the following is the technique applied for the analysis of unstructured data?
    a. Mean
    b. Median
    c. Regression
    d. Text mining

12. The type of data which is not raw but partly structured and has highly irregular pattern
    a. Semi-structured data
    b. Unstructured data
    c. Casual data
    d. Semi-unstructured data

13. Which of the following is not a characteristic of semi-structured data?
    a. Regular pattern
    b. Irregular pattern
    c. Schema less
    d. Heterogeneous

14. OEM stand for
    a. Object exchange model
    b. Organic exchange model
    c. Oriented exchange model
    d. Object engaging model

15. DOM stands for
    a. Document object model
    b. Document oriented model
    c. Digital object model
    d. Direct object model

16. Which of the following is not applied for querying semi-structured data?
    a. SQL
    b. LOREL
    c. XQuery
    d. UnQL

REVIEW QUESTIONS

1. What is understood by data relevance?
2. Discuss how the PLEASE model helps in data governance.
3. What is the importance of data representation?
4. Discuss how the 6C model helps in data representation.
5. Discuss the relevance of unstructured data.

6. Discuss the reasons which make it difficult to analyse the unstructured data.
7. Discuss the analysis aspect of unstructured data.
8. Discuss the relevance of semi-structured data.
9. Discuss the characteristics of semi-structured data.
10. Discuss various techniques of querying of semi-structured data.

ASSIGNMENT

1. "Organisations now are facing the problem of managing the voluminous data rather the scarcity of data". Comment on this statement by discussing relevant examples.
2. Choose any MNC and try to identify the unstructured and semi-structured data which need to be considered for developing appropriate marketing strategies.

PROJECT ACTIVITY

1. Visit an organisation and discuss the PLEASE model with the concerned manager for collection of relevant data.
2. Suppose your department wants to start short-term courses in Banking, IT and Retail. Apply the PLEASE model and the 6C model so as to collect relevant data which are necessary to gauge the future demand of these courses.

CASE STUDY

Need for Data Quality Management

A power supply utility firm provides electricity services to all industrial, commercial and domestic users of North India which is in lakhs. The firm has the following functions.

- Generation, distribution and transmission of electricity
- Ensure reliable and uninterrupted supply to commercial and domestic users
- Maintenance of electricity networks and provides new networks
- Provision of new connections

- Asset management, such as equipments, transformers, etc.
- Complying with government regulations

Due to widespread functions, the firm has an interface with several entities such as government, suppliers, etc. As a result, the firm receives data from different disparate data sources, different lines of business units, multiple users, consumers and all stakeholders. Its current user base is in thousands and the firm employs more than 10,000 employees. Each of such interfaces of the firm results in different sets of data needs such as:

- Periodically reporting to government regarding its compliance with government regulations. It periodically reports to the government about plans, network performance, measures incorporated for public safety and ensuring reliable supply.
- Data arising from network-related tasks
  - These data needs can arise from network layouts such as information about ground cables, routes, aerial routes, etc.
  - Data about network location and assets
  - Data about the performance of each network so that in time steps can be taken to avoid any blackouts (a situation when complete power supply is cut off).
  - Data about feeders to detect faults
- Equipment such as transformers also leads to generation of data, which is related to periodic maintenance of equipment, procurement and maintenance of adequate inventory.
- Sub-stations need to be monitored to match real-time demand and supply, manage frequency and voltage and also provide information regarding load-shedding.

To date, the firm maintained part of its data in legacy systems and part was documented manually. Later, the firm deployed the ERP system for better functioning and analysis and required for mapping of these data onto this ERP-based system. However, the firm experienced difficulties in mapping onto the ERP-based system, as data were not in any set format or standardised, had redundancies, and there was no way to assess its completeness and accuracy. For the same reasons, it was also unable to utilise data for all the above-mentioned functions. Consider, for example, a scenario when an outage occurs (no power supply to a particular area). To manage such an outage, the system should be able to report which network is at fault, its exact location and alternate source to manage the supply till some corrective action can be taken. Besides, the information should be updated, which implies that the system should be able to extract daily operational data of networks. However, on many occasions, the firm could not mitigate the risk of network failure in time due to lack of availability of data which meet all such needs. The firm realised that it required high-quality data, which follows a standard format, is processed and cleansed and is assessed for completeness, accuracy and consistency.

An additional constraint was the hierarchical structure of the firm. The firm's flow of information was inhibited by the lack of clear assignment of roles and responsibilities for data management owing to this hierarchical structure. For example, linemen in the firm have the duty of detecting faulty feeders. But no mechanism is in place to pass on this information to junior engineers who are one up in this hierarchy. Therefore, junior engineers or others up the hierarchy cannot answer any query regarding the faulty feeders, as there is no mechanism for the flow of this information. This also led to delays in fault maintenance in several cases. Another area of concern was the queries posed by the strategic end of the firm. The strategic management frequently demanded high-quality data regarding customer management—their grievances, meter reading and bill generation, etc.; for decision making—which location required new network, which network has been consistently failing and requires maintenance; business intelligence—performance comparison at different locations, seasonal variation in power consumption; and for regulatory compliance. Besides, all the stakeholders such as employees, customers, public authorities have different data requirements; such employees may need to know when their arrears are due. In a nutshell, the firm and its interfaces observed a dire need for data quality management (DQM) which is the process of collection to processing, storing and presentation of high-quality data including change management and defining responsibilities.

In lieu of this, the firm incorporated a data management (DM) team of IT professionals. As a first step for data management, the team ensured that data are collected, stored and processed from different sources, for presentation as and when needed by different stakeholders. For this, the team interviewed managers and users of different systems to understand their data needs and the business outcome. They also studied the current techniques of data management and existing documentation of the firm. The expectation from the team was to come up with a data warehouse which stores only high-quality data. However, the DM team in short time started experiencing problems in DQM. They reported to the firm's management that they are unable to maintain high-quality data because they are facing a number of problems listed below.

- DQM is not solely the responsibility of the IT team. Because data that are maintained by the IT department are received and used corporate wide, an integrated approach is required for data management. The new approach should involve all stakeholders and IT specialists to maintain high-quality data. DQM has to provide balanced data as per needs to different interest groups.
- The team also felt that they had no cooperation from senior management due to non-priority of the DQM task—often their request for data maintenance was ignored due to other works in queue. Also, employees had no knowledge about high-quality data and no standards were communicated to them by the management for the same.

- The DM team was not provided access to all asset data and certain systems, making it difficult to integrate the data and to establish standards.
- No consensus could be reached for data standards—each system has its own pattern and set standards for data, which they were not ready to give up.
- Often, the DM team received no budgetary support, which further provided support to employees' belief that the tasks the DM team asked from them had little importance.
- There was no defined flow of information in the hierarchical structure of the firm. For example, actual fault and the solution lay in the hands of operational staff who had no means to communicate the same to people up the hierarchy in time.

Analysing the above problem, the team proposed that data warehousing is not the only solution to all the problems of the firm, as often it cannot be accomplished on time and is exhaustive in terms of time, money and resources. It was observed that the success of DQM depends on organisational policies rather than technical issues. Therefore, the team proposed the adoption of "data governance". Data governance has two-fold functions—assign corporate-wide responsibilities or accountabilities for DQM and establish guidelines and standards for the same. The literature suggests that data governance can be implemented using three approaches: governance via management in which managers execute decision rights, governance via stewardship in which there exists a hierarchy of roles and rewards and lastly governance via governance where the governor sets rules and stewards follow. Most of the firms commonly adopt the third approach as the entire firm shares the responsibility of maintaining the data quality in this approach. Clearly, to date, the firm was deploying governance via stewardship, which could not produce desired results due to lack of support from people and management. So, the DM team adopted a data governance initiative where the data governance structure had the following roles and responsibilities.

- Data governance council—This included members from strategic level of management who have control over asset data and power to resolve inter-division issue due to their positions. They review the budget for IT and non IT projects and have an interest in asset data management. Therefore, any new changes to be deployed across the firm for data management need an approval from this council.
- Data custodian—The custody of the asset data on behalf of the firm is in the hands of data custodian. They are responsible for planning for data management, such as data-cleansing plan, endorsing a data management plan proposed by the council, change management plan, and stakeholder management and converting strategic plans into tactical plans for actual implementation. Common titles of data custodians are Database administrator, ETL modeler, etc.
- Data stewards—The current DM team of the firm was to function as data stewards. This is because they have in-depth knowledge of current systems

and business processes. They have the technical expertise to handle change management, stakeholder management, project management and asset-related information systems. They act on behalf of the custodian. Everything planned by the custodian is put into action by the stewards. They train and educate users for data management.

- User groups—These were different stakeholders from different interfaces such as customers, vendors and managers from different divisions. They represent the actual sources of data. Therefore, they are responsible for collecting, processing and reporting the data. They report any data-related issues and need for any tools or support required for effective data collection. The firm often calls for user group meetings in the presence of IT staff to handle issues reported by user groups encountered during data collection. They can also ask for urgent meetings in the case of data-handling issues.

Therefore, the operational level for data governance is about the user groups, tactical functioning of data management is handled by data custodians and data stewards, and governance council comprises the strategic level. The creation of such a formal structure was required for effective management of high-quality data. Now, the DM team can propose any new requirements, which can be approved by the council for implementation. Besides, the entire firm is now aware of the importance of high-quality data and shares the responsibility for maintenance of the same. The team can purchase a data profiling and cleansing tool which can discover redundancies in the data. Also, metrics to assess the quality of data can be deployed.

Questions

1. Discuss various data needs of the power supply utility firm.
2. Discuss the problems faced by the power utility firm before incorporating the concept of data management.
3. Comment on the data governance structure adopted by the firm.

REFERENCES

Abiteboul, S. (1997). Querying semi-structured data. In Proceedings of ICDT.

Abiteboul, S., Quass, D., McHugh, J., Wisdom, J., and Weiner. J.L. (1997). The LOREL Query language for semi-structured data. In Journal of Digital Libraries, 1(1).

Baeza-Yates, R.A., and Ribeiro-Neto, B.A. (1999). *Modern Information Retrieval.* ACM Press/Addison-Wesley.

Berglund, A., Boag, S., Chamberlin, D., Fernández, M.F., Kay, M., Robie, J., and Siméon, J. (2007). XML Path Language (XPath) 2.0, W3C Recommendation. http://www.w3.org/TR/xpath 20.

Borgida, A., Casanova, M.A., and Leander, A.H.F. (2009). Logical Database Design: from Conceptual to Logical Schema. In L. Ling and T. M. Özsu (Eds.), Encyclopedia of Database Systems. Springer, Berlin, pp. 1645–1649.

Buneman, P., Davidson, S.B., Fernandez, M., and Suciu, D. (1997). Adding structure to unstructured data. In Proceedings of ICDT.

Clark, R. (2013). New Quantum Archiving Solution Reduces Burden of Unstructured Data Growth on Primary Storage. *Market Watch.* s.l.: http://www.marketwatch.com/story/new-quantum-archiving-solution-reduces-burden-of-unstructured-data-growth-on-primary-storage-2013-11-20?reflink=MW_news_stmp.

Cooper, B.L., et al. (2000). *Data Warehousing Supports Corporate Strategy at First American Corporation.*

Coyne, A. (2013). How the Crime Commission is taking on unstructured data. *ITNews for Australian Business.* s.l.: http://www.itnews.com.au/News/364227,how-the-crime-commission-is-taking-on-unstructured-data.aspx.

Da Silva, A.S., Laender, A.H.F., and Casanova, M.A. (1996). An Approach to Maintaining Optimized Relational Representations of Entity-Relationship Schemas. In B. Thalheim (Ed.), Conceptual Modeling – ER'96. Lecture Notes in Computer Science, vol. 1920. Springer, pp. 292–308, 1996. Dan Suciu, Query decomposition for unstructured query languages. In Proc 22nd VLDB conference.

Davenport, T.H., Harris, J.G., DeLong, D., and Jocobsen, Al. "Data to Knowledge to Results: Building an Analytic Capability", California Management Review 43/2 (Winter 2001): 117–138.

Diche, J., and Levy, E. (2006). Customer Data Integration: Reaching a Single Version of Truth (Hoboken, NJ: John Wiley and Sons).

Friedman, V. "Data Visualization and Info graphics: Smashing Magazine".

Grohser, T. (2008). Global Online Gaming Company Deploying SQL Server 2008 to support 100 Terabytes. *Microsoft Case Studies.* 2: http://www.microsoft.com/casestudies/Microsoft-SQL-Server-2008/bwin/Global-Online-Gaming-Company-Deploying-SQL-Server-2008-to-support-100-Terabytes/4000001470.

Hopwood, P. (2008). "Data Governance: One size does not fit well," *DM Review magazine.*

How a Financial Services Company Developed a Performance Report for Clients, Saved $200K and Sold $167,000,000 of Equity in Just 9 Months. *WinMetrics – BI Case Studies.* [Online] http://www.winmetrics.com/olap_casestudies.html.

Huff, D. (1993). How to lie with Statistics (New York: W.W Norton).

IBM. (2006). NYPD changes the crime control equation by transforming the way it uses information. *Data Warehousing and Business Intelligence – Success Stories.* NY: s.n.

Kawasaki, G. (2000). Rules for Revolutionaries: The Capitalist Manifesto for Creating and Marketing New Products and Services (New York: Harper Business).

Lawson, L. (2013). Three Reasons Why Life Cycle Management Matters More with Big Data. *ITBusinessEdge.* s.l.: http://www.itbusinessedge.com/blogs/integration/three-reasons-why-life-cycle-management-matters-more-with-big-data.html.

Nestorov, S., U4llman, J., Weiner, J., and Chawathe, S. (1997). Representative objects: Concise representations of semi-structured hierarchical data. In Proceedings of the Thirteenth International Conference on Data Engineering, Birmingham, England.

Nazilca, U. Garanti Bank Benefits from 10X Improvement in Reporting. *Oracle.* [Online] http://www.oracle.com/ocom/groups/systemobject/@mktg_admin/documents/webcontent/videoplayer-ocom.html?bctid=1400726933001&playerType=single-social&size=c23.

Online Analytical Processing (OLAP): A Fast and Effective Data Mining Tool for Gene Expression Databases. Alkharouf, N.W., Jamison, D.C. and Matthews, B.F. 2, (2005) s.l.: Journal of Biomedicine and Biotechnology.

Rogers, D., and Sexton, D. (2012). Marketing Measurement in Transition Study, Columbia Business School's Center on Global Brand Leadership and the New York American Marketing Association.

Server, M.S. SQL. Managing Unstructured Data with SQL Server. s.l.: http://www.microsoft.com/sqlserver/2008/en/us/default.aspx, 2008.

Solutions, Alna Business. Implementation OLAP and a Data Warehouse in Elektroskandia. *Alna Business Solutions.* [Online] 2003. http://www.alna.com/alna-business-solutions/about-us/success-stories/implementation-olap-and-a-data-warehouse-in-elektroskandia/.

Stonebraker, M. (2011), NewSQL vs NoSQL for New OLTP, Michael Stonebraker, VoltDB. s.l.: http://www.dataversity.net/newsql-vs-nosql-for-new-oltp/

Tay, L. (2013), Inside eBay's 90PB data warehouse. *IT news for australian business.* 5: http://www.itnews.com.au/News/342615,inside-ebays-90pb-data-warehouse.aspx.

Tresch, M., Palmer, N., and Luniewski, A. (1995), Type classification of semi-structured data, In Proc of Intl. Conf. on very large Data Bases.

Tufle, E. (2001). *The Visual Display of Quantitative Information, Cheshire,* CT: Graphics Press.

Zikopoulos, P.C. et al., (2012). Understanding Big Data: Analytics for Enterprise Class Hadoop and Streaming Data (New York: McGraw-Hill).

CHAPTER 4

Data Warehouse

After going through this chapter, you will be able to

- Understand the importance of data warehouse
- Understand the difference between traditional databases and data warehouse
- Know the data warehouse architecture
- Identify various factors that affect selection of an architecture
- Know the criteria for defining the success of a particular data warehouse design

INTRODUCTION

From the previous chapters, one can easily gauge the importance of data and gets familiarised with the concept of structured and unstructured data. All these structured and unstructured data of the firm act as an input to create data warehouse of a firm which is the next important aspect. Organisations worldwide are acknowledging the importance of data warehouse, because it is the key to provide business users with accurate, timely and relevant information. If the data in an organisation are not properly maintained and organised, it would never be able to make timely decisions. Data warehouse does just that—organise and maintain firm's data. Besides, it augments the firm's decision-making capabilities by allowing them to run business intelligence, such as queries, reporting or analytics on the top of that. There are various important concepts that are related to data warehouse. All these concepts are explained in this chapter. There are two techniques to build a data warehouse—relational modelling and multidimensional modelling. Each of these techniques has been discussed in detail in the next chapters.

Garanti Bank has 10 million customer bases, out of which 1.8 million use Internet banking. More than 50% of the bank is open to the market. The bank started experiencing low customer satisfaction levels owing to delay in user response. The bank decided to switch from mainframes to open systems. For the last 3 years, they have been working on data warehouse and experiencing ten times improvement in user query and therefore higher customer satisfaction.

Data warehouse is a centralised collection of subject-oriented, consistent, historical and secured data which facilitate OLAP applications. Now, in this definition, there are certain keywords which need further explanation.

DATA WAREHOUSE

Earlier, the organisation deployed traditional databases to organise and maintain its data. The problem with traditional databases was the amount of data they could handle. Today's firms deal with massive amounts of data, each in a different format. Therefore, traditional databases neither could handle this ever-increasing volume of data nor were flexible to accommodate different data formats. Besides, its use was limited to operational staff; strategic or managerial level could not base their decisions on the same. It offered no multidimensional view of the data, could not store data according to specific fields and allowed executing only OLTP queries. These databases were also risky because they had limited security options and were not consistent. So, the firms switched to data warehouses which are one-step solution to all the above-stated problems.

1. **Centralised:** The data warehouse facilitates centralised collection of data. Because the data are collected from various functional activities such as human resource, marketing, production, inventory, etc., it is very important that there should be a central repository of data because each department is dependent on other departments for taking critical decisions. For example, the Marketing Department is dependent on the Production Department and the Production Department is dependent on Human Resource and Materials departments. Hence, it is very important that every department should have access to the data. The data warehouse takes care of all these aspects.
2. **Subject-Oriented**: The data come from different sources so that it can help managers to take quick decisions. If all the data are dumped in one place, then it is very difficult to segregate the data and to do the analysis of the data. In data warehouse, the data are stored according to the particular subject such as human resource data, marketing data, financial data, etc., which helps to save time for analysis and facilitates decision-making.
3. **Consistent**: As the same data are viewed by different departments, it is very important that everybody should be able to view the same data, i.e., if the human resource manager views the data, then the same data should be available to the marketing manager and that too in the same format. If there is no consistency in data, then every manager will interpret the information in different ways. The data warehouse maintains the data consistency.
4. **Historical**: Organisations need to consistently change their strategies in the present dynamic environment. For this purpose, it is very important that organisations should have historical data so that it can help in forecasting the future appropriately to amend their strategies accordingly. Data warehouse stores historical data which helps the organisation to properly analyse the data and helps to frame strategies.
5. **Secured**: Data are very precious and no organisation can afford to lose the data. Data warehouse provides the much needed security to the stored data. The users are authenticated before providing access to the data in data warehouse. The authentication also serves as a means to decide the kind of access the user has—such as read-only access where the user can read the data, but cannot delete or modify it, read/write access, write access, etc.

6. **OLAP Queries**: One of the most important aspects of data warehouse is the kinds of queries that data warehouse supports. The traditional Databases support routine translational queries which are known as OLTP, i.e., Online Transaction Processing System. OLTP only supports transactional queries which can access limited records in the database, generally a few hundred records. But considering the kind of competition and dynamic environment, managers need to run complex queries where they need to analyse the information from different aspects, i.e., multidimensional analysis. With the help of multidimensional analysis, managers are able to view the different dimensions of the information which helps in better analysis of the information. The data warehouse provides such a facility of OLAP queries.

New York Police Department (NYPD) has approximately 37,000 police officers. The prime responsibility of the NYPD is to enforce law and investigations. It already had separate crime data systems, and speedy access to information is very important to aid in proactive and effective crime resolution. It incorporated crime data warehouse which delivered information in real times with project trends. It also enabled the efficient gathering and analysis of crime related data.

Hence, from the above discussion, one can understand the importance of data warehouse. Table 4.1 presents the difference between traditional databases and data warehouse.

Table 4.1 Difference between Traditional Databases and Data Warehouse

Traditional Databases	Data Warehouse
Databases support OLTP queries	Data warehouse supports OLAP queries
Traditional databases are meant for only operational control staff	Data warehouse is meant for managers
Traditional databases are not helpful in decision-making	Data warehouse helps in decision-making
Traditional database does not represent the data in a multidimensional view	Data warehouse provides the multidimensional view of the data
Data are stored in a normalised format	Data are stored in a denormalised format
It supports only a limited number of records	It supports a large number of records
Traditional databases can be only accessed by a limited number of users	Data warehouse can be accessed by a large number of users.
Data are not stored according to specific subjects	In data warehouse, the data are stored subject-wise
Traditional databases provide limited security	Data warehouse provides a high level of security
In traditional databases, the data are not in the consistent state	In data warehouse, the data are always in the consistent state

Data warehouse architecture describes how various components of data warehouse are arranged which in turn helps to understand the design of data warehouse.

DATA WAREHOUSE ARCHITECTURE

Data warehouse architecture describes how various components of data warehouse are arranged which in turn helps to understand the design of data warehouse. The knowledge of data warehouse architecture is very important because at the present time the environment is changing rapidly. To cope with this dynamic environment, the manager needs to retrieve different types of data. To accomplish the ever-changing demands of data, the organisation needs different designs of data warehouse. The data warehouse architecture helps to understand the designing of the data warehouse. Because a data warehouse integrates the data from disparate data sources into one common repository, designing of data warehouse often involves ETL tools. ETL stands for extraction, transformation and loading. The purpose of these tools is to extract the data from multiple data sources of the firm and to transform it so that it fits into the structure or format of the data warehouse. Once the input data become suitable for data warehouse, it is loaded into the data warehouse. The concepts of ETL will be discussed in detail in the next chapter. The classification of data warehouse architecture is discussed below.

Single Layer Architecture

As the name suggests, in single layer architecture there is only one layer which is known as source layer (see Exhibit 4.1). Hence, in this type of architecture, there is no distinction between the source layer and the data warehouse layer. Rather in the single layer architecture, the data warehouse is virtual. In the single layer architecture, middleware is used to access the data warehouse. (Note: Middleware is software which is used to connect two separate applications. For example, middleware software is used to connect the HTTP server with scripting engines such as ASP). Generally, such an architecture is deployed in firms which have massive transactional data and need to make real-time decisions based on these data. For example, based on change in weather conditions for a given day and the order history for that day, a pizza chain would modify its material procurement. If it sees that weather forecast is rainy, and it has received a lesser number of orders compared with past records, then it would order fewer raw materials for that day. Also, if a company has disparate data sources, such as legacy systems, data from online or web services, files, etc., then middleware can be used by firms to connect to these disparate sources and access raw data to make decisions. As middleware is used to interpret the queries, the processing speed of single layer architecture is very slow.

In single layer architecture, there is only one layer which is known as source layer.

Two Layer Architecture

In the two layer architecture, there is a proper distinction between the source layer and data warehouse layer which is not present in single layer architecture (see Exhibit 4.2).

Exhibit 4.1 Single layer architecture

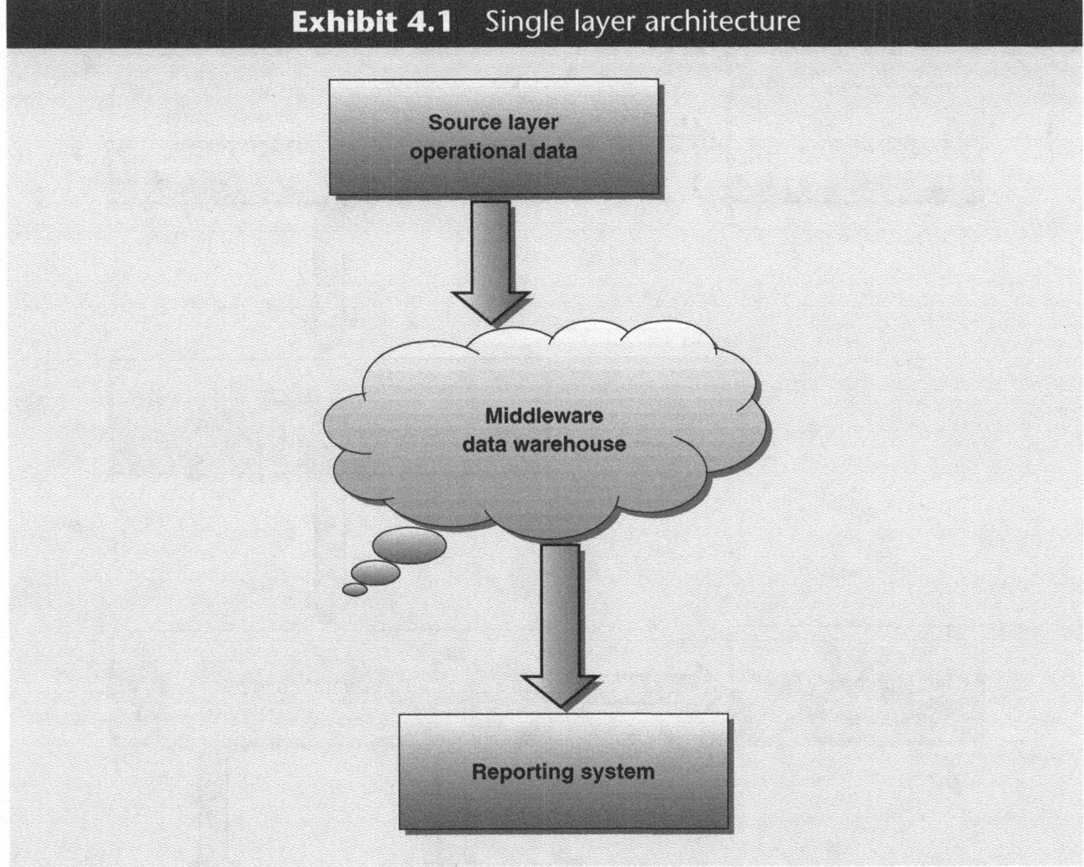

1. **Source Layer**: In the source layer, the data from various sources, i.e., operational data as well as data from external sources are collected. But as these data are not homogenous it is very important to extract, transform and load the data so that there is uniformity in the data. This process is done by applying proper ETL tools (ETL tools will be discussed in detail in the next chapter).
2. **Data Warehouse Layer**: After applying appropriate ETL tools, the Data Warehouse is created. The data in this Data Warehouse are homogenous. With the help of the Data Warehouse, managers are able to apply not only reporting tools but also OLAP tools for proper analysis of data using multidimensional view of data stored in the data warehouse.

Three Layer Architecture

In the two layer architecture, there are two layers, i.e., source layer and data warehouse layer but in three layer architecture there is one additional layer which is known as an operational data store or reconciled layer (see Exhibit 4.3).

Hence, the three layer architecture has the following layers:

In the two layer architecture, there are two layers:

- Source Layer
- Data Warehouse Layer

Exhibit 4.2 Two layer architecture

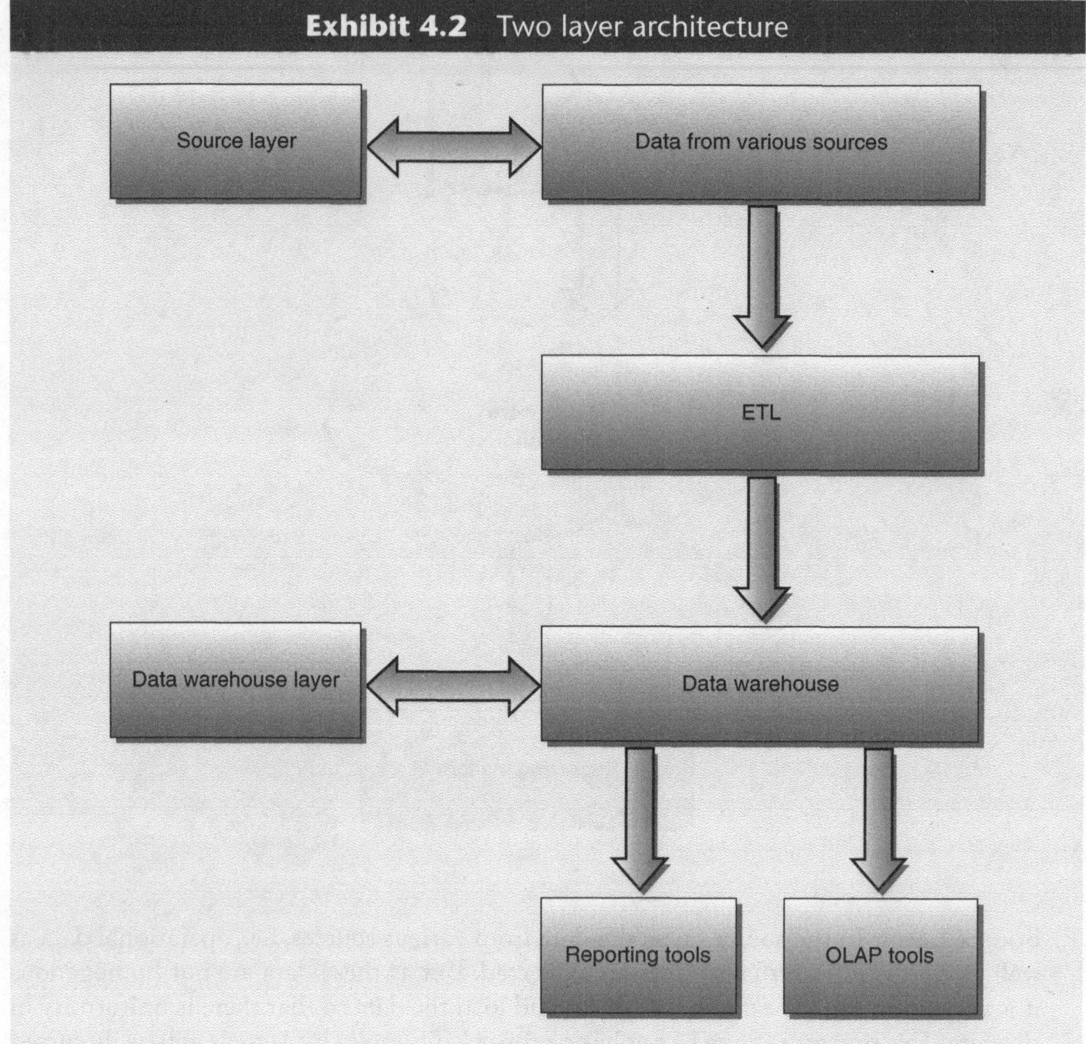

1. ***Source layer***
2. ***Operational Data Store (ODS) layer***
3. ***Data Warehouse layer***

> In three layer architecture, there is one additional layer which is known as operational data store (ODS) or reconciled layer.

1. **Source Layer**: The data from operational and external sources are fed into the source layer. These heterogeneous data are then processed into homogenous data using ETL tools.
2. **Reconciled Layer or ODS Layer**: The operational data layer or reconciled layer stores the current data, i.e., data stored in the ODS layer have a limited prior history. Consider transactional data or real-time data which are

Exhibit 4.3 Three layer architecture

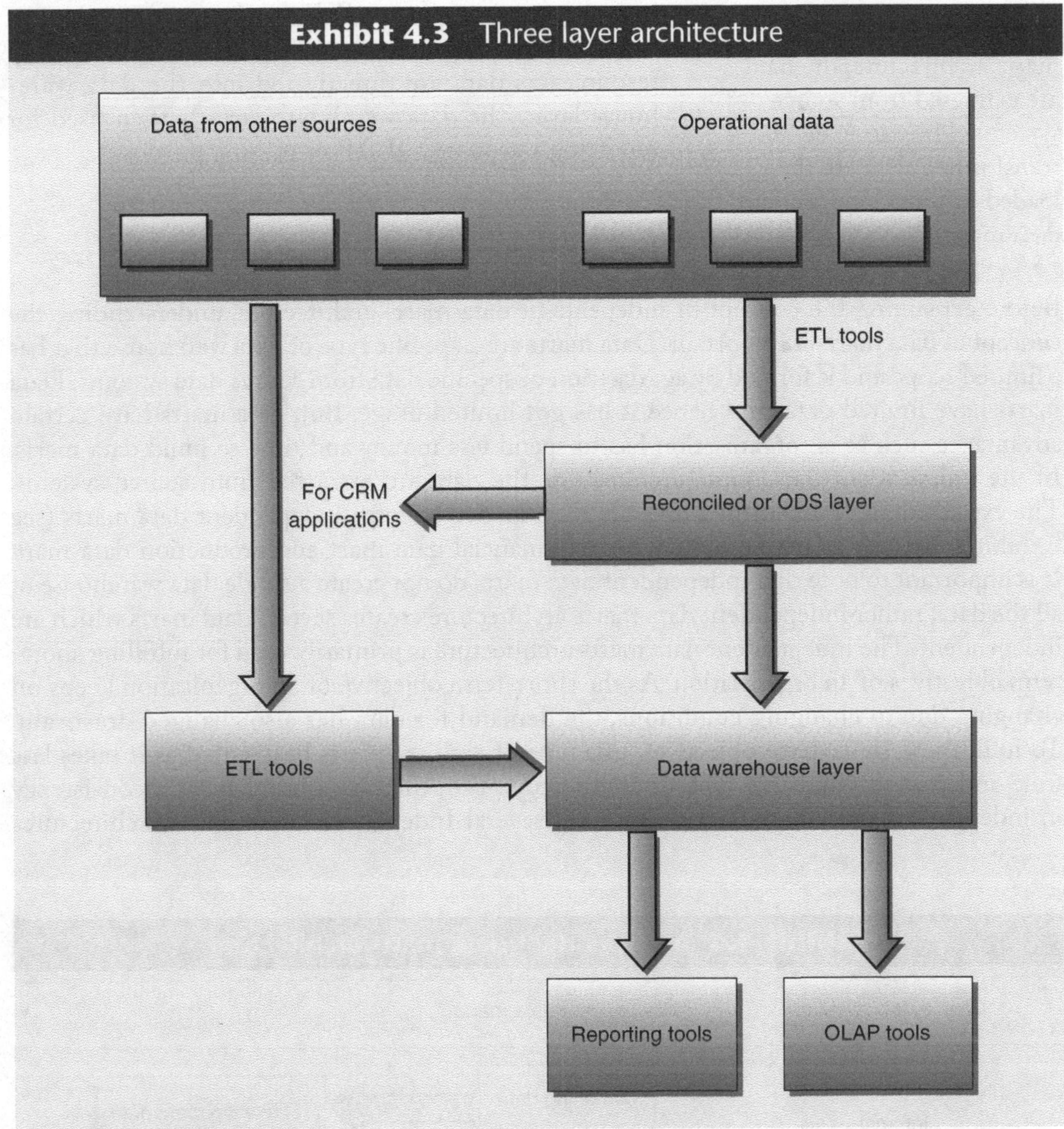

required for decision-making in certain applications of the firm, such as CRM for responding to customer requests. In such cases, ODS stores this chunk of data to be utilised by certain applications. The main advantage of creating ODS is that ODS is a full-fledged system in itself, which allows applications such as CRM to directly access current data. This ODS layer increases the response time of firms by reducing the time to access real-time data which have not yet been processed for storage.

3. **Data Warehouse Layer**: The data warehouse system receives the data from the ODS layer and also from other sources. The data coming from the ODS layer are

In the independent data marts architecture, the data are extracted from source systems. The extracted and transformed data are then loaded to form independent data marts.

homogeneous as proper ETL tools are applied so as to make the data homogenous. This saves time and resources as data are directly fed into the data warehouse layer. The data warehouse layer is then used for reporting purposes, OLAP or mining purposes.

Independent Data Marts Architecture

Before explaining the concept of independent data marts architecture, understanding the concept of data marts is important. Data marts are a specific type of data warehouse that has a limited scope and is formed by aggregation of specific data from source data systems. Data marts have limited data, and hence it has got limited usage. But, data marts have certain advantages such as an organisation has to spend less money and time to build data marts. In the independent data marts architecture, the data are extracted from source systems. The extracted and transformed data are then loaded to form independent data marts (see Exhibit 4.4), such as marketing data mart, financial data mart and production data mart. It is important to note that independent data marts do not create a single data warehouse of all the data; rather independent data marts architecture creates several data marts which are independent. The independent data marts architecture is primarily used for fulfilling short-term objectives of an organisation. As the short-term objective of an organisation keeps on changing due to changing conditions, the demand for data has also changed drastically. To fulfil these short-term objectives, this type of architecture is best suited as it takes less time and cost to build this type of architecture. But, there is a problem of inconsistency in independent data marts architecture. As several Independent data marts architectures

Exhibit 4.4 Independent data marts architecture

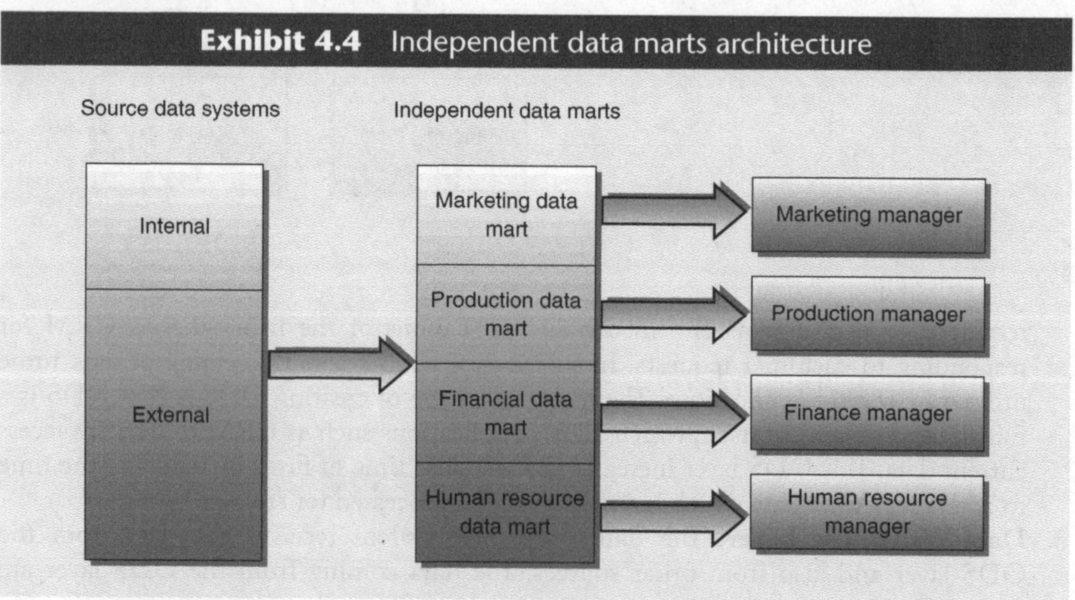

are created with different tools, the data marts are not consistent with each other. Moreover, the independent data marts are not shared because no single data warehouse is created; as a result of which it has got limited capabilities.

In the bus architecture, the independent data marts are linked with each other using appropriate middleware.

To overcome the above-stated limitations, bus architecture design is applied (see Exhibit 4.5). In the bus architecture, the independent data marts are linked with each other using appropriate middleware. Hence, the basic limitation of independent data marts architecture is solved by connecting all the independent data marts. The linking of the various data marts helps to maintain the consistency of the stored data.

Exhibit 4.5 Bus architecture

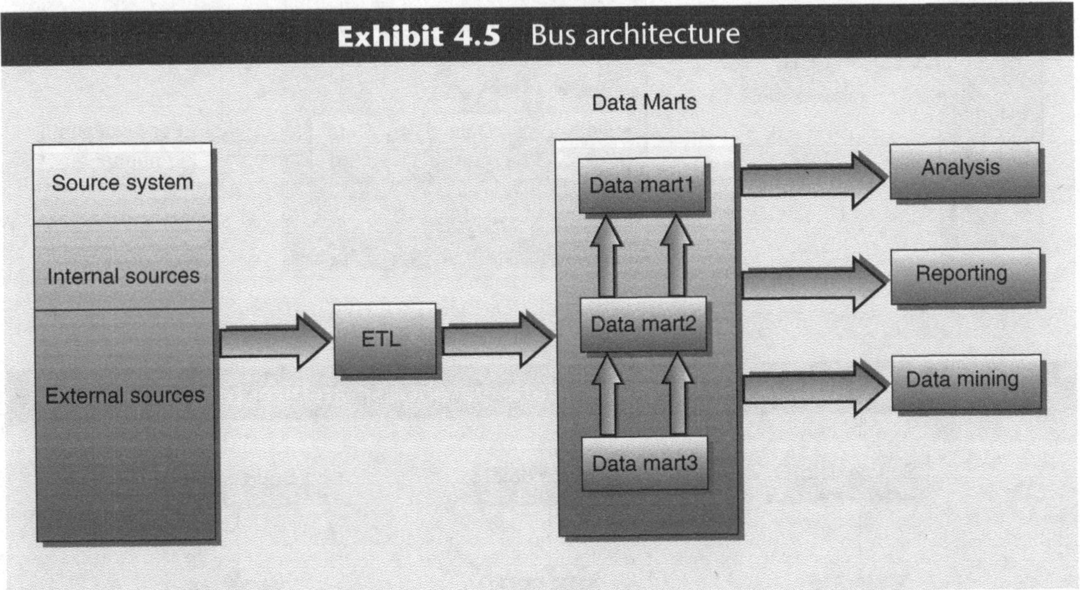

As shown in the exhibit, the data from the source system are extracted, transformed and loaded to build data marts. But here, all the data marts are linked with each other, and these linked data marts are known as bus architecture or dependent data marts.

Hub and Spoke Architecture

In the hub and spoke architecture, the data from source data systems is extracted, transformed and loaded into central data warehouse (CDW).

The hub and spoke architecture is the most widely applied architecture design for the data warehouse (see Exhibit 4.6). In the hub and spoke architecture, the data from source data systems are extracted, transformed and loaded into central data warehouse (CDW). This CDW acts as a hub and the various source systems from which the data are extracted are input spoke of the hub. The data from this CDW is then loaded into various dependent data marts. The specific functional manager such as Marketing Manager can access data from various data marts and when the General Manager wants to analyse the information regarding the organisation the data from CDW can be accessed. The various dependent data marts act as output spokes.

Exhibit 4.6 Hub and spoke architecture

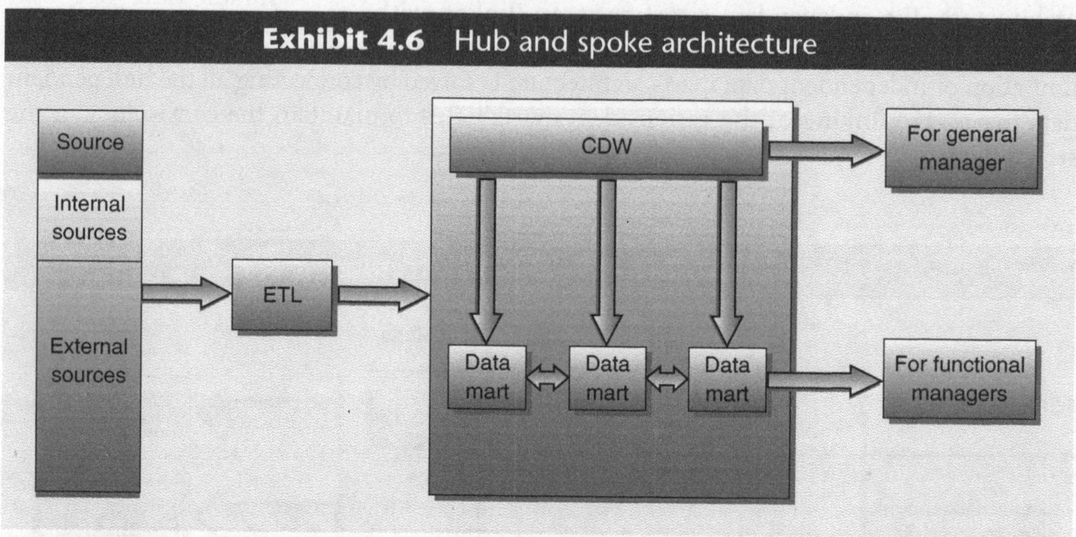

Exhibit 4.7 Federated data warehouse architecture

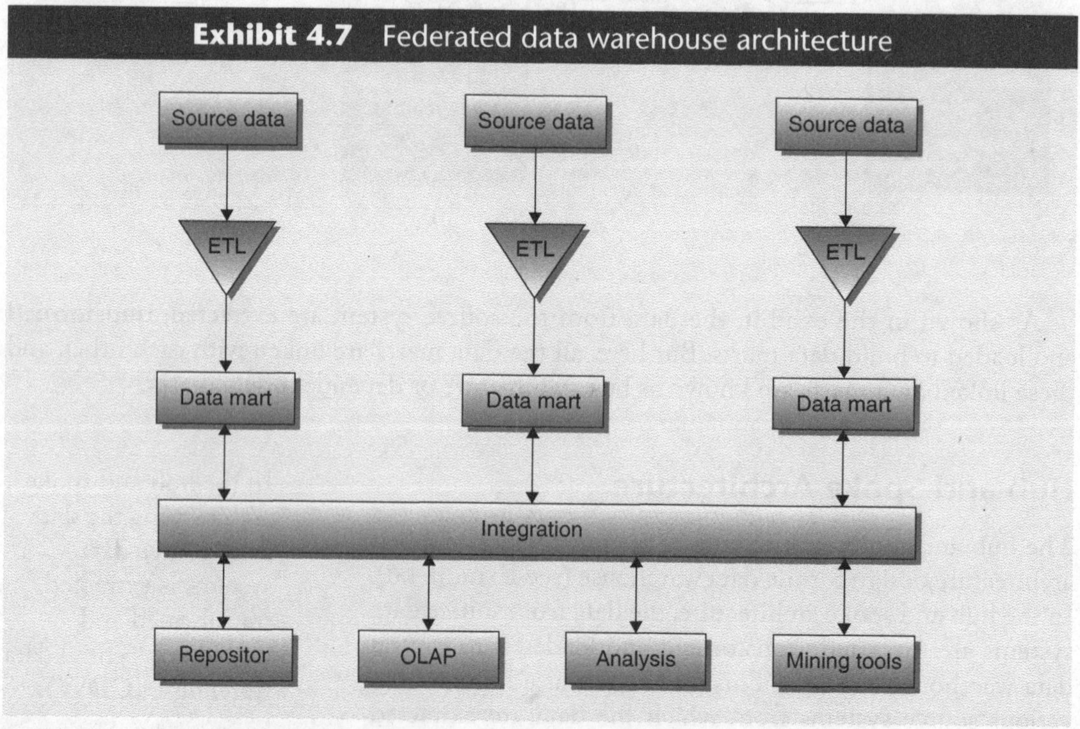

Federated Data Warehouse Architecture

Due to the rapidly changing conditions, the organisational data requirement also changes. In the federated data warehouse architecture (see Exhibit 4.7), the disparate or existing data marts are integrated, unlike bus architecture which integrates independent data marts created from same data sources. The disparate data marts/data warehouse are integrated by the use of either middleware or various advanced technologies such as meta-data interoperability.

In the federated data warehouse architecture, the disparate or existing data marts are integrated.

FACTORS THAT AFFECT SELECTION OF AN ARCHITECTURE

As we have discussed the various types of data warehouse architecture, there are certain factors which govern the choice of the particular architecture. The following are the factors.

1. **Information Interdependence between Organisational Units:** The intensity of interdependence between different units is an important factor which governs the selection of a particular architecture. The organisation should analyse very carefully the amount of interdependence of different units so that an appropriate data warehouse architecture can be selected. For example, if the firm obtains data from a number of disparate data sources which are to be analysed individually to assist in decision-making in the firm, then the federated data marts architecture should be utilised. If the business units make some decisions which are specific to their business functions (such as which digital marketing strategy should be chosen as a core marketing decision) and for some other decisions (such as upgrading an existing product to match customer needs would require data integration from marketing, production, HR units), requiring integrated data from different business units, then hub and spoke architecture would be best suitable.
2. **Information Need**: Every organisation has its own specific needs and it is very important to know the specific needs of functional managers and the top management. For example, the level of drill down capabilities or Roll-up capabilities needed to decide the kind of data warehouse architecture. This implies the ability of the warehouse to present consolidated data such as total annual sales, which can be drilled down to the lowest level of detail to total quarterly sales, monthly sales, weekly sales and day-wise sales. The reverse is roll up that is starting from the lowest level of detail; the warehouse should be able to aggregate or consolidate the data till the highest level.

Factors that affect selection of an architecture:

- Information Interdependence between Organisational Units
- Information Need
- Urgency
- Tasks
- Resources
- Importance
- Expert Opinion
- Compatibility
- In-House Staff
- Sponsorship
- Technical Issues

3. **Urgency**: Some designs take more time as compared with other designs. The urgency of warehouse plays an important role in deciding the particular data warehouse architecture.
4. **Tasks**: Every design helps to analyse the data in a specific manner; moreover, different designs also support different types of queries. Hence, the nature of task that the Data Warehouse should perform matters a lot in deciding the type of architectural design.
5. **Resources**: Every design requires different kinds of resources in the form of IT personnel, cash, hardware and software issues, etc. Hence, before deciding a particular design, every organisation should evaluate its resources.
6. **Importance**: Every organisation views data warehouse in a different manner, e.g., for some organisations, data warehouse is part of the strategic plan whereas for another organisation, data warehouse is seen as support for other applications. The role to be played by data warehouse should be kept in mind before deciding any particular architectural design. For example, if the data warehouse is being designed for a particular application and not for the entire organisation, then the single-layer architecture can be used which is non-strategic.
7. **Expert Opinion**: As development of data warehouse is a costly affair, organisations should take the opinion of different experts. That is, before selecting a particular data warehouse design, the viewpoint of experts should be given due consideration.
8. **Compatibility**: As in the present time, every organisation has a certain information systems, which helps the organisation to run smoothly. The proposed data warehouse architectural design should gel with the existing system so that it could give a synergy effect to the present system. For example, if a firm has a number of disparate systems which act as data sources, then either single layer architecture or federated data marts would be useful.
9. **In-House Staff**: The designing and implementation of Data Warehouse involve many technical issues. Organisations need capable IT staff not only for designing the application of data warehouse but also for smooth running of data warehouse on day-to-day basis. Before choosing a particular design, the organisation should evaluate the capabilities of its in-house staff so that proper decisions can be made as to whether the in-house team can handle the demanding job of designing and maintenance of a data warehouse in an efficient manner or not.
10. **Sponsorship**: As the designing and implementation of data warehouse require much money, the source of sponsorship plays an important factor in deciding a particular design. Different departments act as profit centres or a business unit which can be accounted for profits and revenues of the firm on a standalone basis. So in case the particular profit centre is sponsoring the data warehouse project, then the need and requirement of that particular department will be given more preference and architectural design will be selected according to the needs of the sponsoring department.
11. **Technical Issues**: Data warehouse operations are very much technical in nature. One major technical concern is the amount of data that it can handle. If a firm deals with massive transactional data such as banks or pizza chains, then it needs to deploy three layer architecture. This is because the ODS layer would aid in real-time decision-making, whereas the warehouse layer would aid in strategic decision-making due to

integrated data. Another concern is the analysis part or what kinds of analytical tools and techniques the warehouse can support. Besides, warehouses should be scalable; that is with changes in size of the firm and changes in the environment, it should be able to accommodate larger data and improved analytical tools. These factors should be considered before selecting a particular architecture design because every design of data warehouse has its pros and cons.

CRITERIA FOR DEFINING THE SUCCESS OF A PARTICULAR DATA WAREHOUSE DESIGN

As discussed above, the data warehouse can be created by using any of various architectural designing techniques. Every organisation does take into account various factors into consideration before selecting a particular design. But as the environment is very dynamic and the organisation is spending huge amount of money and resources to build a data warehouse, it is imperative that organisations should review the performance of the selected data warehouse design from time to time. The following are the perspectives that should be considered for the evaluation of the success of a particular design.

1. **Information Perspective**: As every organisation requires timely information for taking quick and relevant decisions, the quality of information is very important for taking accurate decisions. The data warehouse is primarily designed to store data and retrieve information. The data warehouse should provide accurate information to the users. Over the period of time, organisations should evaluate decisions taken on the information retrieved from the data warehouse. If those decisions were appropriate, it means that the quality of information is good. Similarly, as departments are dependent on each other, it is very important that there should be consistency in the information viewed by different departments; otherwise, different departments will retrieve different information that will lead to chaos. Moreover, as the competition is very intense, organisations need to update the information quickly; hence, it is very important that the data warehouse should be updated quickly and all the departments should be able to view the updated information. If the data warehouse is fulfilling all these requirements regarding the information perspective, then it means that the design is appropriate from this perspective.
2. **Technical Perspective**: The data warehouse design needs constant upgradation as an organisation needs to constantly add more users, more applications and diverse queries. The data warehouse should provide the facility of upgradation and that too without any compromise on the final output of the information.
3. **User Perspective**: In spite of the best design and applications if users are not able to use the data warehouse, then the selected design is of no use. Hence, it is very important that the operations of data warehouse should be user-friendly. This feature

Successful data warehouse design criteria:

- Information Perspective
- Technical Perspective
- User Perspective
- Long-Term Perspective
- Access Rate Perspective
- Monetary Perspective

carries more weightage as in any organisation there are many non-technical users. The ease of use of data warehouse not only helps in facilitating the use of data warehouse by nontechnical users, but also helps in quick retrieval of information.

4. **Long-Term Perspective**: The Data Warehouse is designed to fulfil the goals and objectives of an organisation. The data warehouse has a long-lasting impact on the organisation. If the data warehouse is not helping to fulfil the goals and objectives of an organisation, then the organisation should think seriously to change the architectural design of the data warehouse.
5. **Access Rate Perspective**: Time is money for organisations as the managers need to take quick decisions so that they can counter the competition. The data warehouse should provide faster access to the information required by the managers. Any delays in the required information will have a negative effect on the future prospects of the organisation. But at the same time, it is also important that managers should get the complete information because if data warehouse is giving quick but incomplete information then that architectural design is not appropriate.
6. **Monetary Perspective**: Every data warehouse architecture needs resources and before building the data warehouse, the organisation decides the budget regarding the designing, implementation and running of the data warehouse. The architectural design of the data warehouse is only successful when the data warehouse is developed and implemented in that pre-decided budget limit.

DATA WAREHOUSE IMPLEMENTATION

Implementation of data warehouse has been a critical process as even if the data warehouse is designed properly, but not implemented properly then it would not give appropriate results. The implementation defines how the designed data warehouse will be applied practically. It helps to define the steps needed for the execution of the data warehouse. The implementation can be done by the approaches discussed here.

> The implementation defines how the designed data warehouse will be applied practically.

Top-Down Approach

Top-down approach was propagated by Bill Inmon (see Exhibit 4.8). According to him, first the organisation should create a centralised repository of complete data. This means that all the data are stored first in the centralised repository which is known as enterprise data warehouse (EDW). The data stored in EDW will be in a normalised format so as to avoid data duplication and inconsistency. After creating EDW, the organisation depending on its requirements creates subject-specific data marts, for example, marketing data mart, finance

> In top-down approach, firstly the organisation should create a centralised repository of complete data. It means that all the data is stored firstly in the centralised repository which is known as enterprise data warehouse.

Exhibit 4.8 Top-down approach

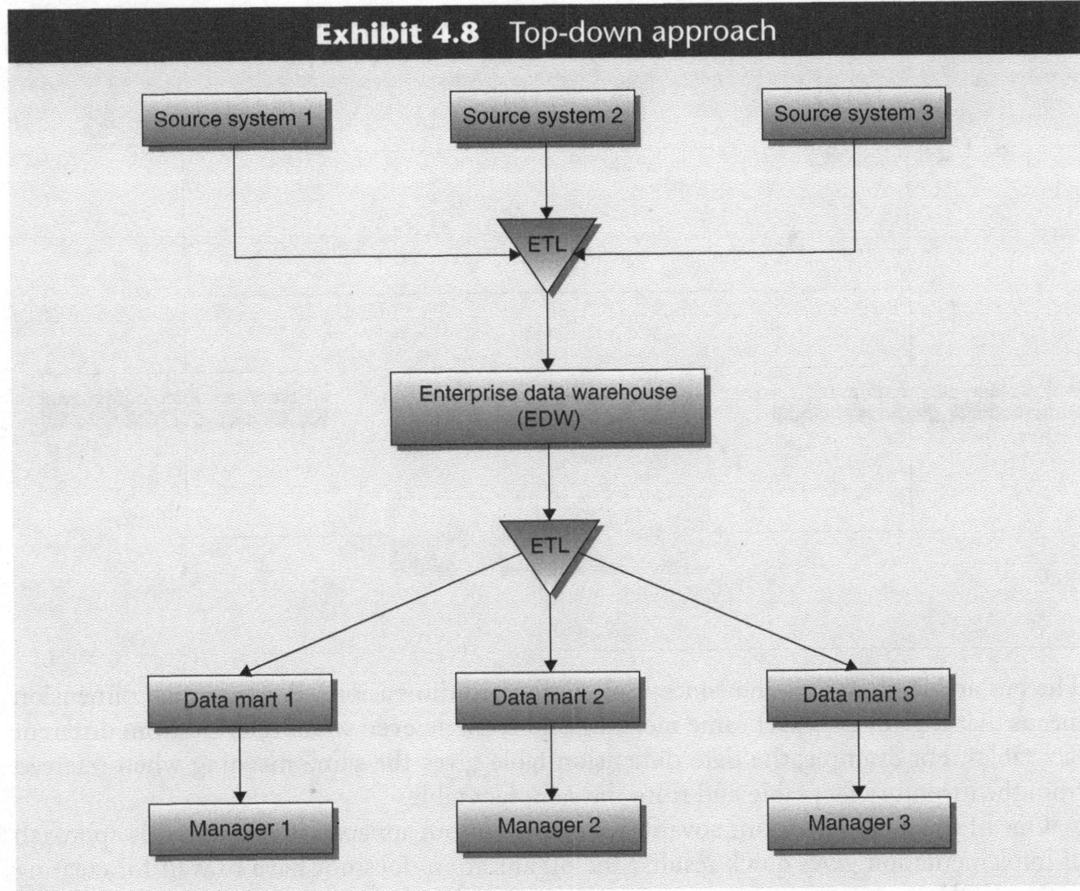

data mart, etc. The data stored in the data marts are in a denormalised form so as to increase the access rate. The top-down approach helps to create single repository, i.e., EDW in a normalised form which helps to enhance consistency in the data. Moreover, as the need arises, using top-down approach, specific data marts can be created in a denormalised form for faster access of data. But on hindsight, it requires more cost and time for implementation as first EDW is created and then subject-oriented data marts are created.

Bottom-Up Approach

Bottom-up approach was propagated by Ralph Kimball (see Exhibit 4.9). In the bottom-up approach, first the organisation creates subject-specific data marts, for example, marketing data mart, human resource data mart, etc. After this process, the integration of individual data marts is done by applying bus architecture.

> In bottom-up approach, firstly organisation creates subject specific data marts, for example, marketing data mart, human resource data mart, etc.

Exhibit 4.9 Bottom-up approach

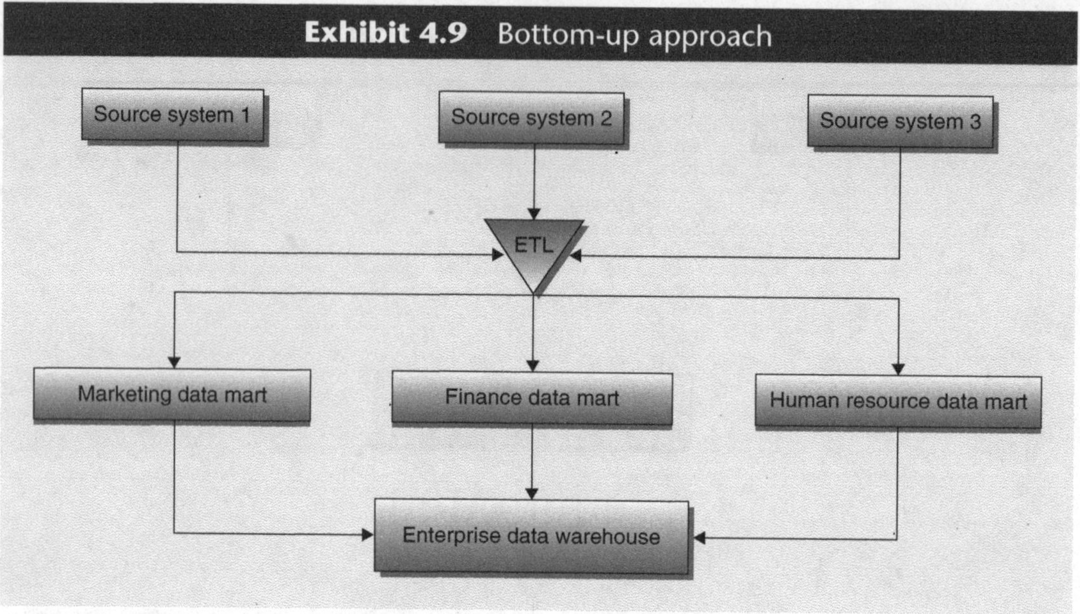

The bus architecture uses the concept of conformed dimensions. A conformed dimension means that it gives the exact same meaning and content, even when refereed from different fact tables. For example, the date dimension table gives the same meaning when refereed from the inventory fact table and from the sales fact table.

One of the most important advantages of the bottom-up approach is that this approach of implementation gives quick results. The organisation does not have to wait for creating entire EDW, but instant reports can be generated from subject-specific data marts. Moreover, as the need arises more data marts can be created. But as the data is stored in the denormalised format, it requires more space for storage and also has less drill-down capabilities as compared with the top-down approach.

Hybrid Approach

Hybrid approach combines above-mentioned approaches, i.e., top-down and bottom-up approaches. Also, it is difficult to know in advance all the data marts, which are needed to create a central repository. Moreover, it is not possible to segment all the data from source systems into subject-specific data marts. Hence, in the hybrid approach, the organisation starts building a centralised source as well as identifies the data marts (see Exhibit 4.10). The data from source systems are extracted, transformed and loaded into data marts as well as in the central repository of data warehouse. The central repository data as well as data from specific data marts are synchronised with each other. The user depending on the need can access data from a central repository as well as from data marts.

> Hybrid approach combines top-down and bottom-up approaches.

Exhibit 4.10 Hybrid approach

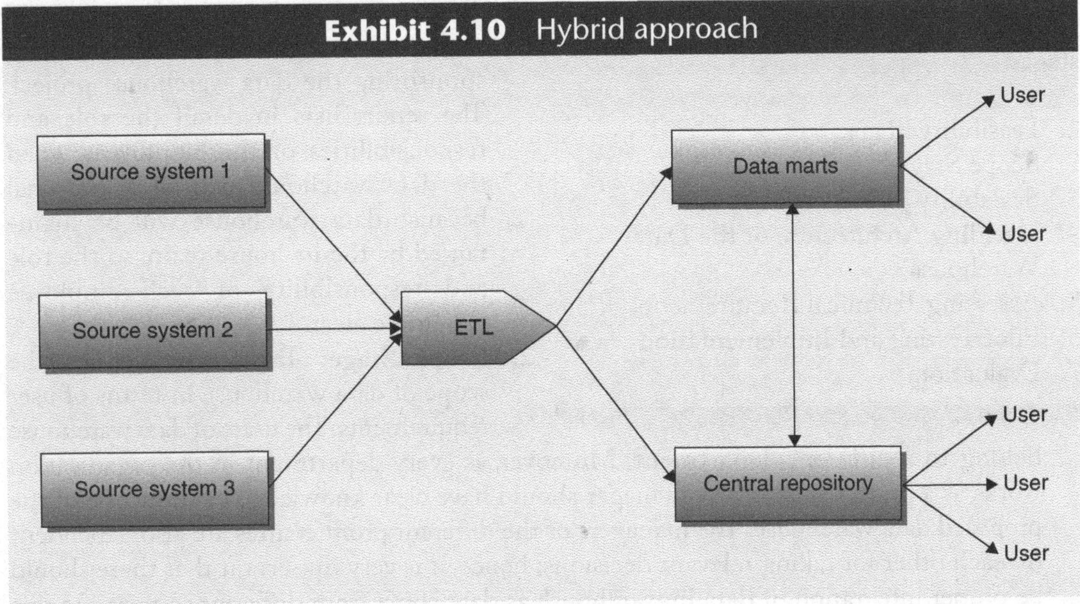

First American Corporation (FAC) in 1990 lost $60 million and launched a drive to centre its customers in all aspects of the company's management. This required the implementation of a data warehouse. For the success of the strategy, they implemented data warehouse called VISION which maintains transactional data and product details, consumer buying preference and profitability. The advantage of the firm is that it could identify the top 20% of customers who contributed to the entire profit and around 50% who were not profitable at all. This enabled the firm to develop relationships with loyal and profitable customers and to aid in business expansion.

DATA WAREHOUSE DEVELOPMENT

The development of data warehouse takes place in different phases. These phases are known as data warehouse development stages. The final data warehouse comes into place after going through all of the following stages. The top management plays a very important role in all the development stages as development of data warehouse involves much cost and resources. Let us discuss the development stages in detail.

1. **Feasibility Stage**: In the first stage of development of data warehouse, the organisation crosschecks the feasibility of the proposed data warehouse. The IT team under the guidance of the top management prepares a detailed feasibility report. This report covers all the operations of the organisation and the areas where data warehouse is needed. This report also covers the financial aspects related to the proposed data warehouse. Sometimes, data marts are also initially created for a certain number of departments.

Data warehouse development stages:

1. Feasibility Stage
2. Scope Stage
3. Scalability
4. Deciding Architecture of the Data Warehouse
5. Assessing Technical Requirements
6. Pilot Testing and Implementation
7. Evaluation

This report also shown to the concerned managers to get their approval for sponsoring the data warehouse project. The report lists in detail the role and responsibilities of the employees when the data warehouse will be operational because data warehouse will be maintained by the in-house team, so the role and responsibility of each employee should be clear.

2. **Scope Stage**: This stage defines the scope of data warehouse in terms of user requirements. The users of data warehouse belong to a different department. Moreover, as every department in the organisation works as a profit centre, every manager should have clear knowledge of the scope of the proposed data warehouse. The managers of the different profit centres are also dependent on each other for taking relevant decisions; hence, it is very important that there should be proper integration of data in warehouse as data come from different sources. At this stage, the scope of the proposed data warehouse is defined precisely after taking into account the demands of different managers.
3. **Scalability**: The next stage in the data warehouse development is the scalability. The organisations are working under highly dynamic and intensely competitive environment. Once the data warehouse is created, it will not work forever. Organisations need to add more applications and more specific data marts in the existing data warehouse. Hence, it is very important that the data warehouse should have scalability. In this stage, the organisation sets rules and procedures for adding new dimensions and applications in the data warehouse. The organisation decides that how the IT team can scale the operations of the data warehouse. Here, the organisation fixes the responsibility of administrators and managers for enhancing the functionality and applications of the data warehouse.
4. **Deciding Architecture of the Data Warehouse**: The data warehouse can be designed by using different architectures. Every architecture design has its own pros and cons and is suitable for the particular situation. The architecture can be categorised as:
   - Single layer
   - Double layer
   - Three layer

   The organisation should have clear knowledge about all the architectures and also requirements in detail so that an appropriate architectural design can be selected.
5. **Assessing Technical Requirements**: Once the architectural design is decided, then for designing and smooth running of data warehouse, support is needed in the form of hardware and software components. The data warehouse should have an appropriate operating system, DBMS and mining tools, so as to get the best results. There are many advances in the technology in the last 10 years; organisations should have knowledge

of various technological advances so that appropriate technology can be selected for developing the data warehouse. For example, there should be a provision for data backup in the data warehouse as in the case of any problem in data warehouse the organisation cannot afford to lose the data. Hence, there should be a provision for data backup and recovery in the data warehouse.

6. **Pilot Testing and Implementation**: After going through all the above stages, the data warehouse is ready for use. But as the practical implementation of data warehouse has a long-term effect on the working of the organisation, it is very important to do pilot testing of the proposed data warehouse. The pilot testing is done under controlled conditions where a select group of managers evaluates the actual performance of the data warehouse. If the results are satisfying, then the complete implementation of data warehouse is done. This implementation is done by using the following approaches.
   (a) Top-down approach
   (b) Bottom-up approach
   (c) Hybrid approach

   Every approach is applied under specific conditions; hence, the organisation should be very clear about its requirements and resources. Depending on these aspects, an appropriate implementation approach is selected.
7. **Evaluation:** This stage is a never-ending stage as the organisation constantly needs to evaluate the performance of the data warehouse in the dynamic environment. For evaluation the organisation should take into account the following factors in detail.
   - Information perspective
   - Technical perspective
   - User perspective
   - Long-term perspective
   - Access rate perspective
   - Monetary perspective

CONCLUSION

At the present time, there is a lot of demand for the data warehouse. There is a drastic shift from traditional databases to data warehouse. Considering the dynamic and competitive environment, the organisations need to store subject-oriented, consistent, historical and secured data which facilitate OLAP applications. The data warehouse provides these features. As the data warehouse can be created by following various architectural techniques such as single layer architecture, two layer architecture, three layer architecture, independent data marts architecture, bus architecture, hub and spoke architecture, federated data warehouse, the knowledge of various concepts of data warehouse is necessary for managers. Each architectural technique is unique and any wrong choice of architectural technique can have a devastating effect on the organisation. Similarly, knowledge of data warehouse implementation techniques is very important for applying the right implementation technique. After the creation of data warehouse, the managers can apply the data mining techniques. In the next chapter, all the concepts regarding data mining will be discussed in detail.

KEY TERMS

- Data warehouse 76
- Single layer architecture 78
- Two layer architecture 78
- Independent data marts architecture 82
- Bus architecture 83
- Hub and spoke architecture 83
- Federated data warehouse architecture 85

SUMMARY

In this chapter, a detailed discussion is done on the various concepts of data warehouse. The chapter starts with the basic definition of data warehouse. Then in detail the difference between traditional databases and data warehouse is explained. To understand data warehouse it is important to understand the data warehouse architecture. All the aspects of data warehouse architecture such as factors that affect selection of an architecture of data warehouse architecture are explained in detail. Then, in the next part, the criteria for defining the success of a particular data warehouse design are discussed. As the data warehouse can be created by using various designing techniques, it is very important to evaluate the created data warehouse. In the closing part of the chapter, two important concepts are explained in detail. The first is the data warehouse implementation approaches. All the approaches of the data warehouse implementation are explained in detail. In the last, the development of data warehouse is discussed. The development of data warehouse takes place in different stages such as

1. Feasibility Stage
2. Scope Stage
3. Scalability
4. Deciding Architecture of the Data Warehouse
5. Assessing Technical Requirements
6. Pilot Testing and Implementation
7. Evaluation

All these stages are discussed in detail. This chapter closes with two case studies, and to have a better understanding of the concepts of data warehouse review, questions and discussion questions are given at the end of the chapter.

MULTIPLE CHOICE QUESTIONS

1. The centralised collection of subject-oriented, consistent, historical and secured data which facilitates OLAP applications is
   a. Data center
   b. Data warehouse
   c. Database
   d. Data store

2. Which of the following is not a characteristic of data warehouse?
   a. Multidimensional
   b. De-normalized format
   c. OLTP
   d. OLAP

3. In the single layer architecture which technology is applied to access the data
   a. Middleware
   b. Centralware
   c. Accessware
   d. Jointware

4. In the three layer architectural design, the third layer is known as
   a. ODS
   b. OBS
   c. OCS
   d. OAS

5. The reconciled layer is applied for
   a. Strategic decisions
   b. Analysis
   c. CRM
   d. OLAP

6. The specific type of dataware that has limited scope and is formed for aggregation of specific data is
   a. Data marts
   b. Data base
   c. Data warehouse
   d. Middleware

7. The architecture which is applied to solve the problems of independent data warehouse architecture is
   a. Bus architecture
   b. Linked architecture
   c. Connected architecture
   d. Interlinked architecture

8. The architecture where one CDW is created and then dependent data marts are formed is known as
   a. Hub and spoke
   b. Dependent and independent architecture
   c. Main and sub part
   d. Primary and secondary architecture

9. For top-down implementation, which architectural design is applied
   a. Hub and spoke
   b. Three layer design
   c. Two layer design
   d. One layer design

10. For bottom-up implementation, which architectural design is applied
    a. Hub and spoke
    b. Bus design
    c. Two layer design
    d. One layer design

11. Bill-Inmon propagated which type of approach
    a. Top-down
    b. Bottom-up
    c. Hybrid
    d. Matrix

12. Ralph Kimball propagated which type of approach
    a. Top-down
    b. Bottom-up
    c. Hybrid
    d. Matrix

13. The approach which combines top-down and bottom-up approaches is
    a. Hybrid
    b. Mixed
    c. Combined
    d. Matrix

14. The architectural design in which disparate data marts/data warehouse is integrated either by use of middleware or meta data interoperability is
    a. Federated
    b. Three layer
    c. Two layer
    d. Hub-spoke design

REVIEW QUESTIONS

1. Define data warehouse.
2. What is the difference between traditional databases and data warehouse?
3. Define single layer architecture.
4. Discuss two layer architecture.
5. Define three layer architecture.
6. Explain independent data marts architecture.
7. Discuss bus architecture.
8. Define hub and spoke architecture.
9. Explain federated data warehouse architecture.
10. List various factors that affect selection of an architecture.
11. What are the criteria for defining the success of a particular data warehouse design?
12. Discuss various data warehouse implementation approaches.
13. Discuss different development phases of data warehouse development.

ASSIGNMENT

1. Discuss the importance of data warehouse.
2. Discuss the limitations of the following architecture designs.
   (a) Single layer architecture
   (b) Two layer architecture
   (c) Three layer architecture
   (d) Independent data marts architecture
   (e) Bus architecture
   (f) Hub and spoke architecture
   (g) Federated data warehouse architecture
3. What are the advantages and limitations of the following implementation approaches?
   (a) Top-down approach
   (b) Bottom-up approach
   (c) Hybrid approach

PROJECT ACTIVITY

1. Visit a company and study its data warehouse structure.
2. You are assigned a project to design the data warehouse for your university. In a group of three students, choose an architecture design and implementation approach which will be best suited for your university.

CASE STUDIES

I. Profitable Bank Data Warehousing

Profitable Bank is a commercial bank operating across the country since 2000. It started with a limited number of branches in Punjab, India. The services provided by the bank gradually expanded beyond the state. The bank massively expanded by acquiring regional banks in the country. Besides basic credit and risk services, it diversified into financial services such as insurance services, foreign trade and money market. By the end of the financial year 2008, the bank had a presence over the majority of the country by operating through 700 branches all over India.

To stay competitive in the present era, the bank offers modern applications such as mobile banking and Internet banking. In its endeavor, to increase physical presence and make debit facilities easier, the bank has more than 1500 ATMs across the country. Today, the bank is a leading bank in the country with very high customer satisfaction and products and services that are tailored to the needs of the customer segments. From regional bank to pan India bank, the journey of Profitable Bank is truly remarkable and in this journey, data warehouse played a very important role for Profitable Bank.

Initially the massive expansion brought lot of problems, as expansion resulted in high number of transactions which meant huge operational and transactional database. Extracting meaningful information from transactional databases was a complex task as updates were very often and data in transactional database was not standardised. Also, the flow of information in the bank across different departments with clients and customers increased. The bank did not have the requisite database to support increasing data. The current technology had limited capabilities in terms of storage, analytical abilities and robustness.

As transactional data were not cleansed, which resulted in redundant data and queries run this data took longer time to execute and therefore reports were delayed. This, in turn, implied that management could not get the requisite information on time which is required to take important decisions, and at certain times this would also obstruct the tactical decisions in the bank. Clearly, the advancement was required in the existing technology and the only viable solution was a ***Data Warehouse.***

Areas of Concern

In 2008, bank realised that the current technology had limited capabilities in terms of the following aspects.

- **Capacity**: The current data capacity had been reached and therefore no new sources of data could be accepted. This implies that data for new clients, new products and new services had no storage space.
- **Technicality limitation**: Analytics could not be deployed on existing database because of the underlying technology. This posed a severe threat to the bank's strategic positioning. To suggest a few benefits that analytics would have provided the bank are to understand its most and least profitable segments against those of competitors and the products that are best and those which are not performing so well.
- **Coverage**: The coverage of the current technology was limited in terms of the dimensions that the bank operates in. For example, it did not adequately cover customers, products, credit, profitability, transactions, channels, etc.

The bank was also experiencing performance issues. The ad-hoc queries run on the transaction database would take extremely longer time than normal to execute and fetch the results. Also, because already the storage limit was reached, extracting information by managers became a tedious task and made them impatient as they could not timely respond to management, client or the situation at hand. The bank had no disaster recovery system in place. A bank cannot operate successfully nationwide if it has no facility to protect the data of its clients and customers. Profitable bank had no system to rollback the data in the case of failure of transactions. There was also no scheme to recover the data or take a backup because of limited storage, which is a huge threat to consumers of the bank.

Another major issue which it faced was integration problem and also there was no mechanism to build data marts. The marketing department could not build its own data mart as there were storage complications, and therefore could not offer the best-in-class customer services and the bank lacked customer relationship management. Similarly, the other departments such as finance or operations could not build their own data marts. There was no way the bank could ascertain the credit worth of an entity because of lack of tools to support the same. Also, there was no provision to entertain a new dimension owing to integration and data storage limitations.

The impact was such that diversification and expansion started looking like a wrong decision for the bank because the cost of operating has increased and the bank could not tap the opportunities in the marketplace. It started losing goodwill among customers due to inefficiency owing to time and resources. Nobody wished to delay the response, but the system would not answer in the given time frame. All it led to frustration and impatience among the employees, clients, customer and the management. Imagine a marketing team trying to segment the customers in a newly acquired region, but has no support the data of its new customers and hence cannot segment them and reach out to them as per their needs.

Finally, the bank decided that data warehouse is necessary and for that three-tier data warehouse architecture would be adopted. This architecture is not only scalable, but also resolved data redundancy issues, enabled disaster recovery, provide front end tools for reporting and provided multidimensional analysis of the bank data.

Three-Tier Architecture of Data Warehouse

Data were integrated from all the transactions and operational databases across the bank and using ETL tools; the data were cleansed, standardised and loaded into the data warehouse (see Exhibit 4.11). A metadata repository contained the standardising rules for the warehouse. The transaction data are updated in real time to reflect the changes in the customer's bank account and to provide access to the same on mobile banking, ATMs or Internet banking.

Exhibit 4.11 Three-tier data warehouse

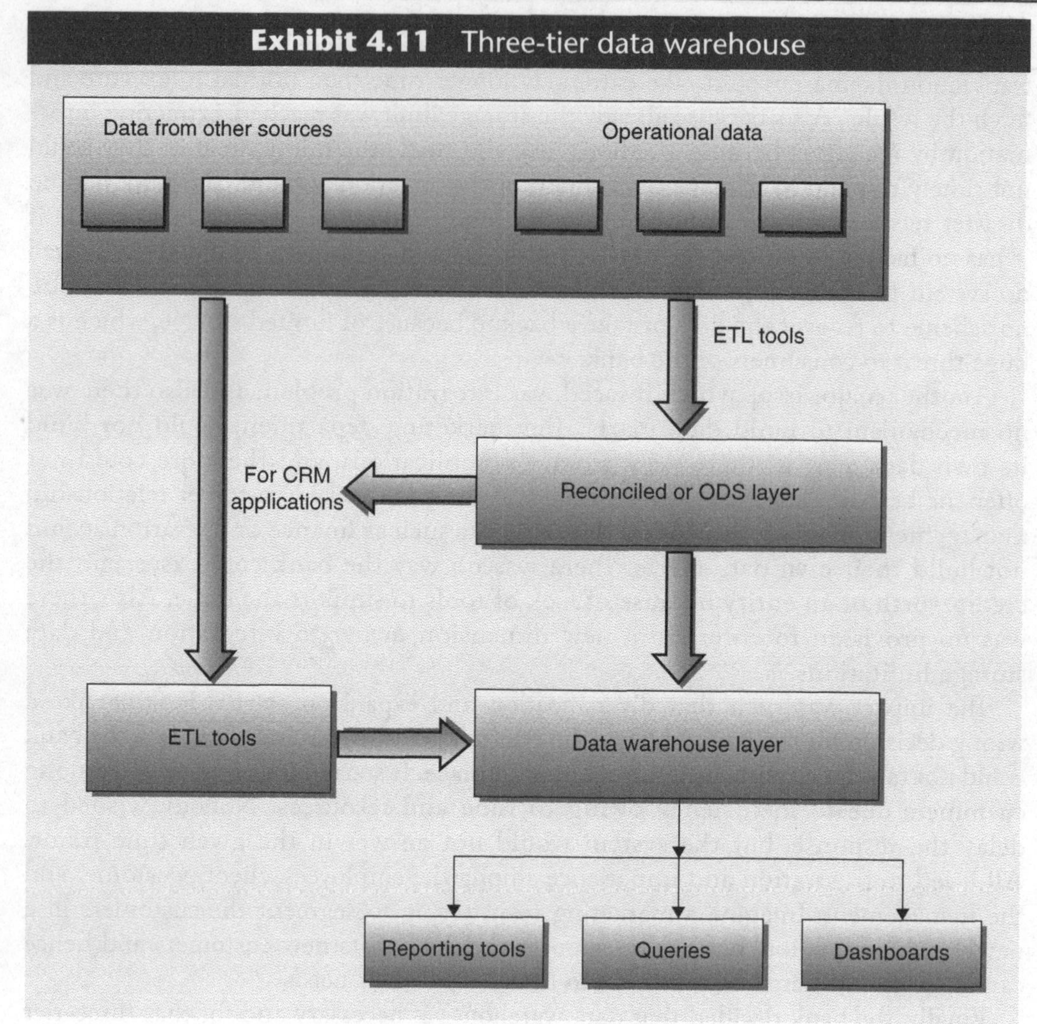

In the data warehouse layer, the data are stored in the form of dependent data marts like marketing data mart, MR data mart, etc. This provided a strategic advantage to the bank because now the analytics were domain specific and hence targeting the customer segments became easier. The bank soon rose in customer satisfaction by providing best-in-class loan facilities, credit and debit card facilities and hassle-free insurance. This provided two-way advantage—one domain-specific data and another integration of specific data. The system supported the building of the multidimensional semantic model to enable analytics to be implemented over the data and gain insights into serving customer better in the marketplace. Further, the system supported front end tools such as reporting, queries, and dashboards using KPIs (key process indicators).

Benefits of Warehousing

The advantages of deploying the three-tier architecture are that the unified data are available to all the users of the banking system, viz., the top management including directors, president of different functional areas and executive customers and middle and lower level management. The user interface and tools are offered as per the user's stature, for example, dashboard tools and access to data from all the departments are given to directors. Data warehouse stores the data in relational databases, while cubes can be built on top of these data marts. Therefore, the sources of data are flexible and consequently the tools are also flexible based on the underlying modelling of the data.

The system now offers a multidimensional view. For example, customer data can be viewed along several dimensions such as at different time periods, what was the frequency of credit or debit, across products—which products are used the most, region of operation and the amount of investment. Such an analysis can enable a manager to easily identify the characteristics of the top selling product or service, or most profitable customer who can then be provided additional services or investment options with more benefits than regularly offered. Other such analysis can be made across different products, insurance services and analysis against competitor's offerings.

CRM is better enabled as a separate data mart in the form of ODS layer is maintained for customers, which contains the information about their assets, personal demographics such as age, marital status, number of children, etc. All this information is also fed into data warehouse layer. Utilising this information, the marketing department can appropriately target the customer, like offering education loans for customers with children in that age group, or home loan for recently married with corresponding address different from mailing address. Using data mining techniques, patterns can be extracted for customer usage of different products.

The user interface for the system is customisable and has drag and drop features to change the layout of reports. For example, simply dragging month and insurance scheme sold would display the total sales for different insurance schemes in each month. The interface for customers enables them to easily navigate across the system and to gain access to their account and policies of the bank and new offerings. Similarly, depending on the employee cadre, different interfaces with reporting tools are enabled.

Complex ad-hoc queries can be executed in a fraction of seconds. The data can be integrated from different data marts to fetch results. For example, which product sells the most in a particular region and which customer segment buys it the most. The system also offers drill-down features, such as previous query fetches the result that education and home loans sell the most in Punjab, then the user can further drill down the result as to in which district of Punjab maximum and minimum sales exist. This enables the management to design effective fact-based strategies to increase sales in the low-sales region.

As in data warehouse layer, all the data are stored in the form of dependent data marts which provided the much needed integration of complete data. The integration brought many advantages to bank, for example, assume that the finance department believes that a particular loan facility is feasible for a given segment of consumers; it can then coordinate with marketing to validate the same and then use the services of marketing to communicate the new facility to its target segment. The reverse is also possible. If the marketing department sees an opportunity in the marketplace, it can communicate the same to finance department to check its feasibility.

This system has made reporting a completely hassle-free job. The data from different departments are now available on a common platform which also provides tools to extract information from them and report them in the standard required by the user. The user has the controls to change the layout of the report as required or export it to other formats such as excel sheets or access database files, etc. Also dashboards can be constructed by using KPIs (key point indicators).

The advanced system has a visible impact on the customers and enabled the bank to effectively counter the competition. The performance of the system is magnificent in terms of speed, data quality and storage ability. The system also provided the strategic competitive advantage to the bank and has made the bank a more customer-oriented bank with offerings pleasing to both the customer and the bank.

Recovery has also become easier with the advent of this system, as it timely generates warnings for the defaulters, communicates them and still if they are non-compliant, adequate measures can be taken to collect the credited amount.

Questions

1. Discuss various problems faced by Profitable Bank before the implementation of data warehouse.
2. Comment on the choice of three-tier architecture adopted by Profitable Bank for implementing data warehouse.
3. Discuss the benefits of data warehouse in Profitable Bank.

II. "Comfort on Wheels" Data Warehousing

"Comfort on Wheels" is a private luxury bus service which operates in major cities and offers comfortable tour across the country. The bus service was started in 2000, generated lot of hype as one of the best luxury bus service but suffered major losses. Although there was no shortage of travelers and the bus was always on tour, but the firm was unable to understand the reason for losses. There were frequent complaints from the customer regarding poor bus services, variable charges and late schedules to name a few. Clearly, the way the firm was being run needed to be changed.

In 2005, the firm identified a few repetitive problems and ascertained that it required a changeover. This plan incorporated the development and deployment of a data warehouse. The case elaborates the issues which the firm identified and how data warehouse enabled to eradicate them and establish the firm as the topmost private luxury bus service. The various areas of concern have been listed below.

Areas of Concern

Earlier, the data from various functional areas were not integrated. Each area generated its own reports and had own standards of communication. This often led to miscommunication across different areas. For example, the bookings made could not be immediately updated across all areas; hence, the availability of seats in the buses could not be exactly ascertained by each area independently.

Also, there was no information regarding historical data, such as which customers have repeatedly travelled over the same routes, or the routes which were less travelled, etc. Moreover, fares and schedules were calculated using conventional techniques adopted in the industry, and no changes were made for special occasions such as festivals, or repeat customers or frequent travellers. The system adopted by the firm did not aid in running any kind of ad-hoc queries such as which are the most profitable routes, which months bring in the largest inflow of customers, etc.

There was no unified or consistent flow of information and the reporting procedure was also not standardised. Each area generated its own format as per convenience due to which management could not make any timely decision. Another problem was due to lack of availability of historical data; no future projections could be made using trend analysis or visualisation.

The firm had no damage control techniques such as if a bus was due for maintenance, there was no method to look for an alternate bus which could cover that route during maintenance. Also, if a bus could not reach by due time due to traffic jam or other such problems on the way, the firm could not immediately arrange for a new bus. This was because there was no way to ascertain whether at a nearby depot a bus is idle for a few hours, which can serve as a replacement or which another bus is on the way that can take the on-board passengers. Implying thereby, the customers had to wait for hours and in the end it leads to loss of image and reputation and dissatisfied passengers.

There was no provision for unified view of data as each department maintained its own list of data which resulted in delay in taking prompt actions. Although decisions were centralised, but by the time information from all areas reached the management it would become stale and hence the decision made on such information has no value in the market.

A major tool for firms in marketing is managing–customer relationships. This can only be done if the firms maintain data about their customers and identify who is loyal to the firm and most profitable. In this way, the firm can offer discounts to such customers or offer travel packages or make arrangements such as a waiting lounge with necessary facilities in the case there is a delay in the arrival of the bus. With the traditional data storage methods, Marketing department of Comfort On Wheels had no information regarding loyal customers, their previous travel history, complete travel itinerary and therefore could not offer loyal passenger seat, newspaper and magazines as per their choice and has no provision to accommodate baggage before boarding the bus.

Even the finance department could never determine when to offer discounts due to lack of knowledge about the maximum inflow of customers. Also, it had no means to determine how much more finance would be required in seasons of high inflow such as festivals so that the firm can hire additional buses to accommodate the increased rush.

Moreover, no financial analysis could be done as complete information about travel journey of a customer is not maintained. In case the customer travels in a cab from Patiala to Chandigarh and then boards the luxury bus from Chandigarh to Delhi, the firm could never offer the customer to board their bus for the complete journey as they have no information about these broken links. Putting two and two together they can offer their services for the entire route of the customer either by opening services on new routes or by making tie-ups with other service providers in the non-operating areas. Going further, Planning Department had no information about profitable and non-profitable routes which made forecasting impossible. Also, due to lack of a common platform for the same, the analysis of competitor strategies and offering could not be done.

The above facts clearly show that the firm had no competitive advantage in the market and all the above factors lead to major losses in the firm.

Implementation of EDW

The only way out was to integrate the data to ensure consistency of information across different departments and to provide access to the same as per needs, unifying the reporting and also providing a platform for viewing the data changes as and when they occur. The solution was to implement as Enterprise Data Warehouse (EDW) which the firm started within 2005.

Three layer data warehouse architecture was adopted in which the ETL (extraction, transformation and load) tools were used to integrate and standardise the data from different departments and loaded into the first tier which is the data warehouse server. This contains a warehouse, a metadata repository which contains the rules for standardisation and data marts, if applicable. The second tier consists of building a cube or a multidimensional model on the top of the database. And the final or topmost tier has front end tools such as dashboards, querying or reporting tools, to name a few.

The process of development and implementation was cumbersome and tedious. All the departments in the firm listed their data requirements and presentation needs. After several rounds of discussion and brainstorming session with each department, the data requirements were finalised and EDW design was done. The common needs were integration of data from different departments into a standardised and interpretable format, access of information to all, visibility of updated data as and when the transaction occurs at the front end and simple reporting tools.

EDW uploads the data from different source systems such as reservations, baggage system, customer care, payroll, KMPL data (to check the mileage of buses), past fare details of various routes, performance of staff on board, etc. The uploads can be real time such as from reservations as and when the transaction occurs, the warehouse is updated at the backend or in the form of batch process such as over weekend or month ends.

Benefits to the Firm

The advantages of implementing EDW are reflected in all the functional areas of business such as marketing, finance or operations.

- **Planning Department**: Planning department gets timely information regarding profitable routes, and thus helps to plan for plying more buses on such routes. The department gets instant access to historical data, such as when a particular route fetches maximum rush or which routes always operate normally. The department can cross check the daily receipts and the KMPL (fuel average) of the buses. The system also enables to get complete information from the start to end journey of the customer so that the firm can establish a complete relationship with the customer. The system also provides access to the agent data, thus ensuring that no agents can make fake reservations and also minimising the probability of fraudulent booking through collaborated work of fraud detection and planning wing.
- In brief, the routes are now planned better without overloading or plying empty buses. Vacant seats are now filled by utilising forecasting and offering discounts in case there is a probability that seats would remain vacant. Theft by fake agents is also removed by maintaining better information about the same.

  The firm also maintains two types of drivers—duty and reserve drivers. In case the duty driver reports a sick leave or emergency leave, the system would immediately arrange for a reserve to take over. This makes a firm proactive and hence prevents any last-minute changes which have the potential of causing loss to the firm.
- **CRM**: All the information regarding customer, their past travels, the problems they faced across the routes, their seating preference or timing preference, repeat passenger which are loyal to the bus service can be adequately fetched

by the CRM wing. This can be utilised to build long-lasting relationship with customers.

- **Effective Customer Segmentation**: EDW Three-layer architecture helps to identify the most profitable customer based on frequency of travel, time gaps of taking bus service and revenue generated from each such boarding. This enables the management to categorise their customer as "top level", "middle" and "random". Top level customers generate maximum profit and hence the firm attempts to build relationships with such customers. The employees who deal with such customers are now better equipped with all possible information about them which is only possible through EDW-enabled analytical tools. For example, now if such a customer calls for reservation, the system reflects the travel history of the same to the employee who can then offer discounts or extra benefits which are available at that time. The customers experience with the employees of the firm; before, during and after the bus travel make them loyal and repeat customers. Middle level customers are those who take the service less often and their decision to travel is based on comparative offering from other competitors. However, they have the potential of turning into top level customers. The system through data mining or querying tools yield the kinds of packages that attract such customers to this firm. Then, the management work out the feasibility of offering such packages more often to attract more segments. Random customers are those who do not travel much or make instant decisions based on the availability of the bus. Applying EDW, now it is possible to manage the buses and drivers in an efficient manner. The result is that all the buses come on time and not even a single route is missed. This helped to tap random customers.

  Another area where the bus service has revamped itself to provide additional comfort to top customers is in the seating arrangement. For example, for top (loyal) customer, within the bus, a separate section is carved out which has recliner seats, separate TVs, magazines and newspapers and baggage handling. Also, the system provides discounts for students on Friday and Monday. To maintain the reputation in case of delay of the bus, the firm now offers discounts to the affected customers on their next travel, and written apologies to all. These small gestures build a lasting relationship with the customers of the firm. All this is only possible due to unified information which is provided by EDW.

- **Fraud Detection and Security**: Now, the system enables crosschecking of daily receipts, KMPL of a particular route, so the staff on board cannot pocket the money of the firm. Also the system enables running instant queries, which can also aid in fraud detection. Earlier, the agents could make fictitious booking or bulk booking to avail discounts. If the seats remain vacant till the scheduled day of travel, their prices are gradually dropped till the last hour to attract customers. This led many employees and agents to do fictitious booking, who would then cancel it on the last day to avail discounts. However, now the system tracks the number of seats reserved against a particular account and does not allow them to exceed a limit. Also, the system time and again checks the accounts which seem suspicious and severely penalises those who are guilty.

- **Strategic Decisions**: Availability of historical data aids the management in making strategic decisions. The top management can now decide which the most profitable route is, and identify the loyal customers and their preferences. The system also suggests the best mode of communication to the customers and hence helps to find out which marketing techniques have highest reach. For example, now the firm proactively arrange for cabs to pick and drop people in Chandigarh who have to travel from Patiala to Delhi as the bus service is available only from Chandigarh to Delhi, or in case the traveler is commuting from a rural area.

Application of analytics (top-tier in EDW) aids in identifying which customers got delayed so that they can be given priority on the next scheduled bus on that route. In a nutshell, the system enables better service delivery to its customer, something which is highly important but relatively unexplored in this field of business.

Comfort On Wheels now diligently applies unity of command and direction with the help of consistency of information across all levels of the firm. The firm has also empowered the employees at the front end to take timely decision, such as if a customer misses one bus, and another bus is scheduled after an hour, the same can be reserved for the customer by paying a fraction of travel amount.

The system also has a feedback mechanism for both employees and customers, and portals where the employees share their unique experiences with both the customer and the top management. The employees can also suggest new ideas based on their experience. If these are implemented, the employees get rewarded by the firm.

Questions

1. Discuss the problems faced by Comfort on Wheels firm before implementation of data warehouse.
2. Discuss the implementation of EDW in the organisation.
3. Discuss how data warehouse has helped the organisation to solve its problems.

REFERENCES

Agosta, L. (2006). "The Data Strategy Adviser: The Year Ahead-Data Warehousing Trends 2006". *DM Review*, 16(1).

Akbay, S. (2006, Quarter 1). "Data Warehousing in Real Time". *Business Intelligence Journal*, 11(1).

Ambeo. (2005). "Ambeo Delivers Proven Data Access Auditing Solution." *Database Trends and Applications*, 19(7).

Ariyachandra, T., and Watson, H. (2005). "Key factors in Selecting a Data Warehouse Architecture", *the Business Intelligence Journal*, 10(2).

Ariyachandra, T., and Watson, H. (2006). "Benchmarks for BI and Data Warehousing Success." *DM Review*, 16(1).

Ariyachandra, T., and Watson, H. (2006). "Which Data Warehouse Architecture is most Successful?" *Business Intelligence Journal*, 11(1).

Ball, S.K. (2005, November 14). "Do You Need a Data Warehouse Layer in Your Business Intelligence Architecture"? Data Warehouse.ittoolbox.com/documents/industry-articles/do-you-need-a-data-warejouse-layer-in-your-business-intelligence architecture-2729.

Barclay, T., Barnes, R., Gray, J., and Sundaresan, P. (1994). "*Loading Databases Using Data Flow Parallelism*", SIGMOD Record, 23(4).

Basu, R. (2003). "Challenges of Real Time Data Warehousing", *DM Review*.

Brown, M. (2004, May 9–12). "8 Characteristics of a Successful Data Warehouse", Proceedings of the twenty-ninth annual SAS users group International Conference (SUGI29), Montreal Canada.

Burdett, J., and Singh, S. (2004). "Challenges and Lessons Learned from Real Time Data Warehousing", *the Business Intelligence Journal*, 9(4).

Chaudhuri, S., and Dayal, U. (1996). "Data Warehousing and OLAP for Decision Support", Tutorials of 22th VLDB Conf., Bombay.

Coffee, P. (2003, June 23). "Active Warehousing". eWeek, 20(25).

Cooper, B.L., et al. (2000). *Data Warehousing Supports Corporate Strategy at First American Corporation.*

Edelstein, H. (1995, December 4). "Faster Data Warehouses: New tools provide high-performance querying through advanced indexing", Information Week Hammer, J., Garcia-Molina, H., Widom, J., Laobio, W., Zhuge, Y. (1995). "*The Stanford Data Warehousing Project*", Data Eng. Bulletin, 18(2).

Hammer, J., Garcia-Molina, H., Widom, J., Labio, W., and Zhuge, Y. (1995). "The Stanford Data Warehousing Project". IEEE Data Engineering Bulletin, Special Issue on Materialized Views and Data Warehousing, 18(2):41–48.

IBM. NYPD changes the crime control equation by transforming the way it uses information. *Data Warehousing and Business Intelligence – Success Stories.* NY: s.n., 2004.

Inmon, W.H. (1996). "*Building the Data Warehouse*", John Wiley & Sons.

Inmon, W.H. (2005). "Building the Data Warehouse", 4th edition, New York, Wiley.

Inmon, W.H. (2006). "Information Management: How Do you Tune a Data Warehouse?" *DM Review*, 16(1).

Kelly, C. (2001, June 14). "Calculating the Data Warehousing ROI", Search SQL Server.com Tips.

Malykhina, E. (2003, January 3). "The Real-Time Imperative", Information Week, Issue 1020.

Martins, C. (2005, December 13). "HP to Consolidate Data Marts into Single Data Warehouse". Compuetrworld.

Nazilca, U. Garanti Bank Benefits from 10X Improvement in Reporting. *Oracle.* [Online] http://www.oracle.com/ocom/groups/systemobject/@mktg_admin/documents/

webcontent/videoplayer-ocom.html?bctid=1400726933001&playerType=single-social&size=c23.

Scheuermann, P., Shim, J., and Vingralek, R. (1996), "WATCHMAN: A Data Warehouse Intelligent Cache Manager", VLDB Conf., Bombay.

Sunders, T. (2009), "Cooking up Data Warehouse", *the Business Intelligence Journal*, 14(2).

Weir, R. (2002). "Best Practices for Implementing Data Warehouse", *Journal of Data Warehousing*, 7(1).

Widom, J. (1995). "Research Problems in Data Warehousing", Int'l Conf. On Info, and Knowledge Management (CIKM).

Wilk, L. (2003). "Data Warehousing and Real-Time Computing". *Business Intelligence Journal*, 8(2).

Zhou, G., Hull, R., King, R., and Franchitti, J.C. (1995). "Supporting Data Integration and Warehousing Using H20", Data Eng. Bulletin, 18(2).

CHAPTER 5

Relational Data Modelling

After going through this chapter, you will be able to

- Understand the concepts and process of data modelling
- Understand the basic of conceptual models
- Understand the basic concepts in ER modelling
- Understand how to resolve many to many relationships
- Understand what is normalisation and its three forms
- Understand the basics of logical data modelling
- Understand physical data modelling

INTRODUCTION

In IT a complex information landscape is made understandable via a data model. Using symbols and text, a data model helps developers and analysts better understand a set of data elements and the corresponding business rules. While a data model can represent a specific functional area, such as order processing, it can also represent the organisation's master plan in the form of an enterprise data model (EDM).

—Steve Hoberman, BI and data modelling practitioner

Data modelling is the plan of the database from the user's perspective. It depicts the structures for data storage, the relationship between them and how the data would be operated upon such as what is the base for loading or extraction of data. The most common and widely used model is the relational data model. The relational data model is a part of database or data warehouse design which inculcates the following steps.

- Plan and analyse information needs for database from end users and existing documentation.
- Conceptual design—This is where data modelling fits in. It is depicted using the ER diagram and provides a description of data objects, associations and rules utilised for database design.
- Logical design—After conceptual design, logical design aids in clearly defining each data object through attributes, primary key and foreign keys.
- Physical design—In physical design, actual allotment of storage space is done for data structures identified in the previous design steps.

Conceptual design is the starting point for creating/building a new data warehouse.

Based on each stage of database design, there are three sub-types of relational data model termed conceptual, logical and physical design models. Each of these models is discussed in detail below.

CONCEPTUAL DESIGN

The organisation might decide to rely more heavily on the conceptual data model (CDM) to provide a high-level overview to the logical data model (LDM). The CDM is about 10% the size of LDM and shows only the most important entities in an LDM and their relationships. For instance, the generalised Teradata Manufacturing Logical Data Model has slightly more than 700 entities, while the manufacturing CDM has about 70 major entities.

—Teradata

Conceptual design helps to

1. Identify the entities
2. Relationship between entities
3. Cardinality of relationship

Conceptual design uses the concept of ER diagrams to depict the relationships between entities. First, let us understand the basic concepts of ER modelling.

Basic Concepts in ER Modelling

ER model is a pictorial representation of structures in the database. This enables easy readability by the end user. It identifies the basic structure in the database, termed entities and the relationships between them. The advantage is that each of these entities can be directly transformed into a relational table.

Database technology has evolved rapidly in the past three decades since the rise and eventual dominance of relational database systems. While many specialised database systems (object oriented, spatial, multimedia, etc.) have found substantial user communities in the science and engineering, relational systems remain the dominant database technology for business enterprises.

—Toby Teorey, Sam Lightstone, Tom Nadeau, H.V. Jagadish, Database Modelling and Design book (5th edition), Elsevier.

Some of the basic concepts of ER modelling are as given below.

ER model is a pictorial representation of structures in the database.

Entities

Anything which has a distinct identity is an entity such as an employee, books, course, student, etc. A key identification of entities is that they require other associative items to describe them. For example, an employee can be identified by her name, employee ID or designation. Similarly, a book has a title, ISBN number, publisher, author to distinguish it from other books. However, time periods such as year 1, year 2 or quarter 1 revenues, quarter 2 revenues cannot be created as distinct entities. Rather, a single entity such as revenue should be categorised using time as an attribute.

> Anything which has a distinct identity is an entity.

Attributes

As understood from entities, attributes are required to define an entity. Those attributes which enable identifying clearly entities are called key attributes. Others are called non-key attributes. Attributes generally should be atomic in nature; that is, they should represent a single fact. For example, certain attributes such as name can be decomposed into first name, last name and middle name. While designing a database, this attribute can be aggregated and used as a single field or decomposed and used as individual attributes. Certain attributes can be simple text fields such as comments or suggestions. These have no specific format and do not fit into a particular data requirement of the model.

> Attributes are required to define an entity.

Relationships

This specifies how the entities are related to each other. For example, an employee works under one supervisor, a course can be taught through many books, etc. Quantification of this relationship is termed cardinality. A "zero" cardinality implies optional relationship, for example, elective subjects which are part of the syllabus, but not opted by any student and hence not taught by any teacher or a book which is not issued by any student or teacher. "One" cardinality implies compulsory relation, for example, each teacher must have at least one course assigned. Here, at least one implies that there can be teachers who take one or more than one subject. Each entity can have one to one (1:1), one to many (1:m) or many to many (m:n) relationships with other entities.

> Relationship specifies how the entities are related to each other.

Having understood the basics of ER modelling, let us now delve into conceptual design with the help of an example of a teaching institute. Consider first two entities: Teacher and Subject. A teacher should teach at least one (one or more than one) subject, while a subject can be taught by zero or more teachers. (There may be certain subjects which are redundant (not part of current curriculum or not being taught currently.) This is therefore an example of many to many relationships. This can be represented as shown below:

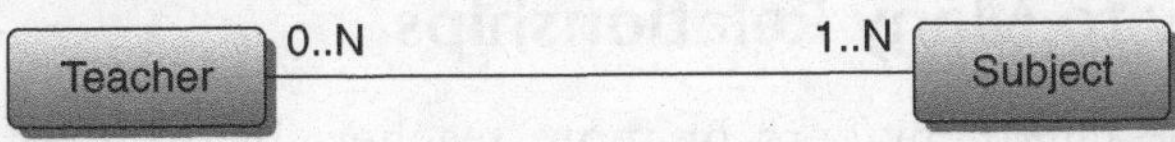

The notation 0..N implies an optional relation for the subjects to teachers. Similarly 1..N implies teacher takes at least one subject. Only 1 against an entity implies a compulsory relation, that is, a record should definitely exist in the corresponding entity. This has been illustrated in the example below between student and books issued entity.

To demonstrate the relationship better between the two entities, consider the following data from the institute:

Teacher
Dr. Sunil
Ms. Mehar
Dr. Rakesh
Dr. Ram

Subject
Management information system
Management science
Business research methods
Business analytics
Operations management
Financial management

The same subject is being taught by many teachers, while a teacher can take more than one subject. For example, a teacher Dr. Sunil is teaching three subjects MIS, MS and Business Research Methods. The subject of MIS is being taught by more than one teacher—Dr. Sunil and Ms. Mehar, and the same applies to other subjects such as Business Analytics and Business Research Methods. Therefore, it is a many to many relationship.

Now assume another set of entities: "Students", containing student details and "Books Issued". The library system of the institute maintains the records of books issued to students and teachers in the entity "Books Issued". Now for a given student, there can be zero or more records of issued books in "Books Issued" entity. In case a student does not get any book issued from the library, zero record would exist for that student in "Books Issued" entity. These cases would be termed optional relationship. However, for a particular record of an issued book in "Books Issued" entity, only one corresponding record of student would exist in "Student" entity (a given book cannot be issued to more than one student!). Hence, this is an example of one to many relationship.

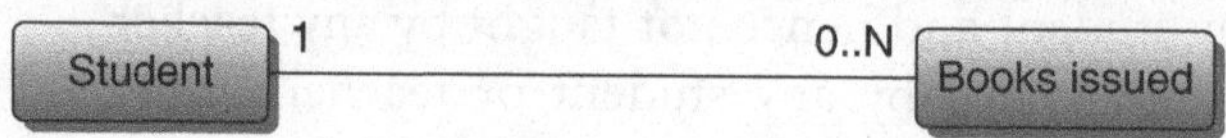

In a similar manner, a particular teacher can get many books issued from the library, while a given book can be issued to one and only one teacher. Therefore, this is also an example of one to many relationship. This relationship would also become optional for those teachers who have not got any book issued from the library, leading to no record against their names, in "Issued books" entity.

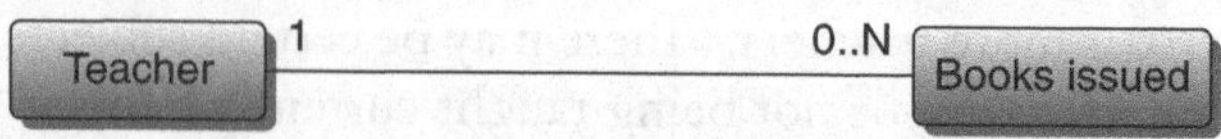

Resolving Many to Many Relationships

Each subject may be taught by zero or more teachers in different classes, while each teacher may take more than one subject. So how do we find out for a particular class, which teacher takes up a particular subject? From the previous illustration of many to many relationship between subjects and teachers, we have the following case: a teacher Dr. Sunil takes up Management Information Systems, Management Science and yet another subject of Business Research Methods. Another teacher Ms. Mehar is taking up a similar course of Management Information Systems in some other class, while Dr. Rakesh is also taking a similar course of Business Research Methods in another class. Therefore, the use of only two entities Subject and Teacher makes the mapping difficult between teachers and subjects taught in different classes. To resolve this situation, the strategy is to identify a link entity and relate that link entity to original entities. In the present example, this link entity would contain the class allocation of teachers for different subjects. Let us assume that Dr. Sunil takes up Management Information Systems in MBA-I (Section A), Business Research Methods in MBA-1 (Section D) and Business Analytics in MBA-II (Section C). Also assume that Ms. Mehar takes up the course of Management Information Systems in MBA-I (Section B), while Dr. Rakesh takes Business Research Methods in MBA-1 (Section A). These data would be contained in the link entity as shown below:

Dr. Sunil	Management Information Systems	MBA – 1 (A)
Dr. Sunil	Bussiness Research Methods	MBA – 1 (D)
Dr. Sunil	Management Science	MBA – 2 (C)
Ms. Mehar	Management Information Systems	MBA – 1 (B)
Dr. Rakesh	Bussiness Research Methods	MBA – 1 (A)

Let us name this link entity as "Class Allocation". Now let us attempt to establish a relationship of the link entity to Subject and Teacher entities. For a given record of class allocation, only one corresponding teacher would exist in Teacher entity. And for a given teacher in Teacher entity, many class allocation records exist, such as for Dr. Sunil. Therefore "Teacher" and "Class Allocation" entities have one to many relationship. Similarly, one subject would be allocated to more than one class, and a particular class allocation would map to only one subject. So "Subject" and "Class Allocation" entities also have one to many relationship. Because there can be certain subjects which are not being taught currently, this relationship becomes optional. This has been depicted in the figure below:

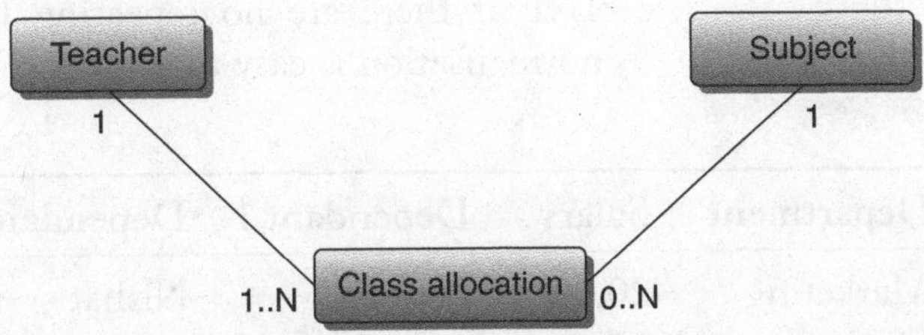

In this way, use of link entity resolves the problem of mapping arising from many to many relationship.

Another entity is "Marks" which contains marks scored by students in multiple subjects. Therefore, this entity would be related to both "Subject" and "Student" entities. Also note its relation to "Teacher" to map which teacher evaluated a particular student's mark sheet. So for a given record in "Marks" entity, it would map to only one corresponding student, subject and teacher (Basically, each data entry in "Marks" entity would answer—which student in which subject evaluated by which teacher and scored how many marks?). Now, as a student is being taught multiple subjects, for each subject that he writes the examination, a corresponding record would exist in the Marks entity. However, in case a student is absent in examinations, the Marks entity may not contain any record of that student. Similarly, a particular teacher would evaluate multiple subjects and multiple students; hence, multiple entries would exist in "Marks" entity for a specific teacher. Similar is the case for Subject and Marks entities. Therefore, Marks entity has one to many relationship with Teacher, Student and Subject entities, as depicted below:

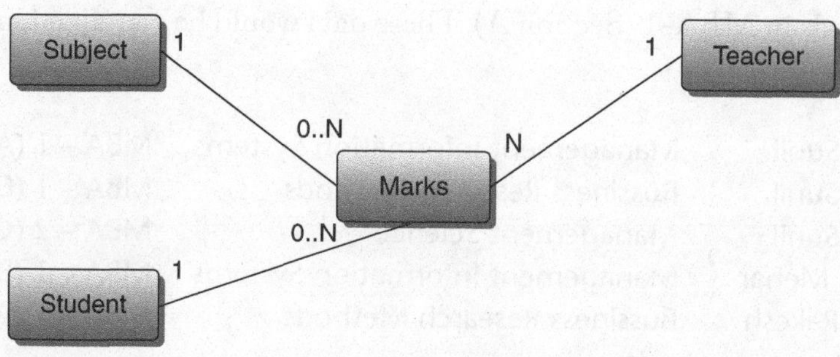

Normalisation technique helps to crosscheck any redundancies in the database and also helps in removing those redundancies.

Normalisation

Normalisation helps to improve the quality of the relational databases. The normalisation technique helps to crosscheck any redundancies in the database and also helps in removing those redundancies. There are three forms of normalisation which helps to check redundancy in the databases.

A table is said to be in first normal form if there are no repeating fields.

1. **First Normal Form (1NF)**: A table is said to be in 1NF if there are no repeating fields. This type of normalisation is easy to achieve. For example,

Emp-name	Department	Salary	Dependant 1	Dependant 2	Dependant 3
Rahul	Marketing	20,000	Naveen	Nishat	Uday
Ravi	Finance	23,000	Satinder	Suraj	Nisha
Varun	HR	29,000	Harry	Pooja	Aasha

The above table is not in the 1NF as the dependant field is a repeated field. So to convert this table in 1NF, the dependency field (repeating field) should be omitted.

> A table is said to be in second normal form if each non-key element is functionally dependent on the entire primary key.

2. **Second Normal Form (2NF)**: A table is said to be in the second normal form if each non-key element is functionally dependent on the entire primary key.

   If a table has two fields, i.e., field A and field B, functional dependency means that for each value of field B there is one corresponding value in field A. For example,

Catalog number	Product number	Price
1	561	2000
2	562	2300
3	563	2000
4	564	3000
5	565	2300

   In the above table, Catalog Number and Product Number are primary key fields. Price is a non-key field. This table is in 2NF as Price (non-key field) is functionally dependent on Catalog Number (Primary Key) and Product Number (Primary Key).

3. **Third Normal Form (3NF)**: A table is said to be in 3NF if no non-key element is functionally dependent on any other non-key element. This means that dependency should be between non-key element and key element.

Order number	Customer number	Unit price	Quantity
1	20	50	3
2	21	40	2
3	23	38	5
4	24	56	6

   In the above table, an example of 3NF is given. Order number is the primary key field. Customer number, Unit price and Quantity are non-key fields. Customer number is non-key field that is dependent on the Order number. Unit Price (non-key field) is dependent on Order number and Quantity (non-key) is also dependent on Order Number. Moreover, no non-key element is functionally dependent on any other non-key field.

> A table is said to be in third normal form if no non-key element is functionally dependent on any other non-key element.

Logical data models enable to graphically depict the data of a firm, using concepts called entities, attributes and relationships.

LOGICAL DATA MODELLING (LDM)

A logical model contains representations of entities and attributes, relationships, unique identifiers, subtypes and supertypes, and constraints between relationships.

—IBM

Logical data models enable graphically depicting the data of a firm, using concepts called entities, attributes and relationships. It expresses the relation between different business constructs or entities, using primary key, foreign key and cardinality. The diagrammatic representation is called LDS or logical data structure.

LDM enables identifying entities, attributes, primary key and foreign key which in turn define the relationship between different entities.

1. The first step in LDS is to identify entities and its attributes. For example, customer, supplier, teachers, student, marks, courses are different entities. Teachers can have the attributes of qualification, gender, experience, teacher name, date of joining and employee number.
2. Next, for each entity, identify the candidate key or unique identifier of that entity. This is called the primary key. For example, employee number for the teacher can be a unique identifier. There can be two types of primary keys:
   (a) *Simple key*: Single key used to identify each data row. For example, employee number can be used to uniquely identify each employee and therefore is a simple primary key. Now, consider the leave system which might have multiple rows for the same employee number for different time periods. In such cases using only employee number as the key would not uniquely identify each data entry in the leave system.
   (b) *Compound key or Composite key*: A candidate key with more than one attribute is termed composite or compound key. In this case, multiple foreign keys in a table (primary keys in other tables) can be clubbed together to form a compound candidate key. Or, foreign keys and a non-key attribute of the current table can be used as a compound candidate key. For example, employee number and date of joining can be a primary key.
3. Next, identify foreign keys which are used to establish the relationship between two entities. When some entity utilises fields from other tables which are primary keys in those tables, they become foreign keys in the current table. To understand this, consider the example of Marks entity. It contains the marks of students in different subjects. Complete detail of students is maintained in Student entity, complete detail of subjects is maintained in Subject entity, so to record marks of a student in a particular subject, Marks entity would contain Student Name, Subject Name and Marks. As Student Name and Subject Name are the primary keys for Student and Subject entity, they are

termed foreign keys in the Marks entity. The use of foreign keys facilitates data access when for a given record in one entity, there exist data in another entity.

Subject
Subject name (PK)

Marks
Student name (FK)
Subject name (FK)
Marks scored

Student
Student name (PK)
Postel address

Say, for example, we would like to post the result to students who failed at their postal addresses. The address is recorded in Student entity, so mapping Student Name from Marks entity to Student Name in Student entity would fetch the desired postal address through which communication can occur.

4. Next, establish relationships, and draw an LDS to complete the modelling. Another key point is that data should be normalised.

The diagram below depicts the logical data model of a system with different entities and its attributes. Following from the above conceptual design of teaching institute, let us identify attributes and primary and foreign keys for each entity and depict it using LDS.

- Student entity should contain details of students such as Name, Address, E-mail, Date of Birth and Class. To identify the candidate key for Student entity, consider Student Name. As names can be the same for more than one student, it cannot be a unique identifier for Student entity. If we consider compound key, such as Student Name, DOB and Class as candidate, there can be situations where more than one student have the same name, DOB and class. Therefore, this compound key would also not be a unique identifier for each student. So another field Student ID, which is numeric, should be used as a primary key in this table.
- Teacher entity would also identify Teacher ID as a primary key. Other attributes can be Name, Age, Experience and Qualification.
- Subject entity should contain names of subject, so one field in this would be Subject Name. The primary key for this can be termed Subject ID.
- Marks entity would contain Marks Scored. It would also contain Student ID, Subject ID and Teacher ID. As these are primary keys for other tables, here they would be foreign keys. All the three foreign keys taken together can uniquely identify marks records; therefore, this entity would have a compound primary key.
- Class allocation entity would contain Teacher ID and Subject ID which would be foreign keys. It would also contain Class. Here, Teacher ID and Subject ID would serve as compound primary key.
- Books Issued entity would contain Book Title, Author, Date of Issue and Date of Return. Besides, Student ID and Teacher ID would be foreign keys in this table. Here, Book Title, Student ID and Teacher ID would serve as compound primary key.

The same has been depicted in Exhibit 5.1:

Exhibit 5.1 Logical data structure

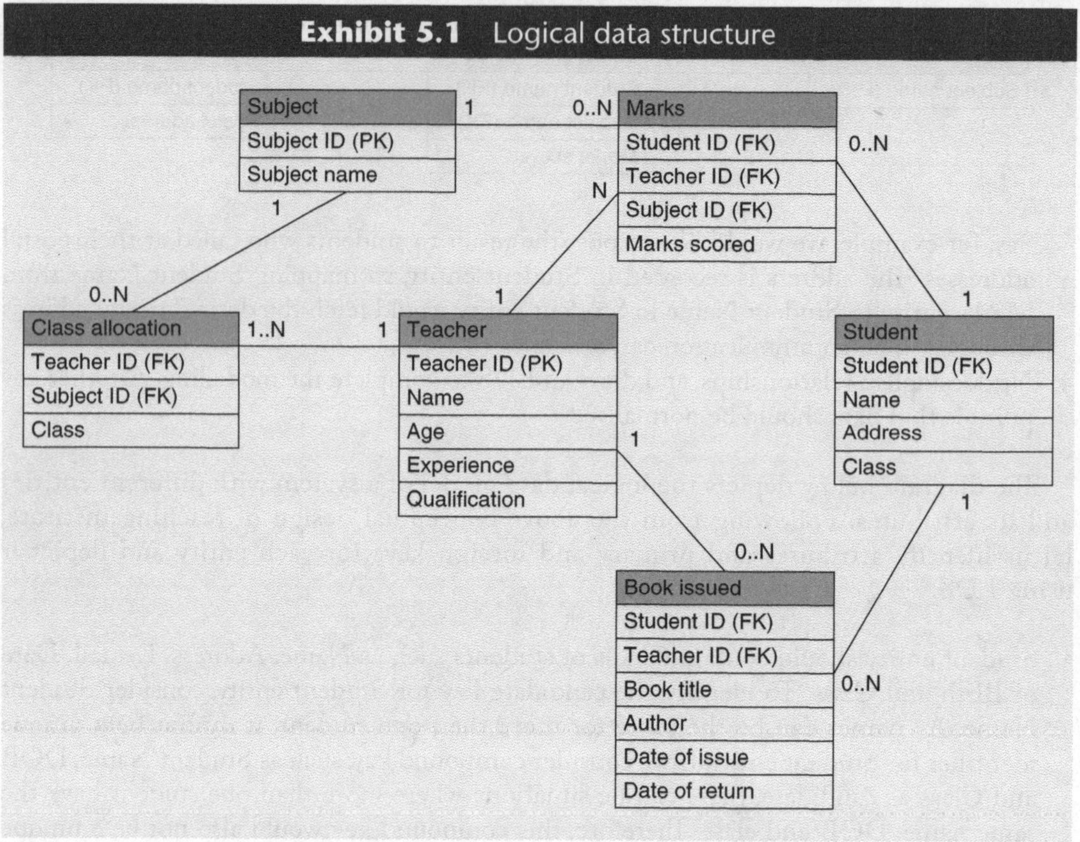

The above are different entities contained in a system. Primary keys have been denoted by PK and foreign keys for each entity have been depicted as FK. Another representation technique for entities is:

Student (Student ID, Name, Address, Class)
Books Issued (Student ID*, Teacher ID*, Book ID, Date of Issue, Date of Return)
Here asterisk * against the fields indicate that they are foreign keys.

PHYSICAL DATA MODELLING

A physical data model is a database-specific model that represents relational data objects (for example, tables, columns, primary and foreign keys) and their relationships.

—IBM

In physical data modelling, actual physical storage space is created for data. In this, entities become table names. For example, Student, Teacher, Class Allocation, Subject, Books Issued and Marks would become individual tables in the database. The attributes for each table would become columns for that table. Here, you also need to decide upon the appropriate data type of each attribute and constraints such as primary key or foreign key. For example, Student ID would be a primary key column with the constraint NOT NULL in "student" table.

In physical data modelling, actual physical storage space is created for data.

Following the similar logical design as shown Exhibit 5.1, let us look at the physical model for each entity.

Student

Column name	Data type	Constraints
Student ID	Int	NOT NULL, Primary Key
Name	nvarchar(50)	NOT NULL
Subject ID	nvarchar(50)	NOT NULL
Class	nchar(10)	NOT NULL

Subject

Column name	Data type	Constraints
Subject ID	Int	NOT NULL, Primary Key
[Subject name]	nvarchar(50)	NOT NULL

Teacher

Column name	Data type	Constraints
Teacher ID	Int	NOT NULL, Primary key
Name	nvarchar(50)	NOT NULL
Age	Int	NULL
Experience	Int	NOT NULL
Qualification	nvarchar(50)	NULL

Marks

Column name	Data type	Constraints
Student ID	Int	NOT NULL
Teacher ID	Int	NOT NULL
Subject ID	Int	NOT NULL
[Marks scored]	Int	NOT NULL

Subject Allocation

Column name	Data type	Constraints
Teacher ID	Int	NOT NULL
Subject ID	Int	NOT NULL
Class	nchar(10)	NOT NULL

Books Issued

Column name	Data type	Constraints
Student ID	Int	NOT NULL
Teacher ID	Int	NOT NULL
Book ID	Int	NOT NULL
[Date of issue]	Date time	NOT NULL
[Date of return]	Date time	NOT NULL

CONCLUSION

The chapter aimed to develop a thorough understanding among readers of data models and the process of developing data models. Managers have to base their decisions on data, but a sound decision can only be made if data have been rightly modelled which eliminates redundancy and inconsistency among data items. Relational models have by far been the most widely used data modelling techniques. OLTP systems are generally relational database systems. Therefore, managers and readers of the books will be skilled enough after going through the chapter to understand and develop relational data models.

KEY TERMS

- Data models 118
- ER diagram 111
- Entities 112
- Attributes 113
- Relationship 113
- Link entity 115
- Normalisation 116
- Logical data structure (LDS) 120
- Logical data model 118

- Primary key **118**
- Compound key **118**
- Foreign key **118**
- Physical data model **120**

SUMMARY

In lieu of relational data models being the most basic and most widely used data models in firms, this chapter discussed what is meant by data models in general and steps undertaken to develop a data model. This chapter also detailed on three stages or types of relational data models. ER diagrams being the most common representation technique of conceptual data models have been discussed in greater detail through examples. The chapter also threw light on logical data models and the logical data structure which is a diagrammatic portrayal of the logical model. Finally, the physical data model has been explained.

MULTIPLE CHOICE QUESTIONS

1. The model in which data are depicted using ER diagram and provides a description of data objects, associations and rules utilised for database design

a. Logical model b. Conceptual model
c. Rational model d. Physical model

2. Anything which has a distinct identity is known as

a. Entity b. Attribute
c. Object d. Unit

3. Those aspects which enable clearly identifying entities are called

a. Key attributes b. Non-key attributes
c. Key-objects d. Non-key object

4. The technique which helps to crosscheck any redundancies in the database and also helps in removing those redundancies is known as

a. Normalisation b. Standardisation
c. Regularisation d. Stabilisation

5. A table in which there are no repeating fields is in which normalised state?

a. First normal form b. Second normal form
c. Third normal form d. General normalised form

6. A table in which each non-key element is functionally dependent on the entire primary key is in which normalised state?
   a. First normal form
   b. Second normal form
   c. Third normal form
   d. General normalised form

7. A table in no non-key element is functionally dependent on any other non-key element is in which normalised state?
   a. First normal form
   b. Second normal form
   c. Third normal form
   d. General normalised form

8. The model which enables graphically depicting the data of a firm, using concepts called entities, attributes and relationships is known as
   a. Logical model
   b. Conceptual model
   c. Rational model
   d. Theoretical model

9. The model in which the entities become table names is known as
   a. Logical model
   b. Conceptual model
   c. Rational model
   d. Physical model

10. A candidate key with more than one attribute is termed
    a. Compound key
    b. Multiple key
    c. Many key
    d. Complex key

REVIEW QUESTIONS

1. What is data modelling? Discuss the steps involved in relational data modelling.
2. What do you understand by conceptual design? What is meant by entities, attributes and relationship in ER modelling?
3. How can you resolve many to many relationships? Discuss normalisation and its orms.
4. What is logical data model and LDS? Discuss in detail the steps involved in depicting LDS.
5. What do you understand by physical data model?

ASSIGNMENT

1. Consider an online book store. Using the concepts discussed in this chapter, develop a relational model for that store.

PROJECT ACTIVITY

1. Visit the library of your department or university. Discuss with the library staff how they maintain library data such as issue records, books records, procurement of books, etc. Understand and document the same and propose a relational model for your library.

CLASS ACTIVITY

A university runs multiple institutes in different fields such as Institute of Engineering, Institute of management, etc. Each institute further runs different courses for a specialisation such as an engineering institute provides courses in electronics, electrical, mechanical, biomedical and civil engineering. Similarly, a management institute provides courses in HR, Business Analytics, General Administration, Marketing, Operations, etc. Each year university conducts its own entrance test to admit students in different institutes and then offers seats in courses based on their merit. The period of admission to all institutes is the same. Notably, the university has only one admission cell to manage all activities related to admission in its various institutes. On request by a student for hostel allocation, after the seat is allotted to that student, hostel allocation is also done by the same cell. The current process is manual and the cell maintains spreadsheets to keep track of seat allotments, seat availability, hostel allotment, and also keeps account of fees details of the students. The section and roll number are not assigned to the student unless the spreadsheet shows the fee status of the student as "Paid". The university runs a total of five institutes, each of which offers graduate, postgraduate and doctorate courses. On average, for each year, an institute's current capacity of student intake is approximately 500 for each department. On the whole, for the university, total student intake exceeds 2000 annually.

With the increase in student intake, admissions at the university became a burden for staff, management and student alike. The foremost issue occurred with conducting and maintaining the results of the entrance test. The number of candidates appearing in test arose, which led to chaos at the backend. It became nearly impossible to maintain records of entrance test results of thousands of aspirants in spreadsheets and to verify from the same when the candidate appears for the admission. Moreover, shortage of staff and lack of technology made it extremely difficult to map which student was admitted to which institute, courses were to be allocated based on rank and availability of seats. This required some form of backend storage, which could answer real-time queries such as for a given course in a given institute how many vacancies are there. The current system was unable to support such cross-tab queries.

Additionally, this situation puts an adverse impact on marketing strategies of the university as it was unable to place appropriate advertisements at the right time due to lack of actual data on seat availability and seat allotted. Students' contacts were also ill maintained and timely notifications such as the due date for fees or hostel allocation could not be sent to students or their parents/guardians. Often, the staff would spend considerable time sorting the records or filtering to answer simple queries such as which student's fee status reads not paid. There were frequent complaints from students that when they had already made the fee payment, the status read not paid. Different versions of spreadsheet data also posed problems for the staff as merging of data became complex. Duplicate records of students existed and these redundant data hindered smooth operations of staff. This posed severe threat to the reputation of this budding university and it needed to fix the problem. Management of the university understood that it would be able to sustain itself only if the current state of affairs was sorted out.

The university decided to hire an analyst to resolve their problems. The analyst interacted with university admission cell staff, management and students to identify the areas of problem that they were facing. Next, he studied the student admission process in detail. The analyst was an expert in database design and concluded that the root of the problem was inappropriate maintenance of data. The university required an integral or central database which could be accessed by all the users of the admission process. He began by modelling the database. To develop a conceptual schema, the analyst identified the following entities for the purpose of the admission process: Entrance, Institutes, Courses, Seat Allotment, Hostel Allotment, Student Detail and Fee detail. Then, ER modelling was carried out to normalise the entities and establish relationships so that cross queries can be run on the data. Attributes, primary and foreign key were identified from the conceptual model to build the logical model. Finally, physical storage space was created for the entities using SQL Server database services and data were loaded onto the tables. Adequate training was provided to the staff to access the database, update, insert and delete the data.

As a result, redundancy and duplicity in the data were removed; this prevented the chaos which occurred earlier. The system is now able to support the ever-increasing data because of adequate storage space. Relationships between entities enable the staff to quickly retrieve answers to their queries such as how many seats are vacant in a particular course in a particular institute. This has also decreased the time to advertise the vacancies and increased the effectiveness of advertising by the university. Versioning of data is no longer a problem as update on the data will occur at central storage and the same data will be available for access to all users at their terminals. Standardised column formats of the tables are to ensure that data entry is appropriate and hence student records can be properly maintained. In a nutshell, the database design has aided the university to sustain itself and its objective of growth and recognition without compromising on quality.

Questions

1. Develop a conceptual design for the university admission process.
2. Implement logical model for university admission process by identifying attributes, primary key and foreign keys.

HANDS-ON PROJECT

Objective of this project is to:

- Identify entities and its attributes
- Identify relationship between them
- Logical modelling
- How to actually create database tables.

Consider the following scenario: You wish to purchase a book on business analytics, but none is available with your local book supplier. So you search the Internet and finally find a website which has a number of leading books on the subject and is also offering lucrative discounts. You finally decide to make a purchase from this website and place an order and you receive an email with the order details and tentative delivery date. What is of interest is what happens at the backend of online bookstore? You and several other users who visited and made a purchase on the website indulged in a "transaction". Each user like you is assigned a unique account for making future offers and saving your personal details for order delivery. This is called a "user account". Then, your "purchase" must have been saved in the online store's database for future reference. Using the order detail the "inventory" must have been checked for availability of the items, listing the cost of the items, and building a tentative delivery date for ordered items.

Now if we were to design a data model for this online ordering, we would first start with the conceptual design which is identifying entities and its relationships. Clearly, the following entities exist in the system:

1. Transaction
2. Purchase
3. User Account
4. Inventory

The next step is to understand the relationships between these entities. For each user account, there can be zero or more transactions (users already present in the database who have not made any transaction cause zero transactions), while each transaction should refer to only one user account. Similarly, a purchase order can emerge from only one transaction while a transaction can create one or more purchase orders. One purchase order can have one or more items from inventory, and an inventory item can also be referred by zero or more purchase orders. Each purchase order can be created by only one user account, while one user account can lead to zero or more purchase orders. From these, we can now depict the ER diagram:

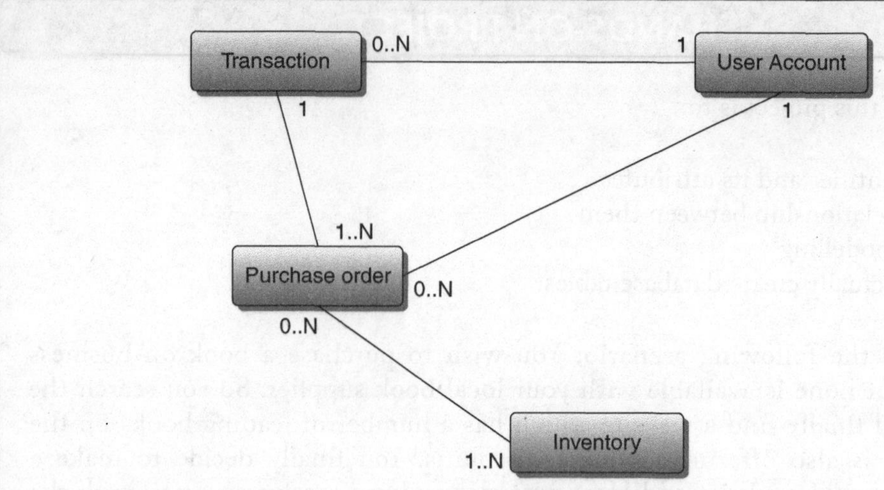

Clearly, the Purchase Order and Inventory entities have M:N (many to many) relationship. Therefore, this needs to be resolved using a link entity which would relate to the original entities. As one purchase order may contain more than one ordered item, mapping of individual item to inventory to check for availability becomes difficult. Therefore, we add a link entity "Itemised Order" which contains the item-wise detail of a purchase order placed by a user. So this entity would contain purchase order number and the name of the ordered item. Intuitively, a purchase order may contain one or more ordered items, while an Itemised Order record can refer to only one purchase order. Similarly, one Itemised Order record refers to only one inventory item, while one inventory item may appear in zero (an item in inventory may have no order at all) or more Itemised Order records for different purchase orders.

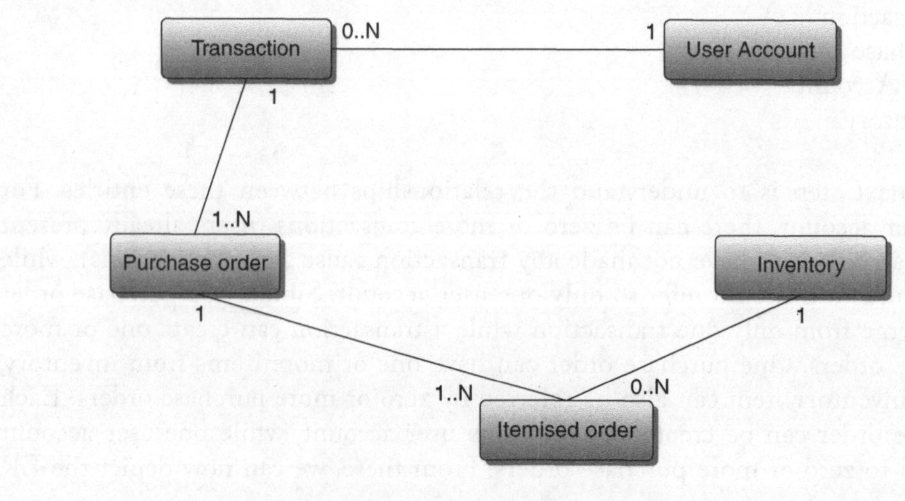

In this way, the many to many relationship is resolved. Now that we understand the ER diagram, we can build a logical model for the same. For this, we need to identify the primary key, attributes and foreign keys for each entity. Intuitively, we can understand the attributes for each entity. The system will generate a User ID for each user account, Transaction ID for each new transaction and Order ID for each purchase order placed by a user. Individual order items for each order will be stored in a separate entity called "ItemisedOrder", which would have a compound candidate key "OrderID + ItemID" as a unique identifier. Each item in "Inventory" will have a unique Item ID.

Transaction can be uniquely identified by Transaction ID and each transaction entry should contain the date of transaction. The transaction leads to a purchase order identified by an order ID and User ID. Similarly, User Account has a unique identifier of User ID, besides other attributes such as Name, Age, Email, Shipping address and mode of payment. In a similar manner, attributes for other entities can also be identified and a logical model can be developed as under:

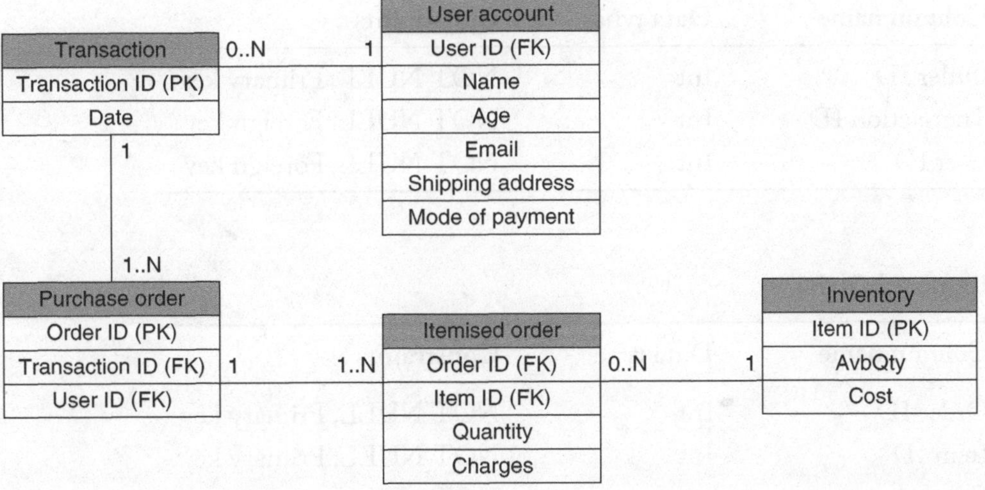

The next step in data modelling is to actually create physical storage for the tables and to identify primary key and attributes for each entity. This has been accomplished using SQL tables.

Transaction

Column name	Data type	Constraints
Transaction ID	Int	NOT NULL, Primary key
Date	Date time	NOT NULL

User account

Column name	Data type	Constraints
User ID	Int	NOT NULL, Primary key
Name	nvarchar(50)	NOT NULL
Age	Int	NULL
Email	nvarchar(50)	NOT NULL
Shipping address	nvarchar(50)	NOT NULL
Mode of payment	Int	NOT NULL

Purchase Order

Column name	Data type	Constraints
Order ID	Int	NOT NULL, Primary key
Transaction ID	Int	NOT NULL, Foreign key
User ID	Int	NOT NULL, Foreign key

Itemised Order

Column name	Data type	Constraints
Order ID	Int	NOT NULL, Primary key
Item ID	Int	NOT NULL, Primary key
Quantity	Int	NOT NULL
Charges	Money	NOT NULL

Inventory

Column name	Data type	Constraints
Item ID	Int	NOT NULL, Primary key
AvbQty	Int	NOT NULL
Cost	Money	NOT NULL

REFERENCES

Batini, C.S. Ceri, S. Kant, and Navathe, B. (1991). *Conceptual Database Design: An Entity Relational Approach.* The Benjamin/Cummings Publishing Company.

Date, C.J. (1990). *An Introduction to Database Systems*, 5th ed. Addison-Wesley.

Fleming, Candace C. and Barbara von Halle. (1989). *Handbook of Relational Database Design*, Addison-Wesley.

Graeme, S. (1994). *Data Modeling Essentials: Analysis, Design, and Innovation.* International Thompson Computer Press.

Kroenke, D. (1989). *Database Processing*, 2nd ed. Science Research Associates, 1983 Martin, James. Information Engineering. Prentice-Hall.

Teory, T.J. (1994). *Database Modeling & Design: The Basic Principles*, 2nd ed. Morgan Kaufmann Publishers, Inc.

CHAPTER 6

Multi-dimensional Modelling

After going through this chapter, you will be able to

- Understand the meaning and need for multidimensional models
- Understand what multidimensional data are
- Understand basic concepts in multidimensional models and how to develop a multidimensional model
- Understand the representation of multidimensional models or schemas
- Understand the different kinds of operations that can be performed on multidimensional model and querying

INTRODUCTION

From school, we know that although most math tasks have plain-English formulation, we still have to state an equation with x, or, sometimes, a system of equations with x, y and maybe even more variables, to find a solution. Similarly, in a decision support system, we have to design a set of data objects, such as dimensions and cubes, according to the business questions formulated in plain English, so that we can get those questions answered.

—Yuli Vasiliev, Cube Development for beginners, Oracle

The earlier chapters focused on the development of concepts of data warehousing and data marts. Readers are already familiar with relational modelling which is one of the tools used to develop a data warehouse. The other tool is multidimensional modelling, which is the focus of this chapter. Multidimensional modelling is used to present information such as key figures or facts of the business in a way which the user can normally understand and in a structure that the business user is familiar with or can easily interpret. Multidimensional models represent this information from various business perspectives or dimensions which are of interest to the user, such as rate of turnover information from department perspective, product perspective, technology perspective, etc. Most firms prefer to design and develop this kind of model on the top of their relational or transactional databases to facilitate the business users such as analysts or managers to dig deeper into the data and answer business problems. This chapter would aid the reader in developing the understanding of basic concepts of multidimensional models, the process of development of these models and representation of multidimensional models.

Multidimensional modelling is based on simple business objects like cubes, measures and dimensions.

NEED FOR MULTIDIMENSIONAL MODELS

The multidimensional data model is important because it enforces simplicity. "The central attraction of the dimensional model of a business is its simplicity... that simplicity is the fundamental key that allows users to understand databases, and allows software to navigate databases efficiently."

—Ralph Kimball, ***The Data Warehouse Toolkit***

Any database can be designed applying two techniques—ER modelling techniques (relational data model) and another approach is dimensional modelling (multidimensional data model). Multidimensional data model emerged around the 1990s to facilitate data analysis rather than performing online transactions. Relational model was developed earlier by Codd in 1970. ER modelling or relational modelling aims to reduce data redundancy, leading to the creation of a larger number of tables in the database. So as the database widens, the number of joins between tables increases to process even simple queries. Besides, the firms today are witnessing a voluminous growth in their data and due to the lack of technical knowledge, many users experience difficulty in querying ER model to find answers to their problems. For example, which customers are yielding maximum profits for the firm? This can be answered by querying the data lying with the firm, only if the manager or the user has the necessary skills to design the query. Sometimes, the query might be correct in syntax, but returns results which are incorrect or do not meet the requirements of the user. Although data are essential for the progress of a firm, it is only the usage of the right tools and schemas to manage the data which provides an actual competitive advantage. So many firms opt for the second solution, i.e., multidimensional modelling which is based on simple business objects such as cubes, measures and dimensions mostly built on the top of relational databases. These models create pre-aggregates or pre-joins of the data objects so that the user does not need to bother about the syntax of the query and retrieves correct results from querying the data. These models also allow the user to drill through the data and analyse trends and patterns.

A huge departure from traditional relational design, OLAP allows the data to be stored and accessed in the most efficient manner—allowing end-users to traverse the edges of a hypothetical "cube" of many dimensions.

—Oracle

Generally, the firms utilise relational databases to maintain transactional data to keep track of their day-to-day affairs. Such databases provide what is termed OLTP or Online Transaction Processing Systems. For example, OLTP for an e-retailer would be required to manage day-to-day order processing. Similarly, OLTP at a bank would manage daily credit, debit transaction made by the customers at the bank or through services offered by the bank such as debit card, credit card, online banking, etc. Relational databases can then house a tremendous amount of firm's data and aid in efficient retrieval and storage of the same. The problem arises when management wishes to analyse these data to find answers to its business problems. For example, usage of relational transactional database can easily answer a simple query like, "What is the total amount debited on 28 July 2014, at a particular ATM of the bank?" This simply involves retrieval of debit records on the given data for a unique ATM. Now consider that management is interested in knowing the answer to: "On weekends, which ATMs record the maximum debit amount and which ATMs record the least debit amount, from all ATMs of the bank in the country?" "Are these findings consistent over time?" This question is not related to one transaction but based on analysis of past performance of ATMs of the bank spread across the country. So firms build multidimensional models on the top of transactional databases which facilitate answers to such business queries. Such findings can be used by the bank to take critical business decisions such as phasing out of certain ATMs or relocating less used ones. This information can also be used to build a re-stocking plan for the ATMs. This is where analytic databases or multidimensional models are required, which provide access to aggregated historical and current data.

Multidimensional models can be thought to have three areas of applications in business data analysis:

1. Data warehousing—Typically modelled using multidimensional techniques
2. Core of OLAP—queries and results are presented in a multidimensional fashion
3. Basis for data mining—To discover knowledge in large databases.

WHAT ARE MULTIDIMENSIONAL DATA?

Visualising the data from different perspectives or along different dimensions gives rise to multidimensional data. Consider the following example: An institute of engineering offers five different courses to the students. The student intake in the year 2012 has been shown in Table 6.1.

Table 6.1 Student intake in five courses

Electronics and communication engineering	Computer science and engineering	Electrical engineering	Civil engineering	Mechanical engineering
185	190	65	29	85

Here, we are visualising the student intake from the perspective of different branches of engineering. Or, in other terms, student intake data are being visualised along one dimension, viz., branch of engineering. Suppose management of the institute is interested in comparing the student intake over a period of time, from the year 2009 to 2012. The data have been depicted in Table 6.2.

Visualising the data from different perspectives or along different dimensions gives rise to multidimensional data.

Table 6.2 Year-wise student intake in five courses

		2009	2010	2011	2012
Branch of engineering	Electronics and communication engineering	50	55	120	185
	Computer science and engineering	75	78	110	190
	Electrical engineering	45	42	80	65
	Civil engineering	25	23	35	29
	Mechanical engineering	37	32	62	85

The table depicts the student intake for each year in different branches of engineering. So now the data are being visualised from two dimensions: branch of engineering and year. Assume that the institute also has campuses spread across different geographical areas. Now let us say that the management would like to compare the student intake across different campuses, for all branches of engineering it offers and over the years 2009 to 2012. This implies adding another dimension to the data: Campus. So now the student intake data would be visualised from three dimensions: Campus, Year and Branch of engineering. This is called multidimensional data.

Often multidimensional data models are also termed cubes, although a cube may have more than three dimensions. In case a cube involves more than 15 dimensions, it is called a hypercube. However, it becomes too difficult to interpret a cube for more than three dimensions. In such cases, cube data are aggregated for two or more dimensions to reduce the viewable number of dimensions in the cube to three.

Exhibit 6.1 below shows a cube which has three dimensions: Year, Branch and Campus. For the purpose of illustration, only two values of each dimension are shown. There can be certain cells in the cubes which are not occupied.

Exhibit 6.1 Three-dimensional cube

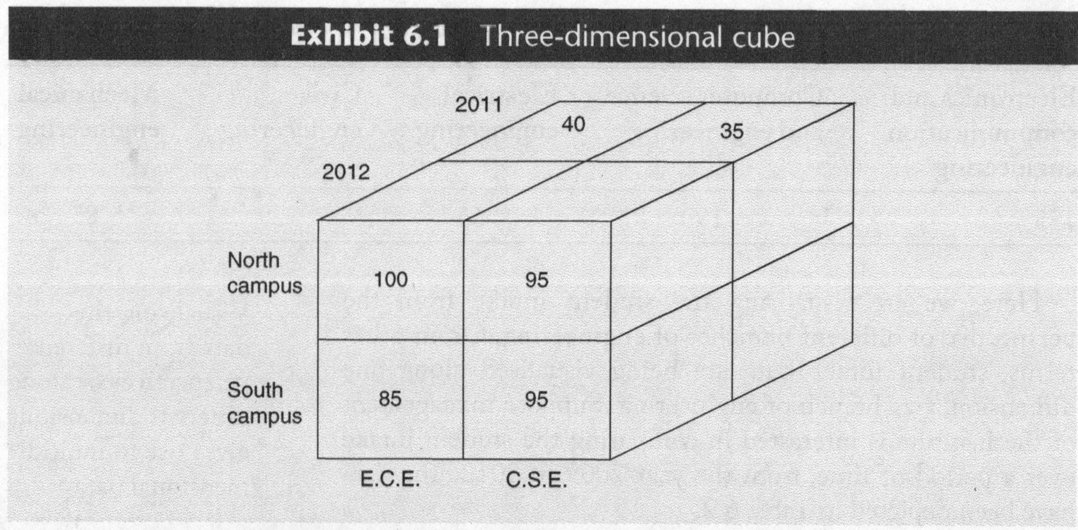

All the cells in a cube which have a value or are "non-empty" are called facts or measures (discussed in detail in the next section).

Here, "student intake" is taken as a fact or measure. All the cubes or multidimensional data models are centred over facts. They are the basis of analysis or the subject of interest for the user which he would like to interpret from different dimensions. For example, the fact "student intake" can be interpreted by the institute's management through time variations, or region such as changes in intake with changes in campus or with branch of engineering.

BASIC CONCEPTS IN MULTIDIMENSIONAL MODELS

"Our first big win, was when we started building our own cubes.....So now, having that skill set within our team – being able to go in and build the cubes with multiple hierarchies within a day or two – has been a huge efficiency gain."

—Jessica Dunn, VP, Bank of America

Measures/Facts

Fact or measure is a numerical quantity which represents some aspect of the firm's performance. Fact is also said to be the subject of interest to be analysed. It can also be a numerical figure which is computed using a formula or the simple functions such as SUM, Average or Count. The business user is interested in studying this fact or measure from different perspectives and utilises this information to make decisions. For example, "Sales" is often the subject of interest for firms which are engaged in sales of any products and services. Management of such firms has been often interested in analysing sales for their products or services. Therefore "Sales" would be a measure for such firms. For example, pizza chains would like to know, "What was the total sale of 'Garlic bread' by end of the day, by end of a week, for a given month, for a given store, etc.?" The matter of interest is the same which is "Sales", while perspective for analysis changes from day to week to month to store, etc. Other examples of measures include incentives, employee turnover, products manufactured, level of inventory, etc.

> Fact or measure is a numerical quantity which represents some aspect of the firm's performance.

Facts can be of three types:

> Facts can be of three types:
>
> - Event facts
> - State facts
> - Cumulative snapshot fact

- Event facts—Event facts are used to numerically represent an event. Event here implies a unique instance of the real world. For example, the sale of a given product at a given store on a particular day would be an event fact. Or student intake for a given semester for a given branch of engineering for a given campus of the institute is also an event fact.

- State facts—State facts are applied to represent the state of a given process at a given time. Like inventory levels at a given point of time, users of the website are such state facts. They are also called snapshot facts.
- Cumulative snapshot fact—Cumulative snapshot facts are facts aggregated or accumulated over a period of time. These represent the state of a process up to a certain amount of time. For example, total sales in a year to date are a cumulative snapshot fact.

Certain measures are additive. This implies that they can be summed like summing up sales along time periods or products or regions, etc. would yield total sales. Similarly, student intake can be summed up along time periods, campuses, branches to impart information about total student intake for the institute. There can be some measures which are completely non-additive, implying that their sum would not yield any meaningful information. For example, sum of average results would not impart any information. Those measures are known as non-additive measures. Yet, another case can be when measures can be summed in certain scenarios while in others they yield no information. For example, sum of inventory levels for a product over a month would not represent the inventory level for that product at the end of the month. Consider this, product 'A' has following weekly stocks in a firm for the month of Februrary.

Week 1 – 25, Week 2 – 30, Week 3 – 40 and Week 4 – 50.

Now at the end of February, stock is 50 and not the sum of all weeks which is 145 (25 + 30 + 40 + 50). However, the sum of inventory levels for a given product at different warehouses would yield information about the total number of that product available in the inventory. Such measures are called semi-additive measures.

Dimension

A dimension is also referred to as a concept. Dimension is the perspective along which the fact is to be analysed. It represents one characteristic of fact along which analysis can be undertaken. For example, total sales for a firm is 120 that does not impart any analytical characteristic to the numerical figure "120". Now consider that total sales for a product of the firm is 120 adds some meaning to the fact "120". Again, consider total sales for a product of the firm in the year 2013 is 120 adds another perspective to the fact "120". Yet, another perspective can be total sales for a product of the firm in the year 2013 in the South region is 120. Here, we have applied different perspectives to the fact "120", such as Product, Year and Region. These different perspectives or characteristics are termed dimensions.

Dimensions not only enable the users to analyse the data, but also aid in slicing and dicing the facts slicing and dicing would facilitate effective decision-making (Slice and dice is explained in detail in section operations on OLAP cube/ multidimensional analysis). Now we are in a position to say that a non-empty cell for a particular combination of multiple dimensions is a "fact". This non-empty value which exists at the intersection of all dimensions of a multidimensional model is also termed *detail* or *leaf-level* value. Following from the above institute example,

> Dimension is the perspective along which the fact is to be analysed.

Student Intake for the branch of E.C.E. in the North Campus for the year 2012 is equal to 100 is a leaf level value. To find the total intake in E.C.E. for the year 2012, we simply need sum Student Intake along the year 2012 yielding a value of 185 students. This is called an additive measure as defined earlier, which uses Sum as an aggregate function to compute the measure.

As of now, remember that each of these dimensions exists as tables in the multidimensional model, which also contains a separate fact table. How these dimensions and fact tables are linked to each other gives rise to the concept of schemas, as discussed in detail in a later section. Based on how a dimension is populated or created, the dimension can be classified as follows.

Fact dimensions

When a dimension is created from a fact table, it is termed as fact dimension. For example, if the Sales fact table contains "Date of Sale", which is used to create a time dimension, then this time dimension would be termed a fact dimension. Because these data are already present in the fact table, this is also termed as "degenerate dimension".

When a dimension is created from a fact table, it is termed as fact dimension.

Sales fact					Dimension time		
Product ID	Customer ID	Date of purchase	Quantity purchased		Date	Month	Year
1	1	13-06-2012	1		13-06-2012	6	2012
2	1	14-06-2012	1		14-06-2012	6	2012
2	5	14-07-2012	2		14-07-2012	7	2012
3	6	16-01-2013	2	⟶	16-01-2013	1	2013
4	3	21-04-2013	1		21-04-2013	4	2013
5	2	17-06-2013	1		17-06-2013	6	2013
5	3	07-09-2013	1		07-09-2013	9	2013
6	4	01-06-2014	1		01-06-2014	6	2014

Parent–child dimension

When a dimension table contains a self-referencing relationship, it yields a parent–child dimension. For such a table, there exists a field which is the primary key for that table and there exists another field which references this primary key. Hence, this second field then becomes the foreign key which points back to the same table. Consider, for example, a book publishing

When a dimension table contains a self referencing relationship, it yields a parent-child dimension.

house has a table of employees who can function in different roles such as author, editor, contributor and reviewer, as shown. This table would have Emp ID as the primary key. Each employee has to report to another employee, and this information is contained in a Reviewer field in the same table. Reviewer field contains the Emp ID of the person who has been designated as a reviewer for a given employee. So, Reviewer field becomes the foreign key and points back to the same table.

Emp ID	Employee name	Role	Reviewer
101	Simmi	Contributor	104
102	Shine	Editor	109
104	Pragati	Author	106
105	Pritam	Contributor	104
106	Udai	Reviewer	107
107	Himani	Editor	109
108	Saurabh	Reviewer	102
109	Gunraj	Chief Editor	

When this dimension table is created, Reviewer ID would be a field in this table. This field is also termed as a parent field or a parent attribute. This type of dimension containing parent–child relationship is called a parent–child dimension and creates its own hierarchy. The number of hierarchy levels in such dimensions is not pre-determined. For each step you move from a child to a parent yields one level in the hierarchy. From the above example, one can understand how a chain of levels can be created in parent–child dimension. Starting from Simmi, who is a contributor, Pragati has been assigned as a reviewer. Pragati's work is reviewed by Udai, Udai's work by Himani and Himani's work by Gunraj, who is the chief editor in the publishing house. So starting from Simmi, the chain yields five levels in the hierarchy. However, if we start with some other person such as Saurabh, then there are only three levels in the hierarchy. And for Shine, there are two levels in the hierarchy.

Role playing dimension

When a dimension is related to the fact table more than once, it is known as a role playing dimension. For each relation to the fact table, it plays a different role. For example, consider the Employee dimension and the Incentives fact table (see Exhibit 6.2). One role of employee dimension would be to approve the incentive, as a supervisor of that employee and another role would be that of an employee who is the receiver of that incentive.

> When a dimension is related to the fact table more than once, it is known as role playing dimension.

For each such role, a new relationship needs to be defined in the data model. Another example is of the Time dimension and Sales fact (see Exhibit 6.3). Here, date in the Time dimension would relate to the Sales fact table for data of sale, for date of shipment and for the date of payment.

Exhibit 6.2 Employee dimension and incentive fact table

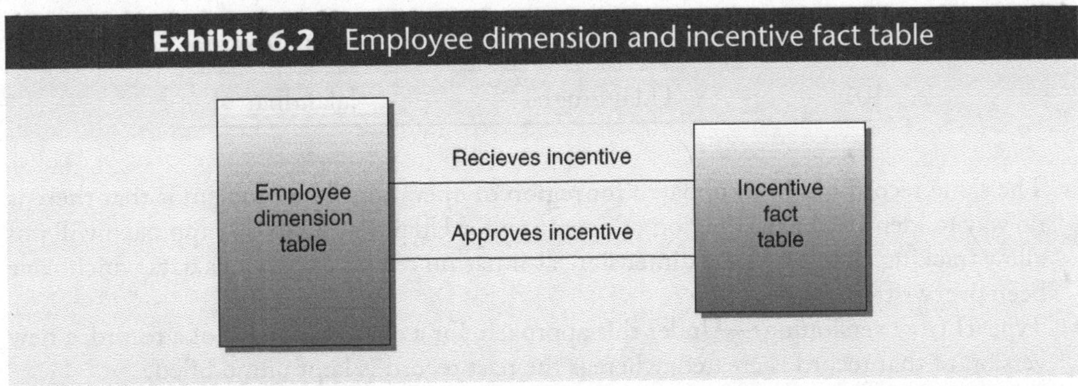

Exhibit 6.3 Time dimension and sales fact table

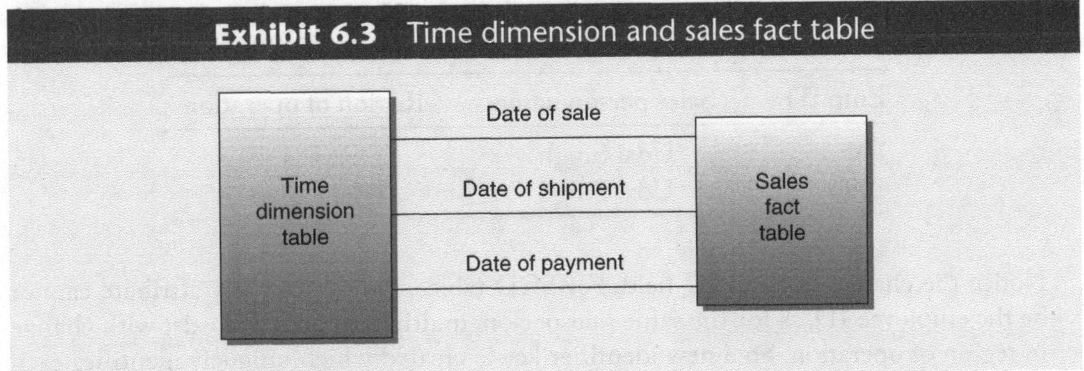

Slowly changing dimensions

Certain dimensions such as salesperson or rating of an album change over time. For example, the region of operation of salesperson changes over time or popularity (rating) of an album changes over time. Employees are promoted to different ranks so their job positions change over time, etc. Such dimensions are called SCD or slowly changing dimensions. As such changes do not occur regularly, rather they occur slowly, they are called slowly changing dimensions. An important point of concern is that database needs to track changes to such dimensions; otherwise, there would be no way to track the past status of the dimension. For example, the database would contain the current region of operation of a salesperson, and hence there would be no means to track the past region of operations and determine the performance of the sales person.

> Certain dimensions such as salesperson or rating of an album change over time; such dimensions are known as slowly changing dimensions (SCD).

There are three approaches to handle a slowly changing dimension:

- Type-I approach (overwrite the old attribute values)—This approach is easiest to implement. For example, a record for the salesperson Udai Singh on change of region of operation from Patiala to Jalandhar would appear as under:

Emp ID	Sales person name	Region of operation
101	Udai Singh	Jalandhar

The same record has been updated for region of operation. The problem is that there is no way to identify the past region of operation for Udai Singh. So this approach will not allow tracking changes in the dimension, as it has no record of previous data which have been overwritten.

- Type-II (row versioning)—Under this approach, for a change in value of a record, a new version of that record is created, whereas the past record is kept unmodified.
For example, a record for the salesperson Udai Singh on change of region of operation would appear as follows:

Emp ID	Sales person name	Region of operation
101	Udai Singh	Patiala
109	Udai Singh	Jalandhar

Notice the change in Emp ID field. For SCD tables, the primary key attribute cannot be the employee ID, as for the same salesperson, multiple records will exist with change in region of operation. So a new identifier key is created which uniquely identifies each new version of the record and aids in tracking historical information. A limitation of this approach is that it increases the size of the dimension table. However, this is the most widely used approach.

- Type-III (versioned columns)—In this approach, a new version of the column is created, which has changed. Rather than creating a new record for the updated value, a new column with an updated value is inserted, thereby not increasing the size of the table.
For example, a record for the salesperson Udai Singh on change of region of operation would appear as follows:

Emp ID	Sales person name	Original region of operation	Current region of operation
101	Udai Singh	Patiala	Jalandhar

Using this scheme, we record the current value and the old value in different columns. This approach is useful only when a limited number of changes would occur. This approach cannot track history for more than one change in the dimension. For example, if the region of operation for Udai Singh changes from Jalandhar to Ludhiana, then past information about Patiala would be lost.

Frequently changing dimensions

If a dimension changes rapidly or frequently, it is termed as frequently changing dimension.

If a dimension changes rapidly or frequently, it is termed as frequently changing dimension. For example, ratings of channels, TV soaps, products or scores in games can be frequently changing dimensions. To handle such dimensions, row versioning would not be suitable because the dimension table would increase manifold, with a new record being inserted for each change in the dimension. So a commonly used approach is to split the dimension into two or more parts also termed mini-dimensions. One part of the dimension would contain the fields or values which are static or change rarely or never like Channel ID, channel name, etc. The second part would hold the rapidly changing part of the dimension like channel rating. In this second mini-dimension table, row versioning can be deployed to track the changes. The same has been depicted in Exhibit 6.4.

Exhibit 6.4 Example of two mini-dimension tables

Channel ID	Channel name
11	EStar
12	FFox
13	Day
14	Health

1 ——— N

Channel ID	Rating	Time
11	A	Mar-12
11	A	Jun-12
11	B	Sep-12
11	C	Dec-12
12	B	Mar-12
12	B	Jun-12
12	B	Sep-12
12	A	Dec-12
13	C	Mar-12
13	B	Jun-12
13	A	Sep-12
13	B	Dec-12
14	A	Mar-12
14	B	Jun-12
14	B	Sep-12
14	A	Dec-12

Here, two mini-dimension tables have been created, one which is static and contains names of channel, its IDs, etc. Another one tracks the frequently changing ratings of these channels. This table utilises row versioning to track the same.

To further reduce the size, rather than directly specifying the value for that field, a range of values is used. For example, for rapid changes in income, use income range to fill in income value in the dimension table. Like Annual income ranges can be "less than 2 lakh", "2 lakh to 4 lakh", "more than 4 lakh", etc. Of course, ranges would be defined based on firm's own data. This way, the number of changes would reduce, as now multiple changes would fall in one range and hence reduce the number of possible rows to be inserted.

Attributes

Attributes provide an additional description about a dimension. For example, Campus dimension can be additionally described by city, state, pin code, etc. All these fields would then become attributes for Campus dimension. Product as a dimension can be characterised by Product ID, which can uniquely identify each product. However, product name, product size, price of the product, nutritional information would provide additional detail.

Attributes can be utilised for a further analysis. For example, which size of the product sells the most could yield an important business insight. Similarly, how pricing of the product is making an impact on the sales of the product can also reveal interesting information for business users. Hence, attributes are added to a dimension table to provide additional information about that dimension.

> Attributes provide additional description about a dimension.

Hierarchies

Each dimension can be further categorised into levels, and the order of these levels is specified by a concept called "hierarchy". In other words, a dimension can have several levels termed hierarchy. For example, for Time dimension, year can be broken down into quarters, quarters into months, months into weeks and weeks into days. This way, time dimension can have five levels: Year, Quarter, Month, Week and Day. Day represents the lowest level of hierarchy. In most of the models, facts are linked to the lowest level of each dimension.

The division of a dimension into hierarchies makes them useful for selection and grouping of data at a desired level. For example, total sales for a product can be analysed across time. Total sales for a given year can be broken down into quarters to compare quarterly sales, into months to analyse which months have the highest and lowest sales and into days to analyse if weekends make an impact on the sale of the product. Here Day, Month, Quarter and Year represent hierarchies of dimension Time.

> Each dimension can be further categorised into levels and the order of these levels is specified by a concept called 'hierarchy'.

All → Year → Quarter → Month → Day

For example, consider the dimension "Location", which can have the following hierarchies:

All → Country → State → City → Village

A hierarchy can be total or partial. If a hierarchy is defined for a dimension which does not cover all the possible levels in that dimension, it would be a partial hierarchy. Consider, for example, time dimension which can have the following hierarchies as depicted in Exhibit 6.5.

Exhibit 6.5 Hierarchies of time dimension

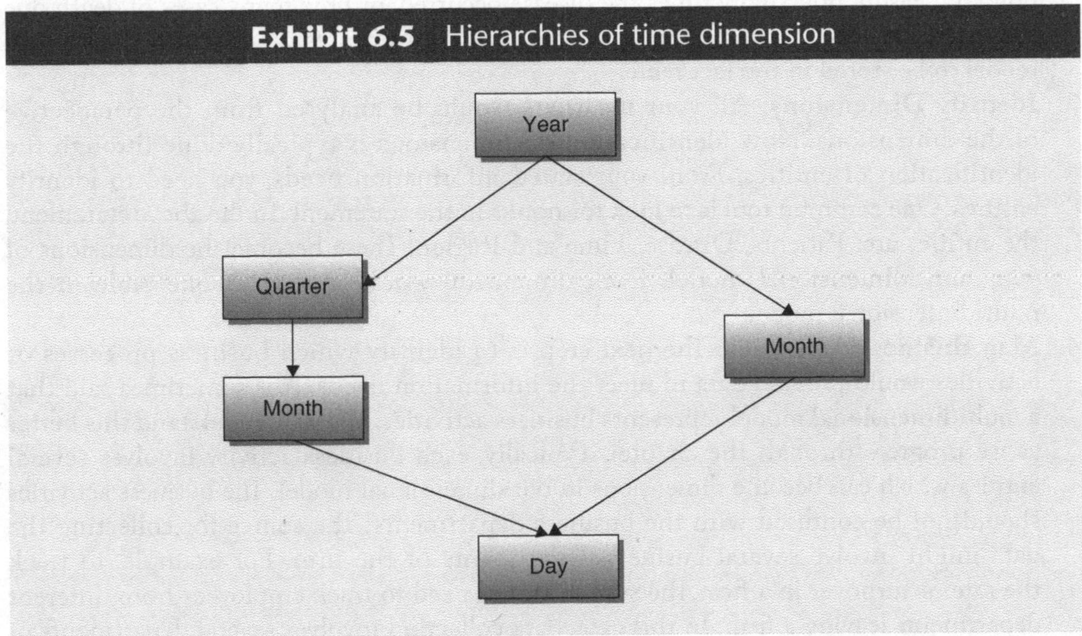

Here, the left hierarchy, viz., Year → Quarter → Month → Day is a total hierarchy while on the right, viz., Year → Month→ Day is a partial hierarchy.

DIMENSIONAL MODELLING PROCESS

Following steps are important for dimensional modelling:

> Dimensional modelling process:
>
> 1. State information needs
> 2. Identify the facts
> 3. Identify dimensions
> 4. Map business activities
> 5. Identification of attributes
> 6. Decide on the level of detail
> 7. Schema

1. **State Information Needs**: The foremost step is to understand why you require a multidimensional model. As a user of that multidimensional model, whether you are a manager or a business analyst, you need to develop a clear picture of your business information needs. As this is exactly what your dimensional model is going to answer. As an example, say your company is involved in research related to healthcare. You state your information need as: "*To track disease occurrence and fatality with respect to time, patients and region.*" As a user of the model, you should be

very careful in stating your requirements. The model cannot answer what you have not specified in the requirements, as it would not contain that sort of data.

2. **Identify the Facts**: Facts are numerical measures such as sales of the product in a location or incentives distributed in a division. Fact is the subject of interest to be analysed. Here, you need to answer how to measure? For example, for the given information need, how to measure how many times the disease occurred, or how many cases of death due to a particular disease were reported? These are the measures of our multidimensional model to be stored in the fact table.
3. **Identify Dimensions**: All your measures would be analysed from the perspective of the dimensions. Now identification of dimensions is typically done through the identification of entities. From your stated information needs, you need to identify entities. One common tool is to look for nouns in the statement. In the above statement, the entities are: Patients, Disease, Time and Region. These become the dimensions of your multidimensional model. Each dimension would appear as one table in the multidimensional model.
4. **Map Business Activities**: The next step is to identify which business processes or activities would provide data to meet the information needs. It is sometimes said that a multidimensional model represents business activities. We will understand this better as we progress through the chapter. Typically, each business activity involves several entities which can become dimensions in our dimensional model. The business activities should not be confused with the business departments. The source for collecting the data might involve several business departments of the firm. For example, to track the rate of turnover in a firm, the system would need to track employees from different departments leaving a firm. In this case, data collection involves several departments of the firm. If the analyst is going to map business activities which are prevalent in multiple departments, a single dimensional model would represent one or more departments. Which business activities in your firm collect patient data, tracks diseases occurrence and incidents of mortality, and region where the disease was found? These can be a data entry form required to fill in by patients and diagnosis of doctors and final status of the disease and the patient.
5. **Identification of Attributes**: In this step, you answer the question, "Which other details you require for each entity or dimension?". These additional details are termed attributes. For example, you might need following detail for patients to analyse what kinds of patients are prone to a given disease: Age, Gender, Marital Status, Existing ailments, etc. Also, the user needs to define hierarchies for each dimension if any in this step. There can be dimensions which have no hierarchies such as Patient as no attribute has underlying levels. Consider the Time dimension which can have the attributes: Year, Quarter, Month and Date. This dimension has a hierarchy as dates are contained in each month, months in each quarter and quarters in each year. Therefore, the hierarchy is Year → Quarter → Month → Date.
6. **Decide on the Level of Detail**: In the terminology of dimensional modelling, the level of detailing is known as the level of granularity. The most basic level of attribute in each dimension would define the granularity of that dimension. In case dimension has hierarchy, then the lowest level in the hierarchy would define its granularity. The

analysis of data, computation of pre-aggregates and stored in a multidimensional model is dependent on granularity of each dimension in the model. For a dimension with no hierarchies, such as Patient dimension, generally an auto-numbered identifier key defines granularity like Patient ID. In a dimension with hierarchies such as Time dimension, the most basic level which is Date defines the granularity.

7. **Schema:** The last step is to develop a complete picture of the multidimensional model which is also termed developing a schema which is the next section of discussion of this chapter.

SCHEMAS FOR MULTIDIMENSIONAL DATA MODELS

How do we represent data diagrammatically in multidimensional model gives rise to the concept of "Schemas". Schemas depict dimensions, facts, attributes and hierarchies in a model clearly. In other words, Multidimensional Data Models are the diagrammatic representation of fact tables and dimension tables and the relationship between them. Depiction of the multidimensional model using schemas enables non-technical persons such as a manager to easily interpret the underlying model. This way, the design analyst can take the feedback from the concerned manager about the data model, which in turn helps to reduce the errors. As to construct a house, you need a blueprint which guides the builder to construct a house according to the specifications. Similarly, Data Models help the analyst to build a DataMart/Data Warehouse according to the specifications provided by the manager. Schemas enable the analyst to map business information needs to entities or dimension, develop relationships between entities or dimensions and then utilise this to track the data sources for the analysis. Depiction using schemas clearly indicates what is to be measured (facts) and how it is to be analysed (using dimensions). This way, it easily facilitates the users to understand whether the given model meets their business requirements or not. Three types of schemas are widely used:

> Schemas depict dimensions, facts, attributes and hierarchies in a model clearly.

Star Schema

Star schema is the most widely applied schema. In star schema, there are one large fact table and multiple dimension tables. The fact table has 1:M relations with each of the dimension tables. One of the most important features of star schema is that the star schema stores data in dimension tables in a denormalised form. The storage of data in a denormalised form helps to increase the access rate of the data because there are fewer linkages and joins. As a result, the star schema is not complex because of the denormalised form of storage, but on the hindsight, the star schema has more redundancies and occupies more space. Intuitively, this type of schema is more appropriate where the dimension table has a less number of rows (occupies less space), but where the dimension table has more rows, then star schema is

> In star schema, there is one large fact table and multiple dimension tables.

not appropriate. The star schema is easier to understand, but it does not capture hierarchies or levels in a dimension. This implies that all the levels within a dimension are stored within one dimension table.

Exhibit 6.6 Star schema

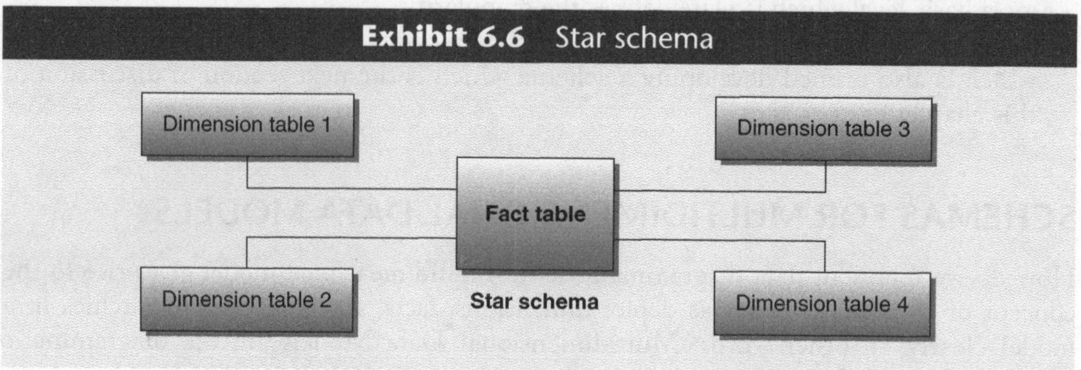

As an example, consider the following star schema which does not capture hierarchies:

Exhibit 6.7 Star schema (Not capturing hierarchies)

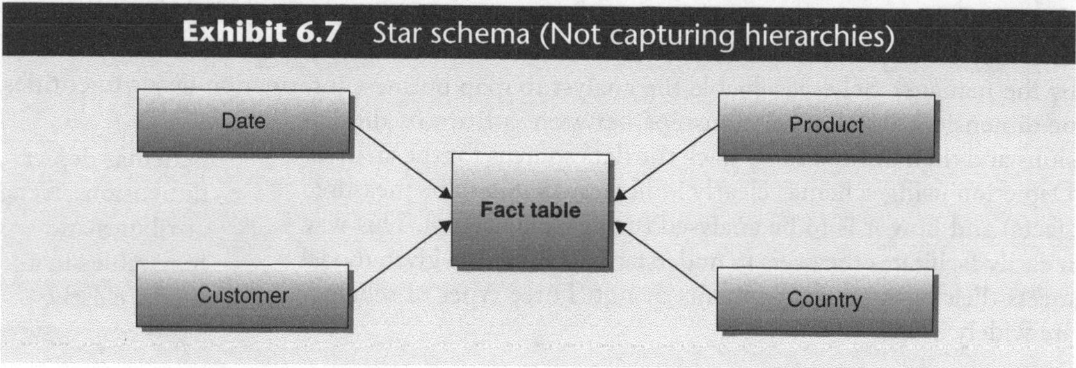

The star schema is practically applied where entities in the dimension table are accessed frequently because the entities are in a denormalised form, i.e., less linkages which increases the access rate. On the flip side, owing to data duplication, it consumes more storage space. Snowflake schema, on the other hand, has a larger number of joins due to the larger number of dimension tables. So access rate is lower, but this reduces storage space requirements.

Consider another example: In star schema depicted in Exhibit 6.8, there is one fact table, i.e., Sales fact table and four Dimension table, i.e., State, Product, Purchase and Employee. The data in the Dimension table are stored in a denormalised form, i.e., without capturing hierarchies and has less joins. The primary key is on Month-ID for Purchase dimension, Employee-ID for employee dimension, Product-ID for Product dimension and State-ID for State dimension.

Exhibit 6.8 Example of star schema

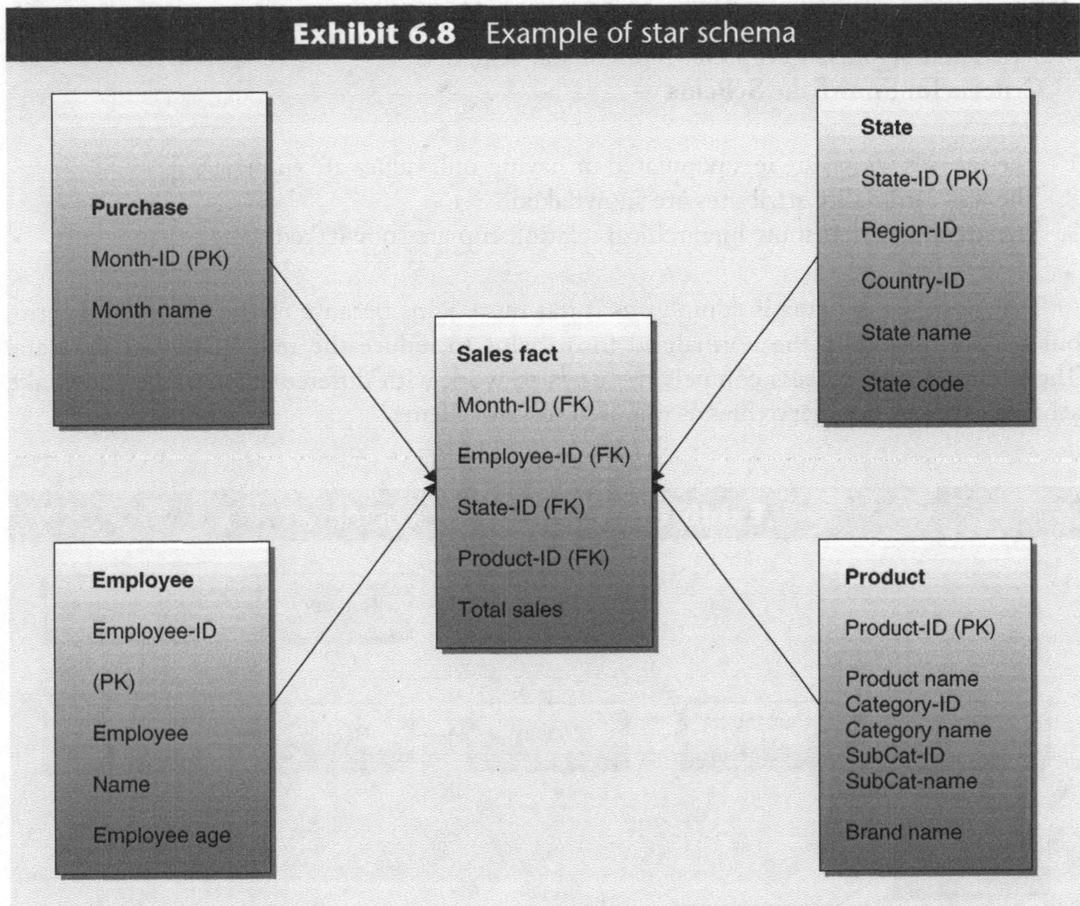

All the primary keys of the dimension tables appear as foreign keys, in fact table leading to 1:M relation between fact and dimension tables. Note that the levels in dimensions are contained in the same table in a star schema. For example, the fields Product, Category and Sub-category are levels in the Product dimension stored within the Product dimension table.

Snowflake Schema

Snowflake schema is the extension of star schema. In the snowflake schema, the Dimension tables are in a normalised form. This implies that for each level of hierarchy in a dimension, a separate table would be created in snowflake schema. The normalised form helps to reduce the storage space, but adversely affects the speed of accessing the data. As in the present scenario, there is no major issue regarding the cost of storage space and organisations are more concerned

Snowflake schema is the extension of star schema. In the snowflake schema, the dimension tables are in normalised form.

regarding the speed of accessing the data. This is a reason that snowflake schema is not preferred and organisations prefer more of star schema.

Criteria for Snowflake Schema

1. The records which are less populated or having null values are snowflaked.
2. The less cardinality attributes are snowflaked.
3. The attributes that show hierarchical relationship are snowflaked.

The snowflake schema is complex as it has more joins because of the normalised form, but on the hindsight, the normalised form helps to reduce the redundancy in the data. The normalisation process compels the users to work with different tables. The snowflake schema captures the hierarchies as opposed to star schema.

Exhibit 6.9 Snowflake schema

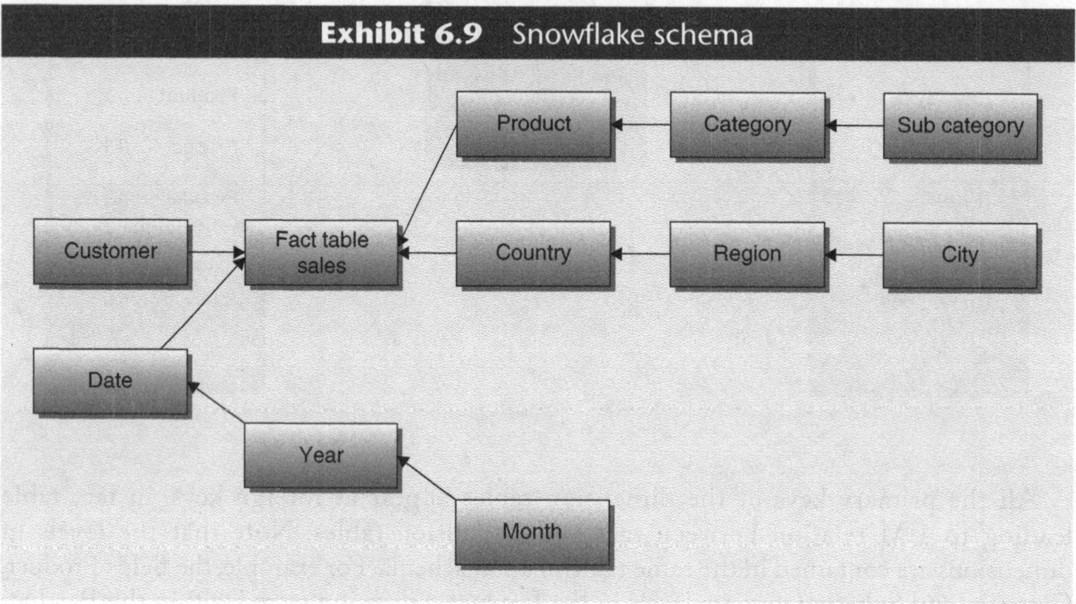

Note in the above example that there is one fact table (the same as that of star schema) but in the Dimension tables are snowflaked to capture hierarchies which leads to more tables and joins. Although this reduces the redundancy, this adversely affects the access speed of data because after snowflaking there are more table and more joins.

Features of Snowflake Schema

1. Snowflake schema shows the hierarchies.
2. 1:M relationships attributes of the dimension tables are separated to show different hierarchies.
3. The Child entity inherits the relationship with Parent entity using key attribute.

Exhibit 6.10 Example of snowflake schema

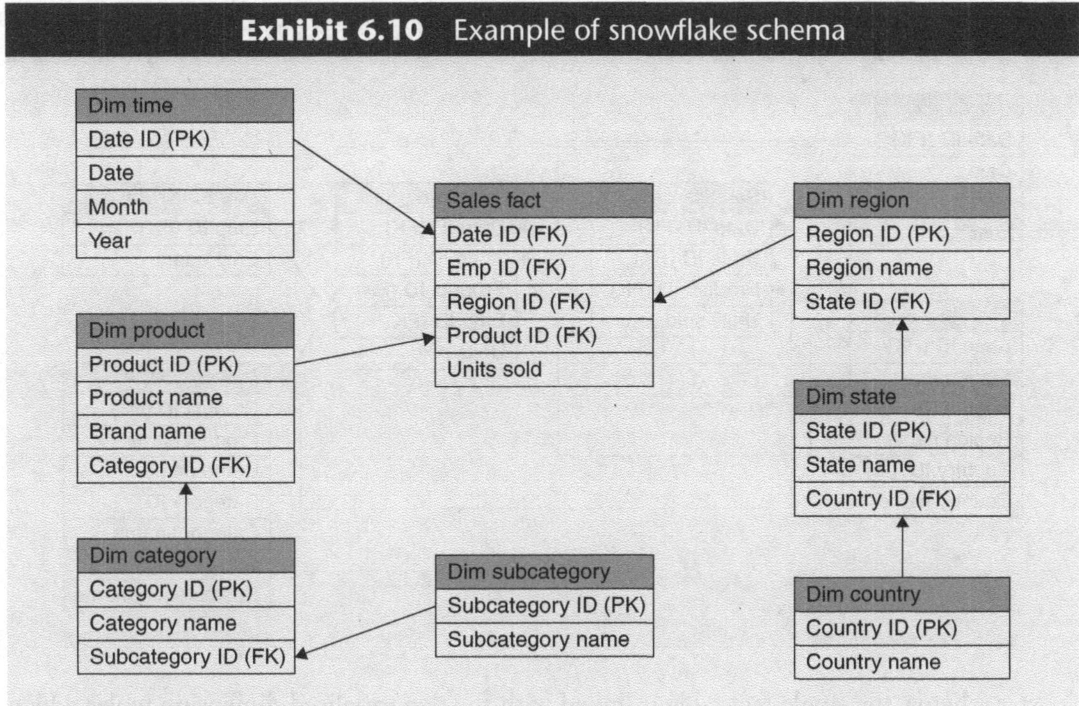

Fact Constellation Schema

Fact constellation schema can be created for both star and snowflake schemas. In the Fact constellation schema, there are multiple facts tables with measures based on existing dimension tables. This helps to share Dimension tables among more than one fact table. This schema is only applicable where some facts are associated with some dimensions and rest of the facts are associated with the other set of dimensions. This creation of multiple schemas generates a complicated layout in the fact constellation schema.

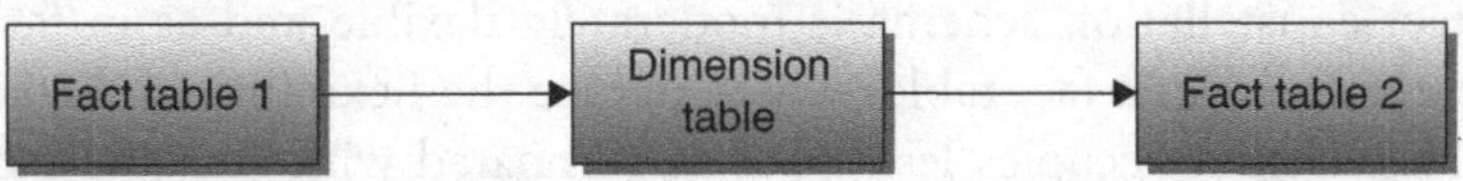

Suppose the firm wants to track which employee generated most of the sales. In such a case, multiple fact tables would be required. In Exhibit 6.11, one fact table is for sales and another is created to map sales to employees.

> In the fact constellation schema, there are multiple facts tables with measures based on existing dimension tables.

Comparison of Fact Constellation, Star and Snowflake schemas

1. Star schema is easy to understand as compared with snowflake schema and fact constellation schema. As in the

Exhibit 6.11 Example of fact constellation schema

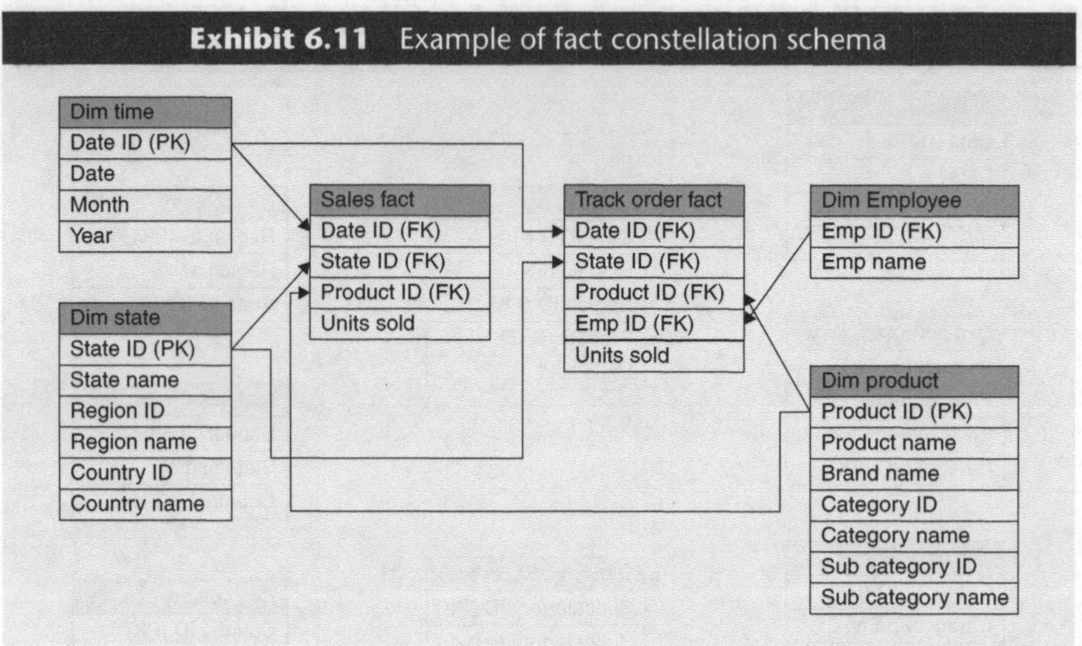

star schema, the single fact table is linked with the denormalised dimension tables which results in less joins and linkages, whereas in case of snowflake schema, the dimension tables are in a normalised form which increases the joins and hence this type of schema is complicated. The fact constellation schema is even more complex as in this schema there are multiple fact tables which increases the complexity of the layout.

2. The star schema is more efficient as compared with snowflake and fact constellation schemas. In the star schema, there are less joins which results in the quick access of data, whereas in case of snowflake and fact constellation schemas there are more joins which although reduce the storage space (specifically in snowflake schema) but reduce the access speed.
3. The star schema is more flexible as data are stored in a denormalised form. The denormalised form helps to add more data without thinking about the redundancy of data. The Fact constellation schema is moderately flexible and as in fact constellation schema there are multiple fact tables which reduce the flexibility of the schema.
4. The snowflake schema occupies less space as compared with star and fact constellation schemas. The data are stored in a normalised form in snowflake schema which reduces the storage space requirement as compared with star and fact constellation schemas.

OPERATIONS ON OLAP CUBE/MULTIDIMENSIONAL ANALYSIS

Some simple summarising operations on the cube are as follows.

1. **Roll Up (Drill Up)**: Roll up implies reducing the dimension hierarchy or entire cube by one or more dimensions. For example, the cube below depicts data over three dimensions,

viz., date, product and country. The data can be rolled up by grouping the data by country and thus by reducing the dimensions to two.

2. **Drill Down (Roll Down)**: It is the reverse of roll up. In this, the data are further detailed to a lower level of hierarchy. For example, total annual sales is presented quarter wise. But, this has been further broken down into quarters as shown in Exhibit 6.12. Either a new concept hierarchy or a new dimension can be added.

Exhibit 6.12 Example of roll up and drill down

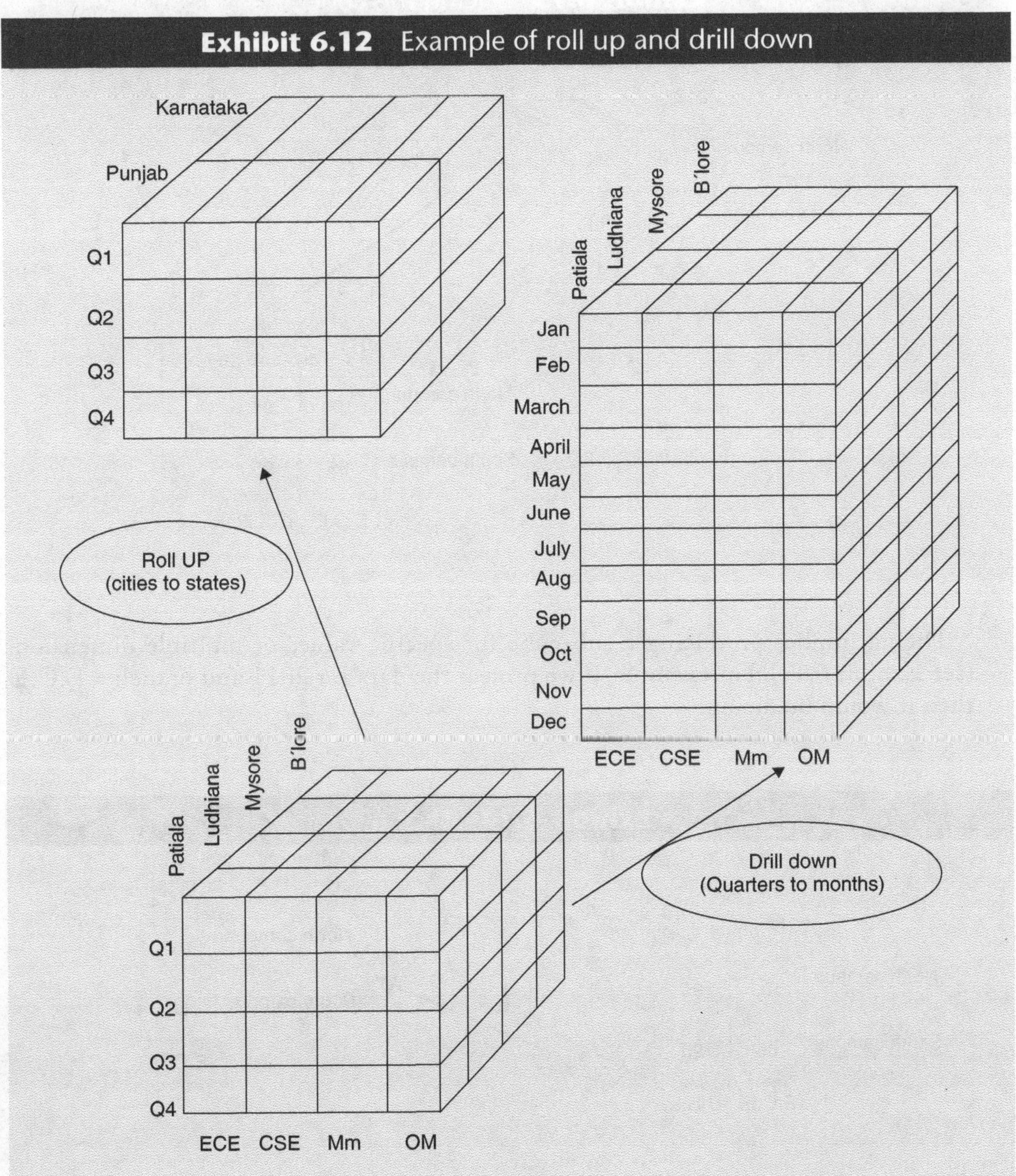

3. **Slice and Dice**: Slice and dice operations are select and project operations. This implies to project the cube for specific or selected values of dimension. When select operation is applied on only one dimension, it is called slicing. If selection is applied on multiple dimensions, it is called dicing. For example, slicing the cube shown in Exhibit 6.13 for the year 2011, keeping everything else the same, produces the following:

Exhibit 6.13 Slicing the cube

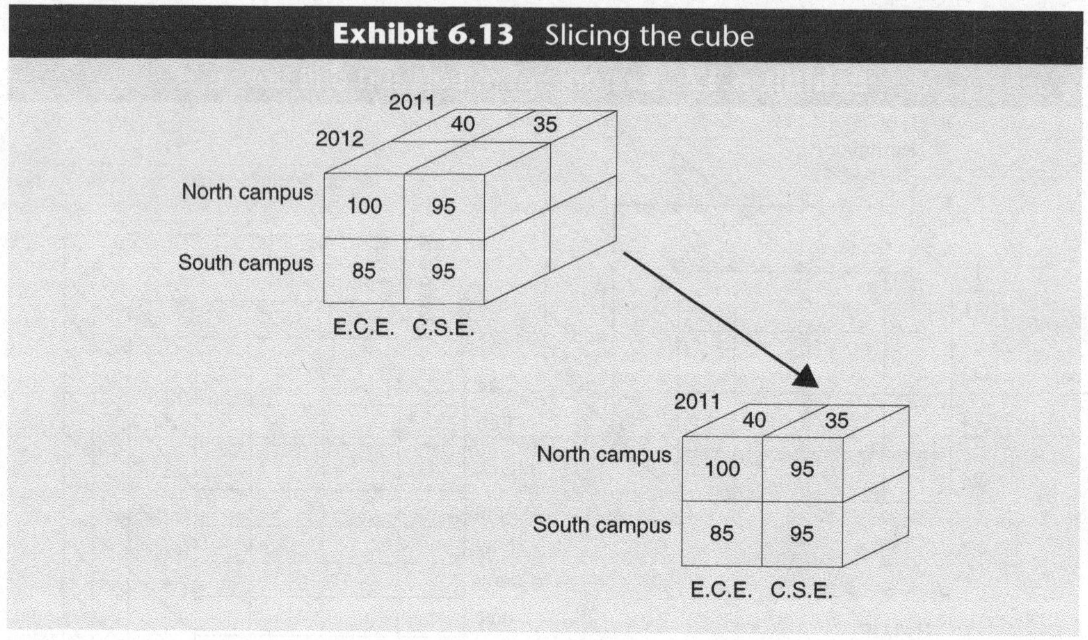

Dicing implies producing a sub-cube for specific values of multiple dimensions (see Exhibit 6.14). For example, if we project the data for 2011 and branch = E.C.E, then it would be dicing.

Exhibit 6.14 Dicing

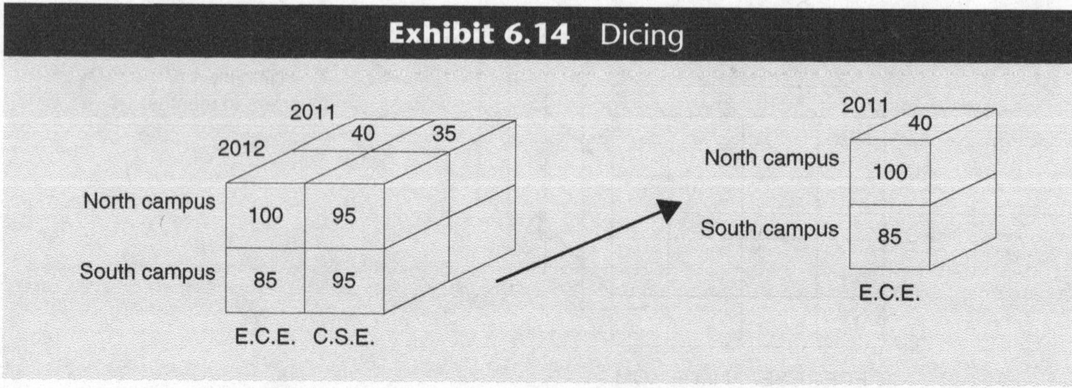

4. **Pivot or Rotate**: Pivot or rotation enables the user to view data from different angles. As the number of dimensions increases, this technique becomes more beneficial, as sometimes it is difficult for the user to interpret the data along the third axis. By rotating, the view is made easier to interpret.

As shown in Exhibit 6.15, the cube is rotated to provide an easier view for the time dimension. The figures for time values would be easier to interpret in the second view.

Exhibit 6.15 Rotate

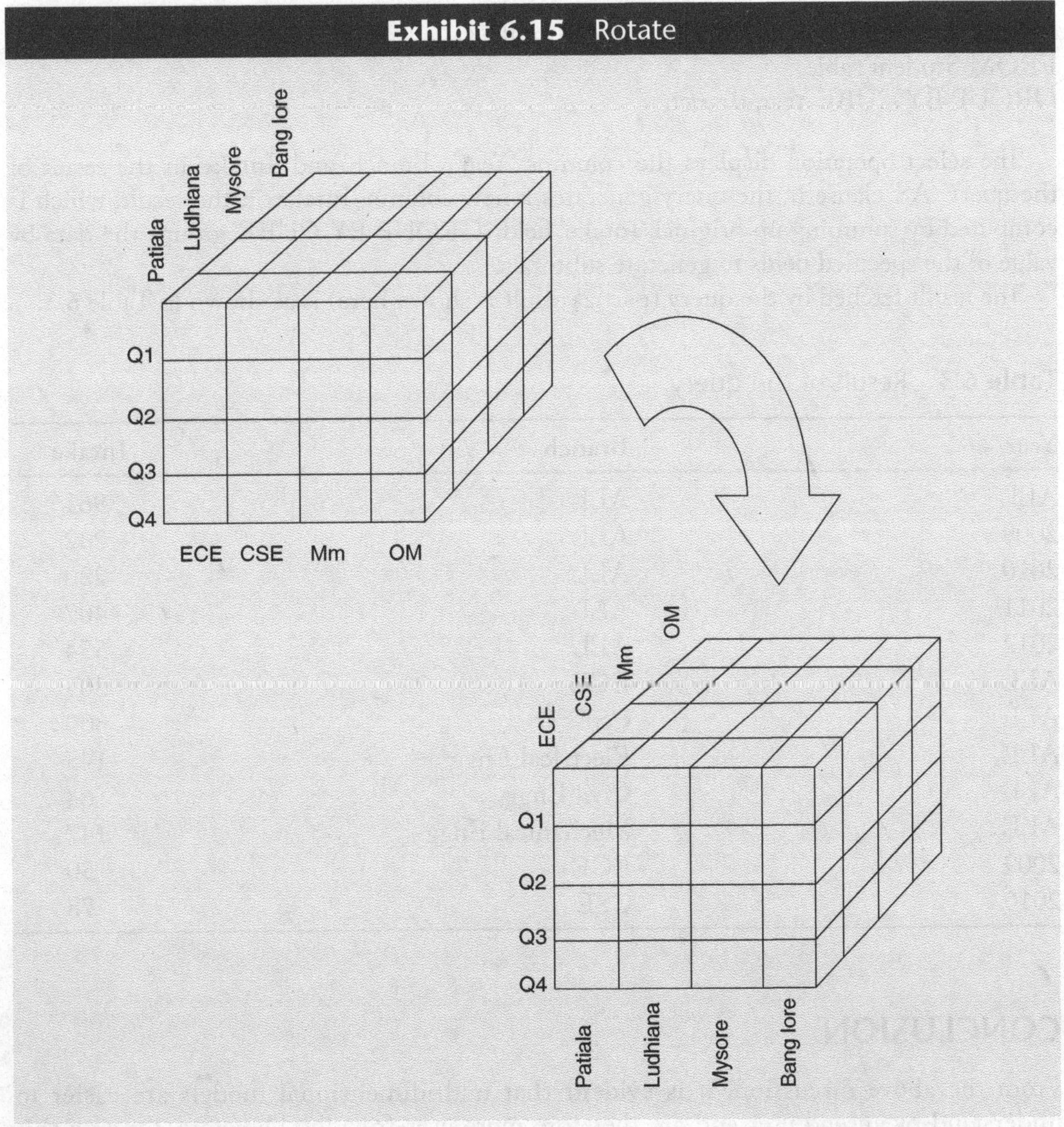

QUERYING IN MULTIDIMENSIONAL MODELS

Multidimensional expression (MDX) is widely used as a query language. In this language, dimension values are called members. The top level of each dimension hierarchy is called "ALL". Members are referred to using dot notation. FROM clause specifies the input cube on which the operation has to be performed. SELECT clause specifies the level of members from which the data are to be retrieved and is denoted as "axes".

For example, the query in Table 6.3 computes the total student intake by year and branch of engineering, with subtotals for both branch and year, and a grand total of all intakes to date. This query also generates ALL values for subtotals and grand totals.

```
SELECT Year, Branch, SUM (Intake) AS Intake
FROM StudentTable
GROUP BY CUBE Year, Branch
```

The select operation displays the columns 'Year', 'Branch' and 'Intake' in the result of the query. 'AS' clause in the query generates a new column 'Intake' in the result, which is computed by summing up original 'Intake' field. 'GROUP BY CUBE' groups the data by value of the specified fields to generate subtotals.

The result fetched by the query (partial result is shown here) is as shown in Table 6.3:

Table 6.3 Result of the query

Year	Branch	Intake
ALL	ALL	961
2009	ALL	232
2010	ALL	230
2011	ALL	407
2012	ALL	554
ALL	ECE	305
ALL	CSE	300
ALL	Electrical Engg	145
ALL	Civil Engg	64
ALL	Mechanical Engg	147
2009	ECE	50
2010	CSE	78

CONCLUSION

From the above discussion, it is evident that multidimensional models are easier to understand by an end user and are therefore more user-friendly. Therefore, through this chapter, the manager is equipped with the essential knowledge to develop a multidimensional model for their business needs. Besides, managers also need to understand what operations they can perform on these models and how to query them.

KEY TERMS

- Measures 137
- Dimensions 138
- Fact dimension 139
- Role playing dimension 140
- Parent–child dimension 139
- Slowly changing dimension 141
- Frequently changing dimensions 143
- Attributes 144
- Hierarchies 144
- Star schema 147
- Snowflake schema 149
- Fact constellation schema 151
- Roll up 152
- Drill down 153
- Slicing 154
- Dicing 154
- Pivoting 155
- MDX queries 156

SUMMARY

In this chapter, we discussed what is multidimensional data and need for multidimensional models. The basic concepts of multidimensional models were discussed in detail such as measures, dimensions, attributes and hierarchies with relevant examples. Once the model is developed, it can be represented using schemas such as star, snowflake and fact constellation which have been explained in detail. The chapter also aids the readers in understanding what kinds of operations they can perform on multidimensional data, such as roll up, drill down, slice, dice and pivoting. It also provides an overview of MDX querying on cubes.

MULTIPLE CHOICE QUESTIONS

1. A numerical quantity which represents some aspect of the organisation's performance is

a. Fact　　b. Truth
c. Aggregation　　d. Dimension

2. Which of the following is not a type of fact?
   a. Event
   b. State
   c. Cumulative
   d. Snap Shot fact

3. The aspect or perspective along which the fact is analysed is known as
   a. Dimension
   b. Measure
   c. Assess
   d. Element

4. Which of the following is not a type of dimension?
   a. Fact dimension
   b. Parent-child dimension
   c. Role playing dimension
   d. SCD (Rapid Changing Dimension)

5. Star Schema has the following attribute
   a. One fact table and multiple dimension tables
   b. Two fact tables and multiple dimension tables
   c. Multiple fact tables and multiple dimension tables
   d. One fact table and one dimension table

6. Which of the following is not an attribute of snowflake schema?
   a. De-normalised dimension tables
   b. Normalised dimension tables
   c. Snowflake show the hierarchies
   d. 1:M relationship attributes of the dimension tables are separated to show different hierarchies

7. Which of the following is not a characteristic of fact constellation schema?
   a. Multiple fact tables
   b. Single fact table
   c. Share dimension tables among more than one fact table
   d. Some facts are associated with some dimensions and rest of the facts is associated with other set of dimensions

8. Which of the following is not an operation on OLAP?
   a. Roll up
   b. Drill down
   c. Slice and dice
   d. Pivot, i.e, Chop and Mix

9. OLAP stands for
   a. Online analytical processing
   b. Offline analytical processing
   c. On-job analytical Processing
   d. Order analytical processing

10. Which of the following is not concept of multi-dimensional model
    a. Measure
    b. Dimension
    c. Technology
    d. Hierarchies

11. OLTP stands for
    a. Online transaction processing
    b. Offline translation processing
    c. Order transaction processing
    d. On job transaction processing

REVIEW QUESTIONS

1. What is understood by facts. Discuss different types of facts which are applied in multidimensional analysis.
2. What is understood by dimension? Discuss different dimensions in detail.
3. Discuss the process of dimensional modelling.
4. Discuss the concept of schemas. How can schemas help in effective dimensional modelling?
5. Discuss various operations that can be applied on OLAP cube.

ASSIGNMENT

1. Visit the placement cell of your department or campus. Identify the different perspectives from which a number of placements can be analysed. Using a number of placements as a fact, and perspectives as dimensions, develop a multidimensional model for student placement. List attributes for the model and hierarchies, if any.

PROJECT ACTIVITY

1. Visit the placement cell of your department or campus. Identify the different perspectives from which a number of placements can be analysed. Using a number of placements as a fact, and perspectives as dimensions, develop a multidimensional model for student placement. List attributes and hierarchies, if any, in the model.

HANDS-ON PROJECT

Toothworks Example

In this project, you will learn how to create data mart (generate schema) for a firm Toothworks. Toothworks is a sales agency, which sells toothpastes of different brands. The agency management wishes to examine the sales of its product from the perspective of product types and customer. The few questions visualised at hand are:

1. What are the total sales of products to date?
2. What are the product sales annually?
3. Which gender prefers which product type?

4. Are the buyers of a particular product married or unmarried?
5. Which size of product sells most?

The agent wishes to analyse using SQL Server 2012 multidimensional analysis services. Therefore, the agent first needs to:

- Identify the underlying schema for the data—dimensions, attributes, measures and hierarchies.
- Develop a database by loading data using ETL tools
- Develop and process the cube
- Run analytics to answer the above questions

This step-by-step guide will let the user develop a cube and run analysis on its own.

Identifying Dimensions, Attributes, Hierarchies and Facts

In the given scenario, clearly there are two dimensions: Product and Customer.

The measure clearly is total sales. The fact table will contain the primary key from each table and total sales would be defined as a measure. Another column in the fact table would be the date of purchase. This would aid in creating and populating time dimension later in the cube.

Now, there are certain parameters which aid in clearly defining the dimensions. These are attributes—Product ID, Product name, Product size for product dimension and Customer ID, Gender, Marital Status (from questions (3) and (4)) for the customer dimension. Both the IDs serve as the primary key and are created by default.

The hierarchy can be defined for time dimension as year → month → date.

Utilising these data, we can create a table for each dimension in the database and the attributes make the fields of the table.

The database is created and stored in SQL Server management studio and analysis is run using SSDT.

Creating Data Mart Using SQL Server Data Tools (SSDT)/ Cube Wizard

The process of creating a schema using the SQL Server management studio is redundant and time-consuming. Therefore, most often SSDT is used which will automatically define a schema (star schema by default) and will aid in creation of dimension and fact tables.

1. The first step is to create a database for Toothworks. For this open SQL Server Management Studio from start programs.

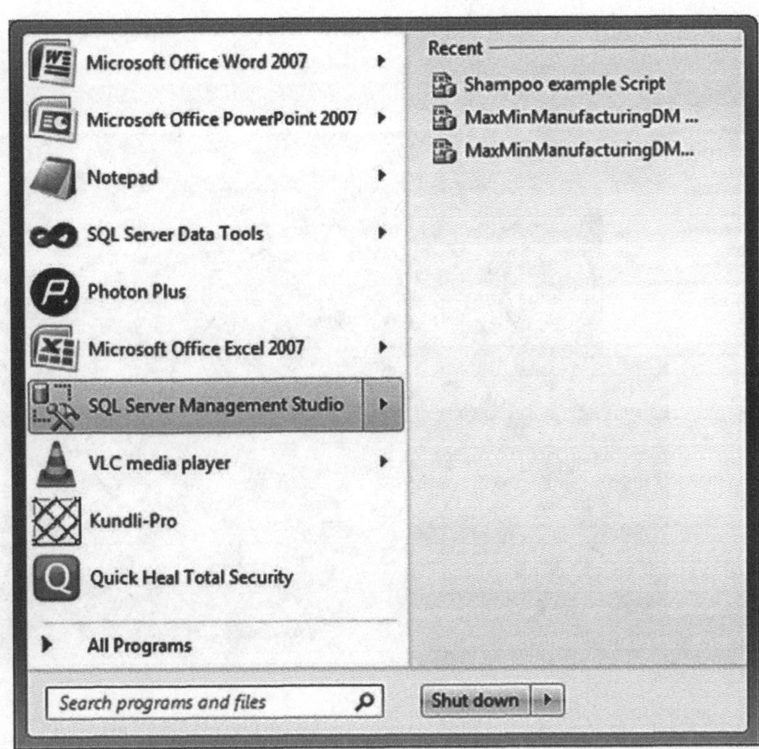

2. The following window opens. Here, the server types should be Database engine, select the appropriate name for the target server. Click Connect.

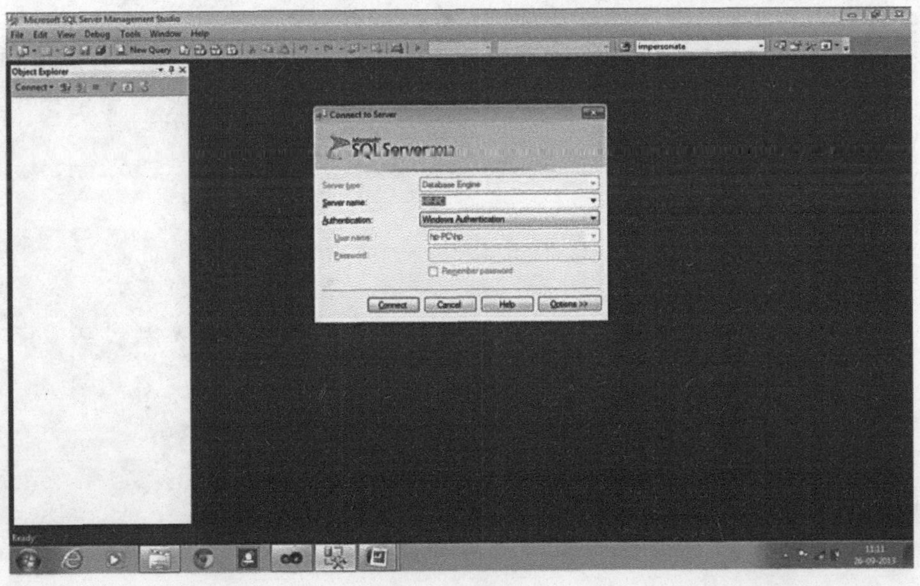

3. In the left pane, right click on databases and select new database.

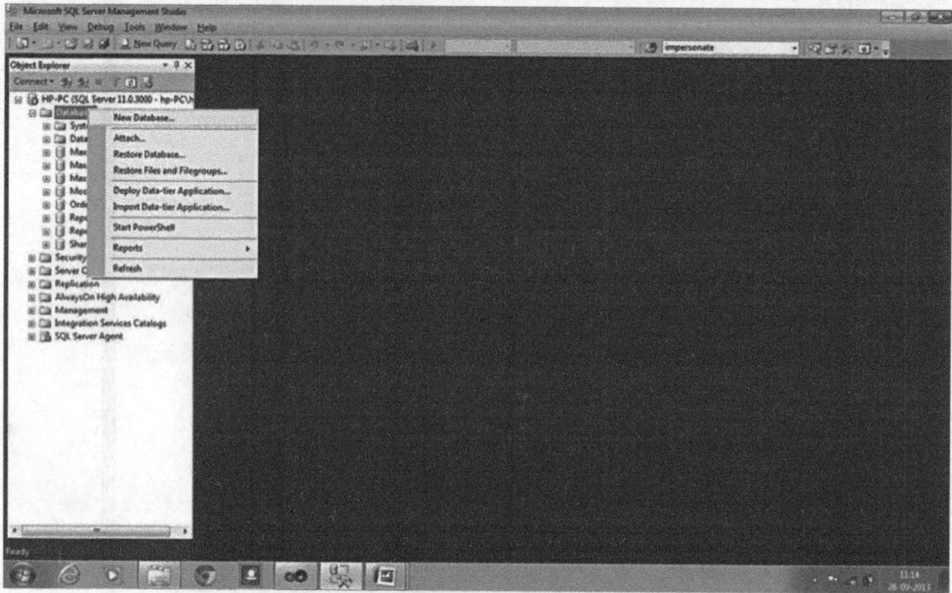

4. In the new database window opened, name the database as "Toothworks". Next, click on Options from the left pane, and change the recovery model to "Simple". Keep the other settings at default. Click OK.

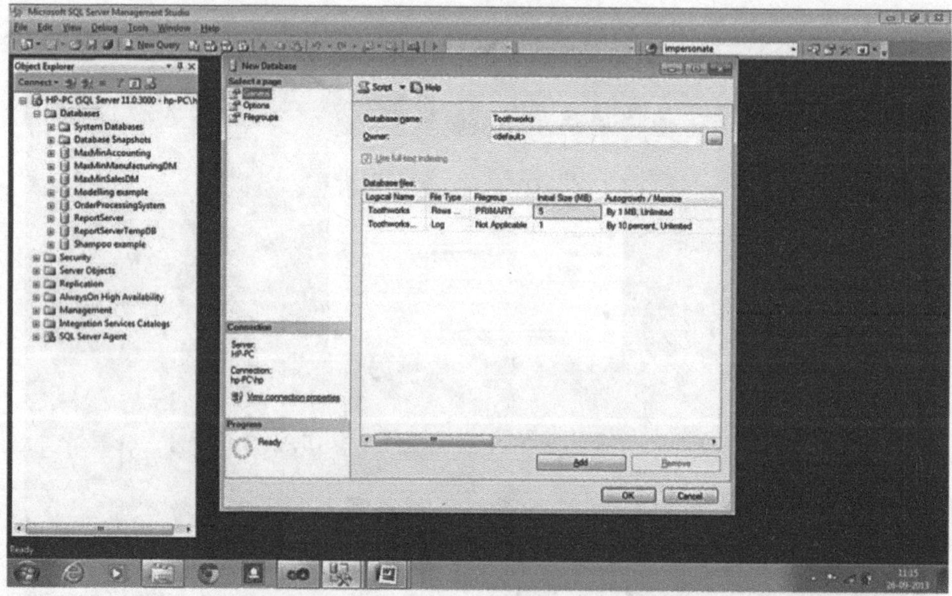

5. This will create a database by the name Toothworks which is now visible in the database drop down list.
6. Next close the management studio and open SSDT from Start.

7. In the start page of SSDT, click on New Project.

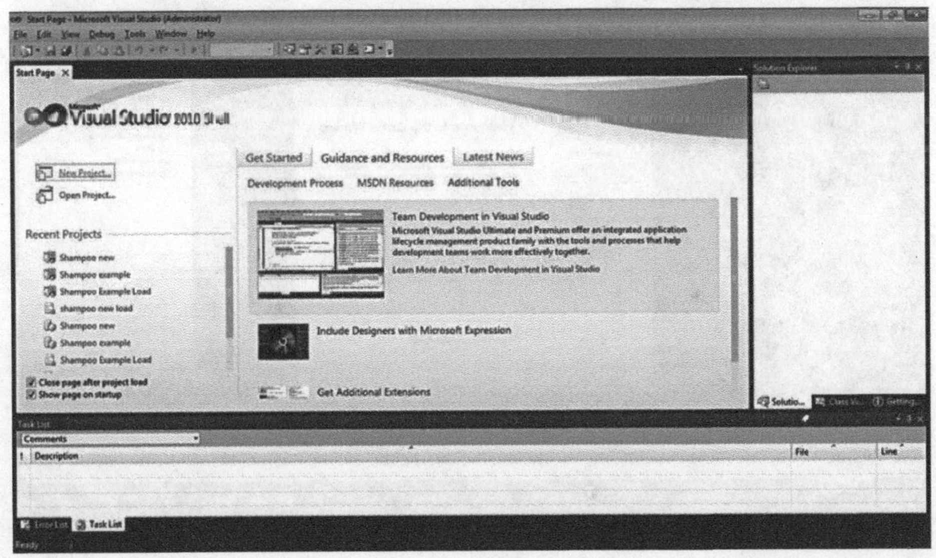

8. Select Analysis Services from Business Intelligence group on the left pane and "Analysis Services Multidimensional and data mining project". Rename it to ToothworksDM. Check Create directory.

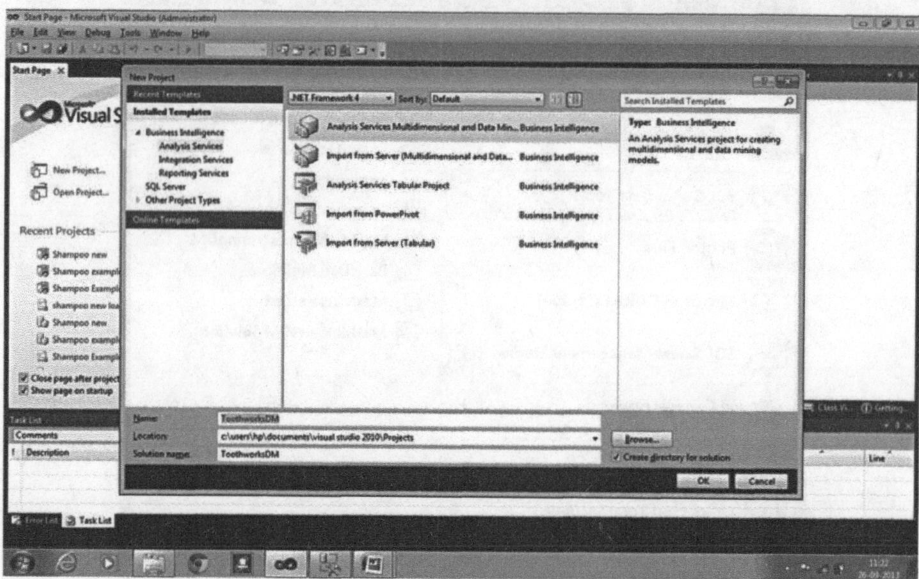

9. Rightclick on new cube from the solution explorer on the right side. This opens the cube wizard as shown:

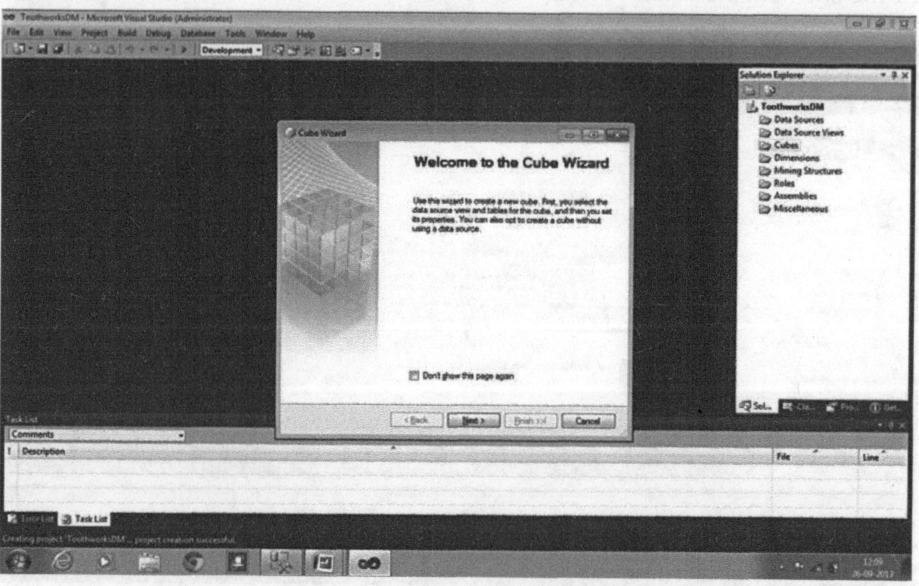

10. Click next on welcome screen. Then select Generate tables in the data source radio button and click next. Now in Define new measures window, add Total Sales in measure name, Sales Information in measure group, change data type to currency and keep aggregation default. All measures have to be grouped into a particular measure group.

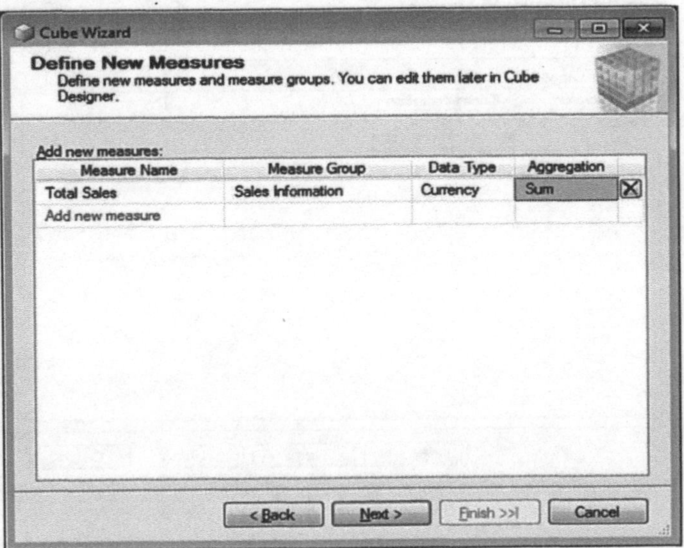

11. The next page allows you to add dimensions to the cube. Uncheck time dimension, we will add this later. In add new dimensions: Write Product, press TAB twice, enter Customer as a second dimension name. Note that all these would automatically create a table with the same name as the dimension name in the database. Click Next.

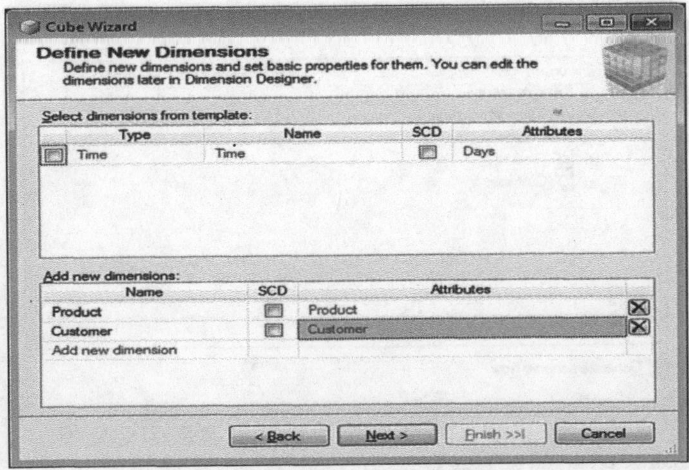

12. The next page lets the user select which dimension relates to which measure group. Remember that we need to analyse total sales by both customer and product dimension. So check against both the fields.

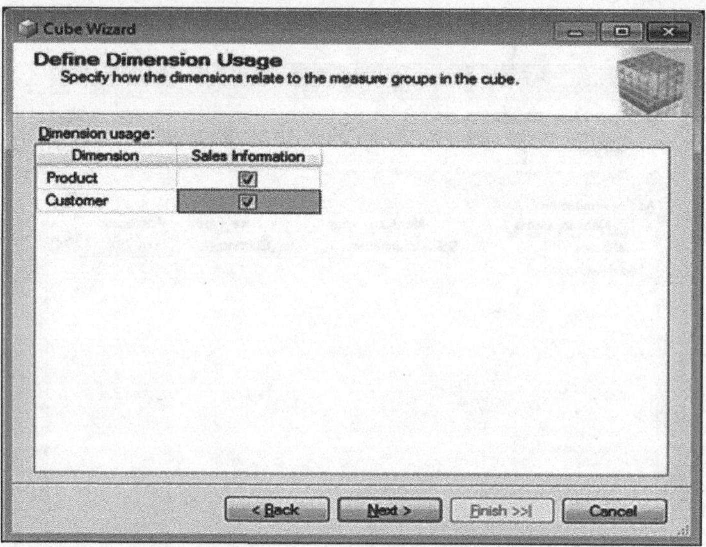

13. Next figure enlists summary of cube. Check "generate schema now", which will enable creation of tables in the database. Click finish.

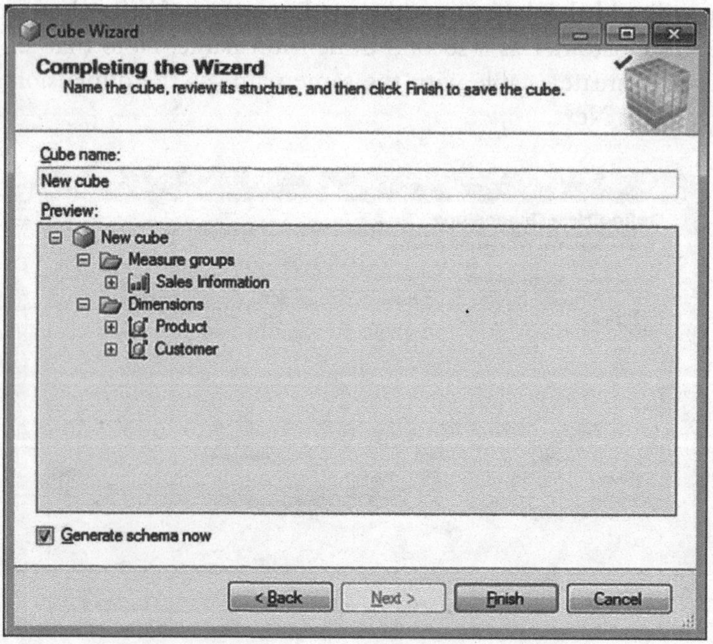

Cube Wizard
Completing the Wizard
Name the cube, review its structure, and then click Finish to save the cube.
Cube name:
New cube
Preview:
New cube
Measure groups
Sales Information
Dimensions
Product
Customer
Generate schema now
< Back
Next >
Finish
Cancel

14. Click next on welcome screen, in specify target window, check on create a new data source view. This is where the schema would be generated and the underlying tables would be created in the database. Click on New in Data Source view.

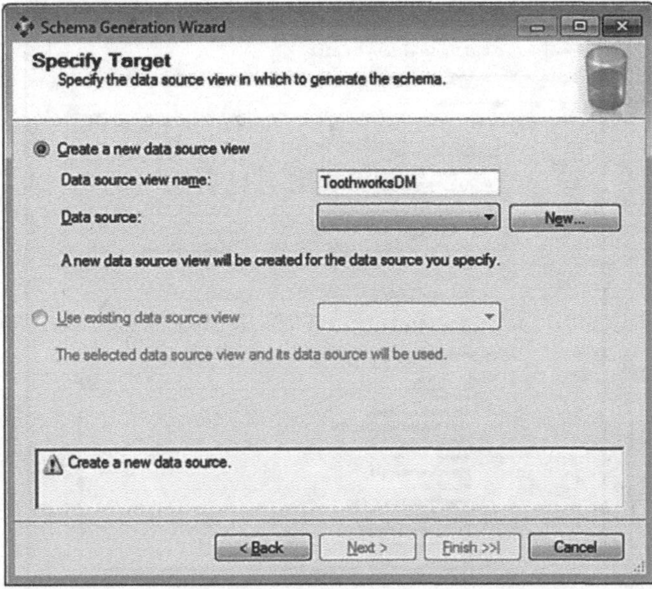

15. This opens the data source wizard. In "how to define the connection", select "Create data source based on existing or new connection" and click on New.

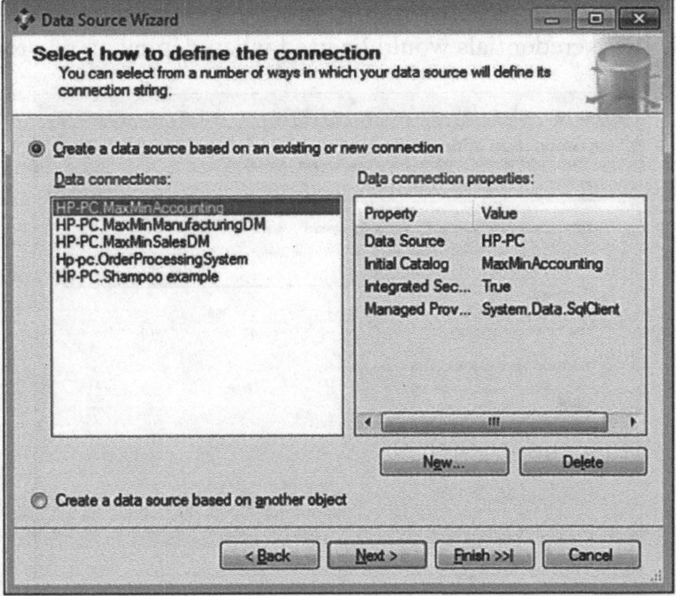

16. This opens the connection manager window which connects to the database. Enter the server name where the database was created. Keep windows authentication checked. For the database name, select toothworks from drop down list:

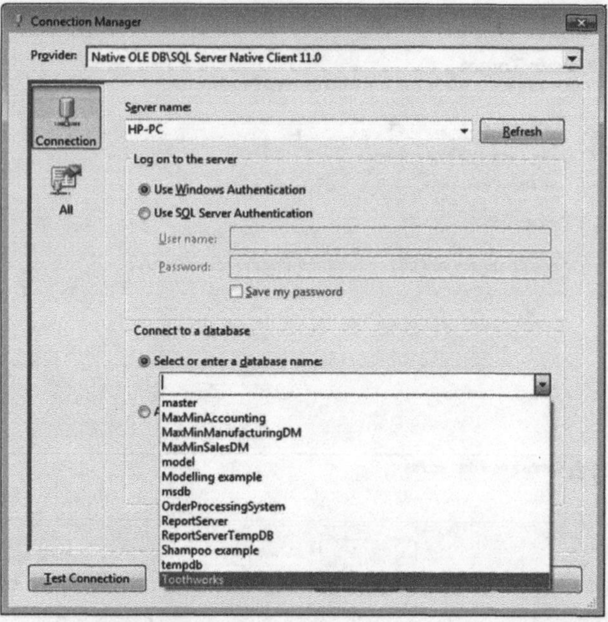

17. Click OK. This takes you back to data source wizard. The connection string with toothworks database should now appear. With this string selected, click Next. In the impersonation window, provide a valid windows user name and password. These credentials would be used when deploying or processing cube.

Data Source Wizard
Impersonation Information
You can define what Windows credentials Analysis Services will use to connect to the data source.
Use a specific Windows user name and password
User name: hp
Password:
Use the service account
Use the credentials of the current user
Inherit
< Back | Next > | Finish >>| | Cancel

18. Click Next and then Finish the wizard. This takes you back to schema generation wizard. The data source "Toothworks" now appears automatically. On the next screen, "Database Schema options", uncheck referential.

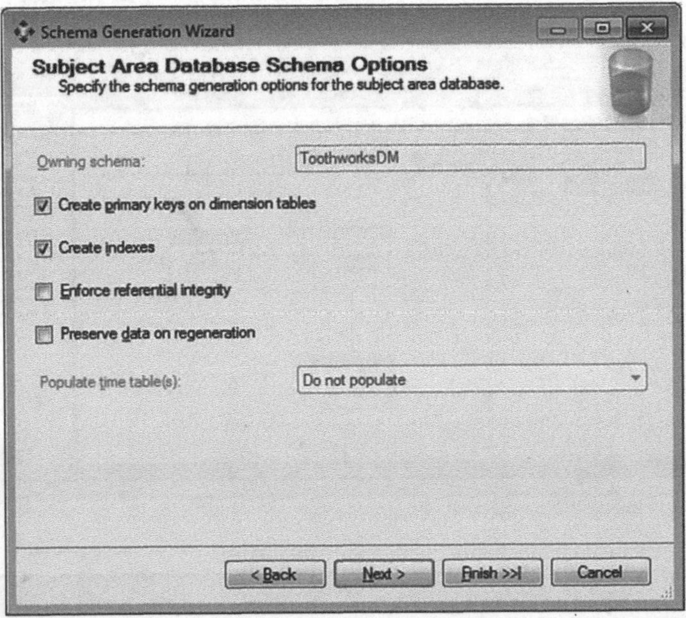

19. We keep the default naming conventions and click Finish. Now the progress for the schema is shown. Once it shows generation complete successfully, click Close.

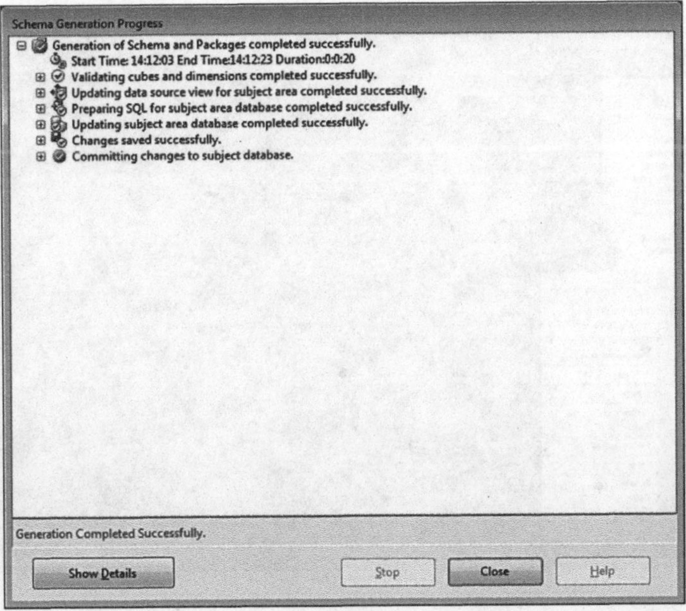

20. The schema created for the cube is as shown below. However, it does not contain the attributes we need. These would be added using the SQL Server management studio. As is evident, the ID keys for each dimension have been generated automatically. Also, the primary key for each dimension is a foreign key in the fact table by default.

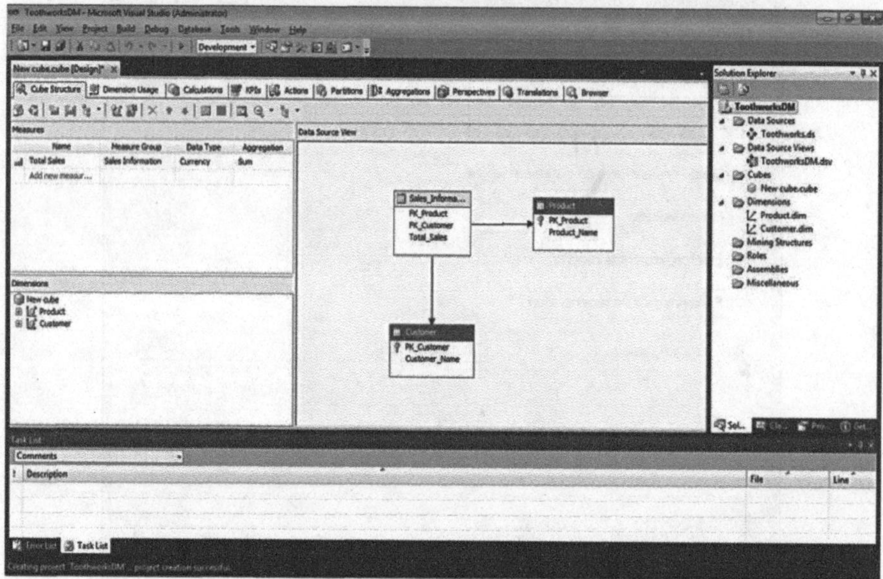

21. Now open SSMS and expand databases. In tables, it has created the tables which we added as dimension in the cube wizard. Now right click on customer table and select design.

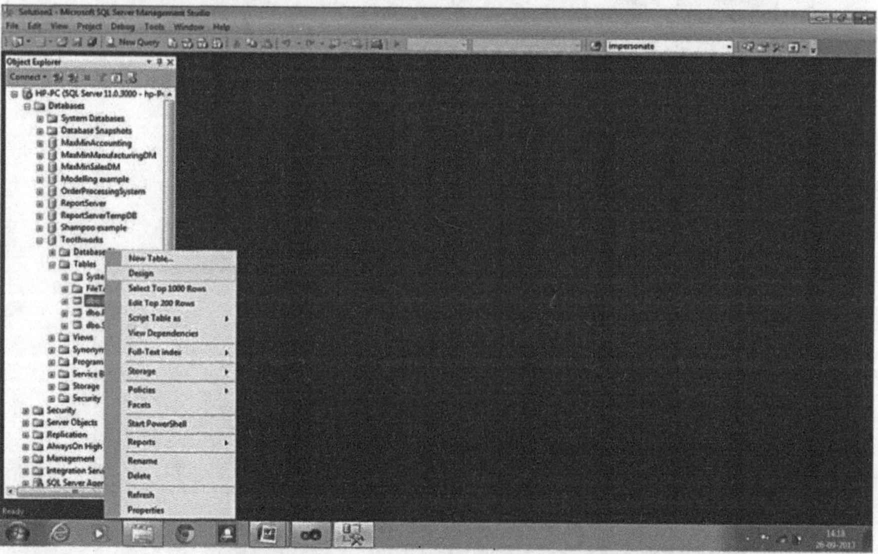

22. Add the following fields: Age, int, allow nulls; Marital Status, char (10), allow nulls.

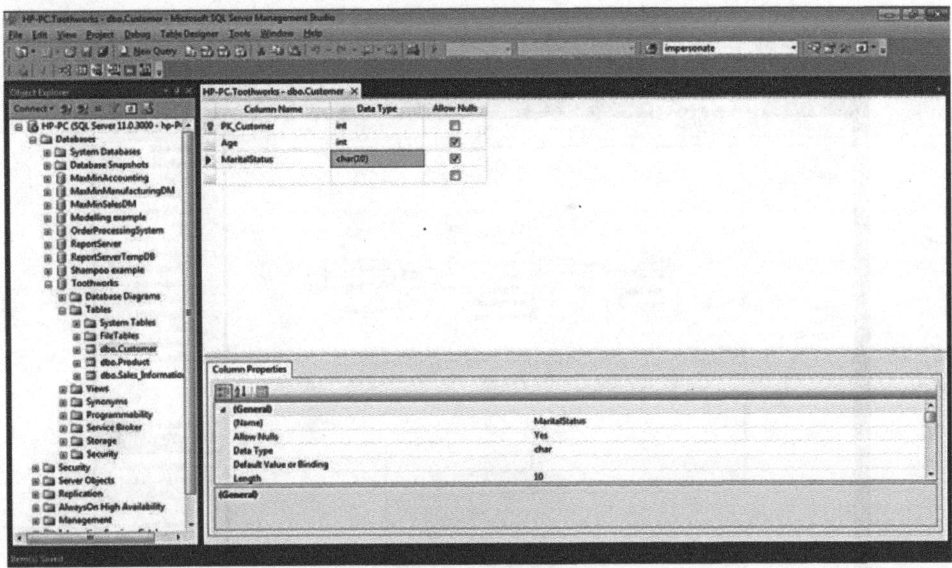

23. In a similar manner, add product name and size as nvarchar(20). For the sales fact table, add Date of Purchase, date and click on save. With the control key held, click on FK_product, FK_Customer and date of purchase, and click on primary key on left side of ribbon. This would be saved as a compound primary key.

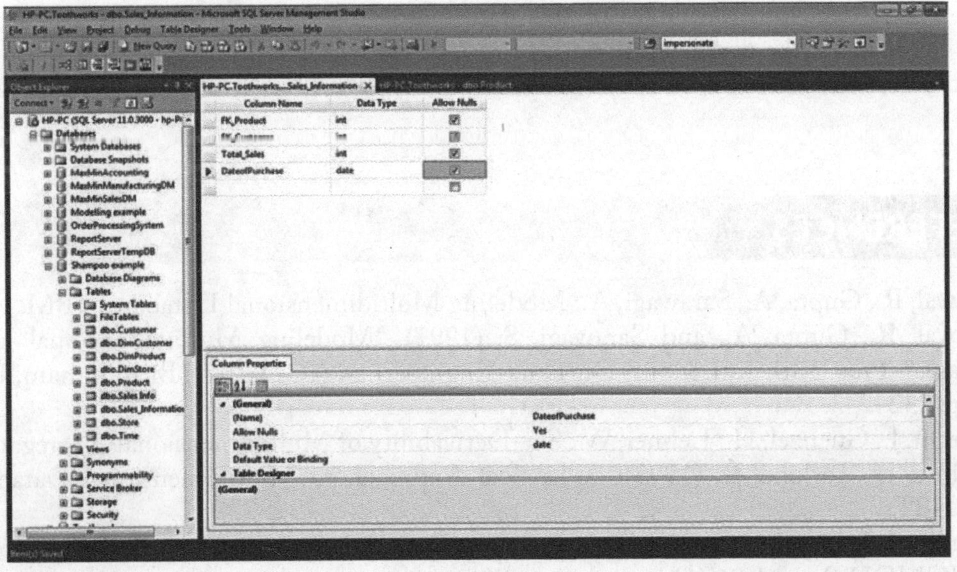

24. Go back to SSDT, double click "ToothworksDM" data source view and right click anywhere in the schema tab. Click on refresh and click OK to accept the changes.

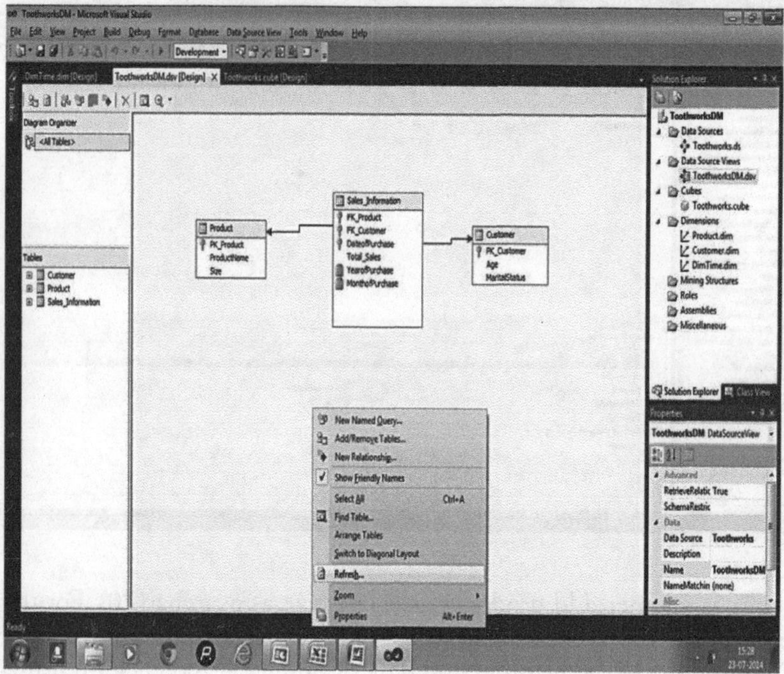

25. The process of building a cube with dimensions is complete. Now we need to load data into the tables or this data mart. This would be done in hands-on project of the next chapter on ETL.

REFERENCES

Agrawal, R., Gupta, A., Sarawagi, A.: Modeling Multidimensional Databases. IBM.

Agrawal, R., Gupta, A., and Sarawagi, S. (1997). "Modeling Multidimensional Databases". Proc. 13th Intl. Conf. On Data Engineering, (ICDE'97), Birmingham, U.K., pp. 232–243.

Albrecht, J., Guenzel, H., Lehner, W.: Set-Derivability of Multidimensional Aggregates.

Cabibbo, L., Torlone, R. (1998): A Logical Approach to Multidimensional Databases. EDBT.

Chaudhuri, S., Dayal, U. (1997): An Overview of Data Warehousing and OLAP Technology. SIGMOD Record, 26 (1).

Codd, E.F., Codd, S.B., Salley, C.T. (1993): Providing OLAP (On-Line Analytical Processing) to user-analysts: An IT mandate. Technical report.

Connolly, T., Begg, C. (1999): Database system: a practical approach to design, implementation, and management. Addison-Wesley Longman, Inc.

Gyssens, M., Lakshmanan, L.V.S.: A foundation for multi-dimensional databases, Proc. VLDB'97.

Gyssens, M., and Lakshmanan, L. (1997). "A Foundation for Multi-Dimensional Databases". Proc. in the 33rd Intl.Conf.On Very Large Database Conference (VLDB'97), Athens, Greece, pp. 106–115.

http://www.sas.com/en_us/customers/bank-of-america-business-analytics.html, Accessed on 2nd July, 2014

http://www.oracle.com/technetwork/articles/sql/11g-dw-olap-100058.html, Accessed on 2nd July, 2014

http://www.oracle.com/technetwork/articles/bi/cube-development-359587.html, Accessed on 2nd July, 2014

Hurtado, C., Mendelzon, A., Vaisman, A.: Maintaining Data Cubes under Dimension Updates. Proc IEEE/ICDE '99.

Mangisengi, O., Tjoa, A M., Wagner, R.R. (1999): Multidimensional Modelling Approaches for OLAP. Proceedings of the Ninth International Database Conference "Heterogeneous and Internet Databases" 1999, ISBN 962-937-046-8. Ed. J. Fong, Hong Kong.

McGuff, F., Kador, J. (1999): Developing Analytical Database Applications. Prentice Hall PTR.

Nguyen, T.B., Tjoa, A.M., Wagner, R.R. (1999): Conceptual Object Oriented Multidimensional Data Model for OLAP. Technical Report, IFS, Vienna.

Research Report, IBM Almaden Research Center, September 1995.

Vassiliadis, P. (1998). "Modeling Multidimensional Databases, cube and cube operations". In proc. of 10th Intl.Conf. on Stadistical and Scientific Databases (SSDBM'98), Capri.

CHAPTER 7

Extraction, Transformation and Loading (ETL)

After going through this chapter, you will be able to

- Understand the Extraction Process
- Understand Different Types of Extraction
- Understand Transformation
- Understand Various Levels of Transformation
- Understand Loading
- Understand Modes for Loading
- Understand Types of Loading

INTRODUCTION

Carriers are being held to more rigorous quality-of-service guarantees, greater transparency on all financial transactions, and vast increases in the number of new business relationships. To compete, you must move faster than ever to capture data from new transaction sources and integrate that information with traditional business data.

—Teradata

From the previous chapters, it is evident that presently organisations are facing rather a peculiar situation. As earlier organisations faced scarcity of data, but now there is an abundance of data. In the present era, the main cause of concern for organisations is to choose the right source of data. It is important that organisations should identify and select the right sources of data so as to extract the right data from those sources. Besides, organisations receive data from a large number of unconventional data sources such as web data, data from sensors, social networking data, all of which are in different formats. This often results in storage complexity owing to different structures of format of data. Hence it is important that data should be transformed in a desired format so that it can be loaded to

As the data come from various heterogeneous source systems, it is very important to extract the relevant data.

perform a final analysis. In this chapter, all the concepts related to extraction, transformation and loading will be discussed with relevant examples and hands-on project.

EXTRACTION

Companies can make better informed decisions when they take into account all available, relevant information. Integrating data from across different parts of your organization brings tremendous value in the form of cross-functional analysis.

—Teradata

Extraction is the first and foremost aspect in business analytics. As the data come from various heterogeneous source systems, it is very important to extract the relevant data. Moreover, not all the available data are meaningful; hence, extraction of relevant data is very important for building appropriate data warehouse. The extraction process is further segmented into two sub-phases:

1. Data discovery phase
2. Data analysis phase

Data Discovery Phase

The first phase in extraction is the data discovery phase. The data discovery phase includes

1. **Identification and Selection**: As organisations are working in a highly dynamic environment, it is imperative that strategies of an organisation should be based on rational analysis of environment and competitors. To formulate appropriate strategies, organisations are collecting huge amount of data available from various source systems. But, it is very important to note that not all the source systems are relevant in extracting the right data for building the specific data warehouse of an organisation. It is imperative to identify the right kind of source systems so that the right kind of data can be extracted from source systems. This identification can only be done if the Business Analytics team knows the end user requirements of the organisation. For this purpose, the top management who is a major end user of the data should actively take part in this phase. Moreover, to get the clear picture regarding the requirements, the Business Analytics team should also conduct interviews of the various managers to know their requirements. On the basis of the above procedure, the Business Analytics team identifies and selects the appropriate source systems.

The extraction process is further segmented into two sub-phases:

1. Data Discovery Phase
2. Data Content Phase

2. **Vigilance**: Once the source systems are identified and selected, the Business Analytics team should keep a vigil eye on the changes occurring in the source systems. As organisations are operating in fast-changing conditions which lead to rapid changes in the source systems, it is essential that these changes should also be reflected in the extraction process. This can only happen if the Business Analytics team takes into account various changes that occur in the source systems. This also includes looking for data sources which are no longer relevant and calls for identification of new data sources, owing to changes in the business environment. For example, if a firm solely conducts business on the Internet compared with business through agents before, then data source responsible for collecting agent data will no longer be relevant, whereas the new source of data—Internet or website data—should be taken into account.
3. **Determining the Origin**: The data in the source systems might be arising from operations being conducted by different departments in a single organisation. Often, these departments manipulate the data at their own end for storage and processing. Most of the firms accumulate these data from departments into a single-storage space called data warehouse. However, this accumulation can result in different versions of the same set of data. To remove this anomaly, it is very important to know the origin of the data so that a single version of the truth can be represented.
4. **Representation**: Once the origin of the source system is determined, it is essential to analyse the data. This analysis will help the Business Analytics team to have in-depth knowledge of the data. This analysis is done by using the Entity Relationship, i.e., ER diagrams.

ER diagrams depict the geographical representation of

- *Various entities*
- *Relationship between entities*
- *Represents the logical structure of the Data Base*

The entities are a concept about which the information is collected. ER diagrams help to depict various entities in detail and also the relationship between entities. This relationship can be mandatory or optional depending on the particular situation. The ER diagrams are helpful in the following manner:

Logical View: With the help of ER diagrams, the Business Analytics team can have a detailed logical view of the various entities. ER diagrams also help to understand the flow of the data and give a complete view of the system.

Data Types: It is very important to know the data types. With the help of ER diagrams, it is possible to identify the data types precisely. As sometimes the name of the column can give the wrong impression of the data type, but when ER diagrams are applied to depict the complete structure it is possible to depict the right data type.

Relationship: The ER diagrams are very helpful in establishing the relationship between various entities (as the entities are not present in isolation, for example, the faculty is related to the course), this in turn helps while retrieving the data from different tables. Degree of relationship also helps to determine the number of instances that participate in a relationship which can be

- **Unary**: Between instances of one entity type
- **Binary**: Between instances of two different entity types
- **Ternary**: Between instances of three different entity types

Cardinality: Cardinality helps to find out the number of instances of one entity associated with each instance of another entity. The instance is the individual occurrence of an entity type. There are two types of cardinality, i.e.,

- Minimum cardinality
- Maximum cardinality

The minimum or maximum cardinality helps to determine the status of a relationship which can be one to one, one to many or many to many.

Data Analysis Phase

The process of detecting and removing or correcting (depending on the quality of data), the corrupt files in the data warehouse are known as data cleansing or data scrubbing.

After the discovery phase, the next step is to analyse the content of the data. In the data analysis phase, the main emphasis is on maintaining the right content of the data. If the data are of poor quality, then it would result in inappropriate design of data warehouse. The process of detecting and removing or correcting (depending on the quality of data) the corrupt files in the data warehouse is known as data cleansing or data scrubbing. Data coming from different source systems might be of poor quality, i.e., there can be various mistakes in the data. These mistakes can occur due to several reasons, most common being errors committed by data entry operators while entering record in the source system, or wrong type and format of data, such as inappropriate date formats, or missing fields in data such as names left blank, etc., can result in corrupt data. It is very important to cleanse or scrub the data so that clean data can be extracted for building the required data warehouse.

Some Common Types of Data Corruption

1. As the organisations are working in different countries, it leads to several regional and cultural variations such as sometimes the name of a person in one country can be very difficult to understand in another country. This can result in the wrong entry of names and even addresses.

2. The wrong entry of address also results in a mismatch between address code and area code or pin code.
3. Sometimes, a non-permissible data value is entered into a particular field. For example, in the field for age, the data entry operator enters telephone number.
4. There may be instances where the same data are duplicated and present at various places in the same file. For example, there can be three records for the same person Mark Andrew, one with the name Mark Andrew, another with only Mark in the name field and a third one with the name Andrew Mark.
5. The most common error occurs in the date field as date data can be entered in a number of different ways or formats, for example, 26-Dec-2008, 26/12/08, 12/26/08, Dec-12-2008 and so on.
6. There may be the problem of inconsistency in the data as sometimes the same data are stored at different levels of detail such as address. At one place, the address can be Punjab, in another place it can be Punjabi University, Patiala, Punjab.

To overcome these problems, data cleansing or scrubbing is done. The data cleansing process has the following stages.

Data Cleansing Stages

1. **Parsing**: In the data cleansing process, first the confusing fields or error-prone fields are parsed or broken to identify each component in detail, for example, name field is broken into first name, middle name and last name.
2. **Correcting**: Applying algorithms, the data cleansing phase corrects the misspelled fields such as name and address.
3. **Standardising**: Following the organisational rules, the data are cleansed so that data can be stored in a standardised format, for example, to store the designation of a senior manager a standardised format is used as SR. Mg.
4. **Reformatting**: In this part, the data are stored in proper data types to avoid any future mistakes.
5. **Merging**: In the merging, first separately extracted parts are matched and merged into one table so as to avoid the duplicity.
6. **Final Correction**: Once the data cleansing is complete, the data records which were in error are logged separately in some file and not passed to output for final storage. These records lead to logging errors. So final correction deals with deleting or correcting logging errors.

> Data cleansing stages:
>
> 1. Parsing
> 2. Correcting
> 3. Standardising
> 4. Reformatting
> 5. Merging
> 6. Final Correction

Data Quality Aspects

There are some critical aspects which describe the quality of data. These aspects are listed below:

> Data quality aspects:
>
> 1. Accuracy
> 2. Explicit
> 3. Reliable
> 4. Compressive

1. **Accuracy**: It is very important that the data should provide a correct description of the entity. For example, if the name of the employee is Harry and designation is Assistant Manager, then the stored data should also show exactly the same record in the same format with proper data type.
2. **Explicit**: The values in the data should convey only one meaning and that too without creating any ambiguity. If there are ten employees working with the name Akash, but only one manager with the name Akash Sharma, then the stored data should provide the exact information about the employee and his designation.
3. **Reliable**: The values in the data should be consistent throughout the entire data warehouse. For example, if for Punjab, PJB abbreviation is used, then at all places, the same abbreviations should be used.
4. **Compressive**: The data should be compressive at both individual and aggregate levels. At the individual level, there should be proper values for each instance, i.e., there should not be any null values and at aggregate level the data should provide the total number of records without losing any individual records.
5. **Consistency**: The data should be synchronised throughout the enterprise. Consistency implies a single version of truth, that is the same data should be available to all users, irrespective of their designation, location, department, etc.

The first step in the mapping exercise requires finding the data within the operational environment to support the extract, transform and load (ETL) design. Here, the complexity of providing an enterprise view of the data is evident: multiple sources often hold duplicate data that should be consolidated. Also, the data needed to support some of the strategic goals may be unavailable, potentially driving the company to use external data sources. For example, if information about competitive activities is needed, the company may seek external sources to provide that data. Once the ETL design is completed, the next step under the mapping exercise is to link the business strategy to the available information in the data warehouse.

—Jonathan G. Gieger, Executive VP, Intelligent Solutions.

Types of Extraction

There are different types of extraction which can be applied by organisations. The different types of extraction are listed below:

Types of extraction:

1. Full Extraction
2. Incremental Extraction
3. Oracle Change Data Capture (CDC)
4. Offline Extraction

1. **Full Extraction**: In the full extraction, complete data are extracted from the source system. This type of extraction does not take into account the subsequent changes that occur in the source system. Hence, its application is also very limited because most times it is very important to track the changes in the source systems and to update those changes.

2. **Incremental Extraction**: In this process, the data are extracted in increments so that any change in the source systems can be detected and updated accordingly. In this process, the current tables are extracted from the source systems and then they are compared with the previous tables to identify the changes. But, this process is lengthy as the only current tables are extracted and compared with the previous table. This process is also very costly as specialised operations are applied to track the changes. This process only captures two values, i.e., start value in the previous table and the end value in the current table but do not cover the intermediary values.
3. **Oracle Change Data Capture (CDC)**: CDC overcomes the limitations of incremental approach. CDC uses synchronous and asynchronous CDC. The synchronous CDC tracks changes when specific operations are used on the data. These operations signify that some change has occurred in the data, for example, Insert, Update and Delete operations, whereas in asynchronous CDC, the changes are tracked from database redo files. Redo files are those files which have a record of all the changes made in the database.
4. **Offline Extraction**: In the offline extraction, data are not directly extracted from the source systems, i.e., the data are extracted from outside source systems such as redo files, flat files and dump files.

TRANSFORMATION

Data after extraction still may be in a different format than what is required by the organisational data warehouse. It is very important to convert the data into one generalised format. The process by which the format of the source data is converted into EDW (enterprise data warehouse) format is known as data transformation. Data transformation specifies rules and regulations for further loading of the data. The data after scrubbing enters the data transformation phase and then it goes to loading phase. Data transformation is a very critical phase as for proper loading of data it is important that data should be present in a desired format. For example, organisation wants to create a data warehouse and the data are coming from Marketing, Finance and Production Departments. Now to integrate the data, it is very important to change the format of data, as the data are coming from various heterogeneous sources.

> The process by which the format of the source data is converted into EDW (Enterprise Data Warehouse) format is known as data transformation.

With 13 million customers across 11 states, 28,000 employees, and annual sales over $5 billion, GST needed help to maintain its commitment to product innovation and personalized customer service. Teradata helped GST consolidate 50 disparate data marts from Oracle, IBM, Informix and Sybase and deliver the service their customers expect.

—Teradata

The data transformation takes place at two levels.

Levels of transformation:

1. Record Level
2. Field Level

Levels of Transformation

Transformation is performed at two levels:

1. **Record Level**: At this level, the records, i.e., field and tables are transformed into the desired format. The data transformation uses various functions to accomplish this task:
   (a) *Select*: If the source system has three columns, i.e., Name, Age and Address, the organisation only needs two columns for EDW. Then by applying the SELECT function one can choose the desired columns.
   (b) *Joining*: Joining helps to combine different fields from different source tables into one table. Joining helps to consolidate the scattered data.
   (c) *Summarisation*: The summarisation helps to convert the detailed information into summarised information, for example, daily transactions can be summarised as total amount received and dispatched.
   (d) *Sorting*: Sorting helps to arrange the data in a specific sequence, for example, salary can be sorted as in the highest to lowest order.
   (e) *Pivoting*: Pivoting helps to transform rows into columns and vice versa. This facility is very helpful in the proper analysis of data.
2. **Field Level**: Field level transformation helps to transform format of field according to the desired format. There are two types of the transformations:
   (a) *Single field*: In this type of field transformation, the same field which is recorded differently from various source systems is transformed according to EDW. For example, same field measurement is recorded in different formats as cm, m, yd, Sq. Yd (see Exhibit 7.1); with the help of single field transformation the field is transformed into one format.

Exhibit 7.1 Single field transformation

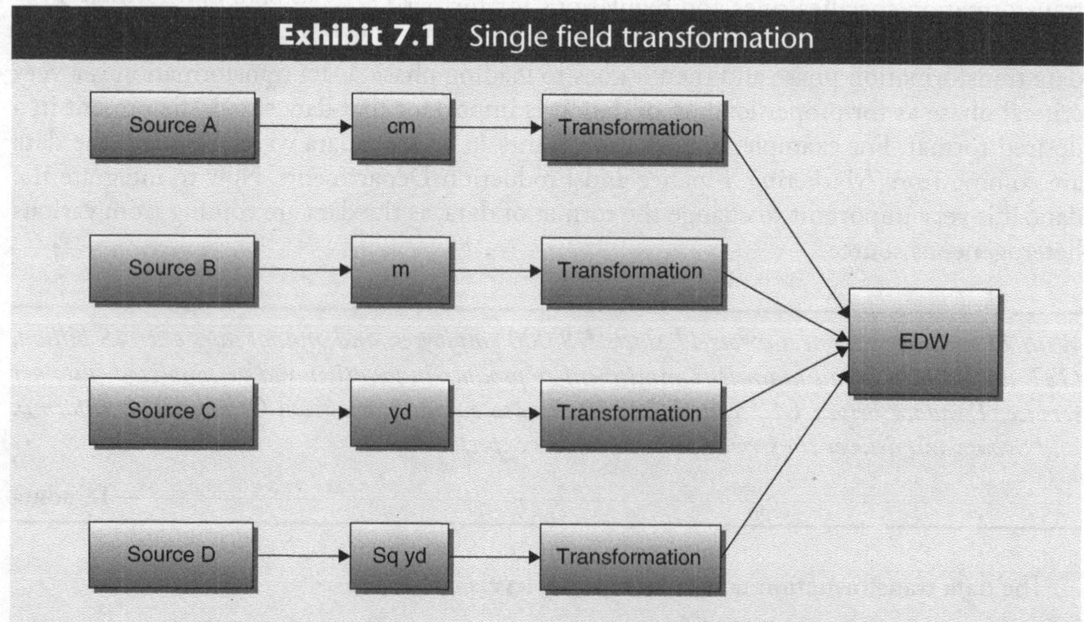

(b) *Multi-field*: In this type, transformation takes place on more than one field, for example, two fields are transformed to create one field, i.e., Stu ID in the target field. This type of transformation is known as many to one transformation, i.e., two source fields are transformed in one field (see Exhibit 7.2).

Exhibit 7.2 Many to one transformation

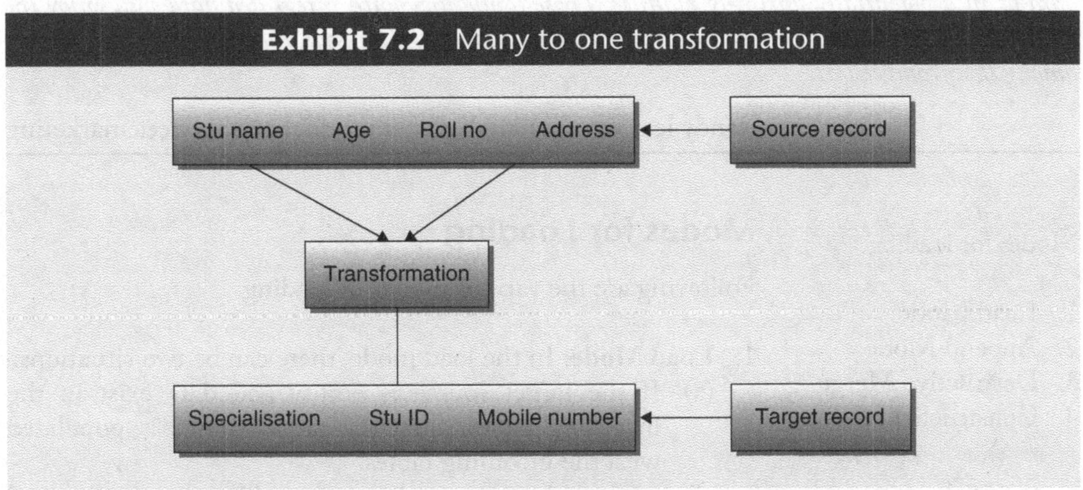

Similarly, there can be one to many transformation, i.e., one source field is transformed into multi-fields, for example, address field in the source is transformed into three fields in the target (see Exhibit 7.3).

Exhibit 7.3 One to many transformation

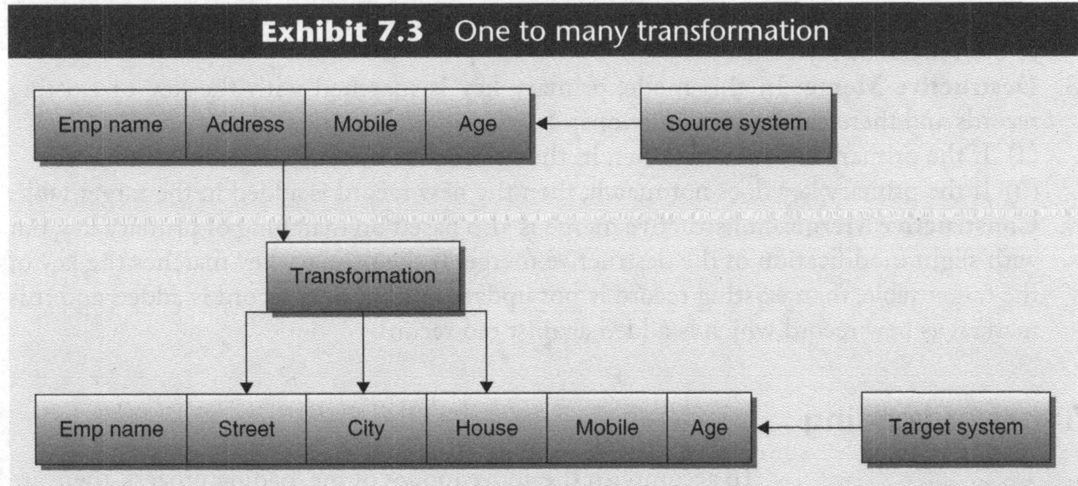

LOADING

The loading is the last phase in the ETL process. After extraction and transformation, finally the data are loaded

After extraction and transformation, finally the data are loaded into the data warehouse.

into the data warehouse. There are three different modes with the help of which loading can be done.

Organizations that lack integrated data will be challenged to make decisions with only partial data or in a potentially untimely manner. Those companies with integrated data will enjoy the ability to make rapid, informed and differentiated decisions. As a result, they will emerge as leaders among their competitors.

—Randy lea, VP, Teradata's global product and services marketing

Modes for loading:

1. Load Mode
2. Append Mode
3. Destructive Merge
4. Constructive Merge

Modes for Loading

Following are the various modes of loading:

1. **Load Mode**: In the load mode, there can be two situations:
   (a) If the target source is empty and data exist in the incoming tables, then the target source is populated with the incoming tables.
   (b) If the target source is full and data also exist in the source tables, then in the load mode the existing data are erased and new data take the place of old data.
2. **Append Mode**: Append mode is a slight modification of load mode. In the append mode, if the target tables are full and data exist in the source tables, then in append mode the incoming data are added to the target tables but at the same time the previous data are not erased. It depends on the situation how to handle the source data. If the source data are copies of already stored data, then the source tables can be marked as duplicate or even it can be rejected.
3. **Destructive Merge**: In this mode, primary key is matched with the key of existing records and there can be two situations:
   (a) If the primary key matches, then in the destructive merge, the record is updated.
   (b) If the primary key does not match, then the new record is added in the target table.
4. **Constructive Merge**: Constructive merge is also based on matching of primary key, but with slight modification of the destructive merge. If the primary key matches the key of the target table, then existing record is not updated rather new record is added and it is marked as new record which is added against old record.

Types of Loading

Types of loading:

1. Initial Load
2. Incremental Load
3. Full Refresh Load

To accomplish the above modes of the loading process, there are three types of loading:

1. **Initial Load**: In this application, the target table is empty and the new data warehouse is to be created. For this purpose, load mode is applied. Even in load mode, case (a) is applicable.

2. **Incremental Load**: As the organisations are working in a highly dynamic environment, it is very important to constantly upgrade the existing data warehouse. In the incremental load, changes occurring in the source system are updated in the existing target system. This updating can be done by applying either destructive or constructive merge.
3. **Full Refresh Load**: In this type of application, all the previous data are erased and new data are added. For this purpose, load mode case (b) is applicable.

CONCLUSION

From the above discussion, it is clear that for getting appropriate results from any business analytics tool, the ETL process is very important. As organisations are collecting huge data from different sources, it is important to identify and select the appropriate source systems. After selecting the appropriate source system, the next aspect is to transform the heterogenous data into one desired format. This is done with the help of the data transformation process. The last part in the ETL process is the loading phase. In loading phase, the data after transformation are loaded into the business analytics tool for further analysis of data. Considering these aspects are very technical, it is important that managers should have knowledge of these aspects for getting the desired results.

KEY TERMS

SUMMARY

In this chapter, various aspects regarding ETL are discussed in detail. The chapter begins with the detailed discussion on extraction process. As many sources of data are available, it is important for organisations to carefully identify and select the appropriate sources of data. In this chapter, all the important issues regarding the extraction process such as data discovery phase and data analysis phase are discussed in detail. The next aspect in the ETL process is transformation process. In this chapter, various aspects of transformation are deliberated. A transformation takes place at two levels, i.e., record level and field level. All the aspects related to these two levels are discussed in detail in this chapter. After transformation, the data are loaded in the business analytics tool. There are three different modes with the help of which loading can be done. These are

- Load mode
- Append
- Destructive merge
- Constructive merge

MULTIPLE CHOICE QUESTIONS

1. Which of the following are the phases of extraction process?
   a. Data discovery
   b. Data analysis
   c. Data modification
   d. Data detection

2. The process of detecting and removing or correcting the corrupt files in the data warehouse is known as
   a. Data cleansing
   b. Data washing
   c. Data rinsing
   d. Data refining

3. Which of the following is not a part of the data cleansing stage?
   a. Parsing
   b. Staging
   c. Correcting
   d. Standardising

4. Which of the following is not a type of extraction?
   a. Full extraction
   b. Incremental extraction
   c. CDC
   d. Online extraction

5. The process by which the format of source data is converted into EDW format is known as
   a. Transformation
   b. Changing
   c. Altering
   d. Shifting

6. Which of the following is not a mode of loading?
   a. Load
   b. Destructive merge
   c. Constructive merge
   d. Offline loading

7. In the load mode, which of the following task is performed
   a. If the target is empty and data exist in the incoming tables, then the target source is populated with data from the incoming tables
   b. If the target is full and data also exist in the incoming tables, then in the load mode the existing data are erased and new data take the place of old data
   c. If the target tables are full and data exist in the incoming tables, the incoming data are added to the target tables without erasing the previous data
   d. None of the above

8. In the append mode, which of the following tasks is performed?
   a. If the target is empty and data exist in the incoming tables, then the target source is populated with the incoming tables
   b. If the target is full and data also exist in the source tables, then in the load mode the existing data are erased and new data take the place of old data
   c. If the target tables are full and data exist in the source tables, the incoming data are added to the target tables, but at the same time the previous data are not erased
   d. Either b or c can happen, depending on the situation

9. In the destructive mode, which of the following tasks is performed?
   a. If the primary key matches, then in the destructive merge, the record is updated
   b. If the primary key does not match, then the new record is added to the target table
   c. If the target source is full and data also exist in the source tables, then the existing data are erased and new data take the place of old data
   d. If the target tables are full and data exist in the source tables, the incoming data are added to the target tables, but at the same time the previous data are not erased

10. In the constructive merge, which of the following tasks is performed?
   a. If the primary key matches the key of the target table, then existing record is not updated rather new record is added and it is marked as new record which is added against old record
   b. If the target tables are full and data exist in the source tables, the incoming data are added to the target tables, but at the same time the previous data are not erased
   c. If the primary key matches, then the record is updated
   d. If the primary key does not match, then the new record is added in the target table

11. Which of the following is not a type of loading?
   a. Initial
   b. Partial
   c. Incremental
   d. Full refresh

12. In the initial load, which type of mode is applicable?
   a. Load mode case (a)
   b. Load mode case (b)
   c. Destructive merge
   d. Constructive merge

13. In the incremental load, which type of mode is applicable?
    a. Load mode case (a)
    b. Load mode case (b)
    c. Destructive merge
    d. Constructive merge
14. In the full refresh load, which type of mode is applicable?
    a. Load mode case (a)
    b. Load mode case (b)
    c. Destructive merge
    d. Constructive merge

REVIEW QUESTIONS

1. What is the relevance of extraction? Discuss sub-phases of extraction in detail.
2. What are the different data cleansing stages?
3. What are various data quality aspects which should be taken into account in judging the quality of data?
4. What are the different types of extraction? Discuss in detail.
5. What is the importance of transformation process? Discuss in detail.
6. What are the different levels of transformations?
7. What do you understand by loading? Discuss various modes and types of loading.

ASSIGNMENT

1. "ETL process is very important for getting desired results from any business analytics tool". Comment on this statement by citing appropriate examples.
2. What are the different types of transformations? Discuss particular situations where these different types of transformations are applicable.

PROJECT ACTIVITY

1. Visit office of your university/college and analyse whether the data are stored in single format or not. Prepare a detailed report of all the fields that are stored in the same format and those formats which are not stored in the same format.

HANDS-ON PROJECT (ETL)

For any effective analysis to be run on Toothworks, we would need to first load the multidimensional model created in previous hands on with the data. This hands-on project would let you do just that.

The fact table has a column "Date of Purchase", which can be used for time-based analysis. For this purpose, we would need to add another dimension "Time". After successfully loading the data, we will add another dimension "Time" from the fact table data to our Toothworks cube, using a feature of SQL Server 2012 called "Named Calculations".

Using Integration Services to Load Data Mart

This hands-on exercise will help you to understand how to load data into fact as well as dimension tables using SQL Server 2012 Integration services. First, we will load the dimension tables and then load fact table. The source of data (extraction) is .csv sheets maintained by Toothworks for each dimension separately. They will be loaded into SQL server tables we created in the previous hands-on exercise. You can save your own datasets by entering the data in an excel datasheet as shown below and by saving it as .csv file. The steps to save an excel datasheet as .csv file are:

Open a new excel sheet. Enter the data. Then from office button, select "Save As" and then select "Other formats":

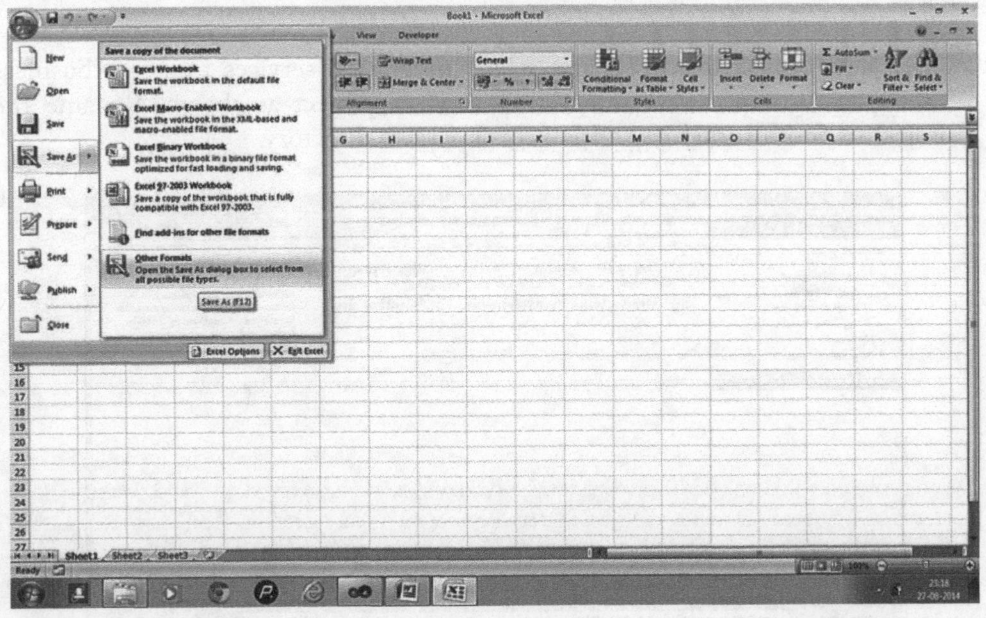

This opens a new SaveAs window. Here, browse to the appropriate location where you want to save your file. Then provide a filename, say Customer.csv and change "Save as Type" to CSV (comma delimited).

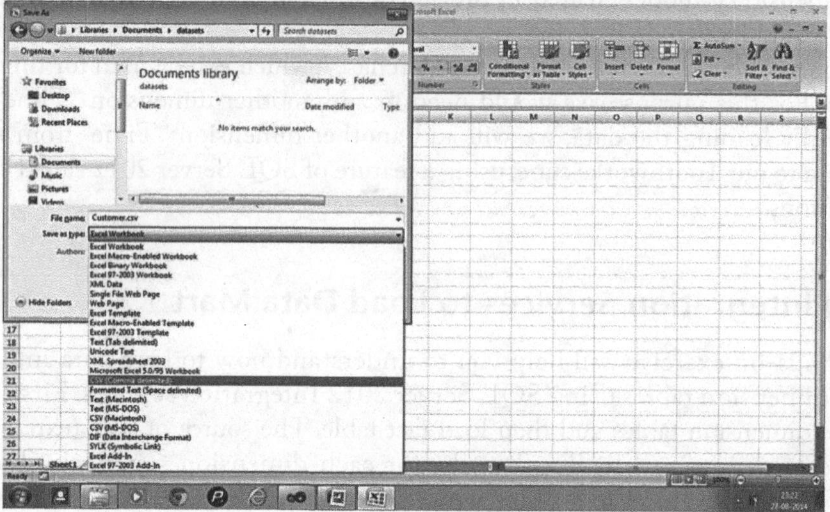

Click OK. The datasets "Customer.csv", "Product.csv" and "SalesFact.csv"are available in the APPENDIX-1 of the book. Save them as csv files in an appropriate location, from where you can use it as a source item later to extract data.

Use the steps listed below to load data into the data mart created in the previous exercise:

1. Open new project in SSDT and select integration services from the business intelligence group. Select integration services project as shown. Rename the project to ToothworksLoad and uncheck Create directory.

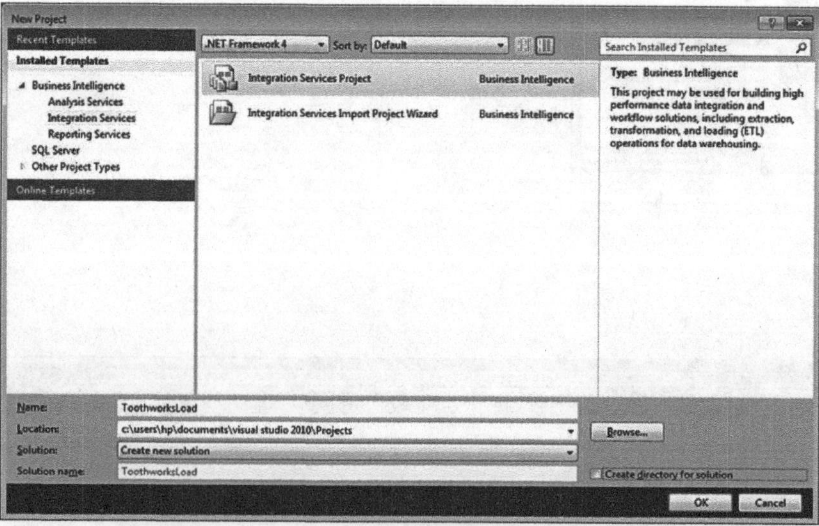

2. In the solution explorer window, rename package.dtsx in SSIS packages to "DimensionLoad.dtsx". Here, we will load the data into dimension tables from csv sheets. So from SSIS toolbox in the left pane, drag and drop data flow task item onto control flow tab.

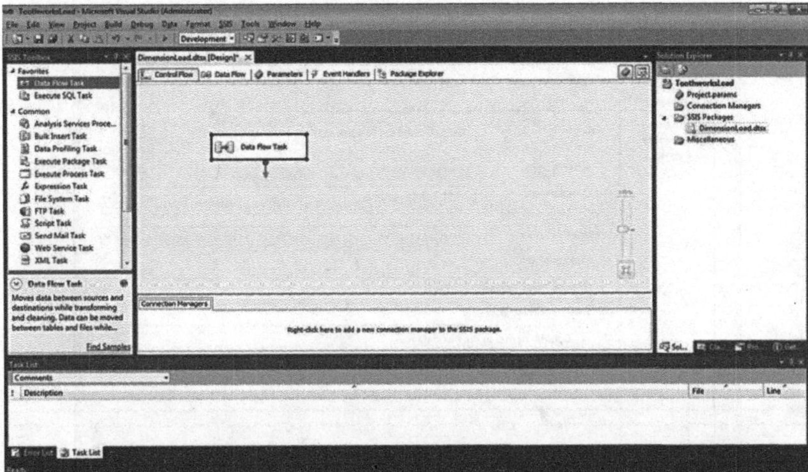

3. Rename it to load customer. Double click on this and data flow tab will open. We wish to load customer table (which is an SQL server or OLEDB destination) from Customer.csv which is a flat file source item. So we need to create a connection for the same. In the connection manager tray below in data flow tab, right click to add the new flat file connection.

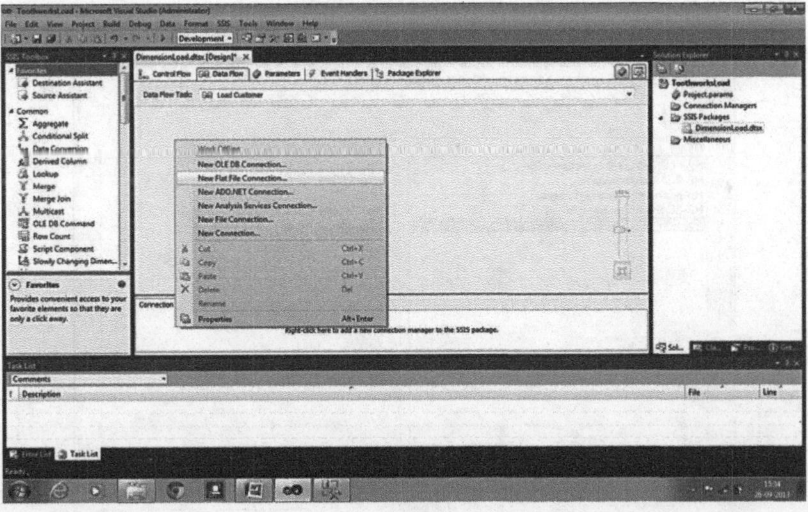

4. Rename the connection manager name to Customer flat file and browse for the appropriate location of customer flat file. Check column names in the first data row. You can preview the data in columns tab. In the advanced tab, you need to

make certain changes. Change the data type of age and customer ID to four byte signed integer. Keep the string data type for marital status. Click OK after changes have been made.

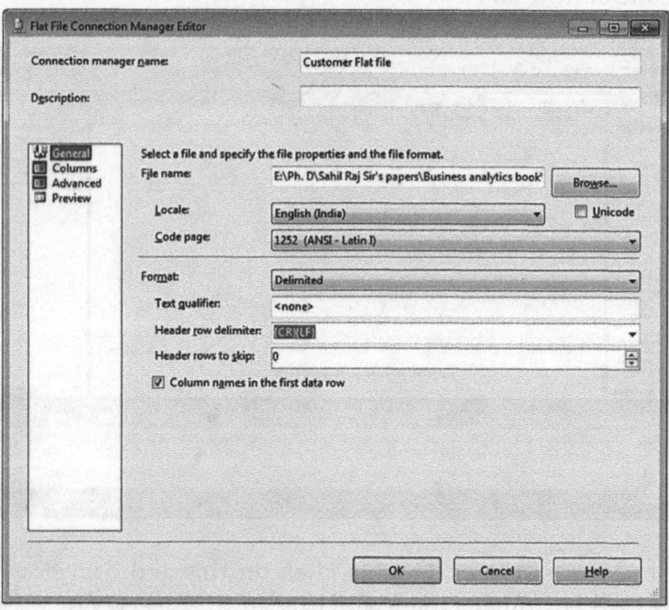

5. Next, create an OLE DB connection for destination table. Again, right click on the connection manager tray and select new OLE DB Connection. Select toothworks database for the same and click OK.

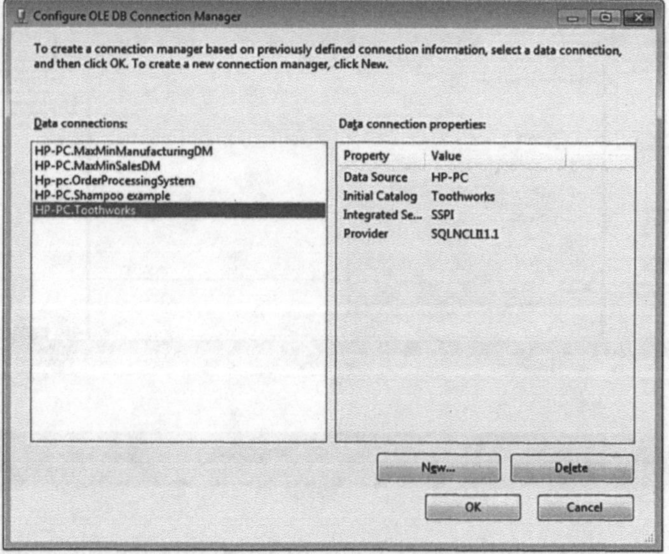

6. From other sources in SSIS toolbox, drag and drop the flat file source item onto the data flow tab. Double click on this and flat file source editor opens. In the columns button, make sure all the columns are checked. You can preview the data using the preview button. Click OK.

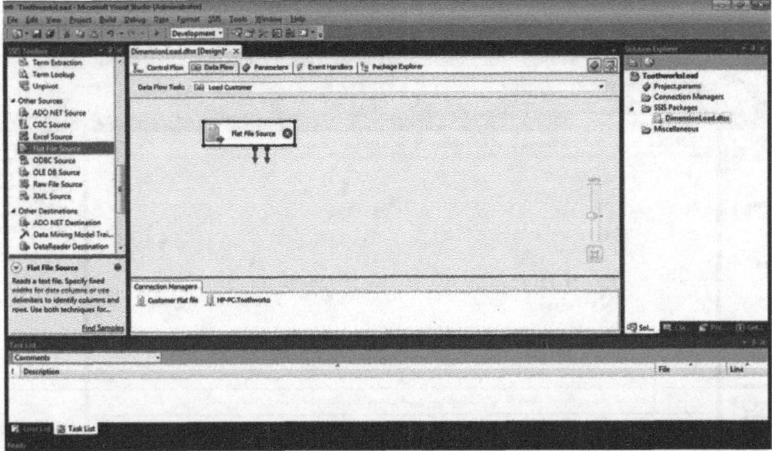

7. Next, drag and drop the OLE DB destination item from destinations and connect with blue arrow from source item. Double click this item. Destination editor window opens. HP-PC.toothworks should already be selected in the OLE DB connection manager. Select dbo.Customer from the name of the table or view. Click mappings from left pane of destination editor. The mappings should be done automatically due to similar names. Else drag and drop from input onto output as shown below.

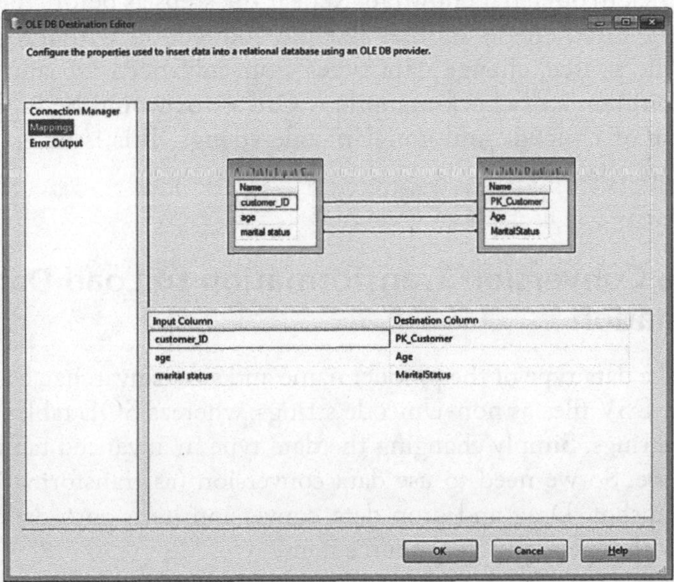

8. Click OK. Go back to control flow tab and drag and drop another data flow task item and rename to LoadProduct. Drag and drop the green arrow dangling from LoadCustomer item onto LoadProduct item. This indicates precedence. Only when loading customer dimension is successfully completed, will loading of product dimension start.

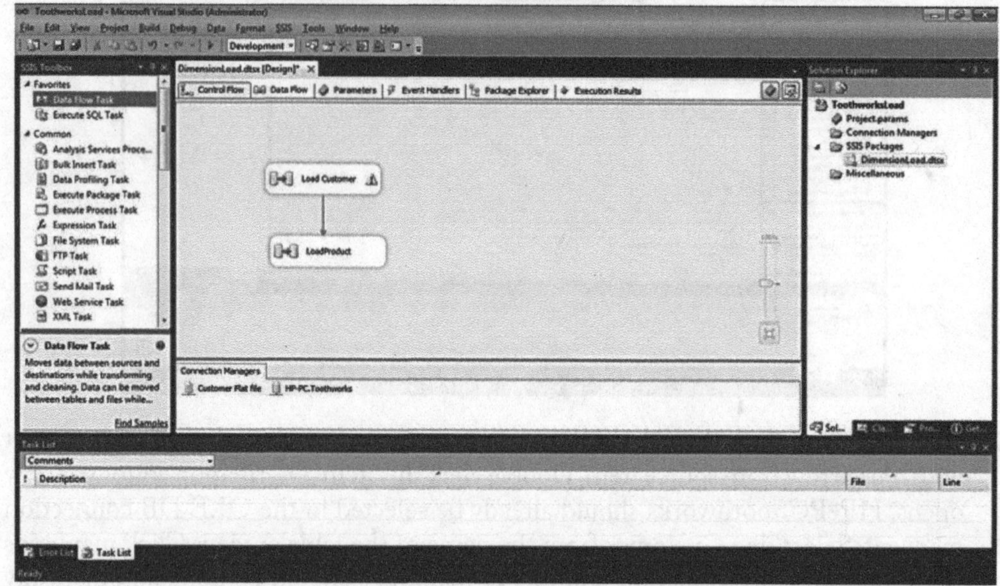

9. Double click to open data flow tab. Repeat the steps as before to load customer dimension. First, create another flat file connection with Product.csv. Then add flat file source, change data types from advanced tab and then add the destination item and check mappings. One error would be highlighted here: conversion of Unicode and non-Unicode strings. This is where the transformations are applicable.

Using Data Conversion Transformation to Load Data Into Destination

10. Because the data type of the product name and size is nvarchar, SSIS treats these data from CSV files as non-Unicode strings, whereas SQL tables are defined as Unicode strings. Simply changing the data type in advanced tab does not serve our purpose. So we need to use data conversion (as transformation) as shown in the snapshot. Drag and drop data conversion item onto data flow tab and connect with blue arrow from source item.

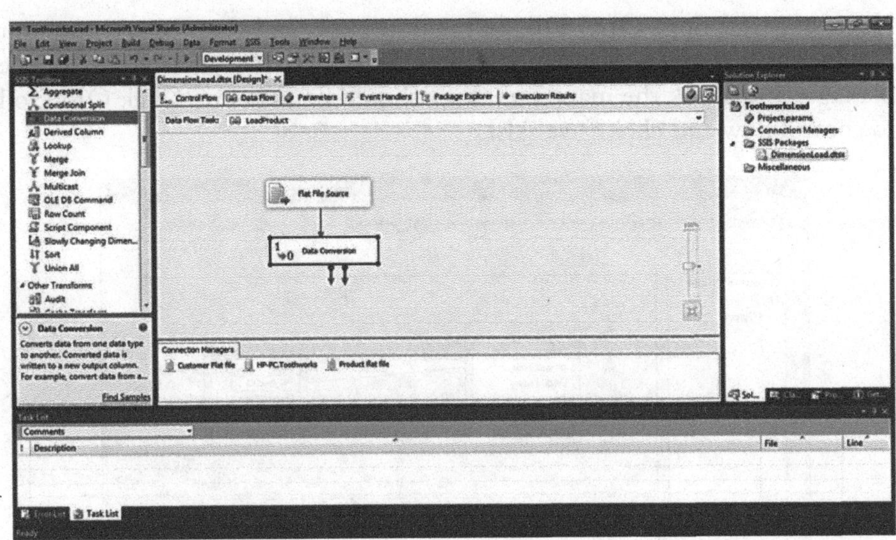

11. Double click this item to open transformation editor window. Here, both product name and product size have non-Unicode string data type. So check the two columns, rename in output alias by prefixing nu. Change the data type to Unicode string [DT_WSTR] and length as required. Click OK.

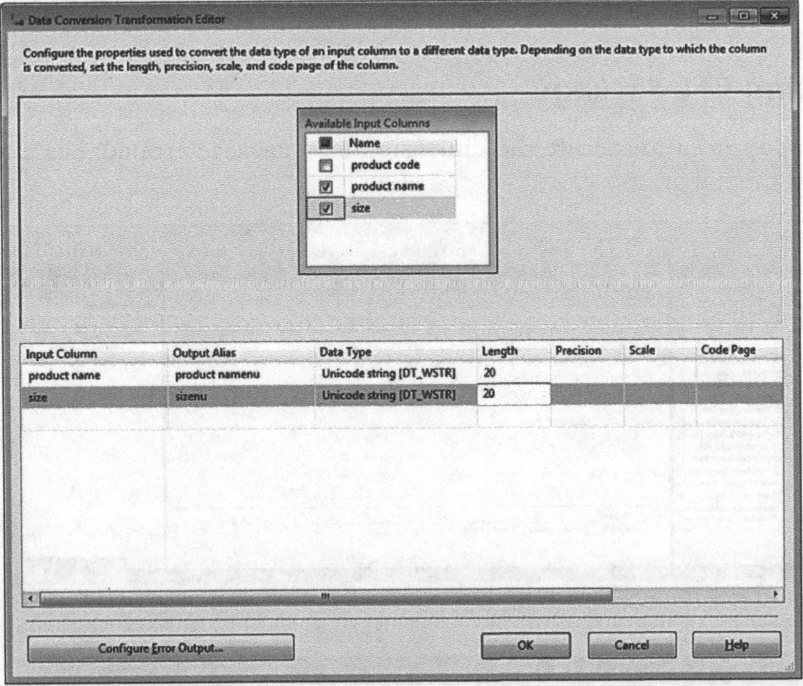

12. Next drag and drop OLE DB destination item, and drop blue arrow onto it. Double click to open destination editor. Select product table from connection manager and check the mappings. They should be as below. Click OK. Go back to control flow and click Save ALL.

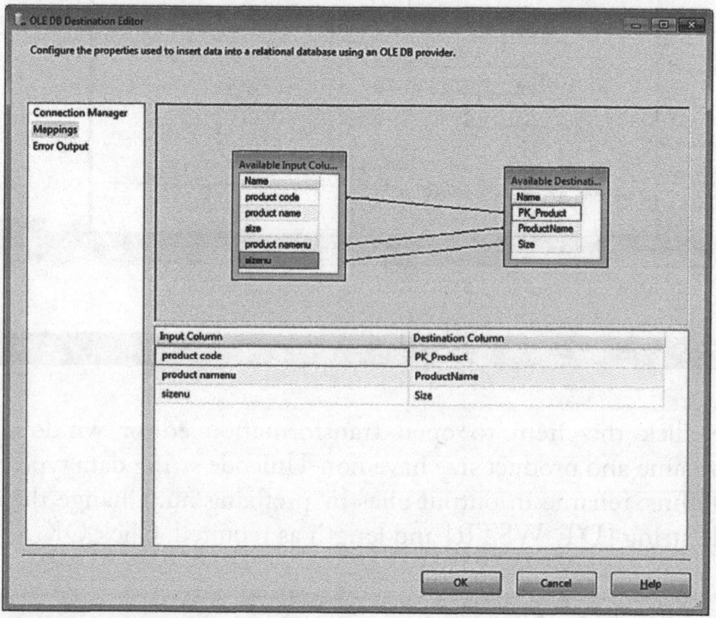

Executing ETL Package

13. Now, we need to execute the dimension load package created. Click on debug from the ribbon above.

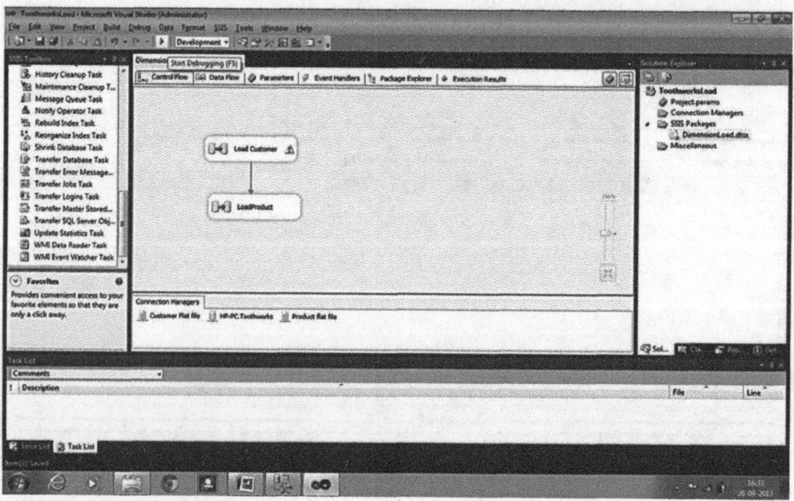

14. Upon successful execution, the window should appear as shown:

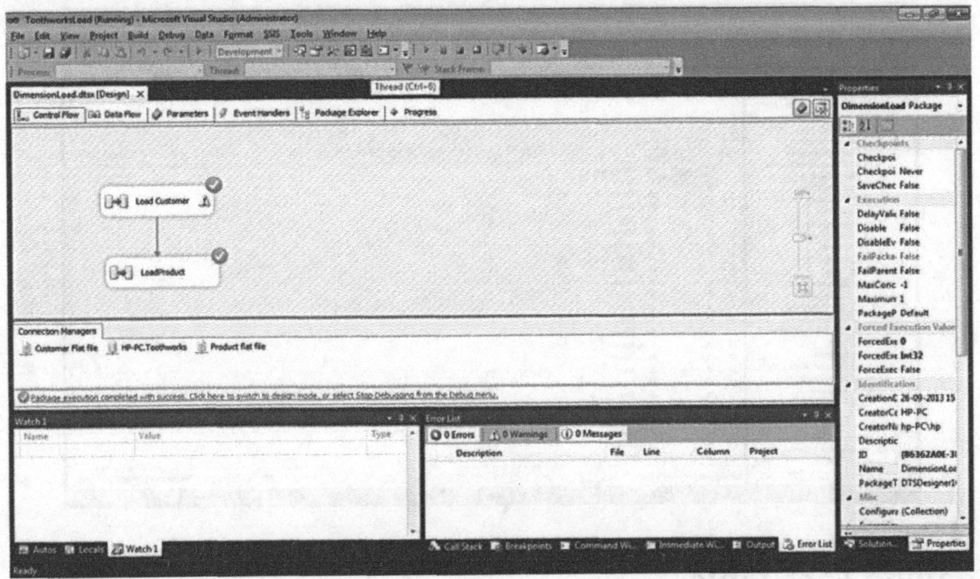

This implies the customer and product dimension have been successfully loaded.

15. You can verify the same in SSMS by right clicking on the table and select top 1000 rows.

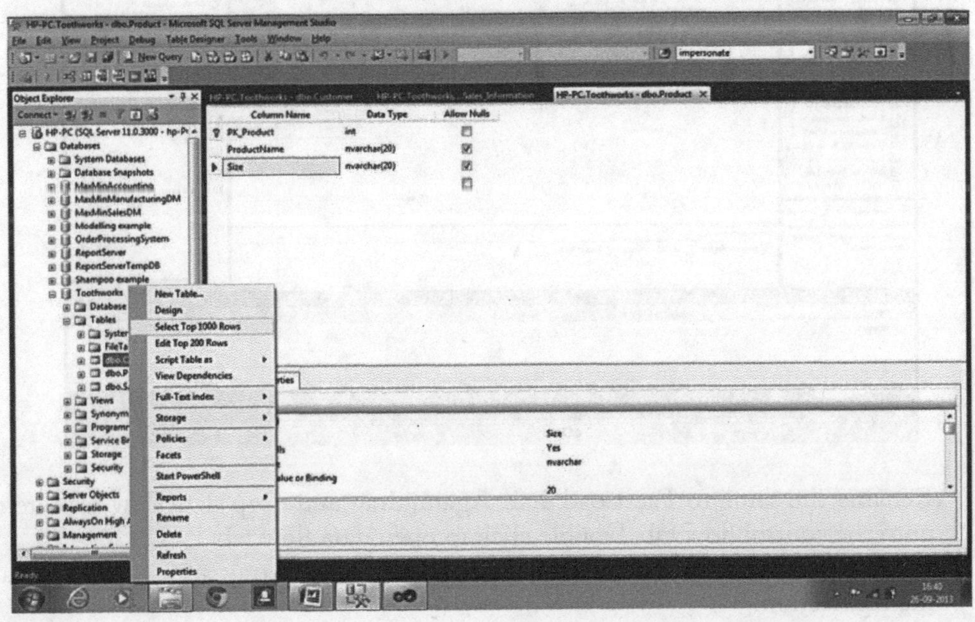

Or create a query as shown in the figure below:

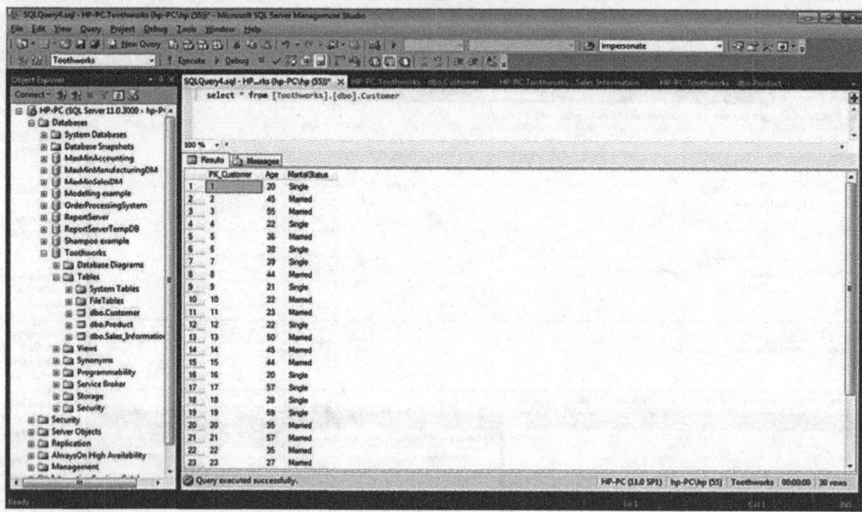

Loading Fact Table

16. Right click on SSIS packages and select new package.

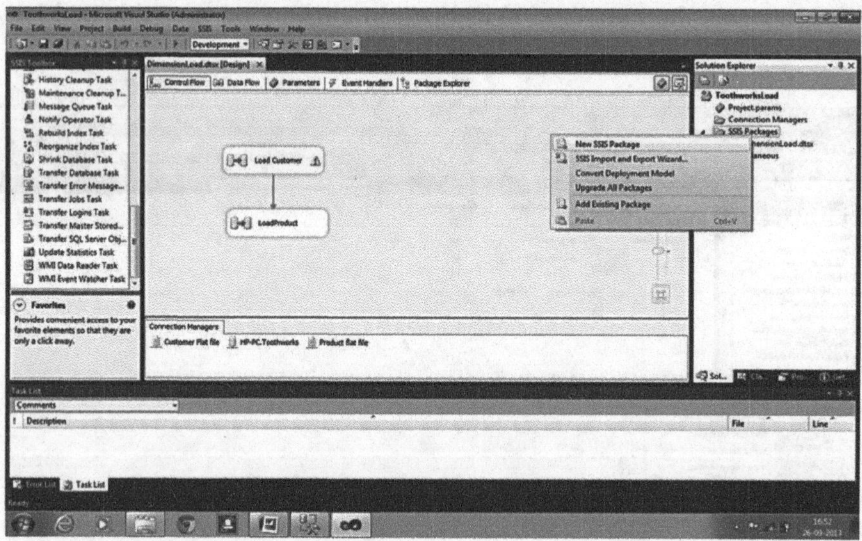

Rename the same to FactLoad.dtsx. Again, drag and drop data flow task item onto the control flow tab. Double click to open data flow tab.

17. In data flow tab, right click in the connection manager tray, and select new flat file connection.

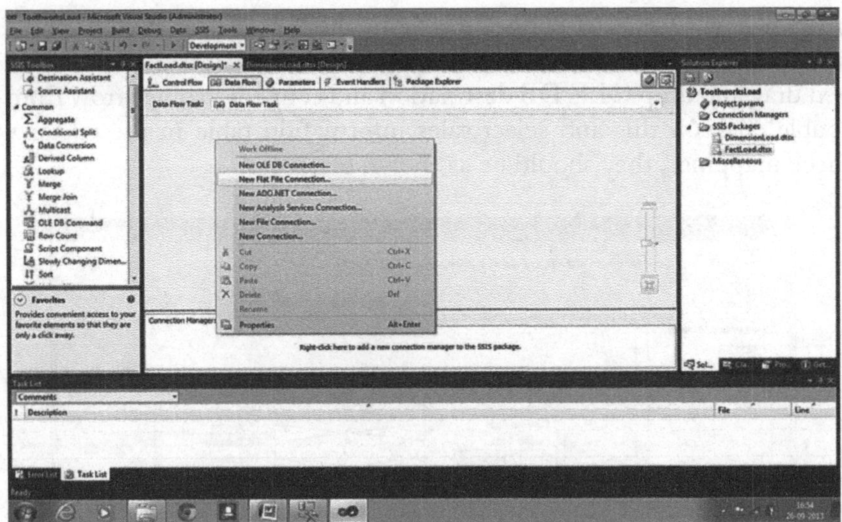

Name the connection manager as sales fact file. Browse for the file, review the columns.

18. In the advanced tab, change the data type of customer id, product id, and total sales to four byte signed integer, and change the date data type to date.

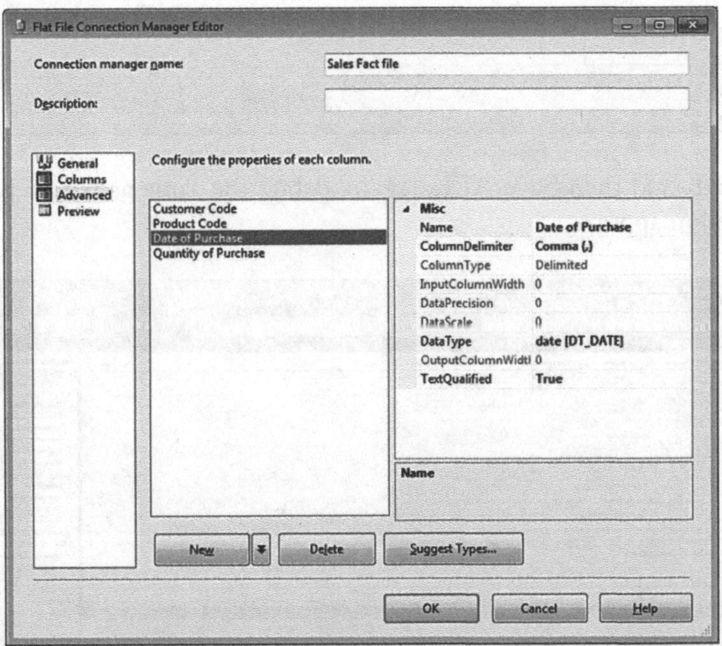

19. Drag and drop flat file source item and double click to connect to sales fact file. Review the columns.

20. Create a new OLE DB connection from the tray. Select toothworks database from the editor window.
21. Next drag and drop OLE DB destination and connect to blue arrow from source. Double click on this and select sales information table in the editor window. Check mappings, they should be as shown below:

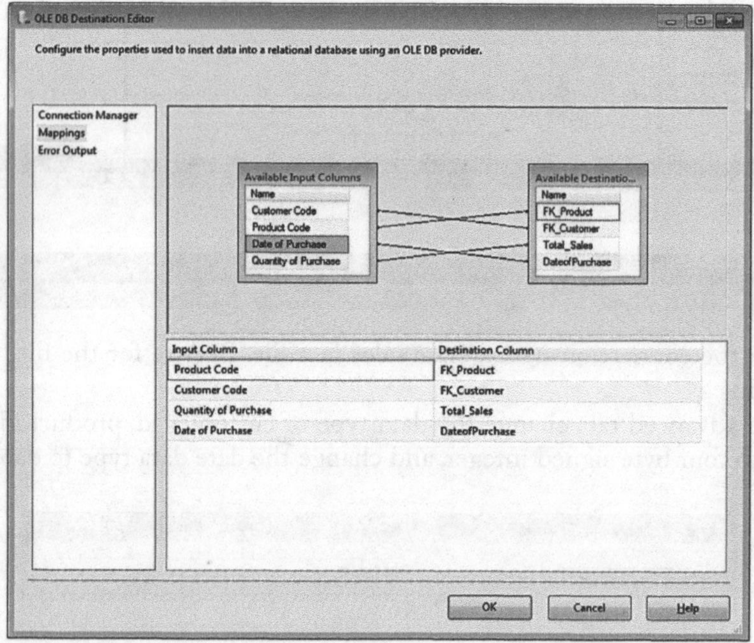

Click OK and then Save ALL. Again, debug the same as before till successful completion appears.

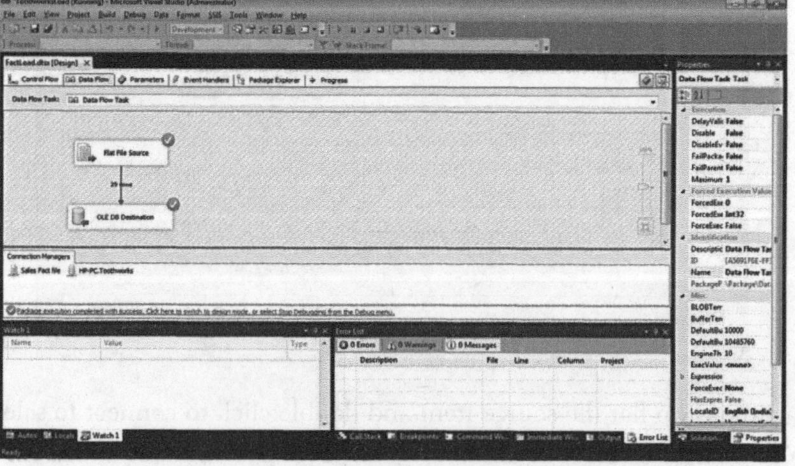

This part of the exercise will let you understand how to add another dimension "Time" to existing cube. This dimension would be created from the field "Date of Purchase" contained in the fact table. This would be done by first creating named calculations and then create time dimension based on this.

- The attributes of this dimension are year, month and date. The hierarchy of time dimension would be as under: Year → Month → Date.
- As year and month are not directly available, they need to be extracted from the date of purchase field using "named calculations" in SQL Server 2012.

Creating Named Calculations

1. Open the analysis services project created earlier "Tooth works DM" multidimensional model from SSDT.
2. From the solution explorer window, open Toothworks.dsv data source view. From tables in lower left pane, right click on Sales_Information table, and select new named calculation.

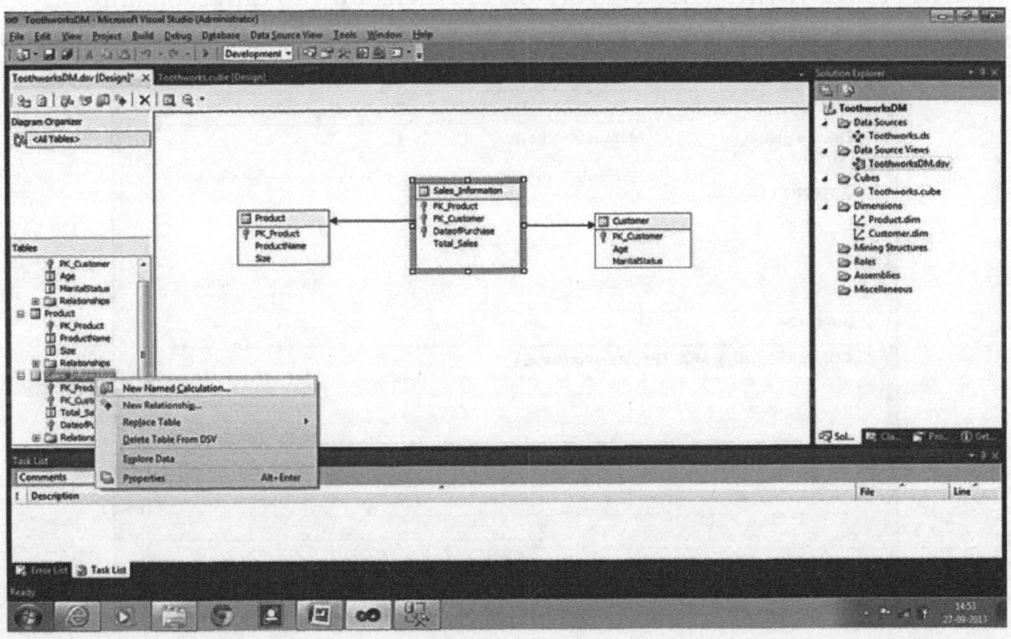

3. The first field is Year. To extract year from date of purchase in sales info table, following expression would be used in named calculation form:
   CONVERT [char(4), YEAR (Date of Purchase)] – to extract year

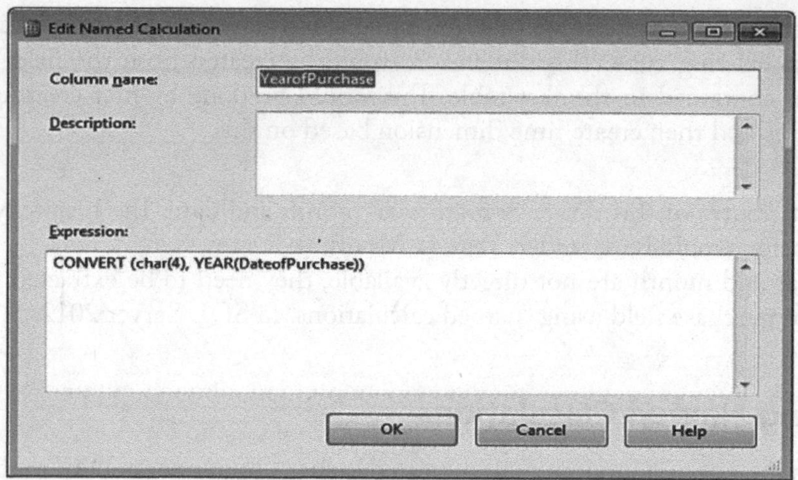

Click OK.

4. Similarly, open another named calculation form for creation of Month filed. To extract month from date of purchase in sales info table, the following expression would be used in named calculation form:
   CONVERT [char(2), MONTH (Date of Purchase)] – to extract month

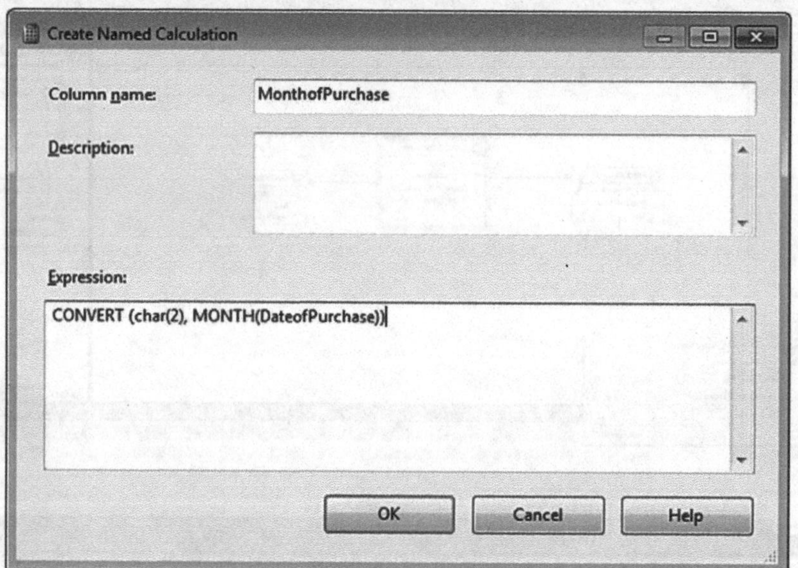

Click OK. This has created two new columns in the data source view of Sales Information table. However, the underlying database is unaffected.

5. You can explore the data for the new columns by right clicking on the same and select explore data:

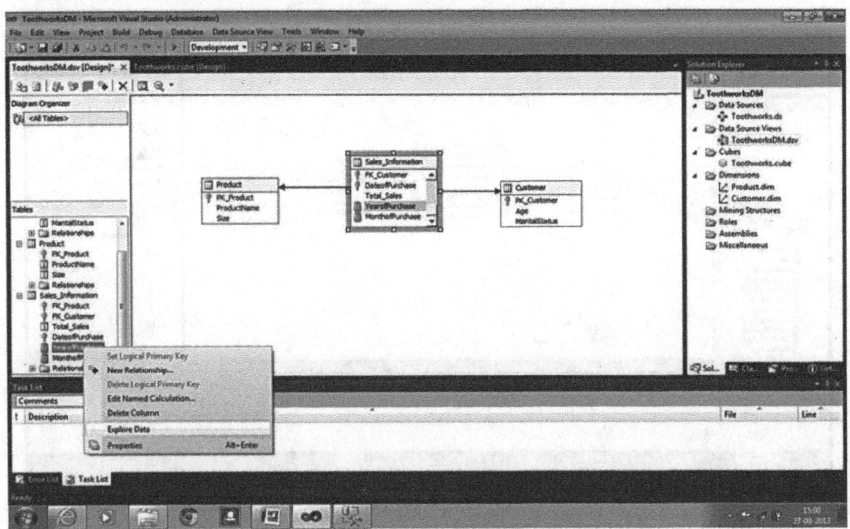

The data are as under:

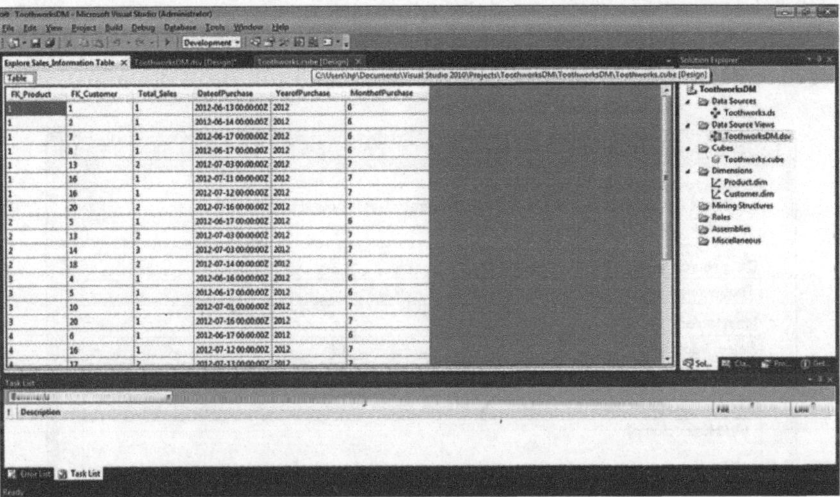

FK_Product	FK_Customer	Total_Sales	DateofPurchase	YearofPurchase	MonthofPurchase
1	1	1	2012-06-13 00:00:00Z	2012	6
1	2	1	2012-06-14 00:00:00Z	2012	6
1	7	1	2012-06-17 00:00:00Z	2012	6
1	8	1	2012-06-17 00:00:00Z	2012	6
1	13	2	2012-07-03 00:00:00Z	2012	7
1	16	1	2012-07-11 00:00:00Z	2012	7
1	16	1	2012-07-12 00:00:00Z	2012	7
1	20	2	2012-07-16 00:00:00Z	2012	7
2	5	1	2012-06-17 00:00:00Z	2012	6
2	13	2	2012-07-03 00:00:00Z	2012	7
2	14	3	2012-07-03 00:00:00Z	2012	7
2	18	2	2012-07-14 00:00:00Z	2012	7
3	4	1	2012-06-16 00:00:00Z	2012	6
3	5	1	2012-06-17 00:00:00Z	2012	6
3	10	1	2012-07-01 00:00:00Z	2012	7
3	20	1	2012-07-16 00:00:00Z	2012	7
4	6	1	2012-06-17 00:00:00Z	2012	6
4	16	1	2012-07-12 00:00:00Z	2012	7

Adding New Dimension: "Time"

The following steps are used to create new dimension "Time" from the fields "Year", "Month" and "DateofPurchase" in the Sales Information table.

6. To add a new dimension, in the SSDT solution explorer window for the ToothworksDM analysis project, right click on the dimensions entry and click new dimension. This opens the dimension wizard.

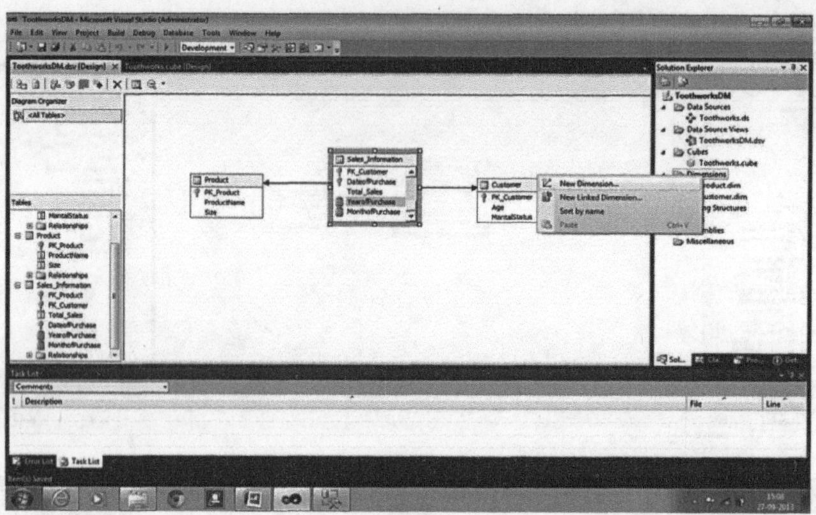

7. Leave Use an existing table selected in select creation method. ToothworksDM should already be selected, next select "sales_Information" in main table drop down list, because this contains date information.
8. Select dateofPurchase as key column and select the blank entry for other columns. Select dateofPurchase column from the name column drop down list.

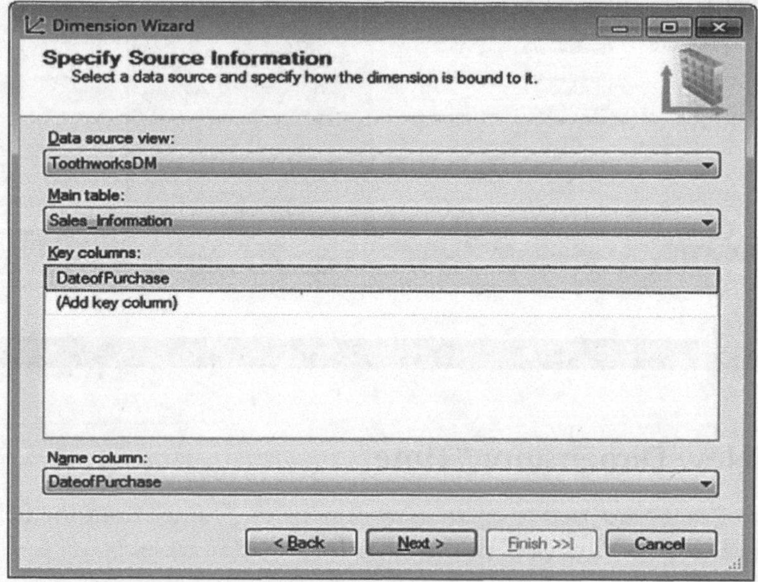

9. Uncheck all items in related tables window. Click next. In select dimension attributes, Check dateofPurchase, yearofPurchase, and monthofPurchase and uncheck all other attributes.

10. Change attribute type of date to date. Click on the drop down in attribute type, expand date, expand calendar and then select date from this. Similarly, select year for yearofpurchase and month for monthofpurchase.
11. Click Next. In completing the wizard, change the name of dimension to DimTime and click Finish.

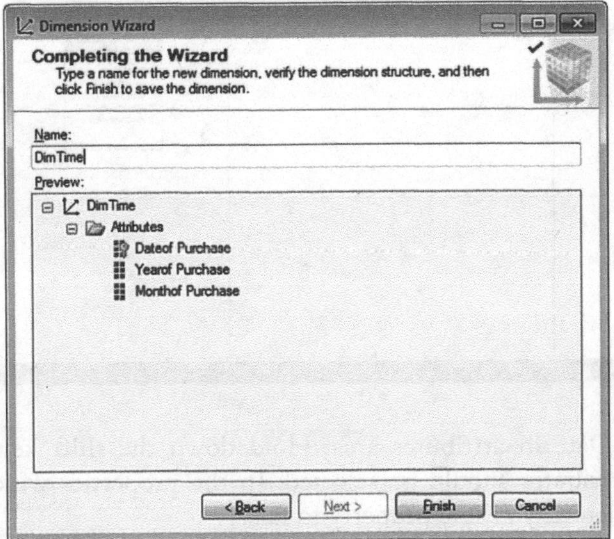

12. Dimension design tab automatically opens. Now right click on Name of date entry in attributes area and change to date.
    Repeat for year and month and day.

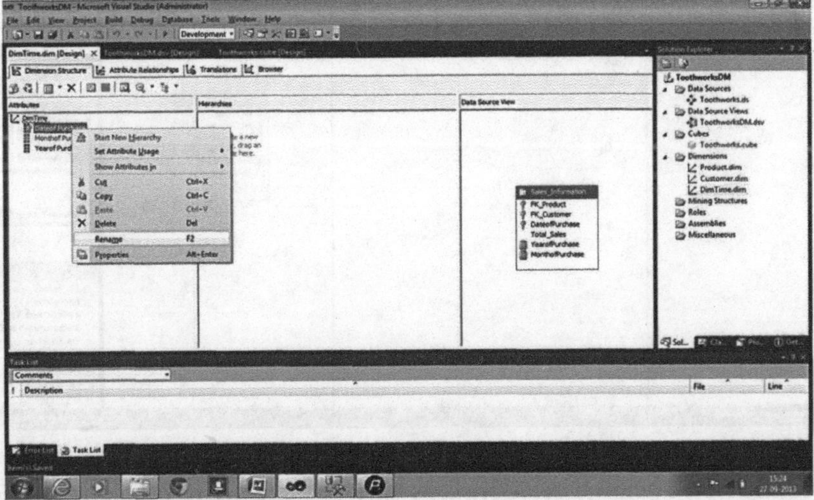

13. Next in the hierarchy tab, drag and drop Year. Next, drag Month and drop it on the new level in hierarchies, and then drop Date. Rename the hierarchy to DateHierarchy.

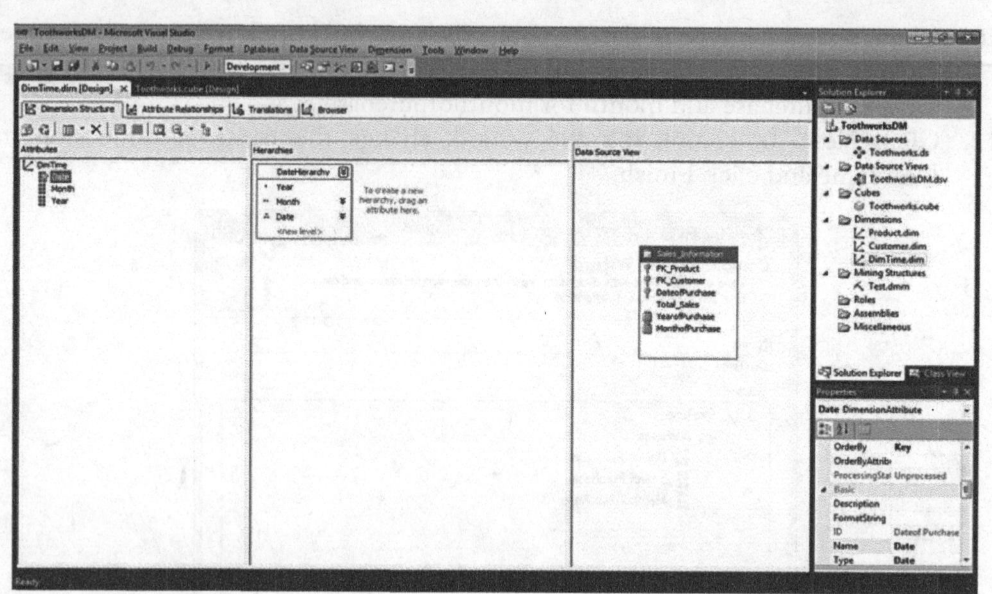

14. Now click Date in attributes area. Hold down the shift key and click Year. All three attributes should be selected. In the properties window, change the AttributeHierarchyVisible property to false.

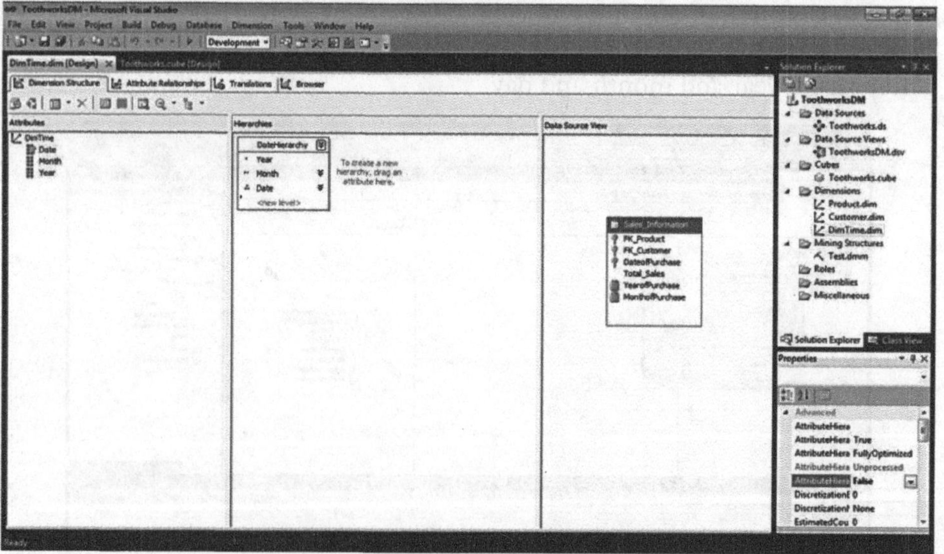

15. Now click on attribute relationships tab. The hierarchy is not mirrored as we should like it to be. Select Month and drop it on Year. Right click on Relationship arrow and change the relationship type to rigid for both arrows. Click Save All.

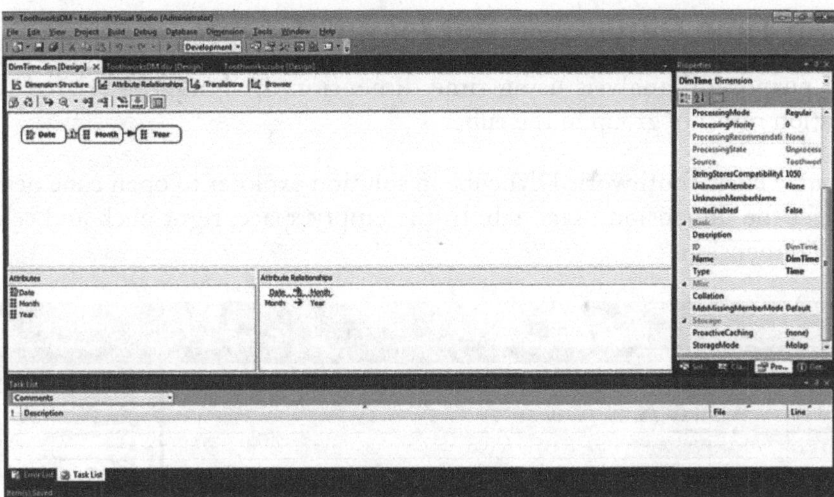

Adding Attributes for Each Dimension

Only those fields of a dimension can be used for analysing the cube which are contained in attributes tab.

16. From solution explorer window, double click Product dimension. Dimension design tab opens. In this, drag and drop all attributes from data source view to attributes area.

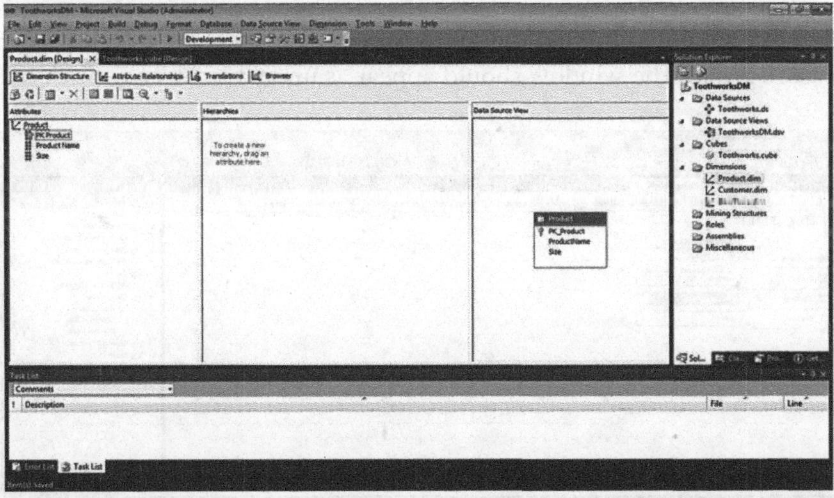

17. From solution explorer window, double click Customer dimension. Dimension design tab opens. In this, again drag and drop all attributes from data source view to attributes area.

Relating Time Dimension to Measure Group

For any purposeful analysis using time dimension, it should be related to Sales Information measure group in the cube.

18. Double click ToothworksDM.cube in solution explorer to open cube design tab. Select the dimension usage tab. In the empty space, right click and select add new dimension.

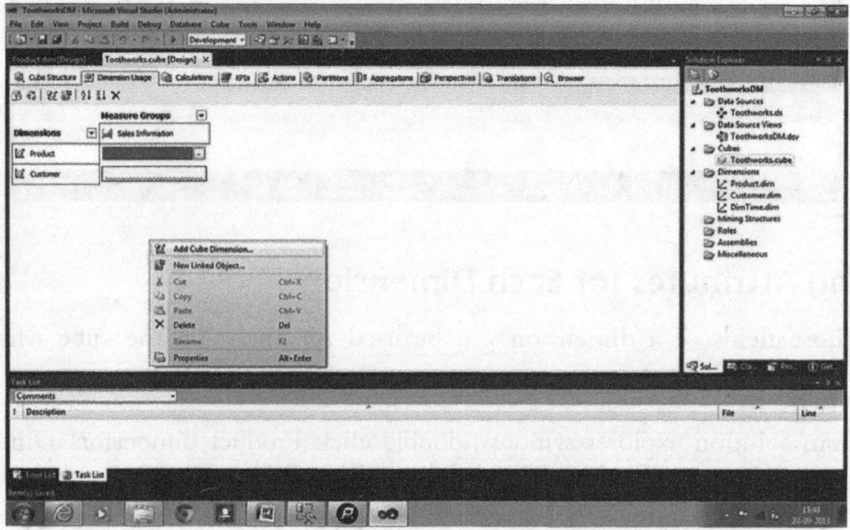

19. Select DimTime and click OK. It automatically relates it to sales information measure group. The window should appear as under:

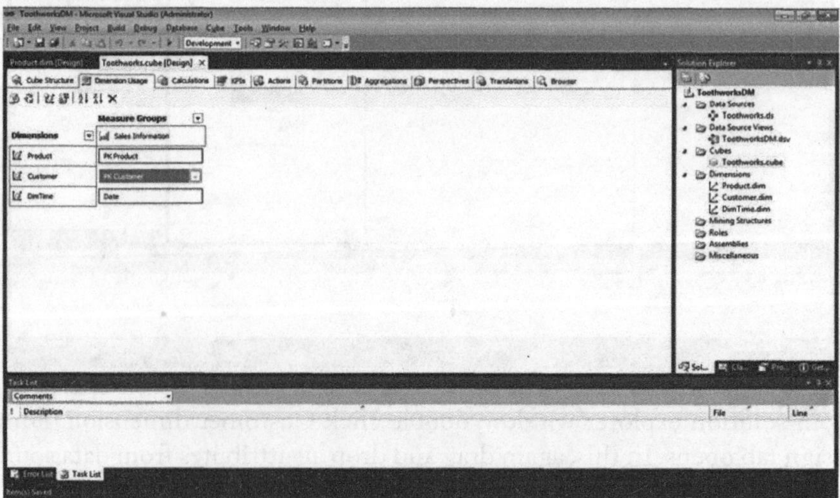

Click Save ALL button.
This has added time dimension to the cube which now has three dimensions—Time, Product and Customer and one fact table.

REFERENCES

Booch, G., Jacobson, I., Rumbaugh, J. (1998). "The Unified Modeling Language User Guide". Addison-Wesley Pub Co; ISBN: 0201571684; 1st edition.

Borkar, V., Deshmuk, K., Sarawagi, S. (2000). "Automatically Extracting Structure from Free Text Addresses. Bulletin of the Technical Committee on Data Engineering", 23(4).

Bouzeghoub, M., Fabret, F., Matulovic, M. (1999). "Modeling Data Warehouse Refreshment Process as a Workflow Application" In Proc. Intl. Workshop on Design and Management of Data Warehouses (DMDW'99), Heidelberg, Germany.

Fundulaki, Averbuch, A. Daskalaki, E. "Overview and analysis of Existing benchmark framework", LDBC Cooperative Project FP7-317548.

Gaur 1, V., Dr. S.S. Sarangdevot 2, Tanwar 3, G. S., Sharma 4, A. "Improve performance of Extract, transform and Load", Vishal Gaur et.al/ International Journal on Computer Science and Engineering, Vol. 02, No.-03, 2010 786–789.

Jun, T., Kai, C., Feng Yu, Gang, T. (2009). "The Research and Application of ETL Tools in Business Intelligence Project," in Proc. International Forum on Information Technology and Applications, IEEE, pp. 620–623.

Kimball, R., Caserta, J. (2004): The Data Warehouse ETL Toolkit: Practical Techniques for Extracting, leaning, Conforming, and Delivering Data. John Wiley & Sons.

Krishna R. and Sreekanth, (2010). "An Object Oriented Modelling and Implementation of web based ETL process", International Journel of computer science and network security, Vol. 10 No. 2.

Qin Hanlin, Jin Xianzhen, Zhang Xianrong, (2012). "Research on Extract,Transform and load in Land and Resources Star Schema Data Warehouses", Computational Intelligence and Design (ISC10), 2012 fifth International Symposium on (Volume 1), 28–29 pp. 120–123.

Rodruez, N. Lawson, K. Molina, E. "Data Warehouses tool Evaluation. ETL Focused", Univesity of Texas-Pan American 1201 W. University Drive, Edinburg, TX (956) 665-UTPA.

Vassiliadis, P. (2009). "A survey of Extract-transform-load technology", International Journel of Dataware Housing & Mining, 5(3), 1–27.

CHAPTER 8

OLTP and OLAP

After going through this chapter, you will be able to

- Understand the concept of OLTP
- Understand the characteristics of OLTP
- Understand the OLTP model
- Understand the concept of OLAP
- Understand the benefits of OLAP
- Understand OLAP architecture
- Understand the difference between OLTP and OLAP

INTRODUCTION

From the previous chapters, one can easily comprehend the importance of business analytics and data. As discussed earlier, business analytics is a powerful tool in the hands of managers with the help of which they can overcome business challenges. Moving ahead, this part starts with fundamentals of OLAP and OLTP, which are the most important concepts of advanced business analytics. While previously the organisations applied OLTP to analyse the online transactions and now as the environment is becoming more and more dynamic, the organisations are applying OLAP to analyse the complex data. The first part of this chapter deals in OLTP, and in the second part all important aspects of OLAP concepts are discussed.

OLTP (ONLINE TRANSACTION PROCESSING SYSTEMS)

OLTP is a class of applications which provides transaction-oriented applications, i.e., data entry, update facility and quick retrieval of information. OLTP applies client–server processing and is used for routine transactions. OLTP is generally applied by lower level or operational-control level staff. For example, in banks, the clerks use OLTP applications for quick update of information and quick retrieval of information. The OLTP application stores data up to certain weeks or months, i.e., routine data that too for a limited

> PayPal's business growth is exponential per year due to the addition of new users, transactions, features and new channels such as mobiles, etc. Database workloads grew 50–100% every year. To meet the demands of the growing business, it implemented fast paced OLTP environment which supports 500+ database instances, 10–130 TB of data, 5000–14000 concurrent processes and 10 GB redo/minute.

time. As OLTP is applied for those routine transactions, which requires an instant update, for example, in case of ATM machines when you withdraw money instantly, your account balance is updated and you get the update information.

The OLTP applications are designed where

- Same database is being referred to fetch information by many users
- When the users want online input and output of information
- The users are not always technical persons
- When the fast retrieval of information is required
- When fast updating of information is required

OLTP applications can be segmented as

1. Transaction Processing
2. Batch Processing
3. Interactive Processing

OLTP applications can be segmented as

1. **Transaction Processing**: This application processes a single item or information as required. In this application, multiple users can fetch the information simultaneously (see Exhibit 8.1). The users do not need to write any technical program, rather this application is very user-friendly. The response rate in this application is also very fast. For example, "How many seats are available on Monday from Delhi to Mumbai"? The user can log in to a website of the particular airline company and can quickly get the information. Moreover, multiple users may want to know same vacancy, and this application provides answers to all the multiple users. To make the things more clear, the following diagram enlists the OLTP model of the ATM machine. Multiple users can operate different ATM machines of the same bank at the same time. The user can get the mini statement; withdraw money, deposit money, etc. It is important to note that this application processes single transaction at a time, i.e., one application at a time.
2. **Batch Processing**: As opposed to the transaction processing, batch processing is applied where the information (or items) is required in batch. Whereas in the transaction processing the requirement is the processing of single information, sometimes there are situations where the information is required in batches. For those situations, batch processing systems are applied. In the batch processing system, the records are collected in a batch and the most important aspect is that this batch is made by presorting of the items (see Exhibit 8.2). This presorting is done by applying some specific rule; for example, payroll generation is a type of batch processing system where the information is required in batch (say, after 30 days or monthly) and the presorting is done,

OLTP stands for Online Transaction Processing systems. OLTP is client/server applications. OLTP provides users direct access to the required information. OLTP helps customers as well as employees to access the information. Using OLTP, the users can access the system online and get the required information.

OLTP finds extensive application in:

- Banks
- Retail stores
- Airline reservation
- Order entry process

Exhibit 8.1 Transaction processing

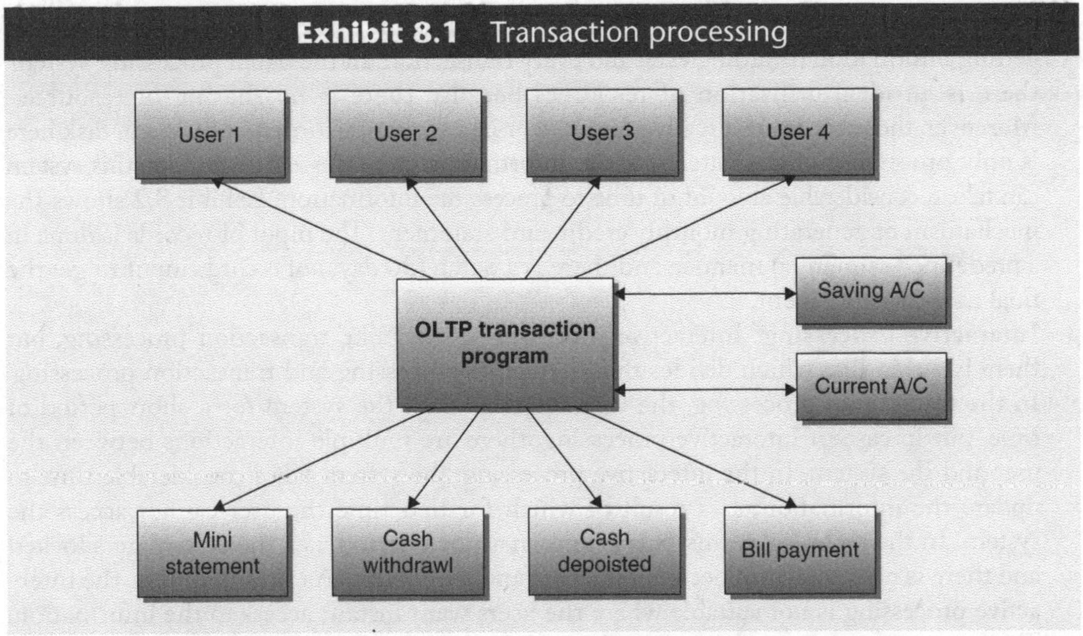

Exhibit 8.2 Batch processing

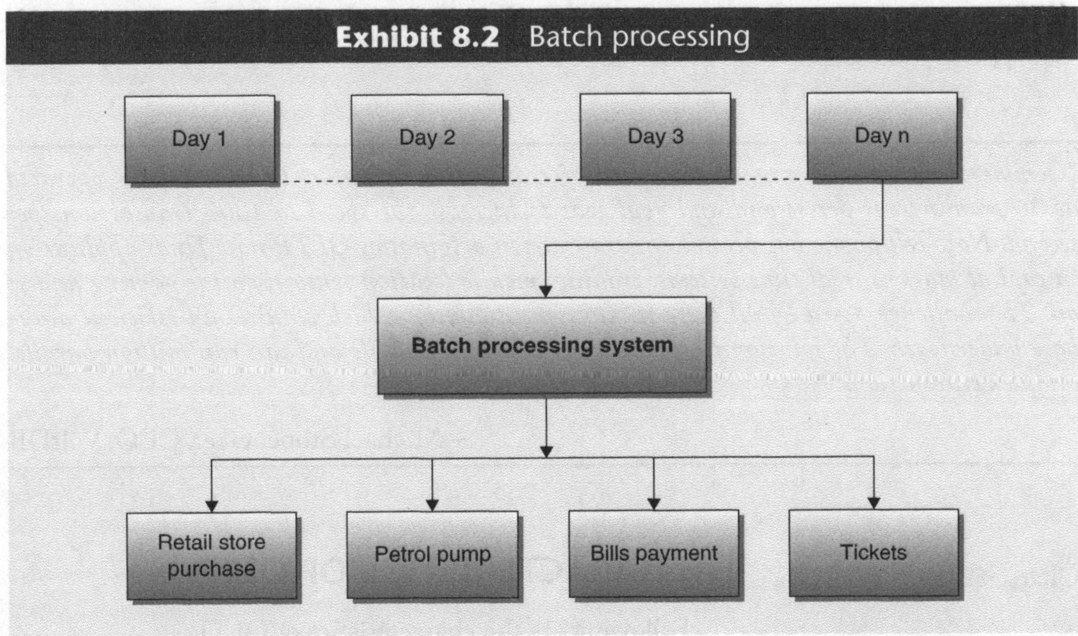

i.e., the information is sorted date wise starting from the first of every month or any other date depending on the policy of the organisation. One of the main differences between transaction processing and batch processing is that while transaction processing is online based, the batch processing has generally offline access to information because batch processing systems are applied in those situations where there is no urgency of getting information regarding each and every transaction. In the batch processing system, there is an ideal utilisation of resources because there is no sharing of resources. Moreover, the records are already presorted or in a sequential order, so the main task here is only processing of the batch. As the information is processed in batches, this system can take a considerable amount of time to process the information. Exhibit 8.2 shows the mechanism of generating monthly credit card statement. The input of records is done in a predefined sequential manner, and there is a batch (30 days) of records input to get the final monthly statement.

3. **Interactive Processing**: Interactive processing is just like transaction processing, but there is a thin line which divides the interactive processing and transaction processing. In the transaction processing, the user interacts with the system for a short period of time, but in case of interactive processing, there are multiple interactions between the user and the system. In the interactive processing, the system takes considerable time to update the information; as a result of which for that time the user cannot access the system. In the technical terms, this is known as lock period, i.e., the system gets locked and there is no interaction between the user and the system. As a result of this, the interactive processing is not suitable where the users want instant access to the information. The interactive processing is generally applied in case of project development where a limited number of users are working and there is no urgency in getting the information. Another area where the interactive processing is applied is the editing and decision support systems.

"Commerce in the 80's ran at the speed of transaction operator. In 90s, OLTP operated at 30 transactions per second and goal was to increase the speed to 1000 transactions/per second. Now cell phone has become the transaction originator. OLTP now finds application in capital markets, real time systems, trading, mobile location sensors, online gaming and so on. The challenge posed by all these is real time analytics which requires an efficient database underneath. The solution to this is SQL which is scalable and can run million parallel complex transactions."

—Michael Stonebraker, CEO, VoltDB

Characteristics of OLTP:

1. Online Connectivity
2. Availability
3. Response Rate
4. Cost
5. Update facility

CHARACTERISTICS OF OLTP

Following are the characteristics of OLTP.

1. **Online Connectivity**: One of the most important characteristics of OLTP is that users can access the system online. This connectivity can be done using LAN or WAN depending on the situation.

2. **Availability**: In the present situation, organisations cannot afford to neglect the customers. The customer can desire to access the information at any time of the day, for example, a customer might want to see his bank record using the Internet banking facility at 11 p.m. Even employees may need to access or update the information at any time of the day; hence, OLTP must be available 24 hours a day. For this, the organisations need a robust OLTP applications which are available 24 hours a day.
3. **Response Rate**: Yet, another important feature of OLTP has been that in OLTP there is a short interaction between the user and the system, which means that OLTP must have a rapid response rate. OLTP should provide proper load balancing by giving priority to the selected transaction over other transactions.
4. **Cost**: OLTP is being extensively applied by organisations. It will be not wrong to say that OLTP is a necessity for organisations in the present time. Hence, it is very important that the cost of the processing of transactions should be low as in any organisation there are thousands of transactions which are processed every day. This cost of processing will add to the running expenses of an organisation, and hence, it is very important that OLTP transaction cost should be less.
5. **Update Facility**: OLTP should provide the facility of instant update of the information. As there are many users who access same Database, there should not be any delays or lock periods. For this purpose, it is very important that OLTP must use the full potential of the hardware and software so that an instant update facility can be provided.

Bwin data management group deployed SQL server 2008 for its international customer base that places more than 1 million bets per day, which leads to more than 30,000 transactions per second. The data size supported is 100 TB and largest table has excess of 1 billion records. "There can be 16 games starting at the exact same moment and ending at the same moment," says Grohser. "You can imagine the demand SQL Server is handling few minutes before these games begin, and in the first few minutes after they end. The traffic is amplified by customers placing wagers on multiple games, and then checking all the results afterwards."

Thomas Grohser, Sr. Database Engineer, Bwin.

OLTP MODEL

For the OLTP application data are stored in the form of the Relational Model. Moreover, the data are normalised in the form of the Relational Model so as to reduce the data redundancy. In the following section, the concept of the OLTP relational table is explained in detail by giving an appropriate example.

> For the OLTP application, data are stored in the form of the relational model.

Relational Data Models Relational data models represent the facts with the help of entities and relationship. Entities are those facts about which the information is collected. The relational data model represents these entities in the form of relations so as to reduce the data redundancy and data duplication. This process of removing the data duplication and redundancy is known as normalisation.

RELATIONAL DATA MODELING HANDS-ON PROJECT

The following example gives a sample of data about a firm XYZ that has various branches in India in different states. Table 8.1 contains the following fields:

1. Employee's name
2. State
3. District
4. City
5. Designation
6. Branch name
7. Manager name
8. Date/Time

The sample data look as under (Table 8.1)
Now with the help of relational tables, we can:

1. Create a group
2. Normalize the table to avoid duplicity in data.
3. Create relationship

A BA analyst in consultation with the manager frames the following rules:

1. Different branches are in one city and each branch is unique.
2. Different cities are in one district and each city is unique.
3. Different districts are in one state and each district is unique.
4. Different states are in one country and each state is unique.
5. One employee can be employed in one branch and can be posted as a manager in another branch.

To achieve the above rules and develop a relational model, following has been identified:

1. The complete data of employee are collected and fringed at one place in 'Employee' table. The data has the fields of branch, employee first name, employee last name, designation, manager id, date/time.
2. To eradicate duplicity in the data, separate tables are created for 'City Info', 'State Info', 'District Info', 'Country Info' and 'Branch Info'. City ID is foreign key to Branch Info table, District ID to City Info table and so on.

Table 8.1 Sample data

State	District	City	Employee first name	Employee last name	Designation	Branch name	Manager name	Manager branch	Date/ Time
Punjab	Patiala	Patiala	Rahul	Sharma	General Manager	XYZP, Punjab	–	XYZ, A.P.	1/1/2009 10:20:00 AM
Punjab	Ludhiana	Ludhiana	Kunal	Sharma	Assistant	XYZL, Punjab	Rahul Sharma	–	1/1/2009 10:20:00 AM
Andhra Pradesh	Anantpur	Hindupur	Sanjiv	Kumar	Sr. Manager	XYZ, A.P.	Rahul Sharma	XYZD, H.P.	1/1/2009 10:20:00 AM
Uttar Pradesh	Allahabad	Dariaganj	Satinder	Kumar	Assistant	XYZA, U.P.	Rahul Sharma	–	1/1/2009 10:20:00 AM
Uttar Pradesh	Aligarh	Biswan	Guruvansh	Kumar	Assistant	XYZB, U.P.	Rahul Sharma	–	1/1/2009 10:20:00 AM
Himachal Pradesh	Simla	Narkanda	Harjit	Singh	Manager	XYZN, H.P.	Sanjiv Kumar	XYZ, Rajasthan	1/1/2009 10:20:00 AM
Himachal Pradesh	Kangra	Dharamsala	Shivam	Srivastava	Assistant	XYZD, H.P.	Sanjiv Kumar	–	1/1/2009 10:20:00 AM
Haryana	Panchkula	Kalka	Manik	Gupta	Assistant	XYZP, Haryana	Sanjiv Kumar	–	1/1/2009 10:20:00 AM

(*Continued*)

Table 8.1 Continued

State	District	City	Employee first name	Employee last name	Designation	Branch name	Manager name	Manager branch	Date/ Time
Rajasthan	Jaipur	Shahpura	Pooja	Garg	Asst. Manager	XYZ, Rajasthan	Harjit Singh	XYZK, TN	1/1/2009 10:20:00 AM
Bihar	Patna	Gaya	Rajiv	Kapoor	Assistant	XYZ, Bihar	Harjit Singh	–	1/1/2009 10:20:00 AM
Maharashtra	Thane	Kalian	Priya	Singh	Assistant	XYZK, Maharashtara	Pooja Garg	–	1/1/2009 10:20:00 AM
Maharashtra	Osmanabad	Tuljapur	Nidhi	Negi	Assistant	XYZO, Maharashtra	Pooja Garg	–	1/1/2009 10:20:00 AM
Tamil Nadu	Coimbatore	Sucur	Harpreet	Singh	Assistant	XYZ, Tamil Nadu	Pooja Garg	–	1/1/2009 10:20:00 AM

3. 'Branch Info' is connected with employee table.
4. All the above made tables are uniquely identified by applying a primary key so that there is no redundancy or duplicate data.
5. Since an employee can be posted as manager in another branch of the firm, another table is created with the name 'Manager Info' table.
6. Manager and designation information in the employee table can be used to retrieve manager details from 'Manager info' table.

The complete relational data model has been depicted below Table 8.2 based on above rules:

Exhibit 8.3 Relational data model

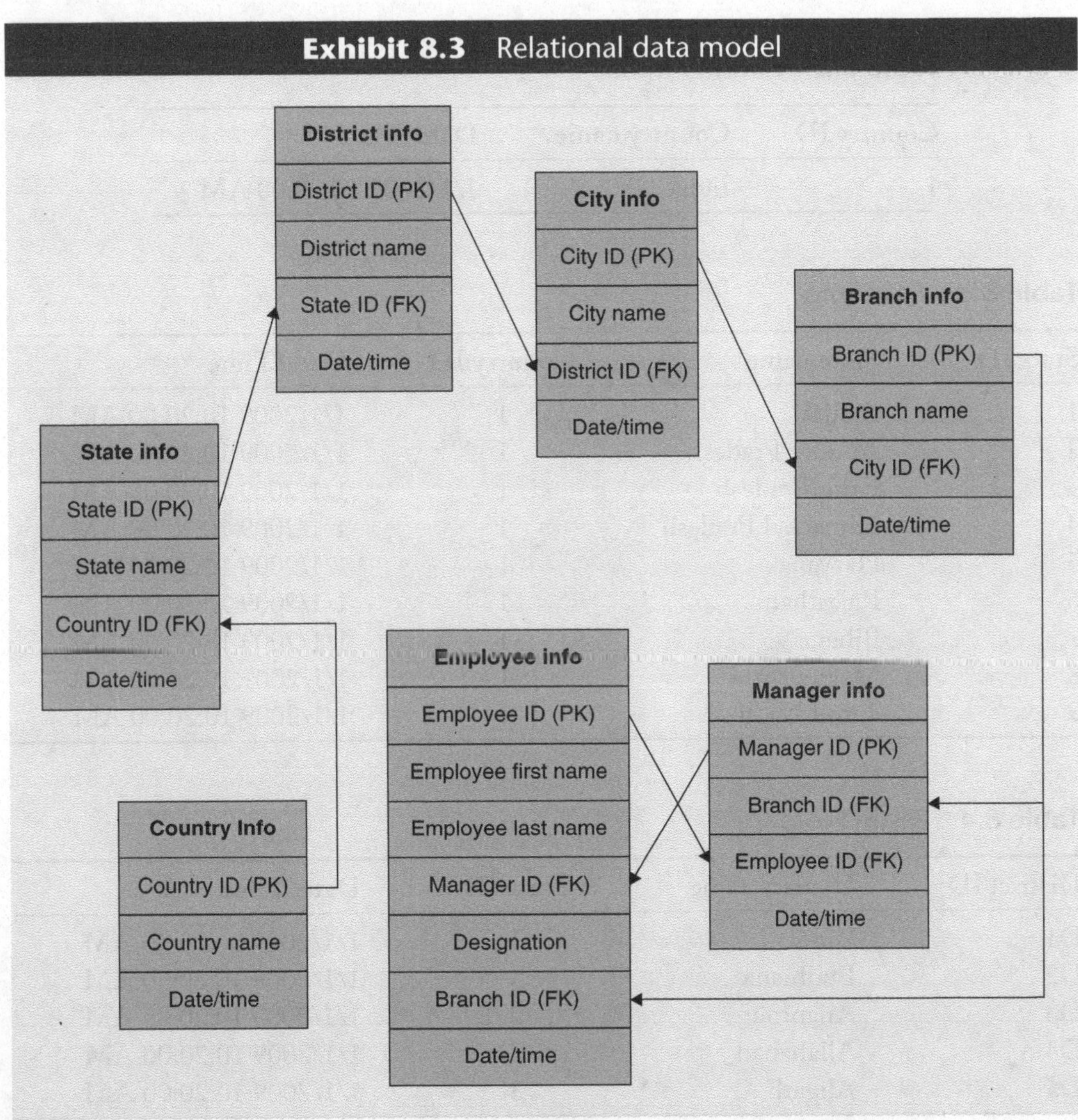

A brief summary of the above relational model is as under

Since several branches exist in one city, so City ID is foreign key to 'Branch Info' table. Similarly, District ID to 'City Info' and so on. If an employee is manager in another branch, then his/her employee details can be fetched from 'Employee Info' table and managerial details such as branch can be fetched from 'ManagerInfo' table. 'Manager Info' table has records for only those employees whose designation is manager. A new 'Manager ID' is generated for each record in this table, which serves as primary key for this table. This table has linkage with both 'Employee Info' and 'Branch Info', using Employee ID and Branch ID as foreign keys.

Based on the above model, complete nomenclature and individual data stored in tables would be as under: (See Table 8.2 to 8.8).

Table 8.2 Country info

Country ID	Country name	Date/Time
1	India	1/1/2009 10:20:00 AM

Table 8.3 State info

State ID	State name	Country ID	Date/Time
1	Punjab	1	1/1/2009 10:20:00 AM
2	Andhra Pradesh	1	1/1/2009 10:20:00 AM
3	Uttar Pradesh	1	1/1/2009 10:20:00 AM
4	Himachal Pradesh	1	1/1/2009 10:20:00 AM
5	Haryana	1	1/1/2009 10:20:00 AM
6	Rajasthan	1	1/1/2009 10:20:00 AM
7	Bihar	1	1/1/2009 10:20:00 AM
8	Maharashtra	1	1/1/2009 10:20:00 AM
9	Tamil Nadu	1	1/1/2009 10:20:00 AM

Table 8.4 District info

District ID	District name	State ID	Date/Time
D1	Patiala	1	1/1/2009 10:20:00 AM
D2	Ludhiana	1	1/1/2009 10:20:00 AM
D3	Anantpur	2	1/1/2009 10:20:00 AM
D4	Allahabad	3	1/1/2009 10:20:00 AM
D5	Aligarh	3	1/1/2009 10:20:00 AM

(*Continued*)

Table 8.4 Continued

District ID	District name	State ID	Date/Time
D6	Simla	4	1/1/2009 10:20:00 AM
D7	Kangra	4	1/1/2009 10:20:00 AM
D8	Panchkula	5	1/1/2009 10:20:00 AM
D9	Jaipur	6	1/1/2009 10:20:00 AM
D10	Patna	7	1/1/2009 10:20:00 AM
D11	Thane	8	1/1/2009 10:20:00 AM
D12	Osmanabad	8	1/1/2009 10:20:00 AM
D13	Coimbatore	9	1/1/2009 10:20:00 AM

Table 8.5 City info

City ID	City name	District ID	Date/Time
c1	Patiala	D1	1/1/2009 10:20:00 AM
c2	Ludhiana	D2	1/1/2009 10:20:00 AM
c3	Hindupur	D3	1/1/2009 10:20:00 AM
c4	Dariaganj	D4	1/1/2009 10:20:00 AM
c5	Biswan	D5	1/1/2009 10:20:00 AM
c6	Narkanda	D6	1/1/2009 10:20:00 AM
c7	Dharamsala	D7	1/1/2009 10:20:00 AM
c8	Kalka	D8	1/1/2009 10:20:00 AM
c9	Shahpura	D9	1/1/2009 10:20:00 AM
c10	Gaya	D10	1/1/2009 10:20:00 AM
c11	Kalian	D11	1/1/2009 10:20:00 AM
c12	Tuljapur	D12	1/1/2009 10:20:00 AM
c13	Sucur	D13	1/1/2009 10:20:00 AM

Table 8.6 Branch info

Branch ID	Branch name	City ID	Date/Time
b1	XYZP, Punjab	c1	1/1/2009 10:20:00 AM
b2	XYZL, Punjab	c2	1/1/2009 10:20:00 AM
b3	XYZ, A.P.	c3	1/1/2009 10:20:00 AM
b4	XYZA, U.P.	c4	1/1/2009 10:20:00 AM
b5	XYZB, U.P.	c5	1/1/2009 10:20:00 AM
b6	XYZN, H.P.	c6	1/1/2009 10:20:00 AM

(Continued)

Table 8.6 Continued

Branch ID	Branch name	City ID	Date/Time
b7	XYZD, H.P.	c7	1/1/2009 10:20:00 AM
b8	XYZP, Haryana	c8	1/1/2009 10:20:00 AM
b9	XYZ, Rajasthan	c9	1/1/2009 10:20:00 AM
b10	XYZ, Bihar	c10	1/1/2009 10:20:00 AM
b11	XYZK, Maharashtara	c11	1/1/2009 10:20:00 AM
b12	XYZO, Maharashtra	c12	1/1/2009 10:20:00 AM
b13	XYZ, Tamil Nadu	c13	1/1/2009 10:20:00 AM

Table 8.7 Employee info

Employee ID	Employee first name	Employee last name	Manager ID	Designation	Branch ID	Date/Time
101	Rahul	Sharma	–	General Manager	b1	1/1/2009 10:20:00 AM
102	Kunal	Sharma	M101	Assistant	b2	1/1/2009 10:20:00 AM
103	Sanjiv	Kumar	M101	Sr. Manager	b3	1/1/2009 10:20:00 AM
104	Satinder	Kumar	M101	Assistant	b4	1/1/2009 10:20:00 AM
105	Guruvansh	Kumar	M101	Assistant	b5	1/1/2009 10:20:00 AM
106	Harjit	Singh	M102	Manager	b6	1/1/2009 10:20:00 AM
107	Shivam	Srivastava	M102	Assistant	b7	1/1/2009 10:20:00 AM
108	Manik	Gupta	M102	Assistant	b8	1/1/2009 10:20:00 AM
109	Pooja	Garg	M103	Asst. Manager	b9	1/1/2009 10:20:00 AM
110	Rajiv	Kapoor	M103	Assistant	b10	1/1/2009 10:20:00 AM
111	Priya	Singh	M104	Assistant	b11	1/1/2009 10:20:00 AM
112	Nidhi	Negi	M104	Assistant	b12	1/1/2009 10:20:00 AM
113	Harpreet	Singh	M104	Assistant	b13	1/1/2009 10:20:00 AM

Table 8.8 Manager info

Manager ID	BranchID	Employee ID	Date/Time
M101	b3	101	1/1/2009 10:20:00 AM
M102	b7	103	1/1/2009 10:20:00 AM
M103	b9	106	1/1/2009 10:20:00 AM
M104	b13	109	1/1/2009 10:20:00 AM

LIMITATIONS OF RELATIONAL MODELS

In OLTP, data are stored in tables in the relational data model; this means that as the volume of data increases, there is a need to create and maintain a large number of tables. The large number of tables seriously hampers the speed of accessing the required information as to run even basic queries it is important to search all the data stored in a large number of tables. Moreover, in present time as, the data are present in an unstructured form, which means that it is not possible to store data in relational tables. As the relational data model is dependent on some denominator, i.e., keys (primary key and foreign key) to store, relate and access the data. But as the volume of data increases, it becomes very difficult to manage the data with that common denominator. In addition to this limitation, tables created in the relational data model are static in nature; that is for each new functionality new tables should be created. Therefore, it is impossible to optimise static tables as in present era organisations need to run dynamic queries.

OLAP

OLAP-Online analytical processing

"Gene expression databases contain a wealth of information, but current data mining tools are limited in their speed and effectiveness in extracting meaningful biological knowledge from them. Compared to traditional cluster analysis of gene expression data, OLAP was more effective and faster in finding biologically meaningful information. OLAP is available from a number of vendors and can work with any relational database management system through OLE DB."

—Dr. Nadim Alkharouf, AP, DCSIS, Towson University, Towson MD

ABC, Inc. is a government debt collection agency based in the US. It prepared 500 pages, "CARE" reports which took more than 24 hours to process and no detail could be added or removed from the same. WinMetrics deployed SQL Server analysis OLAP cube for each process – General Ledger, General Ledger Budget, Payroll, Collector Performance, and Revenue forecasting. The time frame to close ABC's books reduced to 5 days and drill down was enabled on each account to look at the desired level of detail.

OLAP provides multidimensional view of the data.

OLAP is that application which focuses on analysis of data rather than on transactions such as OLTP. OLAP is a specific technology, which enables the managers to view the data from different dimensions. In this definition, the most important word is View. Let us further deliberate on this word.

- **View**: It is very important that managers should be able to view the data. Without proper information managers will not be able to take critical decisions. But simple viewing of data is even possible by using various applications such as MIS or DSS software, but what differentiates OLAP from other applications is that the managers can view the data from different dimensions.

Example

To make the things more clear, just go through the following example very carefully and then try to understand the concept of OLAP.

A retail store manager wants to analyse which brand of shampoo is preferred by its customers. This analysis will help the manager to forecast the demand properly and eventually will help to manage its inventory. The data for OLAP can be visualised in the following manner (see Table 8.9).

Table 8.9 Data visualisation in OLAP

Gender	Product dimension	Location dimension	Sales
1	1	1	71000
2	1	1	45000
1	1	2	50000
2	1	2	46000
1	1	3	29000
2	1	3	25000
Total			**266000**
1	2	1	41000
2	2	1	39900
1	2	2	40000
2	2	2	39000
1	2	3	26000
2	2	3	23000
Total			**208900**

(*Continued*)

Table 8.9 Continued

Gender	Product dimension	Location dimension	Sales
1	3	1	43000
2	3	1	46000
1	3	2	36550
2	3	2	39650
1	3	3	21000
2	3	3	20000
Total			**206200**

- Product dimension represents the different products of shampoo.
  1. Brand A
  2. Brand B
  3. Brand C
- Location dimension represents the different locations where this particular retail store is located.
  1. Punjab
  2. Haryana
  3. U.P
- Gender dimension represents which gender category buys the particular product.
  1. Male
  2. Female
- Sales measure represents the amount of total sales of a particular product at a particular location.

Now when the data are stored in the form of Dimensions then by applying the OLAP application, the manager of the retail store can analyse the information from different dimensions and the following queries can be handled using OLAP.

1. Number of Brand A Shampoo sold in Punjab.
2. Number of Brand A Shampoo sold in Haryana.
3. Number of Brand A Shampoo sold in UP.
4. Number of Brand B Shampoo sold in Punjab.
5. Number of Brand B Shampoo sold in Haryana.
6. Number of Brand B Shampoo sold in UP.
7. Number of Brand C Shampoo sold in Punjab.
8. Number of Brand C Shampoo sold in Haryana.
9. Number of Brand C Shampoo sold in UP.
10. Number of Brand A Shampoo purchased by Males in Punjab.
11. Number of Brand A Shampoo purchased by Females in Punjab.

12. Number of Brand A Shampoo purchased by Males in Haryana.
13. Number of Brand A Shampoo purchased by Females in Haryana.
14. Number of Brand A Shampoo purchased by Males in UP.
15. Number of Brand A Shampoo purchased by Females in UP.
16. Number of Brand B Shampoo purchased by Males in Punjab.
17. Number of Brand B Shampoo purchased by females in Punjab.
18. Number of Brand B Shampoo purchased by Males in Haryana.
19. Number of Brand B Shampoo purchased by Females in Haryana.
20. Number of Brand B Shampoo purchased by Males in UP.
21. Number of Brand B Shampoo purchased by Females in UP.
22. Number of Brand C Shampoo purchased by Males in Punjab.
23. Number of Brand C Shampoo purchased by Females in Punjab.
24. Number of Brand C Shampoo purchased by Males in Haryana.
25. Number of Brand C Shampoo purchased by Females in Haryana.
26. Number of Brand C Shampoo purchased by Males in UP.
27. Number of Brand C Shampoo purchased by Females in UP.
28. Total Sale of Brand A in all locations
29. Total Sale of Brand B in all locations
30. Total Sale of Brand C in all locations

Benefits of OLAP

UAB Elektroskandia is a leading wholesaler of electrical goods. It was experiencing impediments in data analysis due to rapidly increasing amount of data and different databases for stocks, purchases and sales. It then implemented a central data warehouse on the top of which MS SQL OLAP cube was built which allowed rapid analysis, activity tracking and planning.

The benefits of OLAP are discussed in detail.

Benefits of OLAP:

- Multidimensional Analysis
- Centralised Approach
- Fast Retrieval
- Reporting
- Special Features of OLAP
- Pivoting

1. **Multidimensional Analysis**: One of the most important benefits of OLAP is that it allows managers to have a multidimensional view of the data (as explained in the above example). As OLTP where the data are stored in the form of relational tables which do not allow the multidimensional view of data (review the example of OLTP as discussed in the OLTP section). The reason behind the relational model of data in OLTP is that in OLTP the main focus is on the transaction and not on the analysis. Whereas in case of OLAP the main focus is on analysis and not only on transactions. One can even argue that analysis can be possible in OLTP but considering the

kind of competition that an organisation faces it is very important that the concerned manager should be able to view the data from a different dimension so that the manager can perform analysis applying any of the dimensions. As in the above example, the manager can analyse the preferences of a particular gender for a particular brand of shampoo, i.e., gender dimension and product dimension. Similarly, manager can analyse the sale of each type of shampoo in different regions. Moreover, the manager can analyse which product of shampoo is preferred in which region, i.e., product dimension and location dimension. In the multidimensional modeling, the dimension is the attribute of the dataset, for example, product dimension, gender dimension, location dimension and sales dimension. The elements in a particular dimension share common characteristics; for example, in product dimension the elements are codes of different products:

(a) Brand A
(b) Brand B
(c) Brand C

Similarly, in case of gender dimension the elements are:

(a) Male
(b) Female

The dimension modeling provides the facility of representing the elements in a hierarchical manner (see Exhibit 8.4).

Exhibit 8.4 Hierarchial representation of elements

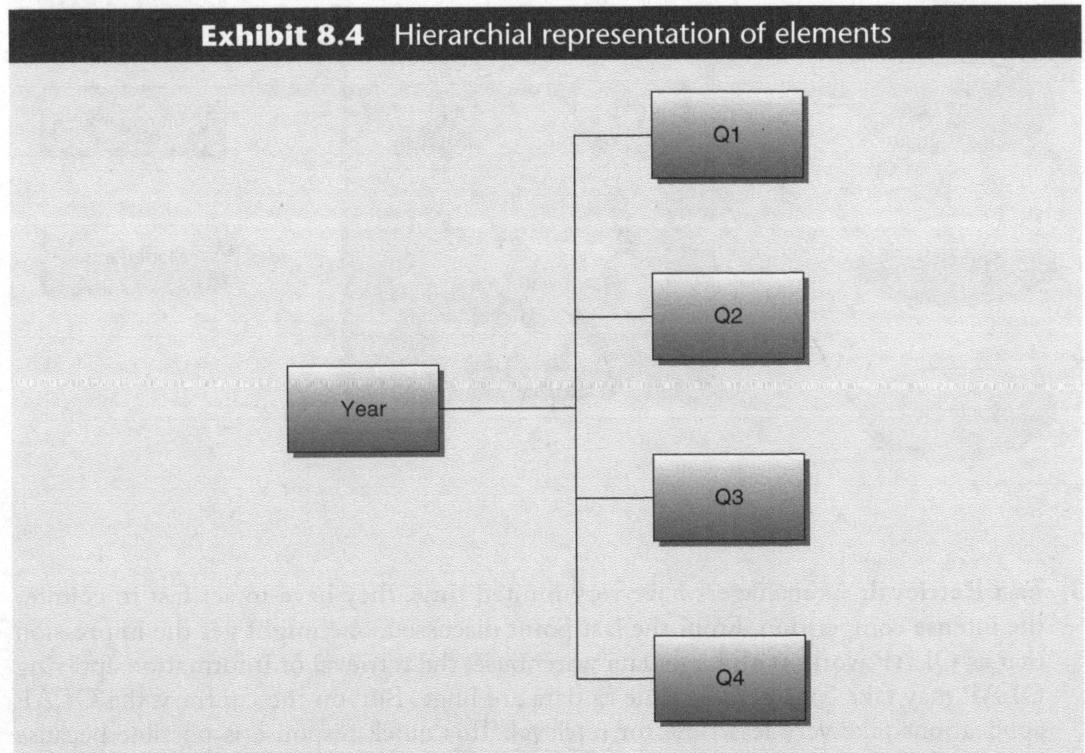

For example, a year can be broken down into a lower hierarchical level of quarters. So this hierarchical representation helps managers to easily view and analyse the complex data for each year by breaking the data and analysis into quarters.

2. **Centralised Approach**: The manager can use different tools to analyse the data, but the problem with the majority of the tools is that most of the tools provide the decentralised approach, for example, MS Excel. Using MS Excel, managers can perform the analysis of data, but major limitation is that the data are not centralised and every employee can use his own metrics to define the data. The different metrics will yield wrong results. The OLAP provides a centralised approach. The data are stored centrally and every employee can access the data using OLAP tools (see Exhibit 8.5). OLAP technology gels with the data warehouse seamlessly; as a result of which OLAP helps in effective utilisation of Data Warehouse. The Data Warehouse collects data from different sources and then these data are extracted, transformed and loaded into the data warehouse. The OLAP technology then helps to run queries on the stored data in data warehouse.

Exhibit 8.5 Centralised approach

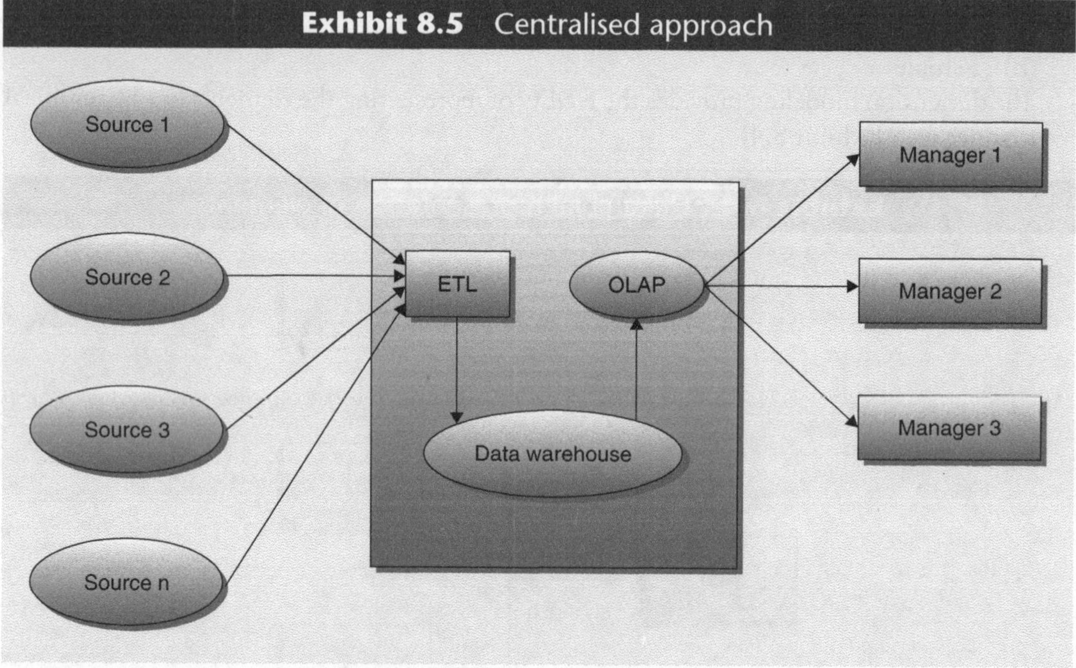

3. **Fast Retrieval**: As managers have very limited time, they have to act fast to counter the intense competition. From the last point discussed, one might get the impression that as OLAP works with large data warehouse, the retrieval of information applying OLAP may take considerable time as data are huge. But, on the contrary, the OLAP applications take very less time for retrieval. This quick response is possible because in the OLAP system the data are stored in a pre-aggregated manner. Pre-aggregated means pre-computing and storing query results that are commonly used by managers. This means that the previous query results are saved and stored which helps in saving

time on calculations. But, there is always a trade-off between the pre-aggregated storage of values and the cost of storage. As there can be thousands of combinations of aggregations, it is not possible to store all the aggregations; moreover, the organisation has to incur the cost to store the aggregated values. Hence, the organisation has to decide up to which limit the level of aggregation is required.

4. **Reporting**: As OLAP is applied for analysis and it is very important that manager should be able to report the findings to his seniors. OLAP provides the facility of creating reports, i.e., the managers can create reports using OLAP. The tools required to create reports in OLAP are very easy to understand and operate. Even a non-technical person applying the tools of OLAP technology can easily create the reports. A simple click of the button creates reports based on the selected dimension (see Exhibit 8.6); for example, reports can be generated region-wise for sales of the product, i.e., in which region a particular product is preferred.

Exhibit 8.6 Reporting by OLAP

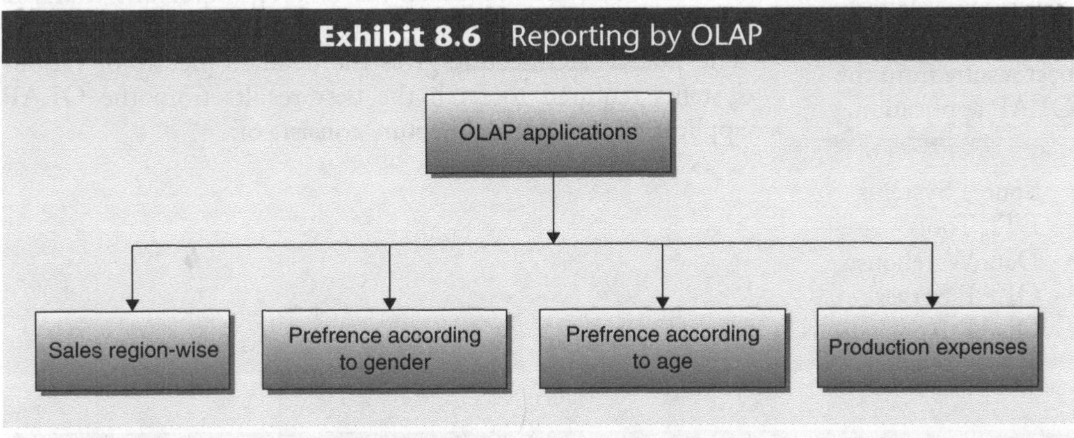

5. **Special Features of OLAP**: There are special features in OLAP which help the managers to analyse the data in an efficient manner. These features are:
   - *Roll-Up:* As the data are stored hierarchically applying dimension modeling in OLAP, roll-up feature allows the analyst to reduce the dimensions. Roll-up feature calculates total for a particular hierarchy of dimension, i.e., it performs aggregation. Roll-up operation helps to summarise the data, for example, when the data are stored in the form of location dimension and location is divided as Punjab, Haryana, UP. In case of Punjab, the data are stored in the form of 10 districts of Punjab. Roll-up facility allows summarising the data from the different districts.
   - *Drill-Down Feature:* The drill-down is just opposite to roll-up feature. Drill-down feature helps the analyst to have the detailed view of the data. For example, for one element Punjab, the drill-down feature helps to break Punjab into, say, five districts so as to view the sales in each district.

- *Slice and Dice Feature:* Managers need to analyse different dimensions for performing analysis of data. The slice and dice feature helps the managers to select one dimension (SLICE) or multiple dimensions (DICE) for in-depth analysis of data.

6. **Pivoting**: Pivot operation helps to rotate the data. This rotation of the data helps to analyse the data from different perspectives. Pivoting can be done by
   - Changing rows into columns
   - Changing one or multiple rows into one or multiple columns
   - Different dimensions can be selected from different tables to make one table and then these dimensions can be rotated.

OLAP Architecture

OLAP architecture gives detailed picture of various systems required to fetch the best results from the OLAP application.

Architecture describes the design of the system. It is essential to know the OLAP Architecture (see Exhibit 8.7) because to avail the benefits of OLAP, it is very important that the appropriate system should be designed with OLAP capabilities. The OLAP architecture gives the detailed picture of various systems required to fetch the best results from the OLAP application. OLAP architecture consists of:

- Source Systems
- ETL Tools
- Data Warehouse
- OLAP Server
- OLAP Applications

Exhibit 8.7 OLAP architecture

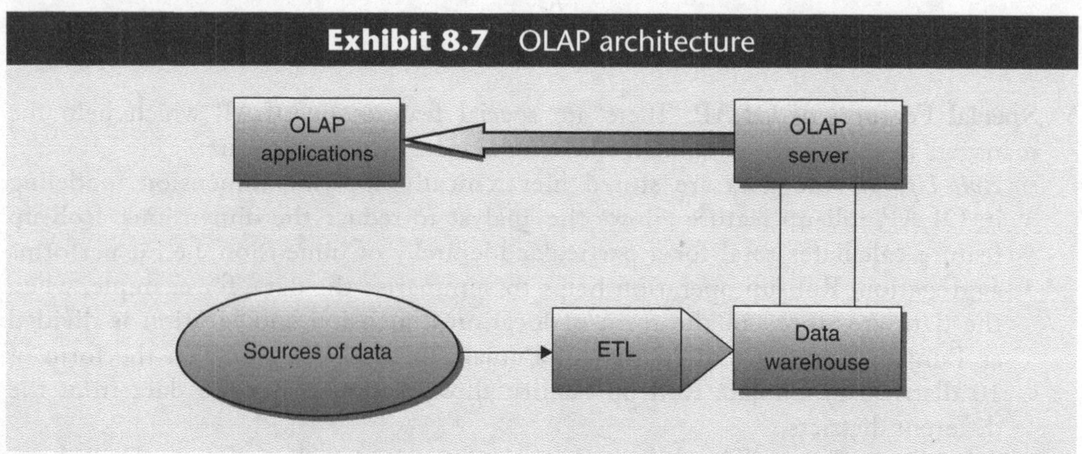

The data from various sources are extracted, transformed and loaded into the data warehouse. In this data warehouse, the OLAP server manages the data and helps managers to establish connection with the data warehouse. Then, in the end with the help of OLAP applications, the manager is able to analyse the data and make reports and charts.

1. ROLAP-Relational OLAP
2. MOLAP-Mutidimensional OLAP
3. HOLAP-Hybrid OLAP

Now, the data in data warehouse can be stored in different forms and each form of storage results in the different form of OLAP applications. Based on different forms of storage, OLAP can be divided as:

- ROLAP
- MOLAP
- HOLAP

In ROLAP, the data is stored in the form of relational tables.

In MOLAP, the data is stored in the form of multidimensional cube.

HOLAP combines the advantages of ROLAP and MOLAP.

1. **ROLAP**: In ROLAP, the data are stored in the form of relational tables. In this type of application, data are not loaded in a cube. The ROLAP application is best suited when the manager needs to have a detailed and in-depth analysis of data. Although ROLAP can handle large data, but the processing of ROLAP is quite slow, i.e., to get an answer the manager has to wait as the data are stored in relational tables and not in a cube.
2. **MOLAP**: In MOLAP, the data are stored in the form of multidimensional cube. Data are stored in the form of pre-calculated aggregations which leads to a faster response rate as compared with the ROLAP. As with the help of pre-calculated aggregation, all possible combinations are made and then the data are stored in the cube which results in a faster response rate. But as the whole data are stored in a cube there is always a limitation up to which limit MOLAP can handle the data. Moreover, the organisation has to spend a substantial amount of resources to run MOLAP applications.
3. **HOLAP**: HOLAP combines the advantages of ROLAP and MOLAP. For example, HOLAP can handle large amount of data and at the same time it provides faster accessibility and other key features of cube technology, i.e., summary reports.

CONCLUSION

There is a lot of difference between OLTP and OLAP applications. The manager should have proper knowledge of the critical aspects of both the applications. The OLTP mainly deals with the routine transactions whereas the OLAP application deals with the processing of the data. The OLAP provides the facility of multidimensional analysis and has a wide range of applications in the present scenario. The knowledge of OLAP helps the managers to properly analyse the complex dynamic environment. To counter the intense competition, managers need to shift focus from OLTP applications on OLAP application, but to realise the full potential of OLAP, it is important that managers should know the difference between OLTP and OLAP applications. Many times managers confuse OLAP applications with OLTP applications. Hence, every manager whether marketing, HR, production or financial needs to have knowledge of OLAP and OLTP applications.

KEY TERMS

- OLTP 211
- Relational Data Models 215
- OLAP 223
- ROLAP 231
- MOLAP 231
- HOLAP 231

SUMMARY

This chapter falls in the category of advanced topics of business analytics. In this chapter, first the concepts of OLTP are discussed in detail. OLTP is a class of applications which provides transaction-oriented applications, i.e., data entry, update facility and quick retrieval of information. OLTP applies client server processing and is applied for routine transactions. OLTP applications can be segmented as:

- Transaction processing
- Batch processing
- Interactive processing

Then various characteristics of OLTP are also discussed in this chapter. As in the OLTP application, data are stored in the form of the relational model, a hands-on project on relational data modeling is discussed in detail. In the second part of the chapter, OLAP is discussed in detail. OLAP is that application which focuses on analysis of data rather than on transactions such as OLTP. OLAP is a specific technology, which enables the managers to view the data from different dimensions. Then, various benefits of OLAP are discussed like.

- Multidimensional analysis
- Centralised approach
- Fast retrieval

- Reporting
- Special features of OLAP
- Pivoting

MULTIPLE CHOICE QUESTIONS

1. OLTP is applied for
a. Analysis
b. Strategy formulation
c. Transaction-oriented application
d. Slice and dice

2. Which of the following is not an OLTP application?
a. Transaction processing
b. Batch processing
c. Interactive processing
d. Analytical processing

3. In OLTP, data is stored in which type of model
a. Relational model
b. Multidimensional model
c. Two-dimensional model
d. One-dimensional model

4. OLAP is applied for
a. Multidimensional analysis
b. Strategy formulation
c. Transaction-oriented application
d. Routine affairs

5. In OLAP, data is stored in which type of model
a. Relational model
b. Multidimensional model
c. Two-dimensional model
d. One-dimensional model

6. Roll-up application in OLAP is applied
a. To calculate totals for different levels of a particular hierarchy of the dimension
b. To have the detailed view of the data
c. Helps the managers to select one dimension and analyse with some other dimension
d. To rotate the data

7. Drill-down application in OLAP is applied
a. To calculate total for different levels of a particular hierarchy of the dimension
b. To have the detailed view of the data
c. To help the managers to select one dimension and analyse with some other dimension
d. To rotate the data

8. Slice and dice application in OLAP is applied
a. To calculate total for a particular hierarchy of the dimension
b. To have the detailed view of the data

c. To help the managers to select one dimension and analyse with some other dimension
d. To rotate the data

9. Pivoting application in OLAP is applied
 a. To calculate total for a particular hierarchy of the dimension
 b. To have the detailed view of the data
 c. To help the managers to select one dimension and analyse with some other dimension
 d. To rotate the data

10. Match the following

Feature	Application
1. The data is stored in the form of relational tables. In this type of application, data are not loaded in a cube	a. MOLAP
2. The data is stored in the form of pre-calculated aggregations in the form of multidimensional cube.	b. HOLAP
3. It combines the advantages of ROLAP and MOLAP	c. ROLAP

REVIEW QUESTIONS

1. Define OLTP and explain in detail the benefits of OLTP.
2. What are the characteristics of OLTP?
3. Discuss the OLTP model in detail.
4. Define OLAP and explain the benefits of OLAP.
5. What is the difference between OLTP and OLAP? Discuss by citing appropriate examples.
6. Explain the OLAP Architecture in detail.

ASSIGNMENT

1. "OLAP has more capabilities as compared with OLTP". Give your opinion regarding this statement based on relevant examples.
2. Identify key application areas of MOLAP, ROLAP and HOLAP.

PROJECT ACTIVITY

1. Visit any organisation in a group of three students and study the working of that organisation in detail. After getting the requisite information, make an OLTP relational model to store and retrieve all the important information.

HANDS-ON PROJECT

Following from the multidimensional model created for Toothworks in the hands-on project of previous chapters, this hands-on will aid in the following:

- Using data mart and data loaded in the previous exercise, finally you would be able to deploy cube to browse through its contents.
- Run queries on the cube.

Deploying Analysis Services Project or Cube Using SSDT

1. Open SSDT and Toothworks DM project. Select Project | Toothworks DM properties from menu. The properties dialog box opens.

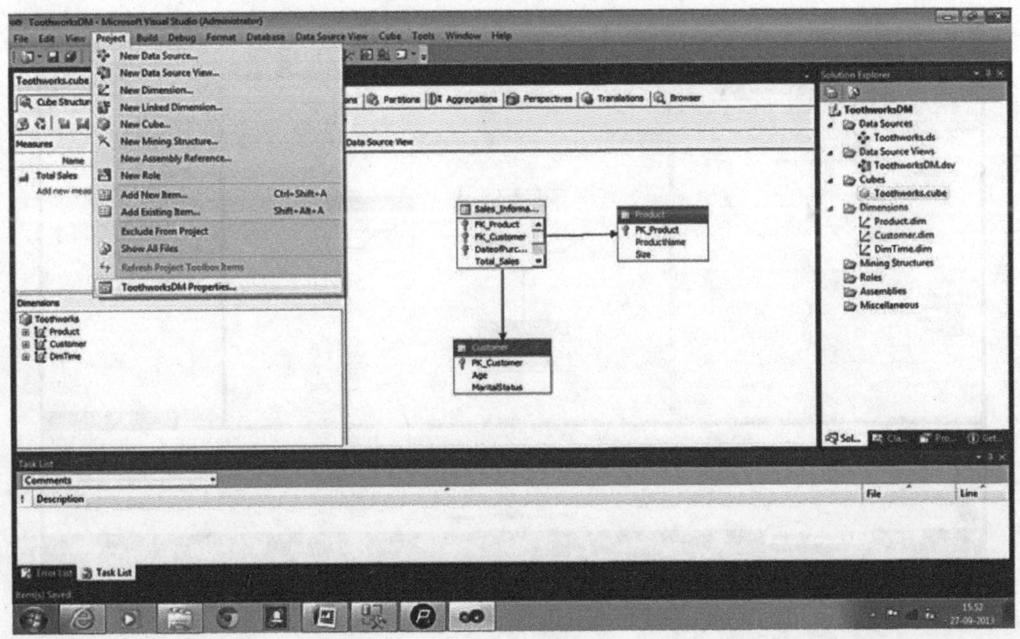

2. In the deployment option, provide the name of the target server where you wish to deploy the analysis services database. Click OK.

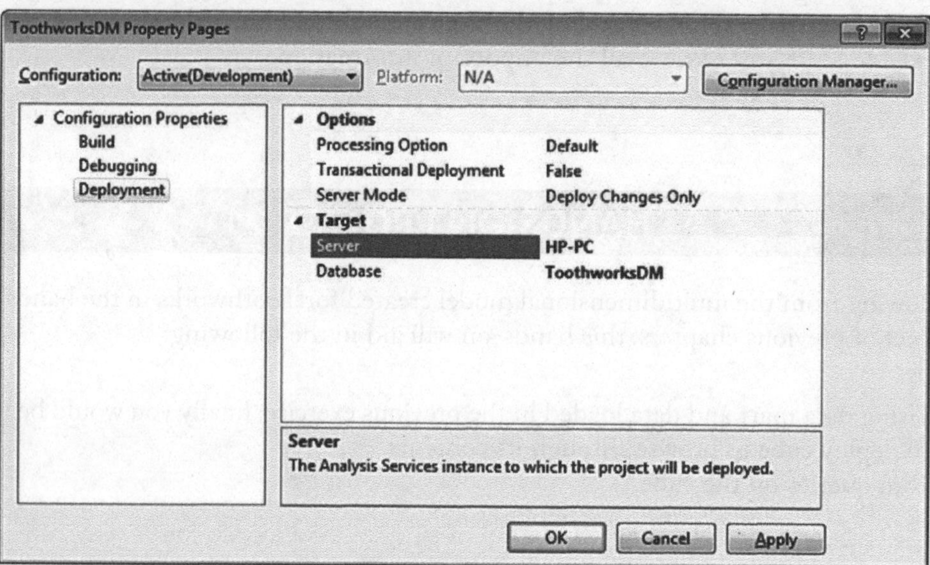

3. From the main menu, select Build | Deploy ToothworksDM. Provide set of credentials of prompted to complete the deployment. Monitor the progress till deployment completed successfully appears.

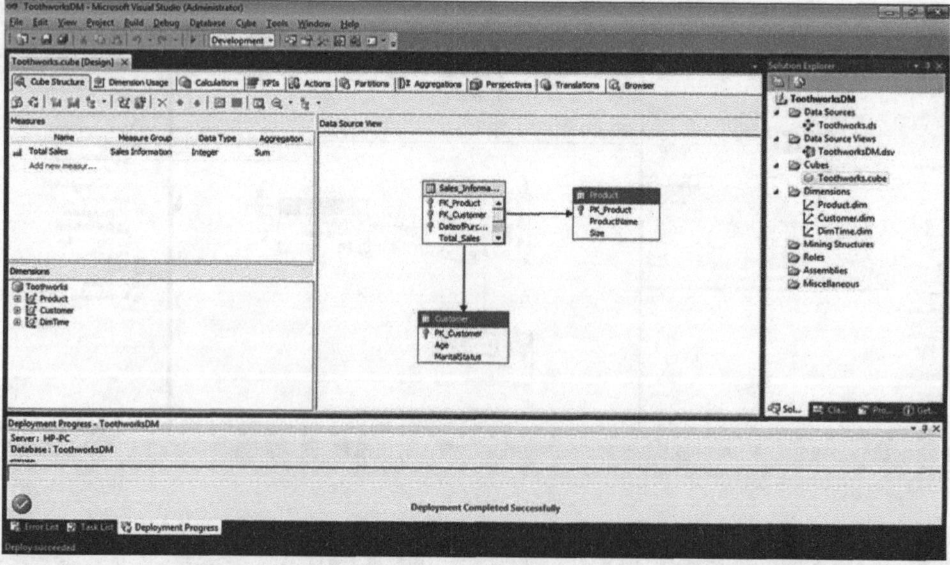

4. The cube is ready to be used for analysis.

Browsing the Cube

You can browse the content of the cube using either SSDT or SSMS analysis database.

5. Open SQL Server Management Studio and connect to analysis service database. (Ensure that SQL Server Browser is started. For this, right click "My Computer" and select manage. In this click Services, double click Services and then trace SQL Server browse. Double click on it and select start.)

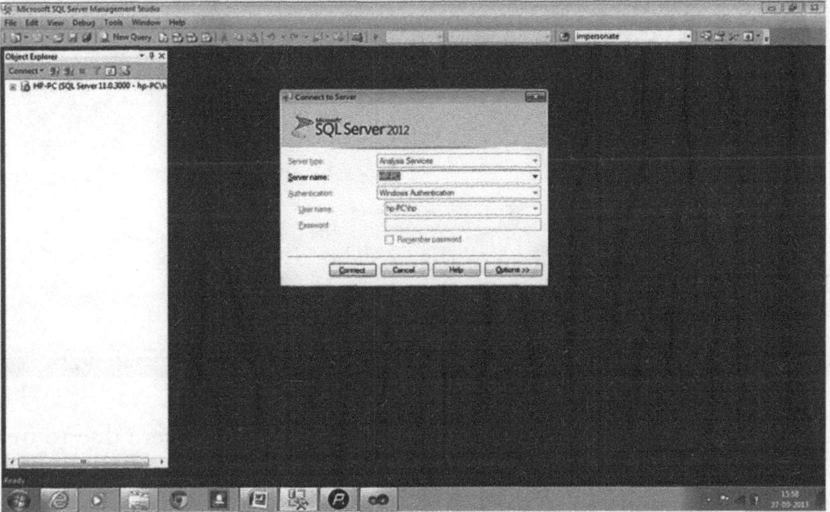

6. Expand databases. Expand ToothworksDM. Expand cubes folder. Right click on Toothworks and select browse.

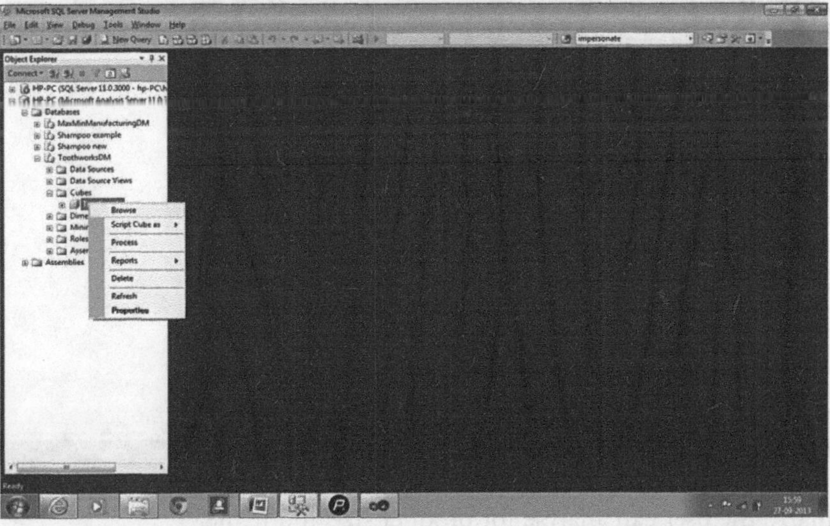

7. Drag and drop total sales from measure group onto the right window. The total sales made by the Toothworks Agent till date is displayed.

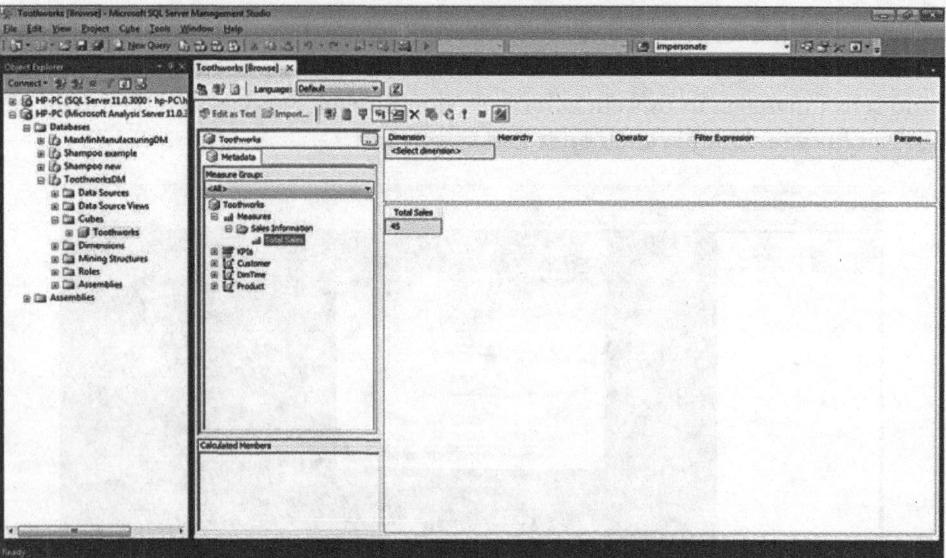

8. Next if the agent wishes to find out how many total sales were due to unmarried customers and how many due to married, just drag and drop marital status attribute from customer dimension to the left of total sales.

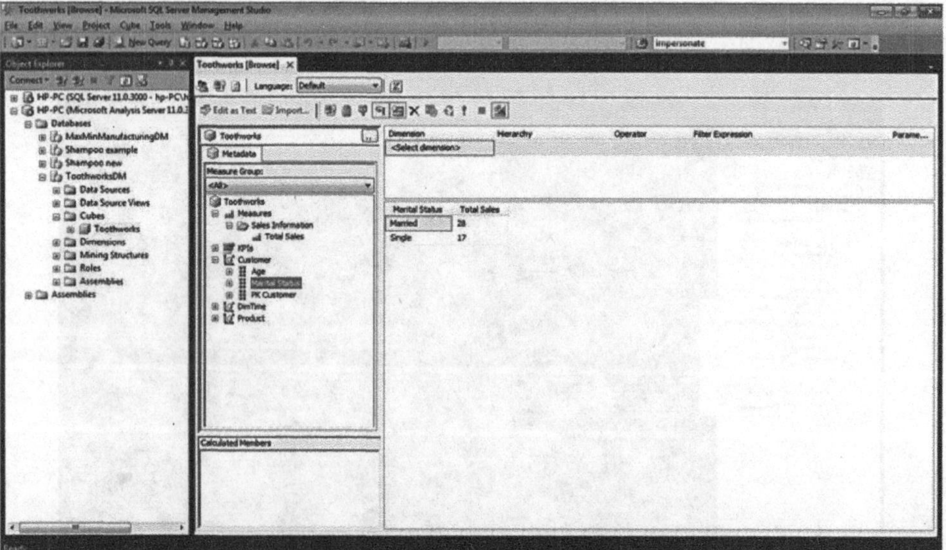

9. Similarly, the user can analyse for product size and name.

10. Or how many sales occurred each month in a year.

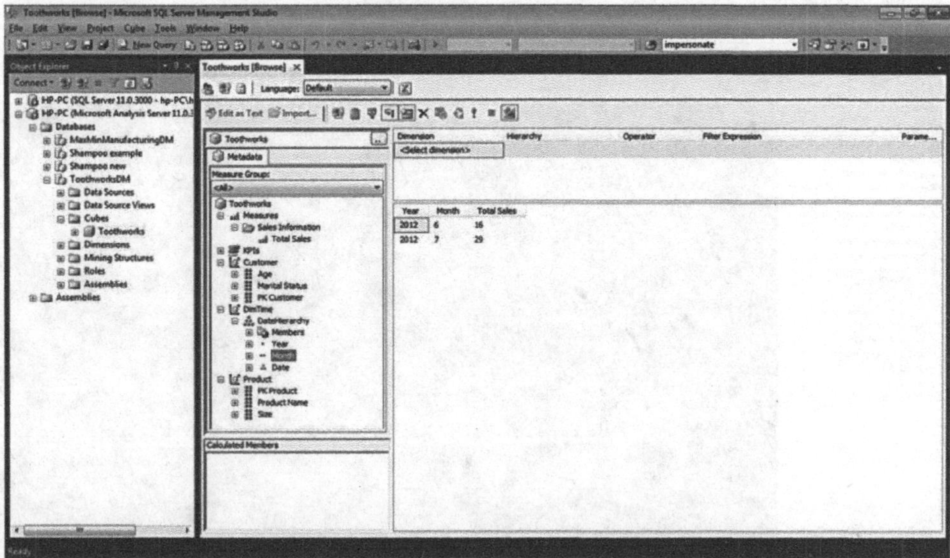

MDX Queries on OLAP

11. To execute queries on a multidimensional cube created, open SQL Server Management Studio. Connect to Analysis services database.

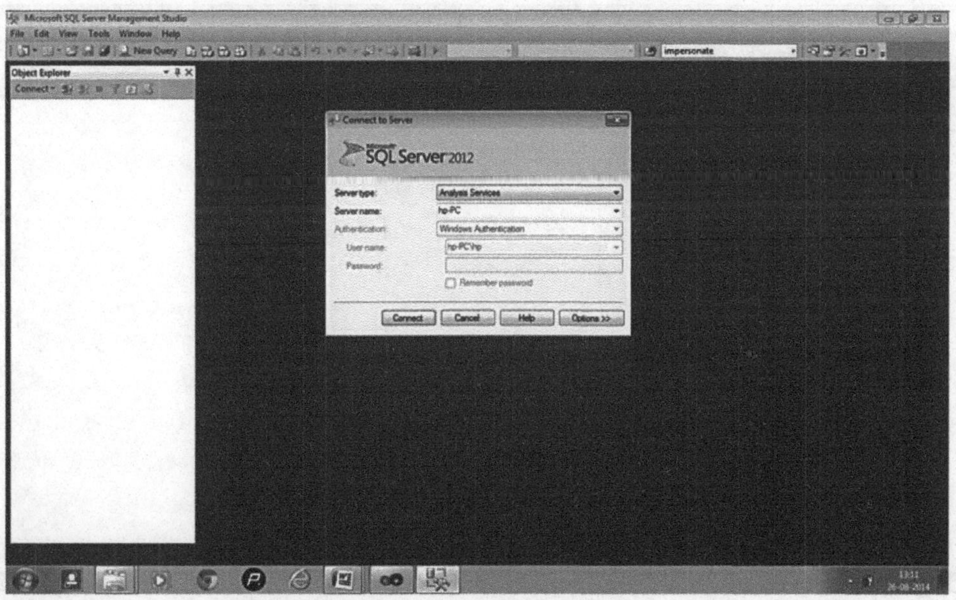

12. Expand databases and select ToothworksDM. Select the new query from upper ribbon:

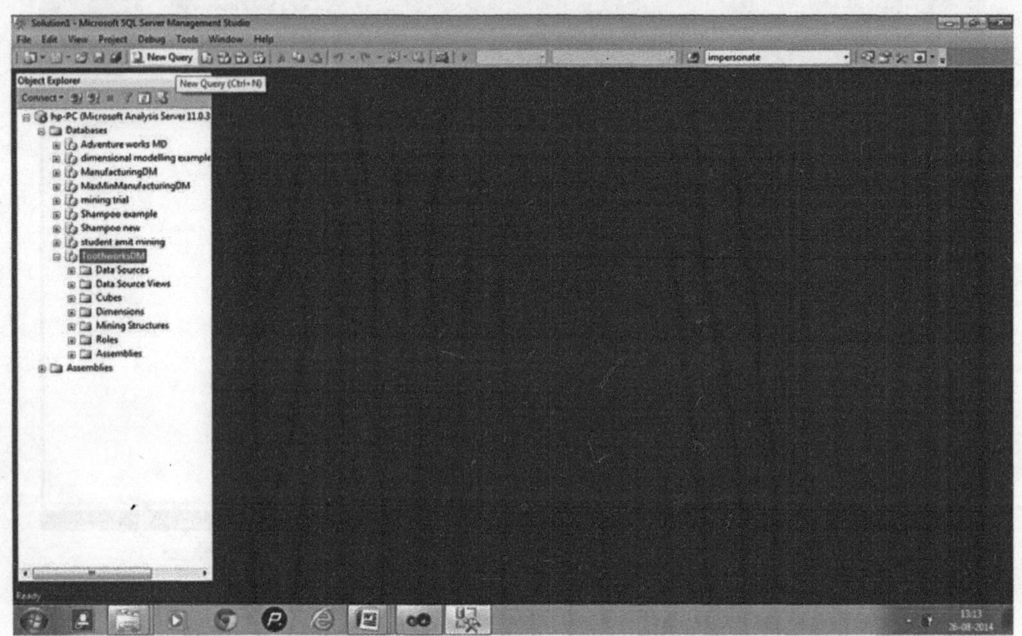

13. A new window opens as shown below.

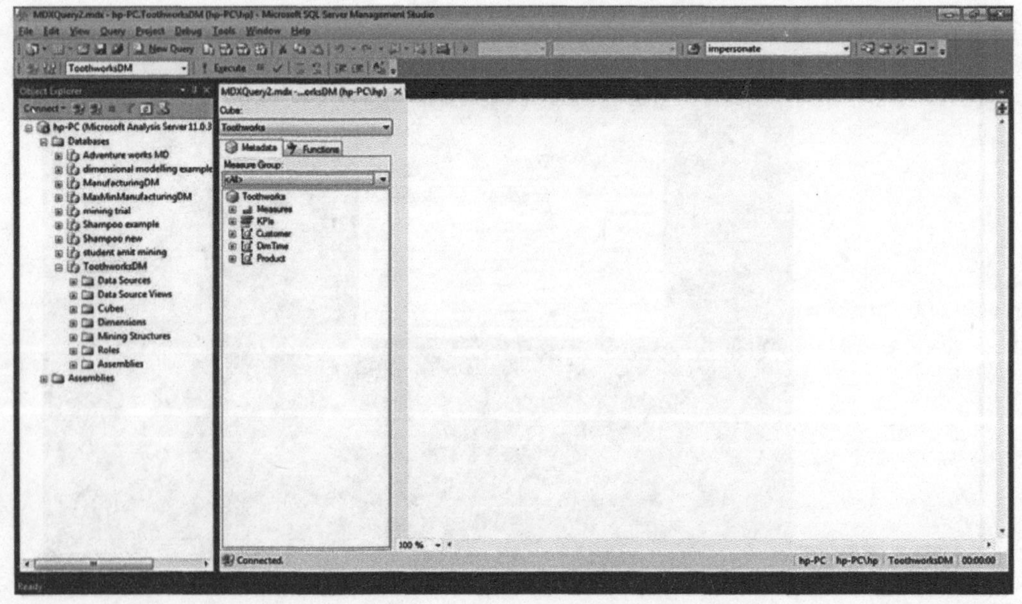

14. First query is to execute the **basic select statement to retrieve all members** from the cube:
Select * From [DatabaseName].[Schema].[TableName]

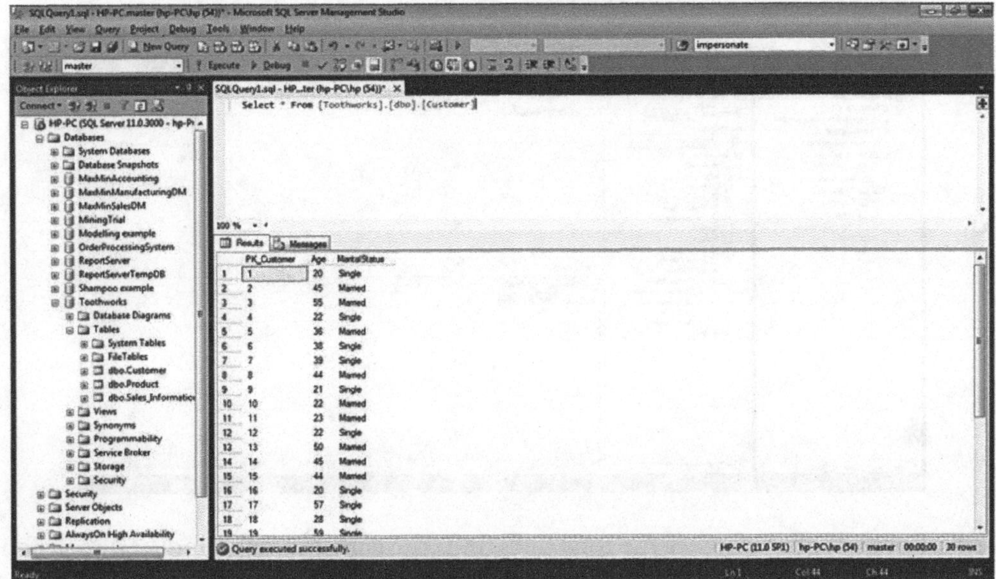

15. Execute the **basic select statement**:
This query retrieves the default measure value.

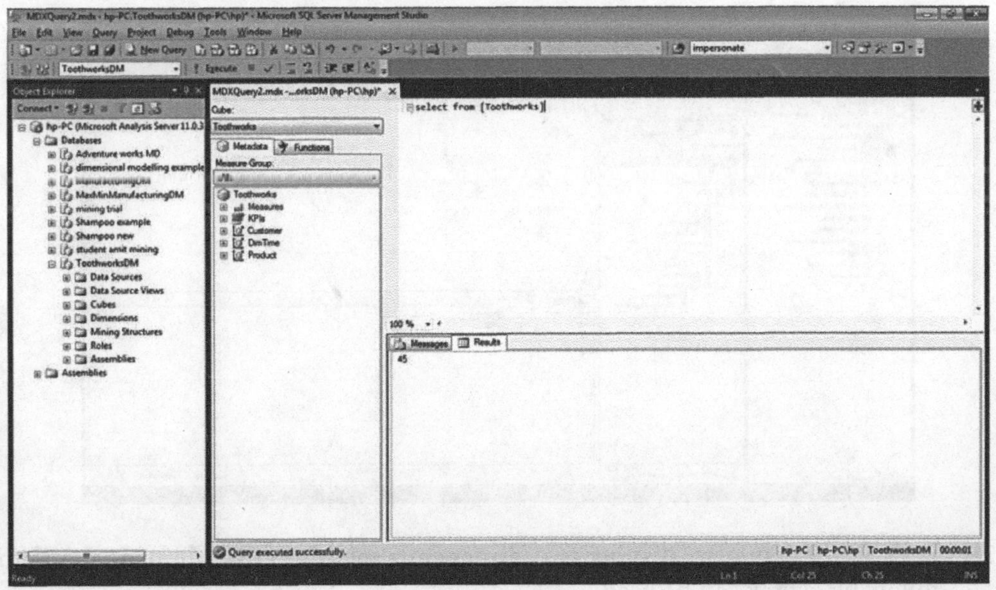

16. **Query dimensions**
SELECT {[set of dimension members]} ON COLUMNS
FROM [cube name]

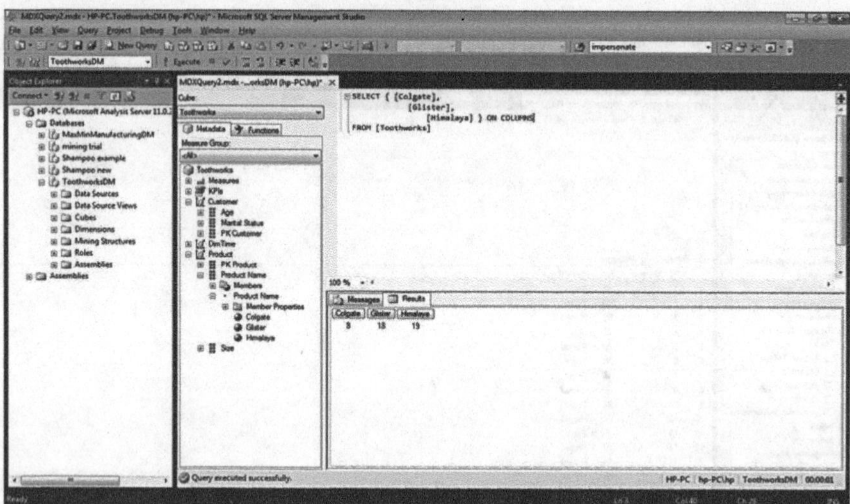

The above query fetches the total sales from the cube for each product dimension member specified which is Colgate, Glister and Himalaya.

17. Rather than explicitly specifying the member name, you can do the following:
SELECT [Product Name].Members ON COLUMNS
FROM [Toothworks]

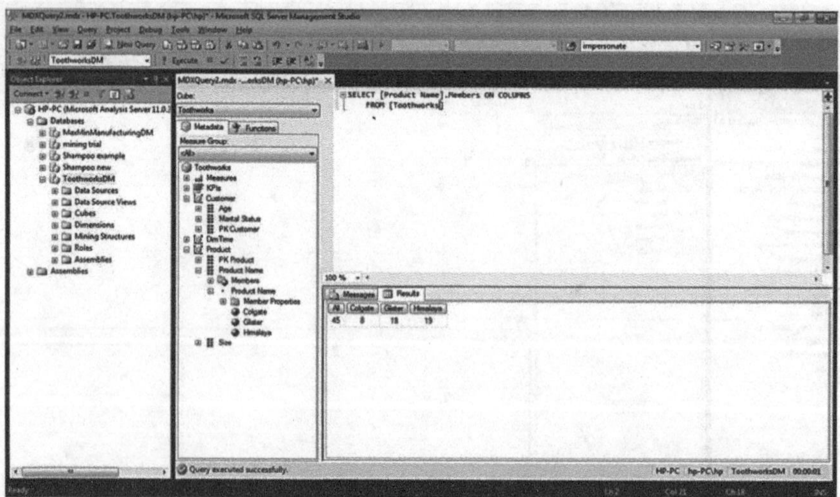

18. If the user wants to **display two dimension members simultaneously**, then following syntax can be used:

SELECT {set of dimension members} ON COLUMNS,
{set of dimension members} ON ROWS
FROM [cube name]

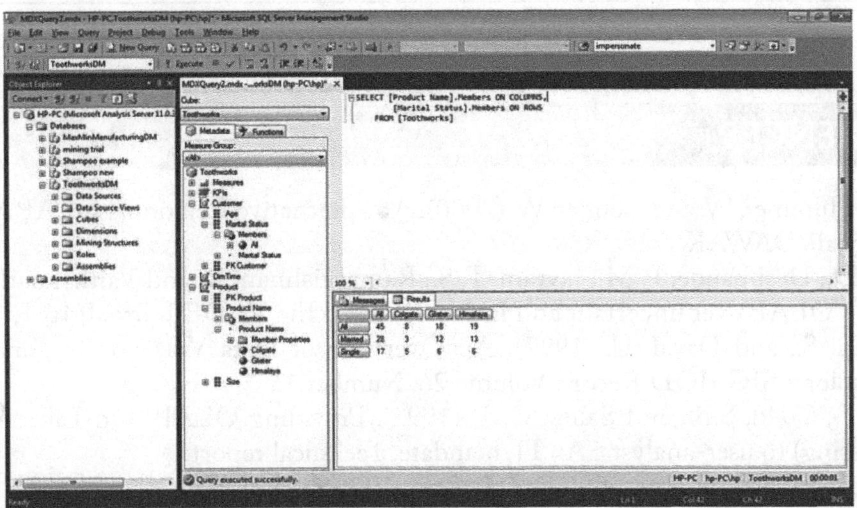

19. **Slicers**

The general syntax for slicer is as under:
SELECT {set of dimension members} ON COLUMNS,
{set of dimension members} ON ROWS,
FROM [Cube Name]
WHERE [Measures or Dimension Member]
For the specified slicer value, this query would fetch all possible combinations of dimension member selected on row and column.

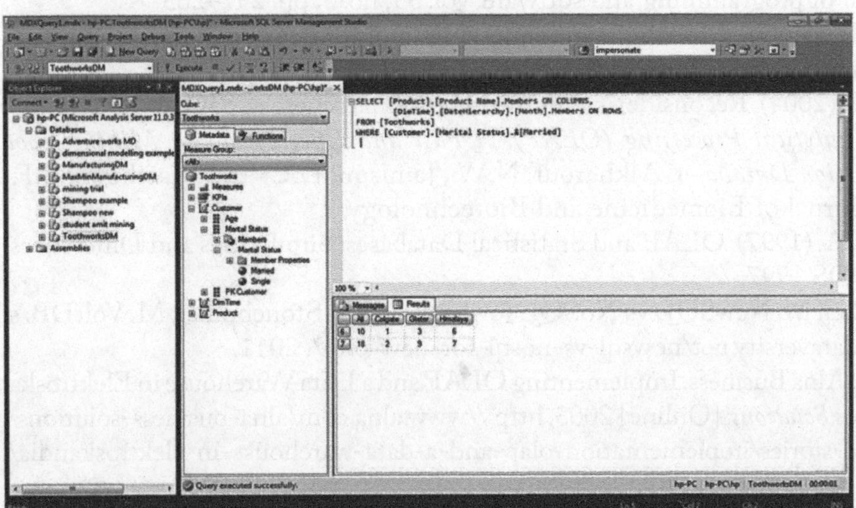

Here, the query fetches how many sales occurred due to married customers for given dimension members. The query also shows the use of "&" operator which is a reference operator.

REFERENCES

Bauer, A. Hummer, W. and Lehner, W. (2000). An Alternative Relational OLAP Modeling Approcah, DAWAK.

Burdick, D., Deshpande, P. M., Jayram, T. S., Ramakrishnan, R. and Vaithyanathan, S. K. (2006). OLAP over uncertain and imprecise data, The VLDB Journal, 16:1, 123–144.

Chaudhuri, S., and Dayal, U. (1997). An Overview of Data Warehousing and OLAP Technology. SIGMOD Record Volume 26, Number 1.

Codd, E.F., Codd, S.B., and Salley, C. T. (1993). Providing OLAP (On-Line Analytical Processing) to user-analysts: An IT mandate. Technical report.

Data Cubes Efficiently, *Proc. of SIGMOD Conf.*, 1996.

Grohser, T. Global Online Gaming Company Deploying SQL Server 2008 to support 100 Terabytes. *Microsoft Case Studies.* 2: http://www.microsoft.com/casestudies/Microsoft-SQL-Server-2008/bwin/Global-Online-Gaming-Company-Deploying-SQL-Server-2008-to-support-100-Terabytes/4000001470, 2008.

How a Financial Services Company Developed a Performance Report for Clients, Saved $200K and Sold $167,000,000 of Equity in Just 9 Months. *WinMetrics – BI Case Studies.* [Online] http://www.winmetrics.com/olap_casestudies.html.

Joe, C. (2006). Analytics and OLAP in SQL.

Kuznetsov, D.Yu., Kudryavtsev, A. (2009). "A mathematical model of the OLAP cubes" journal of programming and software, vol. 35, no. 5, pp. 257–265.

Marcel, P. (1999). Modeling and querying multidimensional databases: An overview, Networking and Information Systems Journal, 2:5, 515–548.

Martyn, T. (2004). Reconsidering multi-dimensional schemas, SIGMOD Rec., 33:1, 83–88.

Online Analytical Processing (OLAP): A Fast and Effective Data Mining Tool for Gene Expression Databases. Alkharouf, N.W., Jamison, D.C. and Matthews, B.F. 2, (2005) s.l.: Journal of Biomedicine and Biotechnology.

Shoshani, A. (1997). OLAP and Statistical Databases: Similarities and Differences. Tutorials of PODS 1997.

Stonebraker, M. NewSQL vs NoSQL for New OLTP, Stonebraker, M. VoltDB. s.l.: http://www.dataversity.net/newsql-vs-nosql-for-new-oltp/, 2011.

Solutions, Alna Business. Implementing OLAP and a Data Warehouse in Elektroskandia. *Alna Business Solutions.* [Online] 2003. http://www.alna.com/alna-business-solutions/about-us/success-stories/implementation-olap-and-a-data-warehouse-in-elektroskandia/.

Trujillo, J., and Palomar, M. (1998). "An Object Oriented Approach to Multidimensional Database Conceptual Modeling (OOMD)". In Proc. of the ACM 1st International Workshop on Data warehousing and OLAP (DOLAP'98), Washington D.C., The USA pp. 16–21.

Vaisman, A. and Mendelzon, A. (2001). A Temporal Query Language for OLAP: Implementation and a Case Study, DBPL.

Yuan Hong, Houcun. H.E. (1999). Online Analysis and Data Warehouse Modeling Technologies [J]. Computer Application Research 12.

CHAPTER 9

Key Performance Indicators

After going through this chapter, you will be able to

- Understand the concept of key performance indicators
- Understand the meaning of balanced scorecard
- Understand the importance of KPI-based balanced scorecard
- Understand the significance of dashboard
- Get the in-depth knowledge of KPI-based dasboards

INTRODUCTION

"Not everything that can be counted counts, and not everything that counts can be counted."

—Albert Einstein

The success of any organisation depends on the constant evaluation of the actions that are taken by the organisation to reach its objectives. In the present era as there is much uncertainty in the business environment, it is essential for any organisation to constantly evaluate its actions to counter the dynamic forces. The KPIs, i.e., key performance indicators are designed to measure the performance of the organisation. Once the analytics is applied and actions are recommended based on the findings of the business analytics tool, it is very important to evaluate the actions taken on the basis of analytics tool to measure the actual performance with the desired performance. This helps not only to crosscheck the results of business analytics but also motivate managers to remain focused. KPIs are based on specific targets which are framed considering the overall objectives of an organisation. KPIs facilitate constant evaluation of the actions taken by the organisation to reach its goal. This, in turn, helps in getting continuous feedback from concerned managers. Moreover, as the organisation need to constantly change its actions because of a changing environment, the KPIs help the organisation to constantly measure its actual performance against desired. The actual performance is measured by applying certain specific metrics, for example, if the overall objective of an organisation is the customer satisfaction. Applying KPI, the metric can be defined so as to measure the complaint resolution time and customer churn rate to measure the performance of an organisation towards its overall objective, i.e., customer satisfaction. Similarly, consider that the objective of an organisation is to increase the sales by 100% in the current financial year. The organisation can frame specific KPI so as to note the number of leads converted into actual sales or number of new leads generated. Organisations can also apply KPI-based Balanced Scorecard and KPI-based Dashboard for measuring the key parameters.

Try to note the above example very carefully, with the help of KPIs; it is possible for organisations to set quantitative metrics which can be measured to gauge the overall performance of the organisation. KPIs help in fixing accountability as every manager knows that his performance will be measured constantly applying KPIs, and in case of any deviation from the set targets, he will be held accountable.

KEY PERFORMANCE INDICATORS (KPIs)

> All KPIs are metrics, but only those metrics are KPIs which measure the specific business objectives of the organisation.

As various organisations are competing for the same set of customers which results in immense competitive environment. The organisation needs to constantly evaluate its performance so as to counter the competitive forces. There is no room for complacency as organisations cannot afford it. Rather, to survive in the present time, organisations need to be proactive. Every organisation needs to constantly change its strategy/actions so as to handle the intense competition. To overcome this situation, organisations are applying KPIs, i.e., key performance indicators, based on metrics, which helps to measure the performance of the organisation. But, it is very important to note that all KPIs are metrics, but all metrics are not KPIs. As metric means quantifiable indicator, KPIs are those quantifiable indicators which help to measure the performance of the organisation. That is why all KPIs are metrics, but only those metrics are KPIs which measure the specific business objectives of the organisation. This means that KPIs are based on overall business objectives, and hence, it is very important that appropriate metrics should be selected for KPIs so that the overall objectives of an organisation can be quantified. For example, to measure the customer loyalty in a store, a retail store can set metrics as

- Measuring the loyalty points earned by customers
- Purchase rate

"Measurements of activity is a vital gear in your business machine."

—John Standaloft

Although the purchase rate is a metric, but in this case it is not KPIs as the overall objective is to measure the customer loyalty. The purchase rate tells the purchasing done by every type of customer, but loyalty points earned metric will give the exact information regarding the points accumulated by loyal customers. When KPIs are based on metrics, it helps the organisation to replace the guess work with certain concrete facts and figures. These facts and figures guide the organisation to formulate the future course of actions. Measuring the objective through specific metric gives the exact information to the manager whether the organisation is moving in the right direction to achieve overall organisational objective or not.

"KPI's should not constitute every company metric for analysis and evaluation. Rather, KPI's should reflect the most important objectives of the business."

—Avinash Kaushik, Co-Founder and Chief Education Officer for Market Motive

---

Example of KPI

A pharmaceutical company has set a business objective which is as follows:

Business Objective – To increase the business by 20% in the year 2014

Once the objective is formulated, by applying business analytics, the organisation chalks out various courses of actions so as to counter the competition and to achieve the business objective. But, it is also important for the organisation to constantly measure the actual performance of the organisation based on the actions suggested by the analytical team. Applying KPI, the pharmaceutical company has framed following metrics:

- Number of new drugs manufactured in 2014
- Increase in sales of drugs in 2014
- Expenses on R&D
- Number of new clients added in 2014
- Number of new/additional manufacturing facilities added in 2014

These metrics are measured at weekly, monthly and quarterly basis so as to measure the overall performance of the organisation.

"Measures that help decision makers define and measure progress toward business goals. KPI metrics translate complex measures into a simple indicator that allows decision makers to assess the current situation and act quickly."

—KAIZEN Analytics

CHARACTERISTICS OF KPI

The KPIs have specific characteristics which are listed below:

Characteristics of KPI:

1. Metric Based
2. Reflection of Top Management Thinking
3. Information
4. Simple
5. Quantifiable
6 Limited Number Approach

1. **Metric Based**: As KPIs should measure the progress of the organisation towards its goals; hence, KPIs are based on metrics. But, it should be noted that all KPIs are based on metrics, but all metrics are not KPI because only those metrics are KPIs which help in measuring the business objectives of an organisation.
2. **Reflection of Top Management Thinking**: As the KPIs are based on overall objectives, it is evident that the top management plays a very important role in defining the KPIs. The overall objectives are defined by the top management and to measure the performance of the organisation based on the overall objectives, KPIs are also framed by active involvement of the top management because any mistake in defining the KPIs will result in the erroneous measurement of the performance. Moreover, the involvement of the top management also sends a positive signal to all the managers that KPIs are very important for measuring progress of organisation towards its overall objective.
3. **Information**: KPIs are meant to measure the actual performance of the organisation. Hence, it is imperative that KPIs should give exact information about the performance of an organisation based on the actions taken by the organisation to reach its goals. Once the organisation sets the objective, the next important task is the implementation of specific actions based on analytics so as to reach the overall objectives, but it is also critical to constantly evaluate its actions. Moreover, the constant competition and dynamic environment often force organisations to change its actions. The KPIs should give exact information regarding the performance of each and every action taken by the organisation so that future strategies/actions can be formulated.
4. **Simple**: KPIs are based on the overall objectives of an organisation for constant evaluation of the performance of an organisation. It is also possible to fix accountability of various managers applying KPIs. KPIs act as track on which the organisation has to trend and that too without any deviation. But, it is essential that the concerned managers should be able to understand KPIs without any ambiguity. Because in case of any ambiguity, it can lead to wrong measurement of the key indicators. The KPIs should be defined considering the business objectives but in a simpler language.
5. **Quantifiable**: KPIs are based on overall objectives which can be measured. Hence, one of the main characteristics of KPI is that it should be quantifiable. The overall objectives may be qualitative in nature, but as KPIs are based on metrics; hence, the organisation should be very careful in defining the KPIs. If KPIs are not quantifiable, then it will not be possible to define metrics, and ultimately it will not be possible to measure the actual performance.
6. **Limited Number Approach**: As KPIs guide the organisation in measuring its performance, sometimes organisations go overboard and try to define the number of KPIs thinking that more the number of KPIs, greater will be accountability. But, it is always advisable to limit the number of KPIs. The large number of KPIs lead to distraction of any manager's attention, hence limiting the number of KPIs results in a better evaluation of performance of an organisation.

KPIs are important because when they are choosing it tells investors what management thinks is important.

—FTSE 100 Company

PROCESS OF SETTING KPIs

Process of setting KPIs:

- Business Objectives
- Communicate
- Take Opinion
- Final Decision

As KPIs are very critical aspect which leads to measurement of actual performance of the organisation, and to get best results from the application of KPIs it is significant that the KPIs should be framed very diligently. The process of setting KPI is as follows:

1. **Business Objectives**: To define KPIs, organisations should have clearly defined objectives. The KPIs are based on objectives and if the objectives are not clearly defined, then it would result in a faulty description of the KPIs. So, the first step in setting the KPIs is the clear definition of the business objectives of an organisation.
2. **Communicate**: It is essential that all the managers should know the business objectives in detail. For this, it is advisable that the top management should call a meeting of all the concerned managers and communicate the business objectives and discuss the rationale behind setting those objectives.
3. **Take Opinion**: The overall objectives can be fulfilled if all the departments work as a team in order to achieve common objectives. This can be achieved only if all the managers feel a sense of belongingness with the organisation. Although the setting of KPIs is the top management's call but all the functional managers should also be part of the entire process. The top management should take opinion from the concerned functional managers so as to know that how the set business objectives can be quantified vis-à-vis various functional parameters. This not only helps to give a sense of belongingness to the managers but also the top management will get advice from those people who know the ground reality which in turn helps in framing accurate KPIs.
4. **Final Decision**: After getting the response from all the functional managers, the top management should take the final decision of setting the KPIs. The KPIs are set considering all the opinions of the managers and the overall objectives of the organisation. After setting the KPIs, the top management should convey the set KPIs to all the concerned managers in the organisation.

In a nutshell, KPIs are:

- Metrics that are quantifiable indicators.
- Quantifiable indicators which measure the progress of the organisation towards the business objective.
- Based on business objectives.

- That guide the organisation to move in the right direction.
- That measure the progress of the organisation towards the set business objectives.

"KPI help organizations achieve organizational goals through the definition and measurement of progress. The key indicators are agreed upon by an organization and are indicators which can be measured that will reflect success factors."

—Bruce Clay, Inc, Global Internet Marketing Solutions

BALANCED SCORECARD

> Balanced scorecard is yet another tool to measure the performance of the organisation. Balanced scorecard was developed by Robert Kaplan and David Norton.

Balanced scorecard is yet another tool for measuring the performance of the organisation. Balanced scorecard was developed by Robert Kaplan and David Norton. Balanced scorecard helps in two aspects; firstly, the organisation can frame the performance objectives, applying the balanced scorecard, and secondly, applying balanced scorecard organizations can also define the measures in order to gauge the performance of the organisation. Every organisation needs to define the precise performance objectives which act as specific guidelines to aid in the execution of the strategies. The balanced scorecard helps to formulate specific performance objectives by considering four perspectives. These four perspectives are (See Exhibit 9.1):

- Customer perspective
- Internal process perspective
- Learning and growth perspective
- Financial perspective

1. **Customer Perspective**: This perspective takes into account all those customers who matter in deciding the overall strategy of an organisation. This perspective defines what is the value proposition in serving the target customer. The organisation should formulate performance objective considering following customer perspectives. According to Treacy and Wiersema (Discipline of Market Leaders), the organisation can attain following excellences to win the customers.

> Four perspectives of balanced scorecard are
>
> - Customer Perspective
> - Internal Process Perspective
> - Learning and Growth Perspective
> - Financial Perspective

   (a) *Operational excellence:* An organisation can decide to attain operational excellence by constant improvement in the basic operational parameters, for example, the organisation can attain the operational excellence by reducing the undue operational expenses. The Wall Mart has attained operational excellence by reducing the expenses on its inventory.

(b) *Product leadership:* An organisation can become a product leader by constant innovation. The customers can be satisfied by providing new and innovative products which satisfy the unfulfilled psychological needs of the customers, e.g., Apple.

(c) *Customer intimacy:* It is not only important to manufacture new products, but also very important to focus on the after-sales service. The organisations can win the confidence of the customers by providing them unmatched after-sales service.

Depending on the above-discussed scenarios, the organisation should formulate specific performance objectives.

2. **Internal Process Perspective**: In the balanced scorecard, this perspective identifies key internal processes which are important to serve the customers in the best possible manner. To deliver any product or service, it is vital that all the internal processes should work in tandem in an organisation. The organisation should question itself that what kinds of internal processes are needed to satisfy the needs of the customer. For example, if delivery time is important for a firm, it should identify which internal processes can be utilised to reduce the delivery time. After doing self-introspection, the organisation should formulate appropriate performance objectives.
3. **Learning and Growth Perspective**: For the successful execution of business strategy, the functional managers require constant learning and growth opportunities. The only mode of survival for today's organisations is to never stop learning and hence growing. In the balanced scorecard, learning and growth perspective takes into account all the learning facilities needed to execute the business strategy. For example, what kind of training needs to be imparted to employees for successful implementation of a strategy? Besides, it also aids the strategist in understanding what is required to sustain a firm in the future, such as how to manage turnover in the firm. The organisation should consider all those capabilities into consideration before formulating performance objective.
4. **Financial Perspective**: Financial perspective in the balanced scorecard identifies all the financial aspects which are needed to execute the business strategy. This perspective helps to consider all the financial policies and strategies needed to accomplish the set business strategy. The organisation should take into account the financial perspective for formulating the performance objective.

Exhibit 9.1 Four quadrants of balanced scorecard

Customer perspective	Internal process
Learning and growth	Financial perspective

From the above discussion, the basic concept of balanced scorecard must be clear to all the readers. But, it is also evident from the above discussion that if all the above four perspectives are not quantifiable, then it will be very difficult to measure the performance of the organisation. Applying KPIs, it is possible to define metrics which measure the overall performance objectives of the organisation considering the above-mentioned four perspectives. The organizations can apply KPIs based balanced scorecard (discussed below) to measure the performance. One of the key features of this kind of balanced scorecard is that it not only helps to formulate the performance objectives, but also helps the organisation to define metrics to measure the performance of the organisation.

KPI-BASED BALANCED SCORECARD

Applying KPIs, it is possible to define metrics which measure the overall performance objectives of the organisation considering the four perspectives.

As KPIs are based on quantitative indicators, applying KPI, the four perspectives of balanced scorecard, can be defined in terms of quantifiable indicators as (see Exhibit 9.2):

1. **Customer Perspective**: The organisation can apply the following KPIs to measure the performance objective based on the customer perspective:
   (a) Customer retention rate
   (b) Number of new customers added
   (c) Total number of customers
   (d) Number of leads converted into sales
   (e) Customer loyalty points earned
   (f) Expense on marketing
   (g) Increase in sales compared with last year
2. **Internal Process**: The following KPIs can be applied to measure performance objective based on the internal processes:
   (a) Average lead time
   (b) New products added
   (c) New patents
   (d) R&D expenses
   (e) Count of unproductive steps removed
   (f) Area of working space
3. **Financial Perspective**: The following KPIs can be applied to measure performance objective based on the financial performance of the organisation:
   (a) Revenue earned
   (b) Return on equity
   (c) Return on investment
   (d) Economic value added
   (e) Market value
   (f) Return on total assets
   (g) Debt on equity ration

Exhibit 9.2 KPI-based balanced scorecard

Customer Perspective **KPI:**	**Internal Process** **KPI:**
(a) Customer retention rate (b) Number of new customers added (c) Total number of customers (d) Number of leads converted into sales (e) Customer loyalty points earned (f) Expense on marketing (g) Increase in sales compared with last year	(a) Average lead time (b) New products added (c) New patents (d) R&D expenses (e) Removal of unproductive steps (f) Optimum utilisation of space rate
Learning and Growth **KPI:**	**Financial Perspective** **KPI:**
(a) Training expenditure (b) Attrition rate (c) Employee participation (d) Number of employees who have improved their qualification (e) Number of suggestions received from employees	(a) Revenue earned (b) Return on equity (c) Return on investment (d) Economic value added (e) Market value (f) Return on total assets (g) Debt on equity ratio

4. **Learning and Growth Perspective**: The following KPIs can be applied to measure performance objective based on the learning and growth of an organisation:
   (a) Training expenditure
   (b) Attrition rate
   (c) Employee participation

Exhibit 9.3 Balanced scorecard in airline company

Customer perspective Performance objective—increase customer retention rate	**Internal process** Performance objective—To have better co-ordination between all the departments
Learning and growth Performance objective—To motivate the ground crew to reduce the turnaround time	**Financial perspective** Performance objective—To increase per seat revenue

(d) Number of employees who have improved their qualification
(e) Number of suggestions received from employees

Example of KPI Based Balanced Scorecard

An airline company can apply the balanced scorecard in the following manner: (See Exhibit 9.3)

1. **Customer Perspective**: Performance objective—increase the customer retention rate
2. **Internal Process**: Performance objective—to have better coordination between all the departments
3. **Financial Perspective**: Performance objective—to increase per seat revenue
4. **Learning and Growth**: Performance objective—to motivate the ground crew so as to reduce the turnaround time

Exhibit 9.4 KPI based balanced scorecard in airline company

Customer perspective KPI: Satisfaction rating	**Internal process** KPI: Target 93% on time departure is fixed
Learning and growth KPI: Number of training programs held, number of applications received for training programme	**Financial perspective** KPI: Profit as percentage of sales

It is evident from the above discussion that the Airline company needs to measure above performance objectives so as to gauge the actual performance of the organisation. This can be only possible by designing the balanced scorecard based on KPIs. Going further same Airline Company can set specific KPIs so as to measure the performance of the company considering four perspectives (See Exhibit 9.4).

DASHBOARD

Presently, managers need to constantly monitor the critical parameters of the organisation. But with the intense competition, the scope of work for managers is increasing with each passing day. Managers have limited time and in this limited time managers need to control diverse functions of the organisation. To overcome this situation, organisations are widely applying the concept of dashboards. The dashboard is one page view of the performance of the organisation. As the

> Dashboard is one page view of the performance of the organisation.

picture speaks a thousand words, applying dashboard, it is possible to visually display the most important information needed for measuring the performance of the organisation. The information is presented with the help of graphs and charts which are easy to interpret. Although the dashboard helps to display information in a concise manner, but only display of the information is not sufficient; managers need to measure the performance of the organisation. This can be done by applying the concept of KPIs in the dashboards. The KPI-based dashboard represents information regarding those metrics which measure the performance of the organisation. When a dashboard is based on KPIs, it helps to monitor the progress of the organisation towards the overall objectives. The KPIs help to identify key measures needed to measure the performance of an organisation and dashboards help to present all the information regarding the key measures in a single view. The concept of dashboard for performance measurement in organizations is derived from dashboards of the cars. As in cars, all the key performance indicators are displayed with the help of dashboard, which guides the driver in analysing the speed, temperature, fuel, average, etc. Similarly, the organisation applies dashboards to display the important information in a concise manner. The KPI-based dashboards help to analyse the key indicators/measures which in turn help in taking quick decisions.

"We have implemented a comprehensive incident management system that is used to drive the lagging KPIs. This feeds into our dashboard at a risk control system level and is rolled up along with the leading indicator performance to drive the top-level management statistics. The system tracks the status and drives improvements just because everyone can see the data."

—Barry Smart, Program Manager, Scottish Power

Features of Good Dashboard

A good dashboard should have the following features:

1. **Understandable**: As the dashboards are designed to give a quick view of the important information, it is imperative that information displayed by the dashboards should be easy to understand. The managers should be able to easily understand and interpret the information displayed by dashboard.
2. **Situation based**: The organisation has to monitor many parameters, it is always advisable to have particular situation/content based dashboards, for example, separate dashboards for Marketing, HR, Manufacturing and Finance.
3. **KPI Based**: Dashboards help to represent all the information in a concise manner; it is always good if the organisation designs the dashboards on the key performance indicators which help to monitor the progress of the organisation towards the overall objectives.

Features of good dashboard:

1. Understandable
2. Situation Based
3. KPI Based
4. Summarised
5. Graphical

4. **Summarised**: The main feature of the dashboard is that it presents the facts in a summarised form, so for a well designed dashboard it is important that the dashboard should present the information in a concise and informative manner.
5. **Graphical**: The managers have limited time and it is always easy to monitor the facts applying the graphs and charts. The dashboards should always be designed applying graphs and charts so that a manager can quickly analyse the performance of the key indicators.

DASHBOARD DESIGN

Dashboard design:

1. Hierarchy Based
2. Functionality Based

As pointed above, managers have to monitor many parameters, so it is always advisable to have a separate dashboard for key parameters. This segregation can be done by the following techniques:

1. **Hierarchy Based**: The dashboards can be designed based on different hierarchies in an organisation, for example, a dashboard for Chief Manager with the roll-up facility to view the consolidated view of the performance of all the departments. Similarly for the team leader, the dashboard displays overall team performance or with the drill-down capabilities to view the performance of a particular team member.
2. **Functionality Based**: The dashboards can also be designed based on functionality like
   - Marketing based dashboards
   - Human resource based dashboards
   - Manufacturing based dashboards
   - Finance based dashboards

   (a) *Applying Marketing Based Dashboards*: The Marketing Manager can view all the important information regarding marketing like
   - New customers added
   - New leads generated
   - Conversion of leads into actual sales

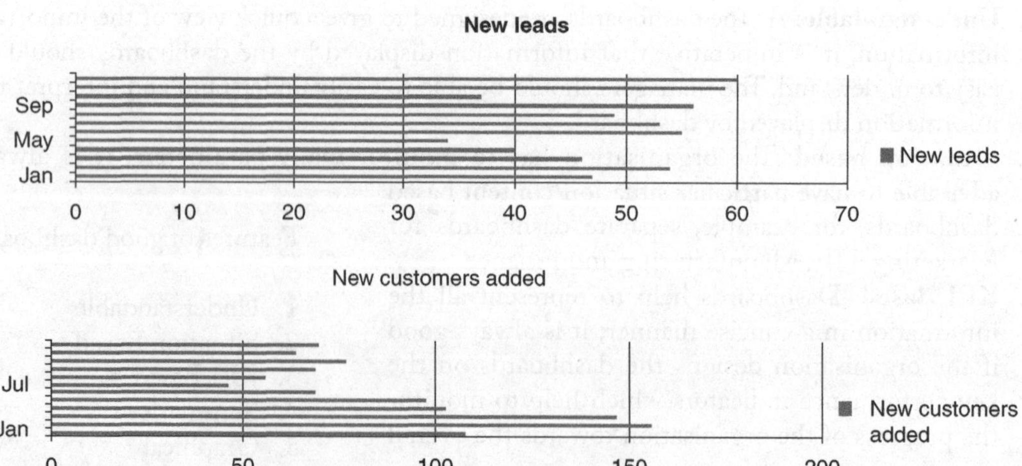

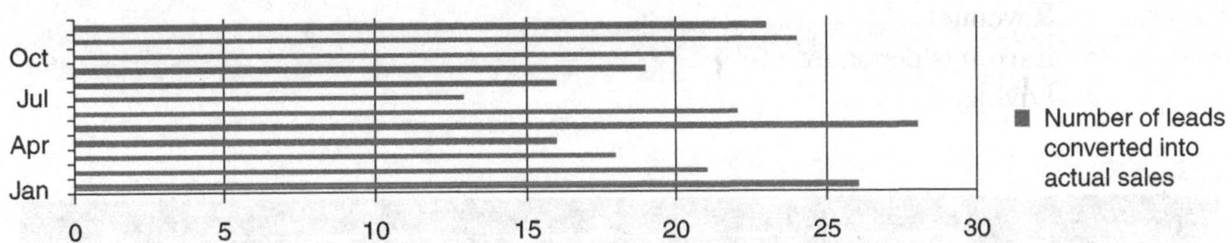

(b) The *Human Resource Based Dashboards:* The HR manager can view all the important information regarding the critical HR metrics like

- Headcount
- Payroll breakdown
- Attrition rate
- Training schedule

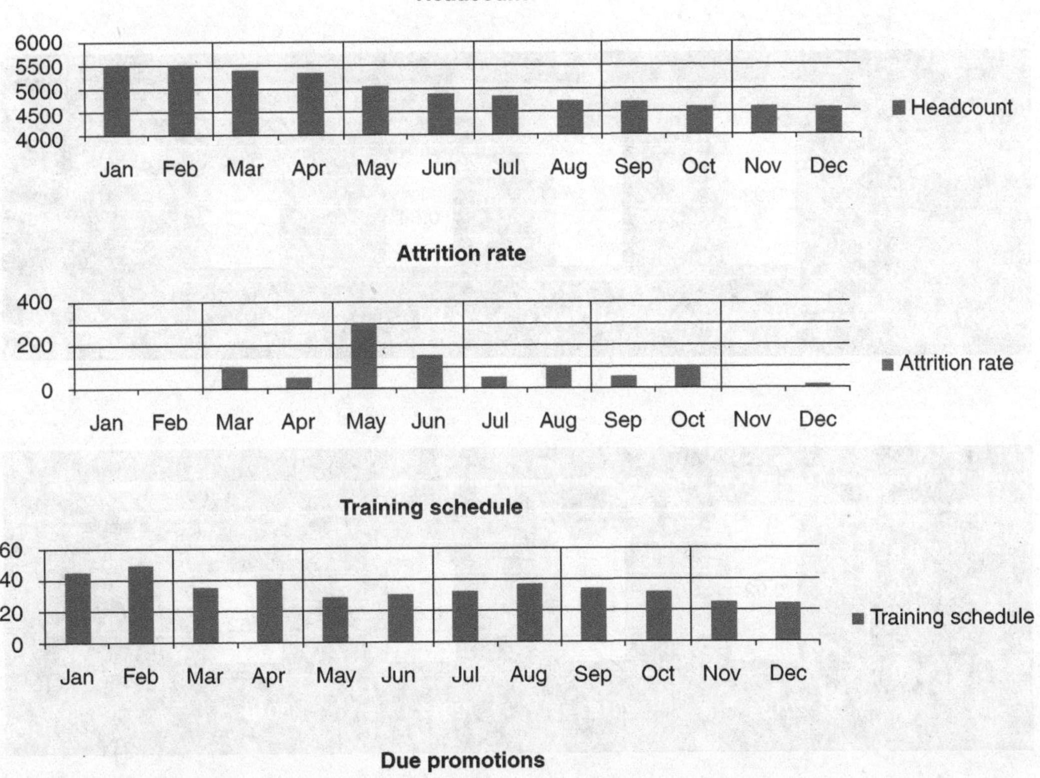

(c) The *Finance Based Dashboards:* The Finance Manager can view all the important information regarding critical financial metrics like

- Revenue
- Earnings per share
- Dividends

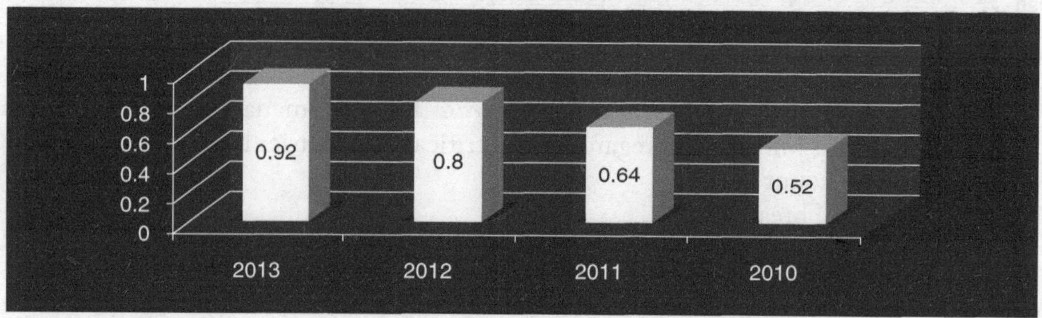

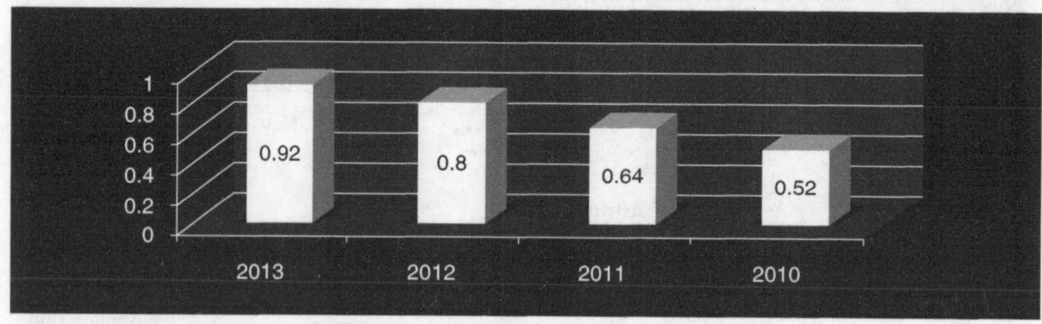

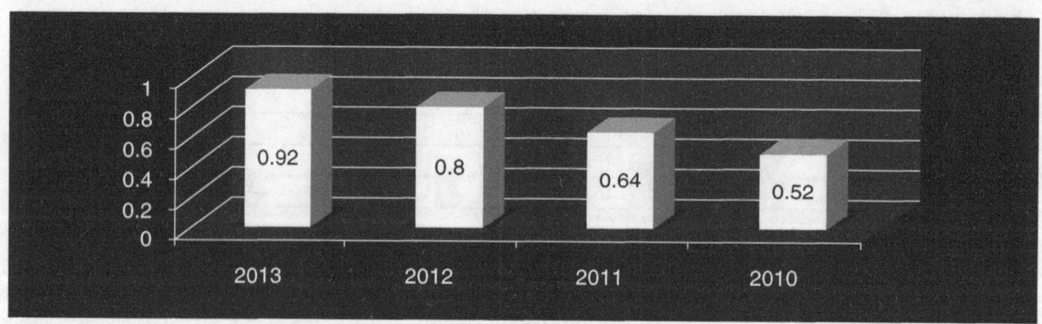

(d) The *Manufacturing-Based Dashboards:* The Production Manager can view all the important information regarding critical production metrics like

- Number of orders

- Orders manufactured location-wise
- Orders manufactured by units in a particular location
- Number of defects in product at a particular location
- Total number of orders shipped from different locations

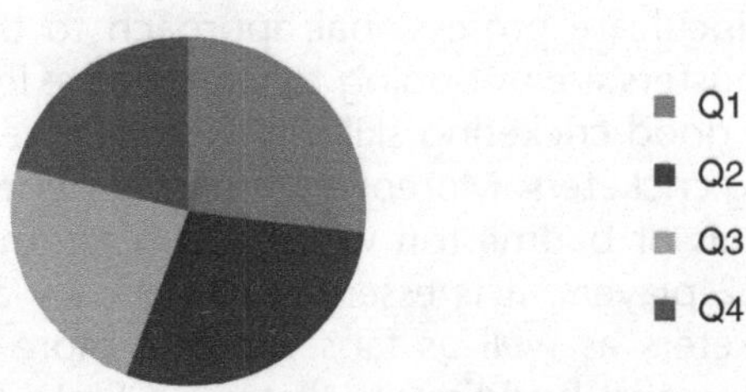

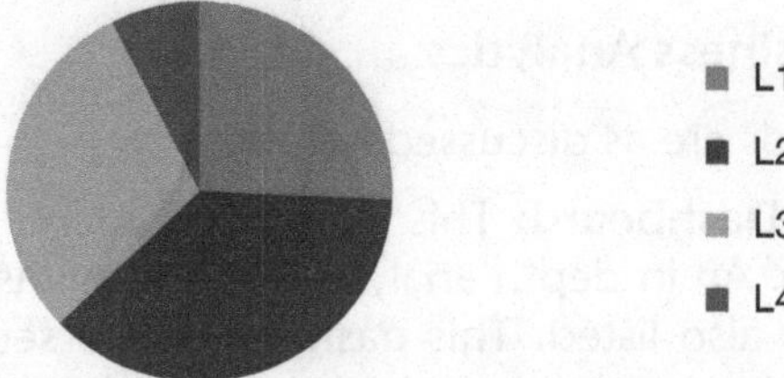

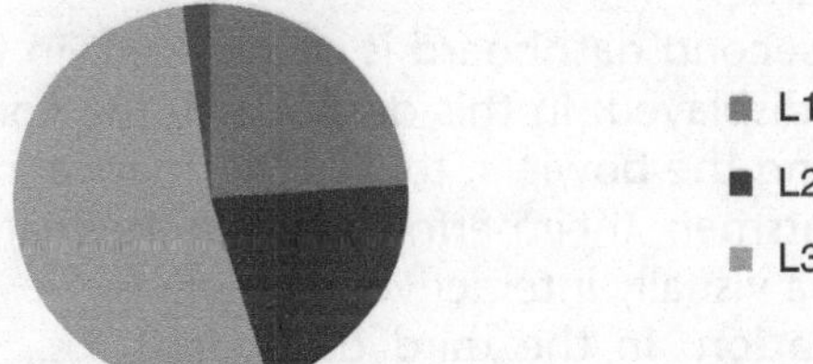

In Practice

Application of Business Analytics in State Cricket Board

Although cricket is the most famous game in India, but at the state level, there is a lukewarm response from the spectators. It is very important that there should be active participation from the spectators not only to revive the game at the state level, but also to inculcate professional approach to the game in the budding players. If the youngsters are not going to watch state level matches then it is not possible to imbibe good cricketing skills in them. There should be more involvement from budding cricketers. Moreover, in cricket there are a lot of data involved as opposed to tennis or badminton where there are maximum 4 players but in cricket there are 22 players. It is essential to critically analyse the huge data so that budding cricketers as well as fans can feel more engaged. To have more interaction with fans and budding cricketers, a State Cricket Board decides to implement business analytics and design an interactive website. The State Cricket Board decides to hire the services of Business Analytical Firm, Insightia, which implemented three dashboards in the website of the state cricket board.

Application of Business Analytics

The three dashboards are as discussed below:

1. **Critical Aspect Dashboard:** This dashboard identifies the critical areas of a particular match. An in-depth analysis of both teams and team's performance in those areas is also listed. This dashboard also sets targets for each critical area which the respective teams should achieve in order to increase the probability of winning the match. These targets are set by considering the past records of teams and present weather conditions. With the help of this dashboard, the budding cricketers get the insight knowledge of the critical aspects of the game.
2. **Live-Feed:** The second dashboard is of live-feed. In this dashboard, live score of the match is displayed. In this dashboard, the comparison of run rate, the statistics regarding the bowlers, their performance in the match, the statistics regarding the batsmen, their performance in the match, remaining overs, etc., are displayed in a visually interactive manner.
3. **Players' Information:** In the third dashboard, i.e., players' information, the statistics' regarding all the 22 players is displayed in visually separate sections for bowlers and batsmen. In the batsmen section, the strike rate of batsmen, number of centuries, a number of half centuries and conditions under which a particular batsman has performed well in the past and performance of particular batsmen on the same ground are displayed. Similarly, in the bowlers' section, the number of matches played by bowler, number of wickets taken by a particular bowler, past performance of a particular bowler on the same ground and the number of times five wickets taken by a particular bowler are also displayed.

Applying these dashboard, State Cricket Board is able to attract more budding players and spectators.

CONCLUSION

From the above discussion, one can comprehend the importance of measuring the performance of the organisation. Key performance indicators and dashboards are designed for this purpose. Not only managers need the application of analytics for taking relevant decisions, but also it is important that the actions suggested by analytics tool must be evaluated so that the effectiveness of analytics can be judged. Organisations also apply key performance indicators to design dashboards which are very beneficial to gauge the performance of the organisation.

KEY TERMS

- Key Performance Indicators (KPIs) 248
- Balanced Scorecard 252
- KPI based Balanced Score Card 254
- Dashboard 256
- Dashboard Design 258

SUMMARY

In this chapter, we have studied how organisations are applying key performance indicators. Going further in this chapter, all the characteristics of KPI are discussed in detail. As KPIs are formulated to measure the performance of an organisation, it is vital that KPIs should be formulated very diligently. All the important aspects related to the setting of KPIs are discussed in detail in this chapter. In the second part of this chapter, balanced scorecard is discussed. Balanced scorecard helps to formulate specific performance objectives by considering four perspectives. All these four perspectives, i.e., customer perspective, internal process perspective, learning and growth perspective and financial perspective are deliberated in this chapter. All the issues regarding application of KPI-based balanced scorecards are discussed in this chapter. In the last part, concept of the dashboard is discussed by taking relevant examples. To have a better understanding of the concepts of KPI and dashboard, review questions, assignment and project activity questions are given at the end of this chapter.

MULTIPLE CHOICE QUESTIONS

1. KPI stands for

a. Key performance indicators
b. Knowledge performance indicators
c. Kind performance indicators
d. Key performance industry

2. Metrics that help the organisation to measure the actions taken by the organisation to reach its business goals
   a. Gauge b. Key performance indicators
   c. Scale d. Measure
3. Which of the following is not a specific characteristic of KPI?
   a. Qualitative b. Quantitative
   c. Metric based d. Reflection of top management thinking
4. Choose the right sequence of setting of KPI.
   a. Business objectives, Take opinion, Communicate, Final decision
   b. Final decision, Take opinion, Communicate, Business objectives
   c. Communicate, Business objectives, Take opinion, Final decision
   d. Business objectives, Communicate, Take opinion, Final decision
5. Which of the following is not a perspective of the balanced scorecard?
   a. Customer perspective b. Internal process perspective
   c. Profit perspective d. Learning and growth perspective
6. Match the following.

Perspective	Feature
(a) Customer perspective	(1) This perspective helps to consider all the monetary policies and strategies needed to accomplish the set business strategy
(b) Internal process perspective	(2) This perspective takes into account all the learning facilities needed to execute the business strategy
(c) Learning and growth perspective	(3) This perspective takes into account all those customers who matter in deciding the overall strategy of an organisation
(d) Financial perspective	(4) In the balanced scorecard, this perspective identifies key internal processes which are important in order to serve the customers in the best possible manner

7. KPI based balanced scorecard is based on
   a. Quantitative indicators b. Qualitative indicators
   c. Same as balanced scorecard d. Measures non-financial aspects
8. Visual display of the performance of the organisation is known as
   a. KPI b. Balanced scorecard
   c. Report d. Dashboard
9. KPI-based dashboard presents
   a. Single view of key aspects b. Single view of non-key aspects
   c. Non-visual display of key aspects d. Same as that of simple dashboard

10. Choose the wrong options for dashboard design.
   a. Hierarchy based   b. Concept based
   c. Functionality based   d. Metric based

REVIEW QUESTIONS

1. What is the relevance of KPIs in the present competitive environment?
2. What are the characteristics of key performance indicators?
3. Discuss the process of framing appropriate key performance indicators for an organisation.
4. What do you understand by balanced scorecard? What is the relevance of KPI-based balanced scorecard?
5. What are KPI-based dashboards? Explain in detail.

ASSIGNMENT

1. Visit a nearby retail store and study the process of setting key performance indicators for measuring the progress of that retail store.
2. Suppose you are the administrator in a leading hospital in your city. Design a KPI-based balanced scorecard for measuring the performance of hospital.

PROJECT ACTIVITY

1. With the help of your concerned teacher, frame appropriate key performance indicators for measuring the performance of students in your course. Present this report to your teacher by using KPI-based Dashboard (based on MS Excel).

CASE STUDY

Building KPI-Based Dashboard for HRM

Key performance indicators enable the manager to graphically analyse the important aspects of an organisation. The manager or the decision maker with the aid of KPIs can monitor key aspects or key attributes of the performance of a firm. For example, for a sales manager, the key performance indicator of different regions under his authority would be total sales or new leads generated in the sales region. For this, the manager needs to establish KPIs region-wise, which would enable a quick glance at the performance of each region. Further, this can be utilised by the manager to take key decisions like which regions are suitable for advertisement or offer discounts. If the manager wishes to know what is the status of sales or expenses in a particular region, no other option would be as beneficial as a dashboard which enables you to slice across different regions and simply look at the sales generated or expenses incurred. The same scenarios could be imagined for managers of different functional areas such as HR, finance, etc.

The decision maker should need to drill through voluminous data or compute massive numbers to determine a specific aspect such as sales or expenses. The case below depicts how KPI-based dashboard can help the HR manager for better functioning of the HR department of a firm and effective decision-making. The HR department of a small firm has maintained the data for its employees in a spreadsheet. However, at times, it becomes difficult to extract meaning from massive columns in the data or relate two different attributes for the same employee together such as which department gets the highest annual performance ranking. The manager, therefore, identifies a number of KPIs for its department such as

- Annual ranking of performance
- Leaves taken annually by the employees
- Salary drawn
- Headcount

With the aid of KPIs, the manager just needs to take a glance at the particular aspect and he is effectively equipped with the information to take a decision.

The following figure depicts the dashboard, which is based on KPI of employee count by the designation of employees in the firm. The firm has trainees, managers and engineers employed. As can be quickly viewed, there are 14 trainees and managers working in the firm whereas the number of engineers is 12.

However, if the manager had to extract this information from the spreadsheet, it would have taken the time to apply filters and do the necessary computation. Now if the manager wishes to know the designation of a particular employee, he just needs to click on the particular employee ID such as "2" and the dashboard displays the related information, as shown on the next page:

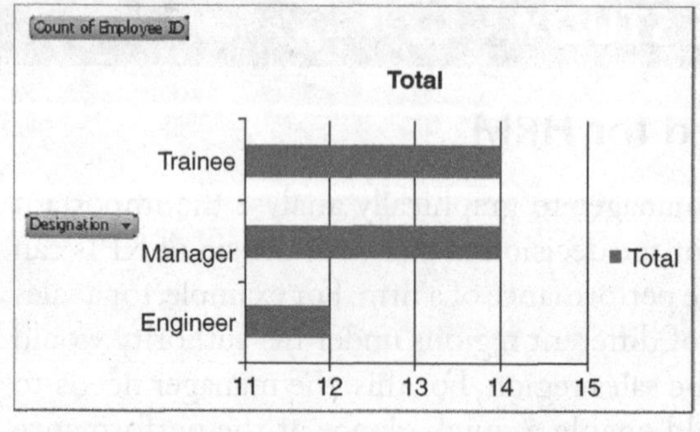

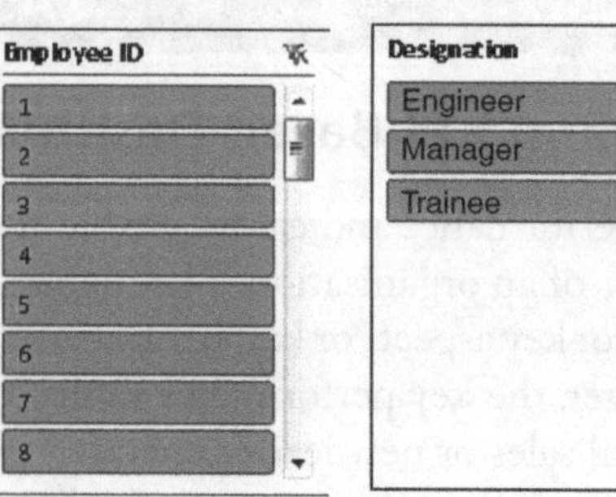

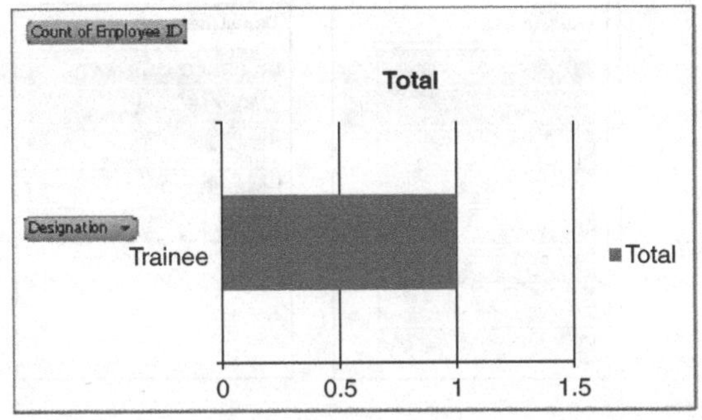

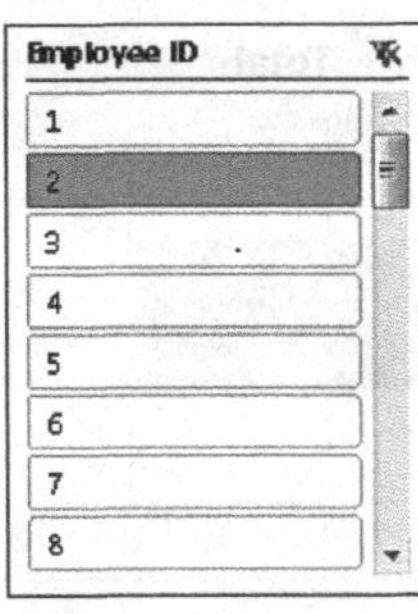

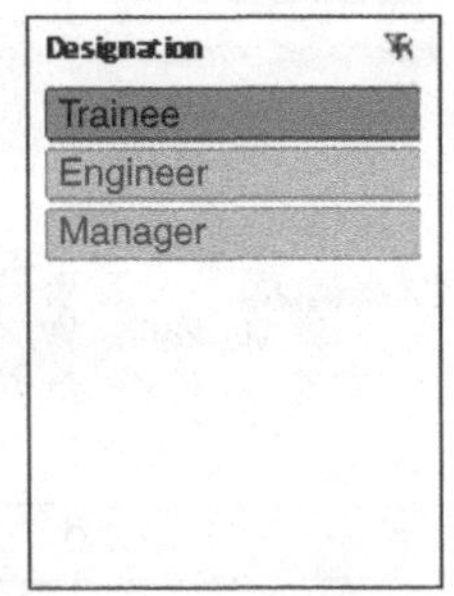

Now, if the decision maker wishes to know the employee count of a particular designation in the entire firm such as of managers or of trainees, etc. all he needs to do is click on the appropriate designation and the information is available at a glance. The figure below displays the headcount for the designation regarding manager.

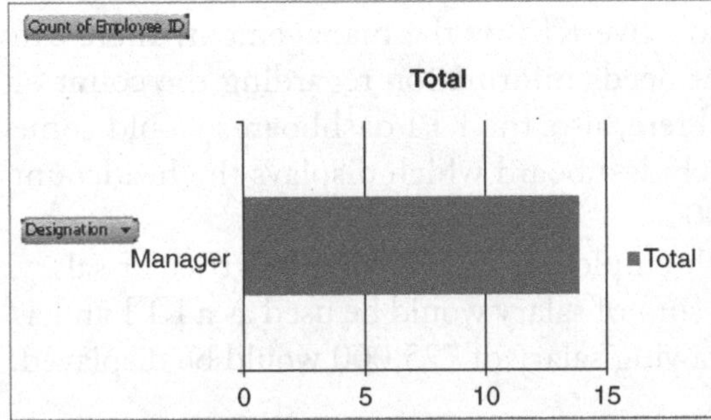

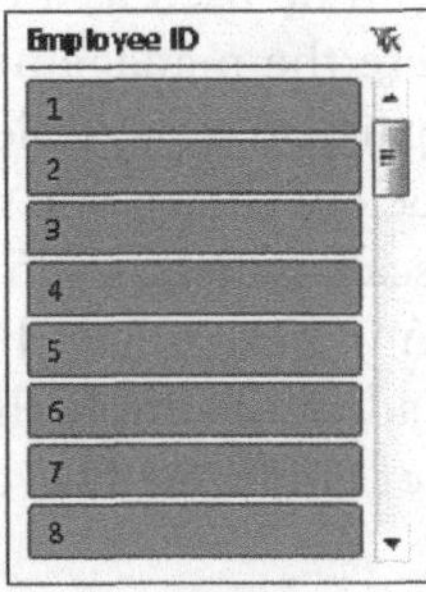

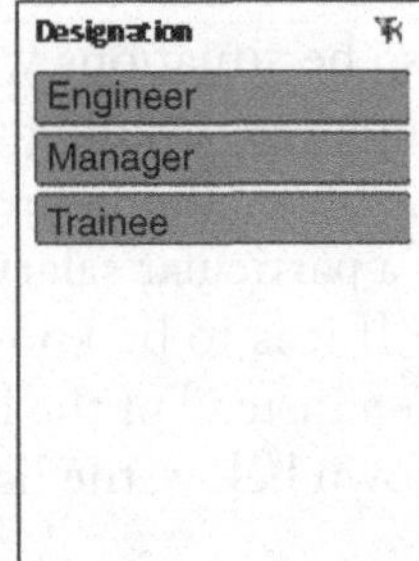

Now, let us assume the firm is on a hiring spree and the management wants to know the existing headcount in the firm. For this, it would not require soliciting information from individual departments. Instead, using headcount as a KPI, the dashboard can provide a quick picture of the employee count department-wise, as shown in the figure.

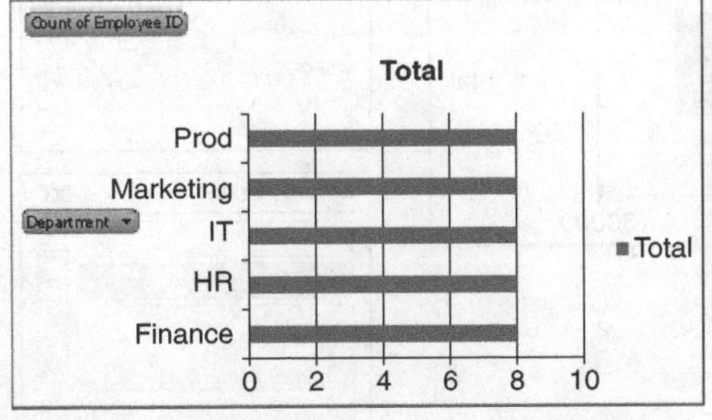

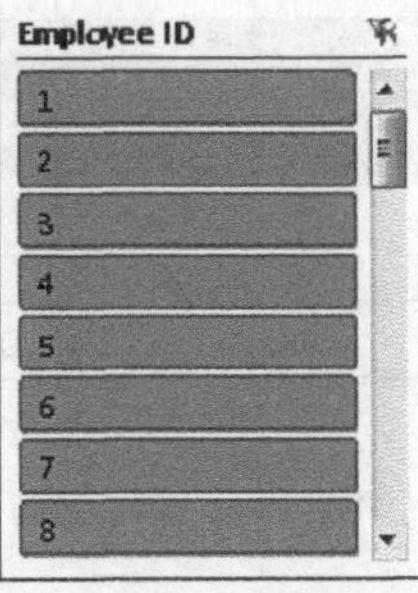

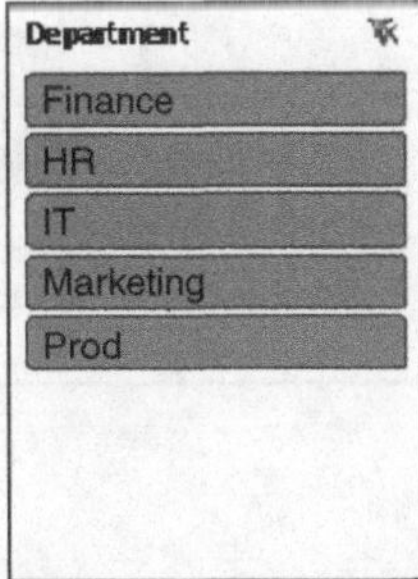

Also, if the management wants the information for a particular department such as headcount in marketing, it just needs to slice that value and dashboard data would change, as shown below.

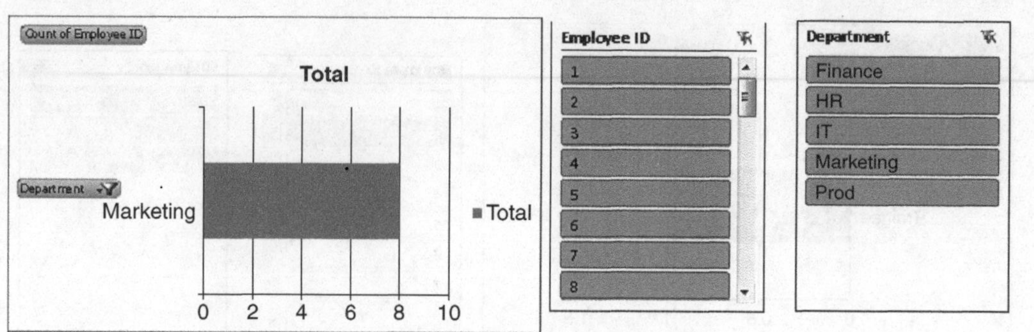

A major issue in any firm, especially small firms, is the cash inflow and outflow. One major outflow of cash is the salary paid to employees. Many a times, the management needs to know which department is drawing maximum salary, so fund allocation can be done accordingly. Or for loan consideration, the management might be interested in knowing the salary drawn by that particular employee who has applied for the loan. For this, salary can be used as an effective KPI by the management. There can also be situations where the management needs information regarding the count of employees availing a particular payscale. Here, also, the KPI dashboards would come to rescue. The figure below shows one such dashboard which displays the headcount of a particular salary scale which is ₹25,000.

If it is to be known in particular which employees are drawing a particular salary, then instead of the headcount simply the sum of salary would be used as a KPI and as shown below, the list of employee IDs drawing salary of ₹25,000 would be displayed.

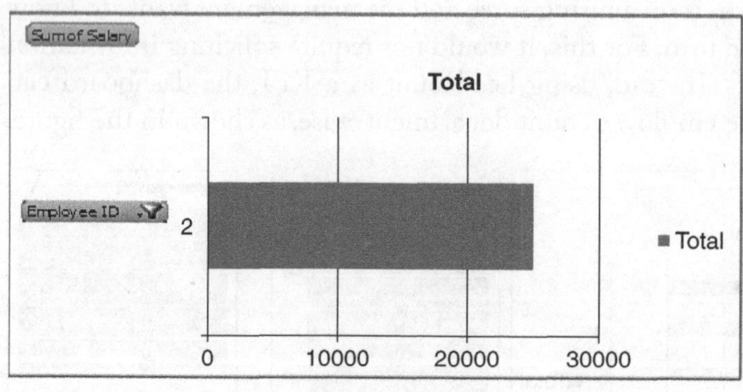

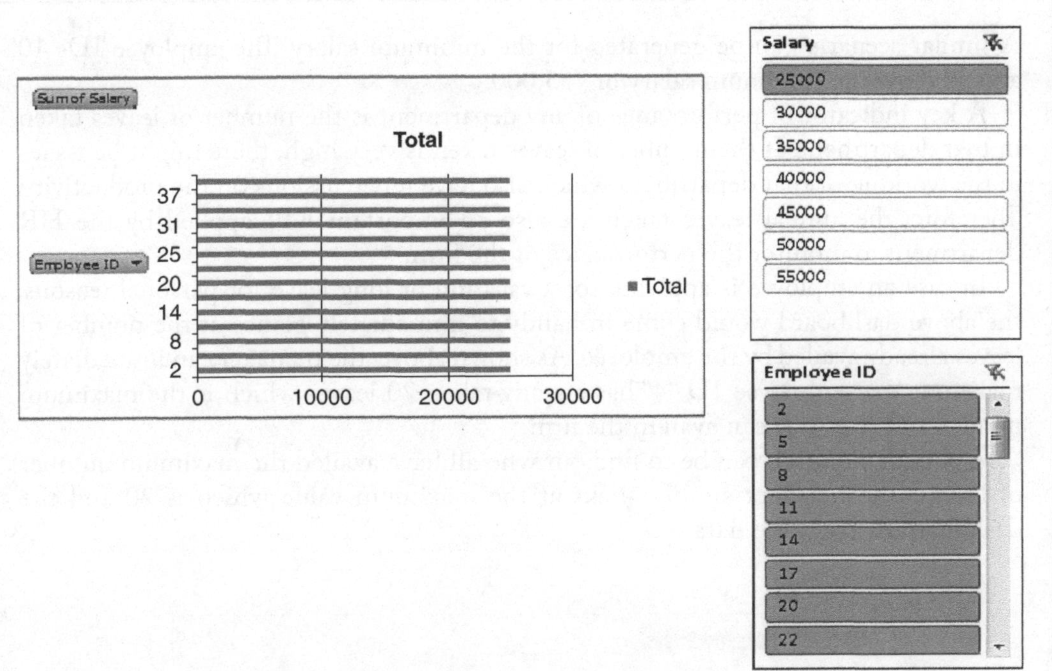

The dashboard automatically arranges the data values of KPIs in ascending or descending order. Therefore, the decision maker can immediately make out the maximum and the least value. Applying the above KPI-based dashboard, the management can take a quick glance at who draws the maximum salary, as shown below.

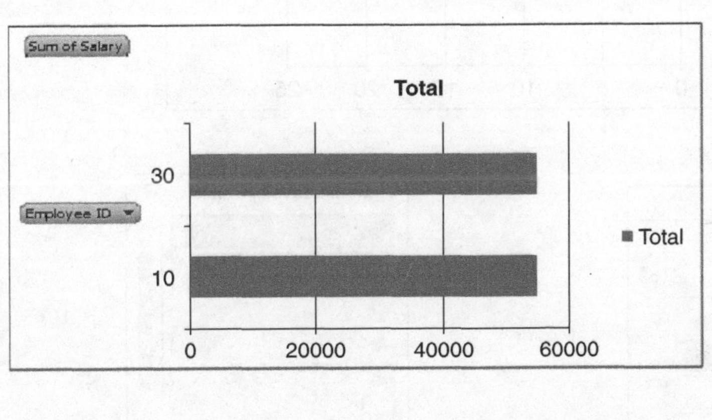

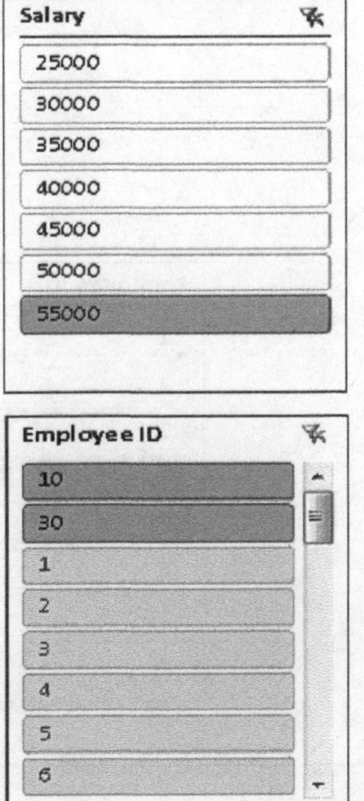

A similar scenario can be generated for the minimum salary. The employee IDs 10 and 30 draw the maximum salary of ₹55,000.

A key indicator of performance of any department is the number of leaves taken in that department. If the number of leaves taken is very high, there might be issues in the working of that department which also have repercussions on the productivity. Therefore, the annual leaves taken are also an important KPI applied by the HR department to monitor the performance of the firm.

In case an employee is applying for a vacation or long leave for personal reasons, the above dashboard would come in handy to immediately glance at the number of leaves already availed by the employee. As shown above, the manager can immediately make out that employee ID "4" has already taken 20 leaves which is the maximum number of leaves one can avail in the firm.

A similar situation can be to find out who all have availed the maximum number of leaves. The manager simply clicks at the maximum value which is 20 and the dashboard displays the data.

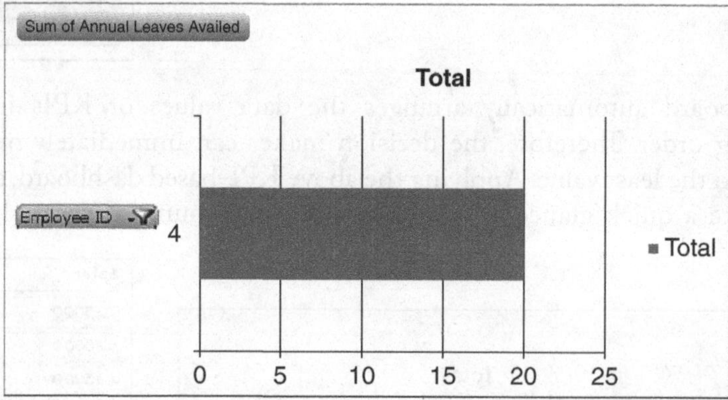

Employee ID
1
2
3
4
5
6
7
8

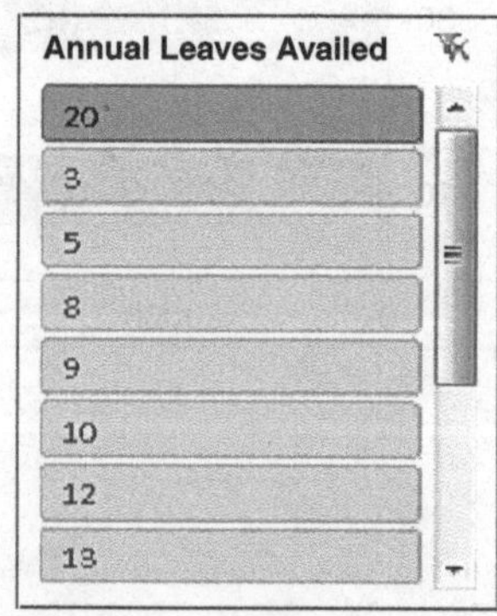

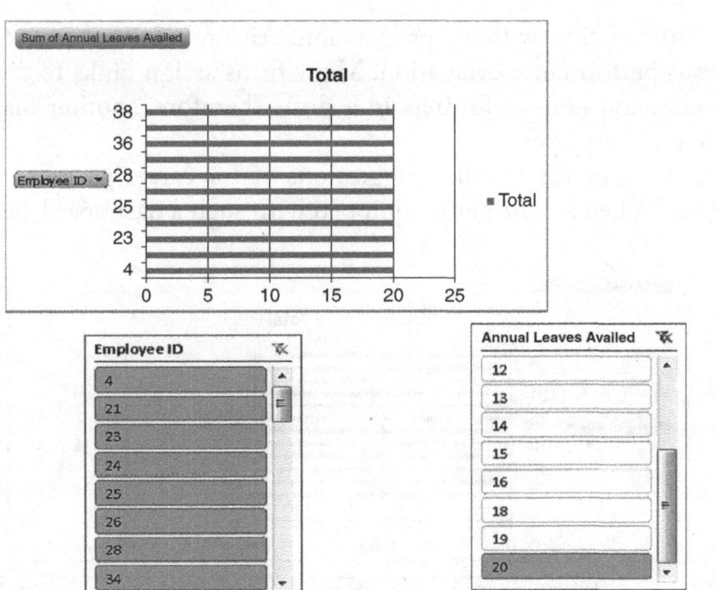

As is prevalent in public sector firms, leaves are enchased; this KPI can also be used to estimate the balance leaves available to an employee. To decrease the absenteeism, this tool can be applied to appreciate those who have availed the least number of leaves and thus set an example for the defaulters. There is only one employee in the present firm who has availed only three leaves.

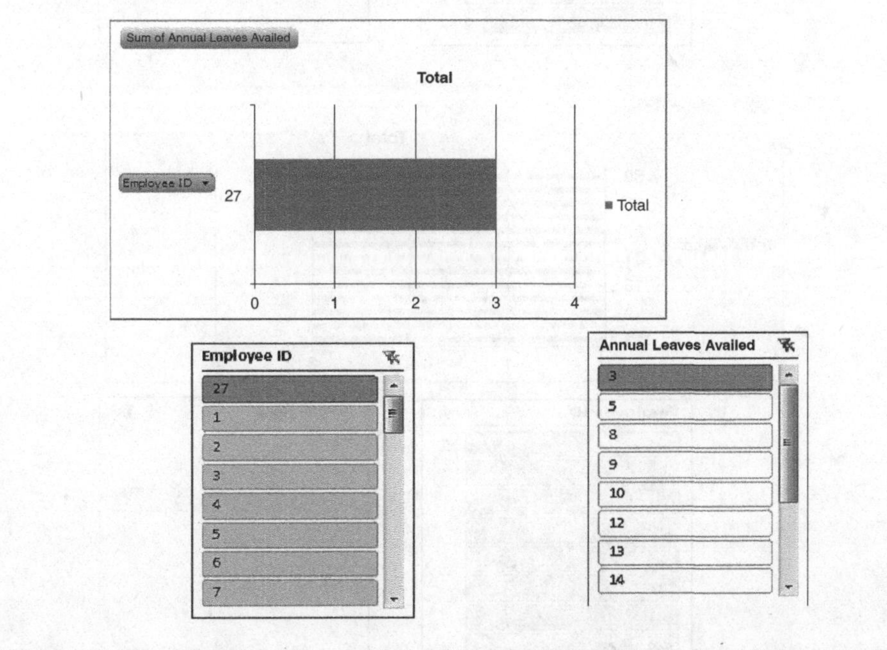

No firm can function without progression. An underlying basis for progression of employees is performance evaluation. Many firms assign ranks to differentiate the high performers and non-performers in a firm. Therefore, another major KPI is an annual ranking of employees.

For promotions, or for training suggestions or for career progression, ranking is very important. When a manager is equipped with such a dashboard, he can immedi-

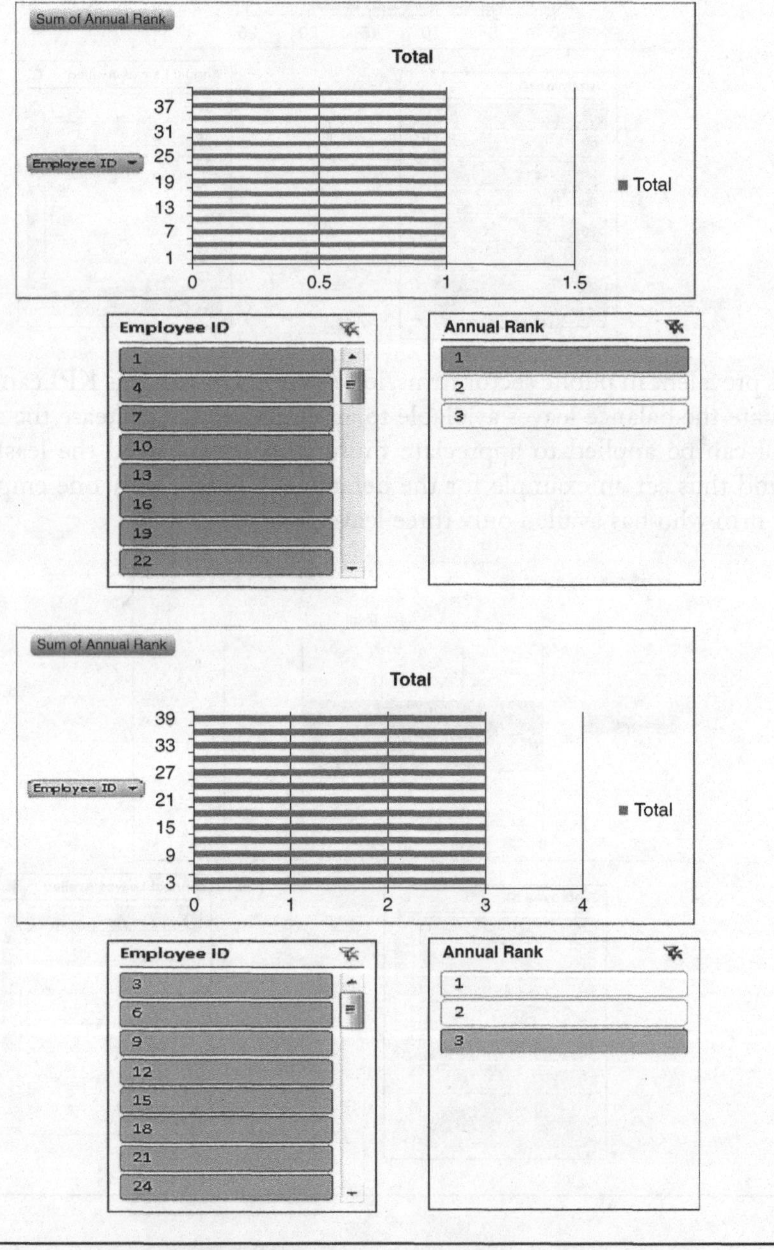

ately decide whether to recommend a particular employee for further training or not. Also a candidate's eligibility can be checked in a matter of a minute for promotion or new job opening within the firm.

Similarly, applying the above information of least rank, the manager can decide to send warnings for performance improvement or counsel the low performers.

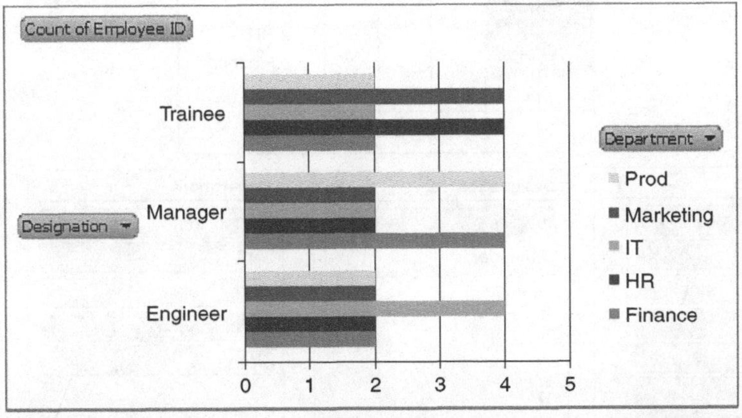

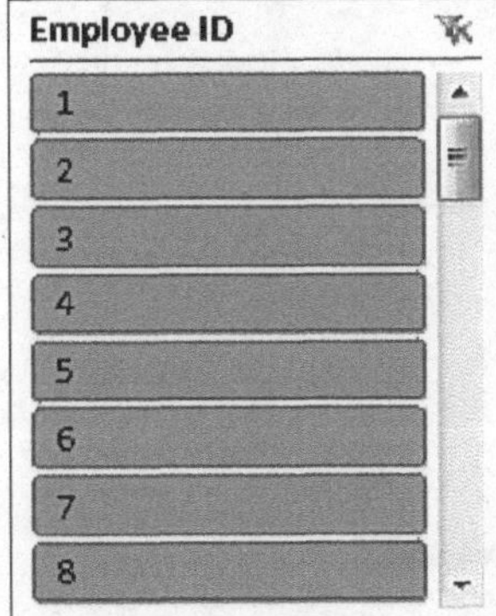

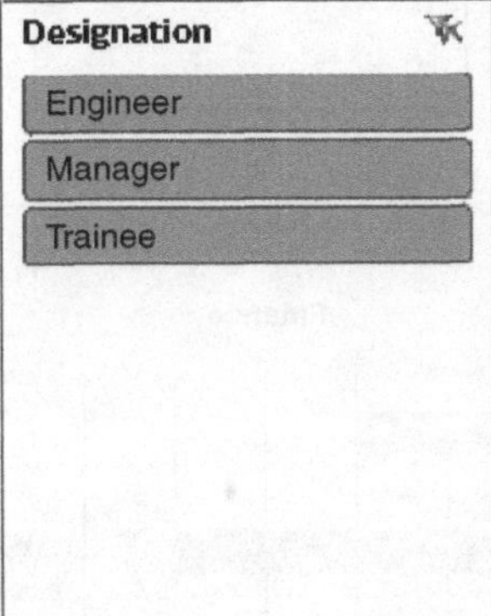

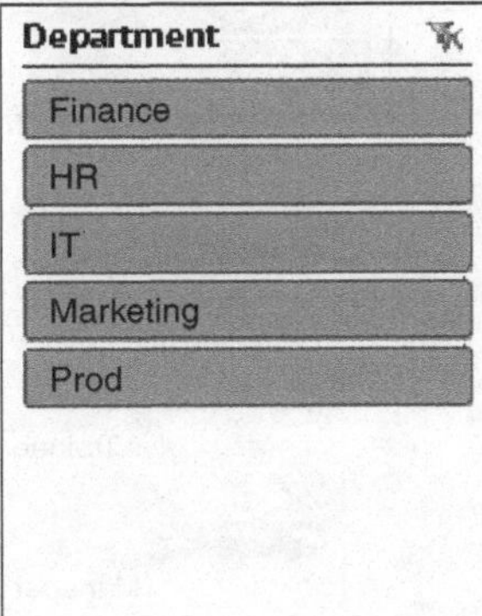

The management can also relate different dimensions to a KPI such as finding the headcount for different departments and designations. For each designation, applying the dashboard shown above, the decision maker can easily determine the headcount in different departments. Now if the manager wishes to find out how many engineers work in each department, slicer can be checked for only engineers who display the required headcount as shown below. Similarly, the headcount for each designation can be seen in different departments in the firm.

The following figure shows the nature of the workforce in the finance department. This can aid in human resource manpower planning. Management may also utilise these statistics to downsize a department in case it has more than required workforce. In other words, many strategies can be built around information extracted from this dashboard.

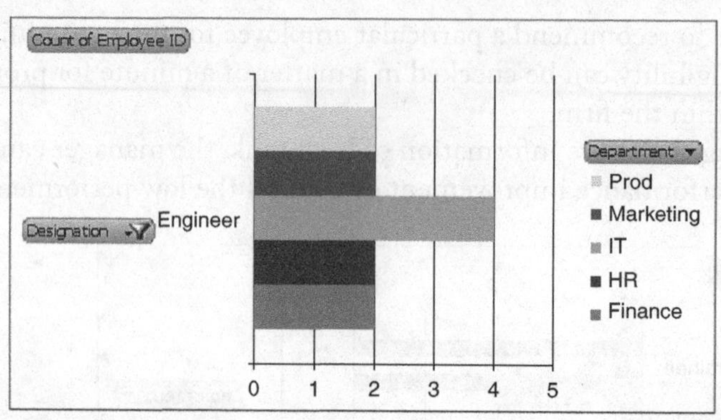

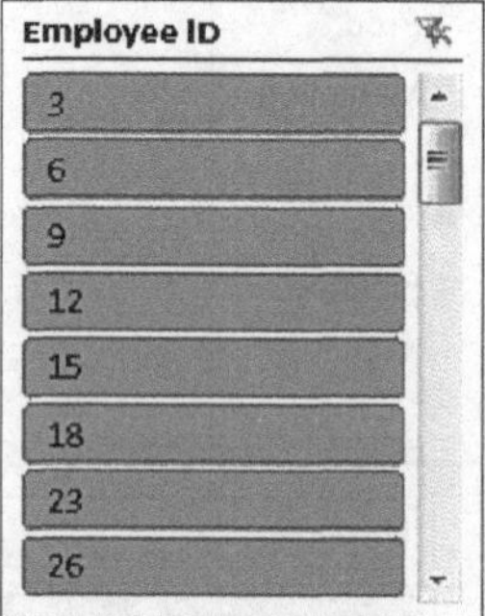

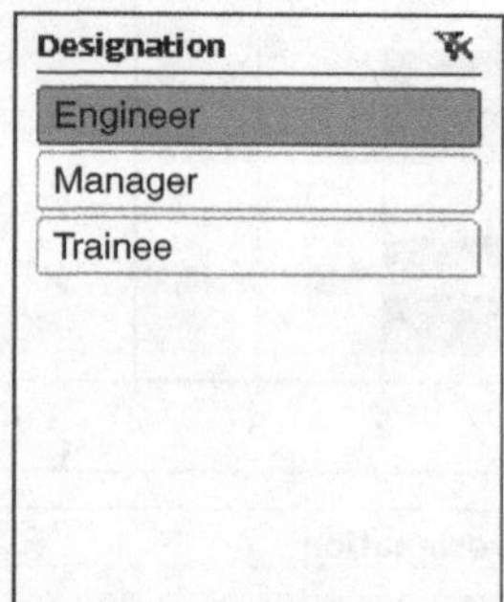

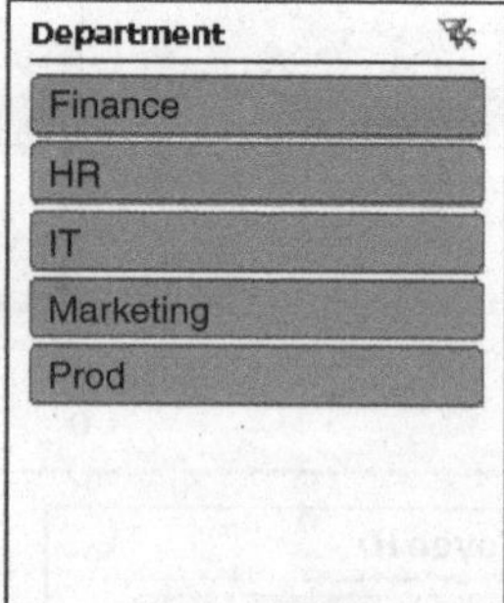

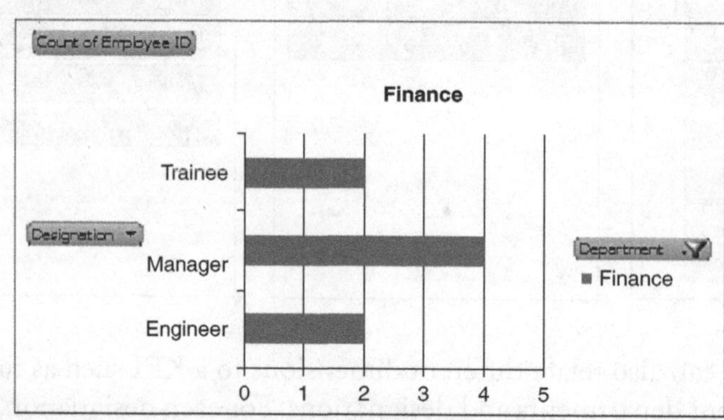

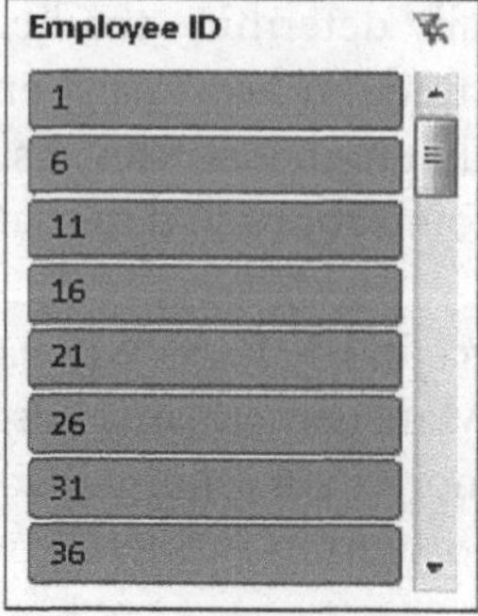

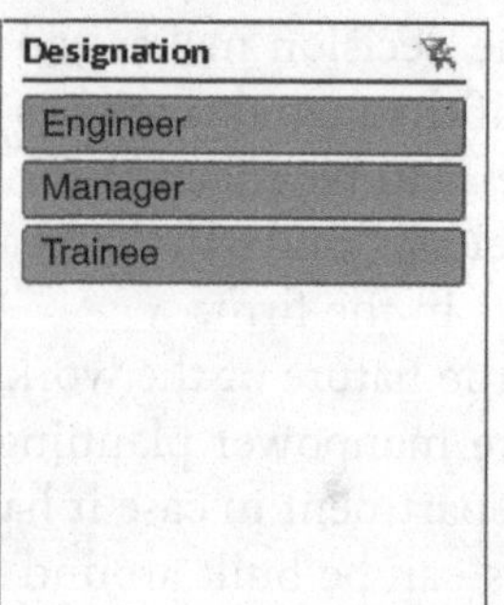

Department
Finance
HR
IT
Marketing
Prod

Similarly, the designation and department of a particular employee can be visualised by applying the employee ID slicer. In the figure shown next to the figure below, the manager can see the designation and department of employee ID "7".

As shown, the employee with ID "7" is an HR manager in the firm.

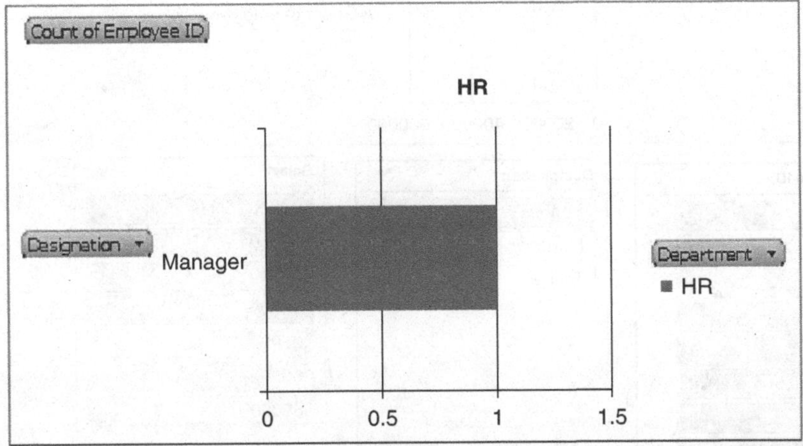

Employee ID
1
2
3
4
5
6
7
8

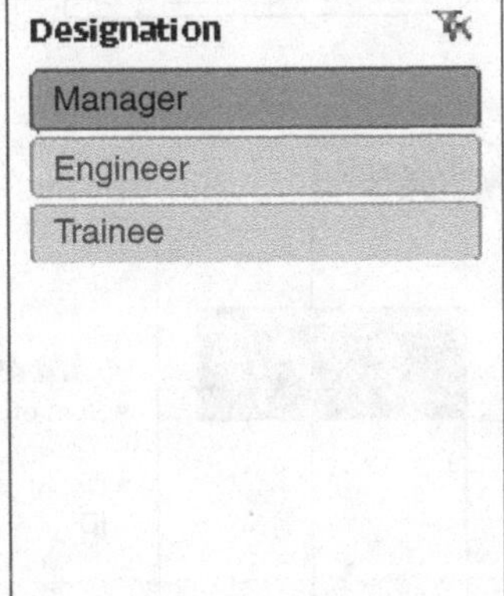

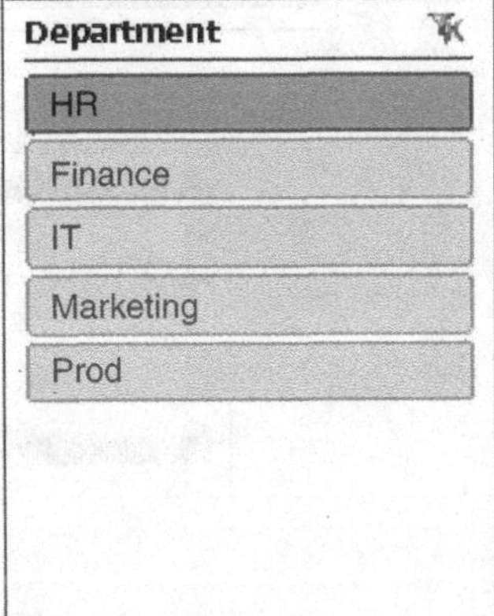

Now, imagine a scenario in which management wishes to know the total salary drawn by a particular designation such as engineers or managers or trainees. Such information can be used by the management to see the polarities in salary drawn by different designations.

As is evident from the figure below, the trainees draw the least amount of salary.

Similarly, it can be interesting to know designation of employees who take the highest and the least number of leaves. From the information seen in the dashboard below, trainees take the maximum number of leaves. Probably, a stricter intervention is needed to maintain discipline for trainees.

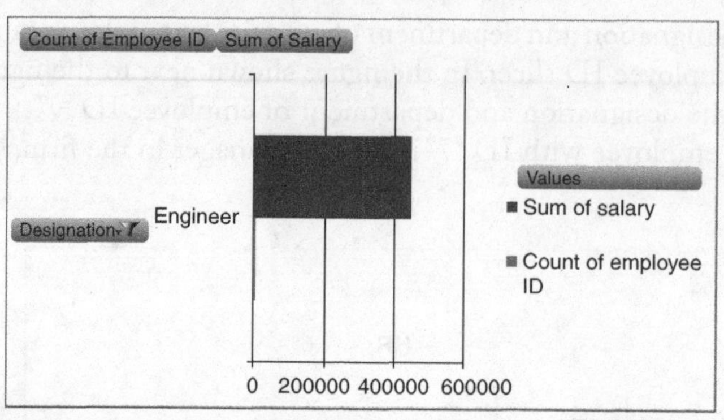

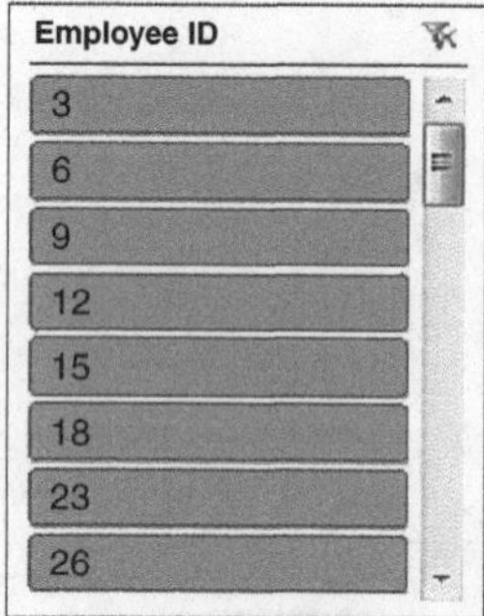

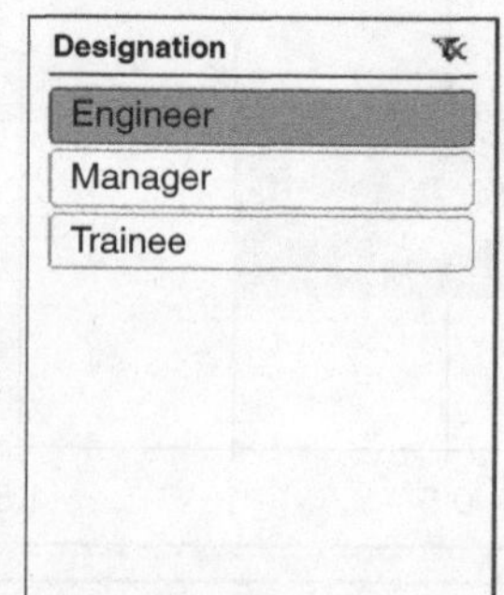

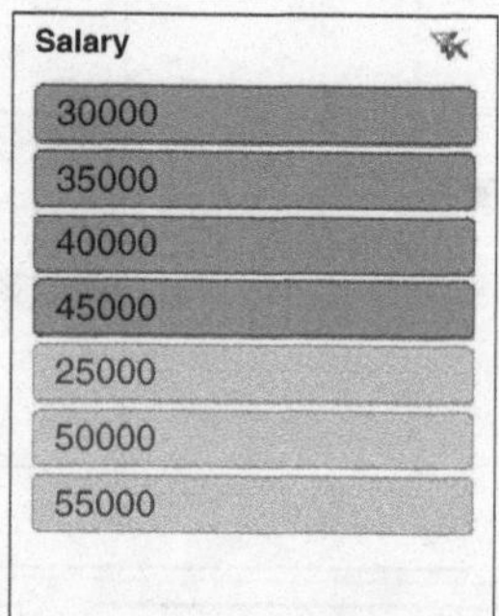

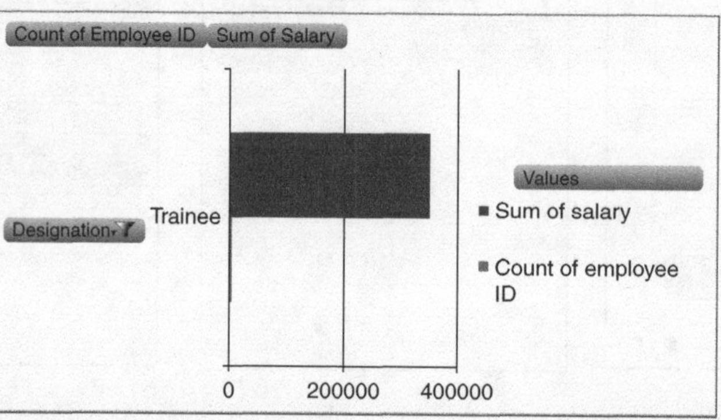

Employee ID
2
5
8
11
14
17
20
22

Designation
Engineer
Manager
Trainee

Salary
25000
30000
35000
40000
45000
50000
55000

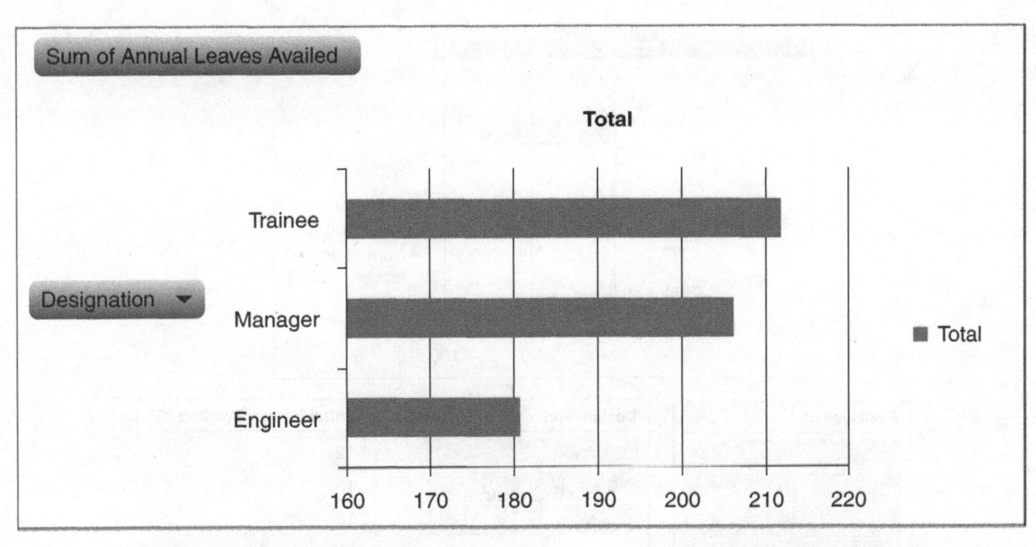

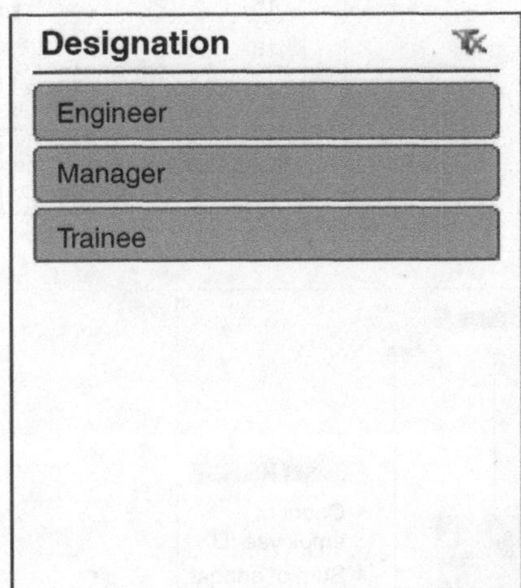

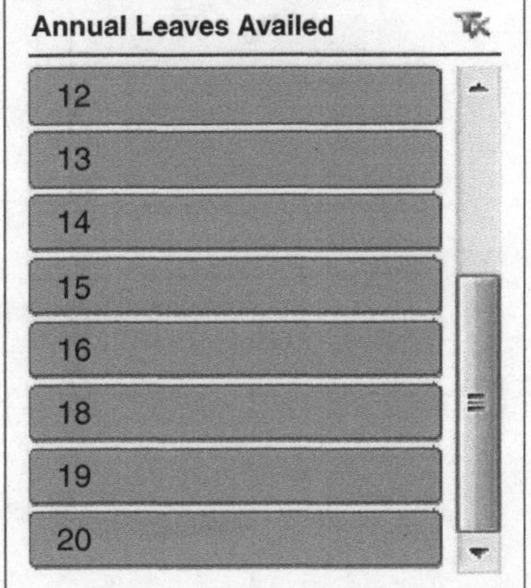

Applying the information shown in the dashboard below, the management can find out the profile of the workforce who has taken the maximum number of leaves. The KPIs shown include the count of employees and sum of annual leaves taken. As shown in the figure on the next page, three managers, four trainees and four managers have taken the highest number of leaves.

Now applying the slicer on employee ID, the management can identify which are those candidates who have taken the maximum number of leaves. Then, it can be related to other dashboards, for example, designation. This is depicted in the figure shown next to this one.

The following figure shows the ID of managers who have taken the maximum number of leaves.

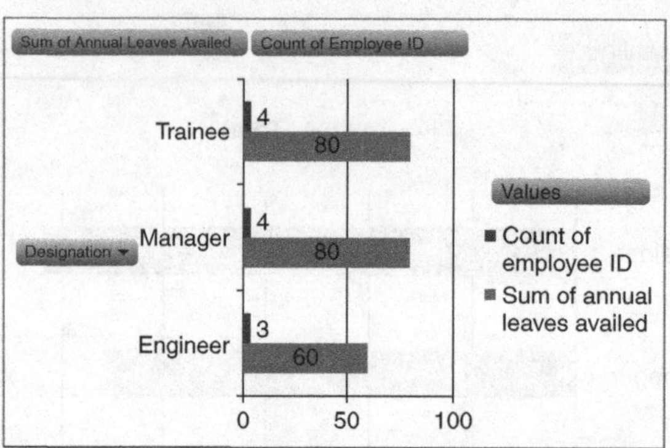

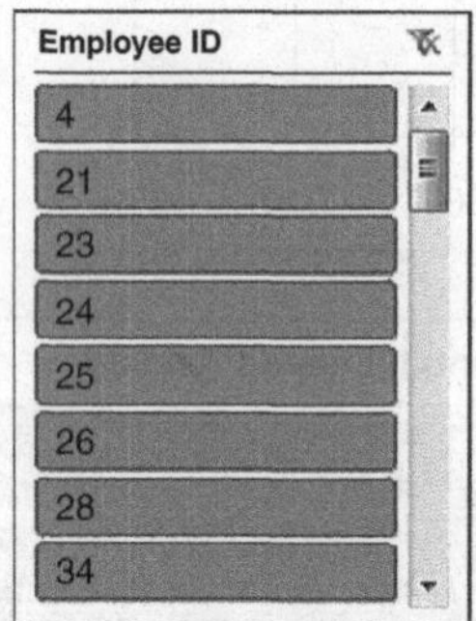

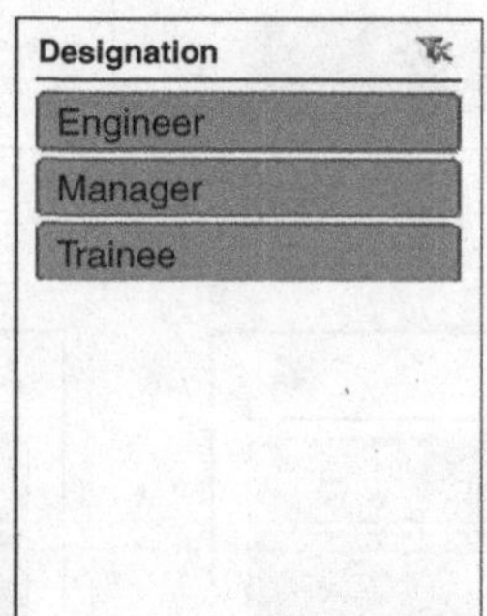

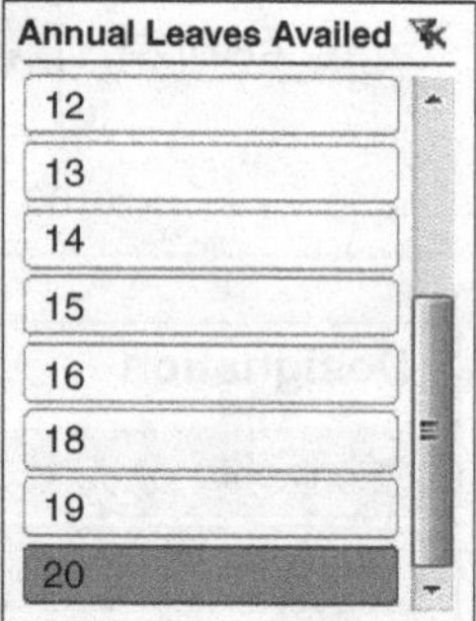

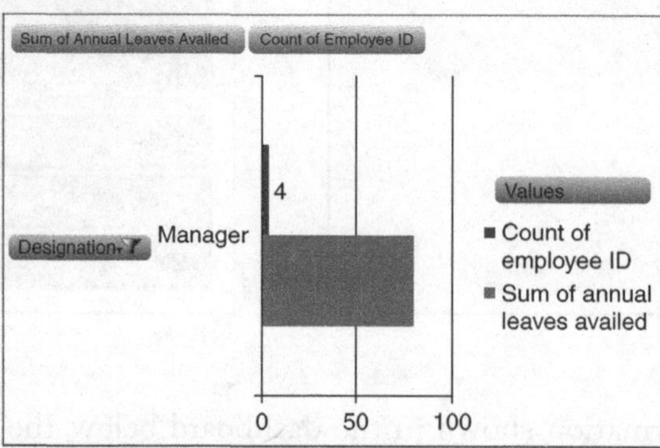

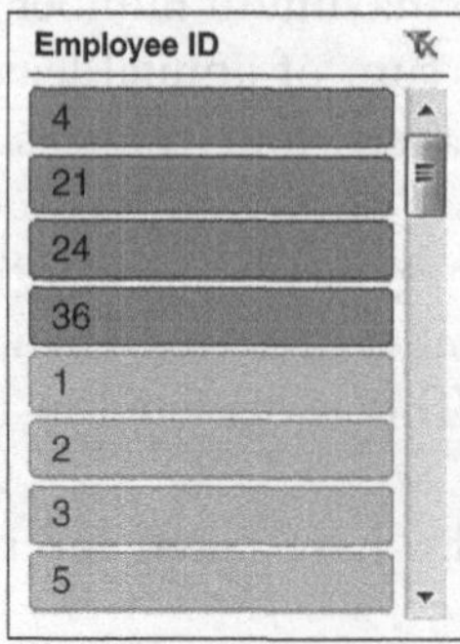

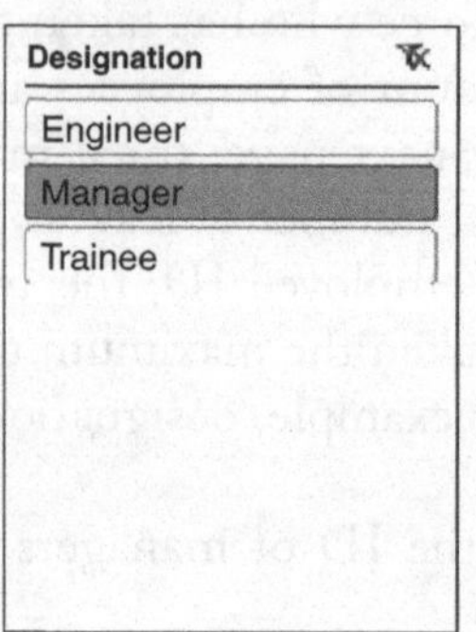

Annual Leaves Availed
14
15
16
19
20
5
8
18

The annual ranking and designation can be clubbed together to jointly assess the performance ratings. For example, none of the trainees performs very low and managers either rank very low or very high. This can be used to see if certain managers are not content with the firm's policies or further discussions can be done with the low ranking managers.

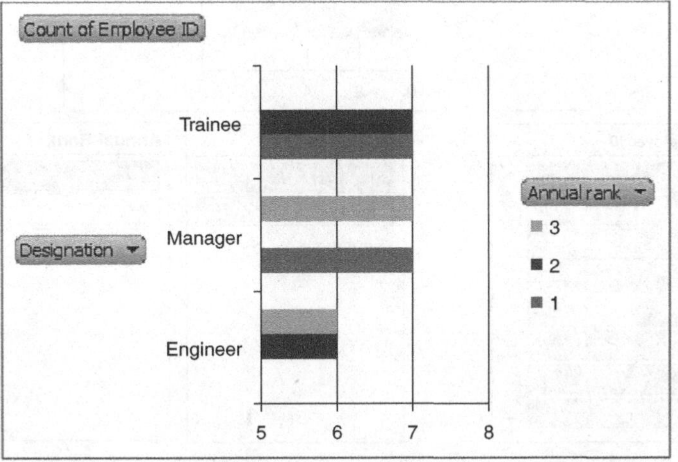

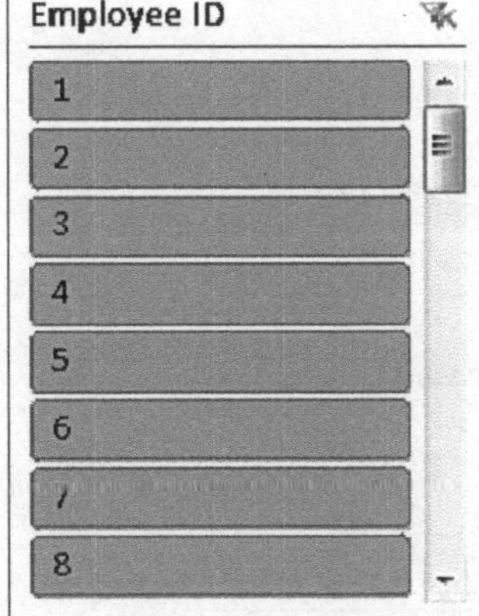

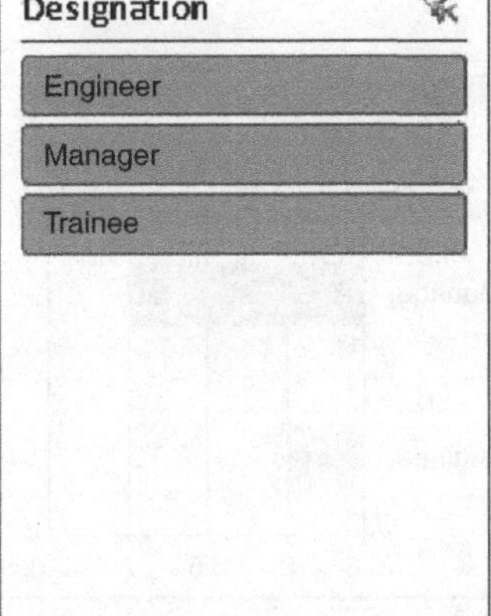

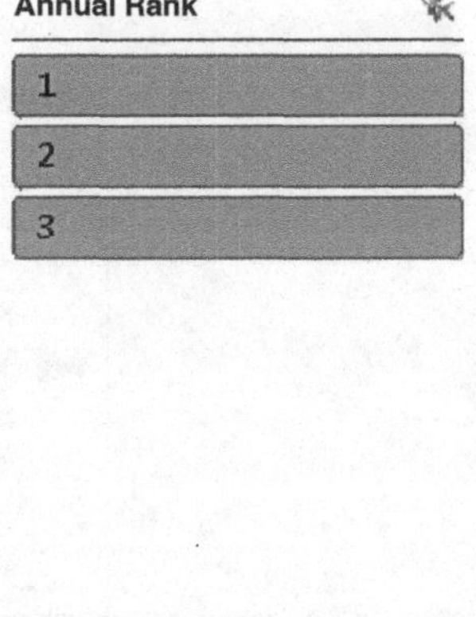

The manager can also check out the profile of the workforce who has the highest rank and the least rank. As shown below, seven managers and seven trainees have the highest rank. The slicer also shows the employee ID of each highest ranker. In the adjacent figure, seven managers and six engineers have the lowest rank. Using the slicer on employee ID, the manager can check out the profile of each candidate individually.

The nature of a workforce with the least rank is depicted in the figure below:

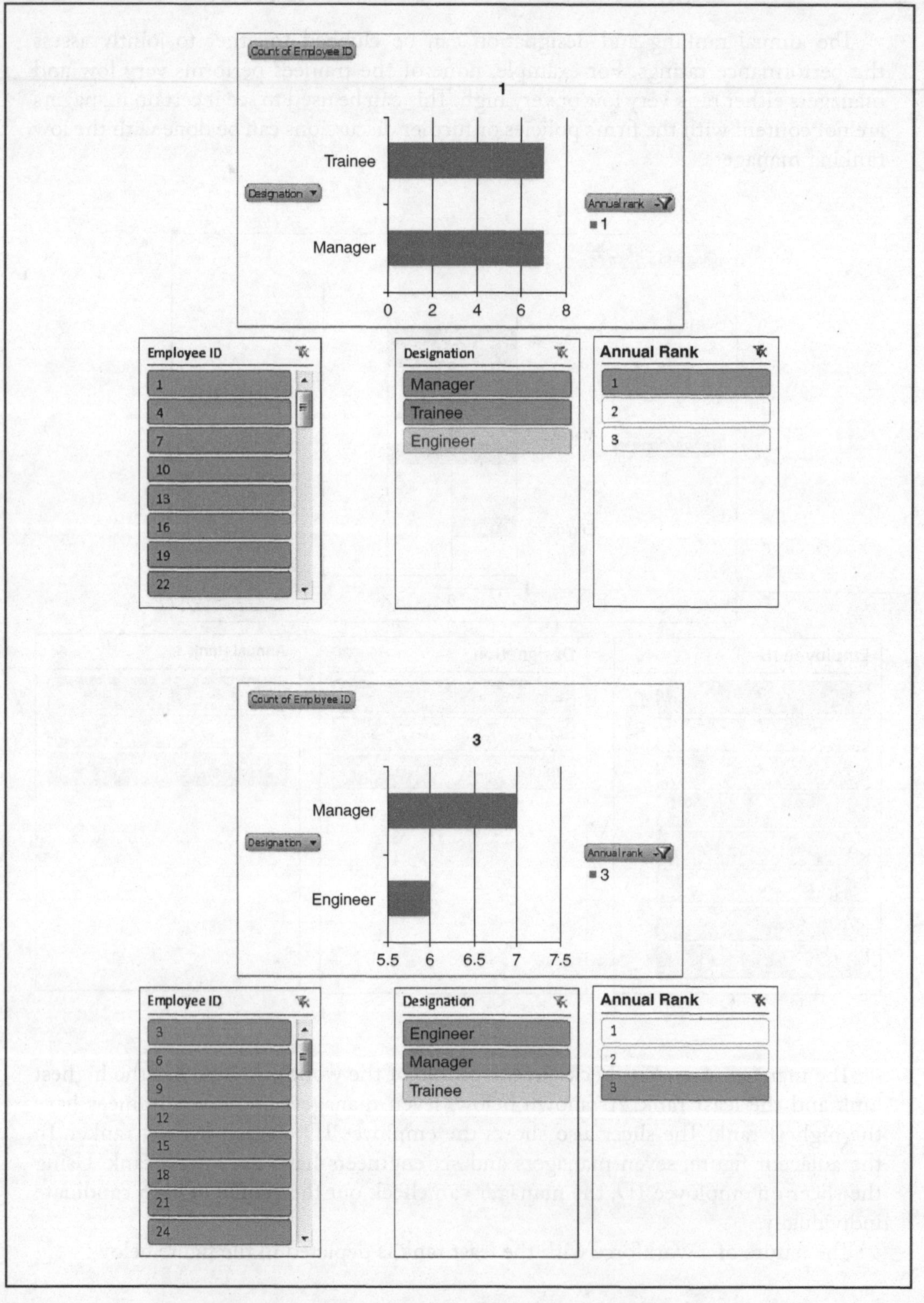
Count of Employee ID
1
Trainee
Manager
Designation
Annual rank
1
0 2 4 6 8
Employee ID
1
4
7
10
13
16
19
22
Designation
Manager
Trainee
Engineer
Annual Rank
1
2
3
Count of Employee ID
3
Manager
Engineer
Designation
Annual rank
3
5.5 6 6.5 7 7.5
Employee ID
3
6
9
12
15
18
21
24
Designation
Engineer
Manager
Trainee
Annual Rank
1
2
3

The KPI of salary can be interrelated with departments to check which departments are drawing maximum salary and to use this information while budgeting. The finance and IT department draws the maximum salary. This can be cross verified with information drawn from previous dashboards such as headcount of the workforce in these departments.

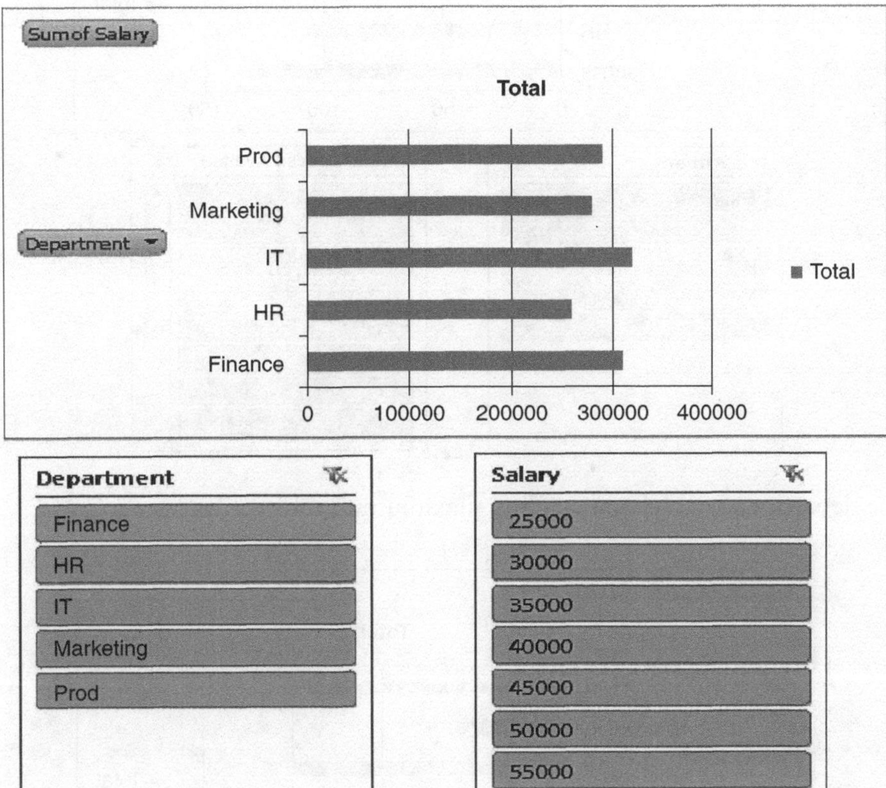

The data can be viewed individually for each department such as for production department applying slicers.

Another major KPI which can be viewed department-wise is the leaves availed. This information can be used to find out the departments where maximum number of leaves is being taken. The management can then assess the performance of these departments so as to identify the impact of leaves on workload and productivity. The figure clearly depicts the total leaves availed in each department in the firm such as finance, IT, HR, etc. Slicers can be used for further analysis such as which department has taken the maximum number of leaves, which department has taken the least number of leaves, and individual statistics for each department can also be seen using slicer on the department. The above scenario is summarised in the two figures below:

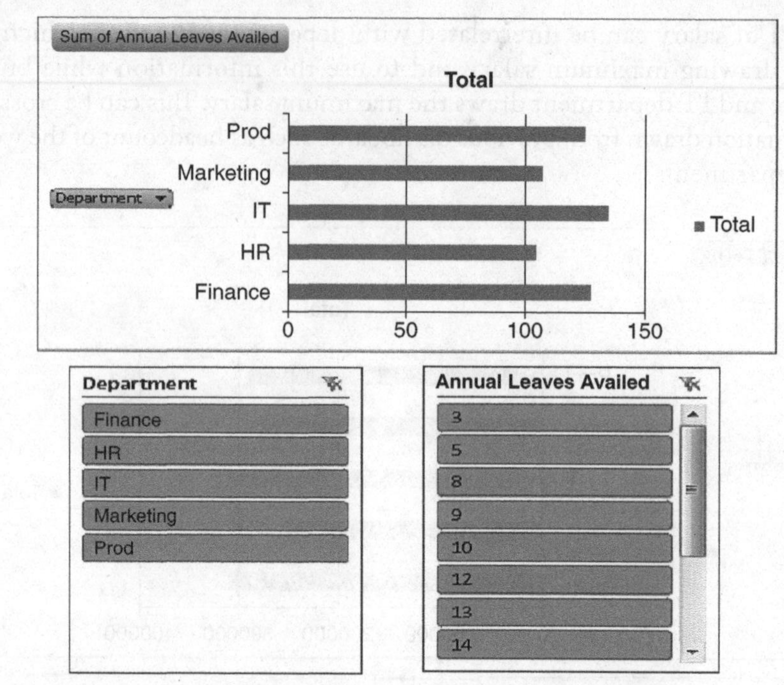

The departments which are availing maximum number of leaves:

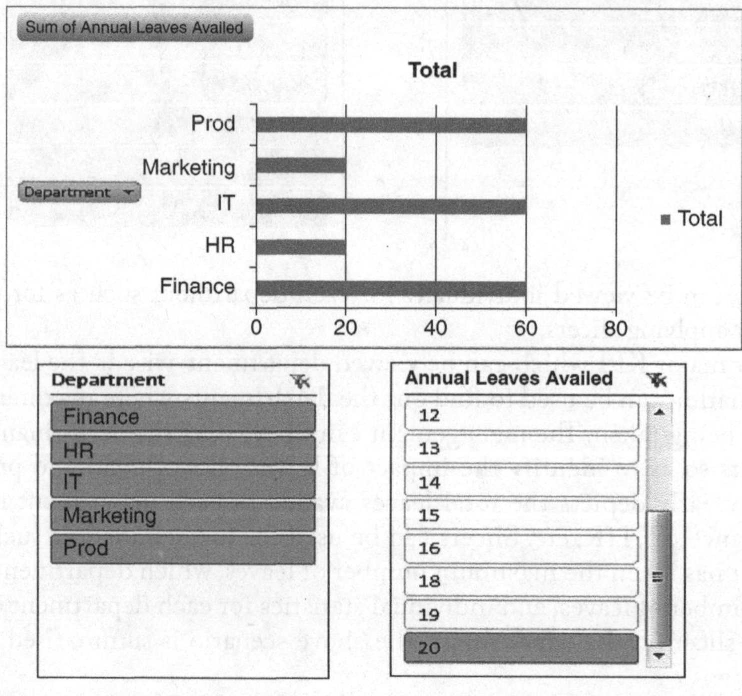

The dashboard shown below with slicers on employee ID, department and annual rank clubs the data from the three fields. This would provide a quick glance to the decision maker about the number of employees at each rank in different departments. Such a summary would readily inform the manager or the decision maker about the high ranking departments and in turn high performing ones. This can also be used for benchmarking.

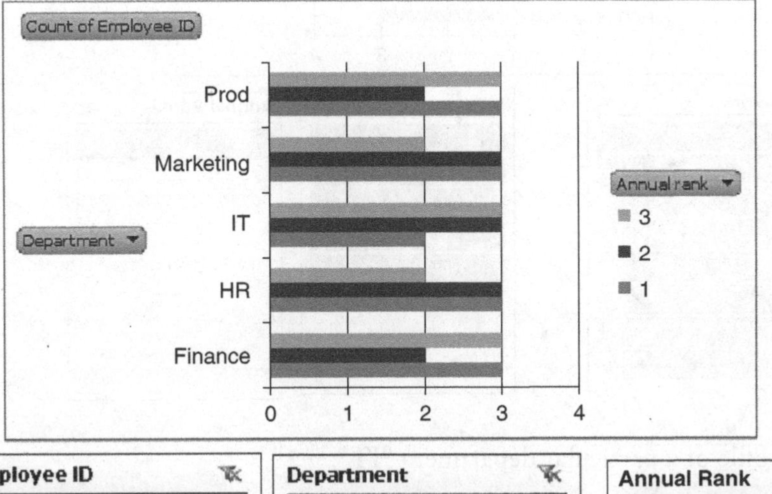

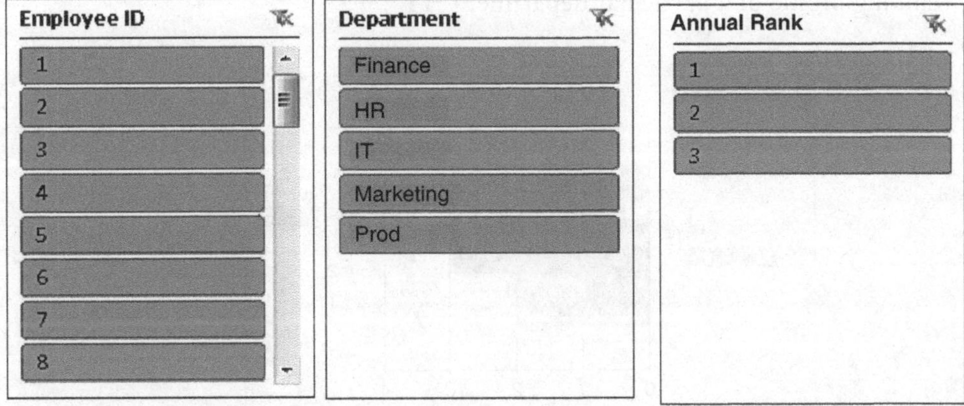

The slicers can be used to drill down the data, such as which departments have the highest rank and how many employees in each department have the highest and least rank. In this case, the user just needs to click rank "1" in the rank slicer. Also to know the ranking profile of "IT" department, slicer on the department can be used. Also, the manager might need to know the rank and department of a particular employee whose employee ID is known such as for employee ID "24"; this information has been extracted in the figure below. All the above situations have been depicted in the figures below:

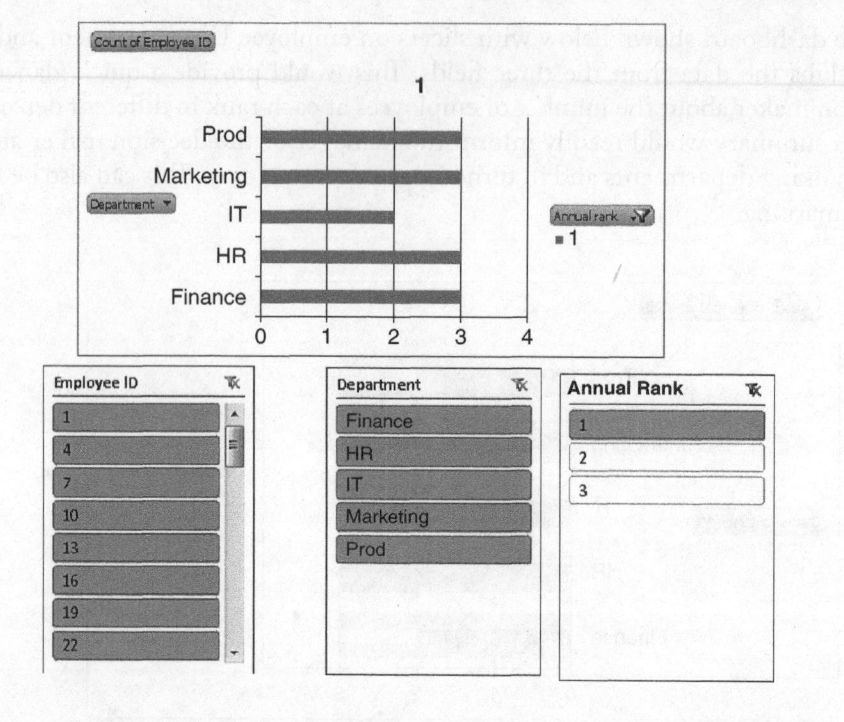

Ranking profile of a particular department "IT":

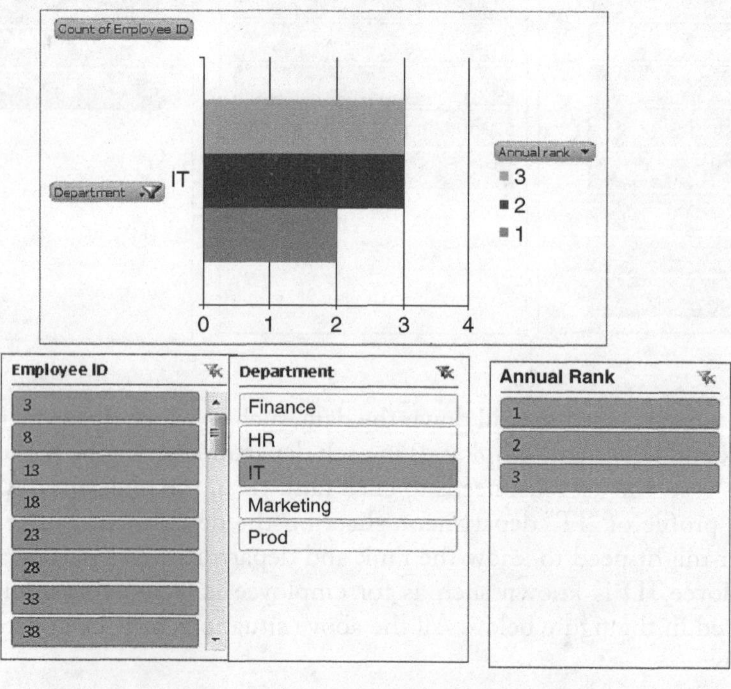

Department and rank of a particular employee: with employee ID "24"

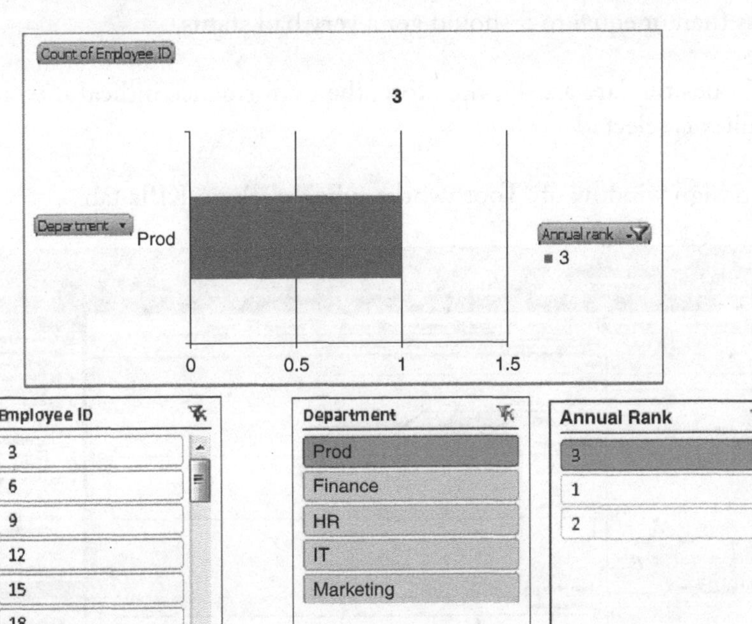

In a nutshell, the above case depicts various KPI-based dashboards, which are very beneficial for the HR manager to take a quick look at the present scenario by equipping him with succinct concrete information. This can be used to reach substantiated decisions.

HANDS-ON PROJECT

SQL Server

Following from the Toothworks example, consider the business need of the retail shop that is minimum ten goods to be sold for each toothpaste brand each month. Therefore, the KPI is calculated for total sales and on consensus with the management, the agents decide that status on the display reflects as under:

- Value greater than or equal to 50 should get a very good status
- Value greater than or equal to 20 and less than 50 should get a good status
- Value greater than or equal to 10 and less than 20 should get a fair status

- Value greater than 5 and less than 10 should get a bad status
- Value less than or equal to 5 should get a very bad status

The total sales till date are 45; therefore, the performance indicator would display good if no filter is selected.

1. In cube design window of "Toothworks.cube", click on KPIs tab.

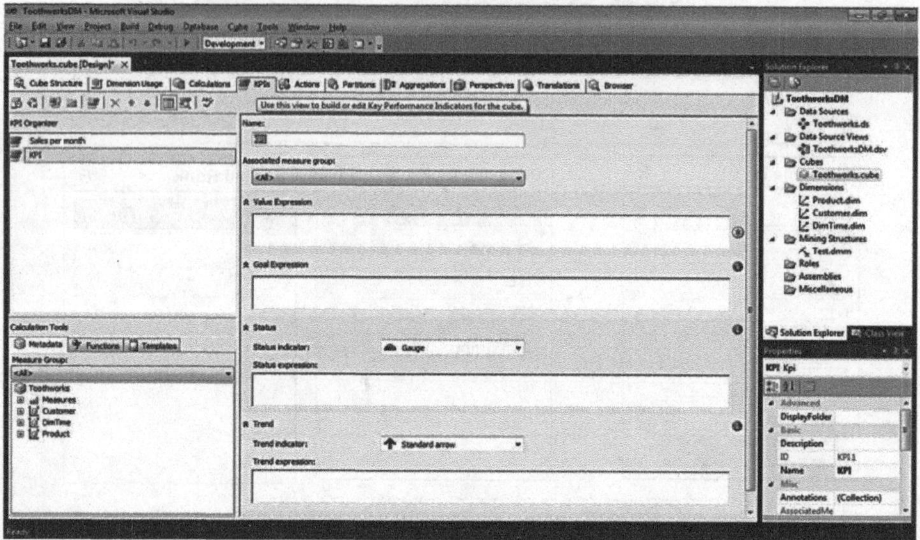

2. In this window, click on new KPI from upper left corner:

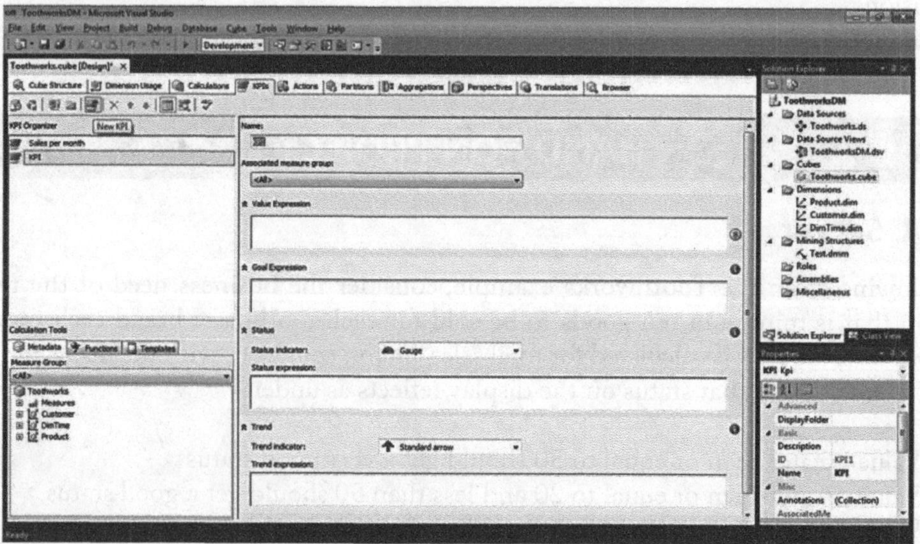

3. A new form opens to create KPI on the existing cube.
   - Provide an appropriate name "Sales per month".
   - In next field, select "Sales Information" from the associated measure group drop-down list.
   - In next field type, the expression used to compute the KPI. Here it is: "[Measures].[Total Sales]". As here KPI is directly based on a column in measures table, you can even drag and drop this "Total Sales" column from "Calculation tools" tab in the lower left pane to Value expression field.
   - Next, you need to specify the target of the KPI or goal field. Simply type the following: "50 units or greater".
   - Keep status indicator at default: Gauge.
   - Status expression is the query which will be used to determine the performance in terms of monthly sales. Enter the following expression in this field:

     Case
     When [Measures].[Total Sales] >=50
     then 1
     When [Measures].[Total Sales] >=20 and [Measures].[Total Sales] < 50
     then .5
     When [Measures].[Total Sales] >=10 and [Measures].[Total Sales] < 20
     then 0
     When [Measures].[Total Sales] >5 and [Measures].[Total Sales] < 10
     then -.5
     else -1
     end

     Leave rest empty. The form should finally appear as below:

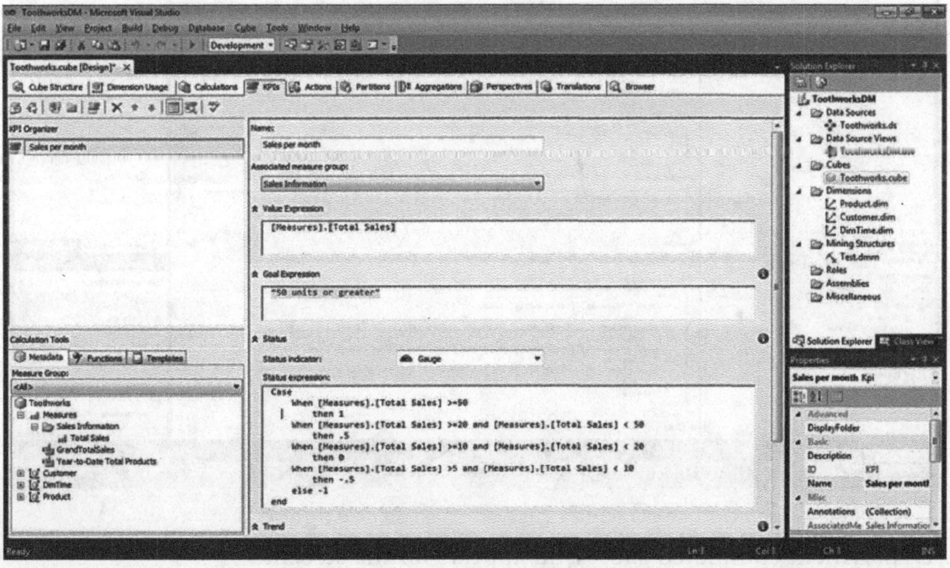

4. Click on Save All. Now, you need to deploy the same to reflect the changes and browse through data. First check for name of server in project deployment properties as done during cube deployment.

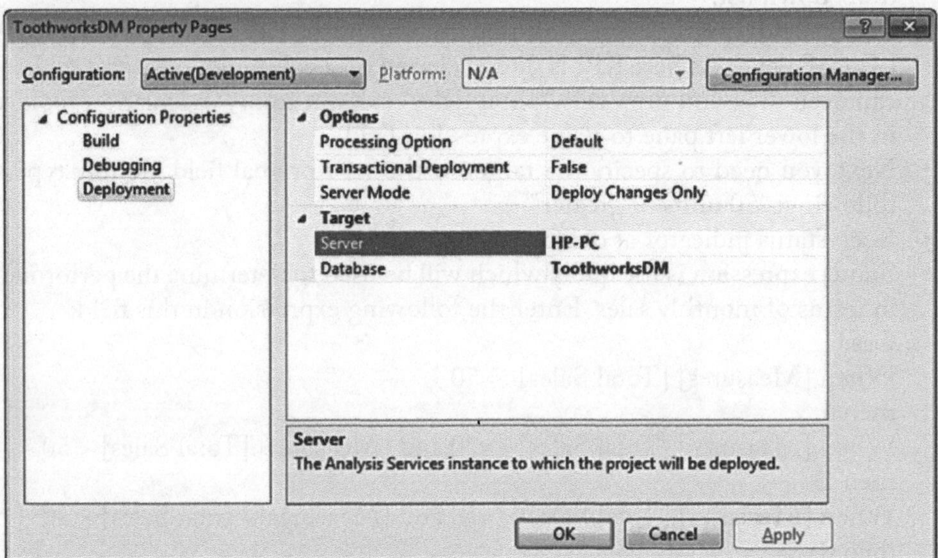

5. Next deploy the project:

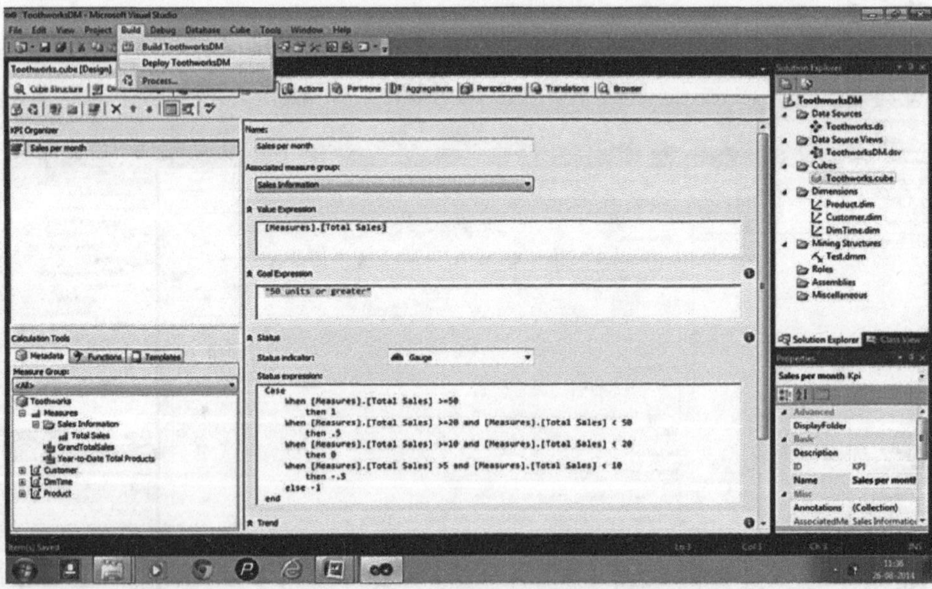

Deployment completed successful appears on the screen.

6. Now you can browse through the KPI. For this, in KPI tab itself, click on browser view:

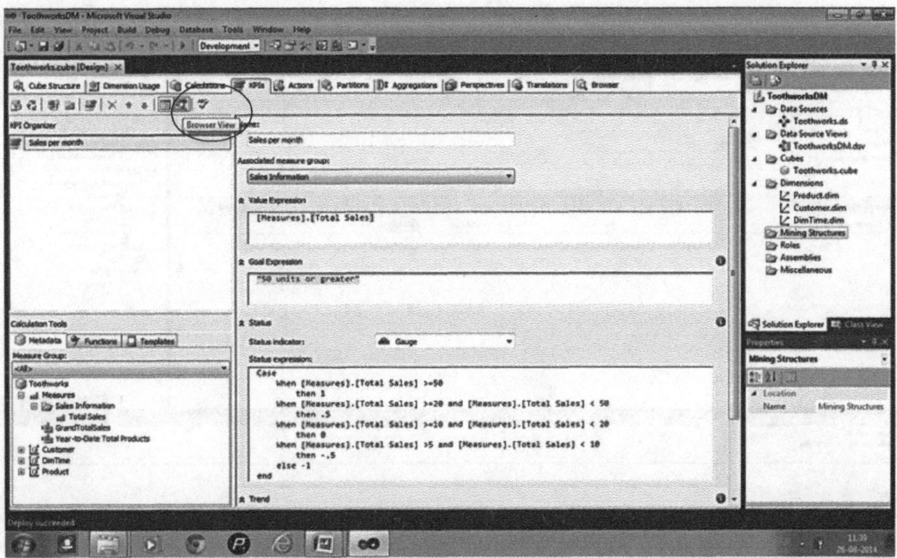

7. Following window appears:

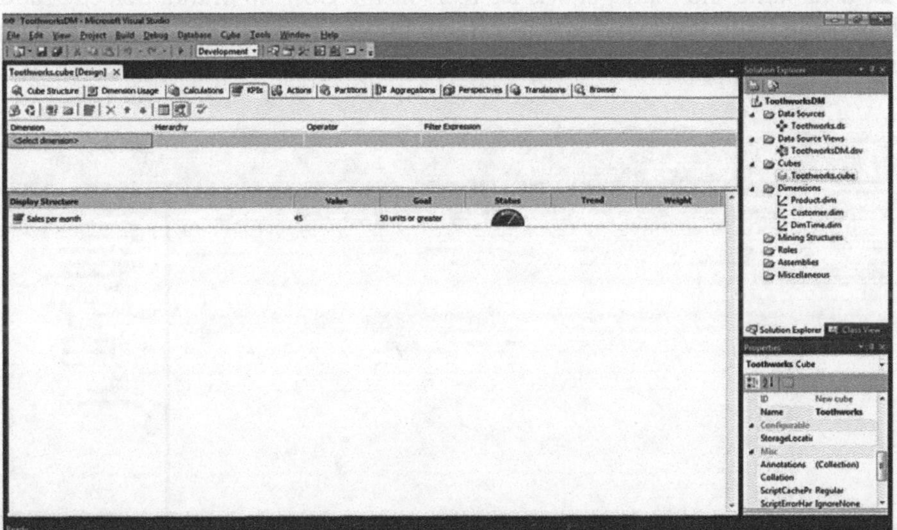

The current status is shown for total sales which is 45, as no filter is selected. So the status is Good.

8. Let us try to run some analysis here. Suppose the manager is interested in showing the status of sixth month, we can apply filter as shown here. Select DimTime

from dimension, DateHierarchy in Hierarchy, Equal as Operator, and 6 in Filter Expression. After this, press Enter.

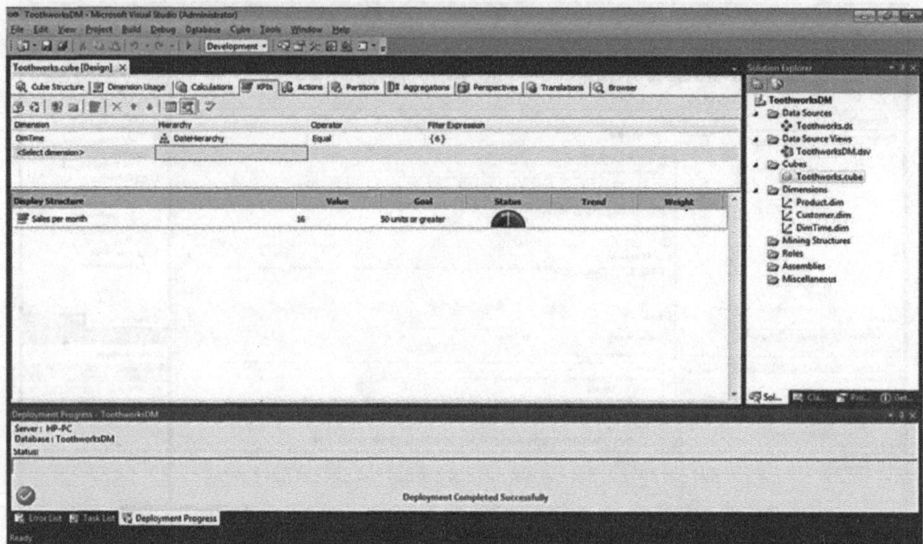

The gauge shows Yellow implies fair performance for the sixth month.

9. Let us assume the manager wishes to look for Colgate brand. Select Product in dimension field, ProductName in Hierarchy, Operator as Equal, and "Colgate" in filter expression.

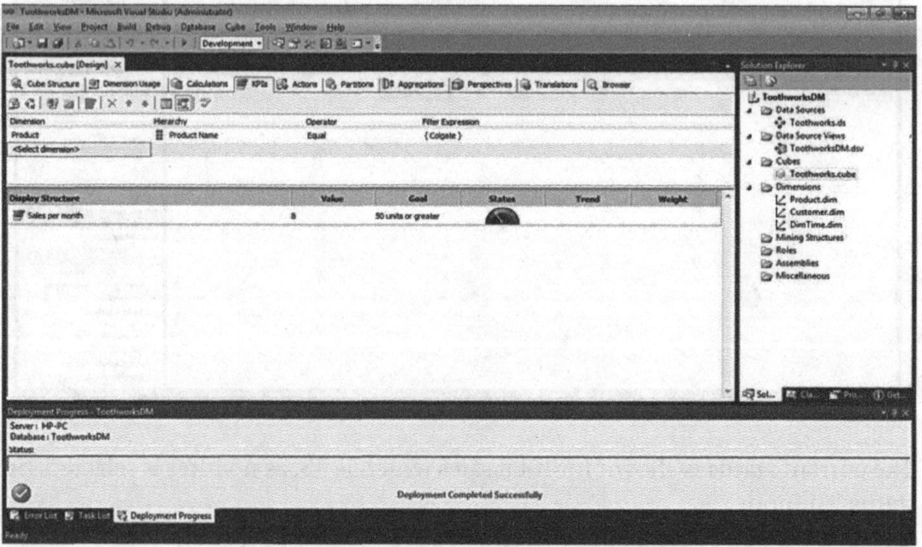

The gauge indicated red implying poor performance. Similarly, Glister has fair performance:

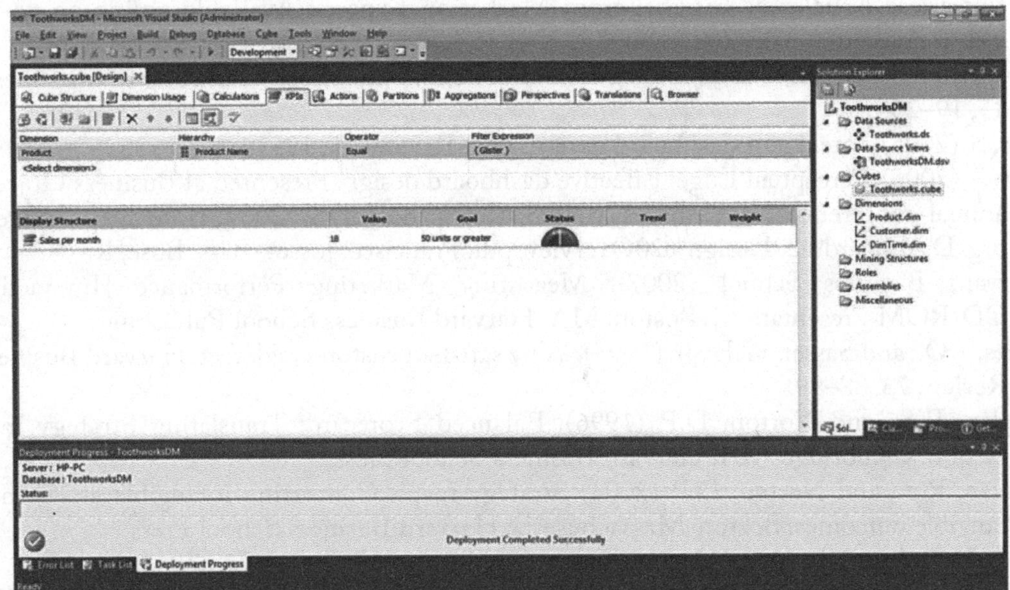

10. Similarly for married customers:

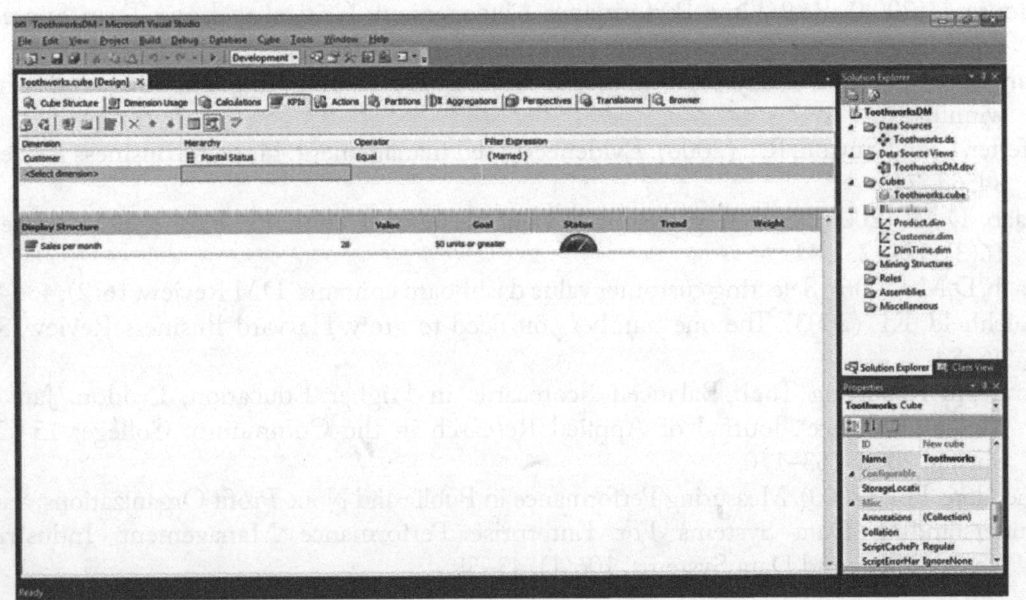

REFERENCES

Bury, J. (2005). Defining Key Performance Indicators, Best of Web Analytics Guide (12 times less Articles & Insights from Marketing Experts; Available online on www.webtrends.com 4 May 2007.

Clark, B.H., Abela, A.V., and Ambler, T. (2006). Behind the wheel. Marketing Management, 15, 19–23.

Few, S. (2005). Intelligent dashboard design. DM Review, 15, 12–14.

Few, S. (2006). Perceptual Edge. Effective dashboard design. Presented at Business Objects annual conference November 17, 2005. Retrieved July 2, 2007, from http://sfarea.org/Dashboard%20Design%20Overview.pdf. Francisco, Jossey-Bass. Bose, R.

Harvard Business School (2007). Measuring Marketing Performance [Interactive CD-ROM Presentation]. Boston, MA: Harvard Business School Publishing.

Jones, T.O., and Sasser, W.E., Jr. (1995). Why satisfied customers defect. Harvard Business Review, 73, 88–99.

Kaplan, R.S., and Norton, D.P. (1996). Balanced Scorecard: Translating Strategy into Action. Cambridge, MA: Harvard Business School Press.

Kaplan, R.S., and Norton, D.P. (2004) Strategy maps. Converting intangible assets into tangible outcomes. Boston-Massachusetts: Harvard Business School Press.

KPIs. Hoboken, NJ: John Wiley & Sons.

LaPointe, P., (2006). Marketing NPV. Three secrets behind successful marketing dashboards. Presented at a MarketingProfs virtual seminar, September 7.

Lewis, M. (2003). Moneyball: The art of winning an unfair game. New York: W. W. Norton & Company.

Moore, J. (2004). Real Time Performance Management: Critical to Long Term Success, Food Engineering.Business News Publishing Company.

Parmenter, D. (2007). Key performance indicators: Developing, implementing, and using winning.

Pfeffer, J., and Sutton, R.I. (2006). Evidence-based management. Harvard Business Review, 84, 62–74.

Raab, D.M. (2006). Selecting customer value dashboard contents, Part 2. DM Review, 16(3), 12–12.

Raab, D.M. (2006). Selecting customer value dashboard contents. DM Review, 16(2), 46–46.

Reichheld, F.F. (2003). The one number you need to grow. Harvard Business Review, 81, 46–54.

Strategic Reporting Tool: Balanced Scorecards in Higher Education, Lyddon, Jan & McComb, Bruce., Journal of Applied Research in the Community College; 15 (2); Spring, 2008, 163–170.

Theodore, H.P. (2003). Measuring Performance in Public and None Profit Organizations: San.

Understanding Data Systems For Enterprise Performance Management, Industrial Management and Data Systems, 106(1), 43–59.

CHAPTER 10

Predictive Analytics

After reading this chapter, you will be able to

- Understand the meaning of predictive analytics
- Understand the factors that led to the emergence of predictive analytics
- Understand how to effectively implement predictive analytics
- Understand applications of predictive analytics
- Understand the limitations of predictive analytics

INTRODUCTION

Gone are the days when managers needed to be active in taking prompt decisions. In the past, the key to success was to wait for the actual data and then take corrective actions. But, in the present business scenario, the managers cannot wait for that long. Managers need to be proactive, i.e., managers need to predict the future and take proactive steps to counter the intense competition and take the maximum benefit from future events. This is far easier than done, as the environment is very dynamic which makes it very difficult to predict and one thing is sure that the prediction cannot based on the gut feeling of managers. Moreover, there is an abundance of data which calls for specialised tools and techniques for analysing the data so that data can be properly analysed to predict the future events. All these factors have led to the emergence of the new specialised field in business analytics, i.e., predictive analytics. In this chapter, all the important aspects related to predictive analytics will be explained in detail.

PREDICTIVE ANALYTICS

> In our most recent research on the predictive analytics, more than half (58%) of participants indicated that predictive analytics is very important to their organisation. Furthermore, it is found that implementing predictive analysis would have a transformational impact in one-third of organisations and a significant positive impact in more than half of other ones.

> Predictive analytics is that specialised field of business analytics with the help of which the organisations can find out unseen patters in the data in order to develop a relationship between various variables by applying different statistical and forecasting models.

Ventana research

In the present time, there is an explosion of data. The data are everywhere and organisations are making deliberate efforts to collect huge volumes of data. In the past, it was very difficult to collect and store data, but with the emergence of digital data and developments in the field of information technology, now it is far easier for the organisations to collect the data. The recent advances have also resulted in the drastic reduction of the storage cost. Organisations now find it very easy and economical to collect and store huge volumes of data. But, the organisations do not fully realise the true potential of huge data. The changing business scenario has shifted the entire focus of the organisations as earlier the focus was only on storing the data and preparing some reports based on pre-decided queries. But with the changing working conditions, it is very important for organisations to have forward-looking approach, i.e., the mere reporting of past events is not sufficient to counter the cut-throat competitive forces. It is important for organisations to search for new avenues of doing business. These new avenues/paths can only be explored by proper analysis of stored data. The organisations need to capitalise the data. Data have immense untapped potential which the organisations need to explore.

Predictive analytics is the technology which helps the organisations to decipher the real potential of the stored data. As discussed, mere reporting of the past events is not sufficient; organisations need to be innovative to change its strategies to counter the dynamic environment. The predictive analytics help the organisations in this aspect. The predictive analytics is that specialised field of business analytics with the help of which the organisations can find out unseen patters in the data to develop the relationship between various variables applying different statistical and forecasting models. The predictive analytics is the forward-looking approach which assists the managers to forecast the future events to take rational decisions. It is important for organisations to be proactive and the predictive analytics help the organisations to discover future trends and patterns.

As knowledge is power and predictive analytics provides knowledge. Applying predictive analytics, it is possible to decipher the hidden patterns in the data. Predictive analytics is rather giving life to otherwise lifeless data. Predictive analytics is a forward-looking approach and often it is treated same like other forward-looking technologies. But, the predictive analytics should not be confused with the other technologies, for example,

- OLAP which tells why something happens
- Query which tells about reasons
- Dashboard which tells about what has happened
- But the predictive analytics tells what will happen by applying various tools like regression analysis, correlation, decision tree, neural networks, etc.

FACTORS THAT LED TO THE EMERGENCE OF PREDICTIVE ANALYTICS

Data is gold and it is important to mine the gold.

There are various factors that led to the growth of Predictive Analytics. These factors are

Factors that led to the emergence of predictive analytics:

1. Technological Advancement
2. Data Availability
3. Dynamic Conditions
4. Competition
5. Customer Retention
6. Image

1. **Technological Advancement**: The rapid and unprecedented advancement in the field of information technology has led to the emergence of predictive analytics. Right from the beginning, the information technology is widely applied in managing business operations. But with the emergence of various tools for forecasting and statistical analysis, the role of information technology has increased drastically. One does not require specialised computer knowledge to operate predictive analytics tools. This has helped the managers to use the tools of predictive analytics in an efficient, yet simple, manner.
2. **Data Availability**: The organisations are collecting and storing huge volumes of data. The emergence of digital data has helped organisations to collect data in a convenient manner, and with the reduction of storage cost it is very economical to store huge volumes of data. So, at the present time, there is no scarcity of data; rather, there is an abundance of data. These huge data store lot of hidden patterns, which can be only unlocked by the application of predictive analytical tools.
3. **Dynamic Conditions**: The environment under which the organisations are operating is becoming more and more dynamic with each passing day. It is very important for organisations to constantly change its strategies to counter the dynamic forces. Moreover, in this dynamic environment, the future is very uncertain. Hence, for organisations it is very important to accurately predict the future. The predictive analytics help the organisations in this aspect.
4. **Competition**: The competition is becoming more and more intense; rather, it will not be wrong to say that nowadays there is cut-throat competition. The customers are not loyal to any organisation and competitors have every chance to entice the ever-demanding customers. The organisations cannot live with the false notion of brand loyality. Organisations need to be innovative and future-oriented to counter competition. The predictive analytics helps the organisation to be future-oriented and guides the organisations to counter the competition by accurately predicting the future. This aids the organisations to be one step ahead of its competitors.
5. **Customer Retention**: No organisation can take customers for granted. The customers are very demanding and want an immediate solution to their problems. Earlier, the organisations used to work on the concept of customer satisfaction. But now the organisations are working on the concept of customer delight. The organisations need to pleasantly delight the customers. For this, the organisation needs to know the untapped patterns and the relationship between various variables (like purchase

> The top use cases for predictive analytics among the active group include direct marketing (58%), cross-sell and upsell (55%) and retention analysis (55%). TDWI Research First Quarter 2014.

pattern) which helps the organisations to satisfy the unfulfilled psychological needs of the customers. The predictive analytics help organisations to decipher the hidden secrets.

6. **Image**: The organisations need to have a very good image in the eyes of customers. Merely manufacturing a product or rendering a service is not the sole aim of the organisations. Organisations need to create a positive image in the eyes of the customers. To achieve this goal, organisations need to go beyond the usual business activities; for example, it is very important for banks to detect any fraud of misuse of the credit card by an imposter. This not only helps to check fraud, but also enhances the credibility of the bank. The predictive analytics help the organisations to detect any unusual patterns like spending through credit cards, and this helps to detect the possible fraud. Similarly, insurance companies are using predictive analytics to find out any fraudulent claims. The predictive analytics also aids the organizations in retaining customers as sometimes customers just shift to some other organisation even without complaining. The predictive analytics helps the organisation to discover the patterns and relationships which lead to the shifting of customers; for example, in case of telecom companies, the predictive analytics helps the organisations to reduce the churn rate by untapping the hidden patterns of shifting. Similarly, by applying the predictive analytics, organisations can predict the future breakdown of machinery which helps to take timely action to avoid the breakdown of machinery. In HR also, with the help of predictive analytics, the HR manager can predict the future attrition and factors which can result in future attrition. Acting proactively, the HR manager can take steps to motivate the staff and in turn negates the future attrition.

IMPORTANT ASPECTS OF EFFECTIVE IMPLEMENTATION OF PREDICTIVE ANALYTICS

From the above discussion, it is clear that predictive analytics plays a significant role in the present time. But to avail the full benefits of the predictive analytics, it is important that there should be proper knowledge of important aspects related to predictive analytics. As the predictive analytics has a long-lasting impact on any organisation, the following section gives the knowledge of the critical aspects of the predictive analytics.

> Important aspects of effective implementation of predictive anaytics:
>
> 1. Clear Objectives
> 2. Collect Data
> 3. Data Mining
> 4. Model Selection
> 5. Model Evaluation

1. **Clear Objectives**: To operate in the present dynamic and highly competitive environment, it is very important that organisations should have clear objectives. The clarity of objectives not only guides the organisation to formulate goals but also helps to design strategies to

fulfil the long-term objectives and goals. The application of predictive analytics depends on these strategies.

2. **Collect Data**: Once the objectives are clear, organisations need to collect and store the relevant data. The results of predictive analytics depend on the quantity and quality of data. Hence, both aspects regarding data are important, i.e., quantity and quality. The organisations need not only to collect huge volumes of data, but also to perform cleansing and transformation of data so that quality of data can be maintained.
3. **Data Mining**: Once the data are collected and stored, the next part is to mine the relevant data out of huge volumes of stored data. The organisation should be clear regarding which functional aspect the predictive analytics should be applied for. Depending on the particular aspect, the specific data are mined from the database.
4. **Model Selection**: After data mining, the next step is the selection of right model of the predictive analytics. There are various models of forecasting and statistics which can be applied to know the future trends, for example, linear regression, partial regression, logit and porbit regression, neural networks, etc. But, it is very important to choose the right tool for getting accurate results from predictive analytics. First, the organisation should select limited number of variables for prediction and then depending on the result, more variables can be added to enhance the functionality of a particular model.
5. **Model Evaluation**: It is very important to evaluate the model. For this purpose, the organisation can choose the technique of selective screening. In this technique, suppose the organisation wants to use the data of previous 52 weeks to predict the future in the coming 4 weeks. In order to test a particular model, first the organisation should use only 40 weeks data and do prediction of 12 weeks. The actual figure is also with the organisation (52 weeks), and hence the organisation can compare actual results with the predicted results to gauge the efficiency of the model.

APPLICATIONS OF PREDICTIVE ANALYTICS

"With Predictive analytics, we were basically able to close a hole in our pocket where money was leaking out steadily. We were also ready to show that this was just the beginning."

—Bill Dibble, SVP of Claims Operations, Infinity Property and Casualty

Predictive analytics is widely applied in various areas of an organisation. Like in marketing, where, although the marketing department gets all the transaction data, but it is very important to unlock the real potential of collected data (as most of the times these data remain unutilised). Moreover, it is also very important for marketing managers to predict the future demands so as to formulate the right strategies. Applying

Applications of predictive anaytics:

1. Airline Industry
2. Insurance Industry
3. Banking Sector
4. Manufacturing Sector
5. Travel Industry
6. Telecom Industry
7. Health Care
8. Retail
9. Online Companies

various models of predictive analytics, it is possible for marketing managers to predict the uncertain future.

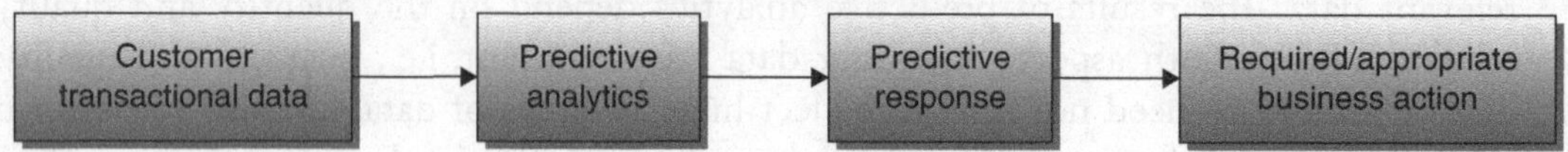

Predictive analytics help the managers in target marketing, customer management, forecasting future demand, cross-selling, budgeting, loyalty, designing appropriate marketing campaigns. Predictive analytics help to eliminate the guess work and provide competitive advantage to the organisations by providing unmatched customer services and fulfilling the needs of customers by predicting the changing preferences of the customers. Similarly, in the HR field also, predictive analytics play an important role. The major resource of any organisation is the workforce. Considering the intense competition, there is much pressure on HR managers to not only hire the right person, but also check the attrition rate. The organisations are applying predictive analytics extensively in the case of hiring. The organisations are taking into account previous factors such as high-performance employees belong to which institute, their selection procedure, age, experience, etc. Considering these factors, with the help of predictive analytics, the HR manager can predict that which type of employee will best fit which job and the best way of selecting that employee. Once hired, the next task of the HR manager is to reduce attrition and motivate staff. Again, applying predictive analytics, the HR manager takes into account various factors such as tenure, performance, leaves availed, age, gender to predict whether a particular employee will leave the organisation or not. This helps organisations to plan proper strategies so as to check the attrition of the employees. In the production field also, predictive analytics play a very important role. Applying predictive models, the production manager can predict the future breakdown of machines and hence can save much time and money for the organisation. For financial firms predictive analytics has become an integral part. Applying predictive analytics the financial firms can see the hidden patterns in spendings and detect any fraud.

"IBM SPSS Predictive Analytic software has exceeded our expectations. The results we obtained in successive mail campaigns during the pilot phase were very good. We are convinced that our success in cross-selling will be much higher, as our database managers gain more experience with the analytical software and build up a richer knowledge of customer needs. With additional data and cross-selling we are expecting improvements of 50% and more."

—Phillippe Neyt, Commercial Director, Corona Direct

To give a clear picture of application of Predictive Analytics, let us discuss industry-wise role of predictive analytics.

1. **Airline Industry**: In the airline industry, it is essential to predict the future demand so that proper planning can be done. Applying predictive analytics, not only forecast of the future demand is possible, but also airline operators can predict which customers are going to defect in the future based on certain past parameters. This helps airline operators to design customer-centric policies and rewards for loyal customers.
2. **Insurance Industry**: One of the major applications of the predictive analytics in the insurance sector is the fraud detection. Applying the predictive analytics, it is possible for insurance companies to decipher the hidden patterns based on proper analysis of past data which helps the insurance companies to decide that which customers are going to default the premium payments. Moreover, as people are taking health-insurance policies applying predictive analytics it is possible for health-insurance companies to find out frauds based on the previous health checkup data of the customers.

"We're committed to profitability and to strengthening our customer relationship thorough every aspect of the way we do business. Predictive Analytics gives us the intelligence and insight we need to follow through on this commitment."

—Dan Marks, Chief Marketing Officer, First Tennessee Bank

---

3. **Banking Sector**: Predictive analytics helps to detect frauds in banking sector. Applying predictive analytics, it is possible to detect the credit card frauds by analysing any drastic change in spending pattern of a particular credit card holder. Similarly, predictive analytics helps to predict the future preference of the customers which helps banks to design specific product and services according to the unfulfilled psychological needs of the customers. Predictive analytics aids in finding out which customers are likely to default the loan payment based on the previous data. This, in turn, assists banks to distribute loans only to those customers who are having a sound track record.
4. **Manufacturing Sector**: In this cut-throat competition era, it is important that organisations should keep on manufacturing the goods without any interruption. Any delay in the production cycle can seriously hamper the future prospects of the organisation. Moreover, any delay in the manufacturing process also results in loss of time and resources, which no organisation can afford. Applying predictive analytics, it is possible for manufacturing organisations to predict the future breakdown of machines which helps organisations to take necessary corrective actions for uninterrupted manufacturing of products.
5. **Travel Industry**: The success of any travel company lies in the fact whether the company provides adequate package and offers to its customers. Applying predictive analytics, it is possible for the travel companies to predict the future demand, and accordingly, the company can design appropriate offers and tour packages for its customers. Moreover, by properly analysing past records, a travel company can provide an appropriate offer to its loyal customers.
6. **Telecom Industry**: Telecom is yet another sector which is witnessing intense competition. When everyday customers are getting tantalising offers from rival

telecom companies, it is very important for any telecom company to stop the churn rate. Applying predictive analytics, it is possible for telecom companies to predict the customers who are going to churn or leave the company. Using the data regarding outgoing calls, bills, messages, incoming calls, it is possible to predict the customers who are likely to churn and accordingly particular telecom company can design appropriate strategies to stop the future churn.

7. **Health Care**: Various big names have entered in the business of health care. As a result of which, nowadays, there is also intense competition in the health-care sector. Various hospitals are taking the help of predictive analytics to find out the re-hospitalisation of patients based on the past health record of patients. Predictive analytics also helps to predict the outbreak of possible future disease and thus guides the invention of new medicines.
8. **Retail**: Retail industry has shown tremendous growth in the last few years, but still there is a lot more in store as we are going to witness more growth in the near future. But even the present rate of growth has resulted in a number of retail stores in the same city and even in the same market. It is very important for retail stores to target the right customers with the right offers. Predictive analytics helps to find out patterns in the purchase so as to predict the future demand. Applying predictive analytics, the retail store manager can perform market basket analysis. Market basket analysis helps to analyse the purchase of more than one item in one basket of a customer. Analysing the basket of the customer and his/her attributes, the retail store manager can provide tailor-made offers to entice its customers (like one plus one offer). The success of any retail store depends on the availability of the items in the store. If the customer does not get the required item, then not only he is going to visit another retail store, but also will tell his acquaintances regarding the non-availability of products, which can have a cascading effect on the retail store. The predictive analytics helps to find out future demand, which helps the retail stores to purchase the items in bulk to avail discounts.
9. **Online Companies**: Predictive analytics plays an important role in the success of online companies. Applying the concept of past purchase patterns, it is possible for online companies to predict the future purchase patterns of customers and also helps in deciding the discounts and combo offers. Even depending on past purchase behaviour, the online companies can cross sell different products to its customers. For example, if a customer has purchased business analytics book from an online bookstore, then the same online bookstore can target that customer to market its books on R and Hadoop.

Limitations of predictive anaytics:

1. Model Selection Prerequisites
2. Data
3. High Cost
4. Knowledge

LIMITATIONS OF PREDICTIVE ANALYTICS

Despite all the above applications, predictive analytics has the following limitations:

1. **Model Selection Prerequisites**: Every model of predictive analytics has pre-requisites. These requirements

should be known to the business analyst before applying particular predictive analytics models. Any wrong decision regarding the choice of predictive analytical tool can have a devastating effect on any organisation. For example, in case of regression, the pre-requisites are

(a) *Linearity* of the relationship between dependent and independent variables
(b) *Independence* of the errors
(c) *Homoscedasticity* (constant variance) of the errors
(d) The errors of prediction are distributed normally

2. **Data**: Data are the lifeline for any business analytics tool. Any inadequacy in the form of quantity and quality can seriously hamper the effectiveness of predictive analytics.
3. **High Cost**: The concept of predictive analytics is still in the nascent stage in India, and hence, the software of predictive analytics are still very costly. For any new organisation, it is very difficult to spend large amounts of money on the tools of predictive analytics.
4. **Knowledge**: To effectively run the software of predictive analytics, one needs proper knowledge of predictive analytics, for example, one needs thorough knowledge of regression analysis to select the appropriate regression tools out of linear regression, partial regression, logit regression, probit regression for proper prediction of the future. Without proper knowledge, predictive analytics will not deliver accurate and desired results.

CONCLUSION

From the above discussion, readers must have realised that managers need to be proactive considering the dynamic environment. Although with the recent advances in technology, it is very easy for organisations to collect and store huge volumes of data, but it is also critical that organisations should decipher the hidden secrets from the stored data. The predictive analytics is that specialised field of business analytics with the help of which the organisations can find out unseen patterns in the data to develop the relationship between various variables applying different statistical and forecasting models. The predictive analytics is the forward-looking approach which assists the managers in forecasting the future events to take rational decisions. The future managers need to have a proper understanding regarding the potential of predictive analytics so that in the future when they are going to manage the organisations they can easily steer the organisation in this dynamic era.

KEY TERMS

SUMMARY

In this chapter, all the important aspects of predictive analytics are explained in detail. Starting from basic concepts of predictive analytics to its applications, all critical aspects of predictive analytics are discussed. As pointed out at the start of this chapter, predictive analytics is the forward-looking approach which assists the managers in forecasting the future events to take rational decisions. Applying predictive analytics, it is possible to decipher the hidden patterns in the data. Predictive analytics is rather giving life to otherwise lifeless data. Moving ahead the chapter has enlisted various factors which led to the growth of predictive analytics. To give a clear picture of predictive analytics, all the important applications and limitations are elucidated. This chapter closes with two case studies and to have a better understanding of the concepts of predictive analytics concept review questions, project activity and assignment questions are given at the end of this chapter.

MULTIPLE CHOICE QUESTIONS

1. Predictive analytics tells
   a. Why something happened in the past?
   b. Why is something happening?
   c. Routine transactions
   d. What will happen

2. Which of the following is not a technique of predictive analytics?
   a. ANOVA
   b. Regression analysis
   c. Market basket analysis
   d. Artificial neural networks

3. Predictive analytics is applied in airline industry to find out
   a. Routine transactions
   b. Summary statements
   c. Which customers are going to defect in the future based on certain past parameters
   d. Reports

4. Predictive analytics is applied in the insurance industry to find out
   a. Which customers are going to default the premium payments
   b. Routine transactions
   c. Summary statements
   d. Reports

5. Predictive analytics is applied in the banking industry to find out
   a. Which customers are likely to default the loan payment based on the previous data
   b. Routine transactions
   c. Summary statements
   d. Reports

6. Predictive analytics is applied in the manufacturing industry to find out
   a. Routine transactions
   b. Summary statements
   c. Reports
   d. The future breakdown of machines

7. Predictive analytics is applied in telecom industry to find out
   a. Customers who are going to churn or leave the particular company
   b. Routine transactions
   c. Summary statements
   d. Reports

8. Predictive analytics is applied in hospitals to find out
   a. Routine transactions
   b. To find out the re-hospitalisation of patients based on the past health record of patients
   c. Summary statements
   d. Reports

9. Predictive analytics is applied in retail industry to find out
   a. Market basket analysis
   b. Routine transactions
   c. Summary statements
   d. Reports

10. Predictive analytics are applied in online retail stores to find out
   a. Cross selling of different products to its customers
   b. Routine transactions
   c. Summary statements
   d. Reports

REVIEW QUESTIONS

1. Discuss how predictive analytics is helping the organisations to operate in the intensely competitive environment.
2. What are the factors which led to the growth of predictive analytics?
3. Discuss the important aspects required for getting best results from predictive analytics.
4. Discuss some of the important applications of predictive analytics.
5. What are the limitations of predictive analytics?

ASSIGNMENT

1. How predictive analytics can be applied in case of campus placements. Make a complete report after discussing the key issues with your university/college placement officer.
2. Search those Indian organisations which are applying predictive analytics in their business. Make a detailed report.

PROJECT ACTIVITY

1. Visit a nearby bank and discuss with the concerned bank manager how the bank applies predictive analytics. In this project activity, include the procedure of fraud detection being applied by that particular bank.

CASE STUDIES

1. Predictive Analytics in Action: IBM Powering Sports Tournaments

IBM is a pioneer in analytics. Apart from providing best analytical solutions to business organisations, IBM has also ventured into the sports arena. IBM recently partnered with US Tennis Open Championship, which is one of the most viewed tennis tournaments. "Our job is to deliver the championship to the world in an innovative way," said John Kent, a technology manager at IBM. "When we do sponsorships, they are a little different. Certainly, the advertising, exposure and hospitality are all very important, but the core of it is showing what we can do with our technology." In order to make US Open as one of the best tournaments, the sponsors provided not only the best facilities to players but also an altogether different technological experience to fans. In the tournament, the organisers of US Open with IBM attempted to engage fans in an interactive manner. IBM offered one of the best visualisation and analytical services to the ardent fans of the US Open. It placed a special feature on the website of the US Open which is known as "IBM Slamtracker". It provides the features of advanced visualisation and real-time analytics. IBM Slamtracker provides a consolidated view of all the matches in a single screen and fans can even get real-time minute details of each ongoing and previous match in the form of player stats, setwise summary of match and that too in an interactive manner. The fans also get a match summary in the form of interactive graphics focussing on each critical parameter of a match like number of aces, double faults, unforced errors and break point conversions.

Live Feed

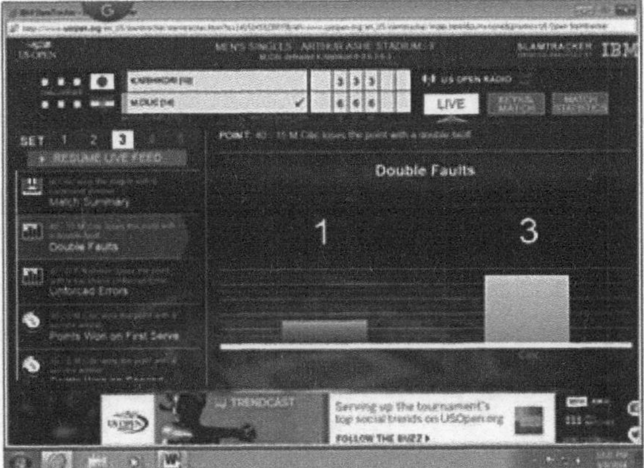

Source: www.usopen.org

Match Summary

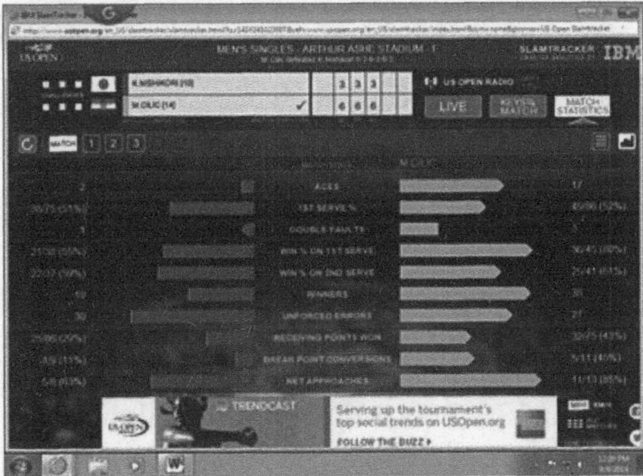

Source: www.usopen.org

Besides this interactive visualisation for the fans, a key feature of IBM Slamtracker is Real Time Analytics. This feature is based on the concept of Predictive Analytics. Applying Real Time Analytics, Slamtracker provides what is termed "Keys to the Match". Slamtracker's "Keys to the Match" feature, built on IBM's predictive analytics technology (SPSS), mines over 8 years of Grand Slam Tennis data (~41 million data points) to determine patterns and styles for players when they win. Before each match, the IBM Keys to the Match system runs an analysis of both competitors' historical head-to-head match-ups, as well as statistics against comparable player styles to determine what each player must do to win the match. By looking at these keys, the fans can predict based on current performance of players the likelihood of winning or losing the game. In short, this tool has proved to be highly engaging. For example, based on the performance of the last three sets, keys to the match provide three keys for player A

- Won more than 50% of medium rallies
- Won 56% on first serve return
- Average between 4.6 and 5.8 points per game serving

Similarly for Player B, the keys to the match are

- Won 54% points on second serve
- Won 30% of first serve return points
- Won 40% points when serving at 15–30

These detailed analyses provide an in-depth view of a match and fans feel more engaged when they have such a detailed analysis of live matches.

Keys to Match

Another classic example of IBM visualisation and real-time analytics service is of the US Open Golf Tournament. IBM has developed iPad apps with advanced visualisation features, which support HD videos from multiple angles, split screens to swipe between different streams and viewing angles on the field. But, the most fascinating feature is "Hole Insights". It is based on real-time analytics to find out which "greens" (area of closely trimmed grass and relatively even ground surrounding the hole) are most difficult and which greens are most costly to miss. Besides, it also suggests what percentage of players recover from these misses to birdie or par the holes. For example, in the following screen shot, it is analysed that 18th hole is the most difficult hole and in the 18th hole, 73% of the shots missed the "green".

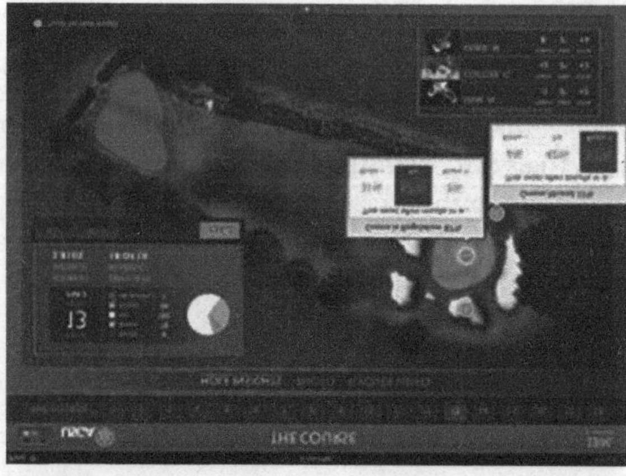

Similarly, the 13th hole is the easiest one with 87% of players reaching green in regulation and only 13% players missed the green and even out of these 13% players, 42% players managed to achieve par and 6% have managed to birdie. Birdie implies to score one under par or one under the number of shots required to complete a hole.

Questions

1. What is IBM Slamtracker? How does it engage fans of the US Open championship?
2. How does IBM Slamtracker apply real-time analytics?
3. How can predictive analytics be applied to golf tournaments?

2. Blue Palms Powering Miami-Dade Police Department

Miami-Dade County is located in the southeastern part of the State of Florida. Miami-Dade is the third largest county in terms of area and with a population of more than 2.5 million citizens, it is the seventh most populous county in the US. The main source of income for the government of this county as well as for citizens is tourism. Tourism provides more than 20 billion US$ per year to the government of Miami-Dade.

To attract an increasing number of tourists from across the world to Miami-Dade, the government intends to foster a safe environment to make the tourists feel at home. With safety as its primary focus area, the Miami-Dade government has specially formulated Robbery Investigation Section (RIS) to control the thefts and ultimately provide a safe environment for tourists as well as local citizens. However, to manage such large area with an equally large population (in millions!) is an arduous job. Of late, RIS is facing many problems in cracking such cases, as RIS is based on the standard procedure or conventional approach of controlling crime. It relies heavily on the experience of its detectives who utilise their skills and experience to generate leads for the case through their informants. The problem is that as number of detectives are getting retired; as they leave, all their skill and experience also go. There is no procedure where this experience of retiring detectives can be utilised to train new recruits. "The standard practices we used to generate leads, like talking to informants or to the community or to patrol officers, haven't changed much if at all. That kind of an approach works OK, but it relies a lot on the experience our detectives carry in their head. When the detectives retire or move on, that experience goes with them" said Lieutenant Arnold Palmer, currently supervising the Robbery Investigations Section.

Many cases could not be cracked in time owing to this problem at RIS of Miami-Dade. However, safety of tourists and citizens could not be compromised at any costs. This is when Palmer decided to take the help of technology to solve the problem and collaborated with IBM. "Our aim is to give investigators factual insights from information we already have that might make a difference, so even if we're successful five percent of the time, we're going to take a lot of offenders off the street", said Lieutenant Arnold Palmer. The aim of this collaboration was not only to find the hotspots where crime is likely to occur and when it is going to occur, but also to pinpoint the persons who have committed the crime, so that in future proper control on crime can be achieved. "I don't need you to tell me that there's going to be a robbery on an afternoon shift in a particular neighborhood. I know it's going to happen," said Lieutenant Arnold Palmer. "I'd much rather you help me narrow down who did it".

Considering the goal of RIS, IBM introduced Blue Palms which is based on predictive analytics. This software operates on a top of a database which contains historical or earlier cases of crime and modulus operandi applied to crack such cases. Additionally, all the information regarding criminals is also stored in the database. To solve a given case, the software Blue Palms take all the data related to crime case and its modus operandi or "crime pattern" as input. The input information is then crosschecked by the software with the historical information and within minutes, the system generates the list of 20 prime suspects who were involved in similar crimes before. Palmer says that, "We are going to save money, resources and catch the offender quicker. We are realizing the power of the program and the analytics, and we are having a conversation we haven't had previously". The software was first tried on 20 cases of crime which had already been solved, to check the accuracy of its predictions. Blue Palms was 73% successful in predicting the criminals. Going by the success of the test run, RIS has now implemented Blue Palms in RIS which is helping a great deal to uncover the cases, even without the retiring detectives. In the words of Palmer, "The fact that we're able to use analytics and intelligence to help us close more cases and keep more criminals off the street is good news for our citizens and our tourist industry".

Questions

1. How does Miami-Dade police ensure a safe environment for tourists?
2. Discuss the problems that the Miami-Dade police was experiencing with its earlier system of investigation.
3. What solution was implemented to overcome the problems? How did predictive analytics provide 73% success rate to the department?

REFERENCES

(2010) Analytics: The New Path to Value; how the smartest organizations are embedding analytics to transform insights into action. IBM Institute for Business Value & MIT Sloan Management Review.

(2011) Analytics: The widening divide; How companies are achieving competitive advantage through analytics. IBM Institute for Business Value & MIT Sloan Management Review.

Davenport, T.H., Harris, J.G. (2007). Competing in Analytics: the new science of winning. Boston, Massachussets: Harvard Business School Press.

Ehrenberg, A.S.C., and Bound, J.A. (1993). "Predictability and Prediction," Journal of the Royal Statistical Society Series A (156:2), 167–206.

Fayyad, U.M, Grinstein, G.G., and Wierse, A. (2002). InformationVisualization in Data Mining and Knowledge Discovery, New York: Morgan Kaufmann.

Forster, M.R. (2002). "Predictive Accuracy as an Achievable Goal of Science," Philosophy of Science (69:3), pp. S124–S134.

Friedman, D.J., and Montgomery, D.C. (1985). "Evaluation of the Predictive Performance of Biased Regression Estimators," Journal of Forecasting (4:2), pp. 153–163.

Harteveldt, H. H., and Stark, E. (2010). "How Travel eBusiness Can Win Friends And Influence Travelers," Forrester Research, Inc.

http://api.ning.com/files/FqkiRUfegCglEZLMZcPW3RDAQs0gVAYbXSis3qa-LTLXxEIL4tWM9OHQr7fRDIgMy9bI0BbmAnF08WfUt5gnIpHKHr64aeD9D/IBMPublicSafetyCaseStudy.pdf. Accessed on Sep 9, 2014.

http://asmarterplanet.com/gamechangers/blog/2013/06/us-open-hole-insights-through-rounds-1-2.html. Accessed on Sep 9, 2014.

http://asmarterplanet.com/gamechangers/files/holeinsights13.jpg. Accessed on 9 September 2014.

http://asmarterplanet.com/gamechangers/files/holeinsights18.jpg. Accessed on 9 September 2014.

http://people4smartercities.com/series/staying-ahead-crime-one-countys-smart-solution-safer-streets. Accessed on 9 September 2014.

http://public.dhe.ibm.com/common/ssi/ecm/en/ytc03062usen/YTC03062USEN.PDF. Accessed on Sep 9, 2014. Accessed on 9 September 2014.

http://siamtechcs.com/index_80.html. Accessed on 9 September 2014.

http://www.forbes.com/sites/ibm/2014/06/09/u-s-open-uses-technology-to-reinvent-golf-fans-experience/. Accessed on 9 September 2014.

http://www.govloop.com/profiles/blogs/leveraging-crime-analytics-miami-dade-county-blue-palm-program. Accessed on 9 September 2014.

http://www.ibm.com/big-data/us/en/big-data-and-analytics/case-studies.html. Accessed on 9 September 2014.

http://www.ibm.com/smarterplanet/us/en/leadership/firsttenbank/assets/pdf/IBM-firstTennBank.pdf. Accessed on 9 September 2014.

http://www.ibm.com/smarterplanet/us/en/leadership/infinity/assets/pdf/IBM_Infinity.pdf. Accessed on 9 September 2014.

http://www.ibmsystemsmag.com/linuxonpower/Business-Strategy/Analytics/grandslam_solution/?page=3. Accessed on 9 September 2014.

http://www.sportsbusinessdaily.com/Journal/Issues/2013/06/17/Events-and-Attractions/US-Open-notebook.aspx. Accessed on 9 September 2014.

http://www.theregister.co.uk/2002/07/24/ibm_talks_big_biz/. Accessed on 9 September 2014.

http://www.usopen.com/en_US/info/partners/ibm.html. Accessed on 9 September 2014.
http://www.usopen.org/en_US/slamtracker/index.html. Accessed on 9 September 2014.
http://www.usopen.org/en_US/slamtracker/slamtracker.html?ts=1410065315297&ref=www.usopen.org/en_US/slamtracker/index.html&syn=none&promo=US%20Open%20Slamtracker. Accessed on 9 September 2014.
https://www.ibm.com/smarterplanet/global/files/us__en_us__leadership__miami_dade.pdf. Accessed on 9 September 2014.
Ko, M., and Osei-Bryson, K.M. (2008). "Reexamining the Impact of Information Technology Investment on Productivity Using Regression Tree and Multivariate Adaptive Regression Splines (MARS)," Information Technology and Management (9:4), pp. 285–299.

CHAPTER 11

Data Mining

After going through this chapter, you will be able to

- Understand the concept and types of data
- Understand the concept and types of data mining
- Understand the fundamentals behind classification techniques such as decision trees, case-based reasoning, regression and neareast neighbour classifier
- Understand what clustering is and its types—partitional and Hierarchical
- Understand how association works

INTRODUCTION

The most important job of any manager is to take quick and rational decisions. But for taking rational decisions, managers need the right information at the right time. The information is obtained when data are processed.

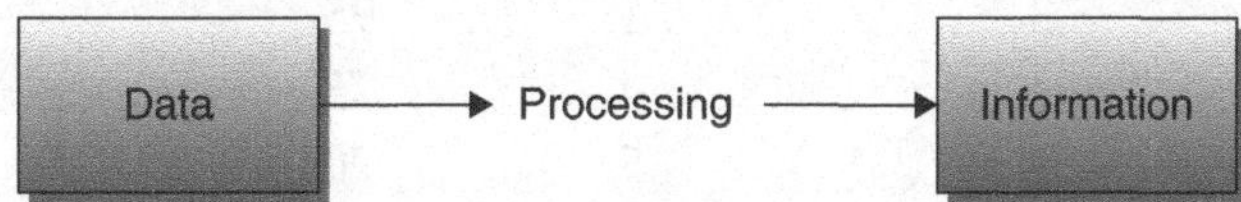

To tackle intense competition, organisations are in dire need to search data for generating right information from the large pool of data to have an edge in over-competitive forces. To extract information, organisations are applying data mining concepts. Data mining is the technique which helps the organisations to mine relevant information from the data. As there is an explosion of data, the organisations need to mine information from large amounts of data. All the concepts of data mining will be explained in this chapter.

DATA TYPES

Data types

1. Nominal Data
2. Ordinal Data
3. Interval data
4. Ratio Data

Before explaining the concepts of data mining, it is important to understand the various types of data in detail. Data are an amalgamation of facts collected from observations or experiments. The data are of the following types:

1. **Nominal Data**: When the data are collected by just assigning codes or labels to classify the objects, it is known as nominal data. The nominal data just categorise the object, for example, jersey numbers of hockey players, marital status, etc. The nominal data does not show the maximum or minimum characteristics possessed by the object. As a hockey player with jersey number 4 does not have a high ranking as compared with a hockey player having jersey number 9. Nominal data just shows the categories or counts.
2. **Ordinal Data**: When the data show the amount of characteristic possessed by an object that data are known as ordinal data. It does not represent the exact numerical value of an attribute; rather, it shows the ranking of objects. For example, Rank 1 student has more marks as compared with Rank 2 student.
3. **Interval Data**: Interval data are collected when the intervals between two objects are taken into account. Interval data differ from the ordinal data. The ordinal data only provide information about the ranking of the objects, but it does not provide information regarding the difference in the interval between the first object and the second object. For example, although the temperature in Celsius, 10°C, is more than 5°C, but there is a problem with interval data as it has no true zero value. For example, ordinal data can be collected by ranking of students, but it does not show the difference of percentage between the first student and the second-rank student. When the data are collected by measuring marks of different students, then that data are known as interval data.

Roll no	Rank	Marks
1	2	90
2	3	85
3	1	95
4	4	75
5	5	70

   Roll number is nominal data as it only classifies the students. Rank is ordinal data which give information regarding particular characteristic possessed by the students, whereas the marks are the interval data which show the difference of that characteristic between students.
4. **Ratio Data**: When data are collected by computing the ratios of the objects, it is categorised as ratio data. The ratio data not only possess the attributes of nominal, ordinal and interval data, but also help to find out the ratio between the objects. In the interval data, the zero is arbitrary; as a result of which, ratios cannot be calculated, but in the ratio data, the zero is non-arbitrary which makes it possible to calculate ratios of the measuring objects.

Data Everywhere and in Different Types

Considering the above facts, it is evident that there are different types of data and with the technological advances organisations are capturing huge volumes of data. But, it is also important that organisations should mine relevant information from the large volumes of different types of data. The data mining has gained more importance in the recent past because at the present time there are lots of avenues available from where organisations can search data and moreover with the reduction in storage space cost, organisations are storing huge amounts of data. Presently, organisations need specific techniques to mine relevant information from the large volumes of stored data. The data mining is the set of techniques which help organisations to mine out relevant information from the large volumes of stored data. These techniques include the concepts of artificial intelligence, artificial neural networks, statistical techniques, management science concepts. The recent advances in the data mining field have enabled organisations to mine out relevant information from the stored data.

DATA MINING TECHNIQUES

There are various techniques of data mining which include the following:

1. Classification
2. Clustering
3. Association

Data mining is the set of techniques which help organisations to mine out relevant information from large volumes of stored data.

In the following section, all the above-mentioned techniques are explained in detail.

CLASSIFICATION

It is the process of organising the item/objects according to the pre-specified categories. In this definition, it is very important to note one word, i.e., pre-specified categories.

Classification is the process of organising items/objects according to the pre-specified categories.

Pre-Specified categories This word is the main difference between classification and clustering. Classification is a supervised learning technique, whereas clustering is unsupervised. Supervised learning implies that target class is known beforehand. So the mining algorithm would then identify patterns from data which fall into each target class. In unsupervised learning, target class is not known beforehand. The algorithm then identifies patterns from data based on distances between them. In clustering, the analyst has no idea about the target or pre-specified categories. On the other hand, classification is an exploratory technique in which the recording/objects are classified according to some selected attributes in a pre-specified classes, e.g., credit card rating agency wants to rate the

The process of searching out the previously unknown facts in the form of information from the large pool of stored database is known as data mining.

customer according to various parameters such as salary, employment status, property, and tax paid and bank statement in high, low credit risk categories. But, the classification is less exploratory as compared with the clustering as in clustering the analyst needs to explore the categories. In classification, the analyst has to decide the predictor (which he wants to predict), like in the above-mentioned example the predictor will be credit risk, and then the analyst categorises the predictor in different classes, i.e., high, medium and low credit (known as target). The model or algorithm is also developed to show the relationship between the predictor and the target. The classification has wide application in the fields of

1. Detection of fraud
2. Loan approval
3. Pattern recognition
4. Image recognition

Tools of Classification

Following are the various tools of classification:

> Decision tree is based on the question and answer method.

1. Decision Tree
2. K-Nearest Neighbor Classifier
3. Case Based Reasoning
4. Regression Models

Decision tree

Decision tree is the most widely applied classification tool. It is a very simple and robust technique. It is based on the question and answer method. Every answer is followed by a question till the final result is reached. This whole sequence of questions and answers is put in the hierarchical structure which shows the entire sequence using nodes and leafs (see Exhibit 11.1). In the terminology of decision tree, **nodes** are of three types:

1. **Root node**: The starting point of the decision tree which has no incoming edges and has only outgoing edges.
2. **Internal node**: The internal node has one incoming edge and two or more outgoing edges. This node represents tests on an attribute. For example, tests gender.
3. **Leaf node**: Leaf has one incoming edge and no outgoing edge. It represents class label of the attribute from which it is branching. Gender can have male or female as class labels.

> **Tools of classification:**
>
> 1. Decision tree
> 2. K-Nearest-neighbour classifier
> 3. Case-based reasoning
> 4. Regression models

The root node is constituted by using pre-specified conditions. At the root node, decision tree chooses an

Exhibit 11.1 Basic structure of decision tree

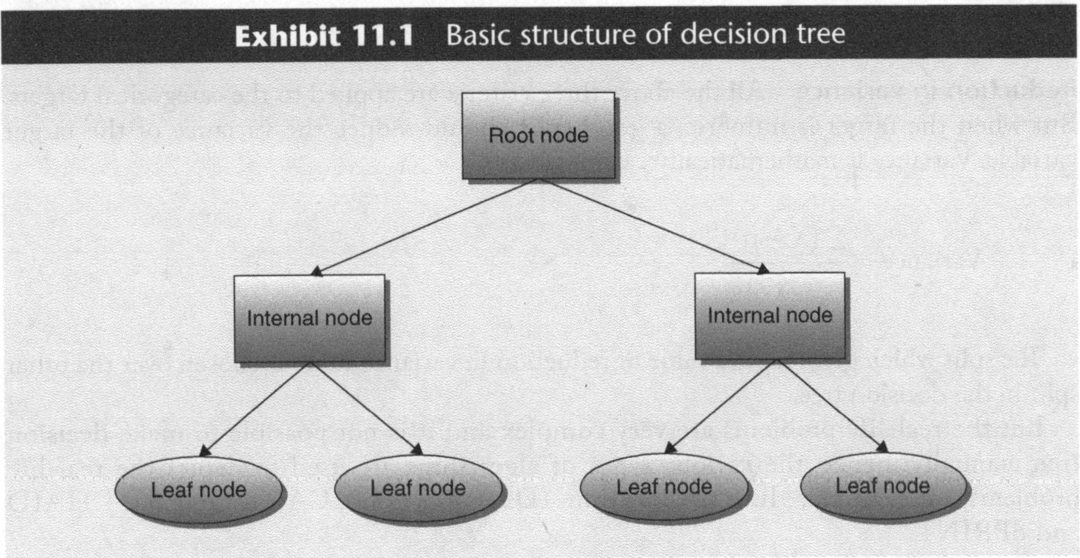

attribute to split the data. As in the above diagram, there are two internal nodes and subsequent leaf nodes. The decision tree applies various splitting criteria to choose the best split among more than one split. A few of important splitting criteria are given below:

Gini index It is one of the most widely applied criteria to choose the best split. The Gini index is applied to calculate the income disparity and gender diversity. The Gini index is named after Italian statistician Corado Gini. The Gini index gives the probability that two items chosen at random from the same population are in the same class.

Chi-square test It is the test of statistical significance developed by Karl Pearson. It is defined as the sum of squares of standardised differences between the expected and observed frequencies of sum occurrences between multiple disjoint samples. In other words, this test is the measure of the probability that an observed difference between samples is due to only chance. When chi-square is applied to measure the purity of decision tree splits, higher value of chi-square means that variation is more significant and not due to mere chance only. A higher score of chi-square signifies that the proposed split successfully splits the population into sub-population with significantly different distributions.

Information gain criteria Information gain criteria is based on the concept of entropy. Entropy is a measure of how disorganised a system is. Entropy is a measure of the number of Yes/No questions, it would take to determine the state of the system. Information gain measures the entropy resolution of a split.

Information Gain = 1 – Entropy of the split

The split having the higher value is chosen over the other split in the decision tree.

Reduction in variance All the above three criteria are applied to the categorical targets. But when the target is numeric, a good split should reduce the variance of the target variable. Variance is mathematically calculated as

$$\text{Variance} = \frac{\Sigma (X - \mu)^2}{N}$$

The split which gives higher value of reduction in variance value is chosen over the other split in the decision tree.

But the real-life problems are very complex and it is not possible to make decision tree manually; hence, the various types of algorithms are used to depict the real-life problems, for example, Hunt's Algorithm, ID3, C4.5, C5.0, CART, QUEST, CHAID and SPRINT.

Detail of decision tree In the decision tree structure, the internal node represents the conditions and the leaf nodes represent the target classes. Internal nodes are built till the classes in the form of the leaf nodes are created.

The tuple/record can be classified by different classes using specific conditions. The attributes of the tuples in the particular class will be the same. Hence, with the help of decision tree, classification of tuples can be done. As shown in Exhibit 11.2, the decision tree classifies the employees who own cars and the pre-specified condition is income. The main advantage of decision tree is that it is very simple and does not need any technical knowledge to understand the decision tree as the decision tree is self-explanatory. But one thing should be kept in mind is that tree size should not be large; otherwise, it would be difficult to show and interpret the tuple in a different classification. Sometimes, a decision tree is overfitted or simply it gets complex as the number of variables increases. To handle such kinds of problems, various tree pruning techniques are available. Pruning reduces the size of tree without affecting the accuracy of the tree. Various pruning techniques are given below:

- Cost-complexity pruning
- Reduced error pruning
- Minimum error pruning (MRP)
- Pessimistic pruning
- Error-based pruning (EBP)
- Optimal pruning
- Minimum description length pruning

Pruning reduces the size of the tree without affecting the accuracy of the tree.

The decision tree represented in Exhibit 11.3 shows the splitting based on age and then classifying the patients (gender-wise) into

Exhibit 11.2 Illustration of decision tree

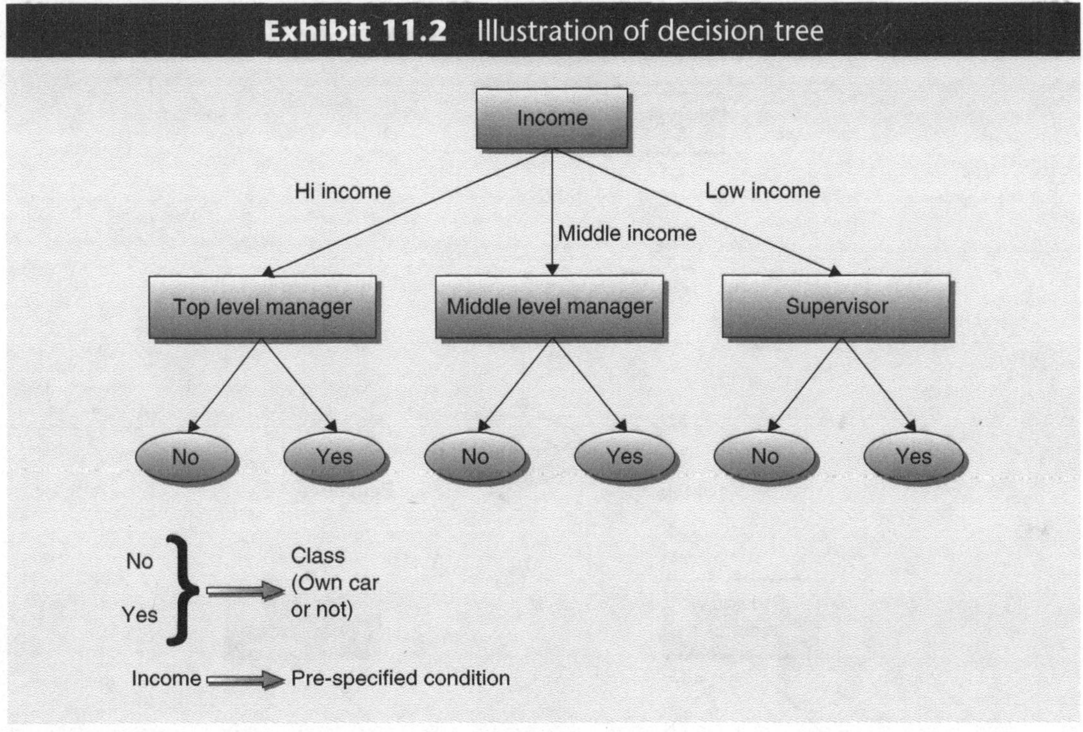

those who are above 60 and are detected with osteoporosis and those patients who do not have osteoporosis.

Important conditions for designing decision tree

1. **Test Condition**: There should be proper test condition which should divide tuple into two parts.
2. **Classes**: The analyst should have accurate knowledge of classes in which he wants to classify the tuple. The classes are important to terminate the decision tree. As the decision tree ends at leaf nodes and leaf nodes represent the classes, there should be proper classes, only then appropriate/suitable decision tree can be built.

K-nearest-neighbour classifier

In the K-nearest neighbour classifier, the sample known as test sample is represented on an n-dimensional space. When the unknown sample comes under k-classifier, the classifier matches the previously mapped patterns, i.e., training set in n-dimensional space. The patterns to which the unknown

In the K-nearest neighbor classifier, the sample known as the test sample is represented on an n-dimensional space.

Exhibit 11.3 Illustration of decision tree

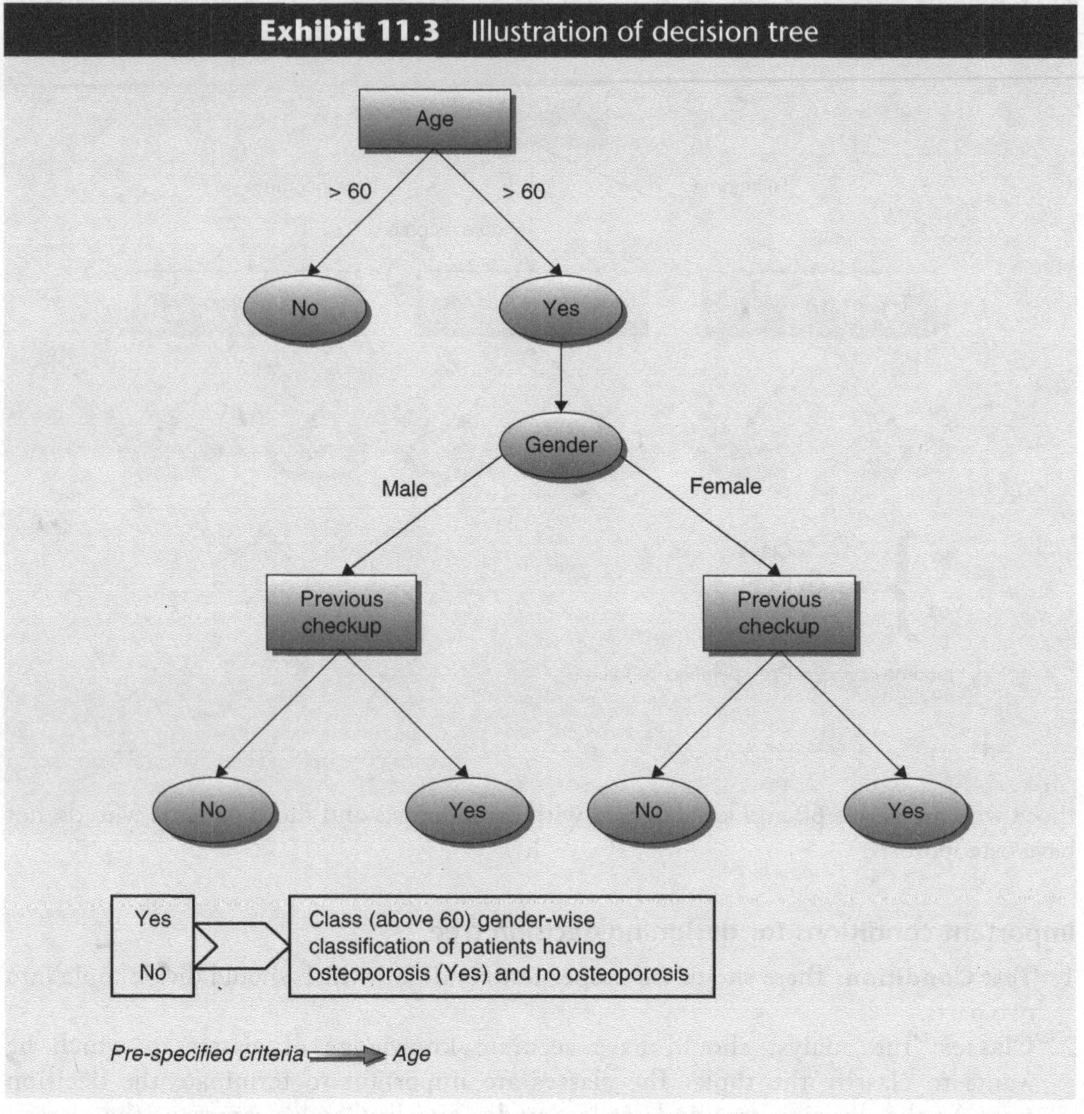

sample is close, it is classified in that pattern. As patterns are mapped in n-dimensional space, closeness to the patterns is defined in the terms of Euclidean distance metric, i.e., distance between two samples X and Y.

$$\text{Dist}\,(X, Y) = \sqrt{\sum_{i=1}^{n} (x_i - y_i)^2}$$

Applications of K-nearest-neighbour classifier K-nearest-neighbour classifier has wide applications in various fields. Some of the key applications of K-nearest neighbour are listed below:

1. **Text Categorisation**: The recent developments in information technology have resulted in the influx of information. Organisations are now finding very difficult to manage the huge volumes of information. This has resulted in the slow and inaccurate information retrieval. It is important that the collected information should be categorised and whenever a new information is to be stored, it should be automatically stored in the appropriate categories. As there are huge volumes of information and it is practically impossible to manually categorise information. To solve this problem, organisations are applying the concept of K-nearest neighbour or KNN classifier. In order to get the accurate results, organisations are applying K-NNFP, i.e., K-nearest neighbour feature projections which is the extension of KNN. KNNFP finds the nearest neighbour separately for each specific feature, whereas KNN finds the nearest neighbour by taking into account all the features.
2. **Medical Field**: KNN is applied in the medical field. The doctors are applying KNN for detection of cancer. As it is very difficult to detect cancer in the early stage, the doctors are applying KNN to match the patterns of sample cells with the cancer-related cells. If there is a match, then doctors can diagnose the cancer at a very early stage.
3. **Graphology**: Graphology deals with the study and analysis of handwriting. KNN is extensively applied in a forensic document examination. The test sample is matched with the training sample and applying KNN experts can tell whether or not a document was written by the person who is thought to have written it.
4. **Human Genome**: Genome, i.e., complete DNA sequence of human being. The human genome contains more than three billion chemical base pairs. Scientists are trying to explain the human genome sequencing. The KNN is widely applied to match the attributes of uncharacterised proteins with the already characterised proteins. The KNN not only helps to identify the attributes of uncharacterised proteins, but in case there is no match, then applying KNN a new category can be created which can be used for further categorisation of uncharacterised proteins.

Case-based reasoning

In the K-nearest classifier, the classification is done by measuring the Euclidean distance. The case-based reasoning is similar to K-nearest classifier; the only difference is that the classification in case-based reasoning is done by classifying the samples in the form of different cases. When a new case comes for classification, the case-based reasoning compares the new case with the already stored cases. If there is a perfect match, then the case-based reasoning classifies the new case automatically with the stored matched case. Even when there is no perfect match, the case-based reasoning matches the specific components which are similar to the stored cases. The matched specific components are known as the new neighbour of the old stored case.

> Case-based reasoning is similar to K-nearest classifier; the only difference is that the classification in case-based reasoning is done by classifying the samples in the form of different cases.

Exhibit 11.4 Case-based reasoning

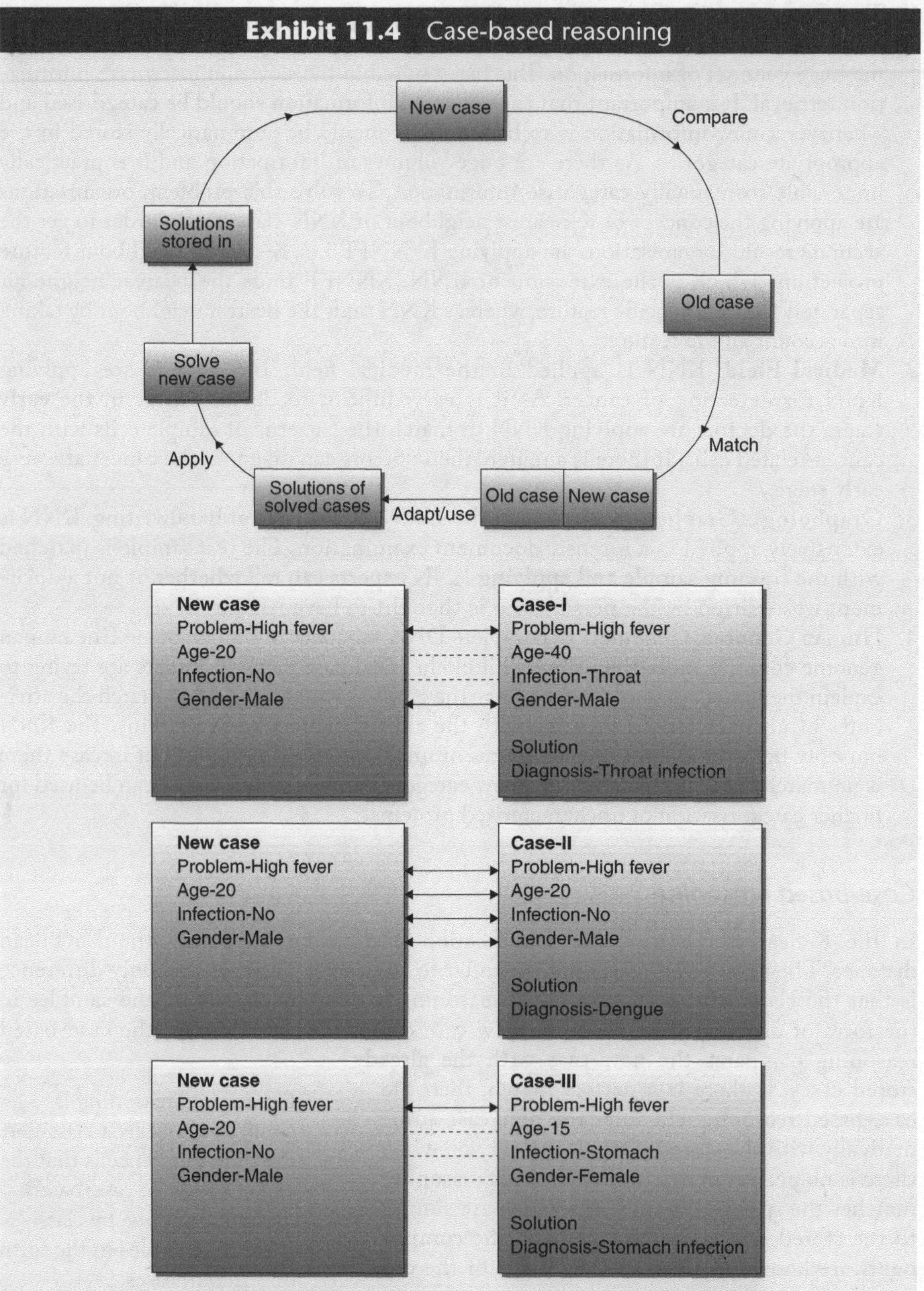

Case-based reasoning has wide application in the area of medical field (Exhibit 11.4). Applying the case-based reasoning, the doctor can classify the new case with the already stored cases. As shown in Exhibit 11.4, there is a perfect match of a new case with already stored Case II, i.e., the new patient is suffering from dengue. Even when there is no perfect match (suppose there is no match even in the second case), the case-based reasoning helps to compare specific symptoms (new neighbour) with already stored cases.

Case-based reasoning is also applied in developing incident reporting system. Incident reporting system records all the failures of critical system and reasons for that failure. Incident reporting is very critical in the safety critical industries such as the navy. Case-based reasoning is applied extensively to index all the previous problems and whenever a new problem comes, the experts take the help from previous/old cases. The experts retrieve past results and apply those results to solve new problems. Moreover, taking clues from old cases, experts can even predict the future breakdown of critical machines. After solving the new cases, the experts add that case in the case-based reasoning database for future reference. Case-based reasoning is even applied to develop Q&A Systems. Q&A system is the most vital component in E-Learning. As E-learning is gaining a lot of popularity, the success of E-learning depends on its Q&A abilities. Any E-learning module should be able to answer the questions of the students. But with the varied topics and a large number of users, it is very difficult to manage the Q&A system. The case-based reasoning is being applied in Q&A system so as to match the new queries with the old queries; this helps in quick answering of the queries.

Another application of case-based reasoning is in supporting strategic decisions in organisations, especially in small and medium enterprises (SME). As large organisations have got ample resources to take strategic decisions, but SMEs have often limited resources to take strategic decisions. Case-based reasoning is widely applied by managers to solve new problems based on the previous cases. Case-based reasoning is also applied in helping desk management. In the era of customer satisfaction, it is very important for organisations to have 24 hours help desk for answering the queries/problems of customers. The help desk executives frequently face influx of queries. Moreover, the help desk executives are often not technical people and the customers at the other end want prompt answers to their queries. No customer likes that help desk executive asks him/her to wait till he/she forwards the query to the concerned department. The case-based reasoning is applied for categorisation of past queries and when a new query comes the help desk executive takes the help from the previous cases to answer new query. Similarly, in molecular biology, which involves a large amount of complex data which have unknown characteristics. The case-based reasoning is being applied by the scientists so as to categorise the complex data of molecules in an efficient manner.

But for getting accurate results applying case-based reasoning it is very important to carefully store the cases with proper indexing so that accurate searching of records can be done. The case-based reasoning can store thousands of cases for future matching but as the case-based reasoning stores more and more cases, the efficiency, although increases, but the speed of retrieval decreases because case-based reasoning takes more time to match the cases. Hence, it is very important to balance the efficiency and speed. To achieve this

Regression analysis is a statistical technique applied to find out the magnitude and direction of a possible causal relationship between an observed pattern and variables, which is assumed to have an impact on the observed pattern.

goal, it is always advisable to delete obsolete and redundant cases so that quick and efficient retrieval can be achieved.

Regression models

Regression analysis is a statistical technique applied to find out the magnitude and direction of possible causal relationship between an observed pattern and variables assumed to have an impact on the observed pattern. In other words, with the help of regression models it is possible to find out the output considering the specific input. The input is taken from the values stored in the database and the output is given by regression models. One of the most common used forms of regression is simple linear regression. In simple linear regression, there are one independent variable and one dependent variable. simple linear regression is represented as

$$Y = A + BX$$

In the above equation, Y is a dependent variable, X is an independent variable, A is intercept and B is the slope.

If we say

$$Y = 9.5 + 0.4\,X$$

It means intercept is 9.5 and slope is 0.4. Slope represents the rate of change of Y when X changes, i.e., the slope 0.4 means that when X changes by 1, Y changes by 0.4. This rate of change will remain the same whether X changes from 5 to 6 or from 100 to 101. This means the change in Y will remain the same that is 0.4. This linear change in Y w.r.t. X is the key feature of simple linear regression. But in case if there is not a linear change in Y w.r.t. X, then it is known as non-linear regression. The non-linear regression is represented as

$$Y = \beta_0 + \beta_1 X + e$$

Y is a dependent variable

X is an independent variable

β_0 is an intercept

β_1 is the slope

e is the error

Y is also known as predicted variable, i.e., whose behaviour we are going to explain

X is also known as predictor, i.e., that variable which influences the dependent variable

Beta Coefficients: Beta coefficients estimate the magnitude of changes in the independent variable on the dependent variable. The beta coefficients are estimated by OLS regression, i.e., ordinary least squares regression technique.

Error: It is the impact of unobserved variables on the dependent variables.

Another widely used classification technique is logistic regression. When the dependent variable is categorical or has classes, then logistic regression is utilised to classify any new observation, based on input or predictor variables. Most of the times, it is used when the dependent variable is binary. The dependent variable can be a success or a failure; or it can be a case or no case. In short, it takes only two values. In this technique, dependent variable Y is not directly used, rather a function of dependent variable called logit is used.

Consider first a linear function of inputs $X_1, X_2, \ldots X_n$ termed "p".

$$p = \beta_0 + \beta_1 X_1 + \beta_2 X_2 + \ldots + \beta_n X_n$$

Then, the logistic response function is defined as:

$$F = \frac{1}{1 + e^{-p}} = \frac{1}{1 + e^{-(\beta 0 + \beta 1\, X1 + \beta 2\, X2 + \ldots + \beta n\, Xn)}}$$

This function indicates the probability of the dependent variable belonging to class 1 or being a success or a case. The odds of belonging to class 1 can be computed as under:

$$\text{Odds} = \frac{F}{1 - F} = e^{(\beta 0 + \beta 1\, X1 + \beta 2\, X2 + \ldots + \beta n\, Xn)}$$

Logit is defined as:

$$\text{Ln (odds)} = \ln(e^{(\beta 0 + \beta 1\, X1 + \beta 2\, X2 + \ldots + \beta n\, Xn)}) = \beta_0 + \beta_1 X_1 + \beta_2 X_2 + \ldots + \beta_n X_n$$

This function can take the values between $-\infty$ to ∞. So, the final outcome is modelled as a linear function of the predictor variables.

Artificial neural networks ANN is basically a mimic of the human brain. The biological brain is a highly interconnected network of trillions of neurons. Several models of the basic functioning of biological neurons called neural networks are available and ANN is built on one of these basic models. It copies the general behaviour of the brain, i.e., to experience and learn and has proven to be highly accurate in forecasting and classification applications.

A neural network in ANN learns the underlying relationship between input and output or just among inputs by using a learning algorithm. The most basic form of neural network is depicted below:

ANN is basically a mimic of the human brain.

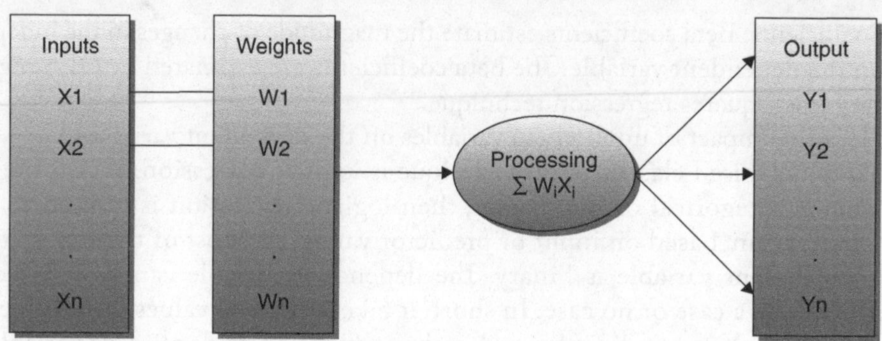

Each input received is multiplied by a weight (weight represents a neuron). This weight represents the strength of the input and its contribution to output. The allocation of weight is done by underlying algorithm. All the weighted inputs are summated and compared with a threshold level, which is used to decide whether to generate or not to generate an output.

To understand how ANN can be used for classification, consider the following example. In this situation, we are trying to classify the consumers based on their credit history into good loans or bad loans. Input data are collected on a set of consumer attributes such as gender, marital status, income is fed as input to ANN to classify. These are predictor variables. The output is whether the borrower turned out to be good (not a defaulter, paid the instalments on time) or bad. The sample data are shown below:

Sr. No.	Gender	Marital Status	Income	Output
1	Male	Married	High	Good
2	Male	Married	Low	Bad
3	Male	Single	High	Good
4	Female	Single	High	Good
5	Female	Married	Medium	Good

If the past history of the borrower is good in terms of loan repayment, then output is coded as good else as bad. In the neural network, the input nodes will take the values from each input attribute. The neural network assigns weights to each input connection and generates an output on its own, which is compared with the actual output. Then, weights are readjusted to match the actual output. This is termed training the neural network. In this manner, the network learns for what range of input values the borrower is classified as good and what range of input values, the borrower is classified as bad. This classification can also be used for prediction of whether a borrower will turn out to be good or bad.

CLUSTERING

> Clustering is similar to classification, but the only difference is that unlike classification, the classes are not known to the analyst.

Clustering is also a data mining technique. Clustering is similar to classification, but the only difference is that unlike classification, the classes are not known to the analyst. It works in an unsupervised manner. In the clustering, first the analyst explores the classes in which he wants to do the classification. Clustering helps to group the objects in different clusters and the objects in each cluster are similar based on the selected attribute and are dissimilar with other objects in other clusters. Practically, Clustering has more application as compared with classification because in many cases it is not possible to know the classes in advance. Clustering is extensively applied in image processing, pattern recognition and marketing research. Especially in marketing, clustering is very useful as with the help of clustering it is possible to segment the customers in different clusters and the customers in one segment are similar based on the selected attribute. This helps to formulate strategies and helps in proper targeting of the customers. The clustering also helps to find out outliers, i.e., the values which do not belong to the particular cluster. In clustering, all the objects are similar but when one particular object does not show similarly on particular selected attribute then that object is known as an outlier. The outliers help to find out the unusual pattern, for example, when credit card is stolen, then outliers help to find out the fraud as suddenly the spending will increase which is shown as outliers in clustering. There are two types of clustering.

1. Partitional clustering
2. Hierarchical clustering

Partitional Clustering

There are various algorithms that are used practically to apply partitional clustering, for example, K-means algorithm and K-medoids algorithm

It is a non-hierarchical type of clustering. In this type of clustering, only one set of clusters is formed. The end user has to define how many clusters he wants to form. There are various techniques to create partition clusters.

> Partitional clustering helps to create clusters in just one step. It constructs K-partitions. The clusters formed by partitional clusters have following characteristics:
>
> 1. Every cluster has at least one object
> 2. Each object belongs to only one specific cluster

1. **Sequential Threshold**: In this method, a cluster centre is determined and all objects that lie within the pre-determined threshold value from the centre are grouped together.
2. **Parallel Threshold Method**: This method is a slight variation of sequential threshold method as in this method several cluster centres are determined simultaneously and then objects which lie in the threshold limit are grouped together.

3. **Optimising Partitioning Method**: In this method, first the objects are clustered applying any of the above-mentioned methods and then the objects are reassigned to optimise the overall criteria.

Cluster in the hierarchical clustering can be created by either

1. Merge or Agglomerative Technique
2. Split or Divisive Technique

Hierarchical Clustering

The partitional clustering helps to partition the objects into different clusters, whereas the hierarchical clustering helps to create hierarchical clusters. The cluster in the hierarchical clustering can be created by either

1. Merge or agglomerative technique
2. Split or divisive technique

The agglomerative or merge technique is the bottom-up approach, i.e., it starts at the lowest level in which each object forms individual cluster and keeps on merging with similar objects till the topmost level is reached, whereas the divisive or split technique is the top-down approach in which all the objects are placed in one big cluster and through iterations the big cluster splits into smaller clusters till the lowest level is reached. Agglomerative clustering has more applications as compared with divisive technique. The agglomerative clusters can be formed by:

1. **Linkage Method**: In this method, the clusters are formed based on the distance between the objects. The distance between objects can be judged by
   (a) *Single Linkage:* In this method, the objects which are having minimum distance with each other are grouped together. The basic governing principle is the nearest-neighbour rule.
   (b) *Complete Linkage:* In this method, the governing principle is the maximum distance rule. In this method, the objects having maximum distance between their farthest points are grouped together.
   (c) *Average Method:* In this method, clustering is based on the average distance between all pairs of objects.
2. **Variance Method**: The main objective of the variance method is to minimise the variance within clusters. The wards's method is commonly applied for minimising the variance within the clusters.
3. **Centroid**: In this method, only those clusters are formed which maximise the distance between the centres of clusters.

ASSOCIATION

The association is the third type of data mining technique. Association in data mining helps to find out the co-occurrence of the item sets (item set means set of two or more items). The association has wide application in the field of marketing. With the help of association, it is possible to do the market basket analysis. As the organisations are collecting huge transactional data and with the help of market basket analysis, it is possible to find the patterns in purchasing. The association helps to find out the co-purchase of items in a particular basket of a customer. It helps to predict the shopping behaviour and even helps to sell different items, i.e., cross-selling of products. Presently, there is retail boom and every retail store is collecting huge transactional data. By applying market basket analysis, it is possible for retail stores to display those items together which show a high association during previous purchases by customers like bread and butter. Market basket analysis also helps in designing proper store layouts, catalogs and combo plans.

Association in data mining helps to find out the co-occurrence of the item sets (item set means set of two or more items).

Technical Terms Used in the Association

1. **Support Count**: It is the number of transactions that contain particular itemset.
2. **Support**: If X and Y are two items in itemset, support tells fraction of transactions that contain both X and Y.
3. **Confidence**: It gives the measurement how often Y is purchased when X is purchased.

Bread ⟶ Butter

For example, 5% support means that of all transactions only 5% transactions show bread and butter are purchased together and 50% confidence means that 50% of customers who purchased bread also purchased butter. The particular itemset should maintain minimum support threshold and minimum confidence threshold limits. These limits are decided on the basis of past purchases.

CONCLUSION

From the above discussion, it is evident that considering the varied nature and quantity of data collected and stored by organisations, data mining is gaining a lot of importance in the present time. Of course, information is gold, but it is necessary to mine information from data just like to mine gold from the gold mine. There are many applications of data mining, but at the same time the managers should be very careful in applying data mining techniques. Every data mining technique is quite distinct from other techniques such as classification is different from clustering. To get the accurate results, it is imperative that managers should have sound knowledge of various techniques and its key features. Any mistake in selecting data mining technique will result in inaccurate results. Hence, due diligence should be given in selecting particular data mining technique. Future managers with sound data mining, knowledge will have an edge in this competitive environment.

KEY TERMS

- Nominal Data 312
- Ordinal Data 312
- Interval data 312
- Ratio Data 312
- Classification 313
- Pre-Specified categories 313
- Decision Tree 314
- K-Nearest-Neighbour Classifier 317
- Case-Based Reasoning 319
- Regression Models 322
- Clustering 325
- Partitional Clustering 325
- Hierarchical Clustering 326
- Association 327

SUMMARY

In this chapter, various aspects regarding data mining are discussed in detail. But before discussing data mining techniques, it is important to know the different types of data. All the types are discussed in detail in this chapter. Data mining involves three important techniques, i.e., classification, clustering and association. All these techniques and detailed aspects of these techniques are discussed in detail in this chapter. This chapter closes with a case study and to have a better understanding of the concepts of data mining review questions, project activity, assignment questions and hands-on project are given at the end of this chapter.

MULTIPLE CHOICE QUESTIONS

1. The technique which helps the organisations to mine relevant information from the data

a. Data discovery
b. Data mining
c. Data excavation
d. Data detection

2. When the data are collected by just assigning codes or labels to classify the objects it is known as

a. Nominal data
b. Interval data
c. Ordinal data
d. Ratio data

3. When the data show the amount of characteristic possessed by an object that data is known as
   a. Nominal data b. Ordinal data
   c. Interval data d. Ratio data

4. In which type of data, zero is arbitrary?
   a. Nominal data b. Ordinal data
   c. Interval data d. Ratio data

5. In which type of data, zero is non arbitrary?
   a. Nominal data b. Ordinal data
   c. Interval data d. Ratio data

6. The process of organising the item/objects according to the pre-specified categories is known as
   a. Classification b. Clustering
   c. Association d. Sorting

7. Decision tree is the tool for
   a. Classification b. Clustering
   c. Association d. Sorting

8. The starting point of the decision tree which has no incoming edges and has only outgoing edges is known as
   a. Starting node b. Root node
   c. Internal node d. Leaf node

9. The node which has one incoming edge and two or more outgoing edges is known as
   a. Starting node b. Root node
   c. Internal node d. Leaf node

10. The node which has one incoming edge and no outgoing edge is known as
    a. Starting node b. Root node
    c. Internal node d. Leaf node

11. The process of reducing the size of tree without affecting the accuracy of the tree is known as
    a. Tree reduction b. Tree pruning
    c. Tree downsizing d. Tree rebuilding

12. The process in which patterns are mapped in n-dimensional space and the closeness to the patterns are defined in terms of Euclidean distance metric is known as
    a. Decision tree b. KNN
    c. Regression d. Case-based reasoning

13. The statistical technique applied to find out the magnitude and direction of possible causal relationship between an observed pattern and variables assumed to have an impact on the observed pattern is known as
    a. Decision tree
    b. KNN
    c. Regression
    d. Case-based reasoning

14. The unsupervised technique in which the analyst has knowledge of classes in which he wants to classify the tuples is known as
    a. Classification
    b. Clustering
    c. Association
    d. Sorting

15. The technique which helps to find out the co-occurrence of the item sets is known as
    a. Classification
    b. Clustering
    c. Association
    d. Sorting

REVIEW QUESTIONS

1. What are the different types of data?
2. What is the relevance of data mining considering the varied nature of the data which are captured by organisations?
3. Explain classification technique by discussing the various tools of classification.
4. Discuss important applications of K-nearest neighbour classifier.
5. What is the difference between classification and clustering? Discuss by taking account different types of clustering.
6. "Association is an important data mining technique which has wide application in marketing". Comment on this statement.

ASSIGNMENT

1. Applying classification, prepare a complete decision tree diagram to mine out information regarding admission in MBA course in your university/college. Choose a pre-specified criteria after discussing with the admission department in-charge.
2. Search the Internet to find out how Indian companies are applying classification, clustering and association techniques for mining relevant information from stored data.

PROJECT ACTIVITY

1. Visit a nearby retail store and discuss with the store manager how he/she is doing the market basket analysis. Collect the actual data to find out whether market basket strategies formulated by the store are working or not.

DETAILED EXAMPLE OF CLUSTERING

The Power Distribution Company wants to implement information technology in the distribution network. The Power Distribution Company has various hierarchies of officials like

- Director
- The Chief Engineer's (CE)
- The Superintendent Engineer's (SE)
- Senior Executive Engineer (XEN)
- Assistant Executive Engineers and Sub-Divisional Officers (SDO)

The company hired a business analyst and the analyst prepared the following questionnaire to know the preference and requirements of various employees of the company from the information systems. The respondent had to agree or disagree with each statement on a scale of 1 to 5, where 1 = Completely Agree, 2 = Agree, 3 = Neutral, 4 = Disagree and 5 = Completely Disagree.

"Following is the list of some areas in which information systems can help in improving the efficiency of the distribution network. Please indicate your assessment of the importance that you may associate with each factor".

	Strongly Agree	**Agree**	**Neutral**	**Disagree**	**Strongly Disagree**
Establishment of a baseline data collection system is an important application area					
Performance benchmarking and appraisal is an important application area					
Improvement in service levels is an important application area					
Customer satisfaction is an important application area					

(continued)

Continued

	Strongly Agree	Agree	Neutral	Disagree	Strongly Disagree
Detection of theft is an important application area					
Network planning is an important application area					
Load scheduling is an important application area					
Consumer feedback is an important application area					
Call centres are an important application area					
Fault detection is an important application area					
Billing is an important application area					
Energy auditing is an important application area					
Feedback is an important application area					
Inventory is an important application area					
Interdepartmental coordination is an important application area					
Matching supply and demand is an important application area					
Mobile networking is an important application area					
Online monitoring of feeders is an important application area					
Consumer indexing is an important application area					
Training and development is an important application area					
Better management is an important application area					
Curtail losses is an important application area					
Proper monitoring is an important application area					
Regulation is an important application area					
E-payments are an important application area					
Better reporting is an important application area					
Easy supervision is an important application area					
Work distribution and assessment is an important application area					
Quick damage control is an important application area					

(*continued*)

Continued

	Strongly Agree	Agree	Neutral	Disagree	Strongly Disagree
Maintaining a timeframe for work is an important application area					
Reduced paperwork is an important application area					
Implementing AMR is an important application area					
Implementing GIS mapping is an important application area					
IT application in reading, collection and billing is an important application area					
Material availability is an important application area					
Regulating flow of information is an important application area					
Critical areas (where losses are increasing and revenues are decreasing) are an important application area					
Introducing SCADA (supervisory control and data acquisition) is an important application area					
Load planning is an important application area					
Demand management is an important application area					
Transparency in administration is an important application area					
Aids strategic planning such as tariff reduction and management is an important application area					
Troubleshooting is an important application area					
A single window system for consumers is an important application area					
Continuous updating of network is an important application area					
Maintenance of network is an important application area					

Based on the collected data, the analyst applied clustering and the following results were derived:

Table 11.1 Cluster analysis

Final Cluster Centres

	Cluster			
	1	2	3	4
f1	2.00	3.26	3.87	3.00
f2	4.00	3.66	2.13	3.00
f3	3.00	3.46	3.87	1.00
f4	3.50	3.46	1.80	5.00
f5	3.50	1.33	3.53	4.00
f6	1.50	4.46	3.87	3.00
f7	1.50	4.40	3.80	4.00
f8	4.00	1.60	3.67	3.00
f9	4.00	3.40	3.93	2.00
f10	5.00	1.34	4.73	4.00
f11	3.00	3.20	1.87	3.00
f12	3.50	3.19	1.80	5.00
f13	4.50	1.66	3.40	4.00
f14	2.00	3.92	3.07	4.00
f15	1.50	4.47	3.73	5.00
f16	2.00	3.13	3.80	4.00
f17	1.50	4.67	4.07	5.00
f18	1.00	3.67	3.07	4.00
f19	2.00	5.00	3.47	4.00
f20	4.00	4.40	1.87	5.00
f21	4.00	4.53	4.00	2.00
f22	4.00	1.53	4.87	4.00
f23	3.50	1.13	3.93	5.00
f24	4.50	1.46	3.93	4.00
f25	2.00	4.47	3.20	5.00
f26	3.00	4.60	1.20	4.00
f27	3.00	1.93	4.47	5.00
f28	3.50	1.40	3.00	5.00
f29	3.50	4.46	2.00	5.00
f30	3.50	4.00	1.93	4.00
f31	2.00	4.67	3.27	5.00

(continued)

Table 11.1 Continued

	Cluster			
	1	2	3	4
f32	3.00	4.13	4.20	2.00
f33	3.00	3.34	4.20	2.00
f34	4.50	4.27	1.93	4.00
f35	3.50	1.20	3.07	4.00
f36	4.00	1.87	3.07	3.00
f37	1.00	4.33	5.00	4.00
f38	3.00	5.00	4.73	1.00
f39	3.00	4.13	1.80	4.00
f40	3.50	4.07	4.87	2.00
f41	2.00	4.27	3.60	4.00
f42	3.50	3.46	3.00	2.00
f43	3.00	3.47	1.13	5.00
f44	1.50	3.27	4.67	5.00
f45	2.00	3.34	4.80	4.00
f46	2.00	3.20	3.87	4.00

From Table 11.1, it is clear that there are four clusters in the final cluster analysis. Now we will describe each and every cluster one by one.

Cluster 1

People belonging to this cluster think that the following variables are important application area.

- Establishment of a baseline data collection system is an important application area.
- Network planning is an important application area.
- Load scheduling is an important application area.
- Inventory is an important application area.
- Interdepartmental coordination is an important application area.
- Matching supply and demand is an important application area.
- Mobile networking is an important application area.
- Online monitoring of feeders is an important application area.
- Consumer indexing is an important application area.
- E-payments are an important application area.

- Reduced paperwork is an important application area.
- Critical areas (where losses are increasing and revenues are decreasing) is an important application area.
- Transparency in administration is an important application area.
- A single window system for consumers is an important application area.
- Continuous updating of network is an important application area.
- Maintenance of network is an important application area.

Cluster 2

People belonging to this cluster think that the following variables are important application area.

- Detection of theft is an important application area.
- Consumer feedback is an important application area.
- Fault detection is an important application area.
- Feedback is an important application area.
- Curtail losses are an important application area.
- Proper monitoring is an important application area.
- Regulation is an important application area.
- Easy supervision is an important application area.
- Work distribution and assessment is an important application area.
- Material availability is an important application area.
- Regulating flow of information is an important application area.

Cluster 3

People belonging to this cluster think that the following variables are important application area.

- Performance benchmarking and appraisal is an important application area.
- Customer satisfaction is an important application area.
- Billing is an important application area.
- Energy auditing is an important application area.
- Training and development is an important application area.
- Better reporting is an important application area.
- Quick damage control is an important application area.
- Maintaining a time frame for work is an important application area.
- IT application in reading, collection and billing is an important application area.
- Load planning is an important application area.
- Troubleshooting is an important application area.

Cluster 4

People belonging to this cluster think that the following variables are important application area.

- Improvement in service levels is an important application area.
- Call centres are an important application area.
- Better management is an important application area.
- Implementing AMR is an important application area.
- Implementing GIS mapping is an important application area.
- Introducing SCADA is an important application area.
- Demand management is an important application area.
- Aids strategic planning such as tariff reduction and management is an important application area.

CASE STUDY

HR Analytics at Nixo (Classification Using ANN)

Nixo is a small manufacturing firm headquartered at Gurgaon, North of India. Nixo produces threads, towels, bed sheets and also exports them internationally. The firm has a headcount of 2000 employees working in various positions like manufacturing staff or line workers, middle level managers and executives. Nixo has invested a large amount of financial and other resources in its IT infrastructure to effectively cater to its domestic and international market. In fact, Nixo has been a leader of sorts in its IT initiatives across the industry. To maintain efficient operation of IT, it has a workforce of around 200 employees dedicated to IT and professionally skilled in information services. There are different tiers of hierarchy (starting as a Level 1 engineer) at which IT staff works and the topmost level is the CIO (Chief Information Officer). So, in this sense, Nixo provides sufficient career growth opportunities for IT workers. Besides, its pay packages are lucrative, competent in the industry and it also provides rigorous training for new joiners to equip them with the skills required for the efficient conduct at workplace.

Despite all this, for the past few years, Nixo has been experiencing considerable turnover of its IT staff, especially of level 1 engineer, who has less than 3 years of service. Although the rate of turnover is comparable to industry rate, Nixo finds this situation daunting. This is because compared with industry practices, Nixo invests sufficiently higher in its employees and hence expects them to stay loyal to the firm. The employees who leave take away the knowledge about sophisticated software deployed in the firm, which is a threat to Nixo, as this knowledge can be exploited by rival firms. Besides, this also increases the burden in terms of expense incurred in training the employees. Therefore, to solve the situation at hand, Nixo's management decided to hire services of business analysts who could dig into the problem and identify reasons for attrition at Nixo.

The team of analysts first probed the organisational factors such as pay structure, policies, career opportunities, etc. and found them to be satisfactory, considering that all the factors were competent and consistent with what the industry was offering. The analysts then conducted interviews of existing staff to find if any organisational parameter was hindering their stay with the firm. However, this exercise yielded no results, as the employees were either reluctant to freely express their views or satisfied with their jobs. So next, they analysed the data from exit interviews conducted by Nixo at the time any employee leaves the firm. They then thematically encoded that data to see if there were some common reasons among those who left the firm. Some interesting revelations were that a large number of people who left the firm have stated that they could not identify with the culture of the firm. Some were not happy with the way the firm framed policies or took decisions. The analysts encoded these viewpoints as "Value congruence" with the firm. Another common factor was encoded "Job embeddedness" which expressed the employee's fit with the firm in terms of job position, networking in the firm or links and willingness to sacrifice the job for any personal or professional reasons. They also deduced that personality emerged out as a major factor as some people were negative about everything in their interviews, whereas some were very timid or inexpressive, and yet others were unable to comprehend the purpose of exit interviews.

To validate their findings, they needed a system to test whether these findings actually related to problem of turnover at Nixo. So, they decided to frame a questionnaire based on these factors to survey the existing employees and those who had left the firm in the past. Besides the factors listed above, the analysts included a few other parameters based on their past experience like "Non-work influences" and demographics like gender, marital status, etc. Utilising the data collected from these questionnaires, they wished to classify the employees into those who have the tendency to stay with the firm and those who have a tendency to leave. This was clearly an application of analytics and analysts decided to use artificial neural networks (ANN) in SQL Server 2012 for this classification.

The questionnaire was administered to 300 respondents in total (both existing and left employees), only 150 valid responses were received by the analysts. Nixo maintains a database of its past employees' records and contact addresses which is frequently updated. So, for the survey, they decided to randomly pick few existing employees and few employees who had left in the past in the position of Level 1 engineers from the firm and mail the questionnaire at their e-mail Ids. The mining model fetched the key influencers for each class of respondents (those who stay and those who leave). The basic results window is as shown below:

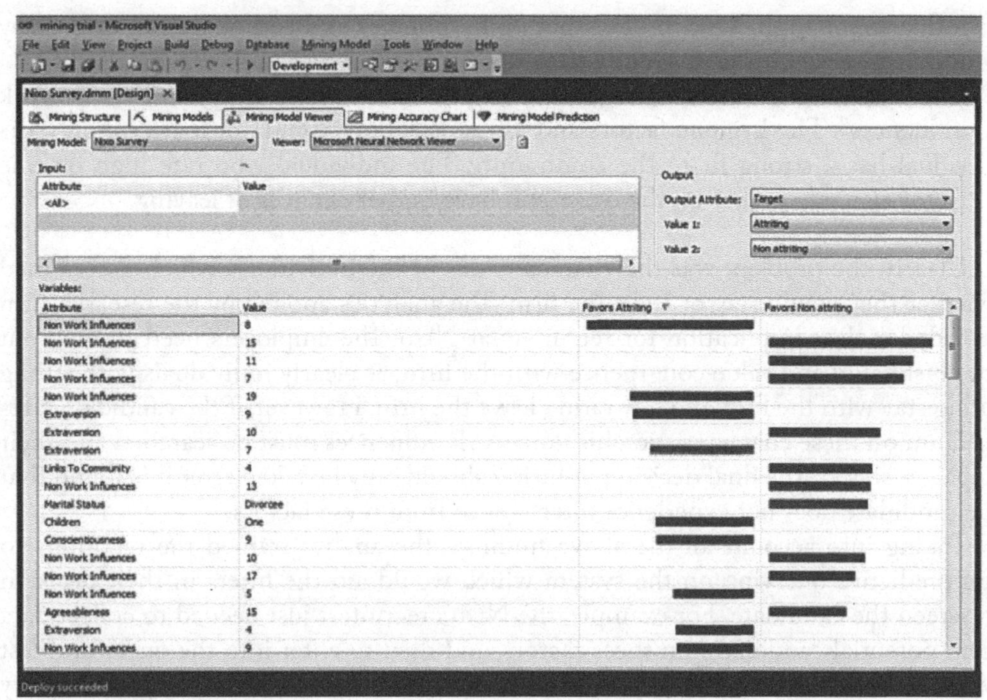

After running deeper analysis on each underlying factor and ANN mining suggestions of key influencers and probability of the contribution of that factor to a target state, the following findings were summarised:

- For individuals with strong personality (who rate high on each dimension), there exists more than 99% probability of non-attrition, irrespective of how they respond to other research variables. Such individuals are highly agreeable, organised and focussed, emotionally stable, outgoing and open to experience.
- If value congruence with the firm is low, the individuals leave the firm. However, most of such individuals identify other contributing factors to aid in the decision to leave which are low fit to the community and high impact of non-work influences. For those with high value congruence, 98% chance of staying with the firm was mined.
- If the impact of non-work influences is high, then the individual would experience work–life imbalance. Research findings support this and key influencer for such individuals is low fit to the community and introversion. Therefore, if a candidate is introvert and unable to adapt to the community, his or her non-work influences should definitely be probed.
- An analysis on job embededness revealed that even if the organisation related sacrifice is high, the individual can leave the firm, given the impact from non-work

influences is high. This implies that perks, policies and compensation offered by the firm serve only as hygiene factors. Similar is the case with organisation fit.

- The clear discriminator emerged out to be "Fit to community" and "Non-work influences". The hygiene factors and job satisfaction would not matter if an individual has a strong fit to the community. The individual who rate high on one factor also rate higher on the other and have higher chances of leaving.

Clearly, the problem was the characteristics of the individuals which determined whether they would stay or leave the firm. The analytics applied by the research firm provided a clear implication for recruiters at Nixo. The employers need to look out for personality and value congruence with the firm, as clearly individuals with strong rating stay with the firm and low rating leave the firm. However, if the candidate rates medium on these characteristics, his non-work influences must be searched and their impact assessed. The final decision of hiring should only be taken after it is found that the candidate does not experience interference from these factors.

Taking into account all the above findings, the analyst trained the recruiters to run predictive querying on the system which would aid the hirers in their decision to screen the candidate. For example, the Nixo's recruiters just needed to collect data from potential candidates on these factors, and then to enter into the query and test whether the candidate is likely to stay in the future or not. Using singleton query input shown below, the recruiter enters the computed value for each factor from the potential candidate and then fetches the result from neural network trained model.

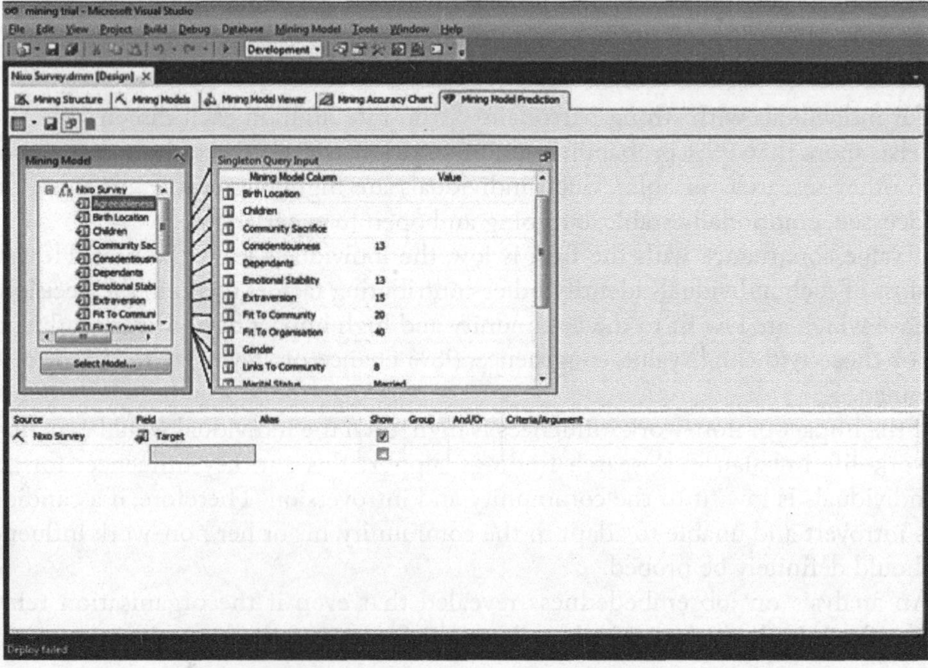

Here, the recruiter has entered high ratings for the candidate on each factor that is a strong personality, strong job embededness, strong value congruence with the firm, low impact of non-work influences, and as expected, the model fetches the following result:

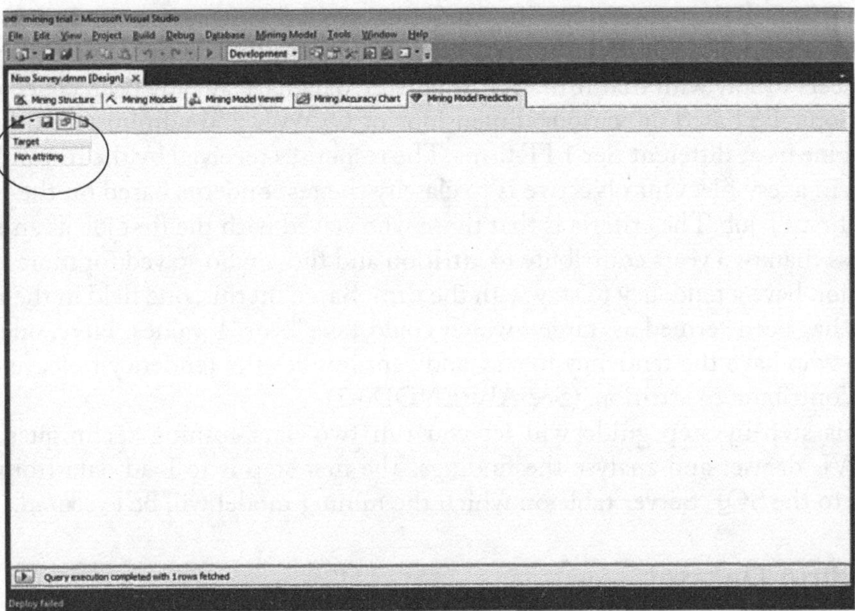

From the past learning, the model implies that the target state for the individual is non-attriting or has a tendency to stay with the job. So, the final decision of hiring can be based on this fact-based prediction. Similarly, for existing employees, HR managers can test their likelihood of staying with the firm. Based on the fetched result, the appropriate retention tool can then be utilised such as counselling, incentives, etc. This exercise has been immensely beneficial to Nixo. Nixo has been able to considerably reduce its rate of turnover, as it can screen the candidates who are likely to leave in the near future. Besides, the system also aids them in looking out for employees who have an intention to quit in the near future and then utilising an appropriate retention strategy to manage its employees.

Questions

1. What were the problems faced by Nixo? What was the role of thematic encoding in this?
2. How did classification overcome the problem at Nixo? From your understanding of the case, list how ANN is used to classify respondents?
3. What were the key findings of the analysts?
4. What can predictive querying do for Nixo and how ANN supports predictive querying?

HANDS-ON PROJECT

Mining Case on QOWL

Scenario: Being researcher in analytics, we are interested in knowing how quality of work life (QOWL) at tier 1 IT firms impact the intention of newly recruited engineers to stay with that firm. In this pursuit, data have already been collected using questionnaire based on various dimensions of QOWL and administered the survey to engineers at different tier 1 IT firms. The responses received by the researcher were saved in a .csv file. Our objective is to classify the respondents based on the tenure in their first IT job. The criteria is that those who stayed with the first job as an engineer for less than two years contribute to attrition and those who stayed for more than this duration have a tendency to stay with the firm. Based on this, one field in the response sheet has been termed as 'target' which could take '0' or '1' values. Here, one implies those who have the tendency to stay and zero implies the tendency to leave or those who contribute to attrition. (See APPENDIX-2)

This step-by-step guide will let you run two data mining techniques on this QOWL dataset and analyse the findings. The first step is to load data from the csv sheet to the SQL Server table on which the mining model will be executed.

Loading Dataset

1. Open SSMS. In any database, which you created in previous exercises, create a table with following fields:

Column Name	Data Type	Allow Nulls
RespondentID	int	☐
[No of children]	bigint	☑
[Personal Satisfaction (30)]	bigint	☑
[Social Satisfaction (30)]	bigint	☑
[Enjoyment at work*(35)]	bigint	☑
[Motivation at work(20)]	bigint	☑
[Mental Satisfaction(30)]	bigint	☑
[Achievement from wor...	bigint	☑
[Occupational Role(25)]	bigint	☑
[Work related (25)]	bigint	☑
[Work involement(5)]	bigint	☑
[Nature of supervision(1...	bigint	☑
[T&D]	bigint	☑
[Growth & job security(1...	bigint	☑
Target	bigint	☑
[Copy of Gender]	nvarchar(50)	☑
[Copy of Birth location]	nvarchar(50)	☑
[Copy of Martial Status]	nvarchar(50)	☑
		☐

2. For the RespondentID field, from Column Properties of Table design tab in SSMS, enter 'Yes' for Identity specification.

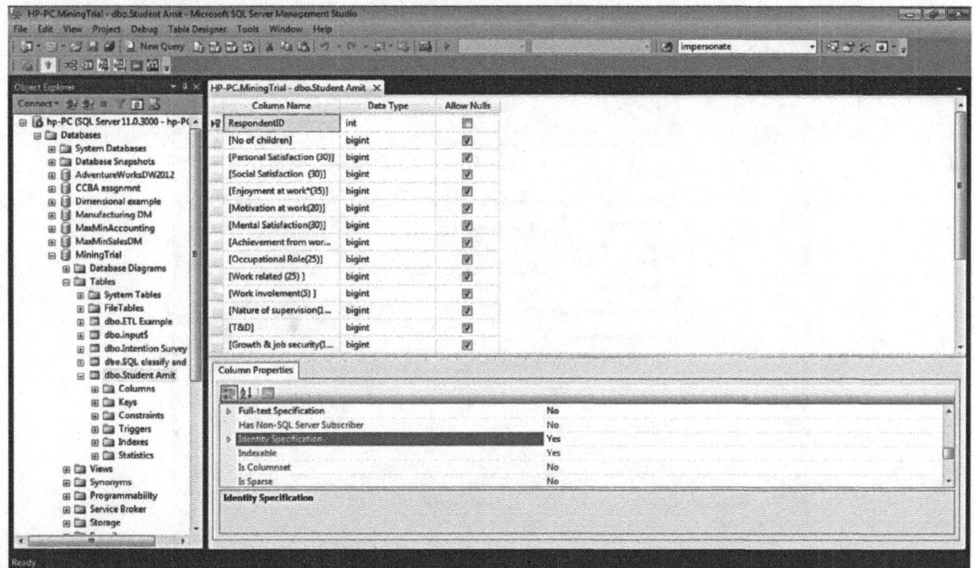

Click Save. Now we need to load data into this table.

3. For this, open SSDT. Open new Integration services project. Give it an appropriate name. The following window opens. Here, drag and drop Data Flow task onto Control Flow tab. Double click this task to open Data Flow tab.

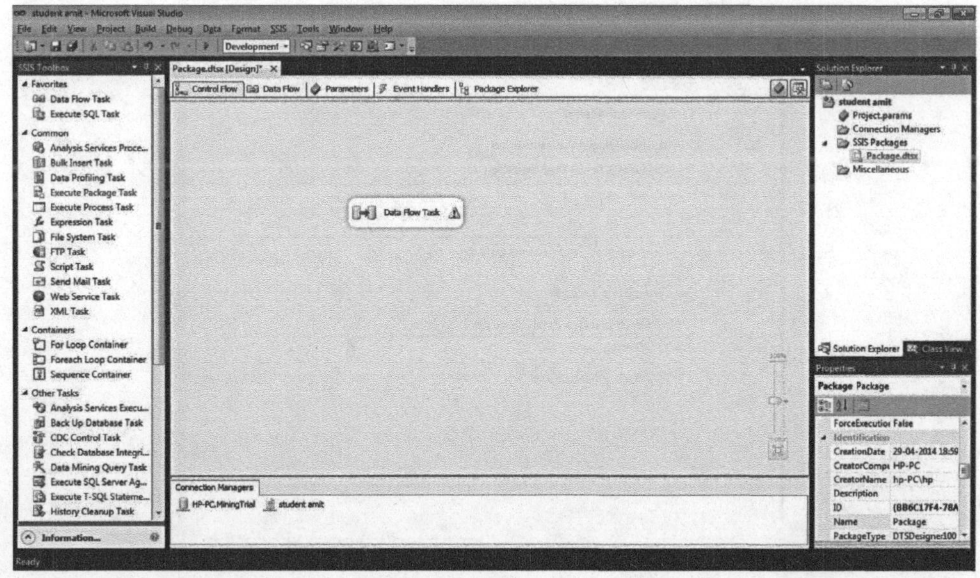

4. In the Data Flow tab, create connection manager for flat file source item. Connect it to .csv dataset where the data is stored.

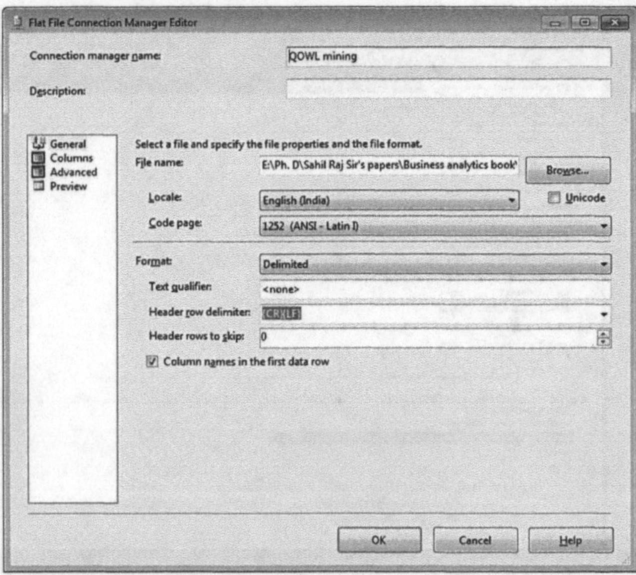

Review the data types in Advanced tab.

5. Similarly, create a connection for the SQL Server table or OLE DB destination item created in the first step, on which the SQL Server 2012 will run data mining.

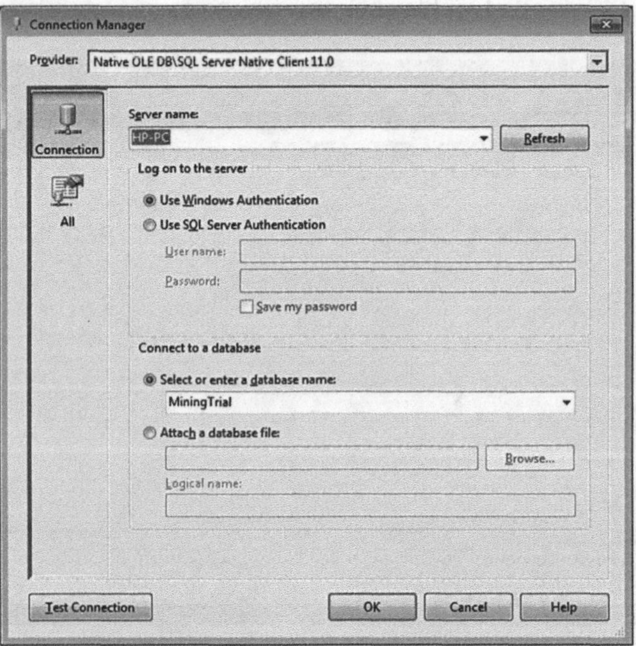

6. Once the connections have been defined, drag and drop a flat file source item onto the Data Flow tab and double click on this to open the source editor window.

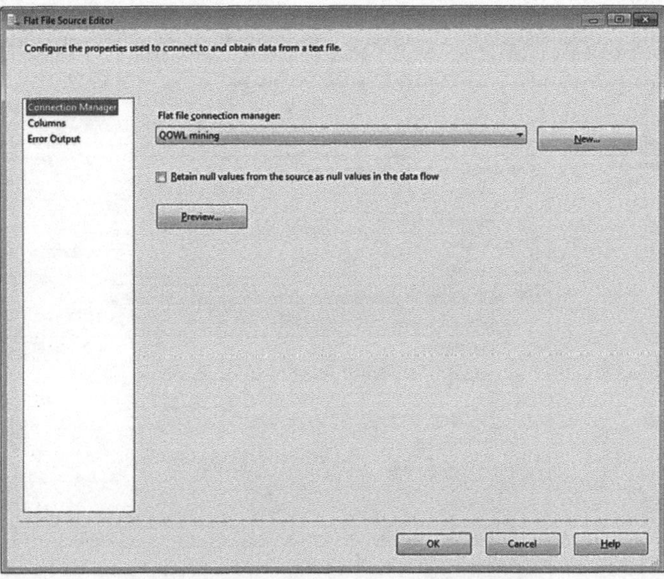

It automatically connects to flat file. Check all columns from Columns tab, since they will be useful for analysis.

7. Below the source item, drag and drop a data conversion item. Drop the blue arrow from the source item onto this data conversion item, for 'Gender', 'Birth Location', and 'Marital Status' as shown below:

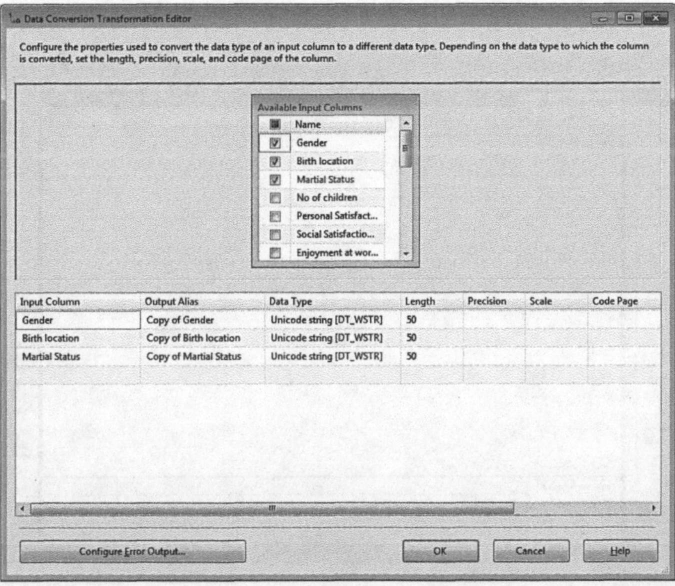

8. Next drag and drop an OLEDB destination item. Drag and drop the blue arrow from the data conversion item onto the destination item. Double click on this to open the destination editor window.

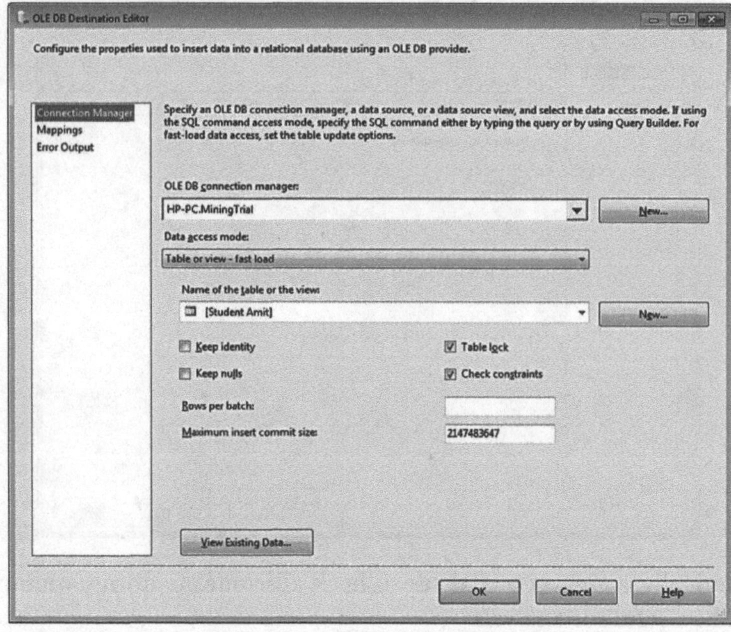

Review mappings page. All columns should be automatically mapped except Respondent Id because this field is auto-sequenced.

9. The Data Flow should finally appear, as shown below:

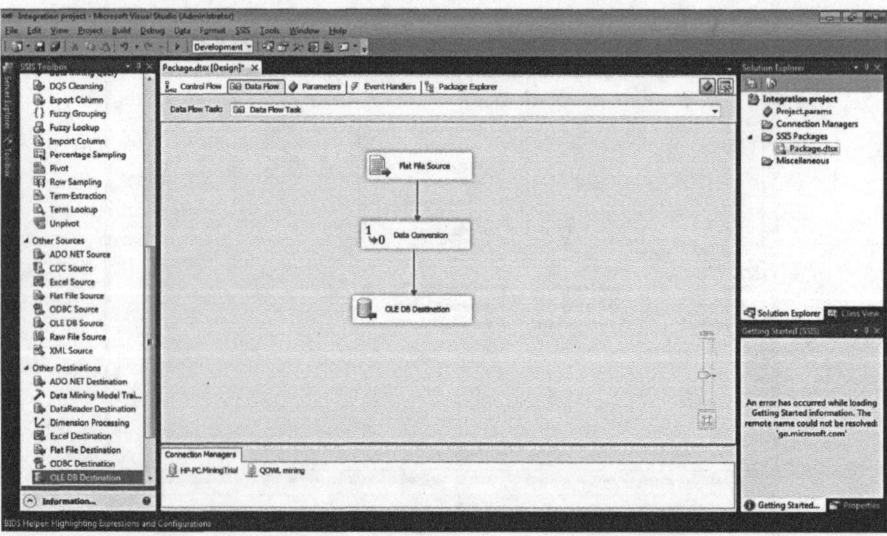

10. Finally execute this ETL package. This would load the data into the SQL table, ready to be analysed.

Running Mining

Here, first create a data source, then a data source view and then create a mining structure on top of it.

1. Create a new analysis services project and name it as 'Mining example hands-on'. Click OK. The following window opens:

2. Right click on the data source in the Solution Explorer window and select a New Data Source:

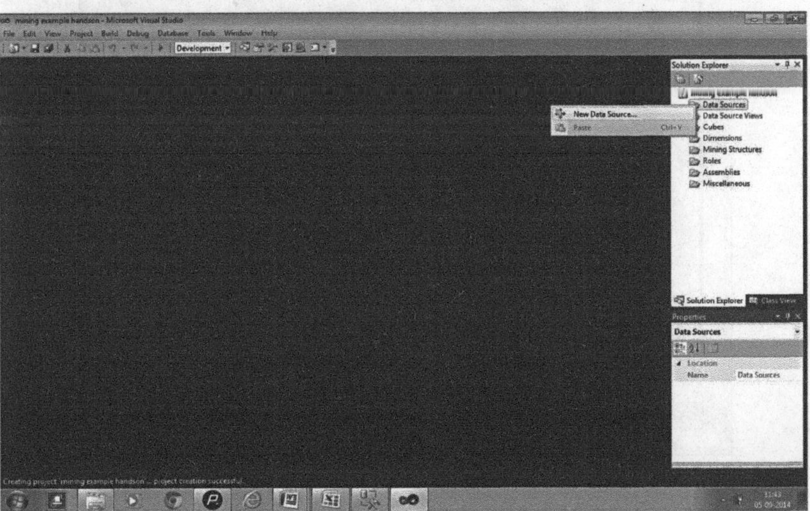

3. This opens Data Source Wizard. Click Next on the welcome screen. In 'how to define new connection' window, select New:

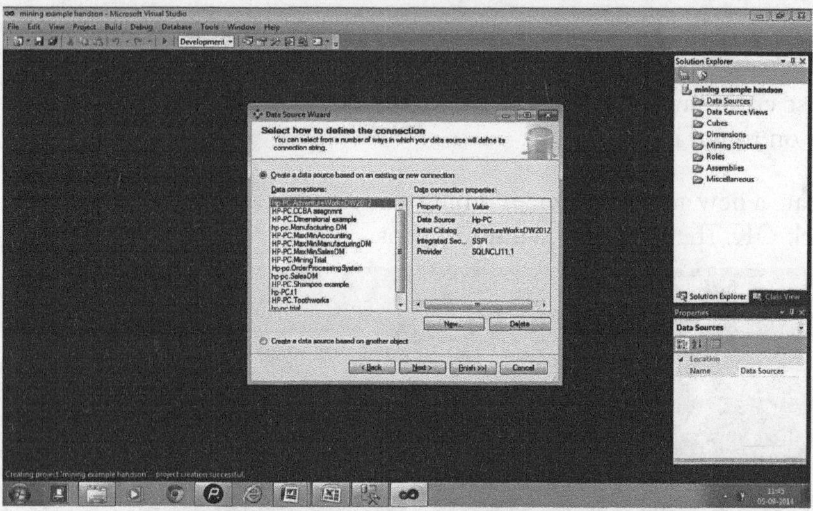

4. In the Connection Manager opened, enter the name of the server where the table resides where we loaded the data:

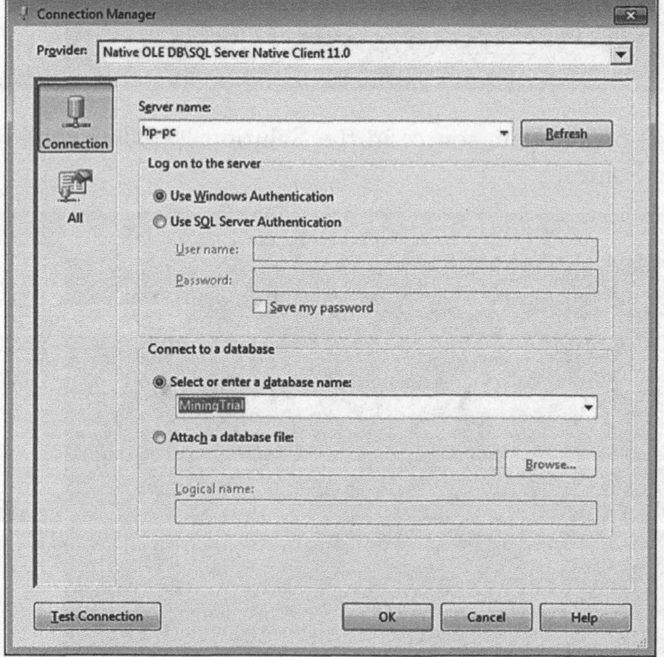

Click OK. Then click next.

5. In the next window, provide Impersonation details for authenticating access to a Data Source:

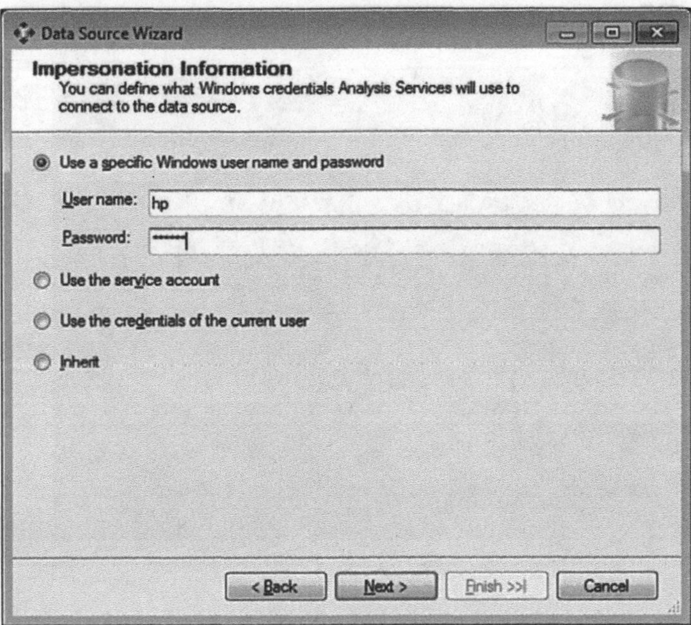

Click Next.

6. Provide an appropriate name to the data source and click Finish.

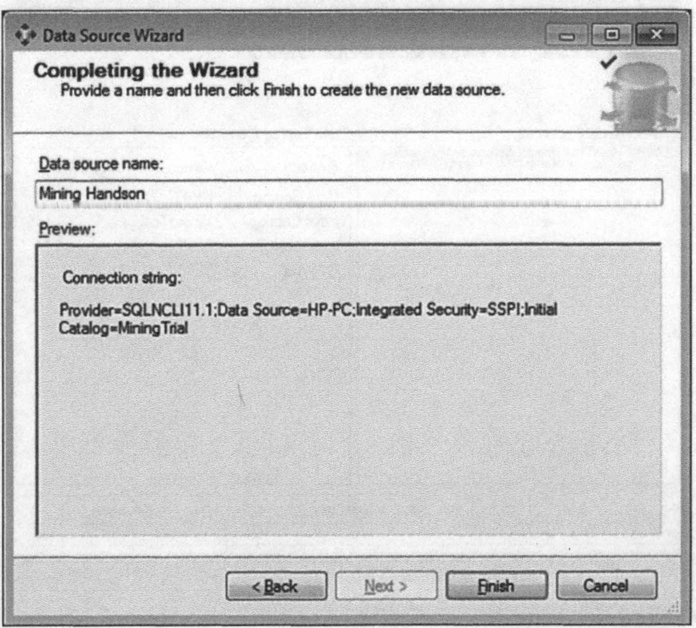

7. Next, right click on the data source view from the Solution Explorer window and select New Data Source view:

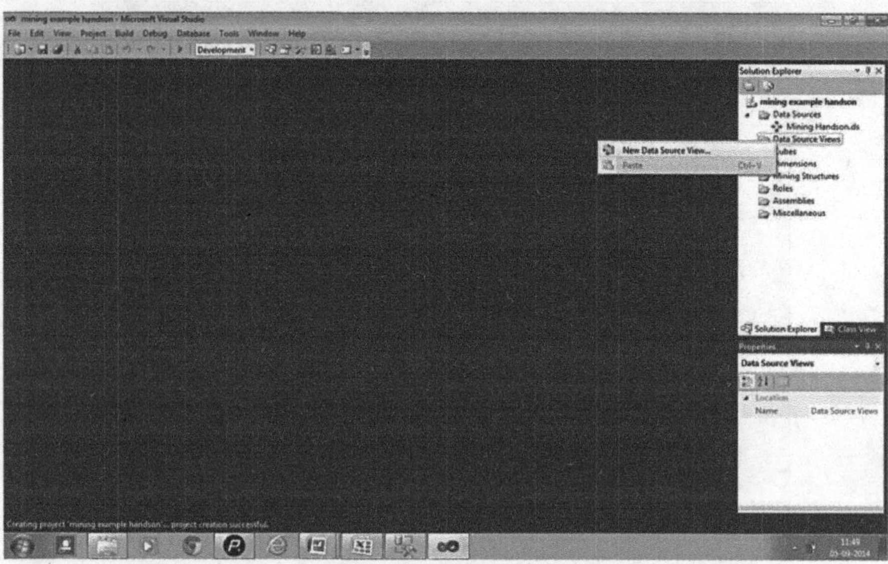

8. Click Next on the welcome screen. The Data Source we created in the previous step, should appear automatically.

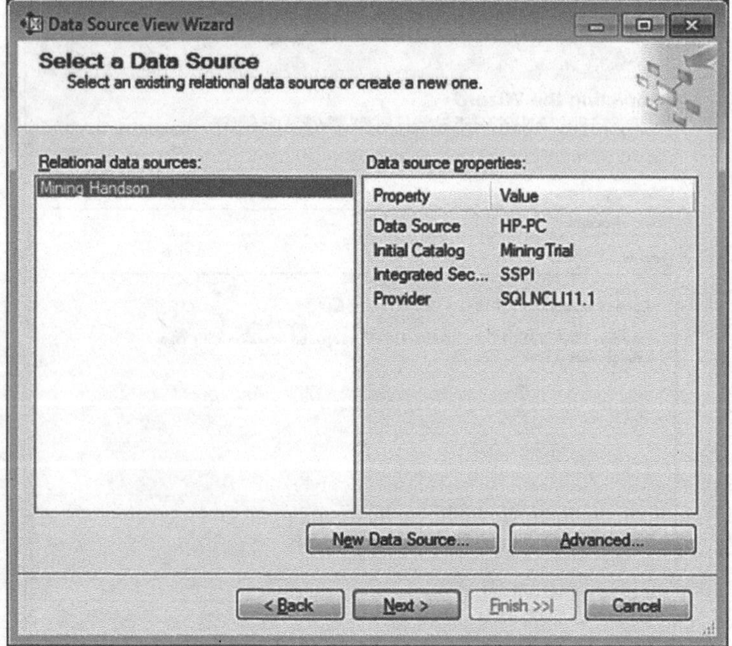

9. Click Next. Keep default for name matching:

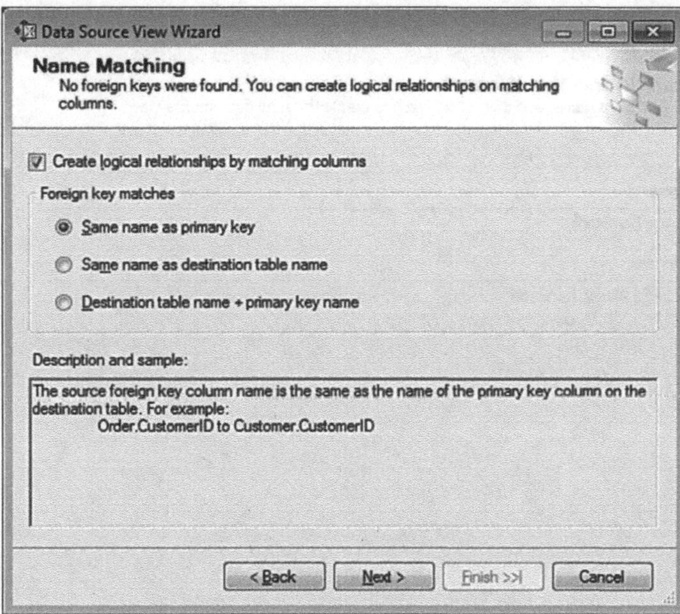

10. In Select Table and Views, select the table where the data are loaded for mining. Click on right arrow on the window:

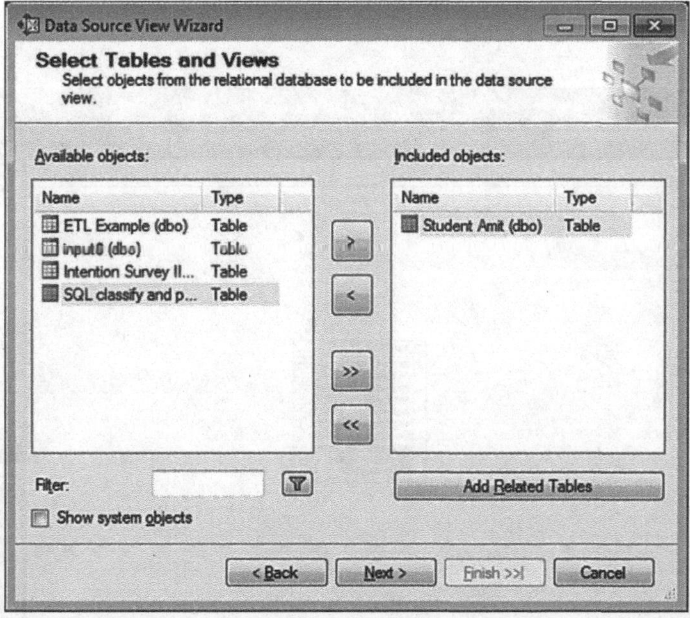

Click next.

11. Give an appropriate name to the view and click Finish:

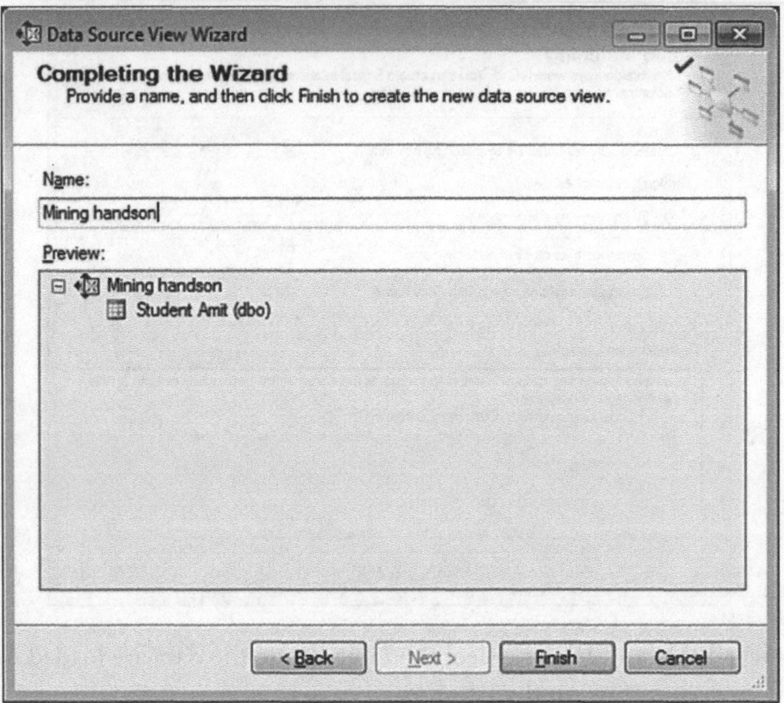

12. The following window appears:

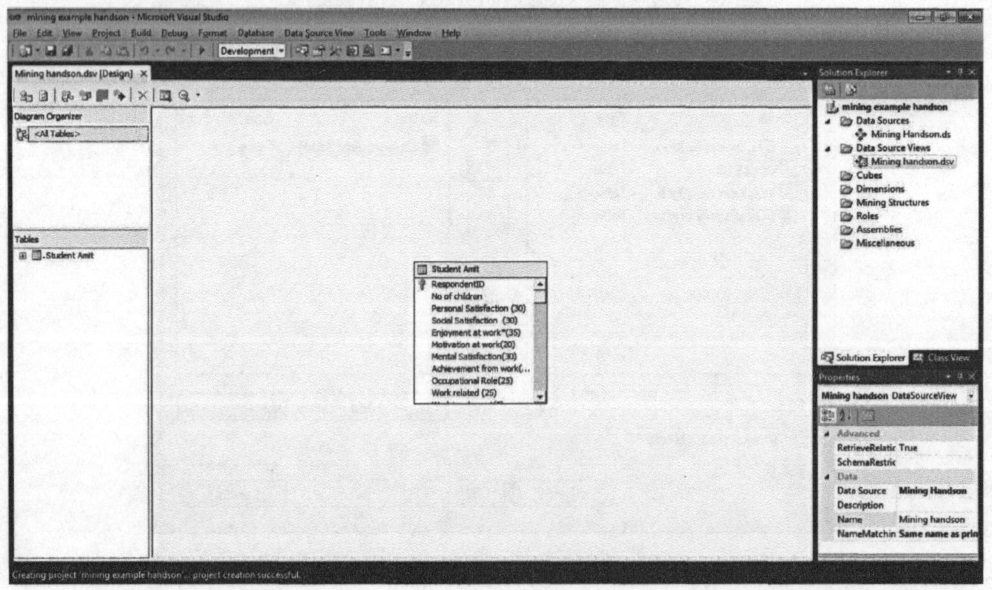

13. Next right click on Mining Structure from Solution Explorer and select:

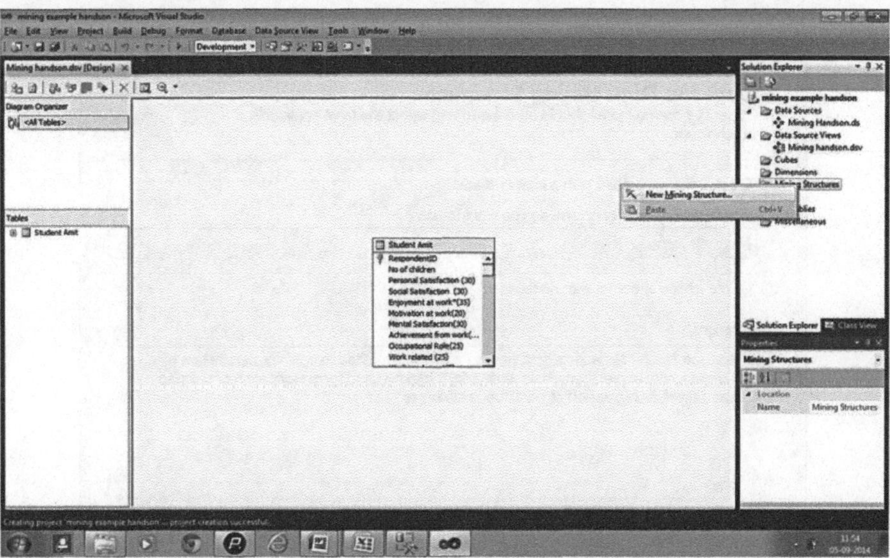

14. Click Next on the welcome screen. In 'Select Define' method, check the radio button against 'use existing relational database or data warehouse'.

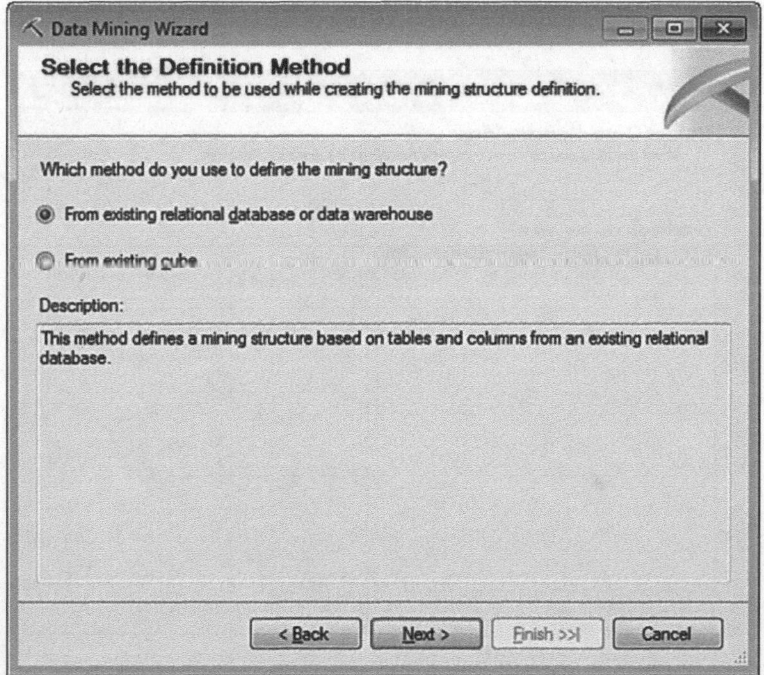

15. Click Next. You are asked to provide inputs for the kind of Mining Structure you want to create. Enter the following:

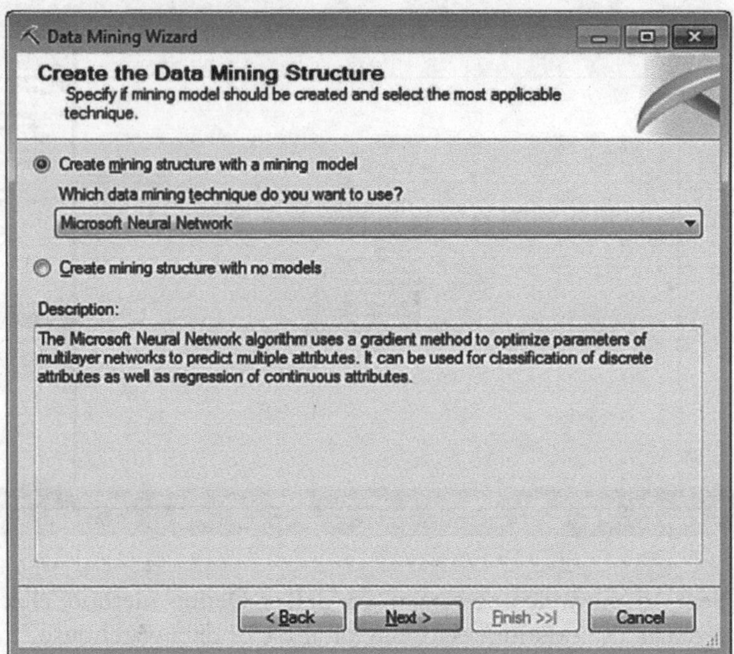

16. In the next screen, add Data Source View:

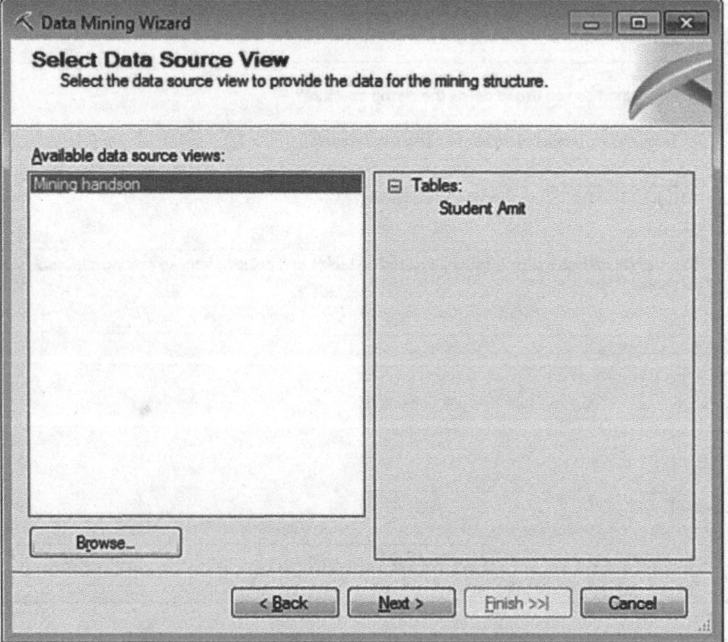

17. Keep the table type as Case, in the next window:

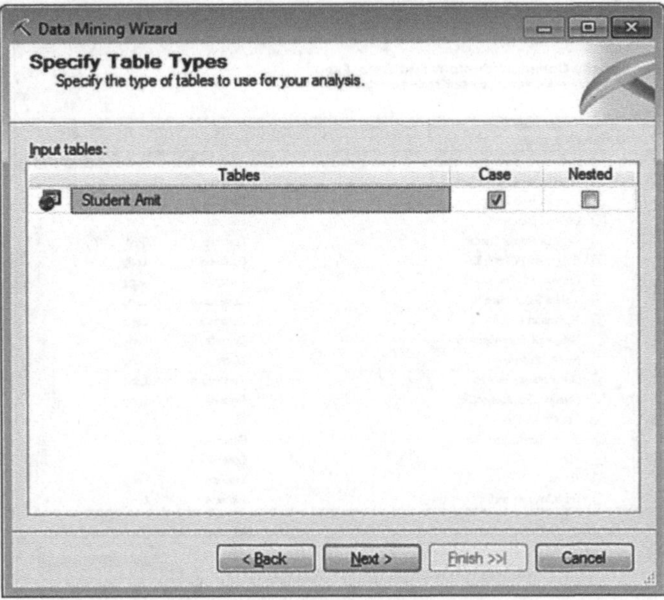

18. In the next screen, specify which field is the Key column, which field is to be predicted, and which fields are to be used as input for prediction:

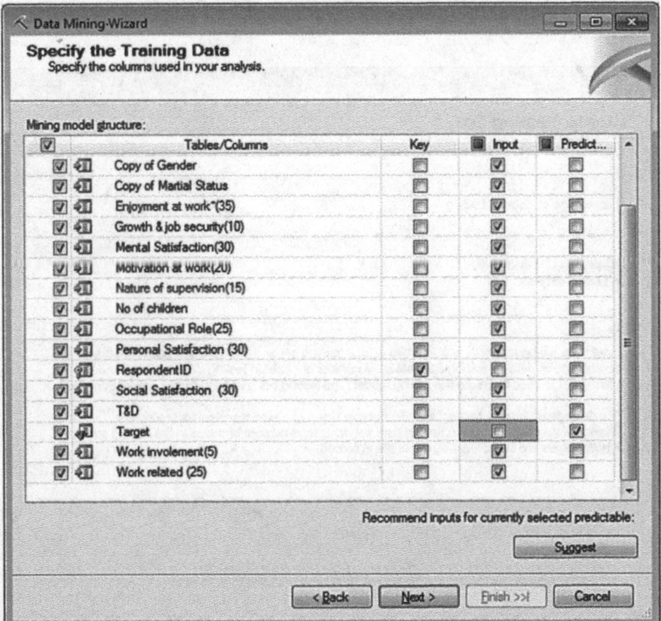

Here, specify 'RespondentID' as Key, 'Target' as Predict and uncheck for Input, and rest all check as Input.

19. In the next screen, click on Detect to specify the data types of the fields as shown below:

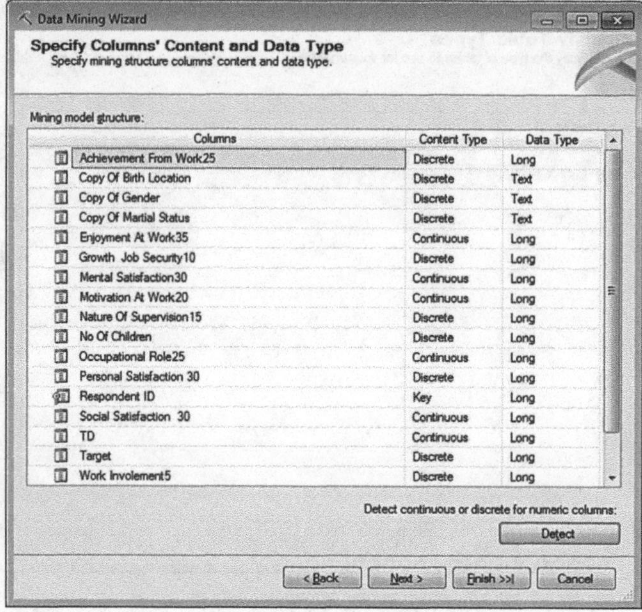

This automatically detects the suitable data type of the fields.

20. Keep default in next screen. This is used to split the input data into training and test data.

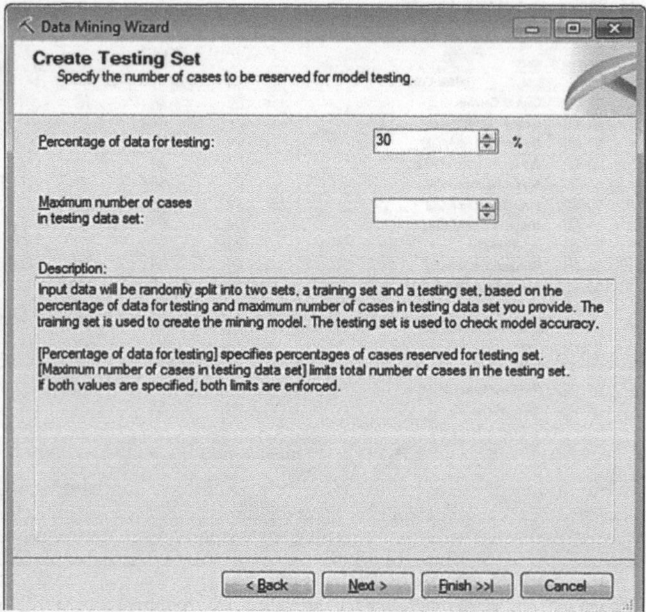

21. Rename as shown below in the next screen:

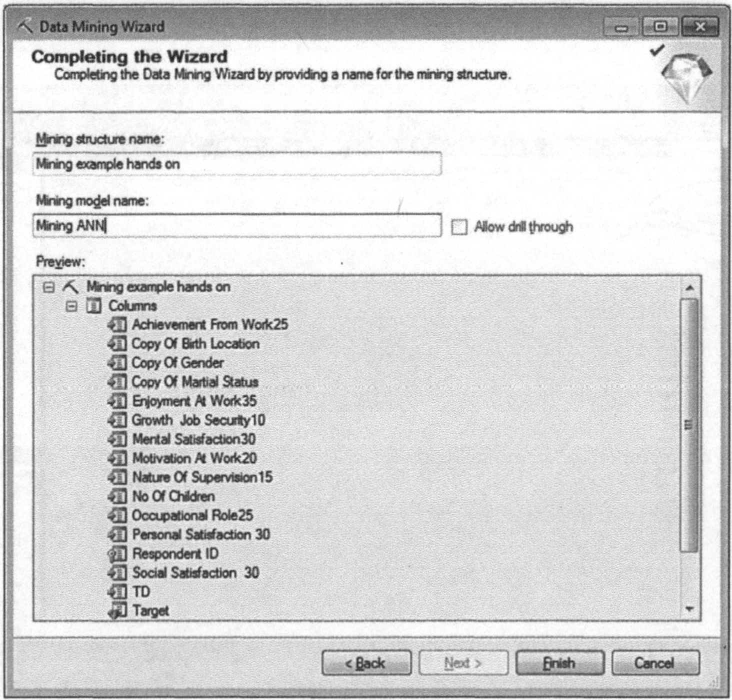

22. Click Finish. The following window opens:

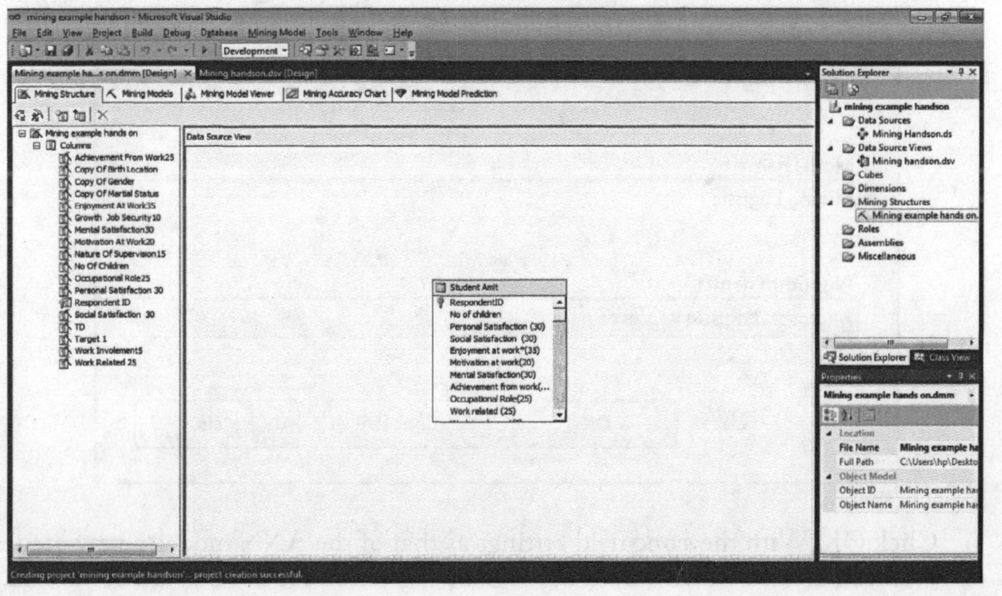

23. In this, click on Mining Models tab. Then click on tab Create a Related Mining Model. We would like to run two mining techniques on these data. ANN has already been added. Another one 'Logistic regression', we would add here:

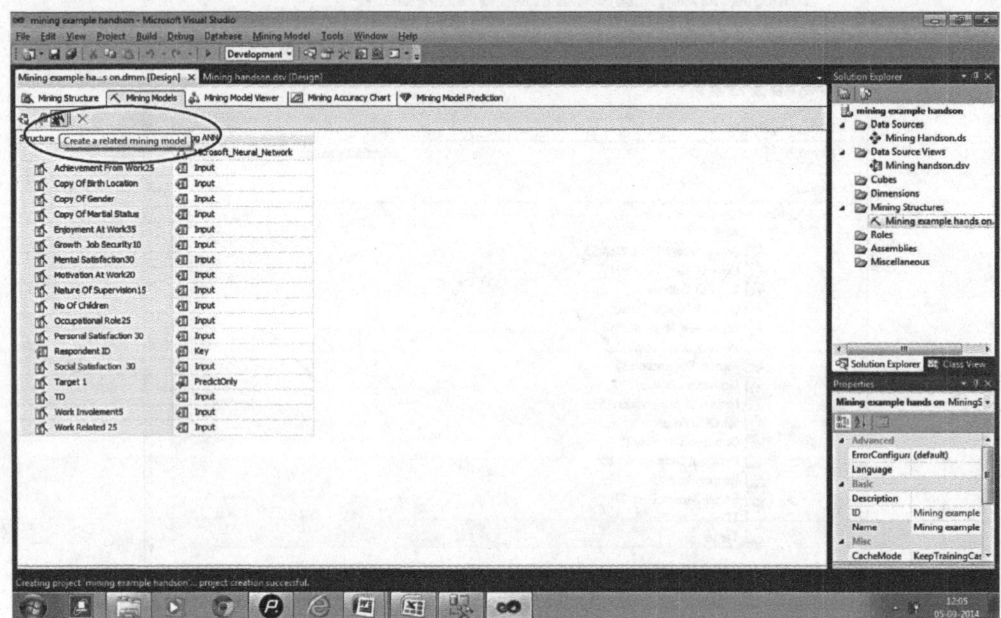

24. This opens the New Mining Model dialog box. Here, name the Mining Model as 'Mining Logistic' and algorithm as 'Microsoft Logistic regression'.

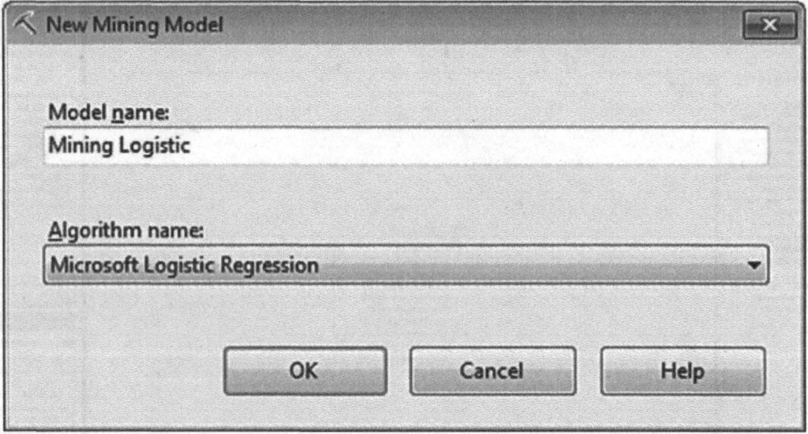

Click OK. With the same field settings as that of the ANN model, a new model has been created which would use logistic regression for mining. Click Save all.

25. Next, you have to deploy this project to view the Mining Model Output. For this, change the deployment server name from Project Properties window:

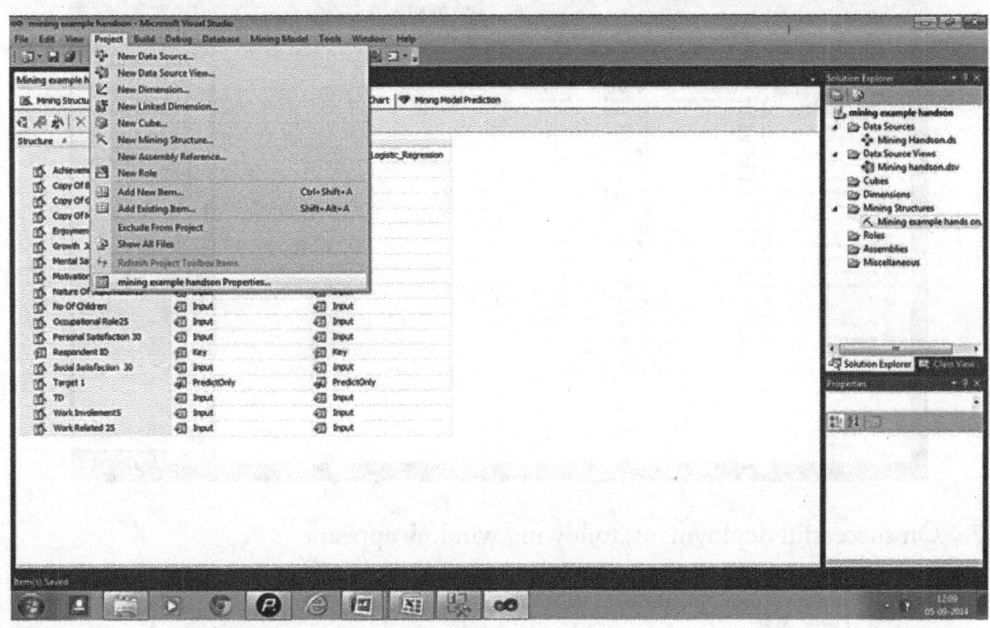

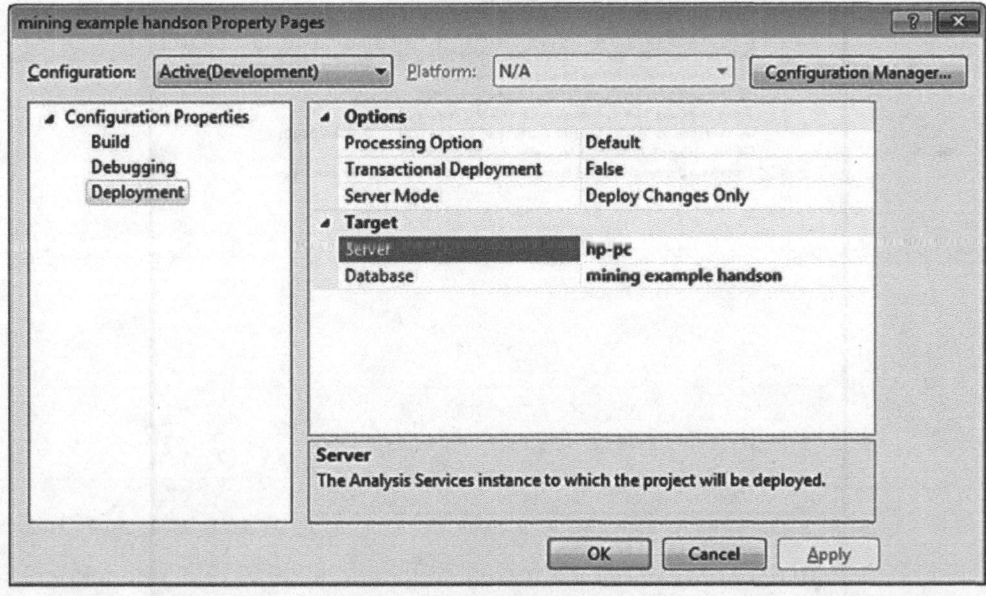

Click OK.

26. Next, deploy the Project from Build menu.

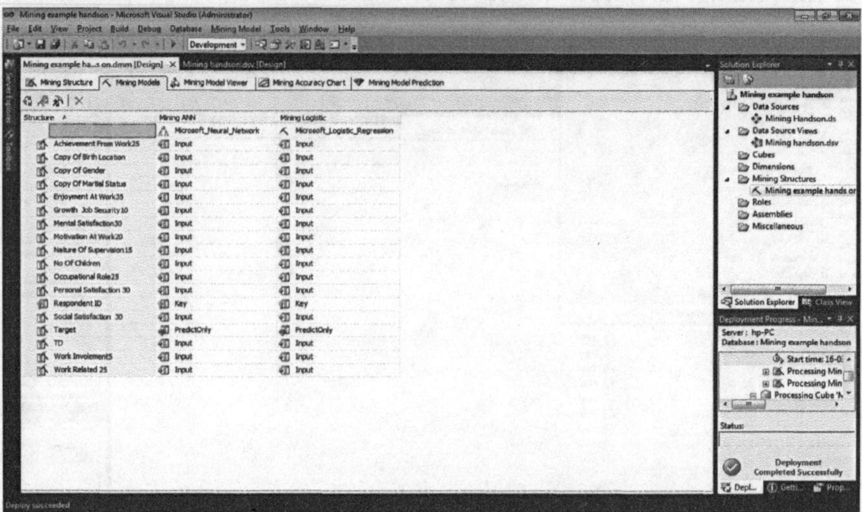

27. On successful deployment, following window appears:

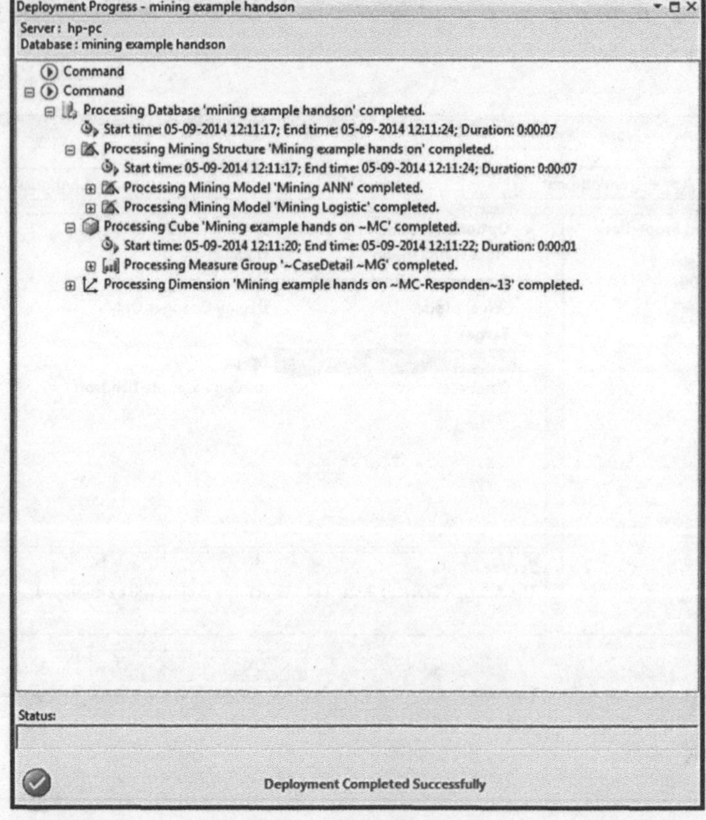

Browsing the Model

28. Now you can browse through Mining Model Output to view the results. Click on Mining Model Viewer:

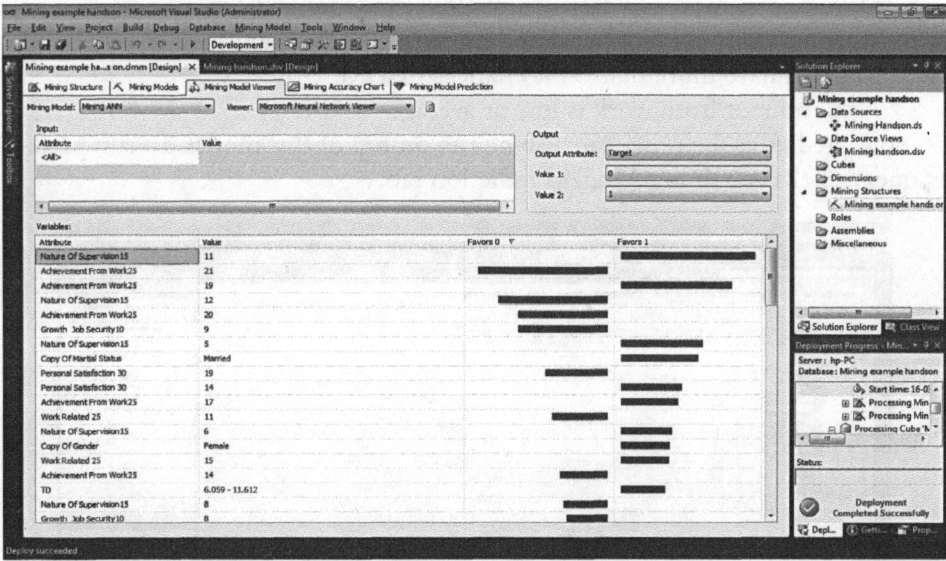

Mining ANN appears by default. You can change to the other Model Mining Logistic by selecting the same from Mining Model drop down list. We will do that shortly. Keep the view at Mining Neural Network viewer.

The output attribute is set at 'Target' (our prediction field). It has only two values, value 1 and value 2. In case the output attribute has more than two values, the view can be changed for any set of two values by choosing the same from drop down appearing against value1 and value 2 fields in the window.

The result window depicts the input variable, their values and the extent to which they favour either state of the target variable. The length of the blue bar indicates how strongly the factor favours a particular target state and hence can predict the same. Hovering the cursor over any bar displays the percentage of cases that favour that state. These attributes which strongly favour a given state are called key influencers. In this manner, the findings can be summarised as under:

Key influencers for those who have a tendency to stay ('Target' state has value 0) as predicted by ANN from a sample of 102 respondents:

- Nature of supervision has a high score (12 or more score out of 15) – more than 92% probability to stay
- Work involvement is high (5 on 5 score) – more than 89% probability to stay
- Achievement from work is high (more than 20 out of 25 score) – 88% probability to stay
- Those who believe growth and job security is high in the current job have very high chances of staying (more than 82%)

For those who have a tendency to leave the firm ('Target' has value 1), the key influencers are:

- Nature of supervision is low or medium (5 or below 12 score out of 15) – more than 96% chances to leave
- Have one or more children – probability to leave is 95%
- Personal satisfaction is average – more than 93% chances to leave
- Married have more than 91% chances to leave
- Achievement from work is low or average

29. Now, predictive querying can also be run on top of this model. To run predictive query, click on Mining Model Prediction tab:

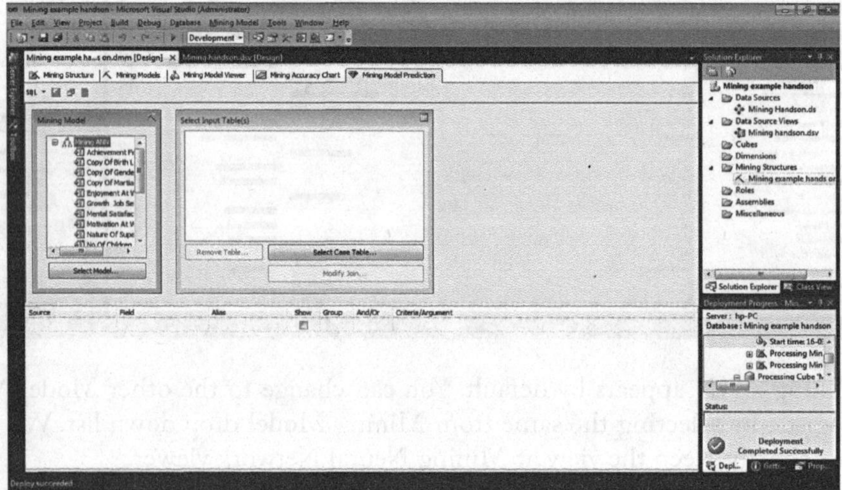

30. In the window thus opened, click on Singleton Query:

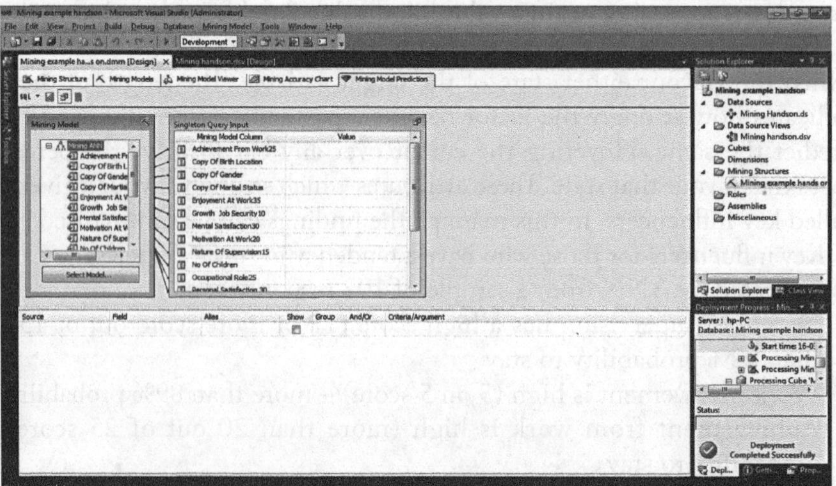

The following window opens. Here, you can enter the values of input variable:

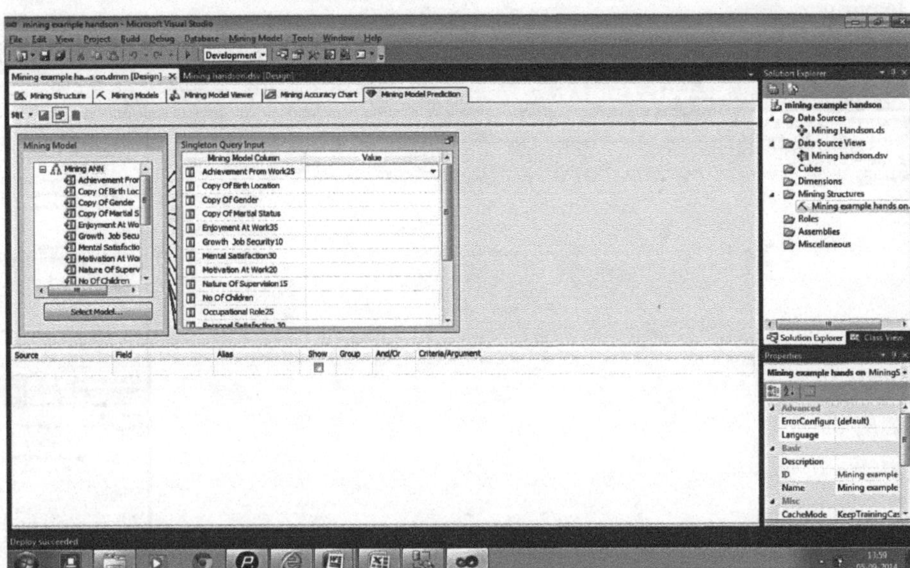

Let us attempt to run some queries, as shown below:

31. *What if the candidate is from an urban location?*

Use Singleton Query where birth location is set to urban (ANN fetches the target state based on past learning from the data). Keep rest empty. Now in the lower half of the window, click in the cell below Source and select the name of data source used for mining. In field, select the output column and check Show. Now from the red circled icon, select Result.

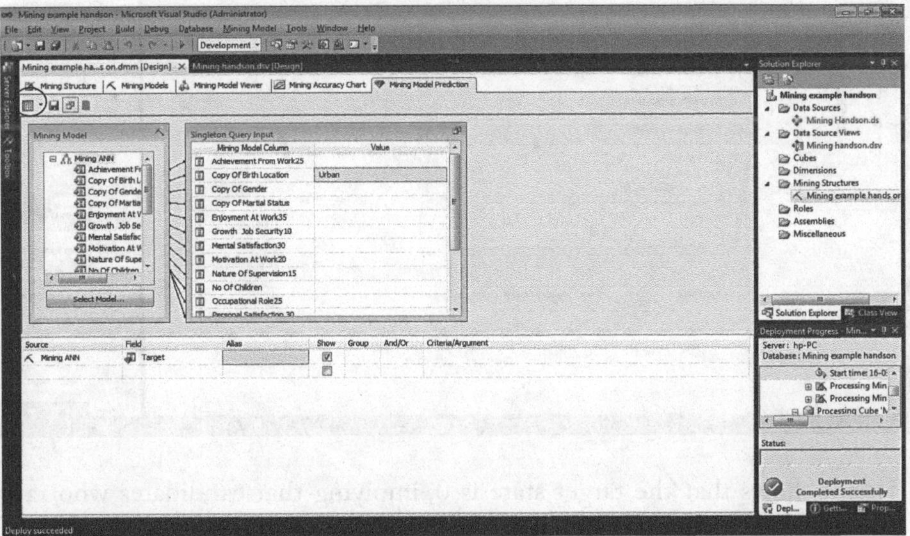

The target state in result is 1, implying the candidate has a high probability of leaving.

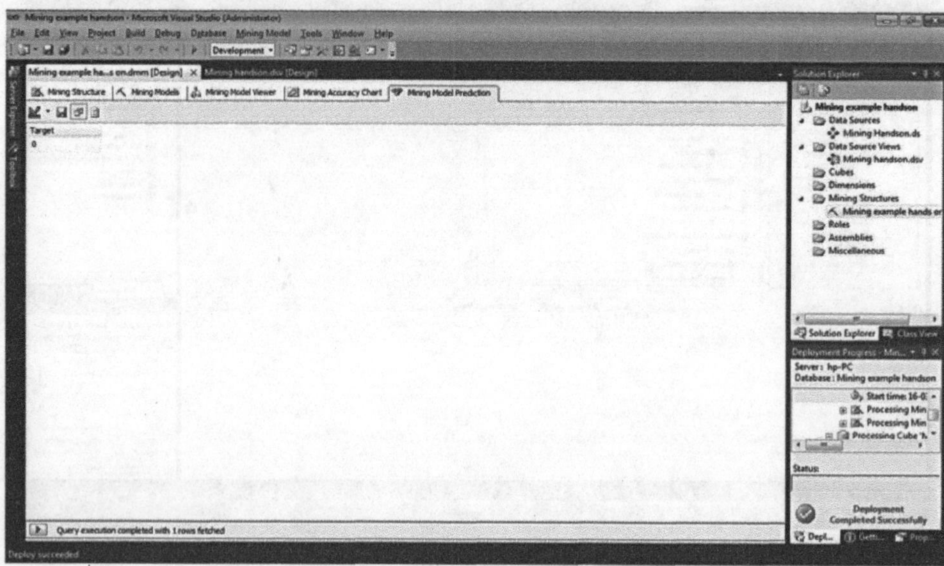

32. *What if a candidate is from a rural location, is married and gives a high score on T&D?*

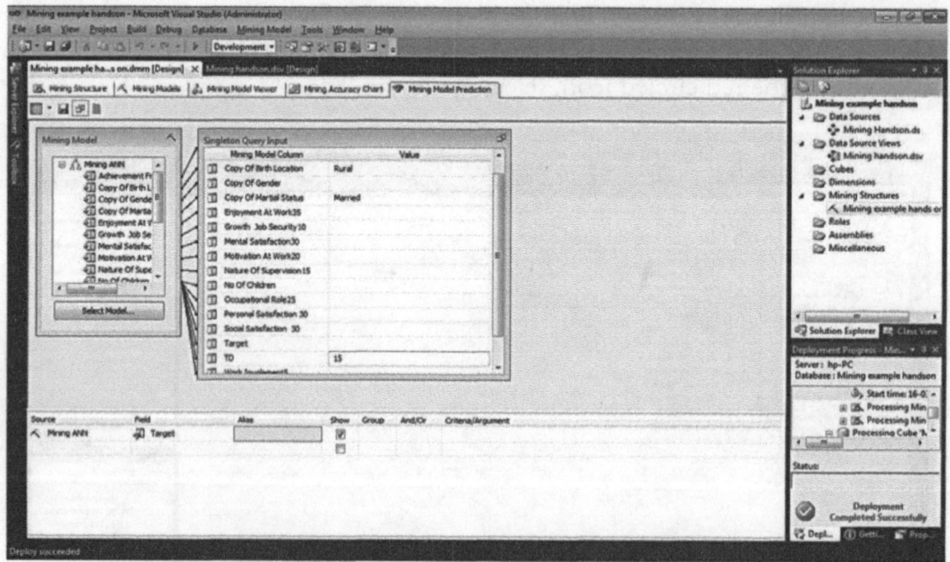

Result shows that the target state is 0, implying that candidates who rate the training and development high in the firm are likely to stay with the firm.

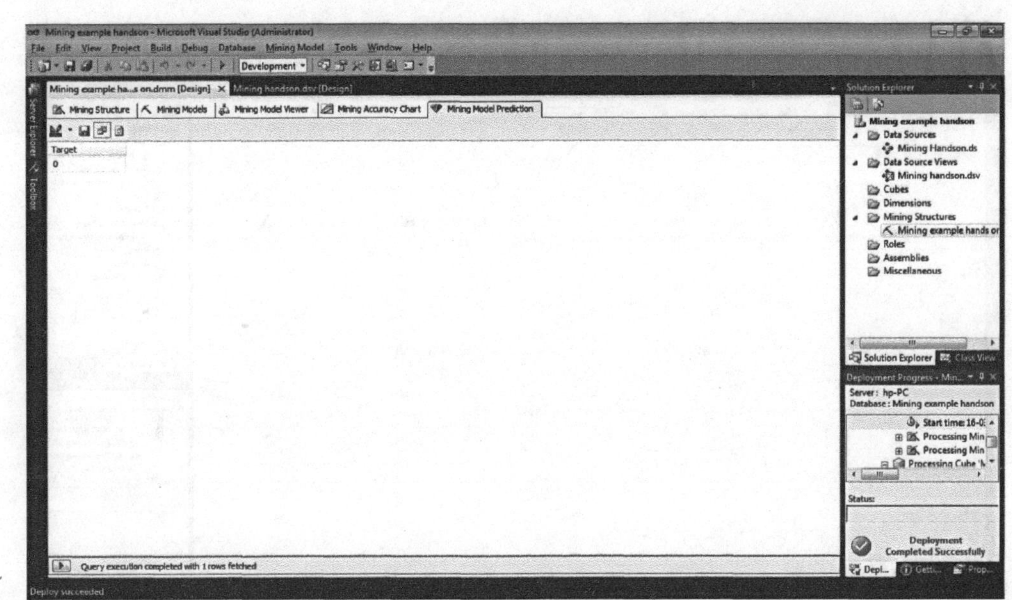

33. *If a candidate is married and from a rural location, but believes that the nature of supervision is high (input 13), achievement from work is high (17), and work involvement is high (5), what are the chances of staying?*

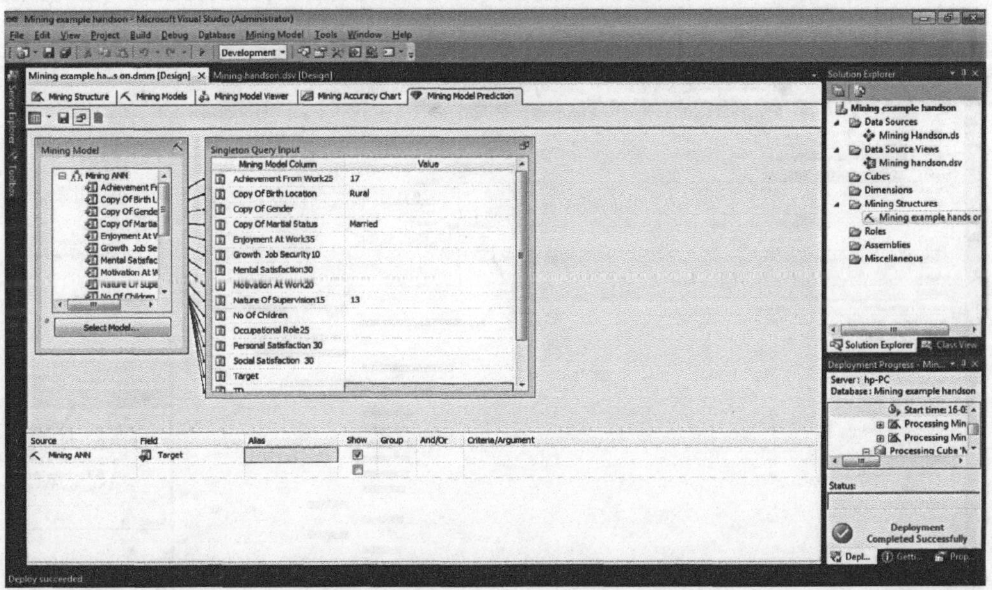

Result fetched by SQL predictive query is target state 1, implying that the candidate is highly likely to leave the firm.

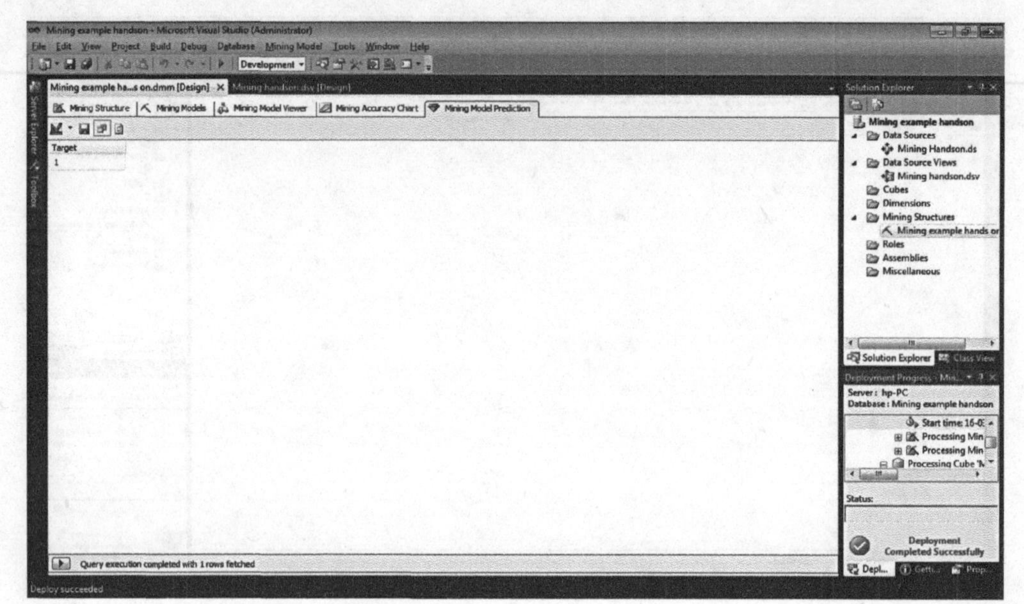

Browsing the other Model 'Mining Logistic'

34. To switch to other Mining Model defined here, click on Mining Model viewer tab. From drop down list of Mining Model in the window, select Mining Logistic.

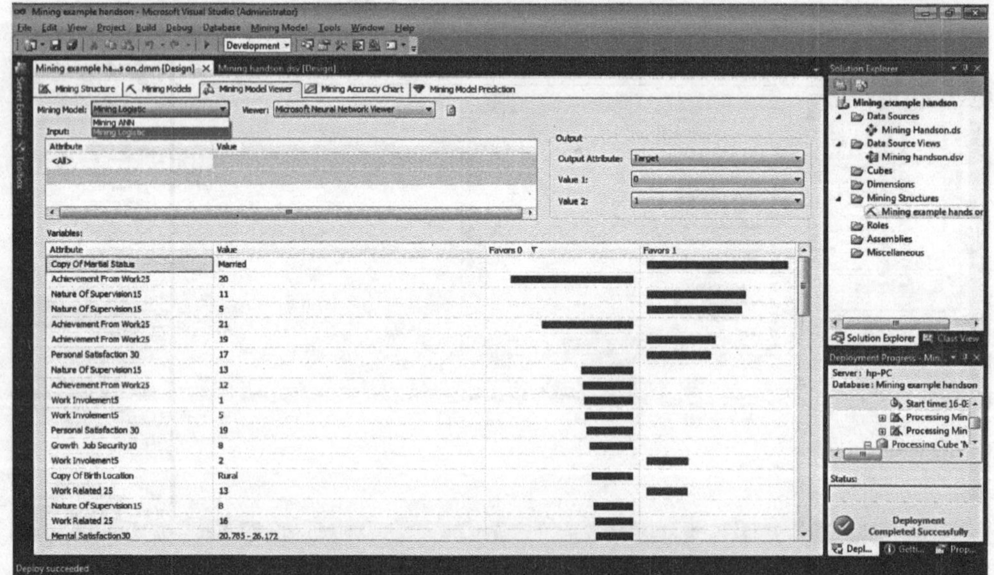

This automatically changes the view and fetches the results for this model.

35. The result is fetched as shown below, which has similar analysis as the ANN viewer tab:

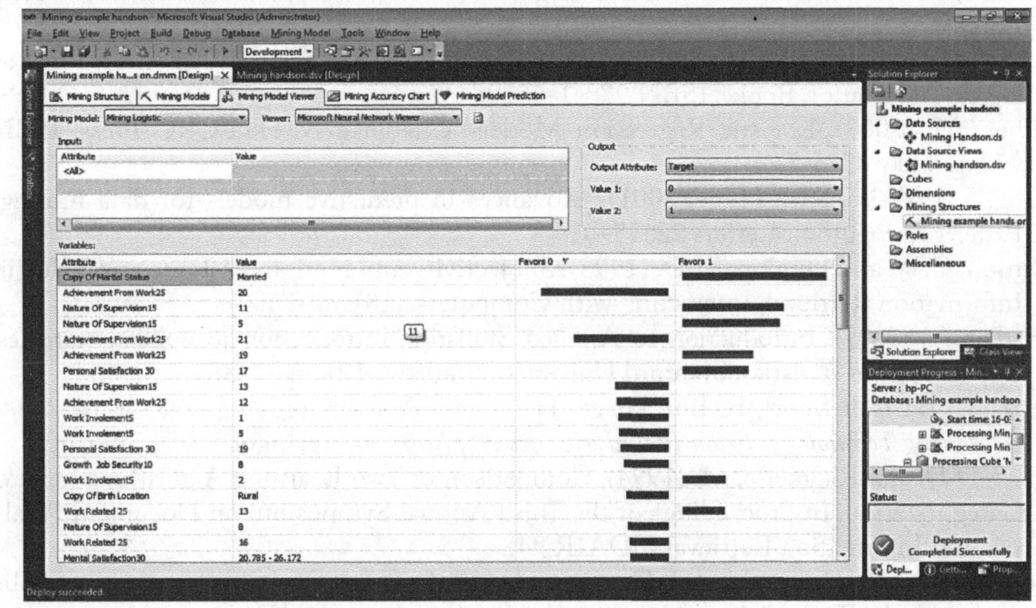

Here, one can also determine key influencers and the probabilities attached and run predictive queries.

REFERENCES

Aha, D., Breslow, L.A. and Munoz-Avila, H. (1999). Conversational Case-Based Reasoning. Journal of Artificial Intelligence (to appear).

Akkus, A. and Guvenir, H.A.K. (1996). Nearest Neighbor Classification on Feature Projections. In Proceedings of ICML 96 Lorenza Saitta (ED) Morgan Kaufmann Bari Italy 12, 19.

Apte, C., Damerau, F. and Weiss, S. (1994). Towards Language Independent Automated Learning of Text Categorization Models. In Proceedings of the 17th Annual ACM_ SIGIR conference.

Apte, C., Grossman, E., Pednault, E., Rosen, B., Tipu, F., and White, B., (1999). Probabilistic estimation based data mining for discovering insurance risks. IEEE Intelligent Syst. 14 (6), 49–58.

Balakrishnan, N. (1991). *Handbook of the Logistic Distribution*. Marcel Dekker, Inc. ISBN 978-0824785871.

Bellazzi, R. and Zupan, B. (2008). "Predictive data mining in clinical medicine: Current issues and guidelines", International Journal of Medical Informatics 77, 81–97.

Breiman, L. (1993). Classification and Regression Trees, Chapman & Hall, New York, London.

Grimm and Yarnold, Reading and understanding multivariate analysis. American Psychological Association Books. ISBN 978-1-55798-273-5.

Hilbe, J.M. (2009). Logistic Regression Models. Chapman & Hall/CRC Press. ISBN 978-1-4200-7575-5.

Hong, S. J. Weiss, S.M. (June, 2001). "Advances in predictive models for data mining" Pattern Recognition Letters 22, 55–61.

Johnson, C.W. and Dunlop, M.D. (1998). Subjectivity and Notions of Time and Value in Information Retrieval, Interacting with Computers, (10): 67–75.

Jonathan, T. (2009). Introduction to Applied Statistics, Introduction to applied statistics, Department of statistics, Stanford University, Statistics 191, pp. 1–38.

Lenz, M. Bartsch-Sporl, B. Burckhard, H.D. and Weiss S. (eds.) (1998), *Case-Based Reasoning Technology: From Foundations to Applications,* Springer Verlag, Berlin.

Lewis, D.D. and Ringuette, M. (1994). Comparison of Two Learning Algorithms for text Categorization. In Proceedings of the Third Annual Symposium on Document Analysis and Information Retrieval (SDAIR 94).

Moulinier, I., Raskinis, G., and Ganascia, J. (1996). Text Categorization:A Symbolic Approach. In Proceedings of the Fifth Annual Symposium on Document Analysis and Information Retrieval.

Owens, C. (1993). *Integrating Extraction and Search.* In J.L. Kolodner (editor) Case-based Learning. Kluwer, London.

Patricia, E.N. Lutu, Engelbrecht, A. P. (2010). "A decision rule-based method for feature selection in predictive data mining", Expert Systems with Applications 37 602–609.

Quinlan, J.R. (1993). C4.5: Programs for Machine Learning, Morgan Kaufmann Publishers, San Mateo, Calif.

Ruggeri, Kennet, Faltin, (2008). Classification and Regression tree methods, In Encyclopaedia of Statistics in Quality and Reliability, Wiley, pp. 315–123.

Ruppert, D. Wand, M.P. and Caroll, R.J. (2003). Generalized Regression Meodels, Journal of the American Statistical Association, STAT902, pp. 1–25.

Sheppard, A.G. (1996). The sequence of factor analysis and cluster analysis: Differences in segmentation and dimensionality through the use of raw and factor scores. Tourism Analysis, 1, 49–57.

Stockwell, I. (2008). Introduction to Correlation and Regression analysis, SAS Global Forum, Paper-364, pp. 1–8.

Tzung-Pei, H., Chyan-Yuan, H., Chih-Hung, W., Shyue-Liang, W. (2009). "An improved data mining approach using predictive itemsets", Expert Systems with Applications 36, 72–80.

Weiss, S. and Indurkhya, N. (1998). Predictive Data Mining: A Practical Guide. Morgan Kaufmann, Los Altos, CA.

Wiener, E., Pedersen, J.O and Weigend, A.S. (1995). A Neural Network Approach to Topic Spotting. In Proceedings of the Fourth Annual Symposium on Document Analysis and Information Retrieval (SDAIR 95).

Yavuz, T. and Guvenir, H. A. Application of k - Nearest Neighbor on Feature Projections Classifer to Text Categorization.

CHAPTER 12

Emerging Analytics

After going through this chapter, you will be able to

- Understand the concept of facial analytics
- Understand the concept of retail analytics
- Understand the applications of social media analytics
- Understand the concept of big data
- Understand the applications of hadoop

INTRODUCTION

At the present time, lot of development is happening in the field of analytics. To survive in this competitive era, organisations are trying to apply analytics in new areas. This has led to the emergence of various new categories of analytics. These are often called emerging analytics as these new applications of analytics are still in the nascent stage, but these are finding much acceptability from organisations slowly and gradually. In this chapter, some of the important emerging analytical applications are discussed to sensitise students regarding the future of analytics.

FACIAL ANALYTICS

Facial expressions can provide a window into a person's unspoken thoughts.

—Jeff Bertolucci is a technology journalist in Los Angeles

Facial analytics is that branch of analytics, which helps to decipher the emotions of humans by studying their facial expressions. Although much emphasis is given to facial analytics (facial analytics is also known as physiognomy) at the present time, the study of facial expression is not a new phenomenon. Rather, the application of facial analytics dates back to fourth century BC when it was known as physiognomy. Physiognomy is a study of assessment of a person's character or personality from his/her outer appearance. In the 19th century, Charles Darwin categorised and grouped the similar facial expression such as low spirits, anxiety, grief, dejection, despair, joy, high spirit, low, tender feeling, devotion, reflection, mediation,

Facial analytics is that branch of analytics, which helps to decipher the emotions of human beings by studying their facial expressions.

ill-temper, determination, hatred, anger, disdain, contempt, disgust, guilt, pride, surprise, astonishment, fear, horror, self-attention, shame, shyness and modesty.

Facial analytics can be performed on 2D and 3D images. When this technology was invented, at that time only 2D images were captured and saved in a database for a further analysis. But with time, the technology changed and now the softwares are able to take the 3D images. 3D facial recognition is a very advanced technique in which real-time images are captured with the camera, and they are analysed at that very moment. Its accuracy is very high than its previous counterpart.

Facial analytics can be done on a single image or a group of images to identify the behaviour of people. Some developers also called it crowd analytics. It is very helpful to check the group behaviour towards any particular subject such as a music video or any product. All the expressions are detected and their average is taken by software to analyse the group behaviour.

Group analytics is also used to detect the potential threats. All the faces in the group are identified first, and then they are scanned to match with the already stored database of faces of criminals. This helps to identify potential threat (such as suicide attacks) in any public place.

Traditionally, facial expressions were studied by clinical, social psychologists and medical practitioners, but of late, many business organisations have started taking interest in observing facial expression of customers. To counter the intense competition in the market, organisations are trying to read the mind of customers by applying the facial analytics, as "face speaks before we actually speak and express ourselves". The advantage of using facial analytics is that organisations do not hamper the privacy of a person as they are not interacting with the person. By applying facial analytics organisations are able to capture the images from a distance without even telling the person. This technology is gaining attention due to its accuracy. Presently, various high-resolution cameras are available in the market. These high-resolution cameras are providing a high rate of accuracy to the facial softwares. Moreover, a face can express many movements such as eye movement, lip movement, jaw movement, eye brow movement and so on. Each of these expressions on a face conveys very important and distinct information to organisations. Imagine that you are in an apparel store and you have just seen your favourite jeans brand in a new colour. Now before you actually speak, your face will reveal what exactly you want to say. But, the problem is that not all the facial expressions are that easy to decipher by naked eyes. Moreover, with hundreds of people visiting big retail stores, it is not feasible to deploy staff just to note down expression of shoppers. This solution is provided by facial analytics. Organisations, particularly big retail stores, are capturing your emotions while you are moving and checking products. Every movement of shopper is recorded to analyse the facial expressions and body language to know what exactly shoppers are thinking. Based on the results of facial analytics, retail stores are offering combo offers. That is why in retail stores we see many cameras and these cameras are not only meant to check theft, but also to record your facial expression so as to provide you the best possible products in best possible combinations.

HOW FACE RECOGNITION TECHNOLOGY WORKS

The human face has approximately 80 nodal points. Most of these nodal points comprise the jaw line, cheekbones, distance between eyes, length and size of nose, depth and curves of the eye sockets, skin texture, etc. The facial software identifies all the nodal points on the face. After that, the software measures all the detected nodal points on a sub-millimetre scale and creates it into a template. Then, this template is converted into a unique code. This unique coding provides a set of numbers to the template to represent all the identified features on a face. These numbers are compared with other images to find the similarity.

There are two types of facial recognition techniques, one is known as static face detection, and the other is known as dynamic face detection technique.

There are two types of facial recognition techniques, one is known as static face detection and the other is known as dynamic face detection technique.

In static face detection, the static images of persons are detected and used for the desired purpose. Most of the times, these images are uploaded in databases and used for analysis or search purposes.

In dynamic face detection, real-time analysis of the image is done with the help of a camera. With this technology, gestures of persons are captured and these gestures are used to detect the mood of shoppers.

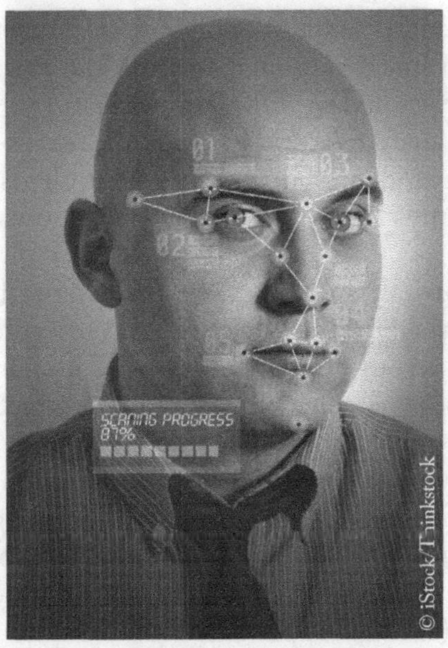

Source: http://www.bk.isy.liu.se/candide/wincandide/

APPLICATIONS OF FACIAL ANALYTICS

Some of us have our feelings written all over our faces. Others may pride themselves on being inscrutable. However, when a computer is analysing our features frame by frame, it can glean insight from even the slightest quirk.

—Michael Steinhart, editor of The Enterprise Cloud Site

Facial analytics has the following applications:

1. Facial analytics has wide applications in retail stores and malls. Through analysis of facial expressions, retail stores are able to display right advertising messages at the right time. For example, by scanning the faces of audience near a billboard in real time, gender-specific advertisements can be displayed on that billboard. If there are more women present near the billboard, a particular advertisement for women can be displayed.
2. Retail stores are also capturing facial expressions of their customers when they are shopping. By doing a complete analysis, the store manager can analyse whether particular combo offers or placements of items are appealing to the customers or not.
3. Similarly, by doing the facial recognition, the customer can get special access to a particular store or a club. This helps the stores and clubs to provide special treatment to its loyal customers.
4. Another wide area of application is in banks. Banks are slowly adopting facial authentication to provide better safety to its customers with the help of face-based biometric technology.
5. The law enforcement agencies are also applying facial analysis to match the images of suspected criminals with images in databases to find out similar or most similar face (facial features) in already-stored record of criminals.
6. In the academics, facial analytic is used to capture reactions of students in a class on various topics. Teachers can identify in which topic students get bored or on which topic students are attentive in the class.

FACS stands for facial action coding system.

Strictly speaking from the perspective of business management, facial analysis is the study and interpretation of facial expressions to find out hidden emotions of humans to judge how a particular person perceives a particular product or a service. This analysis not only helps in deciphering hidden emotions of a customer but also helps to predict the way people will react to given stimuli. Facial analysis is based on the principle of FACS. FACS stands for Facial Action Coding System. FACS, developed by Ekmam and Friesen, is a method of measuring and interpreting the facial expression of humans. FACS helps to note down the changes in the facial muscles which lead to different facial expressions (see the Appendix of this chapter - Appendix-FACS). FACS is measured in action units (AU). For example, AU1 is action of raising the inner brow which is caused by frontalis and para medialis muscles and AU2 is action of raising the outer brow. It is caused by frontalis and para laterals muscles. Based on action unit, FACS helps to note down the change in facial muscle and subsequently to decipher the hidden emotion like for insincere smile—contraction of zygomatic major alone and for the sincere smile—contraction of zygomatic major and the inferior part of orbicullaris oculi (See Appendix-FACS). These days, there is specialised facial analytics software which helps to note down all the changes in facial muscles and to guide the analyst to decipher the hidden emotions of the shoppers, for example, WinCandide, XProject and Face Tracking SDK.

RETAIL ANALYTICS

"We can know when customers walk into a retail location and based on loyalty program activity, we might also know what they were recently looking at online,"

—Jim McHugh, VP of products and solutions marketing for Cisco UCS

Retail analytics deals with the complete analysis of data which are collected by retail stores.

With the proliferation of retail stores, budding managers might think that it is the best time to be retail store managers. But, on the contrary, it is the most difficult situation for any retail manager as there is intense competition among various retail stores. Considering this fact the retail stores have started not only collecting huge amounts of data, but also performing complete analysis of the data. This has led to the emergence of another type of analytics which is specifically meant for the analysis of retail store data. This type of analytics is known as retail analytics. As retail stores are collecting huge amounts of data with the help of which retail stores can find out the following:

1. **The Purchasing Behaviour of Customers**: It is very important for retail store managers to know the purchasing behaviour of its customers. As we see many combo offers in retail stores, these combo offers are the result of the complete analysis of purchasing patterns of customers.
2. **Predict Future Requirement to Judge Optimum Inventory**: The success of any retail store depends on how a particular retail manager manages its inventory. Although a retail store gets huge discounts ordering in advance, but knowing the future requirement is very difficult. With the help of retail analytics, it is possible to predict the future demand and accordingly order the products in advance.
3. **Decide Ideal Store Location**: The location of any retail store is make or break for its success. The location again depends on numerous factors. With the help of analytics, it is possible to decide the ideal store location. The analysis is done on both types of data, i.e., structured data and unstructured data. The structured data are in the form of questionnaires and opinion surveys which a retail store conducts before opening its store. It is also important to collect and analyse huge amounts of unstructured data such as comments and tweets before deciding the ideal location of a retail store.
4. **Provide Personalised Care**: Every customer wants to be treated as a king. This problem is compounded by the fact that every retail store has hundreds of customers. Again with the help of retail analytics, the retail store manager can analyse the huge data and accordingly can offer personalised attention such as loyalty cards and special schemes for its loyal customers.

DELVING FURTHER IN RETAIL ANALYTICS

To highlight the applications of retail analytics, the following points are discussed:

Applications of retail analytics:

1. Shelf Space
2. Touch Points
3. Fraud Detection
4. Future Demand
5. Promotional Campaign
6. Pricing Decisions
7. Workforce Analytics
8. Wi-Fi

1. **Shelf Space**: Applying retail analytics, it is possible to find out at what place which product sells the most. Even it is possible to conduct market basket analysis. Market basket analysis helps to predict which combination of products is frequently bought together by customers. This is also referred to as products in a customer's basket. Applying a detailed analysis, it is possible to find out the hidden pattern in buying and accordingly assortment of goods can be offered to customers. Multinational chains such as Marks and Spencer retail store are able to earn $ 1.5 million through the application of a market basket analysis.
2. **Touch Points**: This refers to the effective points of contact with customers. It is possible to identify right touch points through retail analytics. As each customer's needs are different, hence by studying the purchase behaviour and other personal attributes of a customer, retail stores can identify best touch points to remain in contact with a customer like email, mobile or social networking sites. For example, overstock.com applies targeted emails which have resulted in a 50% increase in their revenue due to effective reach and contact with its consumers.
3. **Fraud Detection**: Fraud is a major concern especially in online purchasing. Retail stores need to do complete analysis to find out any changed pattern in spending. Analytics help in the complete analysis of purchasing patterns through credit cards. Any mismatch in the spending pattern like a sudden spike in purchasing will alert the manager, and accordingly a retail store can contact the customer to verify that whether the purchase is made by that customer or not. For example, Amazon.com is running a complete fraud analysis to check any misuse of credit cards.
4. **Future Demand**: As the environment is highly volatile, it is important that retail stores should do a proper future demand analysis for judging the future demand which in turn helps in optimising its operations. As for any retail stores mere collection of huge data is not important, but it is important to analyse the collected data to find out purchasing trends and any seasonal fluctuations. This, in turn, enables store owners to predict future requirements. For example, office product retailer Staples is analysing eight million data transactions each week to predict weekly and daily sales.
5. **Promotional Campaign**: Presently, there are many channels where a particular retail store can run its marketing activities. But, it is indeed a challenge for retail stores to appropriately choose the right channel and medium for marketing. Complete analysis helps the retail store manager to find out their target customers and then by knowing the demographic profile of its customers, it is possible for retail store managers to formulate right promotion campaign. For example, Dell has made a complete warehouse of 1.5 million records of data regarding print, electronic and social media. Dell does a complete analysis of each medium vis-a-vis its competitors and demographic profile of its customers to formulate an effective promotional campaign.
6. **Pricing Decisions**: As the Indian market is highly price sensitive, it is very important that a retail store manager should perform complete analysis before deciding

the price of products. The retail stores are also selling private labels which make pricing a more important issue. Retail stores apply price optimising softwares to find out products which are most and less price sensitive and accordingly recommend an optimum price of the private labels. This software takes inputs from point of sale information and seasonal sales data. For example, Canadian apparel retailer Northern Group retail store has reported to increase gross margins by 4.5% by applying price optimisation softwares.

7. **Workforce Analytics**: Applying analytics, retail store owners can know the peak sale timing and season. It is also possible to know sales at each display point (season and time) like if there are more sales at sportswear shelf (in winter and especially on Sundays after 2 p.m.); hence, accordingly, it is possible to deploy the right number of staff at right points. For example, Wal-Mart does complete workforce analysis for optimising the workforce and also for predicting the timing and season of peak sales so as to deploy the right number of staff.
8. **Wi-Fi**: Retail stores are applying real-time analytics to analyse the data collected through guest Wi-Fi connection to shoppers. While shopping, retailers can send message to inform shoppers about products and schemes and even shoppers can share their real-time experience with management. For example, retail link provides the guest Wi-Fi connection to its clients. Retail link even integrates all the CRM data, marketing database and loyalty schemes to send customised messages to its shoppers.

SOCIAL MEDIA ANALYTICS

In the next two years, savvy marketers will demand social measurement tools that demonstrate how their social programs are creating marketing and business success.

—Nate Elliott, Forrester

Social media analytics is the practice of monitoring, analysing and interpreting the digital data gathered from blogs and social media websites to take appropriate marketing decisions and for better engagement of customers. But, the question arises as to why do firms need to practice social media analytics? The answer lies in the fact that more and more users are active online and are constantly using social media to express their feelings and emotions about firms' products and services. Besides, social media are emerging as a powerful tool for communication between people. This results in the voluminous digital data which are highly unstructured and dynamic. These data are unstructured as people are communicating using their own slangs and language, which means that these data do not fit in the traditional structure of rows and columns. Another key characteristic of these data is the limited shelf life. Shelf life of social content is very short as people are

Social media analytics is the practice of monitoring, analysing and interpreting the digital data gathered from blogs and social media websites in order to take appropriate marketing decisions and for better engagement of customers.

continuously expressing their feelings and as soon as new emotions come they post their new tweet/FB post or comment. The impact of social content is also far-reaching. Imagine a scenario in which you want to purchase a juicer from Flipkart. Before purchasing that particular juicer you will see comments or reviews of people who have bought the same juicer from Flipkart. After going through all those comments, you will decide whether you want to buy that juicer or not and even if you want to buy that juicer whether to buy that juicer from Flipkart or not. Considering the above facts, it is clear that social media are emerging as a strong tool for communication and organisations cannot afford to neglect the reach of social media, but also acknowledging the fact that these data are voluminous in nature and unstructured type, organisations need special tools for analysing the social data. The branch of analytics, which deals with the analysis of social data, is known as social media analytics. The importance of social media can be judged by the fact that these days organisations have an official Twitter or Facebook page so as to connect with online users. Dell has built an online community known as Idea Storm. In this community, all the users/customers of Dell are invited. The main purpose of this community is to get ideas and feedback from its customers. Dell has implemented more than 550 different ideas that it received from the online community. Even Dell has formulated social media command centre that answers 3500 posts a week in 14 languages, and as a result Dell has 97% resolution rate of complaints.

But for effective use of social media, it is very important that an organisation first should decide its business objectives and end goals. Depending on its objectives and end goals such as increase in revenue, best CRM services, innovation, etc., the organisation then should decide which type of social content it is going to analyse. For example, if the goal is to provide best CRM services, the organisation will only analyse those Tweets and Facebook comments regarding the customer experience on the CRM services provided by the organisation as AT&T (which has bagged the contract to provide network services for iPhone in 2007) is using social media analytics to find out complaints regarding network problems from the tweets, time when the tweet was sent and the location of its sender. It then prioritises the complaints and sends staff to rectify the complaints.

Data processing at massive scale is only now becoming realistic. And data about our wanderings around the web exist on hundreds of random site servers. Data management platforms and exchanges arose to do the piecing-together, and today more (usually anonymised) information is available to marketers than ever before. This will only get better.

—Martin Kihn, Gartner

Social media analytics helps to find out the following:

1. What customers are experiencing about the brand or product—their sentiments, the reach of the firm, the impact of social media on customers, the most liked attribute of the product, the actions taken by competitors?

2. How the customers can be categorised or segmented to identify and reach target audiences?
3. The reputation of a third party to whom the organisation wants to outsource its production.
4. The reputation of vendors from where the organisation is going to source its raw products.

Following are the applications of social media analytics:

1. To find out the social strength of your company and even your competitors.
2. It is possible to identify most influential supporters and their networks. Even the company can find out its detractors and their network.
3. It is possible to perform social research of all the competitors before launching any new product.
4. It is possible to create positive buzz regarding your brand.
5. It is possible to find out the recent trends in your industry and the expectations of the target audience.

Tools and Techniques of Social Media Analytics

The majority of the techniques used to analyse social media content focus on analysing unstructured textual data. Some of them are listed as follows:

> Tools and techniques of social media analytics:
>
> 1. Natural Language Processing (NLP)
> 2. Opinion or Sentiment Mining
> 3. Text Analytics

1. Natural language processing (NLP)—any interaction between humans and computers is processed by applying NLP. Applying NLP, it is possible to interact with your computer in a way as if you are interacting with humans. NLP forms the basis of several advanced analytical techniques. NLP helps in automatic translation of texts, creating new texts by combining information from multiple documents, converting spoken speech into text and automatic subtitling of videos, etc.
2. Opinion or sentiment mining—any text written in natural language contains opinions or sentiments of humans in the form of positive or negative attitude. These sentiments are available on several social media platforms. Firms utilise sentiment mining to extract meaningful patterns of sentiments from social media about their products, brands, promotions or services offered.
3. Text analytics—it refers to the analysis of textual data in terms of frequency counts, patterns, extraction of patterns or trends in text, association of different texts, etc.

Problems of social media analytics

After going through the above text, one can gauge the importance of social media analytics, but at the same time social analytics poses some difficulties. These difficulties are as follows:

Problems of social media analytics:

1. Volume
2. Slangs
3. Shelf Life
4. Storage

1. **Volume**: The main problem with the social media analytics is that in the present time there is an influx of huge amounts of digital data. The result is that it is difficult for organisations to find out the right type of digital data for analysis.
2. **Slangs**: The social content is full of confusing slang as online users are expressing their feelings and communicating using different slangs, which make it very difficult for organisations to appropriately decipher the actual meaning of the tweets/comments.
3. **Shelf Life**: The shelf life of social content is very short which makes it mandatory for organisations to quickly analyse the social content. This means that organisations are always on their toes to collect and decipher the social content quickly.
4. **Storage**: Although with the advancement of technology, organisations are able to store huge data at a very low cost (Moore's law), but with an ever increasing number of digital data and too with short shelf life it becomes very challenging for organisations to store ever-changing digital data.

Key Points

From the above discussion, we can conclude the social media analytics in the following points:

1. Organisations are applying social media analytics to know the perception of their customers regarding their products and services. Moreover, organisations are using social information to know their customers in a better manner like hotels and restaurants can know the birthday, marriage anniversary of their customers and offer special offers to their loyal customers.
2. Organisations are working on the concept of customer engagement rather than customer satisfaction, which makes it important for organisations to have two-way communication with the customers. This is only possible with the help of a social media platform.
3. In the intense competitive environment, it is imperative for organisations to get noticed. Organisations use social media to create buzz regarding their products and services.
4. Organisations are using social media to serve their customers in a better way, for example, the ICICI bank has launched an app that enables Facebook users to link their debit card to their profile to recharge their pre-paid cards.

But, organisations sometimes underestimate the power of social media like Nestle mishandled the social media. Nestle was accused of using palm oil which resulted in the deforestation of rain forest and eventually caused deaths of orangutans. Protestors made a community called Greenpeace and launched an online campaign against Nestle. First, Greenpeace created a video showing eating Kit Kat results in the killing of orangutans. Nestle claimed that this video violated their trademark and removed the video from YouTube, but gave no explanation in its defence. Going ahead, Nestle removed all the negative comments from its official Facebook page, but again never defended its actions. Then, eventually, Nestle realised the growing anger and unrest against brand which could impact the sales of the company. Eventually, Nestle issued an official statement on its Facebook.

Mar 19–Nestle: Hi everyone—we do care and will continue to pressure our suppliers to eliminate any sources of palm oil which are related to rainforest destruction. We have replaced the Indonesian company Sinar Mas as a supplier of palm oil for further shipments.

Apr 13–Nestle: In a letter to Greenpeace today, our Chairman, Peter Brabeck-Letmathe has called for a moratorium on the destruction of rainforests and highlighted how the two organisations can meet this common goal.

BIG DATA

Big data and measurement are starting to gain traction. Big data has long been a technology discussion, but I'm starting to see more and more inquiries about how firms are successfully integrating big data sources into their core consumer measurement techniques.

—Tina Moffett, Forrester

Big data is a term used to define voluminous data that are available in different formats.

Big data is a term used to define voluminous data that are available in different formats. Earlier, organisations had limited data, but with the advent of the Internet and the reduction in storage cost (Moore's law), organisations are storing data in huge quantities. These voluminous data not only are structured but also have semi-structured data and unstructured data as major components. The Internet is the main source of unstructured data and semi-structured data. We can identify two major characteristics of big data, i.e., voluminous amount, i.e., petabytes and exabytes and different formats. Gartner analyst Dong Laney introduced the three-dimensional concept of big data, also termed 3V's model to understand the emergence of big data.

1. **Volume**: The volume represents the amount or large quantity of data. The size "Big data" is forever changing, owing to the increasing volume of data from terabytes to petabytes to zettabytes. Although there is no set rule for defining the volume of data, but a quick look at some facts would enable you to gauge the "volume" of data in present times. Each day, 2.5 quintillion bytes (2.5 trillion gigabytes) of data are created. By 2020, data created would be five times from the data in 2005. Organisations are not reluctant to store this huge volume of data owing to the reduction in storage cost.
   However, these huge data pose a great challenge to managers as they cannot apply conventional methods to analyse such a huge volume.
2. **Variety**: Another characteristic is a variety of different formats in which these data are present. In the past, organisations had structured data, i.e., that type of data which fit into rows and columns. But, the emergence of a large number of non-traditional sources of data has contributed to this variety. The advent

3-dimensional concept of big data:

1. Volume
2. Variety
3. Velocity

of social networking sites has led organisations to collect different varieties of data, i.e., semi-structured data and unstructured data. Contents from Facebook, such as user comments, likes and tweets, are often utilised by firms to plan and execute their business strategies. Each month, 300 billion pieces of content are shared on Facebook. These data are largely unstructured (do not fit into rows and columns) and require special tools for analysis. As discussed earlier, the major component of big data is unstructured data (sometimes semi-structured) and the digital data, i.e., the data which come from social networking sites are essentially unstructured data.

3. **Velocity**: This characteristic of big data has changed the perception of organisations regarding the data. Earlier organisations used to collect data and then conveniently analyse the data thinking that data have long shelf life. But with the advent of social media sites, people are expressing their views and constantly updating and even reposing new comments and tweets. This has resulted in drastic reduction in shelf life of data and organisations are always on its toes so as to quickly capture and analyse the big data.

   At the present time, there is more dimension that is added to the above-mentioned three dimensions.

4. **Veracity**: Veracity refers to uncertainty in data. Most business users do not trust the source of data or information they are presented with. Since data are flowing from versatile sources and are voluminous, uncertainty adds to the complexity of the data.

Big data means every type of data. Big data is a combination of structured data, unstructured data and semi-structured data. These categories depend on the sources from where data are collected. Broadly speaking, the potential sources of collection of big data are

1. Internal sources
2. External sources

1. **Internal Sources**: Internal sources of data collection are the data collected from CRM application, ERP system and transactional data. These types of data are generally structured data. Structured data are that type of data which can be converted into rows and columns, i.e., organised structure. Structured data are in a predefined format like relational databases, legacy databases and multidimensional databases. Conventionally, structured data are analysed by applying the concepts of OLTP. But with the amount of data which are collected and stored, organisations are slowly but gradually moving towards OLAP for a complete multidimensional analysis of data.

2. **External Sources**: External sources of data collection are Internet, market research organisations, mobile data, etc. These types of data are primarily unstructured data (sometimes semi-structured data). Unstructured data are that type of data which do not fit into a set pattern, i.e., columns and rows. The main sources of this type of data are social networking sites. The tweets, comments, blogs

> Internal sources of data collection are the data collected from CRM application, ERP system, and transactional data.
>
> External sources of data collection are the Internet, market research organizations, mobile data.

and photographs are some of the common types of unstructured data. Another type of data is semi-structured data. It is that type of data which do not adhere to some conventional databases. The conventionally structured data are stored in the form of a relational data model, but with the advent of Internet, another type of data that is known as semi-structured data came into being. These data do not fit the relational data model. In this type, the data elements are well understood (that is the main difference between semi-structured and unstructured data), but elements may occur in any order; even some elements may be missing or not in the same format. The semi-structured data are available in database systems, file systems and data exchange formats.

Example of semi-structured data
Case I—Name: Rahul Sharma
Email—rahul@xyz.com
Case II—Name: First name Rehaan
Last Name: Raj
Email - r.raj@xyz.com

Note that in the above example, name appears in different formats like name in the first case and first name and last name in the second case. Similarly, the email address is in different formats like in the first case only first name, i.e., Rahul and second case it is first name and last name, i.e., r.raj

---

Data is the new science. Big Data holds the answers.

—Pat Gelsinger, COO of EMC

PRESENT SITUATION

From the above discussion, it is clear that big data is essentially huge data which are present in different formats, i.e., structured data, unstructured data and semi-structured data. The question is why firms should focus on analysis of big data. The answer lies in the fact that presently organisations are collecting huge amount of big data from the following avenues. It is important for organisations to analyse big data so as to understand feelings and emotions of their customers, which eventually leads to a better customer satisfaction. In the following section, prime sources of big data and advantages of analysis are explained.

1. **Social Networking Sites**: The social networking sites generate huge volumes of unstructured data. The data from social networking sites provide good opportunity for organisations to analyse the buying patterns and customer behaviour. As people are expressing their experience both positive and negative, this makes social networking sites an ideal platform for organisations to know real feelings of customers. Moreover, as it is very difficult for organisations to directly interact with a diverse set of customers, social networking sites provide an ideal medium for interacting with its customers. The examples of social networking sites are Facebook, Twitter, etc.

2. **Geospatial Data**: Apart from the tweets and comments, organisations also collect huge data in the form of location data. The RFID tags and GPS provide vital information regarding the location of items and people. Applying geospatial analytics, it is possible for organisations to track the exact location of people to formulate appropriate strategies. The same product can be perceived in different manners by people residing in different places. The geospatial data help in tracking the exact location of the origin of tweet, which helps in formulating appropriate strategies according to a different set of people.
3. **Routine Data**: Organisations also collect huge transactional data which are being generated by purchasing of products or services. These data are in huge volume because the reduction in storage space cost and rapid advancement in technology have made collection of these data very economical and too hassle free. The big retail stores collect much transactional data which are being collected at point of sales from different stores across different locations. Moreover, with increased penetration and speed of Internet, many people are buying products from online retail stores such as Flipkart and Snapdeal. These online retail stores also capture huge data to understand the buying behaviour of their customers.

ANALYSIS OF UNSTRUCTURED DATA

"Big data is at the foundation of all of the megatrends that are happening today, from social to mobile to the cloud to gaming."

—Chris Lynch, the ex-CEO of Vertica

As discussed, unstructured data do not fit into conventional databases, and as a result, we need to apply special tools for analysing the complex unstructured data. To analyse the ever-changing huge volume of unstructured data, organisations are using Hadoop. Hadoop is open source software which is applied widely to process big data. Hadoop's open source platform is managed by Apache Software Foundation. Hadoop enables distributed processing of large data across a large number of machines that do not share any memory. Hadoop distributes huge data on different servers and then it performs parallel processing on different tasks at distributed systems. Hadoop has many tools and technology such as

Unstructured data do not fit into conventional databases and as a result, we need to apply special tools to analyse the complex unstructured data.

1. HDFS
2. MapReduce
3. Pig
4. Sqoop
5. Hive
6. HBase
7. Flume

Out of the above tools, two fundamental tools of Hadoop are HDFS and MapReduce.

1. **HDFS**: Hadoop Distributed File System (HDFS) is a Java-based file system that helps to store and manage files. HDFS helps to store data in the form of files. The incoming data in the form of files are broken into one or more blocks. These blocks are then stored in the form of data nodes.
2. **MapReduce**: Conventionally in relational databases, SQL is applied to fetch results, but in Hadoop, the data are not stored in conventional databases. Rather, we can say the data in Hadoop are more of the data warehouse system. MapReduce is a framework for parallel processing of large amount of data. MapReduce has two parts Map and Reduce. These two functions depend on the kind of function we want to perform. Suppose we want to count number of times each word has occurred in a set of documents. The map phase counts the words in each document and reduced phase will summate the per document data into word counts in the entire set of documents. A more detailed account of Hadoop is explained in the next section.

HADOOP

"Hadoop is a key ingredient in allowing LinkedIn to build many of our most computationally difficult features, allowing us to harness our incredible data about the professional world for our users".

—Jay Kreps, Principal Engineer, LinkedIn

Hadoop is not just software; rather it is a framework of tools. Hadoop is used to run the applications on big data. It is an open source set of tools and is distributed under Apache licence, i.e., it is maintained by Apache and no particular company controls the Hadoop. The challenges created by big data are addressed by Hadoop. Conventionally, high-end computers were used to handle the big data, but even the high-end computer can handle data up to a certain limit. As the size of data increased, then even these high-end computers in the enterprises failed to handle huge data. The problem is further compounded by the fact that presently organisations are collecting different varieties of data, i.e., apart from structured data organisations are collecting huge volumes of unstructured and semi-structured data. To solve these issues, organisations are applying Hadoop because Hadoop takes a very different approach. To handle big data, Hadoop not even breaks the problem into smaller pieces, but also divides the computation part of the problem. Each part of the problem is having its own computation part and once the computations are finished on divided data, then they are combined together and delivered as an overall result. In other words, Hadoop works on a distributed model. It is based on the Linux operating system. All Linux-based machines have two components.

Hadoop is not just software; rather it is a framework of tools. Hadoop is used to run the applications on big data.

- Job tracker
- Name node

1. **Job tracker**: Job tracker is a service within Hadoop. The primary function of a job tracker is to break the higher tasks into smaller pieces, send each piece of computation to task tracker, manage the task trackers, tracking the progress of tasks and checking the fault tolerance. Job tracker works on the master node and it gives task to the slave node having task trackers. (Client directly interacts with a master node which has name node and secondary name node. The data node is the daemon to the name node. Name node remembers where all the data nodes reside. In contrast to the master node, which is performing the entire supervisory task, the slave node runs all the computations and stores the data.) A task tracker simply follows the order of a job tracker. The task tracker performs the job of processing the task that has been assigned to it. The task tracker is pre-configured with the number of slots which indicates the number of tasks it can accept. It also updates the job tracker about the progress of the tasks from time to time.
2. **Name node**: Name node is the heart of the Hadoop Distributed File System (HDFS). It creates the directory tree of all the file systems present in the HDFS. Name node is responsible for keeping an index of data which are residing on which data node, so when the application contacts the name node, then it tells the application to go on this particular computer to get the corresponding data. This implies that name node has the entire index.

   Name node can be further categorised as follows:

   (a) *Secondary name node*: It is secondary to name node in the sense that it does periodic checkpoints. It is creating a log file of name node so that in case of name node failure, only name node has to be restarted instead of starting all the data nodes.

   (b) *Data node*: The actual data exist in the data nodes and these data nodes do not interact with each other. It provides a heartbeat message to make sure that connectivity is there between the name node and the data node. If no heartbeat signal is given by the data node, then that data node is declared dead and will be unassigned from the task by name node.

ADVANTAGES OF HADOOP

"Twitter's rapid growth means our users are generating more and more data each day. Hadoop enables us to store, process, and derive insights from our data in ways that wouldn't otherwise be possible."

—Kevin Weil, Analytics Lead, Twitter

Hadoop is open-source software. It is freely available on the Internet and is licensed and maintained by Apache. This is the biggest advantage of Hadoop. Anybody can download it from the Internet and can use Hadoop to manage big data.

Hadoop is very useful to store and process the unstructured data. In earlier times, organisations used to downsize the data and then try to classify the relevant data. The rest of the data is deleted by the organisation to save the time and cost to store the data. But if in the future that data are needed, then it is a problem for an organisation to bring back the data. This problem is solved by Hadoop as it can easily manage the big data and easily compute the data for future use and at a very low cost. Moreover, if the big data have to be moved for computing then it is a very cumbersome process as it can cause some failures. Failures can occur due to the transportation of the data as the data can be in petabytes also. So the big data cannot be transported due to the economic and practical reasons. It is easy to compute the data when the computational process is very close to the data. Hadoop gives us the liberty to move the computation process close to the data, which is a very feasible solution. Hadoop directly moves the computational process to the system where the data are kept. It can minimise the movement of data and alongside it also increases the efficiency of the system.

Hadoop ecosystem is applicable for a variety of data. It is very flexible because many types of data can be accessed with Hadoop. The unstructured data available on blogs, email conversation, social networking sites such as Facebook and Twitter, etc., can be analysed for the latest trends and patterns.

Hadoop is very fast as compared with other softwares. It uses a distributed file system known as Hadoop Distributed File System (HDFS) which can trace and connect to the data wherever it is located. It is a very efficient way of storing and computing terabytes of unstructured data as the tools for computing the data are on the same servers on which data are kept.

The biggest advantage of Hadoop is fault tolerance. If any data node fails while computing the data, then that task is given to other data node or it is replicated to another node so that it can be completed in a stipulated time period. Considering the worst case scenario in which there is a failure of name node, the log files for that name node are also made. When the task is shifted to another name node, then only the log files are shifted to the other node.

COMPONENTS OF HADOOP

Following are the main components of Hadoop.

Facebook uses Hadoop and Hive extensively to process large datasets. This infrastructure is used for a variety of different jobs – including adhoc analysis, reporting, index generation and many others.

—Ashish Thusoo, Engineering Manager at Facebook

Components of Hadoop:

1. HDFS
2. MapReduce
3. Pig
4. Sqoop
5. Hive
6. HBase

Hadoop Distributed File System (HDFS)

HDFS is based on Google's white paper known as a Google file system. It is a java-based file system to store large datasets reliably and to deliver dataset to the user application. HDFS is

HDFS is based on Google's white paper known as a Google file system.

a fundamental block in Hadoop. Its main function is to provide reliability, scalability of distributed services. When the file comes for loading, it is stored in forms of blocks. All the meta data are also shared with the data node in this system; for this reason, it is known as a distributed file system. HDFS support read, write, append and rename operations. HDFS is more into the file handling system, so we should also know about clusters and nodes. When we are using the computer, then that single computer will serve as a node. But if many nodes are combined to form a single unit, then that unit is known as a cluster. Cluster is very useful in a distributed file system because it is suitable for handling the failover mechanism. Cluster will form a big eco-system in which big data operations can be handled as all the operations are handled at the cluster level rather than at the node level.

These are two basic commands of HDFS which are used in terminal:

```
$ Hadoop fs
```

It will display all the commands of Hadoop file system.

```
$ Hadoop fs –ls
```

This command will show all the metadata from the Hadoop distributed file system. "ls" will display all the files and directories of the present working directory.

MAPREDUCE

Mapreduce was developed in the early 2000s by engineers of Google to determine the current solution for their applications such as web crawling and query processing. They found that their existing technologies were inadequate for the future as the Internet users were growing at an immense pace. They decided to distribute their work across inexpensive computers. After that, all these computers were connected by the Internet in the form of clusters. Mapreduce is a parallel programming model for processing large datasets. It is a framework for writing applications very easily. Hadoop is based on Java but the Mapreduce can be made in other languages. It divides input datasets into independent pieces, and these pieces are computed with the map tasks in a completely independent manner in a parallel manner. It can also handle unstructured and semi-structured data. Mapreduce simplifies parallel data processing because the functions are automatically parallelised. It allows programmers to utilise the resources of a large distributed system with parallel and distributed systems. Users request the map reduce program to run and results are returned back to Hadoop's distributed file system. Its framework operates on <key, value> pairs.

Mapreduce was developed in early 2000's by engineers of google to determine the current solution for their applications like web crawling and query processing.

Mapreduce job takes input as key value pairs and generates the output as a key value pair. The computation of these input key value pairs produces output key value pairs. Basically, maps are written by users. These maps take input key value pairs and generate intermediate key value pairs. The reduce function will accept the intermediate pairs. These pairs are merged to form a smaller set of values. These values can be zero or there can be single output also.

Below the input is K1 and V1. K2 and V2 are intermediate key value pairs. K3 and V3 is the output from reduce function.

(K1,V1) → Map → (K2,V2)
(K2, V2) → Reduce → (K3,V3)

Mapreduce consists of a single job tracker and one slave task tracker per cluster node. Master node gives the job or task to the slaves and slaves execute the task directed by the master. Master node can re-run the tasks that have failed during computing.

How mapreduce is implemented

To run the mapreduce, code has to be generated, wherein the master node regulates the entire activity such as identifying the data and dividing the data into different workers (Slave Nodes). Mapreduce slave node processes the data which are received from the master and then re-sends the result to the master.

Last, the master will receive the results from the slave nodes, and then it will integrate all the processed results to deliver the final result.

PIG

Pig was initially developed by Yahoo. It has a very interesting fact behind its name. Like a pig can eat anything from garbage to food; in the same way, the pig in Hadoop can handle any kind of data.

Pig is used to create complex mapreduce jobs with the help of a very easy scripting language.

Apache pig is popular among non-developers who are not so much familiar with programming languages. It is a high level processing layer that runs on Hadoop. Pig is a data flow language used for data processing. Pig is used to create complex mapreduce jobs with the help of a very easy scripting language. Its scripting language consists of textual language known as **Pig Latin**. Pig programming can be done in three different ways:

Pig Latin: It is a high level scripting language. The statements in pig latin are translated into mapreduce jobs. The file containing pig latin commands is easily identified by .pig extension. It is a language used for expressing data analysis. It supports a wide variety of types, functions, operators (join, sort, filter) and file system commands. It creates a set of mapreduce jobs. When the user is working on a pig interface, then the user is least bothered about writing code. With a pig user focusing on big data rather than on the code of the custom program, it is also easy to achieve parallel execution of data analysis task.

Grunt: It is an interactive shell. Here, you can enter the command at the grunt command line and the result will be displayed immediately.

Piggybank: This bank is a shared repository for user defined functions (UDF). The UDF can be written in different programming languages. Pig is designed to be used with many programming languages such as python, javascript, Ruby and Java, etc.

In short, the first step is to LOAD the specific set of data from HDFS, on which analysis has to be performed. Then, the data will go through the transformation process under which the operations such as JOIN, FILTER, GROUP and ORDER are performed. To display the result of the transformation process, the user has to DUMP the data; otherwise, the result will not be displayed on the screen. DUMP is used to immediately show the result on the screen, whereas STORE is used to store the result in a file for further analysis.

HIVE

HIVE was originally developed by Facebook team, but now HIVE is the product of the apache Hadoop project.

The size of the industry is growing rapidly, and with the growing industry the size of data is also growing. So with the traditional warehouse solution, it is very expensive to analyse the data because the data are mostly in the unstructured form.

We have discussed about Pig and now we know that it is the product of Google. They developed this product to work on unstructured data. Simultaneously, Facebook also started developing their own warehouse solutions on Hadoop, which is known as Hive.

Although Hive was originally developed by Facebook team, but now Hive is the product of the apache Hadoop project. It provides a data warehousing layer on the top of Hadoop. It allows you to define the structure of your unstructured big data. It simplifies the process of analysis and queries with an SQL-like query language called HiveQL or HQL. This language is helpful for SQL users who want to use query language for data analysis on HDFS. Hive uses a relational database to store metadata, but it stores the processed data in HDFS. The main function of Hive is to take the unstructured data and process it in a way that it can be stored as structured data, which can be viewed by analysts in a simplified manner.

Hive is useful for querying data, or if you want answers to specific questions. Hive is the best solution for those users who are very familiar with the SQL query language. If a user is working with Hive, then the user should not worry about mapreduce jobs because Hive will automatically convert the SQL queries into mapreduce jobs.

Hive structures the data into well understood concepts such as tables, columns, rows and partitions. It supports primitive data types such as integers, float, doubles and strings. Hive also supports map reduce pairs, lists, structures, etc.

Sqoop is the product of the apache project.

SQOOP

Sqoop is the product of the apache project. It is an open source; this means it is freely available on the Internet. With this tool we can easily import the entire database or some part of the database to Hadoop's file system. Sqoop also internally creates mapreduce code of the transferred data. With the help of sqoop, data can be imported directly to the HIVE database. Exports can also be performed with the help of sqoop. Newer versions of sqoop also contain connectors for SQL, postgreSQL, Oracle, Microsoft SQL Server, Netezza. Third-party connectors are also available for NoSQL data stores.

In Exhibit 12.1, it is shown that the sqoop provides connectivity between hadoop distributed file system and relational databases with the assistance of which data can be imported and exported without any difficulty.

Exhibit 12.1 Functionality of sqoop

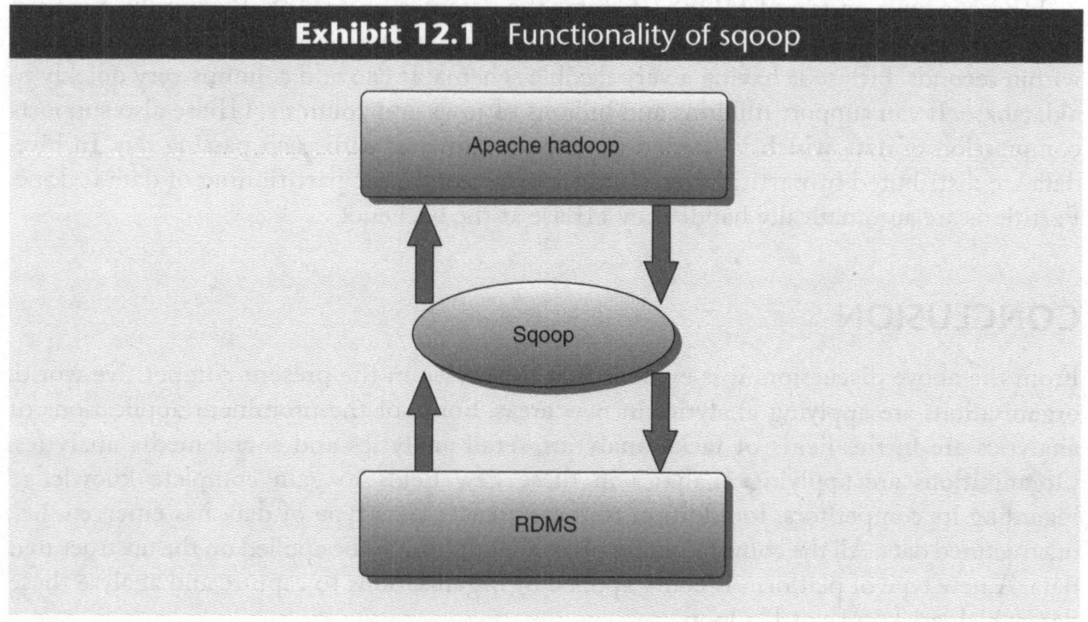

To summarise the key characteristics of sqoop, sqoop is used to easily import the individual tables or entire database to HDFS or can export from HDFS. It can map databases to hive and HBase.

HBase

HBase is based on implementation of Google BigTable distributed data storage system (DDSS). In the present scenario, there are many applications of HBase as there is a need to tackle the real-time data like tweets and other instant messages, which makes the database grow exponentially. If we analyse the capabilities of hive, it can handle the large datasets. But when it comes to real-time data, then hive fails as it cannot load the data quickly. So, there is a need to handle the real-time data which led to the birth of HBase. Table 12.1 shows the development phase of HBase:

HBase is based on implementation of Google BigTable distributed data storage system (DDSS).

Table 12.1 Development phase of HBase

2006	BigTable paper by Google.
2007	Hadoop's contribution started.
2008	Became hadoop's sub product.
2010	Apache Top-level project.
2011	0.92 version of HBase released.

HBase is built on top of HDFS. It stores the database on HDFS. Practically, it is used for two purposes. First, it is used to handle the real-time data. Second, it can make updates within seconds. HBase is having a very flexible schema. It can add columns very quickly to a database. It can support millions and billions of rows and columns. HBase also supports compression of data which is needed as data are growing with each passing day. In hive, data are distributed by partitioning. But in HBase automatic partitioning of data is done. Partitions are automatically handled by HBase at the backend.

CONCLUSION

From the above discussion, it is evident that to survive in the present competitive world, organisations are applying analytics in new areas. Some of the prominent applications of analytics are in the fields of facial analytics, retail analytics and social media analytics. Organisations are applying analytics in these new fields to gain complete knowledge regarding its competitors. In addition to these areas, a new type of data has emerged, i.e., unstructured data. All the conventional tools of analysis cannot be applied on the unstructured data. A new type of platform is being applied by organisations to capture and analyse these data which are known as Hadoop.

DETAILED EXAMPLE

Web analytics has emerged as a powerful tool in the present age of information technology. All firms with a presence on the Internet, whether big or small, are interested in knowing what attracts the visitors to their websites, which promotional campaigns are the most effective, what is the trend or pattern of visiting, which keywords in digital content lead to maximum conversion of prospect visitors into customers, etc. Conventionally, web analytics aided the website owners to perform the following metrics to assess the performance of their websites:

1. **Hits**: This metric helps to find out number of requests generated to a web server for a particular site or web page.
2. **Page View**: Since a website hosts several different pages, this metric helps to find out the popularity of a particular web page by measuring the number of times a page was viewed.

3. **Visit**: This metric is also termed as session which helps to quantify interaction of the user with the website. It is used to track what activity has been done by the user, such as visiting additional pages on the site during a period of time which is usually 30 minutes.
4. **Visitors**: This metric helps to track visitors on a particular website. It also classifies the visitors into new (first-time visitor), repeat (multiple visits in the given time frame) or return (before and within given time frame) visitors.

However, due to increased dependence on the Internet for attracting and retaining customers by firms, there exists an increasing demand for more metrics of the websites. Among the several digital or web analytical solutions present in the market today, Google Analytics has emerged as a leader in the field of web analytics. This powerful digital analysis solution aids website developers, market professionals and executives of site's owner firm to effectively analyse the incoming traffic on their website and to gain several new insights and learning such as:

- Trend of traffic on website,
- Segment visitors/customers on the website,
- Which campaigns on the website are most effective,
- Which pages on the site retain users for the longest time,
- Which search terms will lead visitors to their site.

How does Google Analytics help in doing in-depth analysis of website traffic and guide the site owners to better manage their website? Google Analytics provides the facility of computing ROI, i.e., return on investment for the firms from their digital content. The companies which are advertising on the Internet can actually find out the effectiveness of the content of their website. This metric of effectiveness can be gauged by calculating: (Traffic) *(Conversion Rate). Here, "Traffic" represents how many people visited your website and "Conversion Rate" represents how many leads or visitors to the site are converted into actual sale or customers. Google Analytics, therefore, has to track the number of visitors and conversion rate to compute this metric and find ROI for that site. Google Analytics collects these data by applying two methods. The first method is to monitor web server log data. The web server log data records information regarding time, type, domain and URL of the request generated to that web server hosting a particular site or web page. The second method is utilising Page Tag Data. Page Tag Data works like Web Server Log Data. In addition to information contained in a web server log, it also captures client's browser, operating system, customer ID and conversion data. Once these data are captured, Google Analytics provides complete analysis of site data which can answer several questions such as follows:

- What kind of audience visit your site, where they come from, how they perceive digital content—this information can be used for segmenting visitors, targeting tailored digital campaigns and looking for new opportunities.
- Which operating system do they use—this information can be used to decide about site layout and design.

- Which page user enters the site, what path user takes on the site and which is the exiting page—this information can be used to visualise and design navigation through many pages hosted on the site.
- How much time site takes to load which has an impact on conversion rate. Google Analytics helps in pinpointing slow loading pages which can then be fixed by site developers.
- Generate alerts when there are noticeable spikes in traffic to a site on a particular day or from a particular city.

Another feature provided by Google Analytics is termed "Adword Integration" feature. Google Analytics generates Adword reports which aid the decision maker to see what happens after a user clicks on an adword specified by the website. This analysis helps to find out the effectiveness of key words used in digital promotions and to answer the following questions:

- How effectively adwords in campaigns were able to attract new users?
- Track visitor behaviour—how long they remain with the site after clicking on an ad, which pages they visited?
- Which keywords or ads help to convert leads into actual sales? Google Analytics tracks the amount of money spent by users after clicking on adword to find out how the campaign is performing in terms of revenue generation?

Sometimes, visitors land on a page which they did not intend to visit. This leads to high bounce rate for that webpage and is also used to find out the effectiveness of a web page. High bounce rate indicates that visitors do not like a particular web page. An underlying reason for high bounce rate can be use of inconsistent keywords. The keyword used for that page could be ambiguous. For example, you might be using cortical fracture as a keyword for a site which talks about cortical fracture in hand alone, whereas this keyword would draw users who have cortical fracture elsewhere as well. So, applying Google Analytics, the site owners can track which keywords or search terms lead the maximum users to their website and least bounce rate. They can set this as the keyword for that page. Similarly, site developers can amend those web pages where there is a high bounce rate by modifying the keyword or redesigning the page.

One of the most important features of Google Analytics is Geographic Data Analytics. Geographic Data Analytics helps to find out the areas from where maximum traffic is being generated. This feature also analyses the areas where new leads are being generated. This can be targeted by the firms as new areas of opportunity and use promotions to attract more visitors. This feature is especially beneficial for e-commerce companies which can then utilise these data to generate maximum conversion. Although analysis of data is very important, but representation of data is also equally important. Google Analytics also provides the facility of funnel visualisation of analysed data. Funnel visualisation helps in the effective representation of data in the shape of a funnel, depending on the end goal of the site owner. For example, a new email company has started its operations and wants to know the number of different types of users, based on their visiting and usage pattern. Applying funnel visualisation, the following types of representation of data can be achieved as shown in Exhibit 12.2.

Exhibit 12.2 Types of representation of data

100%	Website visitors
20%	Sign up for trial
10%	Actual login created
5%	Active users
2%	Passive users

KEY TERMS

- Facial Analytics **379**
- Physiognomy **379**
- FACS **382**
- Retail Analytics **383**
- Social Media Analytics **385**
- Natural language processing (NLP) **387**
- Big Data **389**
- Hadoop **393**
- HDFS **395**
- MapReduce **396**
- Pig **397**
- Sqoop **398**
- Hive **398**
- HBase **399**

SUMMARY

In this chapter, emerging analytical applications are discussed in detail. This chapter starts with one of the most emerging analytical techniques, facial analytics, which helps to decipher the emotions of humans by studying their facial expressions. Considering the booming retail sector, retail analytics is finding many applications in big retail stores. All the important aspects of retail analytics are explained in detail in this chapter. Organisations need to monitor, analyse and interpret the digital data gathered from blogs and social media websites to take appropriate marketing decisions and for better engagement of its customers. All the aspects related to social media analytics are explained in the next part of this chapter.

Considering the exponential growth of data, all the aspects related to big data are elucidated in the next part of this chapter. In the last part of the chapter, all the concepts related to analysis of unstructured data are explicated with the help of Hadoop.

MULTIPLE CHOICE QUESTIONS

1. Study of assessment of a person's character or personality from his/her outer appearance is known as
 a. Physiognomy b. Phycology
 c. Physiology d. Psychology

2. FACS stands for
 a. Facial abstract coding system b. Facial accentuate coding system
 c. Facial action coding system d. Facial agile coding system

3. The practice of monitoring, analysing and interpreting the digital data gathered from blogs and social media websites in order to take appropriate marketing decisions and for better engagement of customers is known as
 a. Big data analytics b. Social media analytics
 c. Internet analytics d. Web analytics

4. NLP stands for
 a. Natural language processing b. Nascent language processing
 c. Necessary language processing d. Notable language processing

5. Which of the following term is used to define voluminous data that are available in different formats?
 a. Big data b. Large data
 c. Vast data d. Huge data

6. Which of the following is not part of the three-dimensional concept of big data?
 a. Volume b. Variety
 c. Velocity d. Validate

7. HDFS stands for
 a. Hadoop distributed file system b. Hadoop demographic file system
 c. Hadoop dispatch file system d. Hadoop dissimilar file system

8. Which of the following is not a component of Hadoop?
 a. HDFS b. MapReduce
 c. PIG d. Elephant

9. Which component is a fundamental block in Hadoop?
 a. HDFS b. MapReduce
 c. PIG d. HBase

10. Which component is developed by Yahoo and helps to create MapReduce jobs with the help of very easy scripting language?
    a. Pig
    b. MapReduce
    c. Sqoop
    d. HBase

11. Which component is developed by Facebook and provides a data warehouse layer on the top of Hadoop?
    a. Hive
    b. MapReduce
    c. Sqoop
    d. HBase

12. Which component in Hadoop helps in the easy import of the entire database to a Hadoop file system?
    a. Sqoop
    b. MapReduce
    c. Sqoop
    d. HBase

REVIEW QUESTIONS

1. Discuss the evolution of facial analytics.
2. Discuss in detail the application of facial analytics.
3. Discuss the principle of FACS on which facial analytics is based.
4. Discuss in detail the various applications of retail analytics.
5. What is understood by the term social media analytics? Explain in detail why organisations need to apply social media analytics to survive in a competitive environment.
6. Discuss in detail various tools and techniques of social media analytics.
7. "Although organisations need to apply social media analytics, but at the same time social analytics pose some difficulties". Comment on this statement.
8. What do you understand by the term big data?
9. Discuss 3V model which highlights the emergence of big data.
10. Explain in detail the internal and external sources of big data.
11. Discuss in detail why organisations need to collect and analyse big data.
12. Discuss the applications of Hadoop.
13. Explain in detail various components of Hadoop.

HANDS-ON PROJECT

Twitter Analysis of Mangalyaan

Mars orbiter mission is also known as Mangalyaan. It is the first mission to mars by the Indian Space Research Organisation. This mission was announced on 15 August 2012 by our Prime Minister. The key goal of the mission is to detect the gas in the atmosphere of mars. This mission was launched on 5 November 2013 with the help of PSLV rocket. It was one of the most important missions for India. In the following section, the perceptions of twitter users towards India's indigenous mission of mars, "Mangalyaan", is discussed. The twitter analysis is done with the help of open source R-Studio software. With the help of this software tweets are extracted from twitter and analysis is done on the collected tweets.

The data related to this research are the unstructured data. The unstructured data are extracted from twitter in the form of tweets. For extracting the data from the twitter, first the developer account is created in the twitter, and then the application to mine the text is created. In this application, keys and tokens were generated. With these keys and tokens, authorisation is provided by twitter to extract the tweets. In R-studio software, these tweets are extracted with the help of some text mining packages. After the extraction of tweets, the analysis is done on the set of tweets. In the analysis part, the tweets are categorised into the positive tweets, negative tweets and neutral tweets. It is done with the assistance of text files having the list of positive and negative words. With these lists, tweets are compared and the positive and negative rating is given to the tweets. The rated tweets are plotted on the pie chart to find out social buzz regarding the Mangalyaan project. In the following section, explanation of twitter analysis is given with the help of snapshots.

A Trendwiley2 application has been created to provide authorisation to extract the tweets from twitter.

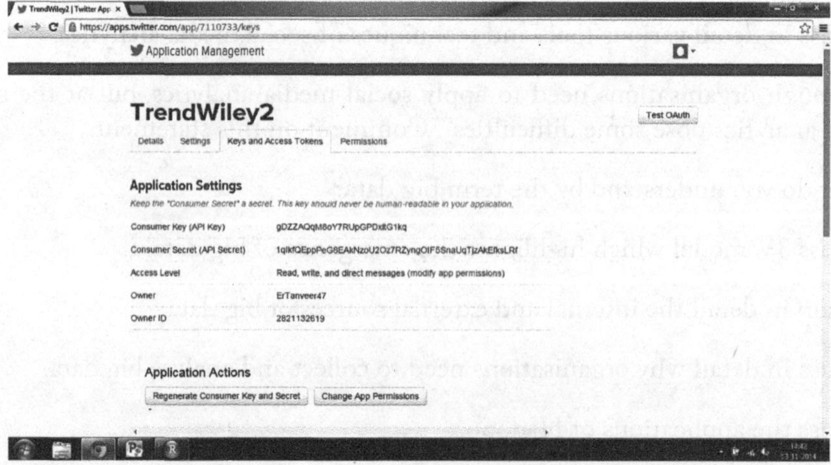

The following packages (highlighted) are used for twitter analysis:

twitteR
It provides an interface to the twitter web API.

ROAuth
It provides interface to the OAuth. Allowing users to authenticate via Oauth.

Plyr
It breaks the problem into manageable pieces.

stringr
It makes string function more consistent, simpler and easy to use. It ensures that function and argument names are more consistent. Output data structure of each function matches the input data structure of other function.

tm
A framework for t ext-mining applications within R-Studio.

RCurl
It allows us to download files from web servers, post forms, use https, upload files, etc.

Consumer key and consumer secret will be copied in R-Studio console.

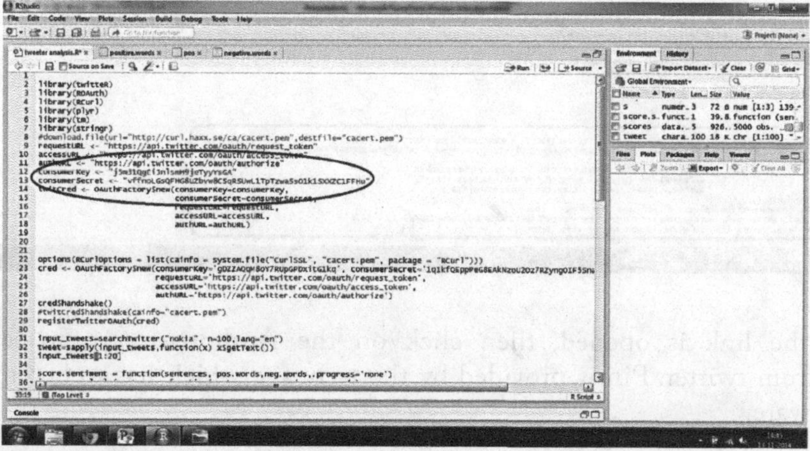

Code is used to perform handshake by using the consumer key and consumer secret of the application.

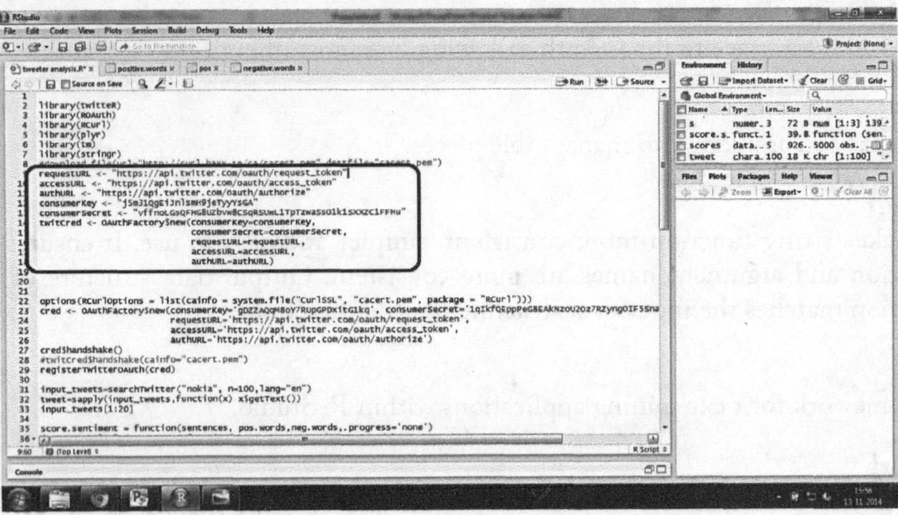

Authorisation and handshake are done with the help of the code below and link is provided for the webpage to authorise the application for fetching the tweets.

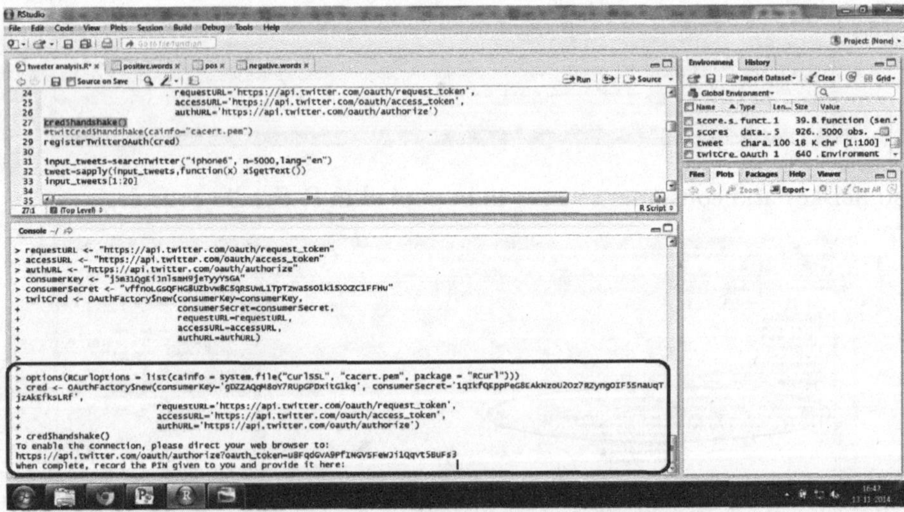

When the link is opened, then click on the Authorise App to fetch the tweets from twitter. Pin is provided by the webpage which has to be entered in the software.

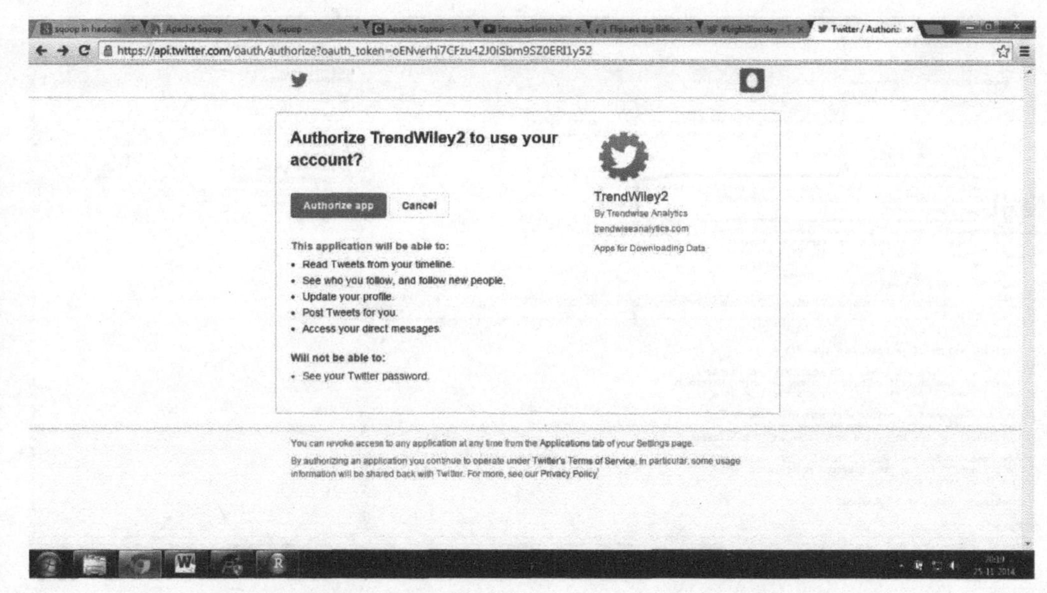

Pin provided in the webpage is entered in the R-Studio software.

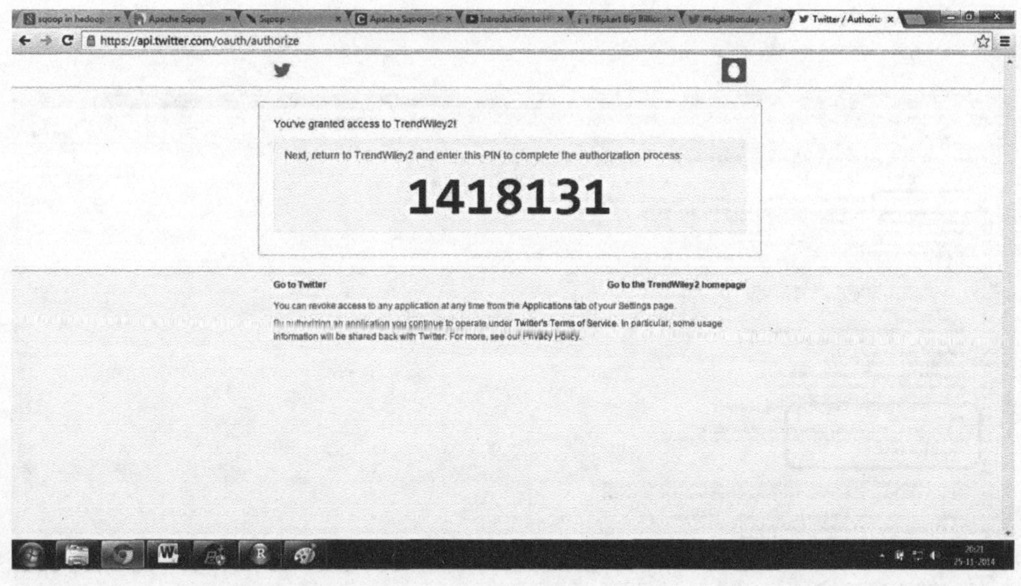

There are three highlighted commands. The first command is used to extract the tweets related to mangalyaan from twitter. The second command is used to get the relevant text out from the tweets. The third command is written to display the first 100 tweets from the result.

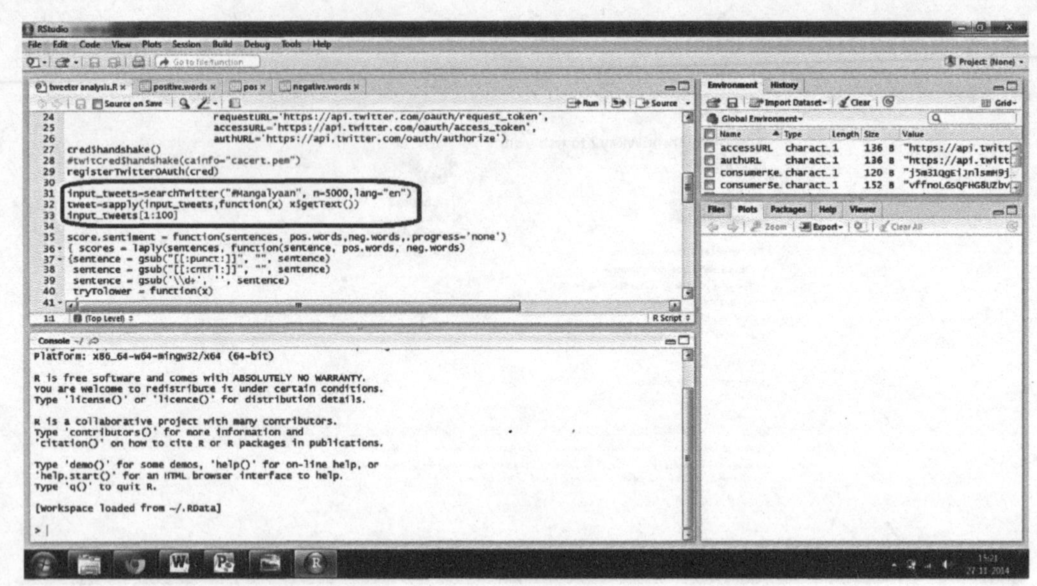

Score.sentiment function converts the text into lower case, removes punctuations and eventually converts the text into data frame to analyse the text for positive and negative words.

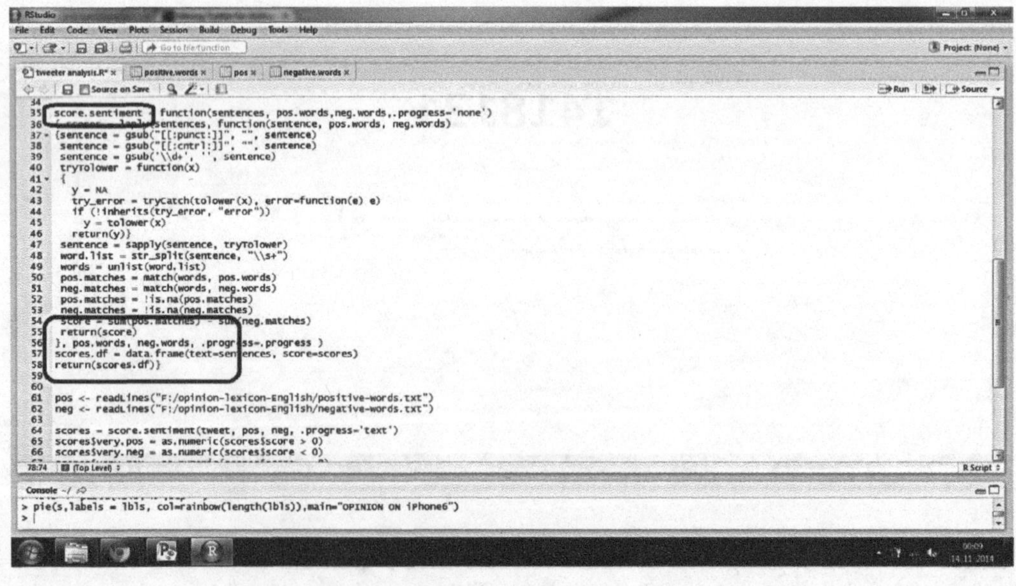

List of positive words is uploaded in the R-Studio software.

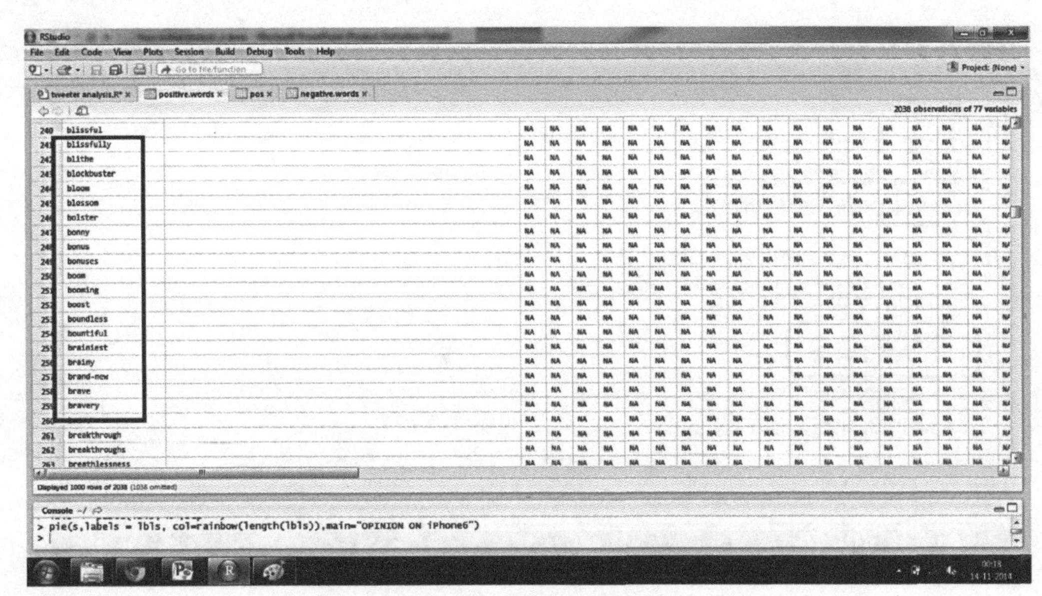

List of negative words is uploaded in the R-Studio software.

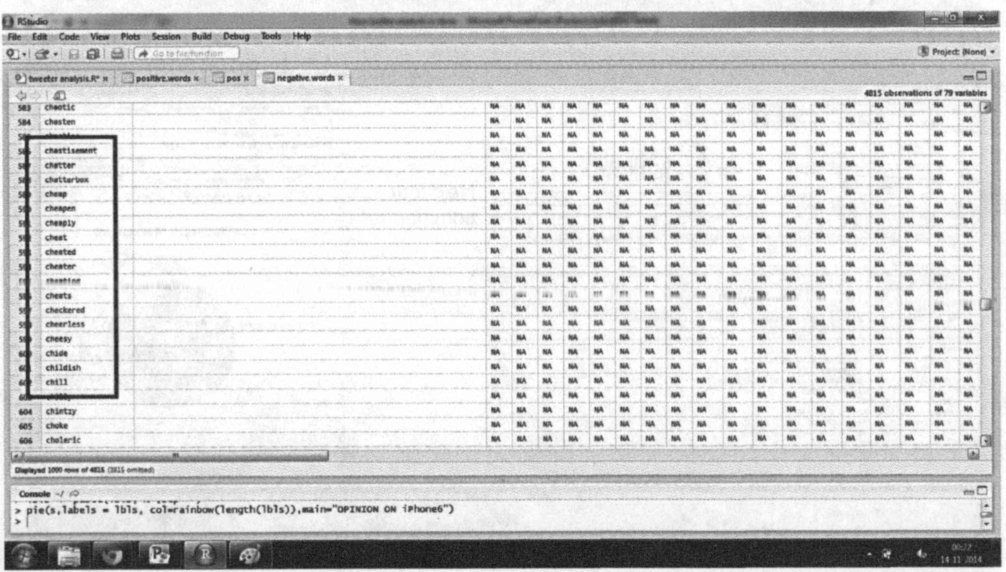

Scores are compared with the words given in positive and negative lists. Positive, negative and neutral scores are stored in numpos, numneg and numneu variables (all highlighted).

```
word.list = str_split(sentence, "\\s+")
words = unlist(word.list)
pos.matches = match(words, pos.words)
neg.matches = match(words, neg.words)
pos.matches = !is.na(pos.matches)
neg.matches = !is.na(neg.matches)
score = sum(pos.matches) - sum(neg.matches)
return(score)
}, pos.words, neg.words, .progress=.progress )
scores.df = data.frame(text=sentences, score=scores)
return(scores.df)}


pos <- readLines("F:/opinion-lexicon-English/positive-words.txt")
neg <- readLines("F:/opinion-lexicon-English/negative-words.txt")

scores = score.sentiment(tweet, pos, neg, .progress='text')
scores$very.pos = as.numeric(scores$score > 0)
scores$very.neg = as.numeric(scores$score < 0)
scores$very.neu = as.numeric(scores$score == 0)

numpos = sum(scores$very.pos)
numneg = sum(scores$very.neg)
numneu = sum(scores$very.neu)

s <- c(numpos,numneg,numneu)
lbls <- c("POSITIVE","NEGATIVE","NEUTRAL")
pct <- round(s/sum(s)*100)
lbls <- paste(lbls, pct)
lbls <- paste(lbls,"%",sep="")
pie(s,labels = lbls, col=rainbow(length(lbls)),main="OPINION ON iPhone6")
```

```
> pie(s,labels = lbls, col=rainbow(length(lbls)),main="OPINION ON iPhone6")
>
```

All the values are stored in s variable and by applying next four commands the result is shown with the help of a pie chart.

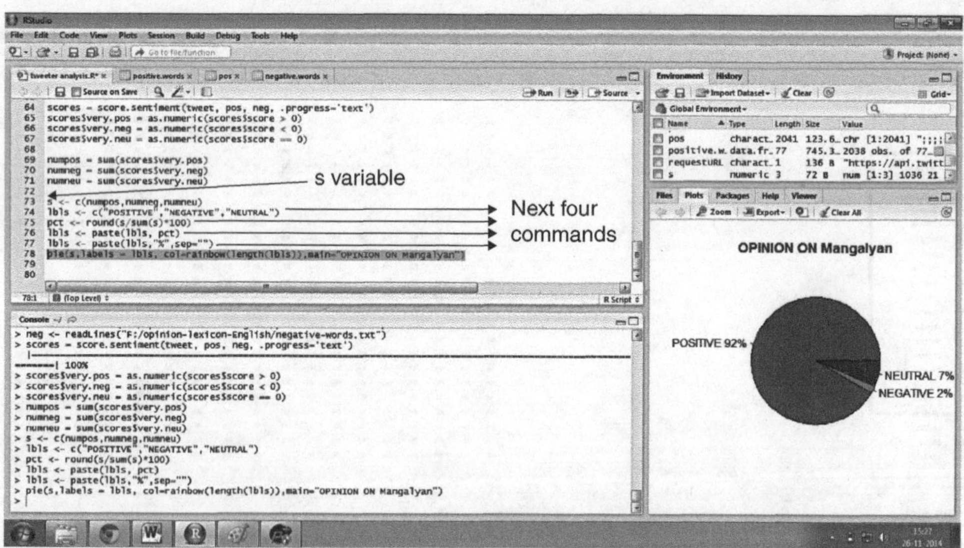

The opinion of tweeter users shows that they are very positive about the mangalyaan mission. Lot of positive tweets have been gathered on mangalyaan mission. Similarly, Tweeter analysis can be performed on any product to know the social buzz regarding that product.

REFERENCES

http://analytics.typepad.com/files/retailanalytics.pdf, (Accessed on 23 August, 2014)

http://briefingsdirectblog.blogspot.in/2014/03/case-study-how-dell-converts-social.html, (Accessed on 23 August, 2014)

http://face-and-emotion.com/dataface/facs/description.jsp, (Accessed on 23 August, 2014)

http://msdn.microsoft.com/en-us/library/jj130970, (Accessed on 23 August, 2014)

http://retailnext.net/products/guest-wi-fi-personalization/, (Accessed on 23 August, 2014)

http://whatis.techtarget.com/definition/3Vs, (Accessed on 23 August, 2014)

http://www.1goodreason.com/blog/blog/2010/05/19/nestles-social-media-meltdown-case-study/, (Accessed on 25 August, 2014)

http://www.aber.ac.uk/~dcswww/Dept/Teaching/CourseNotes/current/CS27020/Lectures/Intro_semistructured_data_and_XML.pdf, (Accessed on 25 August, 2014)

http://www.biogem.org/downloads/notes/Introduction%20to%20R.pdf, (Accessed on 25 August, 2014)

http://www.bk.isy.liu.se/candide/, (Accessed on 29 August, 2014)

http://www.bk.isy.liu.se/candide/wincandide/, (Accessed on 29 August, 2014)

http://www.bk.isy.liu.se/candide/xproject.html, (Accessed on 29 August, 2014)

http://www.cc.gatech.edu/~vbettada/files/FaceExpressionRecSurvey.pdf, (Accessed on 29 August, 2014)

http://www.cc.gatech.edu/~vbettada/files/FaceExpressionRecSurvey.pdf, (Accessed on 29 August, 2014)

http://www.cognitec.com/applications-id-issuance.html, (Accessed on 29 August, 2014)

http://www.cognizant.com/InsightsWhitepapers/How-Banks-Can-Use-Social-Media-Analytics-To-Drive-Business-Advantage.pdf, (Accessed on 29 August, 2014)

http://www.cognizant.com/InsightsWhitepapers/Retail-Analytics-Game-Changer-for-Customer-Loyalty.pdf, (Accessed on 29 August, 2014)

http://www.cs.cmu.edu/~face/facs.htm, (Accessed on 29 August, 2014)

http://www.face-rec.org/interesting-papers/general/imana4facrcg_lu.pdf, (Accessed on 29 August, 2014)

http://www.ibmbigdatahub.com/infographic/four-vs-big-data, (Accessed on 29 August, 2014)

http://www.infoag.org/abstract_papers/papers/abstract_171.pdf, (Accessed on 29 August, 2014)

https://www.dagstuhl.de/Reports/01/01361.pdf, (Accessed on 29 August, 2014)

Appendix-FACS

AU	Description	Facial muscle	Example image
1	Inner Brow Raiser	*Frontalis, pars medialis*	
2	Outer Brow Raiser	*Frontalis, pars lateralis*	
4	Brow Lowerer	*Corrugator supercilii, Depressor supercilii*	
5	Upper Lid Raiser	*Levator palpebrae superioris*	
6	Cheek Raiser	*Orbicularis oculi, pars orbitalis*	
7	Lid Tightener	*Orbicularis oculi, pars palpebralis*	

(*continued*)

Continued

AU	Description	Facial muscle	Example image
9	Nose Wrinkler	*Levator labii superioris alaquae nasi*	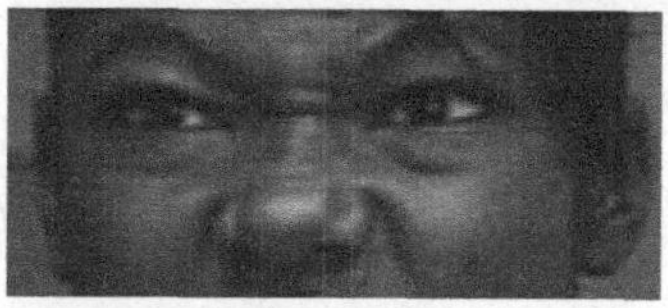
10	Upper Lip Raiser	*Levator labii superioris*	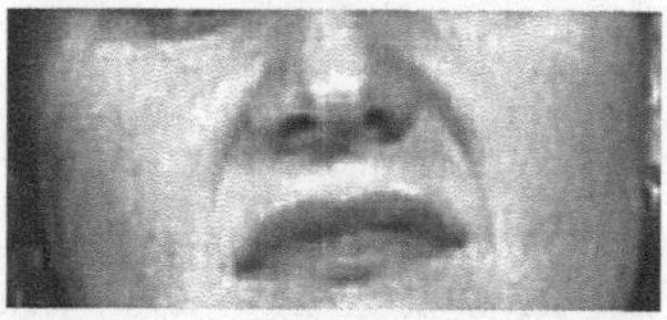
11	Nasolabial Deepener	*Zygomaticus minor*	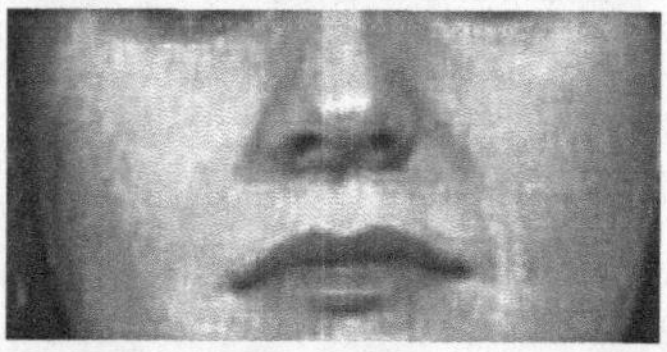
12	Lip Corner Puller	*Zygomaticus major*	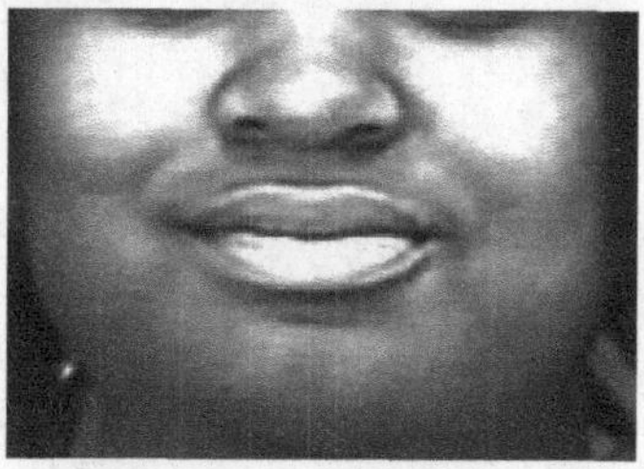
13	Cheek Puffer	*Levator anguli oris (a.k.a. Caninus)*	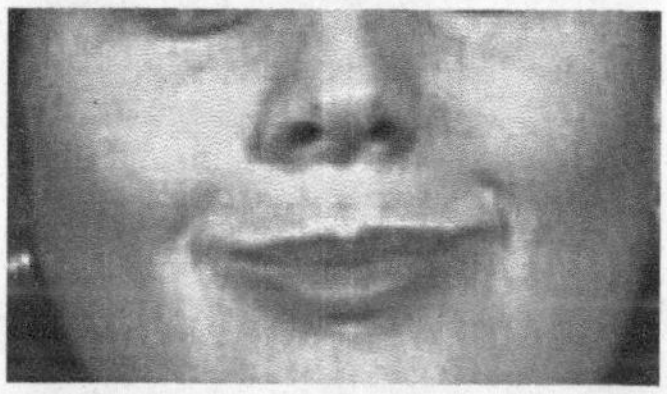
14	Dimpler	*Buccinator*	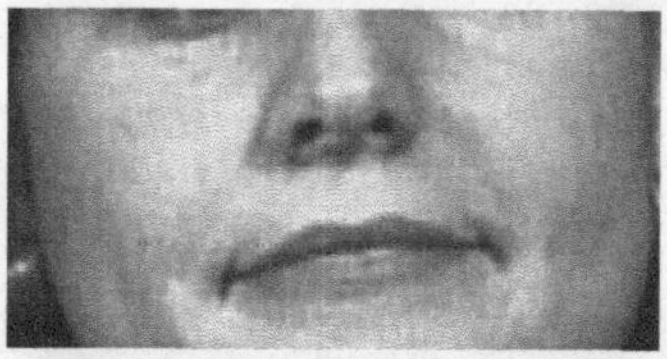
15	Lip Corner Depressor	*Depressor anguli oris (a.k.a. Triangularis)*	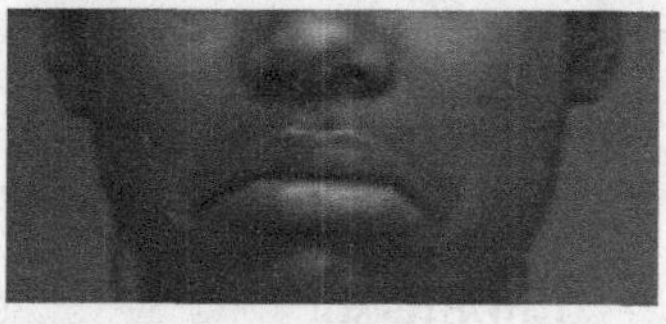

(*continued*)

Continued

AU	Description	Facial muscle	Example image
16	Lower Lip Depressor	*Depressor labii inferioris*	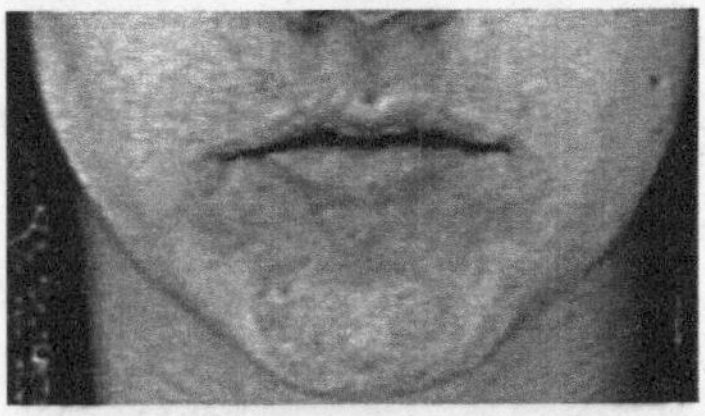
17	Chin Raiser	*Mentalis*	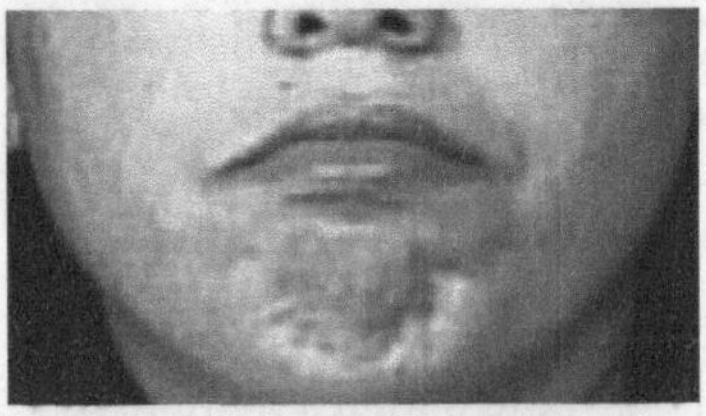
18	Lip Puckerer	*Incisivii labii superioris and Incisivii labii inferioris*	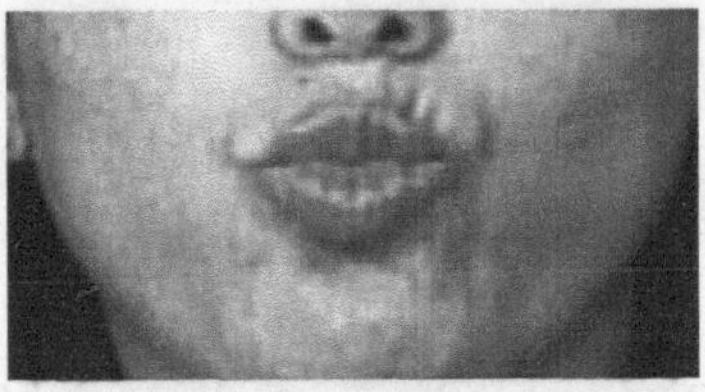
20	Lip stretcher	*Risorius w/ platysma*	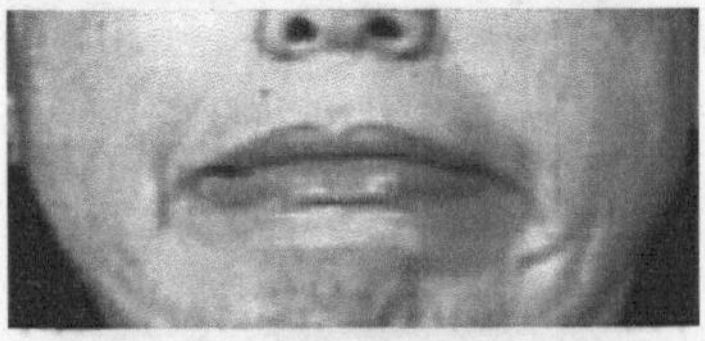
22	Lip Funneler	*Orbicularis oris*	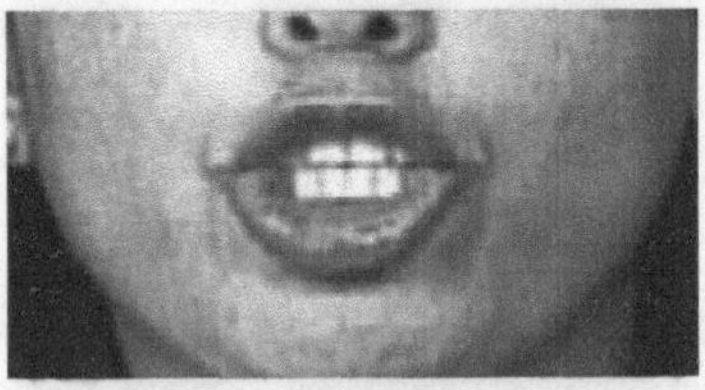
23	Lip Tightener	*Orbicularis oris*	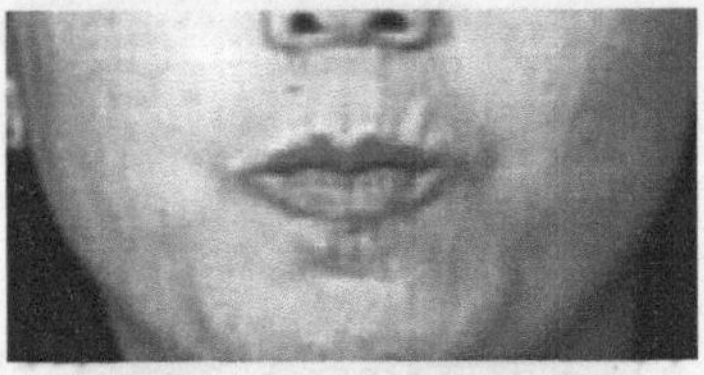
24	Lip Pressor	*Orbicularis oris*	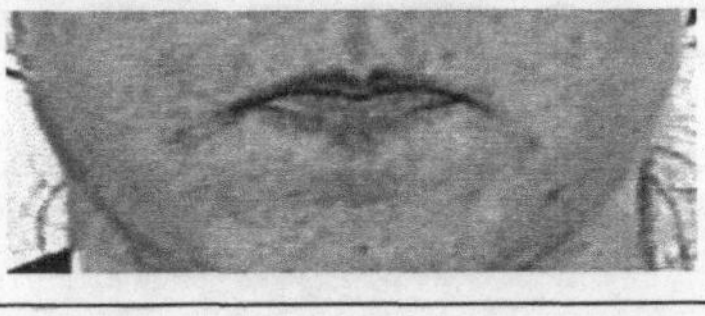

(*continued*)

Continued

AU	Description	Facial muscle	Example image
25	Lips part**	*Depressor labii inferioris or relaxation of Mentalis, or Orbicularis oris*	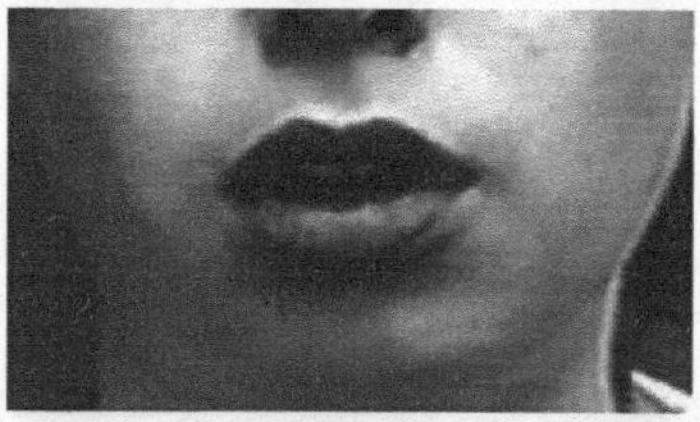
26	Jaw Drop	*Masseter, relaxed Temporalis and internal Pterygoid*	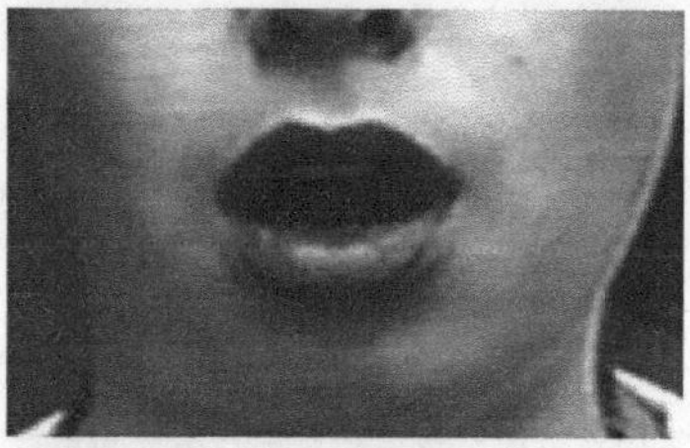
27	Mouth Stretch	*Pterygoids, Digastric*	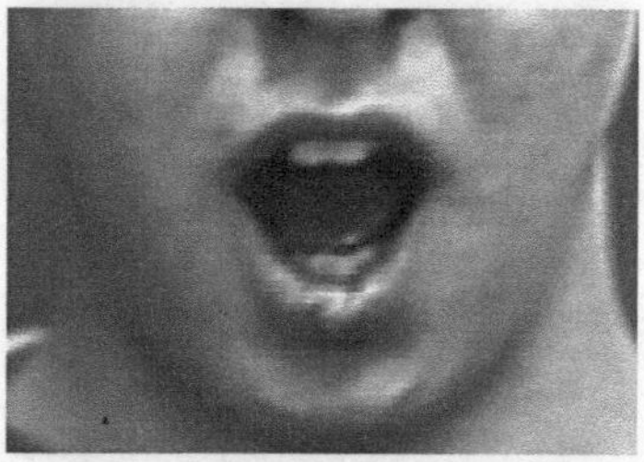
28	Lip Suck	*Orbicularis oris*	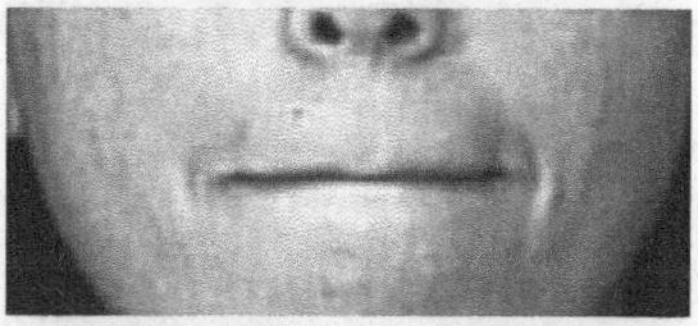
41	Lid droop**	*Relaxation of Levator palpebrae superioris*	
42	Slit	*Orbicularis oculi*	

Source: http://www.cs.cmu.edu/~face/facs.htm

APPENDIX 1

Toothworks

Customer_ID	Age	Marital status
1	20	Single
2	45	Married
3	55	Married
4	22	Single
5	36	Married
6	38	Single
7	39	Single
8	44	Married
9	21	Single
10	22	Married
11	23	Married
12	22	Single
13	50	Married
14	45	Married
15	44	Married
16	20	Single
17	57	Single
18	28	Single
19	59	Single
20	35	Married
21	57	Married
22	35	Married
23	27	Married
24	26	Single
25	48	Married
26	29	Single

(*continued*)

Continued

Customer_ID	Age	Marital status
27	48	Married
28	22	Single
29	39	Married
30	20	Single

Product code	Product name	Size
1	Glister	Travel pack
2	Glister	Family pack
3	Colgate	Travel pack
4	Colgate	Family pack
5	Himalaya	Travel pack
6	Himalaya	Family pack

Customer code	Product code	Date of purchase	Quantity of purchase
1	1	13-06-2012	1
2	1	14-06-2012	1
2	5	14-06-2012	2
3	6	16-06-2012	2
4	3	16-06-2012	1
5	2	17-06-2012	1
5	3	17-06-2012	1
6	4	17-06-2012	1
7	1	17-06-2012	1
8	1	17-06-2012	1
8	5	17-06-2012	2
9	5	17-06-2012	2
10	3	01-07-2012	1
11	5	01-07-2012	4
12	5	02-07-2012	2
13	1	03-07-2012	2
13	2	03-07-2012	2
14	2	03-07-2012	3
14	5	04-07-2012	1

(*continued*)

Continued

Customer code	Product code	Date of purchase	Quantity of purchase
15	6	05-07-2012	1
15	6	11-07-2012	1
16	1	11-07-2012	1
16	4	12-07-2012	1
16	1	12-07-2012	1
17	4	13-07-2012	2
18	2	14-07-2012	2
19	5	15-07-2012	2
20	3	16-07-2012	1
20	1	16-07-2012	2

APPENDIX 2

QOWL

Gender	Birth location	Martial status	No of children	Personal satisfaction (30)	Social satisfaction (30)	Enjoyment at work* (35)	Motivation at work (20)	Mental satisfaction (30)	Achievement from work (25)	Occupational role (25)	Work related (25)	Work involement (5)	Nature of supervision (15)	T&D	Growth & job security (10)	target
Male	Urban	single	0	20	17	26	11	15	13	18	14	1	8	12	6	0
Male	Urban	single	0	20	22	23	14	21	13	18	14	2	9	13	6	1
Male	Urban	single	0	21	21	18	18	22	18	20	14	4	13	15	8	0
Female	Rural	single	0	21	21	12	19	20	19	22	16	5	12	19	5	0
Female	Urban	single	0	21	22	21	17	23	16	18	17	4	11	17	9	0
Male	Rural	single	0	18	20	18	14	18	14	20	17	1	10	16	8	0
Male	Urban	single	0	18	16	21	10	14	14	13	14	2	8	15	5	0
Male	Urban	single	0	19	20	12	15	18	15	18	17	2	9	9	5	0
Male	Rural	single	0	18	19	18	14	18	17	20	17	1	9	15	8	0
Female	Rural	single	0	20	20	24	10	21	18	18	13	1	8	16	7	0
Male	Urban	single	0	17	17	23	11	18	15	16	15	3	8	15	5	0
Female	Urban	Married	1	22	15	27	17	19	17	16	16	4	10	14	6	1
Male	Urban	Married	1	21	19	19	12	28	16	17	17	2	10	14	7	1
Female	Urban	single	0	20	20	23	15	17	19	18	16	2	11	15	6	1
Female	Urban	Married	0	18	22	18	12	18	14	16	12	1	11	16	6	1
Female	Urban	single	0	21	18	22	10	18	13	14	13	2	9	13	6	1
Male	Rural	single	0	18	24	21	16	23	20	21	14	3	7	14	9	0
Female	Urban	single	0	16	12	19	10	22	21	9	11	5	7	16	4	0
Male	Urban	single	0	15	15	18	12	18	16	14	15	4	7	5	5	0
Male	Rural	single	0	18	18	19	14	16	18	16	12	3	7	11	7	1

(*continued*)

Continued

Gender	Birth location	Martial status	No of children	Personal satisfaction (30)	Social satisfaction (30)	Enjoyment at work* (35)	Motivation at work (20)	Mental satisfaction (30)	Achievement from work (25)	Occupational role (25)	Work related (25)	Work involement (5)	Nature of supervision (15)	T&D	Growth & job security (10)	target
Female	Rural	single	0	19	14	21	15	19	15	18	16	1	9	16	6	0
Male	Urban	single	0	16	16	20	13	20	17	15	14	2	6	12	6	0
Male	Urban	single	0	18	19	19	12	17	16	17	12	4	8	13	5	1
Male	Rural	single	0	17	21	22	11	19	19	19	15	3	9	16	4	1
Female	Rural	single	0	20	14	20	10	16	16	16	14	2	5	13	6	1
Male	Urban	single	0	16	16	18	10	18	14	18	16	1	10	14	5	0
Male	Urban	single	0	15	17	17	16	17	15	14	17	2	6	12	4	1
Female	Urban	single	0	19	16	20	11	18	17	16	12	3	10	15	6	0
Female	Urban	Married	1	17	18	22	14	16	19	13	15	1	11	13	5	1
Female	Urban	single	0	20	17	20	15	19	14	18	17	4	9	14	7	0
Female	Urban	single	0	16	20	23	12	20	16	19	14	2	7	16	4	0
Male	Urban	single	0	14	22	18	16	21	15	15	13	3	8	9	5	1
Male	Urban	single	0	16	20	16	12	22	17	20	18	4	10	13	5	1
Female	Rural	single	0	19	18	21	10	21	14	18	16	3	12	15	6	0
Female	Urban	single	0	21	14	16	13	19	16	16	14	3	10	13	7	1
Male	Rural	single	0	18	16	19	11	18	17	14	15	2	7	11	8	0
Male	Urban	single	0	15	18	22	15	20	14	11	18	1	9	10	7	0
Male	Urban	single	0	19	16	24	13	22	12	18	12	4	6	12	8	1
Female	Urban	single	0	21	19	17	14	20	14	16	14	1	10	14	6	0
Female	Urban	single	0	23	20	19	11	21	16	17	11	2	9	15	9	1
Female	Rural	single	0	17	18	20	16	20	18	19	15	2	7	13	5	0
Male	Urban	single	0	19	17	22	14	23	16	14	16	3	6	11	4	1
Male	Urban	single	0	16	19	20	13	19	17	16	13	2	7	8	5	1
Male	Urban	single	0	20	18	22	14	18	20	17	12	3	8	12	6	0
Male	Urban	single	0	22	16	18	12	20	14	19	14	4	5	14	6	0
Male	Urban	single	0	18	20	19	15	22	12	14	11	1	7	11	7	0
Male	Rural	single	0	18	18	21	13	21	16	16	13	1	9	15	5	0
Male	Urban	Married	1	20	21	20	14	19	14	15	15	3	11	16	4	1
Female	Urban	single	0	16	20	15	12	18	15	14	16	2	9	11	5	1
Female	Urban	single	0	17	17	19	14	20	18	17	12	1	10	10	7	0
Male	Urban	single	0	19	16	23	13	22	16	19	13	3	12	13	6	0

(*continued*)

Continued

Gender	Birth location	Martial status	No of children	Personal satisfaction (30)	Social satisfaction (30)	Enjoyment at work* (35)	Motivation at work (20)	Mental satisfaction (30)	Achievement from work (25)	Occupational role (25)	Work related (25)	Work involement (5)	Nature of supervision (15)	T&D	Growth & job security (10)	target
Male	Urban	single	0	20	17	26	11	15	13	18	14	1	8	12	6	0
Male	Urban	single	0	20	22	23	14	21	13	18	14	2	9	13	6	1
Male	Urban	single	0	21	21	18	18	22	18	20	14	4	13	15	8	0
Female	Rural	single	0	21	21	12	19	20	19	22	16	5	12	19	5	0
Female	Urban	single	0	21	22	21	17	23	16	18	17	4	11	17	9	0
Male	Rural	single	0	18	20	18	14	18	14	20	17	1	10	16	8	0
Male	Urban	single	0	18	16	21	10	14	14	13	14	2	8	15	5	0
Male	Urban	single	0	19	20	12	15	18	15	18	17	2	9	9	5	0
Male	Rural	single	0	18	19	18	14	18	17	20	17	1	9	15	8	0
Female	Rural	single	0	20	20	24	10	21	18	18	13	1	8	16	7	0
Male	Urban	single	0	17	17	23	11	18	15	16	15	3	8	15	5	0
Female	Urban	Married	1	22	15	27	17	19	17	16	16	4	10	14	6	1
Male	Urban	Married	1	21	19	19	12	28	16	17	17	2	10	14	7	1
Female	Urban	single	0	20	20	23	15	17	19	18	16	2	11	15	6	1
Female	Urban	Married	0	18	22	18	12	18	14	16	12	1	11	16	6	1
Female	Urban	single	0	21	18	22	10	18	13	14	13	2	9	13	6	1
Male	Rural	single	0	18	24	21	16	23	20	21	14	3	7	14	9	0
Female	Urban	single	0	16	12	19	10	22	21	9	11	5	7	16	4	0
Male	Urban	single	0	15	15	18	12	18	16	14	15	4	7	5	5	0
Male	Rural	single	0	18	18	19	14	16	18	16	12	3	7	11	7	1
Female	Rural	single	0	19	14	21	15	19	15	18	16	1	9	16	6	0
Male	Urban	single	0	16	16	20	13	20	17	15	14	2	6	12	6	0
Male	Urban	single	0	18	19	19	12	17	16	17	12	4	8	13	5	1
Male	Rural	single	0	17	21	22	11	19	19	19	15	3	9	16	4	1
Female	Rural	single	0	20	14	20	10	16	16	16	14	2	5	13	6	1
Male	Urban	single	0	16	16	18	10	18	14	18	16	1	10	14	5	0
Male	Urban	single	0	15	17	17	16	17	15	14	17	2	6	12	4	1
Female	Urban	single	0	19	16	20	11	18	17	16	12	3	10	15	6	0
Female	Urban	Married	1	17	18	22	14	16	19	13	15	1	11	13	5	1
Female	Urban	single	0	20	17	20	15	19	14	18	17	4	9	14	7	0
Female	Urban	single	0	16	20	23	12	20	16	19	14	2	7	16	4	0

(*continued*)

Continued

Gender	Birth location	Martial status	No of children	Personal satisfaction (30)	Social satisfaction (30)	Enjoyment at work* (35)	Motivation at work (20)	Mental satisfaction (30)	Achievement from work (25)	Occupational role (25)	Work related (25)	Work involvement (5)	Nature of supervision (15)	T&D	Growth & job security (10)	target
Male	Urban	single	0	14	22	18	16	21	15	15	13	3	8	9	5	1
Male	Urban	single	0	16	20	16	12	22	17	20	18	4	10	13	5	1
Female	Rural	single	0	19	18	21	10	21	14	18	16	3	12	15	6	0
Female	Urban	single	0	21	14	16	13	19	16	16	14	3	10	13	7	1
Male	Rural	single	0	18	16	19	11	18	17	14	15	2	7	11	8	0
Male	Urban	single	0	15	18	22	15	20	14	11	18	1	9	10	7	0
Male	Urban	single	0	19	16	24	13	22	12	18	12	4	6	12	8	1
Female	Urban	single	0	21	19	17	14	20	14	16	14	1	10	14	6	0
Female	Urban	single	0	23	20	19	11	21	16	17	11	2	9	15	9	1
Female	Rural	single	0	17	18	20	16	20	18	19	15	2	7	13	5	0
Male	Urban	single	0	19	17	22	14	23	16	14	16	3	6	11	4	1
Male	Urban	single	0	16	19	20	13	19	17	16	13	2	7	8	5	1
Male	Urban	single	0	20	18	22	14	18	20	17	12	3	8	12	6	0
Male	Urban	single	0	22	16	18	12	20	14	19	14	4	5	14	6	0
Male	Urban	single	0	18	20	19	15	22	12	14	11	1	7	11	7	0
Male	Rural	single	0	18	18	21	13	21	16	16	13	1	9	15	5	0
Male	Urban	Married	1	20	21	20	14	19	14	15	15	3	11	16	4	1
Female	Urban	single	0	16	20	15	12	18	15	14	16	2	9	11	5	1
Female	Urban	single	0	17	17	19	14	20	18	17	12	1	10	10	7	0
Male	Urban	single	0	19	16	23	13	22	16	19	13	3	12	13	6	0

Index